Fourth Workshop on Financial Technology and Natural Language Processing (FinNLP 2022)

Abu Dhabi, United Arab Emirates and Online
8 December 2022

ISBN: 978-1-7138-9109-3

Printed from e-media with permission by:

Curran Associates, Inc.
57 Morehouse Lane
Red Hook, NY 12571

Some format issues inherent in the e-media version may also appear in this print version.

Printed with permission by Curran Associates, Inc. (2024)

Association for Computational Linguistics
209 N. Eighth Street
Stroudsburg, Pennsylvania 18360

Phone: 1-570-476-8006
Fax: 1-570-476-0860

acl@aclweb.org

Additional copies of this publication are available from:

Curran Associates, Inc.
57 Morehouse Lane
Red Hook, NY 12571 USA
Phone: 845-758-0400
Fax: 845-758-2633
Email: curran@proceedings.com
Web: www.proceedings.com

FinNLP 2022

The Fourth Workshop on Financial Technology and Natural Language Processing

Proceedings of the Workshop

December 8, 2022

Introduction

Welcome to FinNLP-2022, the 4th Workshop on Financial Technology and Natural Language Processing! Since this year, FinNLP has become a twice-a-year workshop and is colocated with IJCAI and EMNLP. This workshop aims to provide a forum for sharing the latest Interdisciplinary results from either the financial domain's or the NLP field's perspective.

In FinNLP-2022, we have a keynote (Knowledge-Based News Event Analysis and Forecasting) from Dr. Oktie Hassanzadeh, a Senior Research Staff Member at IBM T.J. Watson Research Center, and an overview of recent FinNLP studies from the FinNLP organizer. The accepted papers cover various topics, including emerging trend identification, intent classification, market information prediction, sentiment analysis, digital strategy maturity assessment, and so on. Several kinds of financial documents are explored, such as the transcriptions of earnings calls, social media data, and news articles. The shared task participants share several approaches for evaluating the rationales of amateur investors. We hope the audiences of FinNLP-2022 can learn the latest tendency, and also have a comprehensive understanding of where we are now in financial opinion scoring.

FinNLP-2022 is the result of a collaborative effort of the FinNLP community. We would like to thank our Program Committee - Hiroki Sakaji, Emmanuele Chersoni, Kiyoshi Izumi, Pablo Duboue, Juyeon Kang, Paulo Alves, Luciano Del Corro, Chuan-Ju Wang, Ismail El Maarouf, Damir Cavar, Paul Buitelaar, and Jinhang Jiang - for their help in providing feedback on submissions and selecting the papers. We would also like to thank all authors from 10 countries in both academia (16 institutions) and industry (8 companies) for sharing their insightful results in FinNLP-2022.

Welcome and hope you all enjoy FinNLP-2022.

Chung-Chi Chen (AIST, Japan)
Hen-Hsen Huang (Academia Sinica, Taiwan)
Hiroya Takamura (AIST, Japan)
Hsin-Hsi Chen (National Taiwan University, Taiwan)
FinNLP-2022 Organizers

Acknowledgment FinNLP-2022 is supported by a project JPNP20006, commissioned by the New Energy and Industrial Technology Development Organization (NEDO), and was partially supported by National Science and Technology Council, Taiwan, under grants MOST 110-2221-E-002-128-MY3 and MOST 110-2634-F-002-050-.

Organizing Committee

Organizers

Chung-Chi Chen, Artificial Intelligence Research Center, National Institute of Advanced Industrial Science and Technology, Japan
Hen-Hsen Huang, Institute of Information Science, Academia Sinica, Taiwan
Hiroya Takamura, Artificial Intelligence Research Center, National Institute of Advanced Industrial Science and Technology, Japan
Hsin-Hsi Chen, Department of Computer Science and Information Engineering, National Taiwan University, Taiwan

Program Committee

Reviewers

Paulo Alves

Paul Buitelaar

Damir Cavar, Emmanuele Chersoni

Luciano Del Corro, Pablo Duboue

Ismail El Maarouf

Kiyoshi Izumi

Jinhang Jiang

Juyeon Kang

Hiroki Sakaji

Chuan-Ju Wang

Keynote Talk: Knowledge-Based News Event Analysis and Forecasting

Oktie Hassanzadeh
IBM T.J. Watson Research Center

Abstract: In this talk, I will present our ongoing work at IBM Research on building a toolkit for news event analysis and forecasting. The toolkit is powered by a Knowledge Graph (KG) of events curated from structured and textual sources of event-related knowledge. The toolkit provides functions for 1) mapping ongoing news headlines to concepts in the KG, 2) retrieval, reasoning, and visualization for causal analysis and forecasting, and 3) extraction of causal knowledge from text documents to augment the KG with additional domain knowledge. Each function has a number of implementations using state-of-the-art neuro-symbolic techniques. I will go over a number of use cases for the toolkit, including use cases in finance and enterprise risk management.

Bio: Dr. Oktie Hassanzadeh is a Senior Research Staff Member at IBM T.J. Watson Research Center. He is the recipient of several academic and corporate awards, including a top prize at the FinCausal-2022 Shared Task, a top prize at the Semantic Web Challenge at ISWC conference, and two best-paper awards at ESWC conferences. He has received his M.Sc. and Ph.D. degrees from the University of Toronto, where he received the IBM PhD fellowship and the Yahoo! Key Scientific Challenges awards. He is also a two-time recipient of the first prize at the Triplification Challenge at the SEMANTiCS Conference for his projects in the areas of Semantic Technologies and Linked Data. For more information, refer to his home page: http://researcher.watson.ibm.com/person/us-hassanzadeh

Table of Contents

Program

Thursday, December 8, 2022

09:00 - 09:10	*Opening Remarks*
09:10 - 09:45	*Keynote - Knowledge-Based News Event Analysis and Forecasting*
09:45 - 10:00	*Overview of Recent FinNLP Studies*
09:00 - 10:30	*Main Track I*
	Contextualizing Emerging Trends in Financial News Articles Nhu Khoa Nguyen, Thierry Delahaut, Emanuela Boros, Antoine Doucet and Gaël Lejeune
	Contextualizing Emerging Trends in Financial News Articles Nhu Khoa Nguyen, Thierry Delahaut, Emanuela Boros, Antoine Doucet and Gaël Lejeune
10:30 - 11:00	*Coffee Break*
11:00 - 12:30	*Main Track II*
	TweetFinSent: A Dataset of Stock Sentiments on Twitter Yulong Pei, Amarachi Mbakwe, Akshat Gupta, Salwa Alamir, Hanxuan Lin, Xiaomo Liu and Sameena Shah
	Stock Price Volatility Prediction: A Case Study with AutoML Hilal Pataci, Yunyao Li, Yannis Katsis, Yada Zhu and Lucian Popa
	Learning Better Intent Representations for Financial Open Intent Classification Xianzhi Li, Will Aitken, Xiaodan Zhu and Stephen W. Thomas
	Exploring Robustness of Prefix Tuning in Noisy Data: A Case Study in Financial Sentiment Analysis Sudhandar Balakrishnan, Yihao Fang and Xiaodan Zhu
	A Taxonomical NLP Blueprint to Support Financial Decision Making through Information-Centred Interactions Siavash Kazemian, Cosmin Munteanu and Gerald Penn

Thursday, December 8, 2022 (continued)

	Toward Privacy-preserving Text Embedding Similarity with Homomorphic Encryption Donggyu Kim, Garam Lee and Sungwoo Oh
12:30 - 14:00	*Lunch Break*
14:00 - 15:30	*Main Track III and Shared Task I*
	DigiCall: A Benchmark for Measuring the Maturity of Digital Strategy through Company Earning Calls Hilal Pataci, Kexuan Sun and T. Ravichandran
	Disentangled Variational Topic Inference for Topic-Accurate Financial Report Generation Sixing Yan
	Overview of the FinNLP-2022 ERAI Task: Evaluating the Rationales of Amateur Investors Chung-Chi Chen, Hen-Hsen Huang, Hiroya Takamura and Hsin-Hsi Chen
	PromptShots at the FinNLP-2022 ERAI Task: Pairwise Comparison and Unsupervised Ranking Peratham Wiriyathammabhum
	LIPI at the FinNLP-2022 ERAI Task: Ensembling Sentence Transformers for Assessing Maximum Possible Profit and Loss from Online Financial Posts Sohom Ghosh and Sudip Kumar Naskar
	DCU-ML at the FinNLP-2022 ERAI Task: Investigating the Transferability of Sentiment Analysis Data for Evaluating Rationales of Investors Chenyang Lyu, Tianbo Ji and Liting Zhou
	UOA at the FinNLP-2022 ERAI Task: Leveraging the Class Label Description for Financial Opinion Mining Jinan Zou, Haiyao Cao, Yanxi Liu, Lingqiao Liu, Ehsan Abbasnejad and Javen Qinfeng Shi
	aiML at the FinNLP-2022 ERAI Task: Combining Classification and Regression Tasks for Financial Opinion Mining Zhaoxuan Qin, Jinan Zou, Qiaoyang Luo, Haiyao Cao and Yang Jiao
15:30 - 16:00	*Coffee Break*

Thursday, December 8, 2022 (continued)

16:00 - 16:30 *Shared Task II and EMNLP Findings*

Yet at the FinNLP-2022 ERAI Task: Modified models for evaluating the Rationales of Amateur Investors
Yan Zhuang and Fuji Ren

LDPP at the FinNLP-2022 ERAI Task: Determinantal Point Processes and Variational Auto-encoders for Identifying High-Quality Opinions from a pool of Social Media Posts
Paul Trust and Rosane Minghim

Jetsons at the FinNLP-2022 ERAI Task: BERT-Chinese for mining high MPP posts
Alolika Gon, Sihan Zha, Sai Krishna Rallabandi, Parag Pravin Dakle and Preethi Raghavan

16:30 - 16:42 *EMNLP Findings - DialogueGAT: A Graph Attention Network for Financial Risk Prediction by Modeling the Dialogues in Earnings Conference Calls*

16:42 - 16:54 *EMNLP Findings - VarMAE: Pre-training of Variational Masked Autoencoder for Domain-adaptive Language Understanding*

16:54 - 17:06 *EMNLP Findings - ASDOT: Any-Shot Data-to-Text Generation with Pretrained Language Models*

17:06 - 17:18 *EMNLP Findings - DocFiNet: Augmenting Text and Speech Transformers with Semi-structured Document Representations for Financial Tasks*

17:18 - 17:30 *EMNLP Findings - Long Text and Multi-Table Summarization: Dataset and Method*

17:30 - 17:40 *Closing*

Contextualizing Emerging Trends in Financial News Articles

Nhu Khoa Nguyen
University of La Rochelle
F-17000, La Rochelle, France
nhu.nguyen@univ-lr.fr

Emanuela Boros
University of La Rochelle
F-17000, La Rochelle, France
emanuela.boros@univ-lr.fr

Gaël Lejeune
Sorbonne University
F-75006, Paris, France
gael.lejeune@sorbonne-universite.fr

Antoine Doucet
University of La Rochelle,
F-17000, La Rochelle, France
antoine.doucet@univ-lr.fr

Thierry Delahaut
La Banque Postale Asset Management
F-75004, Paris, France
thierry.delahaut@labanquepostale-am.fr

Abstract

Identifying and exploring emerging trends in news is becoming more essential than ever with many changes occurring around the world due to the global health crises. However, most of the recent research has focused mainly on detecting trends in social media, thus, benefiting from social features (e.g. likes and retweets on Twitter) which helped the task as they can be used to measure the engagement and diffusion rate of content. Yet, formal text data, unlike short social media posts, comes with a longer, less restricted writing format, and thus, more challenging. In this paper, we focus our study on emerging trends detection in financial news articles about Microsoft, collected before and during the start of the COVID-19 pandemic (July 2019 to July 2020). We make the dataset accessible and we also propose a strong baseline (*Contextual Leap2Trend*) for exploring the dynamics of similarities between pairs of keywords based on topic modeling and term frequency. Finally, we evaluate against a gold standard (Google Trends) and present noteworthy real-world scenarios regarding the influence of the pandemic on Microsoft.

1 Introduction

Digital news, through many means of diffusion (online publishing platforms, social media, blogs, etc.) is considerably influential, as it not only shapes and forms public opinion but can also be a factor in the decision-making process of many industries that uses technology to improve activities and performance. Therefore, discovering hidden themes and trends residing in news data is essential to improve analyzing and managing development directions for many companies. The importance of identifying new trends before they emerge is further emphasized with the world-changing surrounding the health crisis triggered by the COVID-19 pandemic.

Emerging trend detection is the task of automatically extracting topics that are gaining attention and on the verge of being trending (Dang et al., 2016). Emerging topics usually indicate contents that are more popular in a short period, while growing in interest and utility over time. Moreover, topics that become a trend can either be short-lived or last for a long time depending on the nature of the event (e.g., traffic accidents, natural disasters, election campaigns, regulation enforcement, etc.).

Based on the platform of publication, the data used for detecting emerging trends can be classified into two classes: social media text and formal text. Corpora crawled from social media usually contain text that is short, concise and usually include social features (e.g. likes and retweets in Twitter) which benefits the task as they can be used to measure the engagement and diffusion rate of content. Because of this fact, data from social media has been extensively studied in various research (Peng et al., 2018).

However, formal text data, unlike the short sub-300 characters social media posts, comes with longer, less restricted writing format, yet does not include any social features (e.g., news articles, official documents, reports). Because of these differences, emerging trend detection on such data is rather under-researched. While there exist studies on financial data (Borsje et al., 2010; Malik et al., 2011) and news articles (Liu et al., 2020), most of them are based on techniques such as latent Dirichlet allocation (LDA) topic modelling (Behpour et al., 2021; Bissoyi et al., 2020), term frequency-inverse document frequency (TF-IDF) weighting technique (Zhu et al., 2019; Santis et al., 2020), or different clustering types (Cao et al., 2018; Li et al., 2020) for the identification of either "hot" topics or emerging themes.

Therefore, in this paper, our main contributions of our study are: (1) We build a dataset from the Bloomberg's Event Driven Feeds (EDF), containing news about Microsoft in the time interval from

Proceedings of the Fourth Workshop on Financial Technology and Natural Language Processing (FinNLP), pages 1 - 9
December 8, 2022 ©2022 Association for Computational Linguistics

July 2019 to July 2020, which is the time period from six-month before and six-month after the COVID-19 outbreak. (2) We combine term TF-IDF and LDA for a more precise generation of keywords (bi-grams). (3) We utilize the latest contextual embeddings to represent the real temporality and variation of the semantics during different periods. (4) We make the dataset accessible along with the snapshot of Google Trend data used in our evaluation[1].

The article is organized as follows. Section 2 discusses related work on emerging theme detection. Section 3 describes the data and explains our approach for detecting emerging trends in financial-based data and the experimental setup is established in Section 4 alongside with the evaluation metrics and the detailed analysis regarding the impact of the pandemic on Microsoft. Lastly, Section 5 concludes the article with remarks and points to future work.

2 Related Work

Trend Detection in Formal Datasets The general direction for trend detection in formal text data is to use statistical methods (Hughes et al., 2020; Daud et al., 2021), topic modeling (Bolelli et al., 2009; Behpour et al., 2021), and clustering (Liu et al., 2020; Linger and Hajaiej, 2020) Using financial business patents, the research by Lee and Sohn (2017) aimed to identify emerging technology trends by applying latent Dirichlet allocation (LDA) with an exponentially weighted moving average of LDA probability, which affects whether a topic is "hot" or "cold". A refined version of TF-IDF, proposed by Zhu et al. (2019), aims to discover "hot" topics according to "hot" terms based on time distribution information, user attention, and K-means clustering. Unlike previous work that tackled trend detection in official documents and newspapers, others focused on proposing new approaches using research and scientific papers, documents that generally contain citations and bibliographies that could be considered as additional features (Nie and Sun, 2017; Xu et al., 2019; He et al., 2009; Griol-Barres et al., 2020). However, exploiting bibliographies can have disadvantages in timeliness and content analysis, as discussed by (Dridi et al., 2019). The authors further proposed an approach, called Leap2Trend using *temporal* word embedding that was generated by being trained on the data in an initial period of time, and then fine-tuned in the upcoming time frames. This approach also tracked the similarities between pairs of keywords over time, which yielded results suggesting the robustness and timeliness characteristics of the Leap2Trend.

Detecting Trends in COVID-19 Pandemic Recent works have also been conducted within the period of the COVID-19 pandemic to study emerging trends within certain communities and gauge the impact of the outbreak through social media text (Kassab et al., 2020). Santis et al. (2020) employed term-frequency analysis, calculate nutrition and energy metrics, while also using social features in order to extract hot terms and build a topic graph through co-occurrence analysis using Twitter data in Italy. Another research targeted peer-review papers regarding the COVID-19 virus and apply word embeddings and machine learning models to track novel insight surrounding the spreading of the virus (Pal et al., 2021).

3 Methodology

For the current study, we built a dataset by extracting a portion of the Event-Driven Feeds (EDF) data, a proprietary dataset provided by Bloomberg[2]. Bloomberg L.P. provides financial software tools and enterprise applications such as analytics and equity trading platform, data services, and news to financial companies and organizations. The EDF data is massive and contains more than ten years of news collection that Bloomberg published in multiple languages from 2010 up until the present.

3.1 Data

Considering the scope of the research, specific time frames and a company were chosen as follows: we studied the period from July 2019 to July 2020 - six months before the COVID-19 outbreak up until its peak, split into monthly collections of news. This is a very particular time span since the COVID-19 triggered a massive global health crisis and drastically changed people's lifestyle, which created new trends.

For the specific company, we chose Microsoft which, at the time of writing this article, was known to play a major role in remote working trends dur-

[1] The snapshot of Google Trend used in this paper can be found at: `https://github.com/nnkhoa/ms-edf-evaluation`. Please contact `thierry.delahaut@labanquepostale-am.fr` for the data.

[2] `https://www.bloomberg.com`

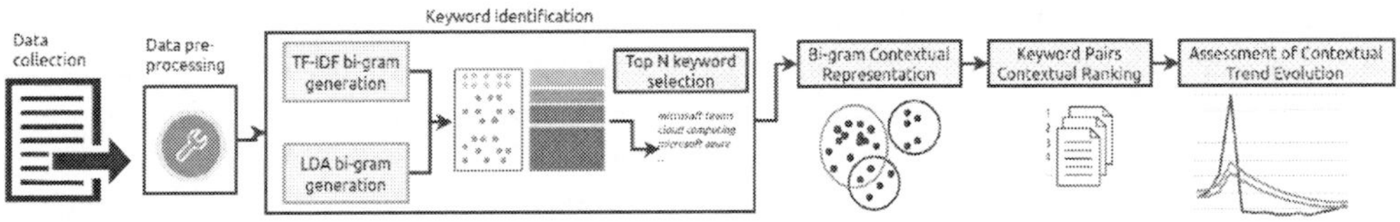

Figure 1: Summary of *Contextual Leap2Trend.*

ing the pandemic by providing a stable and convenient platform for online workplace communication. Moreover, Microsoft is widely known as one of the leading companies in the field of cloud computing. Hence, it is interesting to investigate how trends in Microsoft shifted during the pandemic. It is important to note that while the choice of collecting news involving Microsoft was deliberate, any company could have been selected for our study given enough background knowledge about such company.

With these criteria, we extracted a total of 11,923 news articles about Microsoft within the said time span. The data has an enormous surge in the number of articles during the month of October 2019, which consisted of around 7,500 documents and accounted for more than 60% of the total volume. In contrast, the number of documents during the beginning phase of the COVID-19 pandemic, in the span of 7 months from January 2020 to July 2020, is much lower in comparison. Averaging at about 300 articles per month, the period, the 7-month period only consisted just under 17% of the total amount of articles in the dataset. With these figures, it is expected that October 2019 could be the month that Microsoft started a trend due to the huge spike in news articles volume, while the COVID-19 period may seem uneventful to the company.

3.2 *Contextual Leap2Trend*

Our approach adapts the Leap2Trend method proposed by Dridi et al. (2019) on detecting emerging themes in scientific papers, to financial-based documents in our case, and we refer to it as *Contextual Leap2Trend*. The authors generated keywords representations were in different periods of time using static embeddings. Afterward, they assessed the similarity evolution of keyword pairs over time to depict which keywords are trending, thus forming topics based on the closeness between keywords. Leap2Trend also tackled the matter of lacking a gold standard to evaluate the result of trend detection by using Google Trends[3]. Google Trends collects search data of keywords and present them as interest rate over time, starting from 2004 to the present, which can be used to project emerging trends prediction results to gauge the performance of the system.

Nonetheless, Leap2Trend has some disadvantages that needed to be addressed. First and foremost, Leap2Trend used a straightforward approach to extract the main keywords by inspecting titles of scientific papers for the most frequent bi-grams. The solution is justified by the fact that titles from scientific publications are written with the purpose of being self-explanatory and conveying the methods/problems clearly. The writing style leads to titles often containing a substantial amount of keywords. News articles, on the other hand, have condensed headlines that will only be expanded further in the main content of the documents, where most keywords reside. Thus, using raw frequency to extract keywords is inefficient due to noisy text overshadowing important phrases. Secondly, unlike in the scientific corpus that Leap2Trend used, where the context (which is mostly about the computer science field) is rather consistent, news collection, however, can contain numerous subjects ranging from technology, finance, economy to media.

Thus, with *Contextual Leap2Trend*, we propose to address the aforementioned disadvantages and to adapt them to our dataset an approach that is detailed in Figure 1 with the following steps: First, we pre-process our dataset to remove unwanted text in order to focus on the main content of the news article and divided the whole corpus into monthly sub-corpora (Section 3.3). The next step identify potential keywords from the corpus by calculating the TF-IDF value as well as apply LDA to generate a list of top-rated bi-grams (Section 3.4). Afterward, contextualized representations are generated for these trending keywords for each month (Section 3.5). We then rank the pair of keywords based on their representation similarity (Section

[3]`https://trends.google.com/trends/?geo=US`

3.6). Lastly, we assess the contextual trend evolution in Section 3.7 by analyzing the change in ranking in each pair of keywords over each time span.

3.3 Data Pre-processing

From our analysis of the data, there are text patterns that appear relatively frequent in the corpus and mainly talk about Bloomberg's own publisher's detail, more exactly, the Bloomberg's standardized text as this provides no valuable knowledge to our task. Contrary, this standardized text could actually hinder the performance of a system as they could cause potential keywords to be more subtle, thus harder to be recognized. Moreover, since Bloomberg News is geared towards an audience that is interested in finance, articles usually contain an abundance of words that belong to the financial glossary (e.g. "dividend", "bond", "equity"). The existence of this vocabulary could cause the same problem as with Bloomberg's standardized text, thus is it also removed from the text. Afterward, we perform a lemmatization to return to the canonical form of the token in the text, for reducing the size of the vocabulary to process in later steps. Lastly, any article that has less than ten tokens is considered uninformative and is removed[4].

3.4 Keyword Identification

The research on *keyword identification* discovery originates from the topic detection and tracking (TDT) technology that was first studied by scholars in 1996 and its goal was making new detection and tracking within streams of broadcast news stories (Zhu et al., 2019). Emerging trends are usually signified by terms and phrases that are later considered as defining *keywords* for such themes. Hence, correctly identifying potential keywords will lead to the right direction in discovering promising dormant trends. While keywords can be n-grams, in the scope of this research, only bi-grams were considered due to the fact that compared to uni-grams, they are less ambiguous, while appearing more frequently than other n-grams. Next, we present our methods of extracting potent keywords, using TF-IDF values to generate the list of highly important bi-grams, and utilizing LDA for getting bi-grams that can represent topics.

[4]For this step, we manually checked different values of this threshold and the minimum quality of the remaining perprocessed article.

TF-IDF Bi-gram Generation TF-IDF captures how important a word is in the corpus by considering its frequency and penalizing it for appearing in too many entries in the corpus. Hence, words that are too common have considerably lower TF-IDF values than those that are less frequent. We exploited this method to extract important bi-grams from the corpus. Per month, TF-IDF values are generated for every bi-gram in the news collection and, afterward, we evaluated and produced lists of bi-grams that have either the highest average TF-IDF value in the collection or the highest single TF-IDF value across all documents. A high average TF-IDF value may indicate that a keyword associates closely with the company throughout the month, while a single high TF-IDF value signifies a sudden change in the context surrounding the company.

LDA Bi-gram Generation LDA derives from textual data the probabilities of words belonging to a predetermined number of topics. As such, the method excels at providing easily interpretable insights into what consists of a text corpus. Taking advantage of this fact, we used the results of applying LDA on the collection of texts in each month of our dataset to contextualize bi-grams by topics, which we obtained in the previous step. This is done by searching for topics that contain bi-grams in their list of words with the highest probability that represent topics. To find the optimal number of topics, we built numerous LDA models with different values of the number of topics and measured their topic coherence score (Röder et al., 2015). We chose the topic number that gives the highest coherence value. Coherence is a measure to evaluate to which degree the induced topics of an LDA model are correlated to one another, thus choosing the optimal number of topics that marks the end of the rapid growth of topic coherence usually offers meaningful and interpretable topics.

3.5 Bi-gram Contextual Representation Generation

Unlike static word embeddings that capture the global representations of words in a vocabulary, contextual embeddings aim at representing each word or sub-word in the corpus depending on the words surrounding it. Therefore, each appearance of the word will have a unique vector assigned to it, which differentiates the same token but appears in context. For example, the token "teams" in "Mi-

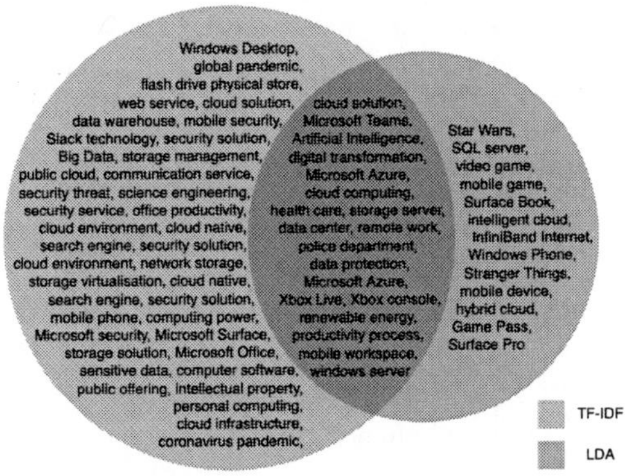

Figure 2: Keywords extracted by TF-IDF and LDA.

crosoft Teams" and "team management" should be represented by distinct vectors, as their context and usage are entirely different. Thus, a contextual embedding is generally better than static word embedding, especially in a scenario where the corpus consists of news articles and not documents containing specialized knowledge.

Because contextual embeddings usually derive vectors for one single token or a character n-gram separately, we employ the following strategy to generate bi-gram embedding to suit our need: for each occurrence of two tokens belonging to a bi-gram appears next to each other and in the right order, we generate FinBERT[5] embeddings for both tokens, and the final vector of the bi-gram is calculated by averaging them.

3.6 Keyword Pairs Contextual Ranking

With the contextual embeddings for the set of chosen keywords, we proceed to compute the similarity between each pair of keywords and rank them based on the value calculated. The idea is that when a number of terms appear frequently together, they usually share the same set of surrounding vocabulary, thus having similar context. For this, we computed the cosine similarity. Regarding how to establish the ranking, we first utilized the algorithm employed by Leap2Trend (Dridi et al., 2019), sorting the similarity of pairs of keywords in descending order, where the higher the similarity is, the lower the rank the pair of keywords has.

3.7 Assessment of Contextual Trend Evolution

Following the ranking calculation for each month, we attempted to assess the contextual evolution of each pair of keywords to identify potential emerging trends relating to the selected keywords. To achieve this, we analyze how much the rank increase/decrease between each month and set a threshold to decide whether changes in ranking signify emerging keywords that can lead to emerging trends. If the differences in ranking between the current month and the previous month of a pair of keywords are greater than the chosen threshold, we identify that this set of keywords will become the emerging terms. On the other hand, if the shift in ranking does not meet the threshold, the pair of keywords is regarded as having no potential in its emergence, either is falling off or is at standstill in terms of growth for being the next trend.

4 Experimental Setup

We present the experiments on previously mentioned dataset from Bloomberg News about Microsoft from July 2019 to July 2020. This includes the description of the evaluation process, the results of our proposed system for emerging trend detection by comparing the shift in similarity ranking of pairs of keywords, and the elaboration of the story behind some keyword pairs that were in trend, and we deemed as interesting.

4.1 Evaluation Metrics

To our knowledge at the current time of writing, there is no annotated dataset that is publicly available to experiment our method on. To produce a gold standard, the process involves examining Google Trends data, a platform for tracking terms/phrases popularity based on Google's search history, of the chosen keywords to identify where their emergence is. This was done by calculating the regression of interest rate evolution from a selected timestamp to N months forward, with a positive value indicating an increase in attention toward the keywords, thus signifying the possibility of the keywords belonging to emerging topics. Formula 1 describes the regression of interest rate evolution in the next N months, denoted as m_{hits}:

$$m_{hits} = \frac{\sum_{i=1}^{N}(x_i - \bar{x})(y_i - \bar{y})}{\sum_{i=1}^{N}(x_i - \bar{x})^2} \quad (1)$$

where x_i and y_i represent the month number and the interest rate of that month, respectively. $\bar{x}$ corresponds to the mean of the month number, while $\bar{y}$ is the mean of interest rate.

[5]https://huggingface.co/ProsusAI/finbert

With the modality Google Trends treats a string in a search query, requesting data on just the literal phrase, we experienced difficulties in extracting interest rate data for combining a pair of keywords. Thus, we devised a solution by looking for data on each keyword separately and averaging the two results to get a final interest rate of the pair of keywords. The hypothesis behind this is the assumption that both keywords are part of the same theme/topic, thus, their evolution should have a similar tendency to rise/fall, albeit having different magnitude, making the combined signal stays relatively close to the two originals in terms of signal progression. Vice versa, phrases that do not fall into the same category cannot produce a good signal, which automatically makes them irrelevant to each other.

After obtaining the gold standard, we proceed to treat the task as a classification problem, where the system will classify whether changes in ranking context can lead to the same type of movement in the gold standard in the next N months. Accordingly, the main evaluation metrics are precision, recall, and F1-measure. Not only do we consider the macro metrics, but we also take into account the aforementioned metrics on the true class detection specifically, since our focus is leaning toward correctly identifying emerging trends, which is signified by the true class. Additionally, we report the receiver operating characteristic (ROC) curves according to the selected time span onward with the purpose of assessing the detection capability on how many months forward can our system detect trends emergent effectively.

4.2 Keyword Generation and Selection

After the keyword generation step (bi-gram generation with TF-IDF and LDA), we noticed that while extracting bi-grams using raw TF-IDF value yielded many potential keywords (68 keywords), the amount of bi-gram that also existed in the LDA results was significantly lower (36 keywords). The intersection of the two lists resulted in a set of 22 keywords. The abundant amount of terms generated by TF-IDF and the high number of intersected keywords between two methods suggests that results from TF-IDF are less specific than that of LDA. From our observation, the semantics of keywords in the intersect region cover not only the general topics and trends such as health care due to COVID-19 pandemic, but also specific development direction of Microsoft. Figure 2 details further on the list of extracted bi-grams and a total number of bi-grams yielded by each method.

4.3 Results

We compare the performance of two systems: the original Leap2Trend that used monthly static Word2Vec embeddings and our *Contextual Leap2Trend*. We set the threshold=0 for both system to imply that any positive change in context can signify potential emerging keywords.

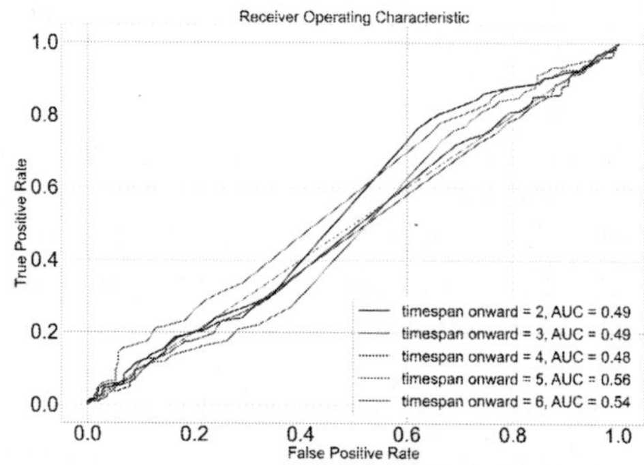

(a) Original Leap2Trend

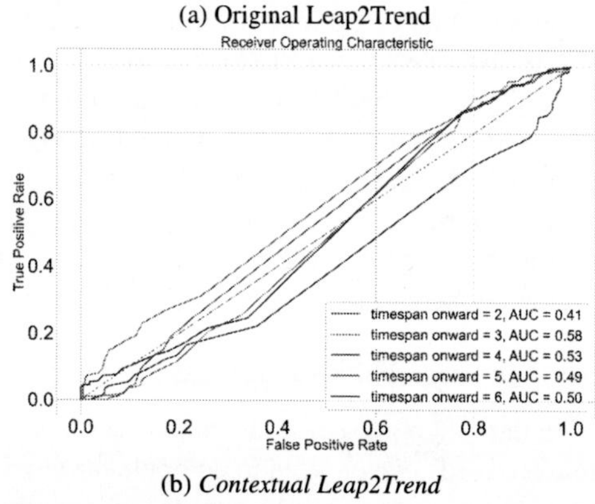

(b) *Contextual Leap2Trend*

Figure 3: Compared ROC curves based on timespan adjustment (threshold = 0).

Figure 3b demonstrates the predictive capability of what is the optimal number of months forward the *Contextual Leap2Trend* respectively can perform the task efficiently. The two system outperformed one another in different timespan onward scenario, with the original Leap2Trend has better area under the curve (AUC) when assessing keywords trendiness potential within the span of 5 and 6 months(0.56 and 0.54 in AUC respectively). However, the *Contextual Leap2Trend* system has the AUC of 0.57 when predicting 3-month forward which not only exceed the original system in the same category (0.49), but also is the best result overall. This observation suggests that by using contextual embeddings, our system surpasses the original Leap2Trend in terms of timeliness property which is crucial for the task of detecting emerging trend. In addition, the *Contextual Leap2Trend* matches the original system in AUC (0.54) in the scenario of timespan forward=6.

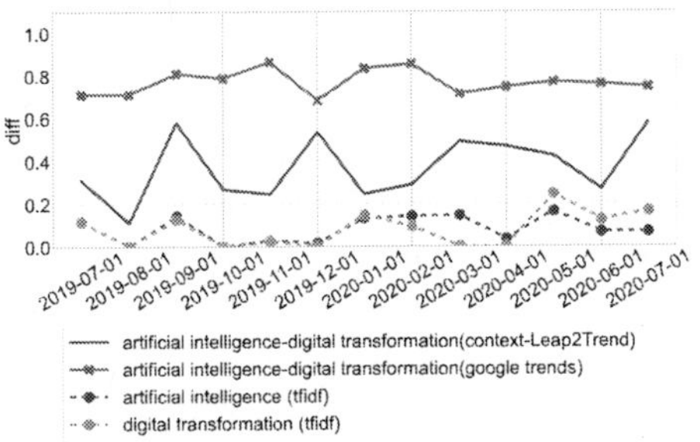

(a) A.I./Digital Transformation

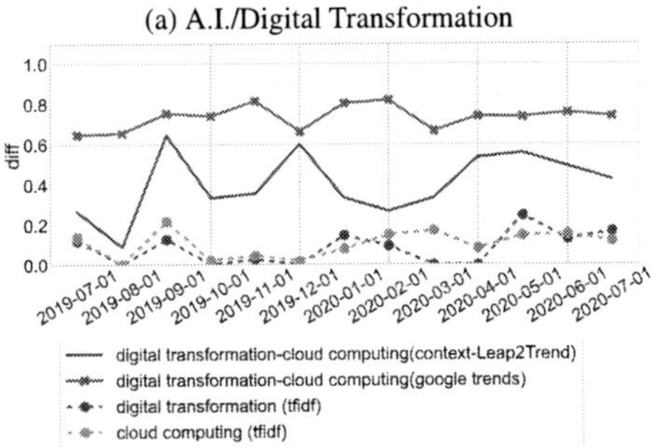

(b) Digital Transformation/Cloud Computing

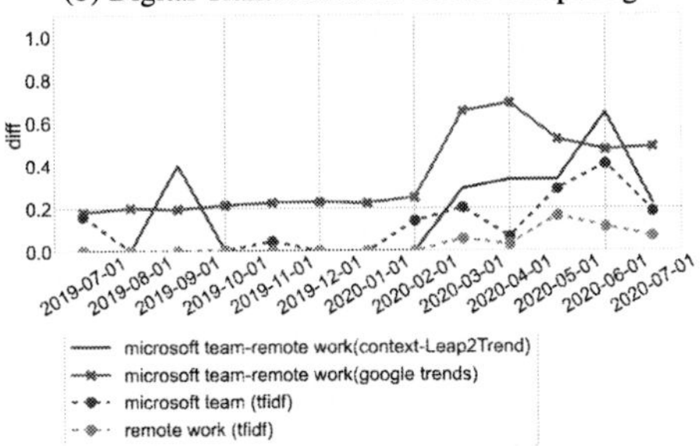

(c) Microsoft Teams/Remote Work

Figure 4: Trends for the chosen pairs of keywords.

While the proposed system is more efficient at predicting trends three months in advance, with the current dataset, the task is considerably challenging. In order to gauge the performance of our system, we compared the results of a system with threshold of 0 to a zero rule baseline where every possible bi-gram was considered as trendy (True class), thus True class metrics were not taken into account for this experiment. Table 1 shows that our system out-performed the zero rule baseline in all three metrics, but are only marginally better in terms of recall and F1 value. This observation further supports the difficulty of the task present using the current data.

Another observation is when comparing the change in ranking to Google Trends data, we notice that delays sometimes exists, usually of one month due to data split in the pre-processing phase, in how soon the ranking change with respect to Google Trends, meaning the timeliness aspect of detecting emerging trends might be affected. One possible explanation is that Bloomberg News could be behind in terms of timing compare to public response as Bloomberg mostly covers big events that were already happened, and does not cover innovations process that can lead to such event.

In following sections, we discuss several example pairs of keywords that signified ongoing trends and emerging ones, mainly about what was happening surround the keywords while comparing the graph between Google Trends and contextual ranking evolution of *Contextual Leap2Trend* system.

Table 1: Proposed approach vs. zero rule baseline, timespan onward =3.

Method	Thresh	Precision	Recall	Macro F1
Zero-rule baseline		0.3000	0.5000	0.3700
Original Leap2Trend	0	0.5384	0.5330	0.5276
Contextual Leap2Trend	0	**0.5600**	**0.5476**	**0.5388**

4.4 A. I. - Digital Transformation

Compared to Google Trends data, for the *artificial intelligence (A.I.) - digital transformation* pair of keywords, our proposed contextual ranking reflects their trends accordingly, as shown in Figure 4a. Digital transformation and artificial intelligence have been an ongoing conversation in technology and business in recent years as the movement seeks an effort to incorporate A.I. into digitizing business processes, customer experiences, etc. This is illustrated through the European Union's strategy to apply A.I. to digital transformation[6]. As for Microsoft, the company supports this trend with multiple projects, one of them being a major col-

[6]`https://ec.europa.eu/commission/presscorner/detail/en/qanda_20_264`

laboration was mentioned in the EDF data[7].

4.5 Digital Transformation - Cloud Computing

Within the context of the corpus, the *digital transformation - cloud computing* pair of keywords describes how Microsoft's cloud computing service contribute to their involvement in advancing Digital Transformation with their business partners by providing Azure, Microsoft's leading cloud platform, to enhance the digital capability of their business partner[8]. According to Figure 4b, the contextual ranking changes of the pair, in general, are in-line with Google Trends data, albeit displayed some level of differences.

One thing to note is that it is the consensus, mentioned throughout the COVID-19 period in our corpus, regarding *Digital Transformation* that because of the pandemic pushing society to stay distant and work remotely, the *Digital Transformation* process will need to be developed faster to adapt to the current situation. In Figures 4b and 4a, it can be seen that this opinion were reflected through an increase in rankings starting March 2020. This period is also where the interest rate on Google Trends on this matter started to increase again after a dip.

4.6 Microsoft Teams - Remote Work

While the magnitude displayed in Figure 4c was definitely lower than Google Trends's signal, Leap2Trend's signal visually still showed signs that the trends of the *Microsoft Teams - remote work* pair of keywords have potential. Remote work, while being lesser known in 2019, has been a staple since the COVID-19 pandemic began. Zoom, a platform for online meetings, was booming at the start of the pandemic, yet fell in popularity due to security reasons. The slump of Zoom paved the way for the rise of Microsoft Teams as the reliable platform for workplace communication[9]. In our EDF dataset, the development of Microsoft Teams with new and better features also aid in its popularity[10].

5 Conclusions

This research addressed the drawback of existing methods in keyword extraction, bi-gram representation due to the differences in writing style between scientific papers and news articles. We, instead, introduced a combination of TF-IDF and LDA for generating potential keywords, and utilized contextual embeddings for the change in temporality. Our *Contextual Leap2Trend* system showed considerable improvements compared to the original method in some scenarios in length of prediction. Moreover, we also presented several examples of emerging trends found in our data and the result also suggested that the approach has a good timeliness characteristic. In future work, we plan to introduce a better variety of data, such as news articles covering more companies and sector, to further experiment and improve our system. Moreover, increasing the time intervals could also uphold the consideration to assess trends longevity.

References

Sahar Behpour, Mohammadmahdi Mohammadi, Mark V. Albert, Zinat S. Alam, Lingling Wang, and Ting Xiao. 2021. Automatic trend detection: Time-biased document clustering. *Knowledge-Based Systems*, 220:106907.

Swarupananda Bissoyi, Brojo Kishore Mishra, and Raghvendra Kumar. 2020. Discovering trending topics from the tweets by odia news media during covid-19.

Levent Bolelli, Seyda Ertekin, and C. Lee Giles. 2009. Topic and trend detection in text collections using latent dirichlet allocation. In *ECIR*.

Jethro Borsje, Frederik Hogenboom, and Flavius Frasincar. 2010. Semi-automatic financial events discovery based on lexico-semantic patterns. *International Journal of Web Engineering and Technology*, 6(2):115–140.

Tuan-Dung Cao, Tat-Huy Tran, and Thanh-Thuy Luu. 2018. Hot topic detection on newspaper. In *Proceedings of the Ninth International Symposium on Information and Communication Technology*, SoICT 2018, page 114–121, New York, NY, USA. Association for Computing Machinery.

[7] https://www.bloomberg.com/press-releases/2020-03-26/c3-ai-microsoft-and-leading-universities-launch-c3-ai-digital-transformation-institute

[8] https://www.bloomberg.com/press-releases/2020-04-07/blackrock-and-microsoft-form-strategic-partnership-to-host-aladdin-on-azure-as-blackrock-readies-aladdin-for-next-chapter-of

[9] https://www.computerweekly.com/news/252485100/Microsoft-Teams-usage-growth-surpasses-Zoom

[10] https://www.bloomberg.com/news/articles/2020-03-19/microsoft-teams-boosts-work-at-home-effort

Qi Dang, Feng Gao, and Yadong Zhou. 2016. Early detection method for emerging topics based on dynamic bayesian networks in micro-blogging networks. *Expert Syst. Appl.*, 57(C):285–295.

Ali Daud, Faizan Abbas, Tehmina Amjad, Abdulrahman A. Alshdadi, and Jalal S. Alowibdi. 2021. Finding rising stars through hot topics detection. *Future Gener. Comput. Syst.*, 115:798–813.

Amna Dridi, M. Gaber, R. Muhammad Atif Azad, and J. Bhogal. 2019. Leap2trend: A temporal word embedding approach for instant detection of emerging scientific trends. *IEEE Access*, 7:176414–176428.

Israel Griol-Barres, Sergio Milla, Antonio Cebrián, Huaan Fan, and Jose Millet. 2020. Detecting weak signals of the future: A system implementation based on text mining and natural language processing. *Sustainability*, 12(19).

Qi He, Bi Chen, Jian Pei, Baojun Qiu, Prasenjit Mitra, and C. Lee Giles. 2009. Detecting topic evolution in scientific literature: how can citations help? *Proceedings of the 18th ACM conference on Information and knowledge management.*

Jack Hughes, Seth Aycock, Andrew Caines, Paula Buttery, and Alice Hutchings. 2020. Detecting trending terms in cybersecurity forum discussions. In *Proceedings of the Sixth Workshop on Noisy User-generated Text (W-NUT 2020)*, pages 107–115, Online. Association for Computational Linguistics.

Lara Kassab, Alona Kryshchenko, Hanbaek Lyu, Denali Molitor, Deanna Needell, and Elizaveta Rebrova. 2020. On nonnegative matrix and tensor decompositions for covid-19 twitter dynamics. *ArXiv*, abs/2010.01600.

Won Sang Lee and So Young Sohn. 2017. Identifying emerging trends of financial business method patents. *Sustainability*, 9(9).

Chuanzhen Li, Minqiao Liu, Juanjuan Cai, Yang Yu, and Hui Wang. 2020. Topic detection and tracking based on windowed dbscan and parallel knn. *IEEE Access.*

Mathis Linger and Mhamed Hajaiej. 2020. Batch clustering for multilingual news streaming. *arXiv preprint arXiv:2004.08123.*

Bang Liu, Fred X. Han, Di Niu, Linglong Kong, Kunfeng Lai, and Yu Xu. 2020. Story forest: Extracting events and telling stories from breaking news. *ACM Trans. Knowl. Discov. Data*, 14(3).

Hassan H. Malik, Vikas S. Bhardwaj, and Huascar Fiorletta. 2011. Accurate information extraction for quantitative financial events. In *Proceedings of the 20th ACM International Conference on Information and Knowledge Management*, CIKM '11, pages 2497–2500, New York, NY, USA. ACM.

Binling Nie and Shouqian Sun. 2017. Using text mining techniques to identify research trends: A case study of design research. *Applied Sciences*, 7:401.

Ridam Pal, Harshit Chopra, Raghav Awasthi, Harsh Bandhey, Aditya Nagori, Arun Gulati, Ponnurangam Kumaraguru, and Tavpritesh Sethi. 2021. Predicting emerging themes in rapidly expanding covid-19 literature with dynamic word embedding networks and machine learning. In *medRxiv*.

Sinya Peng, Vincent S. Tseng, Che-Wei Liang, and M. K. Shan. 2018. Emerging product topics prediction in social media without social structure information. *Companion Proceedings of the The Web Conference 2018.*

Michael Röder, Andreas Both, and Alexander Hinneburg. 2015. Exploring the space of topic coherence measures. *Proceedings of the Eighth ACM International Conference on Web Search and Data Mining.*

Enrico De Santis, A. Martino, and A. Rizzi. 2020. An infoveillance system for detecting and tracking relevant topics from italian tweets during the covid-19 event. *IEEE Access*, 8:132527–132538.

Shuo Xu, Liyuan Hao, Xin An, Guancan Yang, and Feifei Wang. 2019. Emerging research topics detection with multiple machine learning models. *J. Informetrics*, 13.

Zhiliang Zhu, Jie Liang, Deyang Li, Hai Yu, and Guoqi Liu. 2019. Hot topic detection based on a refined tf-idf algorithm. *IEEE Access*, 7:26996–27007.

AstBERT: Enabling Language Model for Financial Code Understanding with Abstract Syntax Trees

Rong Liang
Ant Group
liangrong.liang@antgroup.com

Tiehua Zhang*
Ant Group
zhangtiehua.zth@antgroup.com

Yujie Lu
Ant Group
lyj272836@antgroup.com

Yuze Liu
Ant Group
liuyuze.liuyuze@antgroup.com

Zhen Huang
Ant Group
hz101346@antgroup.com

Xin Chen
Ant Group
jinming.cx@antgroup.com

Abstract

Using the pre-trained language models to understand source codes has attracted increasing attention from financial institutions owing to the great potential to uncover financial risks. However, there are several challenges in applying these language models to solve programming language related problems directly. For instance, the shift of domain knowledge between natural language (NL) and programming language (PL) requires understanding the semantic and syntactic information from the data from different perspectives. To this end, we propose the AstBERT model, a pre-trained PL model aiming to better understand the financial codes using the abstract syntax tree (AST). Specifically, we collect a sheer number of source codes (both Java and Python) from the Alipay code repository and incorporate both syntactic and semantic code knowledge into our model through the help of code parsers, in which AST information of the source codes can be interpreted and integrated. We evaluate the performance of the proposed model on three tasks, including code question answering, code clone detection and code refinement. Experiment results show that our AstBERT achieves promising performance on three different downstream tasks.

1 Introduction

Programming language and source code analysis using deep learning methods have received increasing attention in recent years. Using pre-trained model such as such as BERT (Devlin et al., 2019), AlBERT (Lan et al., 2020) receive a great success on different NLP tasks. Inspired by that, some researchers attempt to apply this technique to comprehend source codes. For instance, CodeBERT (Feng et al., 2020) is a pre-trained model using six different programming languages from GitHub, demonstrating a good performance comparing with different embedding techniques.

Although pre-trained models are now widely used for different purposes, it is rare to see how to apply such techniques to financial service codes. It is believed that re-training the model using financial service code could help uncover the code hazards before being released and circumvent any economic damage (Guo et al., 2021). Existing research points out that the use of domain knowledge is critical when it comes to training a well-performing model, and one way to solve this problem is to pre-train a model using specific domain corpora from scratch (Hellendoorn et al., 2019). However, pre-training a model is generally time-consuming and computationally expensive, and domain corpora are often not enough for pre-training tasks, especially in the financial industry, where the number of open-sourced codes is limited.

To this end, we propose an AstBERT model, a pre-trained language model aiming to better understand the financial codes using abstract syntax trees (AST). To be more specific, AST is a tree structure description of code semantics. Instead of using source code directly, we leverage AST as the prominent input information when training and tuning AstBERT. To overcome the token explosion problem that usually happens when generating the AST from the large-scale code base, a pruning method is applied beforehand, followed by a designated AST-Embedding Layer to encode the pruned code syntax information. To save the training time and resources, we adopt the pre-trained CodeBERT (Feng et al., 2020) as our inception model and continue to train on the large quantity of AST corpus. In this way, AstBERT can capture semantic information for both nature language (NL) and programming language (PL).

We train AstBERT on both Python and Java corpus collected from Alipay code repositories, which contains about 0.2 million functions in java and 0.1 million functions in python. Then we evaluate its performance on different downstream tasks. The

*Corresponding Author

Proceedings of the Fourth Workshop on Financial Technology and Natural Language Processing (FinNLP), pages 10 - 17
December 8, 2022 ©2022 Association for Computational Linguistics

main contributions of this work can be summarized as follows:

- We propose a simple yet effective way to enhance the pre-trained language model's ability to understand programming languages in the financial domain with the help of abstract syntax tree information.
- We conduct extensive experiments to verify the performance of AstBERT on code-related tasks, including code question answering, code clone detection and code refinement. Experiments results show that AstBERT demonstrates a promising performance for all three downstream tasks.

2 Related Work

In this part, we describe existing pre-trained models and datasets in code language interpretation in detail.

2.1 Datasets in Code Understanding

It is inevitable to leverage a high-quality dataset in order to pre-train a model that excels in code understanding. Some researchers have started to build up the dataset needed for the code search task in (Nie et al., 2016), in which different questions and answers are collected from Stack Overflow. Also, a large-scale unlabeled text-code pairs are extracted and formed from GitHub by (Husain et al., 2019). Three benchmark datasets are builed by (Heyman and Van Cutsem, 2020), each of which consists of a code snippet collection and a set of queries. An evaluation dataset developed by (Li et al., 2019) consists of natural language question and code snippet pairs. They manually check whether the questions meet the requirements and filter out the ambiguous pairs. A model trained by (Yin et al., 2018) on a human-annotated dataset is used to automatically mine massive natural language and code pairs from Stack Overflow. Recently, CoSQA dataset constructed by (Huang et al., 2021) that includes 20,604 labels for pairs of natural language queries and codes. CoSQA is annotated by human annotators and it is obtained from real-world queries and Python functions. It is rare to find open-sourced public source code in the financial domain, and we therefore retrieve both Python and Java code from the Alipay code repositories.

2.2 Models in Code Understanding

Using deep learning network to solve language-code tasks has been studied for years. A Multi-Modal Attention Network trained by (Wan et al., 2019) represents unstructured and structured features of source code with two LSTM. A masked language model(Kanade et al., 2019) is trained on massive Python code obtained from GitHub and used to obtain a high-quality embedding for source code. A set of embeddings (Karampatsis and Sutton, 2020) based on ELMo (Peters et al., 2018) and conduct bug detection task. The results prove that even a low-dimensional embedding trained on a small corpus of programs is very useful for downstream task. Svyatkovskiy et al. use GPT-2 framework and train it from scratch on source code data to support code generative task like code completion (Svyatkovskiy et al., 2020). CodeBERT (Feng et al., 2020) is a multi-PL (programming language) pretrained model for code and natural language, and it is trained with the new learning objective based on replaced token detection. C-BERT proposed by (Buratti et al., 2020) is pre-trained from C language source code collected from GitHub to do AST node tagging task.

Different with previous work, AstBERT is a simple yet effective way to use pre-trained model in code interpretation field. Instead of training a large-scale model from scratch, it incorporates AST information into a common language model, from which the code understanding can be derived.

3 AstBERT

In this part, we describe the details about AstBERT.

3.1 Model Architecture

Figure 1 shows the main architecture of AstBERT. Instead of using source code directly, the pruned AST information is used as the input. For each source code token, the AST information is attached in the front, and the position index is used to show the order of the input. There are four embedding modules at the AST embedding layer. Token embedding is similar to what is in BERT (Devlin et al., 2019), one key difference is that the vocabularies used are AST keywords. The token is then encoded to a vector format. Additionally, in AstBERT, AST-segment and AST-position are used to integrate the structure information of AST, the detail of their function will be introduced in subsection 3.3. After the AST embedding layer, the embedding vectors

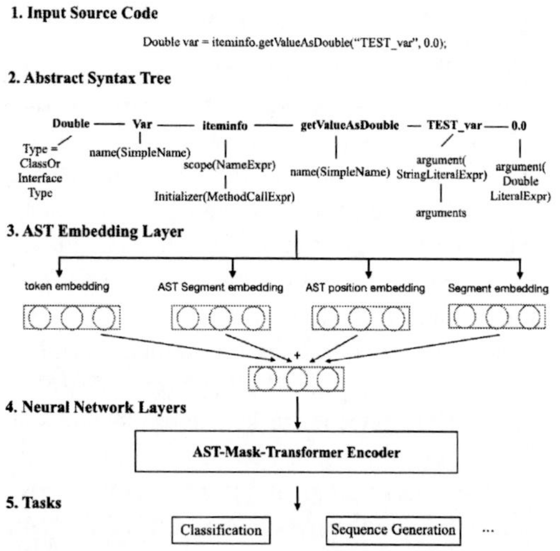

Figure 1: The model structure of AstBERT: An easy and effective way to enhance pre-trained language model's ability for code understanding

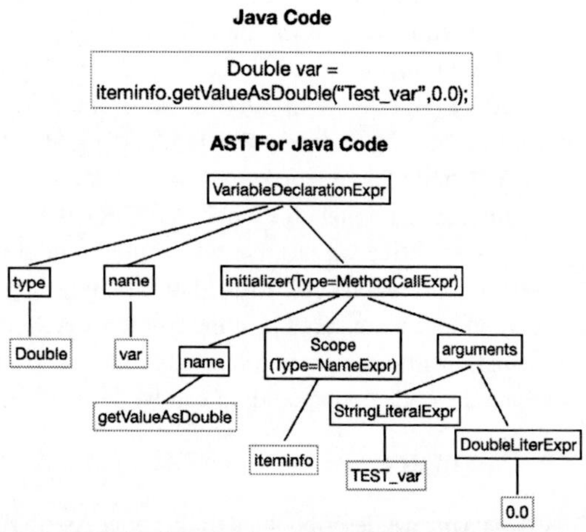

Figure 2: AST-based code representation of a financial code snippet

are then forwarded to a multi-layer bidirectional AST-Mask-Transformer encoder (Vaswani et al., 2017) to generate hidden vectors. The difference is that we use AST-Mask-Self-Attention instead of Self-Attention to calculate the attention score, the detail of which will be unveiled in subsection 3.4. In the output layer, the hidden vectors generated by AST-Mask-Transformer encoder will be used for classification or sequence generation tasks.

3.2 Input and Pruning

We introduce the pruning process in this part. As shown in Figure 2, the AST contains the complete

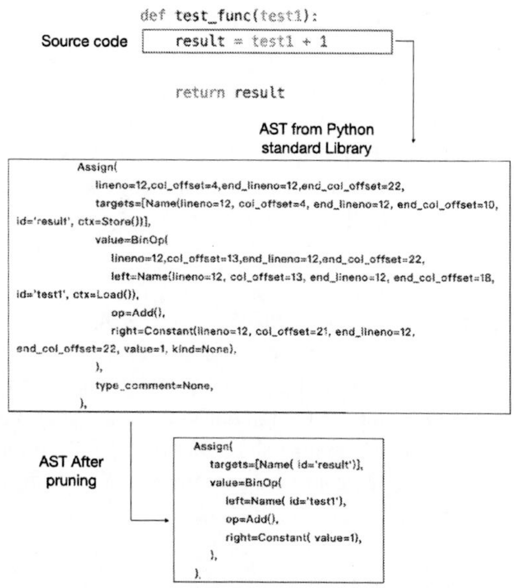

Figure 3: AST pruning process

information of the source code and provide the brief description for each token. For example, the *getValueAsDouble* is the name for *MethodCallExpr* (one of the AST node types) and the *TEST_var* is an argument for *MethodCallExpr*. We know the *Double* is a type of the variable *var* from AST. Such AST information reveals the semantic knowledge of the source code.

In general, the length of AST from the compiled codes is greater than the plain source code, as shown in Figure 3, the AST from Python standard library contains a number of nodes such as *lineno*, *endlineno* and so on. Taking the snippet *result = test1 + 1* as an example, both the original and pruned AST trees can be seen in Figure 3. It is clearly noticed that there exists a large amount of redundant information such as line number and code column offset in the original AST tree, leading to intractable AST exploration problem for large code corpus (Wan et al., 2019). Therefore, after generating AST, we will prune this tree by removing the meaningless and uninformed node to avoid unintended input for the model.

3.3 AST Embedding Layer

As mentioned above, we use the pruned AST as the input for model, and it will pass AST embedding layer first. The details of the AST embedding layer are unveiled in Figure 4, from which token-embedding vectors, AST-segment embedding vectors, AST-position embedding vectors and segment

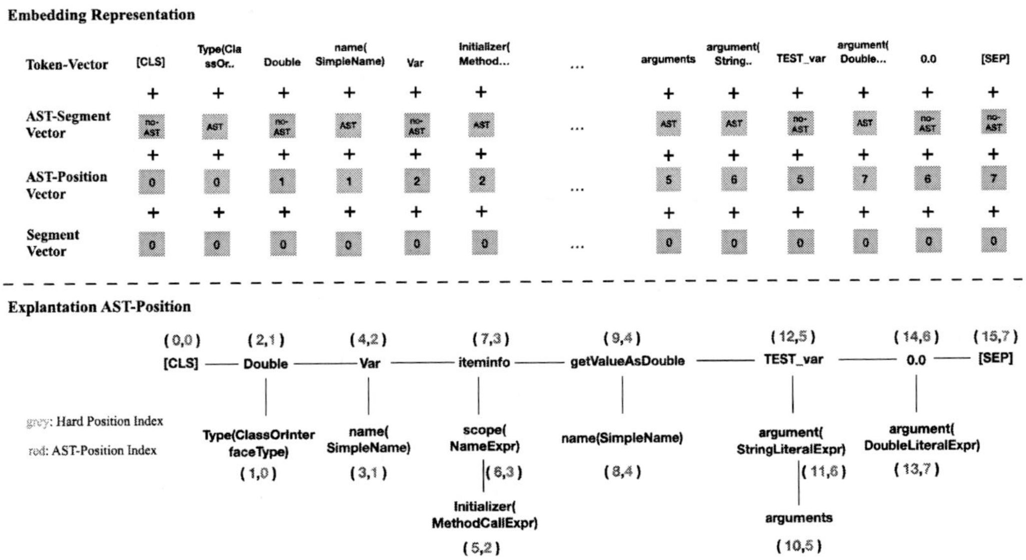

Figure 4: The overview of AST embedding representations

embedding vectors are generated. Taking the code snippet in Figure 2 as an example, we can see the additional AST information account for most of the tokens in the input, which unexpectedly causes changes in the meaning of the original code. To prevent this from happening, we use AST-segment embedding to distinguish between AST tokens and source code tokens. It is known that in BERT all the order information for input sequence is contained in the position embedding, allowing us to add different position information for input. Here, except for the AST-segment, we use an index combination of hard-position and AST-position to convey the order information. As seen in Figure 4, the index combination of *name(SimpleName)* is *(3,1)*, which means it locates at the 3rd position in the input sequence dimension while being the 1st AST token. In the front of *name(SimpleName)*, there is only one extra AST token named *Type(ClassOrInterfaceType)*. Segment embedding is similar to BERT. The output of the embedding layer is simply the sum of all embedding vectors from these four parts. The result is then passed into the AST-Mask transformer encoder to generate hidden vectors.

3.4 AST-Mask Transformer

Since the branch in AST contains the specific semantic knowledge to describe the role of the code token, it is rational to make AST tokens only contribute to the code tokens on the same branch. For example, in

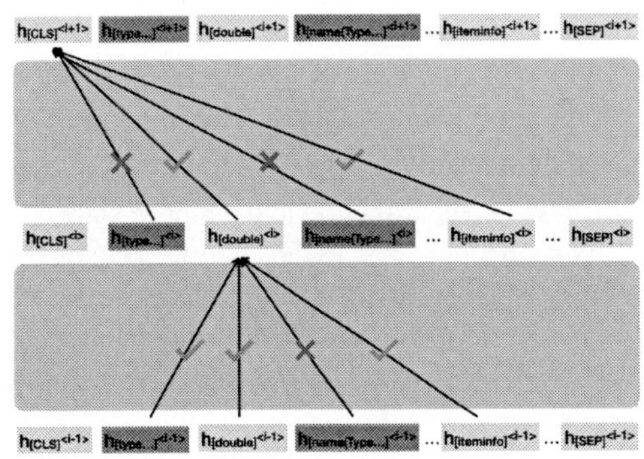
Figure 5: The explanation of AST-Mask-Transformer

Figure 2, [*Type=ClassOrInterfaceType*] only describe the role of the [*Double*] and has nothing to do with [*Var*]. Therefore, the embedding of [*Var*] should not be affected by [*Type=ClassOrInterfaceType*]. As demonstrated in Figure 5, the *Type=ClassOrInterfaceType* should not make a contribution to the embedding of [*CLS*] tag that often used for classification bypass the [*Double*]. This is because that the [*Type=ClassOrInterfaceType*] is a tag in the branch of [*Double*] and should only correlate to [*Double*]. To prevent the AST information injection from changing the semantic of the input, AstBERT employs Mask-Self-Attention(Xu et al., 2021) to limit the self-attention region in Transformer(Vaswani et al., 2017). We use AST matrix M to describe whether the AST token and code token are on the same branch, M_{AST} is defined as follow:

$$M_{AST_{i,j}} = \begin{cases} 1 & w_i \oplus w_j \\ 0 & w_i \otimes w_j \end{cases} \quad (1)$$

where, $w_i \oplus w_j$ indicates that w_i and w_j are on the same AST branch, while $w_i \otimes w_j$ are not. i and j are the AST-position index. The AST mask matrix is then used to calculate the self-attention scores. Formally, the AST-mask-self-attention is defined as follow:

$$Q^{i+1}, K^{i+1}, V^{i+1} = h^i W_q, h^i W_k, h^i W_v \quad (2)$$

$$S^{i+1} = softmax(\frac{K^{i+1^T} Q^{i+1} M_{AST}}{\sqrt{d_k}}) \quad (3)$$

$$h^{i+1} = S^{i+1} V^{i+1} \quad (4)$$

where W_q, W_k, W_v are trainable model parameters. h^i is the hidden state from the ith AST-mask-self-attention blocks. d_k is the scaling factor. If h^i_k and h^i_j are not in same AST branch, the $M_{AST_{kj}}$ will make the attention score S^{i+1}_{kj} to 0, which means h^i_k makes no contribution to the hidden state of h^i_j.

We collect massive Python and Java codes from Alipay code repositories and generate the AST for these source code (Python code using standard AST API, Java code using Javaparser). We use these processed AST information to continue the pre-train of the model. The technique of pre-training is inspired by the masked language modeling (MLM), which is proposed by (Devlin et al., 2019) and proven effective.

4 Experiments

We test the performance of our proposed model on different code understating tasks using the different released test datasets. We also look into the ablation studies.

4.1 Dataset

Code Question Answering CoSQA (Huang et al., 2021) consists of 20,604 query-code pairs collected from the Microsoft Bing search engine. We randomly split CoSQA into 20,000 training and 604 validation examples. We also build AliCoQA dataset based on the code collected from the Alipay code repositories. We use the search logs from AntCode search engine as the source of queries and manually design heuristic rules to find the queries of code searching intent. For example, queries with the word of *tutorial* or *example* are likely to locate a programming description rather than a code function, so we remove such queries. Then, we use the CodeBERT matching model (Feng et al., 2020) to retrieve high-confidence codes for every query and manually check 5,000 query-code pairs to construct AliCoQA. We randomly split AliCoQA into 4,500 training and 500 validation samples.

Code Clone Detection We use BigCloneBench dataset (Svajlenko et al., 2014) and discard samples with no labels. Finally, we randomly split it into 901,724 training set and 416,328 validation set.

Code Refinement BFP (Tufano et al., 2019) dataset constains two subsets based on the code length. For BFP_small dataset, the numbers of training and validation are 46,680 and 5,835, respectively. For the BFP_medium dataset, the numbers of training and validation are 52,364 and 6,545. We collect code from Alipay code repositories and build AliCoRF dataset. Firstly, we identify commits having a message containing the words, such as *fix*, *solve*, *bug*, *problem* and *issue*. Following that, for each bug-fixing commit, we extract the source code before and after the bug-fix. Finally, we manually check 9,000 bug-fix pairs to construct AliCoRF and randomly split it into 8,000 training set and 1,000 validation set.

Evaluation Metric Following the settings in the previous work, we use accuracy as the evaluation metric on code question answering, and F1 score on code clone detection. We also use accuracy as the evaluation metric on code refinement, in which only the example being detected and fixed properly will be considered successfully completing the task. We give one example case for this task in Figure 6. In this example, the model successfully fixes the method name from *getMin* to *getMax*.

4.2 Parameter Settings

We follow the similar parameter settings in previous works (Huang et al., 2021; Svajlenko et al., 2014; Tufano et al., 2019). On code question answering task, we set dropout rate to 0.1, maximum sequence length to 512, learning rate to 1e-5, warm-up rate to 0.1 and batch size to 16. On code clone detection task, learning rate is set to be 2e-5, batch size to be 16 and maximum sequence length to be 512. On code refinement task, we set learning rate to 1e-4, batch size to 32 and maximum

		Datasets					
		ACC					F1
TASK	Model	AliCoQA	CoSQA	BFP_small	BFP_medium	AliCoRF	BigCloneBench
Question Answering	BERT	0.402	0.399	\	\	\	\
	RoBERTA	0.434	0.421	\	\	\	\
	CodeBERT	0.532	0.526	\	\	\	\
	AstBERT	**0.588**	**0.571**	\	\	\	\
Code Refinement	LSTM	\	\	0.100	0.025	0.111	\
	Transformer	\	\	0.147	0.037	0.152	\
	CodeBERT	\	\	0.164	0.052	0.176	\
	GraphCodeBERT	\	\	0.173	**0.091**	0.182	\
	AstBERT	\	\	**0.176**	0.089	**0.183**	\
Code Clone	CDLH	\	\	\	\	\	0.820
	ASTNN	\	\	\	\	\	0.930
	FA-AST-GMN	\	\	\	\	\	0.950
	RoBERTa	\	\	\	\	\	0.957
	CodeBERT	\	\	\	\	\	0.965
	GraphCodeBERT	\	\	\	\	\	0.971
	AstBERT	\	\	\	\	\	**0.973**

Table 1: Experiment results of different tasks on different dataset

buggy code

```
public int getMaxItem(List input_list){
  if(input_list.size() >=0){
      return ListProcesser.getMin(input_list)
  }
  return 0;
}
```

fixed code

```
public int getMaxItem(List input_list){
  if(input_list.size() >=0){
      return ListProcesser.getMax(input_list)
  }
  return null;
}
```

Figure 6: One case of AstBERT output for code refinement task.

sequence length to 256. For all experiments, we use the Adam optimizer to update model parameters (Kingma and Ba, 2015).

4.3 Results of Code Question Answering

We use CoSQA (Junjie Huang et al. 2021) dataset to verify the code question answering task. In this task, the test sample is the query-code pair and labeled as either "1" or "0", indicating whether the code can answer the query. These query-code pairs are collected from Microsoft Bing search engine and annotated by human. We train different benchmark models using our dataset and evaluate the performance of each on CoSQA for code question answering:(i) BERT proposed by (Devlin et al., 2019); (ii) RoBERTA proposed by (Liu et al., 2019); (iii) CodeBERT proposed by (Feng et al., 2020); and (iv) AstBERT. From Table 1, we can see the BERT and RoBERTA achieve a similar yet relative low Acc score in this task. This is because these two models are pre-trained by natural language corpus and not integrated with any code-related domain knowledge. CodeBERT achieves a better performance than the RoBERTA, similar to the results published by (Huang et al., 2021). Our AstBERT achieves the best performance compared with all benchmarks. This clearly demonstrates that the integration of AST information into the model can further improve model's ability for understanding semantic and syntactic information in the codes. We also evaluate our AstBERT on AliCoQA and the results show that in financial domain dataset AstBERT also achieves the best performance.

	Datasets				
	ACC				F1
Model	CoSQA	AliCoQA	BFP	AliCoRF	BigCloneBench
AstBERT	**0.571**	**0.588**	**0.176**	**0.183**	**0.973**
-w/o AST-position	0.552	0.558	0.174	0.181	0.970
-w/o AST-Mask-Self-Attention	0.539	0.544	0.165	0.178	0.966

Table 2: Ablation study

4.4 Results of Code Clone Detection

Code clone detection is an another task when it comes to measuring the similarity of code-code pair, which can help reduce the cost of software maintenance. We use BigCloneBench (Svajlenko et al., 2014) dataset for this task and treat this task as a binary classification to fine-tune AstBert. The experimental results are also shown in the Table 2. The **CDLH** model is proposed by (Wei and Li, 2017) to learn representations of code by AST-based LSTM and use hamming distance as optimization objective. The **ASTNN** model (Zhang et al., 2019) encodes AST subtrees by RNNs to learn representation for code. The **FA-AST-GMN** model (Wang et al., 2020) uses a flow-augmented AST as the input and leverages GNNs to learn the representation for a program. The **GraphCodeBERT** (Guo et al., 2021), which is a pre-trained model using data flow at the pre-training stage to leverage the semantic-level structure of code, learns the representation of code. The experiment shows that our AstBERT achieves the best results in code clone detection task.

4.5 Results of Code Refinement

In general, code refinement is the task of locating code defects and automatically fixing them, which has been considered critical to uncovering any financial risks. We use both BFP_small and BFP_medium datasets (Tufano et al., 2019) to verify the performance of all models and show results in the Table 1. This is a Seq2Seq task, and we record relevant accuracy for each benchmark model. We take the results of **LSTM** and **Transformer** as recorded in (Guo et al., 2021). It is observed in the table that **Transformer** outperforms **LSTM**, which indicates that **Transformer** has a better ability of learning the representation of code. Both **CodeBERT** and **GraphCodeBERT** are pre-trained models, which present state-of-the-art results at their time. Our **AstBERT** achieves a better performance than other pre-trained models on BFP_small dataset, while obtaining the competitive result on BFP_medium dataset. This again demonstrates the effectiveness of incorporating the AST information in the pre-trained model is helpful to the code understanding, including the code refinement task.

4.6 Ablation Studies

In this subsection, we explore the effects of the AST-position and AST-Mask-Self-Attention for AstBERT on three tasks. "**w/o AST-position**" refers to fine-tuning AstBERT without AST-position. "**w/o AST-Mask-Self-attention**" means that each token in input, regardless of its position in the AST tree, calculates the attention scores with other tokens. As shown in Table 2, we have made the following observations: (i) Without AST-position or AST-Mask-Self-Attention, the performance of AstBERT on code question answering has shown a clear decline; (ii) It also can be seen that the model without AST-Mask-Self-Attention demonstrates an even worse performance than without AST-position, which confirms sufficient AST tokens can help incorporate the syntactic structures of the code. The same trend can also be observed on code clone detection and code refinement. We can conclude that the AST-position and the AST-Mask-Self-Attention play a pivotal role in incorporating the AST information into the model.

5 Conclusion

In this paper, we propose AstBERT, a simple and effective way to enable pre-trained language model for financial code understanding by integrating semantic information from the abstract syntax tree (AST). In order to encode the structural information, AstBERT uses a designated AST-Segment and AST-Position in the embedding layer to make model incorporate such AST information. Following that, we propose the AST-Mask-Self-Attention to limit the region when calculating attention scores, preventing the input from deviating from its original meaning. We conduct three different code understanding related tasks to evaluate the performance of the AstBERT. The experiment results show that AstBERT outperforms baseline models on both code question answering and clone detection. For code refinement task, the model achieves state-of-the-art performance on BFP_small dataset and competitive performance on BFP_medium dataset.

References

Luca Buratti, Saurabh Pujar, Mihaela Bornea, Scott McCarley, Yunhui Zheng, Gaetano Rossiello, Alessandro Morari, Jim Laredo, Veronika Thost, Yufan Zhuang, et al. 2020. Exploring software naturalness through neural language models. *arXiv preprint arXiv:2006.12641*.

Jacob Devlin, Ming-Wei Chang, Kenton Lee, and Kristina Toutanova. 2019. Bert: Pre-training of deep bidirectional transformers for language understanding. In *NAACL-HLT*, pages 4171–4186.

Zhangyin Feng, Daya Guo, Duyu Tang, Nan Duan, Xiaocheng Feng, Ming Gong, Linjun Shou, Bing Qin, Ting Liu, Daxin Jiang, et al. 2020. Codebert: A pre-trained model for programming and natural languages. In *EMNLP*, pages 1536–1547.

Daya Guo, Shuo Ren, Shuai Lu, Zhangyin Feng, Duyu Tang, Shujie Liu, Long Zhou, Nan Duan, Alexey Svyatkovskiy, Shengyu Fu, et al. 2021. Graphcodebert:

Pre-training code representations with data flow. In *ICLR*, pages 1–21.

Vincent J Hellendoorn, Charles Sutton, Rishabh Singh, Petros Maniatis, and David Bieber. 2019. Global relational models of source code. In *ICLR*, pages 1–12.

Geert Heyman and Tom Van Cutsem. 2020. Neural code search revisited: Enhancing code snippet retrieval through natural language intent. *arXiv preprint arXiv:2008.12193*.

Junjie Huang, Duyu Tang, Linjun Shou, Ming Gong, Ke Xu, Daxin Jiang, Ming Zhou, and Nan Duan. 2021. Cosqa: 20,000+ web queries for code search and question answering. *arXiv preprint arXiv:2105.13239*.

Hamel Husain, Ho-Hsiang Wu, Tiferet Gazit, Miltiadis Allamanis, and Marc Brockschmidt. 2019. Codesearchnet challenge: Evaluating the state of semantic code search. *arXiv preprint arXiv:1909.09436*.

Aditya Kanade, Petros Maniatis, Gogul Balakrishnan, and Kensen Shi. 2019. Pre-trained contextual embedding of source code. In *arXiv preprint arXiv:2001.00059*.

Rafael-Michael Karampatsis and Charles Sutton. 2020. Scelmo: Source code embeddings from language models. *arXiv preprint arXiv:2004.13214*.

Diederik P Kingma and Jimmy Ba. 2015. Adam: A method for stochastic optimization. In *ICLR*, pages 1269–1272.

Zhenzhong Lan, Mingda Chen, Sebastian Goodman, Kevin Gimpel, Piyush Sharma, and Radu Soricut. 2020. Albert: A lite bert for self-supervised learning of language representations. In *ICLR*, pages 1–17.

Hongyu Li, Seohyun Kim, and Satish Chandra. 2019. Neural code search evaluation dataset. *arXiv preprint arXiv:1908.09804*.

Yinhan Liu, Myle Ott, Naman Goyal, Jingfei Du, Mandar Joshi, Danqi Chen, Omer Levy, Mike Lewis, Luke Zettlemoyer, and Veselin Stoyanov. 2019. Roberta: A robustly optimized bert pretraining approach. *arXiv preprint arXiv:1907.11692*.

Liming Nie, He Jiang, Zhilei Ren, Zeyi Sun, and Xiaochen Li. 2016. Query expansion based on crowd knowledge for code search. *IEEE Transactions on Services Computing*, 9(5):771–783.

Matthew E. Peters, Mark Neumann, Mohit Iyyer, Matt Gardner, Christopher Clark, Kenton Lee, and Luke Zettlemoyer. 2018. Deep contextualized word representations. *arXiv preprint arXiv:1802.05365*.

Jeffrey Svajlenko, Judith F Islam, Iman Keivanloo, Chanchal K Roy, and Mohammad Mamun Mia. 2014. Towards a big data curated benchmark of inter-project code clones. In *ICSME*, pages 476–480.

Alexey Svyatkovskiy, Shao Kun Deng, Shengyu Fu, and Neel Sundaresan. 2020. Intellicode compose: Code generation using transformer. In *ESEC/FSE*, pages 1433–1443.

Michele Tufano, Cody Watson, Gabriele Bavota, Massimiliano Di Penta, Martin White, and Denys Poshyvanyk. 2019. An empirical study on learning bug-fixing patches in the wild via neural machine translation. *ACM Transactions on Software Engineering and Methodology*, 28(4):1–29.

Ashish Vaswani, Noam Shazeer, Niki Parmar, Jakob Uszkoreit, Llion Jones, Aidan N Gomez, Łukasz Kaiser, and Illia Polosukhin. 2017. Attention is all you need. In *NeurIPS*, pages 5998–6008.

Yao Wan, Jingdong Shu, Yulei Sui, Guandong Xu, Zhou Zhao, Jian Wu, and Philip S Yu. 2019. Multi-modal attention network learning for semantic source code retrieval. In *ASE*, pages 13–25.

Wenhan Wang, Ge Li, Bo Ma, Xin Xia, and Zhi Jin. 2020. Detecting code clones with graph neural network and flow-augmented abstract syntax tree. In *SANER*, pages 261–271.

Huihui Wei and Ming Li. 2017. Supervised deep features for software functional clone detection by exploiting lexical and syntactical information in source code. In *IJCAI*, pages 3034–3040.

Wenwen Xu, Mingzhe Fang, Li Yang, Huaxi Jiang, Geng Liang, and Chun Zuo. 2021. Enabling language representation with knowledge graph and structured semantic information. In *CCAI*, pages 91–96.

Pengcheng Yin, Bowen Deng, Edgar Chen, Bogdan Vasilescu, and Graham Neubig. 2018. Learning to mine aligned code and natural language pairs from stack overflow. In *MSR*, pages 476–486.

Jian Zhang, Xu Wang, Hongyu Zhang, Hailong Sun, Kaixuan Wang, and Xudong Liu. 2019. A novel neural source code representation based on abstract syntax tree. In *ICSE*, pages 783–794.

Disentangled Variational Topic Inference for Topic-Accurate Financial Report Generation

Sixing Yan
Department of Computer Science,
Hong Kong Baptist University
Hong Kong SAR, China.
cssxyan@comp.hkbu.edu.hk

Ting Zhu
Research Department, Sales Branch,
TF Securities Co., Ltd.
Shanghai, China.
zhuting@tfzq.com

Abstract

Automatic generating financial report from a set of news is important but challenging. The financial reports is composed of key points of the news and corresponding inferring and reasoning from specialists in financial domain with professional knowledge. The challenges lie in the effective learning of the extra knowledge that is not well presented in the news, and the misalignment between topic of input news and output knowledge in target reports. In this work, we introduce a disentangled variational topic inference approach to learn two latent variables for news and report, respectively. We use a publicly available dataset to evaluate the proposed approach. The results demonstrate its effectiveness of enhancing the language informativeness and the topic accuracy of the generated financial reports.

1 Introduction

Automatically generating long financial reports from a set of macro news have been recently studied with the objective to assist analysts to perform the time-consuming reporting task. A macro news, as shown in Fig. 1, is one paragraph with multiple sentences describing a finance-domain event with supporting details. The corresponding financial report is a longer paragraph with key points of the news and extended analysis, such as inferring and reasoning, with the financial knowledge of analysts. In the literature, long text generation has been well studied in the domain of natural language generation processing (Guo et al., 2018; Guan et al., 2021). Specially, generating long text from the short text with domain-specific settings is still challenging.

The encoder-decoder architecture is commonly employed, where the input news is encoded by a recurrent neural network (RNN) and fed to another RNN model to generate the target report. Some recent works (Beltagy et al., 2020; Chapman et al., 2021) replaced the encoder and decoder with the transformer-based model to learn the long dependency in both news and report text. However, these encoder-decoder models tend to produce generic sentences without the inherent uncertainty in the generated report. This uncertainty arises from the fact that financial reports are written by human specialists with different levels of expertise styles and professional knowledge. Naturally, the reports are very diverse. Probabilistic modeling is reported to be able to learn the uncertainty and diversity of the long texts (Bowman et al., 2016). By learning the stochastic latent variables, the high-level information, such as specialist inference style, is expected to be modeled. Ren et al (Ren et al., 2021b) proposed a variational autoencoder (VAE) method to handle the uncertainty of both news and the report. The background knowledge are learned as the conditional latent variable. In addition, a VAE-based hybrid approach is proposed in (Hu et al., 2020; Ren et al., 2021a) where the report outline is employed as latent variable for VAE decoder. These approaches alleviated the challenges of long text generation. However, the topic of both news and reports are not explicitly learned, where the coherence and coverage of the generated reports are not guaranteed. Recently, in the data-to-report generation domain, Najdenkoska et al (Najdenkoska et al., 2021) proposed a variational model with topic inference to enhance the topic alignment, where a set of latent variables of sentence-level topics are employed. Nevertheless, the topic misalignment between input data and corresponding reports still exists and makes the model hard to be learned.

To address the existing issues of topic modeling and alignment in a unify way, we propose a **D**isentangled **V**ariational **T**opic **I**nference (**DeVTI**) approach to generate financial reports by the probabilistic latent variable model. In particular, we learn two disentangled latent variables as the topics of input news and target reports, respectively. The news-related topic represents the context in-

Proceedings of the Fourth Workshop on Financial Technology and Natural Language Processing (FinNLP), pages 18 - 24
December 8, 2022 ©2022 Association for Computational Linguistics

News	The European sovereign debt crisis is the manifestation of the "sequelae" of the financial crisis relief policy. The global economy may fall into the stage of "high debt and low growth" due to the sovereign debt crisis or slowdown of the European five countries (PIIGS). The market demand will be weakened, and the process of global recovery from the crisis will be correspondingly prolonged. The window of the Federal Reserve to raise interest rates will be extended to 2011.
Financial Report	The superposition of the external forces of the global economic "rebalancing" and the internal forces of China's economic structural adjustment makes the traditional economic growth mode of China relying on "investment + export" face "passive" adjustment. Under the influence of "real estate regulation + inflation expectation management + European sovereign debt crisis" and other factors, the small cycle of economic downturn has been established; The domestic economic recovery is facing tortuous "Foxconn incident", which will lead to the rise of labor cost and the slow growth of the world economy, which will lead to the decline of China's future economic growth potential. Unlike the economic picture of "two highs and one low" (high unemployment rate, high debt rate and low growth rate) of Western economies, the future picture of China's economy will be: the era of high growth has passed, and it will return from the previous high growth of 11% to the medium growth of 8-10%, The multiple perplexities of "moderate economic growth, moderate structural inflation and low-level overcapacity" are accompanied by controllable inflation: under the background of the establishment of a small cycle of economic downturn, the fall of commodity prices and the lifting of the economic overheating alarm, prices rose in the middle of the year, but inflation is controllable, and the expectation of interest rate increase is weakened. At present, China's macroeconomic policy regulation may be trapped in a "perplexity": China's economy seems to have entered the most contradictory and complex situation, On the one hand, the story of high growth is still expected. On the other hand, the micro operation contradictions highlight the accumulation of many problems, which are almost irreconcilable. In the multi-level goal oriented macro-economic decision-making or the future policy orientation trapped in the macro-economic "maze": (1) the "Chinese version of the national income doubling plan" to stimulate consumption is the key to the switch of economic growth momentum; (2) Economic restructuring: a strategic choice that must be made; (3) The monetary cycle, the economic cycle and the inflation cycle are not synchronized. The economic downturn and policy tightening (liquidity tightening) continued until the end of the third quarter and the beginning of the fourth quarter of 2010. It is expected that the policy will be moderately relaxed at the end of the year; (4) The exchange rate reform was launched, and the interest rate increase was postponed.

Figure 1: An example of news and the corresponding financial report. The co-occurred topics are highlighted.

formation while the report-related topic maintains the prior knowledge of inference and reasoning of human specialists. To summarize, the contributions of this work are three folds,

- We propose a disentangled variational topic inference based approach to generate the topic-accurate financial reports.
- We study the misalignment of the variational topic inference in the short-to-long text generation under the domain-specific setting, and apply disentangled variational inference to learn the latent variables of source and target knowledge individually.
- We demonstrate that our approach achieves comparable performance on a public large-scale news-and-report dataset under a broad range of natural language generation and keyword accuracy evaluation criteria.

2 Methodology

2.1 Preliminaries

Problem Formulation Given the input news X, the goal is to generate a report $Y = \{y_1, y_2, ..\}_{n=1}^{N}$ where y_n refers to the nth sentence. We aim to maximize the conditional log-likelihood as,

$$\theta^* = \arg\max \sum_{n=1}^{N} \log p_\theta(y_n|x), \quad (1)$$

where θ stands for the model parameters.

Variational Topic Inference To learn to generate report toward the input news, the generation is formulated as a conditional variational inference problem where a set of latent variables z are employed to represent the topics of the report. We incorporate z into the conditional probability of news-based report $\log p_\theta(y|x)$ as,

$$\log p_\theta(y_t|x) = \int \log p_\theta(y_t|x,z) p_\theta(z|x) \mathrm{d}x, \quad (2)$$

where $p_\theta(z|x)$ is the prior distribution condition to the input news x. A variational posterior $q_\phi(z)$ is defined to approximate the intractable true posterior $p_\theta(z|y,x)$ of inferring latent variables z from the input news and the target report. By approximating $D_{\mathrm{KL}}[q_\phi(z)||p_\theta(z|x,y)]$, we can obtain $\mathbb{E}[\log q_\phi(z) - \log p_\theta(y|z,x)p_\theta(z|x)/p_\theta(y|x)] \geq 0$. Following Najdenkoska et al (Najdenkoska et al., 2021), the ELBO of the report generation log-likelihood $\log p_\theta(y|x)$ to be maximized as

$$\log p_\theta(y|x) \geq \mathbb{E}[p_\theta(y|z,x)] - \mathcal{K}_0, \quad (3)$$

where $\mathcal{K}_0 = D_{\mathrm{KL}}[q_\phi(z|y)||p_\theta(z|x)]$. z is sampled from the variational posterior distribution $z_{train} \sim q_\phi(z_t \mid y)$ in the training, and sampled from the prior distribution $z_{test} \sim p_\theta(z \mid x)$ in the inference.

Misaligned Topic Inference In Eq.(3), the information covered by report y, i.e., $\mathcal{I}(y)$ is assumed to be $\mathcal{I}(y) \subseteq \mathcal{I}(x)$ which is too strong and not hold in practice. The financial news is usually about a particular domain event. However, the financial report is intuitively composed of key points of that event and conclusive inference from business analysts. The logical analysis presented by the financial report is depended on the analyst knowledge and common sense which are not well presented in the input news. Thus, only $\mathcal{I}(y) \cap \mathcal{I}(x) \neq \emptyset$ is guaranteed such that aligning $\mathcal{I}(y)$ and $\mathcal{I}(x)$ by the same latent variable z will incur the misaligned topics.

2.2 Disentangled Variational Topic Inference

The proposed DeVTI model is illustrated in Fig. 2. We first disentangle the topic of news and report from the single latent z by using another VAE to learn the extra knowledge z_y in the target report y. The corresponding ELBO is given following (Bai et al., 2020),

$$\begin{aligned}\mathcal{O} =&\frac{1}{2}(\mathbb{E}_{z_y \sim q_\psi}[\log p_\theta(y|z_y)] \\ &+ \mathbb{E}_{z_x \sim q_\phi}[\log p_\theta(y|z_x)]) - \mathcal{K}_1,\end{aligned} \tag{4}$$

where $\mathcal{K}_1 = D_{\mathrm{KL}}[q_\psi(z_y|y)||q_\phi(z_x|x)]$. The first term encourages the report reconstruction by z_y while the second term encourages the report generation by z_x. $\mathcal{K}_1$ penalizes the KL divergence between the approximated distribution $q_\psi(z_y|y)$ and $q_\phi(z_x|x)$ which are conditional to y and x. The knowledge l, which is related to news x and extracted from report y, is expected to be aligned as

$$\begin{aligned}\mathcal{K}_2 =& D_{\mathrm{KL}}[p_\theta(l|z_y)||p_\theta(l|z_x)] \\ =& \mathbb{E}_{q_\phi}[\log p_\theta(z_y|l)] - \mathbb{E}_{q_\psi}[\log p_\theta(z_x|l)] - \mathcal{K}_3\end{aligned} \tag{5}$$

where $\mathcal{K}_3 = D_{\mathrm{KL}}[q_\psi(z_x)||q_\phi(z_y)]$. Given that the knowledge is covered by reports as $\mathcal{I}(l) \subset \mathcal{I}(y)$, $\mathbb{E}[\log p(z_y|l)] \leq \mathbb{E}[\log p(z_y|y)]$ is hold,

$$\mathcal{K}_2 \leq \mathbb{E}_{q_\phi}[\log p_\theta(z_y|y)] - \mathbb{E}_{q_\psi}[\log p_\theta(z_x|l)] - \mathcal{K}_3. \tag{6}$$

Thus, a higher lower bound is conducted as,

$$\begin{aligned}\mathcal{O} \leq& \frac{1}{2}(\mathbb{E}_{q_\psi}[\log p_\theta(y|z_y)] \\ &+ \mathbb{E}_{q_\phi}[\log p_\theta(y|z_x)]) - \mathcal{K}_4 - \mathcal{K}_2 - \mathcal{K}_3\end{aligned} \tag{7}$$

where $\mathcal{K}_4 = D_{\mathrm{KL}}[p_\theta(z_x|x)||p_\theta(z_x|l)]$. The right-hand-side is the lower bound of objective function Eq.(4) where $\mathcal{K}_4$ penalizes the KL divergence between the approximated distribution $p_\theta(z_x|x)$ and $p_\theta(z_x|l)$. In this way, z_x is disentangled to focus on learning the topic information from input financial news, while z_y is focusing on learning the domain knowledge of target reports. Finally, we are able to learn the model by maximizing a new ELBO as,

$$\begin{aligned}&\frac{1}{2}(\mathbb{E}_{q_\psi}[\log p_\theta(y|z_y)] + \mathbb{E}_{q_\phi}[\log p_\theta(y|z_x)]) \\ &-\beta_2\mathcal{K}_2 - \beta_3\mathcal{K}_3 - \beta_4\mathcal{K}_4\end{aligned} \tag{8}$$

where β_* is the hyper-parameter to control the similarity between several Gaussian distributions (Bai et al., 2020). The $\mathcal{K}_2$ penalizes the KL divergence between the predicted label from generated report and image, which enforces the uncertainty of report to be close to the observed image. The $\mathcal{K}_3$ penalizes the KL divergence between language latent variable $q_\psi(z_y)$ and topic latent variable $q_\phi(z_x)$, which releases the conditions in $\mathcal{K}_1$ and encourages two distribution contain the shared topic knowledge.

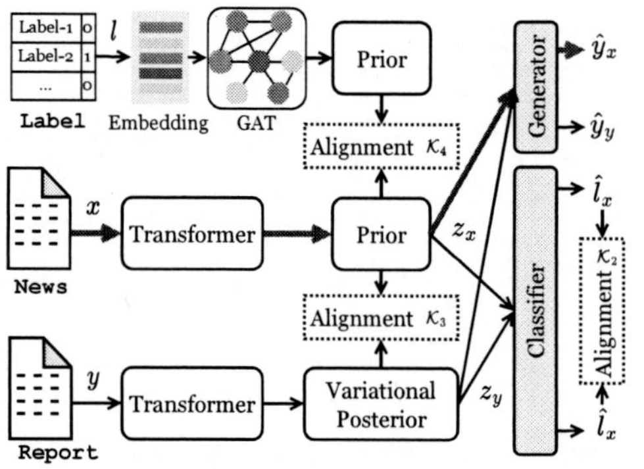

Figure 2: The deep model architecture. In the training, the workflow in black and blue arrow lines are applied while only blue arrow lines are applied in the testing.

	Avg. (Std.)	Percentile	
		5%	95%
# tokens per news	92.6 (±55.5)	58	183
# tokens per report	412.7 (±233.2)	81	784
# sent. per news	1.4 (±1.8)	1	3
# sent. per report	2.1 (±4.4)	1	10
sent. len. per news	66.6 (±41.8)	11	139
sent. len. per report	198.0 (±233.8)	11	635

Table 1: The statistics of the benchmark dataset, including the number of token, sentences, and sentence length for input news and target reports, respectively.

3 Experiments

3.1 Data and Evaluation Criteria

Data We evaluate the proposed approach on the large-scale news-and-report dataset (Ren et al., 2021b). The raw dataset[1] is composed of 10,707 pairs of macro news and corresponding financial reports. We tokenize all news and reports, and filter out frequency least than 5 by an open-source toolkit [2]. This results in 16,052 unique tokens including four special tokens <pad>, <start>, <end> and <unk> (related statistics is shown in Table. 1).

There is no existing topic annotations provided by the raw dataset, so we further automatically annotate each new-and-report pair by the public available tools. We apply a event parser, which is pretrained on financial knowledge graph data (Wang et al., 2021) , to extract 10 types of entities and 19 types of relationships, and apply a sentiment classifier (Tian et al., 2020) to predict their sentiment polarity (details could be found in A.2). We utilize event subject-predicate-object (SPO) triple

[1] https://github.com/papersharing/news-and-reports-dataset

[2] https://github.com/hankcs/HanLP

Model	NLG Metrics						CA Metrics			
	B.-1	**B.-2**	**B.-3**	**B.-4**	**R.**	**C.**	**E.**	**S-E.**	**ER.**	**S-ER.**
SEQ. (Bahdanau et al., 2014)	32.69	7.65	4.85	2.75	3.59	-	-	-	-	-
SEQA. (Bahdanau et al., 2014)	33.64	13.85	9.89	6.92	3.89	-	-	-	-	-
POINTERNET (See et al., 2017)	36.45	9.51	5.75	2.45	3.44	-	-	-	-	-
CVAE (Zhao et al., 2017)	33.50	14.07	10.04	6.97	4.65	-	-	-	-	-
CVAE-KD (Ren et al., 2021b)	46.67	20.32	12.81	8.00	6.95	-	-	-	-	-
TRANS. (Vaswani et al., 2017)	**48.00**	25.30	9.22	10.65	4.05	<u>39.67</u>	<u>25.10</u>	15.44	9.56	8.03
T-CVAE (Wang and Wan, 2019)	43.01	19.00	13.00	<u>10.98</u>	7.03	34.76	20.33	16.66	13.90	8.47
VTI (Najdenkoska et al., 2021)	40.88	23.43	12.90	10.91	**10.09**	30.65	19.40	17.32	14.89	<u>11.03</u>
DEVTI W/ E.	39.09	**26.70**	12.51	5.57	7.87	33.43	**25.66**	20.30	12.03	10.02
DEVTI W/ S-E.	39.50	22.77	11.32	6.01	6.99	31.32	<u>25.10</u>	**21.30**	12.41	11.02
DEVTI W/ ER.	38.01	20.35	10.32	8.93	6.56	39.03	19.43	17.93	<u>14.90</u>	10.30
DEVTI W/ S-ER. (proposed)	41.70	24.01	**13.90**	**11.11**	<u>9.69</u>	**39.86**	23.59	<u>20.43</u>	**15.09**	**12.33**

Table 2: Performance comparison of report generation models. The experimental results in first section is directly cited from Ren et al (Ren et al., 2021b). The experimental results in second section is our replicated results using their codes. The best scores are in bold face and the second best are underlined."B.", "R." and "C." stand for BLEU, ROUGE and CIDEr scores, respectively. "E.", "S-E.", "ER." and "S-ER." stand for the F-1 measure score of entity, entity with sentimental polarity, entity relationship and entity relationship with sentimental polarity, respectively.

with sentiment polarity to construct labels of the news and report data, respectively.

Evaluation Criteria For report quality, we adopt the natural language generation metrics[3] including BLEU (Papineni et al., 2002), ROUGE-L (Lin, 2004) and CIDEr (Vedantam et al., 2015). To measure the topic accuracy, we adopt the F-1 measure for evaluating the entity and entity relationship with or without sentimental polarity that are extracted from the generated report and ground truth. The micro-avg percentage scores are reported.

3.2 Baseline model and Experiment Setting

We compare the proposed approach with several generation models, including SEQ. (Sutskever et al., 2014), SEQA. (Bahdanau et al., 2014), TRANS. (Vaswani et al., 2017), POINTERNET (See et al., 2017), CVAE (Wang and Wan, 2019), T-CVAE (Wang and Wan, 2019), CVAE-KD (Ren et al., 2021b) and VTI (Najdenkoska et al., 2021). For the proposed DEVTI model, we apply entity relationship with sentimental polarity to optimize the generator, denoted as DEVTI W/ S-ER. The dimensions of hidden state and number of heads in MHA are set as 512 and 8. The model is trained with the learning rate 1e-5 with the mini-batch size of 16. We run the experiments three times with different random seeds and report the average scores. The Implementation details could be found in A.1.

3.3 Experimental Results and Analysis

We evaluate baseline and the proposed approaches by the NLG metrics and classification accuracy metrics in Table 2 1st and 2nd sections.

Performance of Report Generation The proposed DEVTI achieves comparative performances in most of the NLG metrics. In addition, DEVTI achieves best scores in accuracy of entity relationship with sentimental polarity which is more challenging but critical for report usability and reliability. Both results indicate the effectiveness of learning disentangled latent variables for aligning the topics between input news and target reports while ensuring the language informativeness. One possible reason could be that the relationship between entities with sentimental polarity mainly determines the style and topic of the report reasoning and inference. Thus, the latent variable of domain knowledge could enhance the both language fluency and topic accuracy coordinately.

Sensitivity Analysis To analyze how the label affects the report generation performance, we conduct the experiments of learning DEVTI with different labels (as shown in 3rd section). The results consistent with the commonsense that rich semantic knowledge benefit the generation of long and topic-accurate texts with domain-specific setting.

4 Conclusion

In this work, we propose a disentangled variational topic inference (DeVTI) approach to enhance the topic-accurate financial report generation. Two latent variables are learned for the topic of news and extra knowledge of reports. The experiments show the effectiveness of the proposed DeVTI is able to generate descriptive report with correct topics.

[3] `https://github.com/tylin/coco-caption`

References

Jimmy Lei Ba, Jamie Ryan Kiros, and Geoffrey E Hinton. 2016. Layer normalization. *arXiv preprint arXiv:1607.06450*.

Dzmitry Bahdanau, Kyunghyun Cho, and Yoshua Bengio. 2014. Neural machine translation by jointly learning to align and translate. *arXiv preprint arXiv:1409.0473*.

Junwen Bai, Shufeng Kong, and Carla Gomes. 2020. Disentangled variational autoencoder based multi-label classification with covariance-aware multivariate probit model. In *Proceedings of the Twenty-Ninth International Joint Conference on Artificial Intelligence (IJCAI-20)*.

Iz Beltagy, Matthew E Peters, and Arman Cohan. 2020. Longformer: The long-document transformer. *arXiv preprint arXiv:2004.05150*.

Samuel R Bowman, Luke Vilnis, Oriol Vinyals, Andrew M Dai, Rafal Jozefowicz, and Samy Bengio. 2016. Generating sentences from a continuous space. In *20th SIGNLL Conference on Computational Natural Language Learning, CoNLL 2016*, pages 10–21. Association for Computational Linguistics (ACL).

Clayton Chapman, Lars Hillebrand, Marc Robin Stenzel, Tobias Deusser, Christian Bauckhage, and Rafet Sifa. 2021. Towards generating financial reports from table data using transformers.

Marcella Cornia, Matteo Stefanini, Lorenzo Baraldi, and Rita Cucchiara. 2020. Meshed-memory transformer for image captioning. In *Proceedings of the IEEE/CVF Conference on Computer Vision and Pattern Recognition*, pages 10578–10587.

Jian Guan, Xiaoxi Mao, Changjie Fan, Zitao Liu, Wenbiao Ding, and Minlie Huang. 2021. Long text generation by modeling sentence-level and discourse-level coherence. In *Proceedings of the 59th Annual Meeting of the Association for Computational Linguistics and the 11th International Joint Conference on Natural Language Processing (Volume 1: Long Papers)*, pages 6379–6393.

Jiaxian Guo, Sidi Lu, Han Cai, Weinan Zhang, Yong Yu, and Jun Wang. 2018. Long text generation via adversarial training with leaked information. In *Proceedings of the AAAI conference on artificial intelligence*, volume 32.

Kaiming He, Xiangyu Zhang, Shaoqing Ren, and Jian Sun. 2016. Deep residual learning for image recognition. In *Proceedings of the IEEE conference on computer vision and pattern recognition*, pages 770–778.

Wenxin Hu, Xiaofeng Zhang, and Yunpeng Ren. 2020. Generating financial reports from macro news via multiple edits neural networks. In *Joint European Conference on Machine Learning and Knowledge Discovery in Databases*, pages 667–682. Springer.

Diederik P Kingma and Max Welling. 2013. Auto-encoding variational bayes. *arXiv preprint arXiv:1312.6114*.

Chin-Yew Lin. 2004. Rouge: A package for automatic evaluation of summaries. In *Text summarization branches out*, pages 74–81.

Ivona Najdenkoska, Xiantong Zhen, Marcel Worring, and Ling Shao. 2021. Variational topic inference for chest x-ray report generation. In *International Conference on Medical Image Computing and Computer-Assisted Intervention*, pages 625–635. Springer.

Kishore Papineni, Salim Roukos, Todd Ward, and Wei-Jing Zhu. 2002. Bleu: a method for automatic evaluation of machine translation. In *Proceedings of the 40th Annual Meeting of the Association for Computational Linguistics*, pages 311–318.

Yunpeng Ren, Wenxin Hu, Ziao Wang, Xiaofeng Zhang, Yiyuan Wang, and Xuan Wang. 2021a. A hybrid deep generative neural model for financial report generation. *Knowledge-Based Systems*, 227:107093.

Yunpeng Ren, Ziao Wang, Yiyuan Wang, and Xiaofeng Zhang. 2021b. Generating long financial report using conditional variational autoencoders with knowledge distillation. In *Proceedings of the AAAI Conference on Artificial Intelligence*, volume 35, pages 15879–15880.

Abigail See, Peter J Liu, and Christopher D Manning. 2017. Get to the point: Summarization with pointer-generator networks. *arXiv preprint arXiv:1704.04368*.

Ilya Sutskever, Oriol Vinyals, and Quoc V Le. 2014. Sequence to sequence learning with neural networks. *Advances in neural information processing systems*, 27.

Hao Tian, Can Gao, Xinyan Xiao, Hao Liu, Bolei He, Hua Wu, Haifeng Wang, and Feng Wu. 2020. Skep: Sentiment knowledge enhanced pre-training for sentiment analysis. In *Proceedings of the 58th Annual Meeting of the Association for Computational Linguistics*, pages 4067–4076.

Ashish Vaswani, Noam Shazeer, Niki Parmar, Jakob Uszkoreit, Llion Jones, Aidan N Gomez, Łukasz Kaiser, and Illia Polosukhin. 2017. Attention is all you need. *Advances in neural information processing systems*, 30.

Ramakrishna Vedantam, C Lawrence Zitnick, and Devi Parikh. 2015. Cider: Consensus-based image description evaluation. In *Proceedings of the 28th IEEE Conference on Computer Vision and Pattern Recognition*, pages 4566–4575.

Petar Veličković, Guillem Cucurull, Arantxa Casanova, Adriana Romero, Pietro Lio, and Yoshua Bengio. 2017. Graph attention networks. *arXiv preprint arXiv:1710.10903*.

Tianming Wang and Xiaojun Wan. 2019. T-cvae: Transformer-based conditioned variational autoencoder for story completion. In *IJCAI*, pages 5233–5239.

Wenguang Wang, Yonglin Xu, Chunhui Du, Yunwen Chen, Yijie Wang, and Hui Wen. 2021. Data set and evaluation of automated construction of financial knowledge graph. *Data Intelligence*, 3(3):418–443.

Di You, Fenglin Liu, Shen Ge, Xiaoxia Xie, Jing Zhang, and Xian Wu. 2021. Aligntransformer: Hierarchical alignment of visual regions and disease tags for medical report generation. In *International Conference on Medical Image Computing and Computer-Assisted Intervention*, pages 72–82. Springer.

Tiancheng Zhao, Ran Zhao, and Maxine Eskenazi. 2017. Learning discourse-level diversity for neural dialog models using conditional variational autoencoders. *arXiv preprint arXiv:1703.10960*.

A Appendix

A.1 Implementation via Deep Neural Network

As common practice in similar research (Kingma and Welling, 2013; Najdenkoska et al., 2021), $q_\phi(z_x|x)$, $q_\phi(z_y|l)$ and $q_\psi(z_y|y)$ are all parameterized as fully factorized Gaussian distributions and inferred by multi-layer perceptrons (MLPs). They are denoted as language prior module, label posterior module and the language posterior module. The proposed DeVTI model is illustrated in Fig. 2. The log-likelihood is implemented as a cross entropy loss based on the generated report and ground-truth reports.

Topic Posterior Modules A matrix E is applied to learn the pre-defined topic embedding. In addition, we also learn the relationship between the topics by the graph attention layer (Veličković et al., 2017). A pair of topics are connected refer to their co-occurrence in the same news-and-report pairs.

Language Prior and Posterior Modules A pre-trained Financial BERT model is employed to learn the token embedding of input text. The input news is fed to the prior module while the target report is fed to the posterior module. Noted that, the posterior module produce the latent topics for guiding the learning the generation, which only applied in the training stage.

Report Generator Module We employ the transformer (Vaswani et al., 2017) as the decoder to generate report. The transformer is composed of multi-head attention module which is able to learn the long dependency in news, report and news-to-report. For each decoding step t, the hidden stats h_t is encoded from the input word features x_t by the standard encoder from Transformer,

$$x_t = w_t + e_t; h_t = \mathrm{MHA}(x_t, x_{1:t}), \quad (9)$$

where w_t and e_t are the word embedding and positional embedding, respectively. A multi-layers transformer decoder is employed to generate the proper report by the latent variable z, following (Cornia et al., 2020; You et al., 2021), h'_t is calculated as,

$$h'_t = \mathrm{MHA}(h_t, z). \quad (10)$$

We apply L-layer MHA where each layer is followed by the operations of residual connection (He et al., 2016) and layer normalization (Ba et al., 2016). Each word is predicted by $y'_t \sim p_t = \mathrm{Softmax}(h'_t W^R)$ where $W^R \in \mathbb{R}^{\mathrm{D}\times\mathrm{W}}$ is the linear projection to transform latent feature into word embedding.

Report Classification Module We employ the fully-connected network with the *Sigmoid* function as the binary classifier to predict each topic from latent variable z,

$$p = \mathrm{Sigmoid}(\max(0, zW_1 + b_1)W_2 + b_2), \quad (11)$$

where $W*$ and $b*$ are learnable parameters. The classifiers are learned by weighted binary cross entropy losses to reduce the label imbalance issue.

A.2 Label Construction

Entity-relationship Extraction We apply a financial research report-based knowledge graph[4] to extract the financial entities and their relationships. The 10 entity types include Industry, Organization, Research report, Risk, Person, Product, Service, Brand, Article and Indicator. The SPO triples of 19 entity relationships include (Industry, subordinate of, Industry), (Organization, belong to, Industry), (Research report, be related to, Industry), (Industry, has, Risk), (Organization, has, Risks), (Organization, be affiliated with, Organization), (Organization, invest, Organization), (Organization, merge, Organization), (Organization, be the customer of, Organization), (Person, work for, Organization), (Person, invest, Organization), (Research report, be related to, Organization), (Organization, produce and sale, Product), (Organization, purchase, Product), (Organization, provide, Service), (Organization, has, Brand), (Product, belong to, Brand),

[4]http://openkg.cn/dataset/fr2kg

(Organization, publish, Article) and (Research report, use, Indicators).

A financial BERT [5] followed a Conditional Random Fields (CRF) model is learned to tag the token with entities and predict the corresponding relationships. The tagging model is trained by the official code[6]. After that, the pre-trained tagging model is applied to extract the entities and their relationships from each sentence of the news-and-report data.

Sentiment Analysis We apply a open-source sentiment analysis toolkit[7] to predict the sentimental polarity of each sentence of the news-and-report data. We set threshold as 0.9 such that one sentence is predicted to be "Positive" or "Negative" only if the related predicted probability is larger than 0.9; otherwise it is predicted to be "Neutral".

The extracted entities and their relationships with the sentimental polarity of each sentence is employed as a label of that sentence, while labels of all sentences are constructed to be the multiple labels of one news or report.

[5]https://github.com/valuesimplex/FinBERT

[6]https://github.com/wgwang/ccks2020-baseline

[7]https://github.com/baidu/Senta

Toward Privacy-preserving Text Embedding Similarity with Homomorphic Encryption

Donggyu Kim*[1] **Garam Lee***[2] **Sungwoo Oh***[1]
KB Kookmin Bank[1], CryptoLab[2]
{donggyukimc, david.oh0126}@gmail.com, garamlee@cryptolab.co.kr

Abstract

Text embedding is an essential component to build efficient natural language applications based on text similarities such as search engines and chatbots. Certain industries like finance and healthcare demand strict privacy-preserving conditions that user's data should not be exposed to any potential malicious users even including service providers. From a privacy standpoint, text embeddings seem impossible to be interpreted but there is still a privacy risk that they can be recovered to original texts through inversion attacks. To satisfy such privacy requirements, in this paper, we study a Homomorphic Encryption (HE) based text similarity inference. To validate our method, we perform extensive experiments on two vital text similarity tasks. Through text embedding inversion tests, we prove that the benchmark datasets are vulnerable to inversion attacks and another privacy preserving approach, $d\chi$-privacy, a relaxed version of Local Differential Privacy method fails to prevent them. We show that our approach preserves the performance of models compared to that the baseline has degradation up to 10% of scores for the minimum security.

1 Introduction

Recently, various industries provide enhanced user experiences through natural language processing (NLP) applications. AI assistants such as Amazon's Alexa and Google Assistant are representative examples that help users to achieve their purposes with a wide range of intentions. To build such complex applications, it is common to utilize machine-learned text representations, i.e., text embeddings to infer similarities between texts (Cer et al., 2018). Text embeddings facilitate the efficient implementations of various NLP functions like document search (Karpukhin et al., 2020), intent decision (Humeau et al., 2020), and dialogue response selection (Gu et al., 2020) by leveraging precomputed embeddings for real-time applications. However, such usage of text embeddings poses emerging privacy risks so-called *inversion attacks* that recover the original texts from embeddings (Song and Raghunathan, 2020).

No.	Query Text
1	*I'm 13*. Can I buy supplies at a pet store without a parent/adult present?
2	I earn *\$75K*, have *\$30K in savings, no debt, rent from my parents* who are losing home. Should I buy home now or save?
3	How do I *fold side-income into our budget* so my husband doesn't know?

Table 1: Examples of query text containing sensitive information from FIQA-2018 dataset. Sensitive texts are marked with red color.

User texts such as *Know-Your-Customer*[1] inquiries in the finance domain frequently contain privacy-sensitive data. The sensitive data include not only personal information which can identify users, but also their assets and clues or intentions about their future behaviors (Wheatley et al., 2016; Schwartz and Solove, 2011). Table 1 shows example texts with information that causes infringements on user's privacy if they are leaked to unauthorized users. We define malicious users without authorization for user's privacy information into two categories. First, external malicious users perform attacks from outside of services by accessing data or servers. Second, in certain domains that require strict privacy preservation such as finance, the data access from internal malicious users even including service providers should be prevented.

In this paper, we propose Homomorphic

*Equal contribution

[1]https://en.wikipedia.org/wiki/Know_your_customer

Proceedings of the Fourth Workshop on Financial Technology and Natural Language Processing (FinNLP), pages 25 - 36
December 8, 2022 ©2022 Association for Computational Linguistics

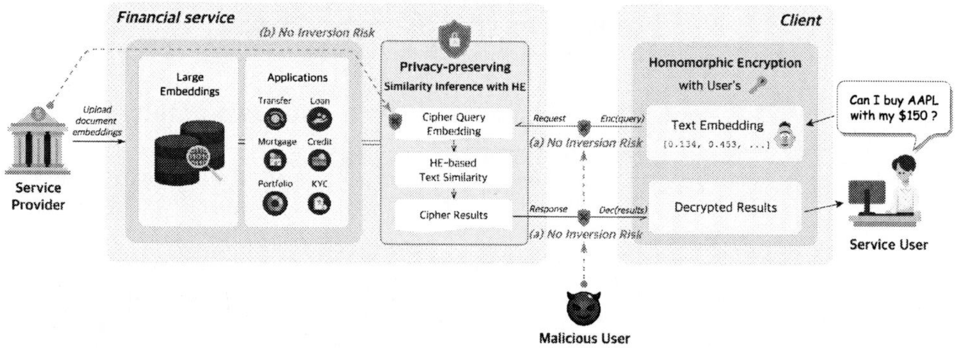

Figure 1: An example of text embedding based finance service with privacy preservation. Our Homomorphic Encryption method protects user data from *(a) external* and *(b) internal* malicious user attacks.

Encryption (HE) based text similarity inference secure from inversion attacks by both external and internal malicious users. It is possible to satisfy such rigorous privacy-preserving mechanism because HE approach enables all computations to be performed without decryption of the data (Cheon et al., 2017). Other cryptographic technologies do not meet the requirements because they need server-side decryption for computation (Acar et al., 2018). Another candidate method to resolve the above problem like d_χ-privacy, a variant of Local Differential Privacy (LDP) should consider a privacy-utility trade-off (Qu et al., 2021) in our tasks.

Figure 1 shows an example of text embedding based financial services using our HE method to protect user's query embedding from inversion attacks. First, a large number of server-side text embeddings such as documents for search were precomputed and uploaded to a centralized server in advance. Here, we assume that server-side text embeddings are not encrypted since service providers can access the database. Service users generate a public key and a secret key for homomorphic encryption. Then they convert their query texts into embeddings and encrypt them using HE with their public key. When the users send the encrypted query embedding to the server, no external malicious user can access the original data because of encryption. As a result, we can protect an inversion attack at *(a)*. Once the encrypted query embeddings reach the server, services can perform inference without decrypting the data due to our HE-based similarity function. During the inference, the service provider cannot extract any information from encrypted data because the HE secret key is owned by the user only. Therefore, the inversion attack point *(b)* is secure. Finally, the server sends the still encrypted result securely, and the user decrypts the result with the secret key.

We perform extensive tests using well-known benchmarks on two text similarity tasks, semantic textual similarity and text retrieval. The results on inversion attacks indicate that text embeddings can be easily recovered to original texts. Furthermore, we observe our d_χ-privacy baselines are not suitable to prevent such attacks completely while maintaining the performance of models. Specifically, it loses up to 10% of scores at minor noise settings and still shows information leakage. In contrast, our method guarantees the protection from inversion attacks and do not hurt performances. To summarize, our contributions are:

- We demonstrate that well-known bechmarks and pretrained text embedding models are vulnerable to inversion attacks.
- We implement HE based text similarity functions that can precisely approximate original performance while preventing any potential information leakage.
- Through extensive experiments, we prove that our method achieves complete privacy-preserving similarity tasks without hurting the performance.

2 Related Work

2.1 Text similarity with embeddings

Measuring text similarity is a fundamental functionality for many NLP applications. To overcome the limitation of lexical matching (Robertson and Zaragoza, 2009) such as TF-IDF and BM25, it is common to convert natural language text into text embeddings (Reimers and Gurevych, 2019) capturing the semantic meaning of texts as a form of vectors because it can represent rich contextual information. Using text embeddings, the similarity between texts can be interpreted as distances between data points in a vector space. These properties facilitate efficient computations of large-scale text similarity inference because embeddings can be precomputed and used in real-time applications without inference considering many parameters (Karpukhin et al., 2020). In practice, large amounts of texts such as search documents are precomputed whereas real-time data from users such as short search-queries require the embedding process on the fly. The relevancy between query and documents can be calculated with similarity functions such as cosine similarity or dot product. Formally (1), given text embeddings for query and document, E_q and E_d, the similarity between query q and each document d is computed with a similarity function:

$$sim = funct(E_q(q), E_d(d)) \tag{1}$$

2.2 Privacy-preserving in NLP

Although homomorphic computation basically takes numerical data as its input, much recent research shows attempts to apply HE to text data (Lee et al., 2022; Chen et al., 2022). However, these works mainly consider encrypted *classification* tasks on text embeddings. In this study, we focus on the text embedding based text similarity applications. Compared to classification task settings, the service scenario using text similarity is more suitable to take the advantage of using HE. This is because huge text embeddings are stored in a centralized server and users need to send query texts to the server to get inference results. In the process of it, they want their queries, which may contain sensitive information, not to be exposed to the server and still receive a response as expected.

The authors in (Feyisetan et al., 2020) proposed $d_\mathcal{X}$-privacy for privacy-preserving approach on textual data. However, their method requires to select a privacy parameter ϵ very carefully. Our baseline experiment results using $d_\mathcal{X}$-privacy showed low performance. The work in (Xiong et al., 2022) proposed how to evaluate a privacy risk on text data using semantic correlation. Our HE-based method using CKKS provides a practically complete security in terms of this privacy risk assessment since it ensures a 128-bit level of security and no information leakage occurs without decryption using a secret key. Other prior HE-based works such as (Yu et al., 2017) and (Nautsch et al., 2018) do not compute cosine similarity directly because the HE schemes they use do not support bootstrapping.

3 Method

In this section, we propose our Homomorphic Encryption (HE) based method to protect text data privacy. To achieve this, our goal is to approximate text similarity functions for given text embeddings in an encrypted state using the CKKS scheme. Formally, similar to the definition in (1), we implement encrypted similarity function $funct_*$ that computes the encrypted similarity result sim_* from encrypted text embeddings in order to achieve $sim_* \approx sim_{(1)}$ as much as possible.[2]

$$sim_* = funct_*(Enc(E_q(q)), E_d(d))$$

3.1 Homomorphic Encryption : CKKS Scheme

Homomorphic Encryption is a cryptographic primitive that can support computations on encrypted data without decryption. After performing computations in encrypted state, the decrypted output is the same as if we performed the computations in plaintext.

We adopt the CKKS scheme (Cheon et al., 2017, 2018a, 2019) that supports *approximate* arithmetic operations over encrypted real-valued vectors. While other HE schemes

[2] Asterisks(*) indicate a ciphertext or a computation in ciphertext.

such as BGV (Brakerski et al., 2011) and BFV (Fan and Vercauteren, 2012) can be applied for computations over integers, the fourth generation HE scheme, CKKS supports encrypted computations over real and complex numbers. This advantage provides scalability of encrypted computation to many applications in the real world. More details of the CKKS scheme can be found in (Cheon et al., 2017).

CKKS is a *leveled* HE scheme (Lee et al., 2022). This implies that a given ciphertext has a bounded depth to perform operations; the number of operations we can perform repeatedly is limited due to noise increase in computation. If we multiply two ciphertexts of level l, the output is a ciphertext of level $l-1$, which means the remained number of operations is reduced by 1. For this reason, we need a unique operation called *bootstrapping* to resolve this level reduction. The bootstrapping operation refreshes a ciphertext increasing its level higher so the number of possible operation times increases. The following HE operations are available over ciphertexts of given real-valued vectors pt_1 and pt_2 in plaintext.

- Add(ct_1, ct_2): output a ciphertext of pt_1+pt_2, where $+$ is the slot-wise addition.
- Mult(ct_1, ct_2): output a ciphertext of $pt_1 \odot pt_2$, where $\odot$ is the slot-wise multiplication.
- Bootstrap(ct_1): output a ciphertext of pt_1 at refreshed level.

In addition, it is worth to note that homomorphic operations can be performed on a plaintext and a ciphertext together as the operands of operations (Carpov and Sirdey, 2015). We can take the advantage of a plaintext-ciphertext operation because the noise increase is less than that of between both ciphertext operation. This flexibility enables us to consider various user scenarios depending on what to be protected.

For our tasks, we adopt the cosine similarity as our relevance score. Recall the cosine similarity of two vectors is defined as follows:

$$\cos\theta = \frac{\mathbf{u}\cdot\mathbf{v}}{\|\mathbf{u}\|\|\mathbf{v}\|} = \frac{u_1v_1+\cdots+u_nv_n}{\sqrt{(u_1^2+\cdots+u_n^2)\times(v_1^2+\cdots+v_n^2)}}$$

where u and v are n-dimensional vectors and θ is the angle between them, which indicates how close they are. Since HE supports addition and multiplication only, it is essential to approximate an arbitrary operation with an appropriate polynomial. In our task, the approximation we need is the square root inverse function. To implement this, we apply Newton's method (Panda, 2021) of the following form to approximate the square root inverse in an encrypted state.

$$y_{n+1} = \frac{1}{2}y_n(3 - xy_n^2)$$

The input domain of the function is $1 \le x \le 2^{22}$ and precision is 3×10^{-7}. For each iteration, the polynomial equation is updated recursively. Note that the function converges with an initial value y_0 satisfying $|1 - xy_0^2| < 1$. Here is a brief error analysis of the approximation:

$$\begin{aligned} 1 - xy_{n+1}^2 &= \frac{1}{4}xy_n^2(3 - xy_n^2)^2 \\ &= (1 - xy_n^2)^2(1 - \frac{xy_n^2}{4}) \\ &\vdots \\ &= (1 - xy_0^2)^{2^{n+1}}\prod_{k=0}^{n}(1 - \frac{xy_k^2}{4})^{2^{n-k}} \end{aligned}$$

where n denotes the number of iterations.

Inference In a real-world scenario for HE based similarity inference, the workflow requires the procedure for en/decryption of data. Procedure 1 describes how a client and a server can communicate in the process of a document search service while achieving privacy-preserving. One might concern that the most relevant document index with decrypted at the end might imply information about the query. To resolve this concern, a client can generate random indices and send the target index with them to the server.

Security Lastly, we emphasize that our HE parameters ensure 128-bit security level, which implies 2^{128} operations are required to recover the plaintext from a ciphertext with the current best algorithm (Cheon et al., 2022). Thus, a homomorphically encrypted ciphertext is securely protected and cannot be revealed without access to the secret key for decryption.

Procedure 1 Find most relevant document

Initialize

D *//service documents for search*
E_d, E_q *//text embedding models*
$funct_*$ *//HE based similarity function*
$D_{emb} \leftarrow E_d(D)$

Client

Generate a public key pk and a secret key sk
$Q_{text} \leftarrow$ *User input query text*
$Q_{emb} \leftarrow E_q(Q_{text})$
$Q_{emb*} \leftarrow Enc_{pk}(Q_{emb})$
$Q_{emb*}, pk \rightarrow Server$

Server

return $sim_* \leftarrow funct_*(Q_{emb*}, D_{emb})$ with pk

Client

$sim \leftarrow Dec_{sk}(sim_*)$ with sk
$index \leftarrow argmax(sim)$
$index \rightarrow Server$

Server

return $document \leftarrow D[index]$

4 Experiments

4.1 Text Similarity Tasks

To evaluate our approach, we consider two text similarity task settings: **STS** (Semantic textual similarity) and **Text retrieval**. We provide the brief descriptions on the tasks.

- **STS (Semantic textual similarity):** The task assesses the ability to inference the semantic similarity of given text pairs. Specifically, we measure the correlation between ground truth labels judged by human, and similarity scores predicted by models. Following previous studies (Reimers and Gurevych, 2019), we consider a set of seven well-known semantic textual similarity datasets, STS 2012–2016 (Agirre et al., 2012, 2013, 2014, 2015, 2016), STS Benchmark (Cer et al., 2017) and SICK-Relatedness (Marelli et al., 2014). Each dataset has a set of text pairs and the corresponding ground truth labels indicating semantic relevances. We compute the cosine similarity between text embeddings and measure the correlation between the similarities and the ground truth labels. Following Gao et al. (2021), we utilize Spearman's correlation evaluation script from the SentEval toolkit[3] (Conneau and Kiela, 2018).

- **Text Retrieval:** The task computes list-wise relevance scores i.e. dot product between a query and documents to be searched. The documents are sorted according to the scores and the task assesses text retrieval quality based on the rank of correct documents. Following the recent works (Gao and Callan, 2021; Santhanam et al., 2022), we evaluate text retrieval performances with the BEIR benchmark (Thakur et al., 2021), which aims to evaluate zero-shot retrieval performance of text embedding models. We consider five datasets: FiQA-2018, NFCorpus, ArguAna, SCIDOCS, and SciFact. Each dataset contains domain-specific text data. For instance, FiQA-2018 consists of finance search queries which are representative examples of privacy-sensitive texts.

We use publicly open text embedding models without additional fine-tuning to demonstrate that our approach can be applied generally to any existing text embedding models. For STS and text retrieval, we use *SimCSE*[4] and *DistilBERT*[5] checkpoints from huggingface transformers (Wolf et al., 2020) as our backbone models, respectively. More details about evaluation settings can be found in Appendix A.

4.2 Privacy-Preserving Baseline

1. **Plaintext:** The results from text embeddings without privacy-preserving schemes are obvious counterparts to be compared with privacy-preserved ones. In the rest of this paper, we denote them as *plaintext*. The common objective of our method and other privacy-preserving baselines is to precisely approximate the performances of *plaintext* while preventing the exposure of original information.

2. **d_χ-privacy:** Following Qu et al. (2021) and Lee et al. (2022), we consider d_χ-privacy, which is a relaxed variant of noise-based local differential privacy (LDP) methods as our baseline. The method prevents information leakage of text embeddings

[3]https://github.com/facebookresearch/SentEval

[4]https://huggingface.co/princeton-nlp/sup-simcse-bert-base-uncased

[5]https://huggingface.co/sentence-transformers/msmarco-distilbert-base-v3

	SentEval							BEIR benchmark				
	STS12	STS13	STS14	STS15	STS16	STS-B	SICK-R	FiQA-2018	NFCorpus	ArguAna	SCIDOCS	SciFact
Plaintext	**0.1617**	**0.1381**	**0.1493**	**0.1496**	**0.1033**	**0.2489**	**0.1325**	**0.6281**	**0.4731**	**0.0797**	**0.1556**	**0.6098**
$\eta = 175$	0.0492	0.0546	0.0466	0.0441	0.0321	0.0699	0.0232	0.5718	0.3237	0.0694	0.1132	0.4806
$\eta = 150$	0.0407	0.0505	0.0425	0.0392	0.0318	0.0592	0.0262	0.5715	0.3175	0.0638	0.1154	0.5101
$\eta = 125$	0.0333	0.0406	0.0344	0.0296	0.0254	0.0465	0.0178	0.5603	0.3225	0.0560	0.0984	0.4756
$\eta = 100$	0.0248	0.0280	0.0235	0.0211	0.0152	0.0350	0.0114	0.5060	0.2245	0.0494	0.0823	0.4175
$\eta = 75$	0.0139	0.0141	0.0115	0.0101	0.0075	0.0190	0.0040	0.4347	0.1827	0.0375	0.0558	0.2844
$\eta = 50$	0.0031	0.0027	0.0019	0.0016	0.0017	0.0049	0.0007	0.3204	0.0910	0.0249	0.0283	0.1439

Table 2: **Performance of Text Embedding Inversion.** Black-box inversion on text embeddings with text data from SentEval and BEIR benchmark. We report the F1 scores of multi-label classifiers predicting words in original text from given text embeddings.

	SentEval							BEIR benchmark				
Name	STS12	STS13	STS14	STS15	STS16	STSB	SICK-R	FiQA-2018	NFCorpus	ArguAna	SCIDOCS	SciFact
#Texts	3,108	1,500	3,750	3,000	1,186	1,379	4,927	648	323	1,406	1,000	300
#Avg words	6.33	6.48	6.09	5.88	5.96	5.76	4.94	6.48	2.59	108.38	7.80	9.12

Table 3: **Statistics of evaluation text data.** #Texts indicates the number of sentence pairs and queries. #Avg words show the number of average words per sentence and query.

through the noise injection privatization. For a given embedding x and sampled noise N, the privatized embedding is $P(x) = x + N$. We sample $N \in \mathbb{R}^n$ by $N = rp$ where r is sampled from the Gamma distribution $\Gamma(n, \frac{1}{\eta})$ and p is sampled from the uniform distribution $\mathbb{B}^n$. Same as Lee et al. (2022), we measure performances at six noise levels (η = 175, 150, 125, 100, 75, 50). Lower η indicates higher noise to embeddings and better privacy-preserving.

4.3 Text Embedding Inversion

We investigate inversion risk existing in text similarity tasks. Song and Raghunathan (2020) suggests two methods for embedding inversion attack, namely, white-box and black-box inversion. We choose **black-box inversion** since it assumes that an attacker only can access text embeddings but no access to model itself. This property is suitable for our privacy-preserving concerns on the applications which utilize precomputed embeddings for text similarity inference. Black-box inversion, in a nutshell, trains a multi-label classifier which takes text embeddings as inputs and predicts words in original texts.

$$\max_{\phi} \sum_{s \in S} \sum_{w \in W} \log p_{\phi}(w|E(s))$$

Formally, for any pretrained text embedding model E, we train an inversion model ϕ by maximizing the log-likelihood where S and W are a set of training sentences and a set of words in a sentence, respectively.

Implementation As an inversion model, we use a simple 1-layer MLP which shows enough performance to extract meaningful information from given text embeddings in our test. To train the inversion model, we sample sentences from BookCorpus (Zhu et al., 2015) and take the train-split texts from benchmark datasets. To choose the best checkpoints and the thresholds for classifiers, we also make the validation data by using BookCorpus and the development split of benchmark datasets. For more detail settings on text embedding inversion test, see Appendix B.

Result Table 2 shows the performances (F1 measurement) of inversion models. We measure F1 scores for the extracted words filtered by the best threshold selected by validation data. Note that our HE approach is not included in the test because it provides complete security (see Section 3.1). First, we can find the inversion models successfully extract original texts from plaintext embeddings. However, compared to typical classification tasks, the models show poor performances (less than 0.5 point) on overall F1 scores (except for FIQA-2018 and SciFact). This is because the model should perform extreme multi-label classification (Chalkidis et al., 2019) with a large number of classes i.e. the vocab size, which is roughly 20,000 words. We can see that inversion models show worst performance on the ArguAna retrieval dataset, it is because ArguAna consists of search queries much longer than other datasets (presented in Table 3).

Original text from **FIQA-2018**:	
15 year mortgage vs 30 year paid off in 15	
Plaintext	vs, year, mortgag, 30, paid, 15
$\eta = 175$	vs, paid, mortgag, year, loan, 30
$\eta = 150$	vs, mortgag, paid, year, pay, 15
$\eta = 125$	vs, paid, month, bore, 30, pay
$\eta = 100$	vs, mortgag, 30, paid, pay
$\eta = 75$	vs, 30, paid, spare, mortgag, tore
$\eta = 50$	paid, vs, common, pay, hunch

Original text from **STS-B:**	
a man is singing and playing a guitar	
Plaintext	guitar, sing, man, play, fluid
$\eta = 175$	guitar, play, man, banana, trampolin, sing
$\eta = 150$	guitar, play, man, banana, trampolin, afghanistan
$\eta = 125$	guitar, play, banana, man, afghanistan, nadia
$\eta = 100$	guitar, banana, afghanistan, play, nadia, afghan
$\eta = 75$	guitar
$\eta = 50$	-

Table 4: **Result of Text Embedding Inversion with texts from FIQA-2018 and STS-B.** The words with red color are correctly predicted ones.

Meanwhile, inversion models show different overall performances on STS and text retrieval benchmarks. This might be due to two factors, which are: 1) SentEval and BEIR benchmark have different domains of texts i.e. sentences on common domain and search queries for diverse domains such as finance science; 2) most importantly, they use their own text embedding models, *SimCSE* and *DistilBERT*. Even though the overall performance on STS does not reach that of text retrieval, inversion models still extract unneglectable amount of original information. At lowest noise value ($\eta = 175$), the model loses more than half of its performance in the plaintext setting. After that, the results clearly show that the more noise we add the less original information extracted. When a noise reaches the highest value ($\eta = 50$), inversion model shows F1 scores less than 0.01 point on all STS datasets. On the other hand, for text retrieval, the model still has moderate performances (greater than 0.3 point at most).

Qualitative Analysis We analyze two examples of text embedding inversion in order to provide an qualitative analysis. We bring two examples of texts from FIQA-2018 and STS-B shown in Table 4. We enumerate extracted words up to Top-6 words ordered by their likelihood scores. We set the number of top words based on the analysis from Table 3, which shows the number of average tokens on most datasets is about 6. We first see the example from FIQA-2018. From the plaintext embedding, the inversion model successfully extracts a set of words (*vs, year, mortgag, 30, paid, 15*) that represent the semantic information of original text and have no false positive words. After we add lowest noise ($\eta = 175$) to the embedding, the model starts to confuse semantically related words (*mortgag* $\rightarrow$ *loan, paid* $\rightarrow$ *pay*). At highest noise ($\eta = 50$), the model starts to extract completely unrelated words such as *common, hunch.* We can observe similar patterns on the example of STS-B. The inversion model extracts all important words (*guitar, sing, man, play*) and only one false positive word (*fluid*) from the plaintext embedding. After we maximize the noise, the model failed to extract any words (filtered by a threshold). By using d_χ-privacy, it is possible to alleviate the embedding inversion but not enough to prevent it completely. These results demonstrate how vulnerable text embeddings are in terms of potential information leakages. For more examples on other datasets, see Appendix C.

4.4 Text Similarity Evaluation

Implementation We implemented HE methods with the full residual number system (RNS) of the CKKS scheme (Cheon et al., 2018b) that supports bootstrapping on GPU. We utilized approximation of the square root inverse with a vector-vector multiplication in STS and a vector-matrix multiplication to compute dot products in Text Retrieval. Note that we only encrypt query texts in retrieval settings since we suppose a situation where documents are open to the public and need not to be protected. Similar to computing cosine similarity, other similarity functions like dot product can be easily implemented with additions and multiplications in an encrypted state. For detailed descriptions of our HE parameters, refer to Appendix D.

Semantic Textual Similarity Table 5 shows the performance results on STS datasets. To accurately validate the approximation performance of our HE method, we report the Spearman's correlation scores displaying floating point numbers up to seven decimal point. At the first step of noise ($\eta = 175$), the noise-based perturbation, d_χ privacy loses about 10% of plaintext performance in average. It shows the largest drop at STS-12 (75.2961809

	STS-12	STS-13	STS-14	STS-15	STS-16	STS-B	SICK-R	Avg
Plaintext	75.2961809	84.6670451	80.1894789	**85.3988064**	**80.8192094**	84.1348744	80.3869902	81.5561381
$\eta = 175$	51.7546246	74.0075826	67.1210473	81.6210128	69.9514644	78.9265977	78.1727766	71.6507294
$\eta = 150$	48.2063251	71.9283803	64.6684534	80.4148958	67.3609882	77.2761905	77.0743311	69.5613663
$\eta = 125$	44.3021020	69.2406938	61.6506406	78.6018538	63.8953096	74.9027321	75.2612661	66.8363711
$\eta = 100$	39.9374092	65.3637801	57.6159417	75.5333165	58.9898118	71.1861685	72.0707709	62.9567427
$\eta = 75$	34.4587947	58.1591253	50.9218122	69.1092061	51.0846282	64.1191090	65.5976507	56.2071895
$\eta = 50$	25.1756964	41.6619297	36.5166211	52.4056402	35.6048580	47.1511518	49.2968972	41.1161135
HE (Ours)	**75.2984575**	84.6670451	**80.1894864**	85.3988015	80.8192093	**84.1348781**	**80.3870014**	**81.5564113**
diff. w plaintext	0.0022766	-	0.0000075	-0.0000049	-0.0000001	0.0000036	0.0000112	0.0003277

Table 5: **Performance of Semantic Textual Similarity task.** We report Spearman's correlation scores using the SentEval toolkit. At the bottom of the table, we show the gap between Plaintext results and HE approximations. Values in bold denote better scores.

	FiQA-2018	NFCorpus	ArguAna	SCIDOCS	SciFact
Plaintext	0.2569705	**0.2564896**	**0.4261360**	0.1332835	**0.5378220**
$\eta = 175$	0.2384545	0.2568275	0.4177632	0.1263631	0.5305757
$\eta = 150$	0.2327629	0.2533514	0.4136059	0.1252494	0.4925842
$\eta = 125$	0.2262708	0.2521192	0.4073824	0.1204473	0.5075745
$\eta = 100$	0.2142368	0.2478810	0.3909309	0.1112396	0.4824138
$\eta = 75$	0.1850581	0.2281045	0.3484871	0.0938708	0.4300155
$\eta = 50$	0.1071001	0.1670855	0.2334603	0.0499934	0.2653896
HE (Ours)	0.2569705	0.2564895	0.4259367	0.1332835	0.5378219
diff. w plaintext	-	-0.0000001	-0.0001993	-	-0.0000001

Table 6: **Performance of Text Retrieval task.** We report nDCG@10 scores.

$\rightarrow$ 51.7546246). After the representation of text embeddings are highly collapsed with large noise ($\eta = 50$), the average correlation scores down to the half of the original score (81.5561381 $\rightarrow$ 41.1161135). On the other hand, we can see that our HE method preserves the performance of plaintext almost completely. The method lose scores less than 10^{-5} point from plaintext (at most 0.0000049 point on STS-15). We can also observe the increase of scores at STS-12, STS-14, STS-B and SICK-R datasets. This happens to occur because the noises during encryption may influence in a positive way to compute the scores. As a result, in terms of average score, plaintext and our approach have almost the same scores (less than 10^{-3} point difference between them). In particular, the average absolute deviation between the plaintext cosine similarity scores and the ciphertext cosine similarity scores is from 3.89×10^{-8} in STS15 (lowest) to 5.08×10^{-8} in STS12 (highest).

Text Retrieval Table 5 shows the experimental results on text retrieval datasets. We report nDCG(Normalized Discounted Cumulative Gain) scores. Different from the results on STS datasets, the d_{χ}-privacy method shows relatively robust performances on text retrieval. We can observe little performance degradation (less than 5%) on most datasets (except for FIQA-2018). Even if we increase noise further, it still maintain small degradation (less than 10%). We think theses differences comes from their evaluation metrics (spearman's correlation and nDCG). Since the correlation measures the difference between ground truth similarities and predicted ones, the noise directly affects the final correlation scores although the noise is small. In contrast, nDCG is measured by the rank of documents which remain the same if the noise only affects to the relevance scores but not to the rank of documents. However, at the last noise step (η = 50), the scores drop under 50% of original scores similar to the results on STS datasets. On the other hand, same as the STS result, our HE method maintains plaintext performance with little degradation (at most 0.0001993 point on ArguAna). More precisely, the average absolute deviation between the dot-products in plaintext and those in ciphertext lies from 3.67×10^{-8} in SciFact (lowest) to 3.94×10^{-8} in NFCorpus (highest).

5 Conclusions

In this paper, we proposed homomorphic encryption based text similarity inference with text embeddings. With our method, users can utilize text embedding based services without revealing the original text, which can be recovered through inversion attacks as we demonstrated in the experiment 4.3. Extensive experiments 4.4 on two text similarity tasks proved that our approach does not harm the performance of models. In contrast, the d_{χ}-privacy baselines fail to achieve protection from inversion attacks without performance degradation. We hope that this work lays the groundwork for the secure usage of text embeddings in privacy-sensitive industries like finance and more future works on the practical usage of our HE approach by resolving the current limitations.

Limitations

Our HE-based methods report that a vector-vector multiplication in STS takes roughly 30 to 40 ms per text on average. For text retrieval, a vector-matrix multiplication per query takes approximately 0.6 to 0.7 seconds against 1,000 documents in our benchmark datasets on average. The computation time increases linearly depending on the number of documents. Since operations in an encrypted state are computationally expensive, efficiency need to improve in computing time to provide document search services over large amounts of corpora for a practical use.

For efficient search with text embedding similarities, modern applications equip with approximate search frameworks like faiss[6]. Such method becomes more crucial when handling open-domain search corpus like Wikipedia (larger than 5 million of documents). Since the HE implementation in this paper focuses on relatively simple similarity functions like cosine similarity, it is non-trivial to be directly incorporated with existing frameworks and algorithms that utilize complex data structures and operations like hashing and graph-based search. Therefore, one of our future works will be the research on the implementation of the HE based efficient search methods.

Acknowledgements

We thank our anonymous reviewers for their constructive comments. Lee was supported by Institute of Information & communications Technology Planning & Evaluation (IITP) grant funded by the Korea government (MSIT) [NO.2022-0-01047, Development of statistical analysis algorithm and module using homomorphic encryption based on real number operation].

[6]https://github.com/facebookresearch/faiss

References

Abbas Acar, Hidayet Aksu, A. Selcuk Uluagac, and Mauro Conti. 2018. A survey on homomorphic encryption schemes: Theory and implementation. *ACM Comput. Surv.*, 51(4).

Eneko Agirre, Carmen Banea, Claire Cardie, Daniel Cer, Mona Diab, Aitor Gonzalez-Agirre, Weiwei Guo, Iñigo Lopez-Gazpio, Montse Maritxalar, Rada Mihalcea, German Rigau, Larraitz Uria, and Janyce Wiebe. 2015. SemEval-2015 task 2: Semantic textual similarity, English, Spanish and pilot on interpretability. In *Proceedings of the 9th International Workshop on Semantic Evaluation (SemEval 2015)*, pages 252–263, Denver, Colorado. Association for Computational Linguistics.

Eneko Agirre, Carmen Banea, Claire Cardie, Daniel Cer, Mona Diab, Aitor Gonzalez-Agirre, Weiwei Guo, Rada Mihalcea, German Rigau, and Janyce Wiebe. 2014. SemEval-2014 task 10: Multilingual semantic textual similarity. In *Proceedings of the 8th International Workshop on Semantic Evaluation (SemEval 2014)*, pages 81–91, Dublin, Ireland. Association for Computational Linguistics.

Eneko Agirre, Carmen Banea, Daniel Cer, Mona Diab, Aitor Gonzalez-Agirre, Rada Mihalcea, German Rigau, and Janyce Wiebe. 2016. SemEval-2016 task 1: Semantic textual similarity, monolingual and cross-lingual evaluation. In *Proceedings of the 10th International Workshop on Semantic Evaluation (SemEval-2016)*, pages 497–511, San Diego, California. Association for Computational Linguistics.

Eneko Agirre, Daniel Cer, Mona Diab, and Aitor Gonzalez-Agirre. 2012. SemEval-2012 task 6: A pilot on semantic textual similarity. In **SEM 2012: The First Joint Conference on Lexical and Computational Semantics – Volume 1: Proceedings of the main conference and the shared task, and Volume 2: Proceedings of the Sixth International Workshop on Semantic Evaluation (SemEval 2012)*, pages 385–393, Montréal, Canada. Association for Computational Linguistics.

Eneko Agirre, Daniel Cer, Mona Diab, Aitor Gonzalez-Agirre, and Weiwei Guo. 2013. *SEM 2013 shared task: Semantic textual similarity. In *Second Joint Conference on Lexical and Computational Semantics (*SEM), Volume 1: Proceedings of the Main Conference and the Shared Task: Semantic Textual Similarity*, pages 32–43, Atlanta, Georgia, USA. Association for Computational Linguistics.

Zvika Brakerski, Craig Gentry, and Vinod Vaikuntanathan. 2011. Fully homomorphic encryption without bootstrapping. Cryptology ePrint Archive, Paper 2011/277. `https://eprint.iacr.org/2011/277`.

Sergiu Carpov and Renaud Sirdey. 2015. A compression method for homomorphic ciphertexts. *IACR Cryptol. ePrint Arch.*, 2015:1199.

Daniel Cer, Mona Diab, Eneko Agirre, Iñigo Lopez-Gazpio, and Lucia Specia. 2017. SemEval-2017 task 1: Semantic textual similarity multilingual and crosslingual focused evaluation. In *Proceedings of the 11th International Workshop on Semantic Evaluation (SemEval-2017)*, pages 1–14, Vancouver, Canada. Association for Computational Linguistics.

Daniel Cer, Yinfei Yang, Sheng-yi Kong, Nan Hua, Nicole Limtiaco, Rhomni St. John, Noah Constant, Mario Guajardo-Cespedes, Steve Yuan, Chris Tar, Brian Strope, and Ray Kurzweil. 2018. Universal sentence encoder for English. In *Proceedings of the 2018 Conference on Empirical Methods in Natural Language Processing: System Demonstrations*, pages 169–174, Brussels, Belgium. Association for Computational Linguistics.

Ilias Chalkidis, Emmanouil Fergadiotis, Prodromos Malakasiotis, Nikolaos Aletras, and Ion Androutsopoulos. 2019. Extreme multi-label legal text classification: A case study in EU legislation. In *Proceedings of the Natural Legal Language Processing Workshop 2019*, pages 78–87, Minneapolis, Minnesota. Association for Computational Linguistics.

Tianyu Chen, Hangbo Bao, Shaohan Huang, Li Dong, Binxing Jiao, Daxin Jiang, Haoyi Zhou, Jianxin Li, and Furu Wei. 2022. THE-X: Privacy-preserving transformer inference with homomorphic encryption. In *Findings of the Association for Computational Linguistics: ACL 2022*, pages 3510–3520, Dublin, Ireland. Association for Computational Linguistics.

Jung Hee Cheon, Kyoohyung Han, Andrey Kim, Miran Kim, and Yongsoo Song. 2018a. Bootstrapping for approximate homomorphic encryption. In *Advances in Cryptology – EUROCRYPT 2018*, pages 360–384, Cham. Springer International Publishing.

Jung Hee Cheon, Kyoohyung Han, Andrey Kim, Miran Kim, and Yongsoo Song. 2018b. A full RNS variant of approximate homomorphic encryption. In *International Conference on Selected Areas in Cryptography*, pages 347–368. Springer.

Jung Hee Cheon, Kyoohyung Han, Andrey Kim, Miran Kim, and Yongsoo Song. 2019. A full rns variant of approximate homomorphic encryption. In *Selected Areas in Cryptography – SAC 2018*, pages 347–368, Cham. Springer International Publishing.

Jung Hee Cheon, Andrey Kim, Miran Kim, and Yongsoo Song. 2017. Homomorphic encryption for arithmetic of approximate numbers. In *Advances in Cryptology – ASIACRYPT 2017*, pages 409–437, Cham. Springer International Publishing.

Jung Hee Cheon, Yongha Son, and Donggeon Yhee. 2022. Practical FHE parameters against lattice attacks. *Journal of the Korean Mathematical Society*, 59(1):35–51.

Alexis Conneau and Douwe Kiela. 2018. SentEval: An evaluation toolkit for universal sentence representations. In *Proceedings of the Eleventh International Conference on Language Resources and Evaluation (LREC 2018)*, Miyazaki, Japan. European Language Resources Association (ELRA).

Junfeng Fan and Frederik Vercauteren. 2012. Somewhat practical fully homomorphic encryption. Cryptology ePrint Archive, Paper 2012/144. `https://eprint.iacr.org/2012/144`.

Oluwaseyi Feyisetan, Borja Balle, Thomas Drake, and Tom Diethe. 2020. Privacy- and utility-preserving textual analysis via calibrated multivariate perturbations. In *WSDM '20: The Thirteenth ACM International Conference on Web Search and Data Mining, Houston, TX, USA, February 3-7, 2020*, pages 178–186. ACM.

Luyu Gao and Jamie Callan. 2021. Condenser: a pre-training architecture for dense retrieval. In *Proceedings of the 2021 Conference on Empirical Methods in Natural Language Processing*, pages 981–993, Online and Punta Cana, Dominican Republic. Association for Computational Linguistics.

Tianyu Gao, Xingcheng Yao, and Danqi Chen. 2021. SimCSE: Simple contrastive learning of sentence embeddings. In *Proceedings of the 2021 Conference on Empirical Methods in Natural Language Processing*, pages 6894–6910, Online and Punta Cana, Dominican Republic. Association for Computational Linguistics.

Craig Gentry. 2009. Fully homomorphic encryption using ideal lattices. volume 9, pages 169–178.

Jia-Chen Gu, Tianda Li, Quan Liu, Zhen-Hua Ling, Zhiming Su, Si Wei, and Xiaodan Zhu. 2020. Speaker-aware bert for multi-turn response selection in retrieval-based chatbots. In *Proceedings of the 29th ACM International Conference on Information and Knowledge Management*, CIKM '20, pages 2041–2044. ACM.

Samuel Humeau, Kurt Shuster, Marie-Anne Lachaux, and Jason Weston. 2020. Poly-encoders: Architectures and pre-training strategies for fast and accurate multi-sentence scoring. In *International Conference on Learning Representations*.

Vladimir Karpukhin, Barlas Oguz, Sewon Min, Patrick Lewis, Ledell Wu, Sergey Edunov, Danqi Chen, and Wen-tau Yih. 2020. Dense passage retrieval for open-domain question answering. In *Proceedings of the 2020 Conference on Empirical Methods in Natural Language Processing (EMNLP)*, pages 6769–6781, Online. Association for Computational Linguistics.

Garam Lee, Minsoo Kim, Jai Hyun Park, Seung-won Hwang, and Jung Hee Cheon. 2022. Privacy-preserving text classification on BERT embeddings with homomorphic encryption. In *Proceedings of the 2022 Conference of the North American Chapter of the Association for Computational Linguistics: Human Language Technologies*, pages 3169–3175, Seattle, United States. Association for Computational Linguistics.

Marco Marelli, Stefano Menini, Marco Baroni, Luisa Bentivogli, Raffaella Bernardi, and Roberto Zamparelli. 2014. A SICK cure for the evaluation of compositional distributional semantic models. In *Proceedings of the Ninth International Conference on Language Resources and Evaluation (LREC'14)*, pages 216–223, Reykjavik, Iceland. European Language Resources Association (ELRA).

Andreas Nautsch, Sergey Isadskiy, Jascha Kolberg, Marta Gomez-Barrero, and Christoph Busch. 2018. Homomorphic encryption for speaker recognition: Protection of biometric templates and vendor model parameters. pages 16–23.

Samanvaya Panda. 2021. *Principal Component Analysis Using CKKS Homomorphic Scheme*, pages 52–70.

Chen Qu, Weize Kong, Liu Yang, Mingyang Zhang, Michael Bendersky, and Marc Najork. 2021. Natural language understanding with privacy-preserving bert. In *Proceedings of the 30th ACM International Conference on Information Knowledge Management*, CIKM '21, page 1488–1497, New York, NY, USA. Association for Computing Machinery.

Nils Reimers and Iryna Gurevych. 2019. Sentence-BERT: Sentence embeddings using Siamese BERT-networks. In *Proceedings of the 2019 Conference on Empirical Methods in Natural Language Processing and the 9th International Joint Conference on Natural Language Processing (EMNLP-IJCNLP)*, pages 3982–3992, Hong Kong, China. Association for Computational Linguistics.

Stephen Robertson and Hugo Zaragoza. 2009. The probabilistic relevance framework: Bm25 and beyond. *Found. Trends Inf. Retr.*, 3(4):333–389.

Keshav Santhanam, Omar Khattab, Jon Saad-Falcon, Christopher Potts, and Matei Zaharia. 2022. ColBERTv2: Effective and efficient retrieval via lightweight late interaction. In *Proceedings of the 2022 Conference of the North American Chapter of the Association for Computational Linguistics: Human Language Technologies*, pages 3715–3734, Seattle, United States. Association for Computational Linguistics.

Paul M. Schwartz and Daniel J. Solove. 2011. The PII Problem: Privacy and a New Concept of Personally Identifiable Information. *NYUL Rev.*, 86:1814–1894.

Congzheng Song and Ananth Raghunathan. 2020. Information leakage in embedding models. In *Proceedings of the 2020 ACM SIGSAC Conference on Computer and Communications Security*, CCS '20, page 377–390, New York, NY, USA. Association for Computing Machinery.

Nandan Thakur, Nils Reimers, Andreas Rücklé, Abhishek Srivastava, and Iryna Gurevych. 2021. BEIR: A heterogeneous benchmark for zero-shot evaluation of information retrieval models. In *Thirty-fifth Conference on Neural Information Processing Systems Datasets and Benchmarks Track (Round 2)*.

Spencer Wheatley, Thomas Maillart, and Didier Sornette. 2016. The extreme risk of personal data breaches and the erosion of privacy. *The European Physical Journal B*, 89(1):1–12.

Thomas Wolf, Lysandre Debut, Victor Sanh, Julien Chaumond, Clement Delangue, Anthony Moi, Pierric Cistac, Tim Rault, Rémi Louf, Morgan Funtowicz, Joe Davison, Sam Shleifer, Patrick von Platen, Clara Ma, Yacine Jernite, Julien Plu, Canwen Xu, Teven Le Scao, Sylvain Gugger, Mariama Drame, Quentin Lhoest, and Alexander M. Rush. 2020. Transformers: State-of-the-art natural language processing. In *Proceedings of the 2020 Conference on Empirical Methods in Natural Language Processing: System Demonstrations*, pages 38–45, Online. Association for Computational Linguistics.

Ping Xiong, Lin Liang, Yunli Zhu, and Tianqing Zhu. 2022. Pritxt: A privacy risk assessment method for text data based on semantic correlation learning. *Concurrency and Computation: Practice and Experience*, 34(5):e6680.

Xiaojie Yu, Xiaojun Chen, and Jinqiao Shi. 2017. Vector based privacy-preserving document similarity with lsa. In *2017 IEEE 9th International Conference on Communication Software and Networks (ICCSN)*, pages 1383–1387.

Yukun Zhu, Ryan Kiros, Rich Zemel, Ruslan Salakhutdinov, Raquel Urtasun, Antonio Torralba, and Sanja Fidler. 2015. Aligning books and movies: Towards story-like visual explanations by watching movies and reading books. In *The IEEE International Conference on Computer Vision (ICCV)*.

A Experimental Settings for Text Similarity Tasks

Hyperparameters for text embedding models are shown in Table 7. We only report the parameters necessary for inference because we do not fine-tune the models at all. The models used for two text similarity tasks have differences on 1) their pooling strategies which decides the way to aggregate transformer hidden states to single text embedding, 2) the similarity functions to calculate the relevancy between text embeddings.

Hyperparams	SimCSE	DistilBERT
Pooling strategy	[CLS]	mean
Max sequence length	512	512
Embedding size	768	768
Similarity	cosine	dot product

Table 7: Hyperparams for text embedding model test.

B Experimental Settings for Text Embedding Inversion

Hyperparameters for inversion model are shown in Table 8. We sample 100k sentences from BookCorpus as train data. We choose the best threshold parameter based on the results with thresholds from 0.6 to 1.0 with an interval 0.05. As a result, 0.90 and 0.95 thresholds are selected for SentEval and BEIR benchmark, respectively. To build the vocabulary for inversion model predictions, we tokenize given texts with spacy[7] and postprocess them by removing stopwords and normalizing words with lemmatization[8].

Hyperparams	Inversion Model
Learning rate	0.001
Max epoch	100
Batch size	64
Hidden size	768
Threshold range	[0.6, 1.0]

Table 8: Hyperparams for inversion model training and test.

[7]https://spacy.io/

[8]https://www.nltk.org/index.html

C Text Embedding Inversion Results

Table 9 shows additional text embedding inversion results from NFCorpus, SCIDOCS, SciFact, and SICK-R.

Original text from **NFCorpus:** *Do Cholesterol Statin Drugs Cause Breast Cancer?*	
Plaintext	cholesterol, cancer, caus, statin, drug, breast
$\eta = 175$	cholesterol, caus, statin, cancer, breast, **exact**
$\eta = 150$	cholesterol, cancer, statin, breast, drug, caus
$\eta = 125$	cholesterol, cancer, statin, breast, caus
$\eta = 100$	cholesterol, breast, caus, cancer, statin
$\eta = 75$	cholesterol, cancer, statin, breast, drug, **induc**
$\eta = 50$	cholesterol, cancer, statin, breast, **soar**
Original text from **SCIDOCS:** *Digital image forensics: a booklet for beginners*	
Plaintext	beginn, digit, imag, begin, **twelv**
$\eta = 175$	digit, beginn, **photograph**, **slowli**, **fascin**, **pictur**
$\eta = 150$	digit, beginn, **photograph**, **fool**, **examin**, **pictur**
$\eta = 125$	beginn, digit, **photograph**, **photo**, imag, **dive**
$\eta = 100$	**photograph**, **pictur**, imag, digit, beginn, **studi**
$\eta = 75$	**photograph**, digit, **absorb**, **prod**, **fascin**
$\eta = 50$	**drawer**, **manual**, **photo**, **examin**, **lectur**, **memor**
Original text from **SciFact:** *0-dimensional biomaterials show inductive properties.*	
Plaintext	biomateri, dimension, induct, properti
$\eta = 175$	dimension, biomateri, induct, properti, **note**
$\eta = 150$	induct, dimension, biomateri, **feminin**, **tight**, **close**
$\eta = 125$	biomateri, dimension, properti
$\eta = 100$	biomateri, dimension, induct, **element**, **feminin**, **announc**
$\eta = 75$	induct, **scrub**, **tentat**, **dealt**, **project**, show
$\eta = 50$	dimension, **agon**, **daze**, biomateri, induct, **darren**
Original text from **SICK-R:** *A black dog on a leash is walking in the water*	
Plaintext	dog, black, **collar**
$\eta = 175$	black, **bella**
$\eta = 150$	black, **bella**
$\eta = 125$	black, **bella**
$\eta = 100$	black, **bella**
$\eta = 75$	**mall**, **daypack**
$\eta = 50$	-

Table 9: Result of Text Embedding Inversion

D Our HE parameter selection

For STS, we selected CKKS parameter whose dimension $N = 2^{16}$ and its modulus q is 2^{1555}. For text retrieval, since dot products only require additions and multiplications, we select a ciphertext parameter preset for Somewhat Homomorphic Encryption (Gentry, 2009) for efficiency in computation. We choose a parameter set where dimension N is 2^{13} so each ciphertext block consists of $2^{13-1} = 4,096$ slots and its modulus $q \approx 2^{217}$ guarantees a 128-bit security level under SparseLWE-estimator.

TweetFinSent: A Dataset of Stock Sentiments on Twitter

Yulong Pei[1], **Amarachi Mbakwe**[2], **Akshat Gupta**[2], **Salwa Alamir**[1]
Hanxuan Lin[3], **Xiaomo Liu**[2], **Sameena Shah**[2]
[1]JP Morgan AI Research, London, UK
[2]JP Morgan AI Research, New York, USA
[3]JP Morgan, Shanghai, China
{yulong.pei,xiaomo.liu}@jpmchase.com

Abstract

Stock sentiment has strong correlations with the stock market but traditional sentiment analysis task classifies sentiment according to having feelings and emotions of good or bad. This definition of sentiment is not an accurate indicator of public opinion about specific stocks. To bridge this gap, we introduce a new task of stock sentiment analysis and present a new dataset for this task named TweetFinSent. In TweetFinSent, tweets are annotated based on if one gained or expected to gain positive or negative return from a stock. Experiments on TweetFinSent with several sentiment analysis models from lexicon-based to transformer-based have been conducted. Experimental results show that TweetFinSent dataset constitutes a challenging problem and there is ample room for improvement on the stock sentiment analysis task. TweetFinSent is available at https://github.com/jpmcair/tweetfinsent.

1 Introduction

Sentiment analysis, as a classical research problem in machine learning and natural language processing, aims to analyze peoples opinions, sentiments, and emotions towards entities such as products, services, organizations, individuals, and their attributes (Liu, 2012). A large amount of attention in industry and research community has been given to analysing sentiment of Twitter feeds. This has been done to analyse the effectiveness and predicting the result of election campaigns (Wang et al., 2012; Ramteke et al., 2016), analyse Twitter mood during the Covid-19 outbreak (Manguri et al., 2020; Dubey, 2020) and to analyse and predict the stock market. It has been repeatedly shown in literature that the Twitter sentiment has strong correlations with the stock market, with several works on predicting the stock market movement based on Twitter sentiment (Bollen and Mao, 2011; Bollen et al., 2011; Mittal and Goel, 2012). For instance, recent discussions of meme stocks on social media such as Twitter and Reddit have attracted significant attention and influenced the sentiment of investors especially young and inexperienced investors[1]. Therefore, it is of great value to analyse stock sentiment in both practice and research.

Despite the wide interest and importance, most existing research on sentiment analysis focused on distinguishing if the text contains or a user has feelings or emotions of good or bad. However, in the financial domain, we would like to analyse more specific and concrete sentiment, i.e., we aim to re-calibrate the definition of sentiment to include this desired property such as gaining or expecting to gain positive or negative return from a stock. Although traditional sentiment analysis of Twitter feeds correlates with the stock market dynamics to some extent, it is not an accurate indicator of public opinion about financial returns of specific stocks. In worst case, traditional sentiment analysis methods may classify tweets into controversy sentiment due to various factors such as finance-specific terms. Some representative examples are shown in Table 1. To bridge the gap, we introduce the concept of *stock sentiment*, where a positive sentiment indicates the opinion of a stock value increasing, a negative sentiment indicates the opinion of a stock value decreasing, and a neutral sentiment indicating that the given sentence does not make predictions for either. Stock sentiment is inherently related to the mention of a specific stock in the sentence. Based on the new definition of stock sentiment, we introduce the task of stock sentiment analysis, underlining the need for moving away from the traditional sentiment analysis definition.

[1] https://en.wikipedia.org/wiki/Meme_stock

Proceedings of the Fourth Workshop on Financial Technology and Natural Language Processing (FinNLP), pages 37 - 47
December 8, 2022 ©2022 Association for Computational Linguistics

Table 1: Some examples showing the differences between traditional sentiment and stock sentiment. For the traditional sentiment analysis, RoBERTa-base model trained on 124M tweets and fine-tuned for sentiment analysis with the TweetEval benchmark (Loureiro et al., 2022) is used.

Tweet	Target Ticker	Traditional Sentiment	Stock Sentiment
Bubbles burst an any given moment. Maybe $TSLA bubble will burst with the Bitcoin buy.	$TSLA	Neutral	Negative
$BABA is on yolo status and I almost sold $BIDU lol.	$BABA	Neutral	Positive
$SOFI Not touching it. I love the company though. We all know the rules, and know what happens during the lockup expiry	$SOFI	Positive	Negative
*Buy the f*cking dip! Hold the line! $AMC $GME $NOK*	$AMC	Negative	Positive

We then construct an expert-annotated dataset for stock sentiment analysis called TweetFinSent which will be made publicly available to the research community. We benchmark this dataset with various state-of-the-art baselines. Experimental results show that TweetFinSent dataset constitutes a challenging problem and there is ample room for improvement on the stock sentiment analysis task.

In summary, our main contributions are three-fold:

- We construct and release TweetFinSent, a new Twitter stock sentiment dataset. To the best of our knowledge, this is the first resource for stock sentiment analysis.
- We demonstrate the utility of the TweetFinSent dataset by evaluating different types of state-of-the-art sentiment analysis models on our dataset.
- We investigate the performance of different baselines and outline the challenge of the stock sentiment analysis task and future directions.

2 Related Work

The tremendous growth of unstructured text data has spurred research in NLP, especially in the area of sentiment analysis, which involves classifying and analyzing of people's opinions, emotions, and sentiments from textual data (Liu, 2012). In NLP, sentiment analysis plays a significant role in analyzing the emotions or feelings behind written texts which serve different purposes depending on the domain of its applications. Since sentiment analysis is an increasingly valuable tool for many organisations to enhances their decision-making, it has been extended to variety of use cases. However, we'd like to argue the use case of this study is unique in the sense that stock sentiment on Twitter is considerably different from traditional sentiment analysis. In the following, we review most relevant prior work and then highlight the value of our study and dataset.

Twitter sentiment analysis: Twitter sentiment analysis is an important area and has attracted much attention. It is considered a more challenging problem than general sentiment analysis on conventional texts because of the frequent use of slang, irregular words, informal words, and a vast number of tweets on various topics. Twitter sentiment analysis has applications in business management, public actions understanding, political analysis, and other domains. Previous works in Twitter sentiment analysis include sentiment analysis to assist stock prediction (Qasem et al., 2015; Pagolu et al., 2016), discovering brand perception (Arora et al., 2015; Gursoy et al., 2017), and analyzing and predicting election results (Xia et al., 2021; Budiharto and Meiliana, 2018). Researchers proposed different methods to solve this problem including lexicon-based (Elbagir and Yang, 2019), machine learning (Qasem et al., 2015), and hybrid methods (Kolchyna et al., 2015). Recent works (Bozanta et al., 2021; Mathew and Bindu, 2020) have applied transformers for sentiment analysis tasks.

Stock sentiment analysis: stock sentiment analysis significantly differs from general sentiment. It differs in terms of domain and purpose. The purpose behind stock sentiment analysis is usually to predict the stock markets reaction to the sentiments hidden in the text. Previous works have attempted to forecast stock prices using price history. Recent works have begun using textual data for predicting the stock markets reaction. For example, stock market values were predicted using news articles (Kalyani et al., 2016), news headlines (Nemes and Kiss, 2021), and sentiments on social media (Qasem et al., 2015; Mittal and Goel, 2012). Apple Inc. companys news data were collected by (Kalyani et al., 2016) and performed sentiment analysis using supervised machine learning to understand the relationship between news and stock trend. Sentiment analysis of economic news headlines was used by (Nemes and Kiss, 2021) to predict the stock value changes for giant tech companies. (Xing et al., 2020) investigated the error patterns of some widely acknowledged sentiment analysis methods in the finance domain. There have been several sources of data for stock sentiment analysis. Popular sources of data include Financial PhraseBank (Araci, 2019), Yahoo Finance (Koukaras et al., 2022), Finviz (Nemes and Kiss, 2021), StockTwits Data (Araci, 2019), and SemEval (Cortis et al., 2017).

Twitter sentiment for stock analysis: Since Twitter provides a real-time information channel that can generate information about the market even before the leading newswires, it has been investigated for stock analysis. For example, (Souza et al., 2015) showed that social media can be a valuable source in the analysis of the financial dynamics in the retail sector. Also, the collective mood states (happy, calm) derived from large-scale Twitter feeds were correlated to the value of the Dow Jones industrial average over time (Bollen and Mao, 2011). Likewise, the rise and fall in stock prices and public sentiments in tweets were shown in (Pagolu et al., 2016; Smailović et al., 2013) to be strongly related. One of the challenges in Twitter sentiment analysis is lack of labeled data. Most recent works (Pagolu et al., 2016; Aattouchi et al., 2022; Nousi and Tjortjis, 2021) extracted tweets from the Twitter platform. Although some of these datasets are usually prepared by automatic sentiment detection of messages or manually determining the sentiments (Skuza and Romanowski, 2015), they are still in realm of traditional definition ("good" and "bad") of sentiments for stock movements. However, this study is more about retail investors' expected gain or loss from their investments as "stock sentiment" (please refer to Section 3.1 for the formal definition).

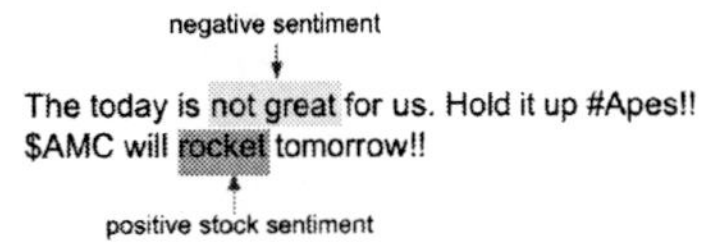

Figure 1: Sentiment vs Stock Sentiment

To the best of our knowledge, no labeled Twitter stock sentiment analysis dataset exists so far. In this paper, we construct and release an expert-annotated Twitter stock sentiment analysis dataset for the downstream stock analysis. This dataset is an essential step toward addressing the missing link of such a dataset in financial industry. The goal of releasing this dataset is to spur the development of more advanced algorithms and for the effective comparisons of these algorithms.

3 The TweetFinSent Dataset

3.1 Task Definition

This study concentrates on a hypothetical use case that financial analysts need conduct equity analyses for a list of stocks and would like to take into account impact of online meme stock communities, in which these stocks may gain popularity on social media platforms like Twitter. Retail investors may rally on these platforms and have collective investment actions on them. Therefore, it can be important for financial analysts to understand the online stock sentiments which are defined as follows.

- **Positive**: Gained or expected to gain positive return from a stock
- **Negative**: Received or expected to receive negative return from a stock
- **Neutral**: Other situations

As one can observe, the stock sentiment in this study correlates but also differentiates from the ordinary sentiment which has been well studied in various scenarios such as product reviews and public opinions etc. These commonly discussed sentiments are more about feelings and emotions of good and bad (Liu, 2012). Nonetheless, the stock sentiment is more about price moving up and down. Stock sentiment and ordinary sentiment can certainly be the same thing. But they sometimes also can be completely unrelated. Figure 1 shows such an example where the indicators for different sentiments are highlighted. In this tweet, the ordinary sentiment to the market is negative,

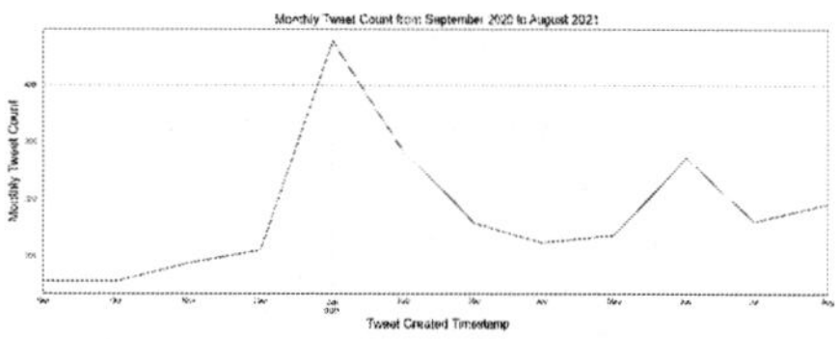

(a) Number of tweets per month.

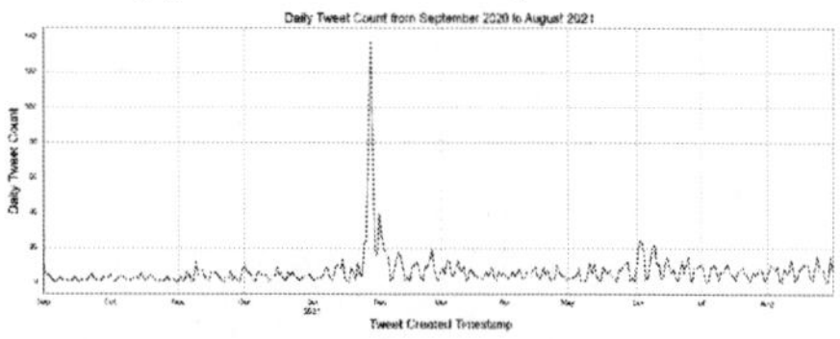

(b) Number of tweets per day.

Figure 2: Number of tweets in TweetFinSent during the time. The number of tweets spike correlates with the GameStop short squeeze in January 2021. The subreddit r/WallStreetBets posts, comments, and Twitter tweets by retail investors related to four meme stocks (GameStop, Nokia, AMC, and Blackberry) initiated the GameStop short squeeze in January, 2021 (tefan Lyócsa et al., 2022; Didier et al., 2022; Chohan, 2021).

but it also expects a specific stock $AMC to rise, which indicates positive stock sentiment. More examples can be found in Table 1.

In the context of social media, an online post such as a tweet P may contain the discussions of multiple stock tickers $G = \{g_1, g_2, ..., g_n\}$, we are interested in calculating the stock sentiment $S(g|G, P)$ towards a target ticker g within a post P. For example, given the following tweet:

> *@PhoShoBro I sold $1000 worth today of my $CLOV and threw it in my $FUBO position and some in $LGHL*

if the target ticker is $CLOV, the stock sentiment is *negative* because this user sold $CLOV. However, if the target ticker is $FUBO or $LGHL, the sentiment is *positive* because she bought $FUBO and $LGHL which indicates that she expected positive return from them. Note that in our TweetFinSent dataset, given a tweet, the target ticker is also provided.

3.2 Data Preparation

We collected 300 stock tickers of interests covering technology, consumer goods and energy etc. various sectors. We then used Twitter's standard search API[2] to retrieve recent 7 days' tweets containing one or multiple stock tickers of interests. Due to the rate limit of Twitter API, at most 17,280 tweets can be collected everyday. The data collection process was ongoing for 12 months from Sep., 2020 to Aug., 2021. Since this study only focuses on the English content, non-English tweets were filtered by the language tag in tweet metadata from API and also using some heuristics developed by authors. After that, a random sample of 2,113 tweets were selected for stock sentiment annotation to construct the TweetFinSent dataset. The volume of tweets per month and per day in TweetFinSent are shown in Figure 2. It is observed that there are two peaks in Figure 2a and 2b. This is consistent with the fact that retail investors initially gathered on r/wallstreetbets[3] and then on Twitter to start a short squeeze on GameStop, pushing their stock prices up significantly from January 22, 2021[4].

3.3 Annotation Procedure

The annotation procedure consists of three steps: (1) annotation guideline discussion to establish criteria of assigning sentiment labels; (2) pilot annotation exercise to resolve annotators' discrepancy (if there is any) of understanding annotation guideline; (3) and final annotation on the entire dataset.

Annotation guideline. Since stock sentiment is notably distinct from ordinary sentiment, a professional financial analyst who is an expert of equity research helped to establish the annotation guidelines on detailed rules of POSITIVE, NEGATIVE, NEUTRAL based on the definition of stock sentiment described earlier. 5 other domain experts were recruited to annotate the entire dataset. To guarantee they are on the same page, the annotators discussed the labeling rules in the guideline with the financial analyst. Through this process, we found some of labeling rules are not straightforward because of the complexity of the languages to express expectations of financial returns on social media. Some labeling rules and non-trivial examples are shown in Appendix.

Pilot annotation. Due to the challenges to be consistent with the labeling rules as shown above, we decided to incorporate an extra step

[2]https://developer.twitter.com/en/docs/twitter-api/v1/tweets/search

[3]https://www.reddit.com/r/wallstreetbets/

[4]https://en.wikipedia.org/wiki/R/wallstreetbets

Table 2: TweetFinSent inter-annotator agreement before and after conflict resolution.

	before	after
Positive	80.4%	90.0%
Neutral	77.8%	90.2%
Negative	67.8%	77.5%
Overall	77.5%	88.5%

for pilot annotation, which is unusual in other annotation tasks (Conforti et al., 2020; Orbach et al., 2020). Our financial analyst expert who created the guideline annotated 50 random samples by himself as the gold label set. They were assigned to every annotator as a pilot annotation exercise. The annotation disagreement (about 20%) with gold labels were discussed among annotators to align with the guideline and avoid potential ambiguity in the final annotation process.

Final annotation. During the final annotation process, 5 domain experts went through the pilot annotation and became the final annotators. 4 of them were assigned to annotate the whole dataset, in which each tweet was independently labeled by at least 2 annotators. The 5th annotator was used to resolve the conflicts in other 4 as a mean of controlling the data quality. If labels of 3 annotators are different, then that data point will be discarded.

3.4 Data Quality Assessment

In order to assess inter-annotator agreement, we calculate the pairwise Cohen's Kappa (κ). The average κ obtained was 0.67, which is substantial (Cohen, 1960) and interpreted as the moderate level of agreement (McHugh, 2012). To guarantee the data quality, we introduce an additional step to resolve the conflicts in annotations. Instead of adding new annotators with potential noise, we utilize an existing annotator. In practice, our conflict resolution step requires two annotators who have conflicted labels to discuss the annotations with a third annotator in order to achieve the agreement. We calculate the inter-annotator agreement ratio overall and at the class level before and after the conflict resolution. The results are presented in Table 2. In this comparison, it can be observed that with this conflict resolution step, we can achieve higher inter-annotator agreement as well as higher data quality. In fact, our overall agreement (88.5%) is higher than some previous sentiment analysis datasets; e.g., the

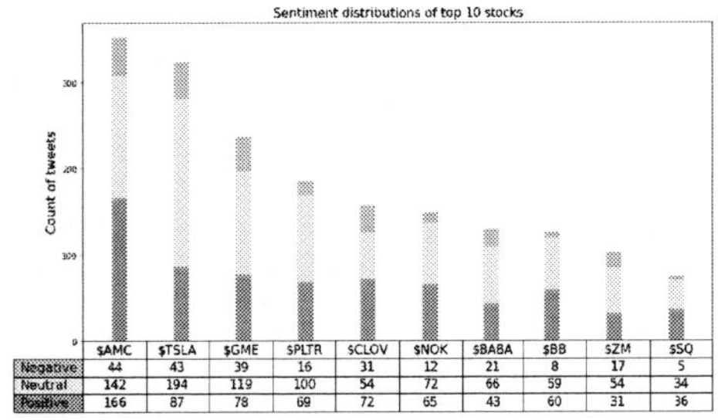

Figure 3: Sentiment distributions of top 10 stocks in TweetFinSent dataset.

inter-annotator agreement in Obama-McCain Debate dataset is 83.7% (Speriosu et al., 2011).

Moreover, in the cases where annotators disagree, we investigate the extent of the disagreement by measuring the distance between classes. If a Positive sentiment has value 1, Negative as -1 and Neutral as 0. Then we subtract the difference between the annotators and find that in 86.7% of the disagreements, it was with a difference of 1. In other words, it is more likely to differ on a Positive versus a Neutral sentiment than a Negative one, which happened to be the exact case for 67.9% of the disagreements. Another observation is that even after conflict resolution, the agreement in negative samples is still lower than that in positive and neutral samples. By investigating some cases, the possible reasons are: (1) the number of negative samples is smaller, so a small number of conflict can increase the disagreement, and (2) it is more difficult to determine if a tweet is negative due to various factors such as sarcasm, complicated emotions, and lack of context. For instance, given the tweet

> *Too many people drank the Kool aid. Telling you ....take your profits. Stack your cash. $tsla $zm $aapl*

the annotation conflict happens between *Positive* and *Negative.* This tweet contains complicated sentiments: being positive because the user gained positive return (with **profits**) while being negative because the user expected to gain negative return in the future (taking *cash* instead of buying stocks).

3.5 Data & Label Analysis

TweetFinSent dataset contains 2,113 tweets where the numbers of positive, neutral, and negative samples are 816, 1,030, and 267, re-

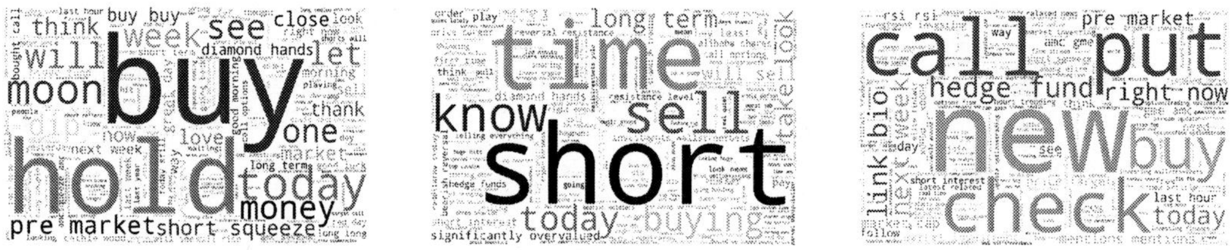

(a) Most frequent positive terms. (b) Most frequent negative terms. (c) Most frequent neutral terms.

Figure 4: Most frequent terms in TweetFinSent with different sentiment classes.

spectively. The distribution of different sentiment classes is quite imbalanced, i.e., there are much less negative samples. This imbalance may influence the performance of sentiment analysis methods and we will show more details in the experiments. We also show the sentiment distribution of 10 most discussed stocks in the dataset in Figure 3. One can observe that they are the meme stocks gaining most popularity among retail investors on social media during the period of data collection.

The most frequent terms in positive, negative, and neutral tweets in TweetFinSent dataset are shown in Figure 4. In positive samples, Twitter users talked more about 1) actions including to **buy** and **hold** stocks, 2) finance-specific expressions such as **to the moon**, **buy the dip** and **short squeeze** which was a hot topic during the period of data collection. All these discussions indicate positive (expected) return. In negative samples, more discussions are related to **sell** or **short** certain stocks and some stocks were **significantly overvalued**. They show the negative (expected) return. In neutral tweets, more tweets shared news or statistics about stock market, e.g., **pre-market stocks trend** and both **call** and **put** have been discussed.

4 Experimental Studies

4.1 Experimental Setup

We first preprocess the dataset by removing URLs and username (mentioning using @ notation)[5]. Hashtags are not processed because we observe that in financial domain some hashtags are indicators for special sentiment, e.g., *#YOLO* and *#WSB*[6]. Furthermore, it is common for a hashtag to refer to a particular stock ticker which represents the target for the sentiment analyzer. The data is split into training and test set with 1,113 and 1,000 tweets respectively. To make a fair comparison, we will keep the train-test split for all baselines.

4.2 Baselines

Since the task of stock sentiment analysis is different from traditional sentiment analysis and existing methods are not directly suitable for this task, we adopt several architectures that are commonly used in text classification and Twitter analysis for this problem. In details, three types of methods have been tested:

Lexicon-based methods In this experiment we adopt *Vader*[7] (Hutto and Gilbert, 2014) for our lexicon-based baseline because as the valence-based lexicon, *Vader* provides not just the binary polarity, but also the strength of the sentiment expressed in the given text. *Vader* is a rule-based sentiment analyzer that utilizes lexicons specifically trained on social media data. We were able to extract the lexicons list that contains a sentiment both English words and emoticons. Domain experts in Finance provided us a list of key words along with a sentiment class of 'Positive' or 'Negative'. We therefore modified the lexicon list we extracted based on the words provided, and gave a higher weighting to these relevant financial keywords. For example the sentiment scores in the lexicon file ranged from +3.4 to -3.9, and words like 'long' and 'short', were not present in the list as these words were classed as 'Neutral'. However in the financial context they would be 'Positive' and 'Negative' respectively. We enforce this by assigning a +5.0 score for pos-

[5] Note that there are more complicated preprocessing steps that could improve the performance especially in methods relying on feature engineering. We highlight our contributions on dataset construction and leave these preprocessing steps for future work.

[6] https://en.wikipedia.org/wiki/R/wallstreetbets

[7] https://github.com/cjhutto/vaderSentiment

itive keywords and -5.0 for negative ones. To be consistent with supervised methods, we use the lexicon-based methods only on the test set.

Pre-trained embedding. To conduct a comprehensive evaluation, both context-independent and context-dependent pre-trained word embeddings are compared. For each type of word embedding approach, we select different pre-trained embeddings that have been trained on general corpus and Twitter data. Specifically,

- For context-independent approaches, GloVe (Pennington et al., 2014) (including the original model *GloVe* pre-trained on general corpus like Wikipedia and the domain-specific model *GloVe-Twitter* pre-trained on Twitter) is selected.
- For context-dependent models, we use *DistilBERT* (Sanh et al., 2019), *FinBERT* (Araci, 2019), and RoBERTa (Liu et al., 2019) (including the original *RoBERTa* model pre-trained on general corpus and specific *RoBERTa-Twitter* model pre-trained on Twitter and fine-tuned for sentiment analysis task (Loureiro et al., 2022)).

After getting the embeddings, SVM and Gradient Boosted Decision Trees are employed to classify the sentiment using pre-trained embeddings as features.

Fine-tuned embedding models. Intuitively, due to the different patterns in our stock sentiment analysis task, general sentiment lexicons and pre-trained models may not perform well. Therefore, we fine-tune these pre-trained embedding models to verify the performance. Considering the advances of pre-trained language models, we only fine-tune these transformer models, i.e., DistilBERT, FinBERT, and RoBERTa. To make a fair comparison, we use the same train-test split, i.e., we use the training set to fine-tune the model and report the results on the test data.

4.3 Evaluation Metrics

The stock sentiment analysis is a typical multi-class classification task, so commonly used classification evaluation metrics can be easily adapted. Thus, following previous studies, in the experiments we utilize *Accuracy* and *F1* as the evaluation metrics. In particular, for *F1* scores, we report both macro average and weighted average versions.

It's worth noting that our constructed dataset contains more positive and neutral tweets than negative ones. To better understand the performance of different methods, we also calculate the F1 score for each class.

4.4 Benchmark Results

Benchmark results on these baselines are shown in Table 3. It can be observed that fine-tuned RoBERTa-Twitter achieved the best performance w.r.t all metrics. It makes sense because this model has been pre-trained on Twitter and fine-tuned for sentiment analysis task. By continuing to fine-tune on task-specific data, i.e., stock sentiment tweets in our experiments, the performance can be further improved.

Another observation is that in machine learning models, more advanced models generally achieve better performance which is consistent with other tasks. For example, context-dependent models are superior to context-independent models. One interesting and counter-intuitive result is that FinBERT performed worse than DistilBERT. This observation is consistent with previous study (Peng et al., 2021). A possible reason is that although FinBERT is trained for the financial domain, content from Twitter has different patterns from regular documents such as financial news texts and company press releases that FinBERT has been pre-trained on (Malo et al., 2014). However, fine-tuning cannot always guarantee better performance. After fine-tuning, although overall performance of DistilBERT and FinBERT has been improved, both F-1 scores for Negative tweets decreased.

It is also worth mentioning is that performance degradation can be observed for all models on negative tweets compared to positive and neutral ones. The major reason is that in the dataset, the size of negative samples is much smaller than that of positive and neutral ones. Such imbalance may make the models learn less representative information from the negative samples. Another reason is that there are different ways to express negative sentiment in financial domains including 1) using finance-specific terms, e.g., *put* and *short*, 2) using negation, and 3) using sarcasm or irony.

It is surprising that lexicon-based methods performed quite well compared to advanced deep learning models. In particular, finance

Table 3: Benchmark results of stock sentiment analysis using different baselines.

Methods	Overall performance			Per-class F-1		
	accuracy	macro avg F1	weighted avg F1	Positive	Neutral	Negative
Vader lexicon	0.4760	0.3592	0.3972	0.1840	0.6154	0.2781
Vader+Finance lexicon	0.5810	0.5269	0.5727	0.5342	0.6503	0.3962
GloVe+SVM	0.5340	0.4312	0.5157	0.4821	0.6275	0.1839
GloVe+GDBT	0.5420	0.4551	0.5335	0.4993	0.6397	0.2262
GloVe-Twitter+SVM	0.5140	0.3828	0.4872	0.5681	0.5215	0.0588
GloVe-Twitter+GDBT	0.5600	0.4823	0.5488	0.5248	0.6348	0.2872
DistilBERT+SVM	0.6020	0.5607	0.6017	0.5857	0.6557	0.4408
DistilBERT+GBDT	0.5920	0.5340	0.5871	0.5548	0.6667	0.3805
FinBERT+SVM	0.5750	0.5098	0.5694	0.5479	0.6465	0.3348
FinBERT+GBDT	0.5820	0.5262	0.5782	0.5537	0.6500	0.3750
RoBERTa-Twitter+SVM	0.5980	0.5594	0.5991	0.5982	0.6391	0.4409
RoBERTa-Twitter+GBDT	0.6320	0.5868	0.6306	0.6349	0.6701	0.4554
Fine-tuned DistilBERT	0.6180	0.5271	0.6095	0.6345	0.6838	0.2629
Fine-tuned FinBERT	0.6190	0.4923	0.5967	0.6390	0.6830	0.1548
Fine-tuned RoBERTa-Twitter	**0.7230**	**0.6785**	**0.7196**	**0.7436**	**0.7482**	**0.5439**

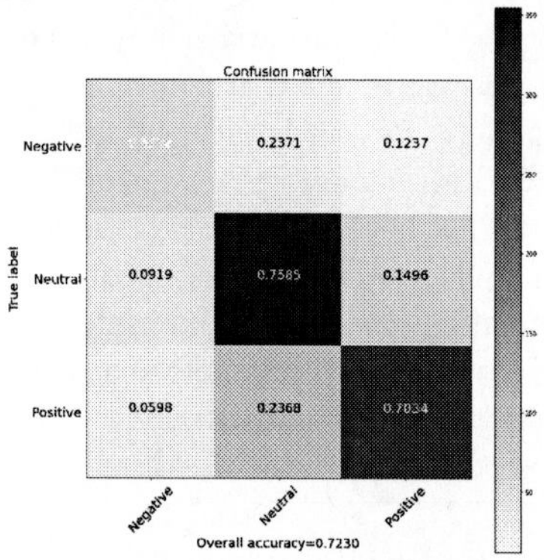

Figure 5: Confusion matrix of model output.

lexicons even outperformed GloVe including original one and GloVe pre-trained on Twitter data. Besides, Vader+finance lexicon performed better than general Vader lexicon. This comparison not only indicates the special characteristics of our constructed dataset and challenges of the stock sentiment analysis problem but also demonstrates the importance of prior knowledge in domain-specific tasks.

4.5 Discussions

To better understand the task of stock sentiment and TweetFinSent dataset, we select Fine-tuned RoBERTa-Twitter, the baseline achieving best performance, to further analyse. The confusion matrix of the prediction is shown in Figure 5. We can see that it performed poor on negative samples and achieved similar results on positive and neutral samples. Although Fine-tuned RoBERTa-Twitter outperformed other baselines with 0.72 accuracy, compared to existing Twitter sentiment analysis studies, the performance is acceptable but far from good. For example, different datasets and methods have been evaluated in (Saif et al., 2013) where the accuracy can reach to 0.8 even to 0.9 in some datasets. Therefore, on the one hand, this shows that TweetFinSent constitutes a challenging problem. On the other hand, there is ample room for improvement on the stock sentiment analysis task. Some research directions may be of interest for future work. From the data perspective, how to handle the data imbalance and improve the performance on negative data may improve the effectiveness of proposed models. From the methodological perspective, since finance lexicon showed its effectiveness, integrating prior knowledge of finance and stock into advanced machine learning models may boost the performance. Release of the TweetFinSent dataset enables researchers to further explore these directions.

5 Conclusions

We presented TweetFinSent, a new dataset for stock sentiment analysis and it contains 2,113 expert-annotated tweets covering different stocks. Different from existing sentiment analysis dataset, TweetFinSent defines sentiment based on whether a user gained or expected to gain positive or negative return from a stock rather than having feelings and emotions of good or bad. Our experiments with several sentiment analysis models indicated that there is a huge gap between machine learning models and human annotations. Thus, the TweetFinSent dataset constitutes a challenging problem and there is ample room for improvement on the stock sentiment analysis task.

References

Issam Aattouchi, Ait Mounir, Saida el Mendili, and Fatna Elmendili. 2022. Financial sentiment analysis of tweets based on deep learning approach. *Indonesian Journal of Electrical Engineering and Computer Science*, 25:1759–1770.

Dogu Araci. 2019. Finbert: Financial sentiment analysis with pre-trained language models. *arXiv preprint arXiv:1908.10063*.

Deepali Arora, Kin Fun Li, and Stephen W Neville. 2015. Consumers' sentiment analysis of popular phone brands and operating system preference using twitter data: A feasibility study. In *2015 IEEE 29th International Conference on Advanced Information Networking and Applications*, pages 680–686. IEEE.

J. Bollen and H. Mao. 2011. Twitter mood as a stock market predictor. *Computer*, 44(10):91–94.

Johan Bollen, Huina Mao, and Xiaojun Zeng. 2011. Twitter mood predicts the stock market. *Journal of computational science*, 2(1):1–8.

Aysun Bozanta, Sabrina Angco, Mucahit Cevik, and Ayse Basar. 2021. Sentiment analysis of stocktwits using transformer models. In *2021 20th IEEE International Conference on Machine Learning and Applications (ICMLA)*, pages 1253–1258. IEEE.

Widodo Budiharto and Meiliana Meiliana. 2018. Prediction and analysis of indonesia presidential election from twitter using sentiment analysis. *Journal of Big data*, 5(1):1–10.

Usman W Chohan. 2021. Counter-hegemonic finance: The gamestop short squeeze. *Available at SSRN 3775127*.

Jacob Cohen. 1960. A coefficient of agreement for nominal scales. *Educational and psychological measurement*, 20(1):37–46.

Costanza Conforti, Jakob Berndt, Mohammad Taher Pilehvar, Chryssi Giannitsarou, Flavio Toxvaerd, and Nigel Collier. 2020. Will-they-won't-they: A very large dataset for stance detection on twitter. *arXiv preprint arXiv:2005.00388*.

Keith Cortis, André Freitas, Tobias Daudert, Manuela Huerlimann, Manel Zarrouk, Siegfried Handschuh, and Brian Davis. 2017. Semeval-2017 task 5: Fine-grained sentiment analysis on financial microblogs and news. Association for Computational Linguistics (ACL).

Sornette Didier, Sandro Lera, Jianhong Lin, and Ke Wu. 2022. Non-normal interactions create socio-economic bubbles. *arXiv preprint arXiv:2205.08661*.

Akash Dutt Dubey. 2020. Twitter sentiment analysis during covid-19 outbreak. *Available at SSRN 3572023*.

Shihab Elbagir and Jing Yang. 2019. Twitter sentiment analysis using natural language toolkit and vader sentiment. In *Proceedings of the international multiconference of engineers and computer scientists*, volume 122, page 16.

Umman Tugba Gursoy, Diren Bulut, and Cemil Yigit. 2017. Social media mining and sentiment analysis for brand management. *Global Journal of Emerging Trends in e-Business, Marketing and Consumer Psychology*, 3(1):497–551.

Clayton Hutto and Eric Gilbert. 2014. Vader: A parsimonious rule-based model for sentiment analysis of social media text. In *Proceedings of the international AAAI conference on web and social media*, volume 8, pages 216–225.

Joshi Kalyani, Prof Bharathi, Prof Jyothi, et al. 2016. Stock trend prediction using news sentiment analysis. *arXiv preprint arXiv:1607.01958*.

Olga Kolchyna, Tharsis TP Souza, Philip Treleaven, and Tomaso Aste. 2015. Twitter sentiment analysis: Lexicon method, machine learning method and their combination. *arXiv preprint arXiv:1507.00955*.

Paraskevas Koukaras, Christina Nousi, and Christos Tjortjis. 2022. Stock market prediction using microblogging sentiment analysis and machine learning. In *Telecom*, volume 3, pages 358–378. MDPI.

Bing Liu. 2012. Sentiment analysis and opinion mining. *Synthesis lectures on human language technologies*, 5(1):1–167.

Yinhan Liu, Myle Ott, Naman Goyal, Jingfei Du, Mandar Joshi, Danqi Chen, Omer Levy, Mike Lewis, Luke Zettlemoyer, and Veselin Stoyanov. 2019. Roberta: A robustly optimized bert pretraining approach. *arXiv preprint arXiv:1907.11692*.

Daniel Loureiro, Francesco Barbieri, Leonardo Neves, Luis Espinosa Anke, and Jose Camacho-Collados. 2022. Timelms: Diachronic language models from twitter. In *Proceedings of the 60th Annual Meeting of the Association for Computational Linguistics: System Demonstrations*, pages 251–260.

Pekka Malo, Ankur Sinha, Pekka Korhonen, Jyrki Wallenius, and Pyry Takala. 2014. Good debt or bad debt: Detecting semantic orientations in economic texts. *Journal of the Association for Information Science and Technology*, 65(4):782–796.

Kamaran H Manguri, Rebaz N Ramadhan, and Pshko R Mohammed Amin. 2020. Twitter sentiment analysis on worldwide covid-19 outbreaks.

Kurdistan Journal of Applied Research, pages 54–65.

Leeja Mathew and VR Bindu. 2020. A review of natural language processing techniques for sentiment analysis using pre-trained models. In *2020 Fourth International Conference on Computing Methodologies and Communication (ICCMC)*, pages 340–345. IEEE.

Mary L McHugh. 2012. Interrater reliability: the kappa statistic. *Biochemia medica*, 22(3):276–282.

Anshul Mittal and Arpit Goel. 2012. Stock prediction using twitter sentiment analysis. *Standford University, CS229 (2011 http://cs229. stanford. edu/proj2011/GoelMittal-StockMarketPredictionUsingTwitterSentimentAnalysis. pdf)*, 15:2352.

László Nemes and Attila Kiss. 2021. Prediction of stock values changes using sentiment analysis of stock news headlines. *Journal of Information and Telecommunication*, 5(3):375–394.

Christina Nousi and Christos Tjortjis. 2021. A methodology for stock movement prediction using sentiment analysis on twitter and stocktwits data. In *2021 6th South-East Europe Design Automation, Computer Engineering, Computer Networks and Social Media Conference (SEEDA-CECNSM)*, pages 1–7.

Matan Orbach, Orith Toledo-Ronen, Artem Spector, Ranit Aharonov, Yoav Katz, and Noam Slonim. 2020. Yaso: A targeted sentiment analysis evaluation dataset for open-domain reviews. *arXiv preprint arXiv:2012.14541*.

Venkata Sasank Pagolu, Kamal Nayan Reddy, Ganapati Panda, and Babita Majhi. 2016. Sentiment analysis of twitter data for predicting stock market movements. In *2016 International Conference on Signal Processing, Communication, Power and Embedded System (SCOPES)*, pages 1345–1350.

Bo Peng, Emmanuele Chersoni, Yu-Yin Hsu, and Chu-Ren Huang. 2021. Is domain adaptation worth your investment? comparing bert and finbert on financial tasks. In *Proceedings of the Third Workshop on Economics and Natural Language Processing*, pages 37–44.

Jeffrey Pennington, Richard Socher, and Christopher D Manning. 2014. Glove: Global vectors for word representation. In *Proceedings of the 2014 conference on empirical methods in natural language processing (EMNLP)*, pages 1532–1543.

Mohammed Qasem, Ruppa Thulasiram, and Parimala Thulasiram. 2015. Twitter sentiment classification using machine learning techniques for stock markets. In *2015 International Conference on Advances in Computing, Communications and Informatics (ICACCI)*, pages 834–840. IEEE.

Jyoti Ramteke, Samarth Shah, Darshan Godhia, and Aadil Shaikh. 2016. Election result prediction using twitter sentiment analysis. In *2016 international conference on inventive computation technologies (ICICT)*, volume 1, pages 1–5. IEEE.

Hassan Saif, Miriam Fernandez, Yulan He, and Harith Alani. 2013. Evaluation datasets for twitter sentiment analysis. *Emotion and Sentiment in Social and Expressive Media*, page 9.

Victor Sanh, Lysandre Debut, Julien Chaumond, and Thomas Wolf. 2019. Distilbert, a distilled version of bert: smaller, faster, cheaper and lighter. *arXiv preprint arXiv:1910.01108*.

Michał Skuza and Andrzej Romanowski. 2015. Sentiment analysis of twitter data within big data distributed environment for stock prediction. In *2015 Federated Conference on Computer Science and Information Systems (FedCSIS)*, pages 1349–1354. IEEE.

Jasmina Smailović, Miha Grčar, Nada Lavrač, and Martin Žnidaršič. 2013. Predictive sentiment analysis of tweets: A stock market application. In *International workshop on human-computer interaction and knowledge discovery in complex, unstructured, big data*, pages 77–88. Springer.

Thársis Souza, Olga Kolchyna, Philip Treleaven, and Tomaso Aste. 2015. Twitter sentiment analysis applied to finance: A case study in the retail industry.

Michael Speriosu, Nikita Sudan, Sid Upadhyay, and Jason Baldridge. 2011. Twitter polarity classification with label propagation over lexical links and the follower graph. In *Proceedings of the First workshop on Unsupervised Learning in NLP*, pages 53–63.

Hao Wang, Doğan Can, Abe Kazemzadeh, François Bar, and Shrikanth Narayanan. 2012. A system for real-time twitter sentiment analysis of 2012 us presidential election cycle. In *Proceedings of the ACL 2012 system demonstrations*, pages 115–120.

Ethan Xia, Han Yue, and Hongfu Liu. 2021. Tweet sentiment analysis of the 2020 us presidential election. In *Companion Proceedings of the Web Conference 2021*, pages 367–371.

Frank Xing, Lorenzo Malandri, Yue Zhang, and Erik Cambria. 2020. Financial sentiment analysis: an investigation into common mistakes and silver bullets. In *Proceedings of the 28th international conference on computational linguistics*, pages 978–987.

tefan Lyócsa, Eduard Baumöhl, and Tomá Výrost. 2022. Yolo trading: Riding with the herd during the gamestop episode. *Finance Research Letters*, 46:102359.

A Appendix

A.1 Annotation Rules and Examples

1. [RULE]: Stock sentiment of a target ticker should be assessed only based on its own context. If there are multiple tickers in the same tweet, contexts of other tickers should have no impact to the target ticker.

   [EXAMPLE]: *"$AMC rocketed today! $BB $NOK $TSLA $GME."* The sentiment to $AMC is clearly POSITIVE. If the target is $GME though, then the sentiment should be NEUTRAL.

2. [RULE]: The assessment of sentiment should follow the subjective expectation. When both current and future returns are discussed, the focus should be on the future return.

   [EXAMPLE]: *"$TSLA revenue failed expectation, indicating a red day. However I will still buy at the dip"* should be POSITIVE. Because although the fact of $TSLA has negative return currently, the user still expects positive return in future and thus wants to keep buying.

3. [RULE]: Besides the normal buy or sell trades, other trade types like call vs put or long vs short can also reflect the expectation of positive or negative return.

   EXAMPLE: *"short $clov at this point"* is NEGATIVE. *"$ABIO ought $5 call options June 2021... easy buy, trading at book value."* is POSITIVE.

4. [RULE]: Besides the normal textual content, some slangs and hashtags indicating buy or sell, up or down are salient signals of stock sentiment and should contribute to the final sentiment assessment of the whole tweet.

   [EXAMPLE]: *Apes, to the moon, diamond hand* (risk tolerant, hold positions for long time), *#squeeze, #toMoon* are POSITIVE signals. Meanwhile *paper hand* (sell too early) is an example of NEGATIVE signals.

5. [RULE]: Some emojis in social media indicating "up"/"down" trend or expectation are salient signals of stock sentiment.

   [EXAMPLE]: 🚀 🔥 📈 are POSITIVE signals and 📉 is a NEGATIVE signal.

6. [RULE]: The received or expected return should be directional, i.e. either up or down. Ambiguous direction should be considered as NEUTRAL.

   [EXAMPLE]: *"$AMC cannot stop!"* or *"Looks like $tsla having its typical Tuesday."* are NEUTRAL since the content in the tweet is not enough to tell the direction.

A.2 Implementation Details

We use spaCy[8] to extract pre-trained *GloVe* embedding and obtain *GloVe-Twitter* embedding from the original paper[9] (Pennington et al., 2014). For classifiers, we use the implementations of linear SVM[10] and Gradient Boosting classifier[11] in scikit-learn. We use PyTorch and Hugging Face to obtain and fine-tune pre-trained transformers including *DistilBERT*[12], *FinBERT*[13] and *RoBERTa*[14]. The settings of major hyper-parameters for transformers are: batch size is 16, max training epochs is 5, and max sequence length is 256. We use Adam as the optimizer with learning rate 2e-5 and the dropout rate is 0.1. The other hyper-parameters are set by default. e.g., hidden size is 768 and number of attention heads is 12.

[8] https://spacy.io/usage/embeddings-transformers

[9] https://nlp.stanford.edu/projects/glove/

[10] https://scikit-learn.org/stable/modules/generated/sklearn.svm.LinearSVC.html

[11] https://scikit-learn.org/stable/modules/generated/sklearn.ensemble.GradientBoostingClassifier.html

[12] https://huggingface.co/distilbert-base-uncased-finetuned-sst-2-english

[13] https://huggingface.co/ProsusAI/finbert

[14] https://huggingface.co/cardiffnlp/twitter-roberta-base-sentiment-latest

Stock Price Volatility Prediction: A Case Study with AutoML

Hilal Pataci
Rensselaer Polytechnic Institute, USA
patach@rpi.edu

Yannis Katsis
IBM Research, USA
yannis.katsis@ibm.com

Yunyao Li *
Apple, USA
yunyaoli@apple.com

Yada Zhu
IBM Research, USA
yzhu@us.ibm.com

Lucian Popa
IBM Research, USA
lpopa@us.ibm.com

Abstract

Accurate prediction of stock price volatility, the rate at which the price of a stock increases or decreases over a particular period, is an important problem in finance. Inaccurate prediction of stock price volatility might lead to investment risk and financial loss, while accurate prediction might generate significant returns for investors. Several studies investigated stock price volatility prediction as a regression task using the transcripts of earnings calls (quarterly conference calls held by public companies) with Natural Language Processing (NLP) techniques. Existing studies use the entire transcript, which can degrade performance due to noise caused by irrelevant information that may not have a significant impact on stock price volatility. In order to overcome these limitations, by considering stock price volatility prediction as a classification task, we explore several denoising approaches, ranging from general-purpose approaches to techniques specific to finance to remove the noise, and leverage AutoML systems that enable auto-exploration of a wide variety of models. Our preliminary findings indicate that domain-specific denoising approaches provide better results than general-purpose approaches, while AutoML systems show promising results.

1 Introduction

Predicting stock price volatility is of great interest to researchers and seems to remain one of the interesting open problems. Volatility is about information disclosure, and how unexpected the information is to the market; therefore, volatility persists in the market until the future values of stock reflect the information provided. According to (Fama, 1998), markets are informationally efficient if prices at each moment incorporate all available information about future values. Such that if there is an information disclosure, not yet incorporated in market prices, the future values will be volatile until the price fully reflects the disclosed information. (Lang and Lundholm, 1993; Baumann et al., 2004) Any information disclosed to the market by competitors, suppliers, customers, and regulators creates volatility, in addition to the internal information the company voluntarily discloses. Every quarter the executive leadership of a public company holds an earnings call meeting with investors and analysts to inform them about the company's status. As executives inform the investors about the company's current status and future outlook, earnings conference calls may result in stock price volatility. In finance and accounting research, the high volatility following an earnings conference call is conceptualized as Post-earnings Announcement Drift (PEAD) (Ball and Brown, 1968; Bernard and Thomas, 1989), which refers to the drift of a company's stock price for an extended period. Stock prices tend to drift upward (or downward) when the announcements are above (or below) expectations following an earnings conference call. Depending on how unexpected the information shared during earnings conference calls is, stock prices and firm valuations change, and markets become more 'informationally efficient' by absorbing this information over the long run (Fama, 1998; Fink, 2021).

In this work, we study the problem of leveraging the textual transcripts of companies' earnings calls and building Natural Language Processing (NLP) models to predict the volatility of their stock prices for a period of time following the earnings calls. While this problem has been studied in the literature, prior works exhibit these limitations:

- First, they model the problem as a regression task trying to predict the exact value of the stock price volatility. While this can be valuable in some settings, financial analysts are often interested in identifying the stocks with abnormally low or high volatility rather than identifying their exact value. This implies

* The work was done when the author was at IBM Research.

Proceedings of the Fourth Workshop on Financial Technology and Natural Language Processing (FinNLP), pages 48 - 57
December 8, 2022 ©2022 Association for Computational Linguistics

the need to consider the problem as a classification task rather than a regression task as evaluated in prior work.

- Second, existing works typically leverage the earnings call transcripts as-is. However, transcripts contain a lot of irrelevant information for the purpose of stock price volatility prediction. This raises the question of whether this affects the performance of NLP models and whether there is an opportunity for improving such approaches by appropriately distilling these documents before feeding them into NLP models.

In this work, we address the aforementioned challenges as follows:

- We model the problem as a text classification task, where given the transcript of an earnings call one is asked to predict the stock price volatility as being low, medium, or high (Li and Lin, 2003). Considering this as a classification task also enables us to experiment with AutoML systems and democratization of this task by giving access to a wider user base that includes those without specialized knowledge of AI. To the best of our knowledge, this is the first work that models the stock price volatility prediction problem from earnings call transcripts as a classification problem and leverages associated NLP techniques.

- Earnings call transcripts include information that has almost no impact on the stock price volatility, and we conceptualize such irrelevant information as noise in our analysis. To improve the signal coming from the transcripts, we propose and experiment with an entire spectrum of denoising approaches, ranging from domain-agnostic denoising techniques to domain-specific approaches that utilize domain knowledge to improve the denoising process further. Our experimental evaluation shows that domain-specific denoising approaches outperform domain-agnostic techniques, which points to the importance of incorporating domain knowledge into the denoising process.

The rest of this paper is structured as follows: We start by reviewing related work in Section 2. In Section 3, we describe the problem definition and data preparation. We propose a range of denoising approaches in Section 4 and explain how we discover appropriate NLP models by leveraging an AutoML system in Section 5. Finally, we present the experimental evaluation results and associated insights in Section 6 and conclude the paper in Section 7.

2 Related Work

Information is one of the most valuable and highly sought assets in financial markets (Vlastakis and Markellos, 2012; Grossman and Stiglitz, 1980; French and Roll, 1986; Antweiler and Frank, 2004) and is found to be impacting stock price volatility in several studies. Moreover, as posited by the mixture of distributions hypothesis, the sequential arrival of new information generates trading volume and price movements (Clark, 1973; Tauchen and Pitts, 1983; Bessembinder and Seguin, 1992) (i.e. information shocks). Briefly stated, the impact of information disclosure on the volatility of stock prices has been investigated from several angles in the literature.

Four types of textual data have been mainly used for stock volatility prediction: Annual Statements, News, Social Media data, and Earnings calls transcripts.

Annual statements (10-K reports): Annual statements include historical data about a company's financial performance and a future outlook that can be valuable in predicting the volatility of its stock. For instance, Kogan et al. (2009) formulate a "text regression problem", where information from the 10-K reports is used to predict the volatility of stock returns in the periods following the reports. Loughran and McDonald's (Loughran and McDonald, 2011) financial lexicon generated from fourteen years of historical annual statements (10-K reports) is one of the major and initial attempts that utilize language resources to predict stock price volatility.

News data: News data often provide important information about events related to a company. For instance, Tetlock (2007) uses daily content from the Wall Street Journal to predict volatility. In a similar vein, Ding et al. (2014) adapt Open IE technology for event-based stock price movement prediction by extracting structured events from large-scale public news.

Social media data: Social media data often capture public sentiment about a company that can be an important indicator for the future price of its stock. Bollen et al. (2011) use behavioral economics to investigate how societal moods affect collective decision-making for Dow Jones Industrial Average (DJIA)'s values.

Earnings calls transcripts: Several works have found that earnings calls (as captured through their transcripts) can be predictive of investor sentiment for stock price volatility prediction tasks (Frankel et al., 1999; Bowen et al., 2002; Cohen and Lou, 2012; Matsumoto et al., 2011). Recent studies also combined the textual transcripts with additional verbal and vocal cues from audio recordings of earnings call events and leveraged multi-modal learning to predict stock price volatility (Qin and Yang, 2019; Li et al., 2020). Most of the existing research models the stock price volatility prediction as a regression task, with the exception of Keith and Stent's work (Keith and Stent, 2019), which - similar to our work - models it as a classification task. However, they use classification to predict the analysts' recommendations to buy/sell/hold a stock. In contrast, we predict the market reaction itself by predicting the actual stock price volatility (classified as low, medium, and high volatility).

Our work makes multiple novel contributions: First, we consider stock price volatility prediction as a text classification task different from existing work (Qin and Yang, 2019; Li et al., 2020). Second, instead of using the earnings call transcripts as-is, we employ denoising techniques designed to separate the signal from the noise caused by irrelevant information in the transcripts and improve the performance of the resulting NLP models. We design and test several denoising approaches and report the results of their effectiveness. Third, AutoML systems have been used in several text classification tasks (Estevez-Velarde et al., 2019; Bisong, 2019; Blohm et al., 2020), however, there is little effort in the literature to use AutoML systems for the stock price volatility prediction task. Using AutoML systems to predict stock price volatility enables non-AI expert users (who may not be proficient in AI/NLP techniques) to create NLP models for the stock volatility prediction task quickly.

3 Problem Definition & Data Preparation

In this paper, we aim to predict the magnitude of volatility from earnings call transcripts and formulate this as a classification problem. In line with that purpose, we combine earnings call transcripts (text data) with their corresponding volatility labels (financial data).

3.1 Text Data

After each conference event, recordings of earnings conference calls are shared as audio and text files. In this work we focus on the transcripts of calls and leverage the earnings call transcripts dataset of Qin and Yang (Qin and Yang, 2019). Their dataset was built by collecting all S&P 500 companies' quarterly earnings conference call transcripts in 2017 from Seeking Alpha with written consent. It contains 576 conference calls, totaling 88,829 sentences. In order to avoid interference among different speakers, previous work (Qin and Yang, 2019) only processes the sentences of the most spoken executive (usually the CEO or CFO of the company). In the next stage, we use company names and earnings call dates collected from the dataset to retrieve the associated stock price information and compute the stock price volatility labels.

3.2 Financial Data

We manually collect the ticker symbols (an abbreviation used to uniquely identify publicly traded shares of a particular stock in a specific stock market) of these companies from Yahoo Finance with their corresponding company names obtained from the earnings call dataset (Qin and Yang, 2019). We use the ticker symbols of companies to extract their financial data and calculate stock price volatility labels by leveraging the Yahoo Finance API (Rekabsaz et al., 2017). Although Qin & Yang (Qin and Yang, 2019)'s dataset contains 576 conference call transcripts, due to missing financial information data on Yahoo Finance, we drop 27 transcripts, resulting in 549 transcripts that we use for our subsequent analysis.

We define stock price volatility prediction as a 3-class classification task; high-volatility, medium-volatility, or low-volatility for the respective company stock; similar to (Li and Lin, 2003). If the market reaction is almost neutral, we expect the stock price volatility to be low, so we label it as 'low volatility'. If the market reaction is high because there was too much unexpected news in the call, we expect the stock volatility to be high, so we label it as 'high volatility'. If the market reaction is mixed and in between neutral to high, we expect the stock volatility also to be in between, and therefore we label it as 'medium volatility'.

$$v_{[0,n]} = \ln\left(\sqrt{\left(\frac{\sum_{i=1}^{n}(r_i - \bar{r})^2}{n}\right.}\right) \quad (1)$$

Consistent with prior work, we compute stock volatility for a period of n days following the earnings call event. We first calculate the absolute value of volatility as shown in Equation 1. In this equation, r_i is the stock return on day i and $\bar{r}$ is the average stock return in a window of n days. The return is defined as $r_i = (P_i - P_{i-1})/P_{i-1}$, where P_i is the adjusted closing price of a stock on day i.

Using this equation, we first calculate stock price volatility for four time periods of n = 3, 7, 15, and 30 days. Once the stock price volatility is calculated for 3 days using Equation 1, we calculate the thresholds for the high volatility, medium volatility, and low volatility labels by considering the distribution of volatility within our corpus for 3-days. Once we identify the range of stock price volatility for each category for 3-days, we apply the same range for 7-days, 15-days, and 30-days and label accordingly. Given that each stock volatility will fade over time, we use 3-days volatility ranges to identify the ranges for each class.

In particular, following an earnings call conference of Company A, if the stock price volatility of Company A is at the lowest 33% of the stock price volatility distribution, the transcript of that call is labeled as low-volatility. If the stock price volatility of Company B is between the 33% to 66% of the stock price volatility distribution, the transcript of that call is labeled as medium-volatility. Finally, if the stock price volatility of Company C is at the highest 33% of the volatility distribution, the transcript of that call is labeled as high-volatility for 3-days. Through this process, we identify the stock price volatility ranges that correspond to high, medium, and low volatility for 3-days and we use the same ranges to generate the volatility labels for the 7-day, 15-day, and 30-day stock price volatility. Figure 1 shows the resulting distribution of volatility labels for 3-days, 7-days, 15-days, and 30-days.

		Volatility over the following n-days			
		3-days	7-days	15-days	30-days
Labels	Low volatility	186	137	129	102
	Medium volatility	182	255	292	335
	High volatility	181	157	128	112

Figure 1: Distribution of volatility labels

4 Denoising Approaches

Earnings call transcripts are typically long documents containing a lot of information. While some of this information is valuable for predicting stock price volatility, another part of it can be irrelevant for the stock price volatility prediction task and can thus introduce unwanted noise. To address this problem, we experiment with several approaches of denoising the transcripts as a pre-processing step. We propose a spectrum of approaches, ranging from generic domain-agnostic approaches that are used in different tasks to more domain and task-specific approaches related to finance.

We start by using raw earnings call transcripts without further processing (which we use as our baseline). In the second approach, we use a general domain-agnostic denoising approach by leveraging the T5 summarization model (Raffel et al., 2019) to create a summary of the earnings call transcript. In the third approach, we experiment with a more domain and task-specific approach by borrowing a finance domain-specific dictionary (Loughran and McDonald, 2011), which we use to identify the sentences with important information. In the fourth approach, we create an intermediate domain-specific NLP model to identify the sentences containing important information that has the potential of affecting the stock price volatility.

4.1 Full document processing

In our first approach, we experiment with the full documents provided in (Qin and Yang, 2019) without any further processing. In this setting, we use the volatility labels calculated above and process the raw documents. The full document processing approach helps us identify how accurate stock price volatility prediction is when we process the earnings call transcripts without denoising or preprocessing. By considering full document processing as our baseline, we can also observe how other denoising approaches improve the model predictions.

4.2 General-purpose summarization of documents through T5

Sentences in a conference call have an order and relationships, leading to high dependency. Such that, a company executive answers a question and then motivates his/her answer with additional information in the following sentences. Drawing on this dependency, distilling the overall information from the earnings call transcripts by summarizing the transcripts could potentially be an appropriate approach for removing the noise from an input document. Text-to-Text Transfer Transformer (T5) is an encoder-decoder model pre-trained on a multi-task mixture of unsupervised and supervised tasks (Raffel et al., 2019). T5 provides state-of-the-art results for various tasks such as translation and summarization. In this work, we implement summarization with Text-to-Text Transfer Transformer (T5) and consider this a domain-agnostic approach since it does not require domain-specific finance knowledge. We process each input paragraph separately while limiting the number of tokens in each iteration to less than 512. We then concatenate the summarized versions of subsequent paragraphs to create a summary of the entire earnings call transcript.

4.3 Application of the domain-specific dictionary of Loughran - McDonald

Even though there may be relations and dependency among sentences, some may not provide any information relevant to the stock price volatility, such as "good morning" or "thank you for your question." Moreover, some sentences might provide relatively more important information, while previous or following sentences may just be minor clarifications of the previous message. In this denoising technique, we leverage a domain-specific dictionary developed particularly for financial documents to identify sentences with relatively more important information. The dictionary of Loughran and McDonald (Loughran and McDonald, 2011) is one of the most recognized dictionaries in the financial literature and has been used for several different tasks (Keith and Stent, 2019; Rekabsaz et al., 2017). The LM dictionary provides the list of words with positive, negative, uncertainty, litigious, strong modal, weak modal, constraining, and complexity that exist in annual company statements (10-K documents). In this work, we use this dictionary as a benchmark to identify the sentences that contain relatively more important information that may impact stock price volatility. We search for words from the LM dictionary at the sentence level in each earnings call transcript and drop the sentences that do not contain any matching words with the LM dictionary. Finally, we append the filtered sentences and create a new distilled document for each earnings call transcript.

Label	Sentence
0: irrelevant	Thank you and good morning
1: buy	In Q4 we generated worldwide revenue growth of 7%.
2: sell	{our} prices declined 1% in Q4.

Table 1: Examples of labels for intermediate model

4.4 Creating an intermediate model to filter irrelevant data

Given that domain-specific knowledge can often help improve model performance, we also experiment by filtering sentences containing irrelevant information by building an intermediate task-specific filtering model. In this approach, we trained a separate model specifically for filtering out information that we believe may be irrelevant for the stock price volatility prediction task. To this end, we randomly selected 1,000 sentences from our corpus and labeled them to be used for training, validating, and testing purposes [1]. During labeling, sentences were labeled as 'buy', 'sell', or 'irrelevant'. As illustrated in Table 1, similar to previous research (Keith and Stent, 2019), sentences that provide positive information about the company were labeled as 'buy', sentences that provide negative information about the company were labeled as 'sell', and finally sentences that are generic or do not create an impact on the analysts' decision making were labeled as 'irrelevant'. We trained a BERT(base-cased) model by fine-tuning it on 70% of the labeled data (700 sentences) and used the remaining 15 % for test (150 sentences), and 15% for validation (150 sentences). We used the fine-tuned model to get 'buy'/'sell'/'irrelevant' predictions for the remaining sentences in the corpus (87,829 sentences in 549 earnings call transcripts). In a similar vein to the training data, sentences with similar positive information are expected to be labeled as 'buy' (1), sentences with negative information are expected to be labeled as 'sell' (2), and sentences with generic information are expected to be labeled as 'irrelevant' (0). In the final stage, we dropped sentences with generic information ('irrelevant'), and kept only sentences with 'buy' or 'sell' labels in each earnings call transcript with their corre-

[1]The labeling process was performed by one of the authors of this paper with relevant background.

sponding volatility label [2].

5 Building Classification Models through AutoAI for Text

Building models for NLP tasks, such as the stock price volatility classification task considered in this work, requires significant technical expertise, effort, and resources. To lower the barrier of entry and accelerate the model development process, the research and industrial community have developed AutoML/AutoAI techniques to automate parts of this process (Hutter et al., 2019; He et al., 2021; Wang et al., 2020). Multiple AutoML techniques suggested in the literature target different parts of the model development process. These include neural architecture search (He et al., 2021), hyperparameter optimization (Weidele et al., 2020), and others.

While previous works on stock volatility prediction using textual data leverage a small set of hand-picked NLP models, we explore AutoML techniques to select the best NLP model for the stock price volatility prediction task in this work. The goal behind this choice is twofold: First, we want to investigate how domain experts (in our case, financial analysts) can create NLP models for their tasks. Second, we want to explore multiple NLP model architectures and gain insights into which model architectures work best for the stock volatility prediction task.

We feed the denoised earnings calls transcripts and their corresponding labels into AutoAI for Text (Chaudhary et al., 2021). AutoAI for Text is a comprehensive end-to-end AutoML system for text classification tasks, which given a labeled text classification dataset explores a large search space of models for the provided dataset. During this search, AutoAI for Text explores multiple *featurizers* (such as GloVe, TFIDF, etc.), *estimators/transformers* (such as SVC, CNN, LSTM, etc.), and *hyperparameters*. The result of this optimization process is a set of NLP models for the given dataset (referred to as *pipelines*), ranked based on a chosen optimization metric (such as accuracy, precision, recall, F1, etc.). As we explain when describing the experimental evaluation in Section 6, AutoAI for Text also allows for various configuration options, including a specification of the set of models to explore, time budget that can be used for optimization purposes, the maximum number of candidate models to be trained, and others [3].

6 Experimental Evaluation

Experimental setting. For each earnings call transcript, we compute its volatility label for four different time periods, corresponding to 3, 7, 15, and 30 days following the earnings call. Through this process we obtain four different sets of labels for our earnings call transcripts (one per time period). In parallel, we run each transcript through the four denoising approaches outlined in Section 4. This leads to four sets of documents (one per denoising approach). For each (time period, denoising approach) pair, we combine the denoised transcript with the corresponding volatility label to generate a labeled dataset corresponding to the given time period and denoising approach. This labeled dataset is then fed into AutoAI for Text, which is tasked with discovering the best NLP model for the given pair.

Each labeled dataset is split into a 90% combined train and validation split and 10% test split. This split is done sequentially based on the timestamp of the earnings calls to ensure that we do not include in the train split any information about the time periods included in the test split (i.e., we want to avoid giving the model at training time information about the future). The combined train and test split is then further split by AutoAI for Text into train and validation utilizing another 90/10 split. In addition to the train/validation split ratio, we use the following configuration for AutoAI for Text: We assign an optimization time budget of 2 hours (i.e., instructing it to use up to 2 hours for optimization purposes) and ask it to explore and train at most 81 candidate models. We also select accuracy as the metric used both internally for optimization purposes and externally to report model performance. Finally, we instruct AutoAI for Text to explore a variety of estimators/transformers, which include SVC, CNN, LSTM, and BERT, and a variety of featurizers, which include GLoVe and TFIDF [4]. For

[2]Note that we modeled filtering as a ternary classification task, distinguishing between 'buy', 'sell', and 'irrelevant' sentences, to ensure that each class is homogeneous. However, in an alternative formulation, one could also model filtering as binary classification (with sentences labeled simply as 'relevant' or 'irrelevant').

[3]The focus of this work is not a comprehensive review of AutoAI for Text, but an investigation of how it can be used to solve the stock price volatility prediction task.

[4]It should be noted that all experiments were ran utilizing CPU (i.e., without GPU support), which may have affected the choice of BERT (which as we will see did not appear in

each (time period, denoising approach) pair, we select the model that AutoAI for Text has identified as having the highest accuracy on the validation set (which we refer to as the *best model*). The best model is then evaluated on the test set, computing its accuracy, which is the metric that we present in our evaluation results.

Baseline. Existing works on stock price volatility prediction from earnings call transcripts model the problem as a regression problem, however, as a baseline we use a simple approach that assigns to all transcripts the same label. For each (time period, denoising approach) pair, we report three versions of this baseline, depending on which is the common label assigned to all transcripts: L (low), M (medium), or H (high). For instance, in the L-baseline, all transcripts are predicted as being low volatility. While this is an admittedly simple baseline, it still allows us to understand whether the discovered models have identified a signal in the data or have simply learned to predict the most common label.

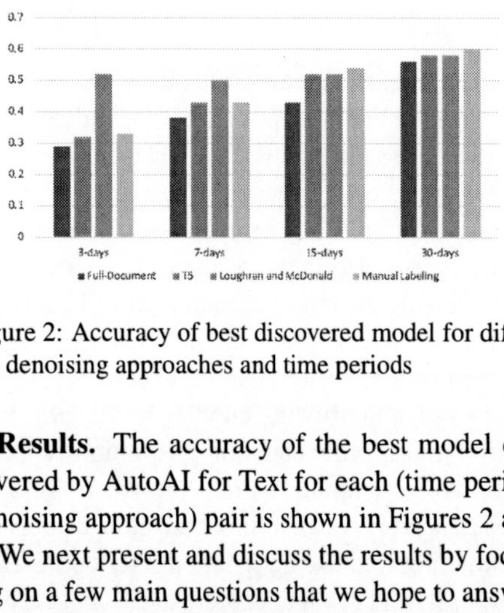

Figure 2: Accuracy of best discovered model for different denoising approaches and time periods

Results. The accuracy of the best model discovered by AutoAI for Text for each (time period, denoising approach) pair is shown in Figures 2 and 3. We next present and discuss the results by focusing on a few main questions that we hope to answer from this experimental evaluation.

Are the models able to identify a signal in the data? The first question we hope to answer is whether the discovered models have identified a signal in the input transcripts that allows them to predict the stock price volatility or whether they have simply learned to predict the most common label. This is a non-trivial question, as transcripts are long documents that in addition to information that may affect the stock price often contain a lot of irrelevant information. To answer this question, we compare in Figure 3 the accuracy of the best model discovered for each time period (shown in bold) with the accuracy of the best baseline (shown in italics).

As we can see, for all time periods, the former is always higher than the latter. Thus the best models seem to have successfully identified a signal in the transcripts that allows them to perform better than the baseline. For instance, the best model for the 3-day time period has an accuracy of 0.52, which is higher than the best baseline accuracy of 0.43 (which corresponds to predicting for every input transcript the most common label, which in this case is the high volatility). The gap between the best model and the baseline closes as the time period increases. While this is an interesting phenomenon that needs to be investigated further, a potential explanation is that transcripts may be more useful in predicting volatility for time periods immediately following the earnings calls, rather than for longer time periods [5].

Which denoising approaches perform best? The next question is identifying the best denoising approach for the studied problem. Which of the proposed denoising approaches should one choose for predicting stock price volatility and does the choice of the approach make a difference? Comparing the performance of the denoising approaches provides some interesting insights:

First, utilizing the full document (without any denoising) always yields the lowest performance. This shows that denoising approaches are important for distilling the long transcripts and making them more amenable for being used as training data for an NLP model.

Second, domain-agnostic denoising (such as the one provided by the T5 summarization approach) consistently underperforms domain-specific denoising approaches (such as the use of the domain-specific dictionary or the intermediate model). This shows that further applying domain knowledge to distill input documents can improve model performance.

Finally, while the best denoising approaches are the two domain-specific approaches, we observe that using the domain-specific dictionary of Loughran - McDonald is better for shorter time periods (i.e., time periods of 3 and 7 days), while using the intermediate denoising model based on

the results).

[5]The stock price may fluctuate due to other causes beyond what has been reported at the earnings call.

Denoising Approach	3-days volatility	7-days volatility	15-days volatility	30-days volatility
Baseline	L:0.25/M:0.30/*H:0.43*	L:0.12/*M:0.43*/*H:0.43*	L:0.10/*M:0.50*/H:0.38	L:0.12/*M:0.58*/H:0.29
Full Document	TFIDF+SVC (0.29)	TFIDF+SVC (0.38)	TFIDF+SVC (0.50)	GloVe+CNN (0.56)
T5	TFIDF+SVC (0.32)	GloVe+CNN (0.43)	TFIDF+SVC (0.52)	GloVe+CNN (0.58)
Loughran McDonald	**GloVe+CNN (0.52)**	**TFIDF+SVC(0.50)**	GloVe+CNN (0.52)	TFIDF+SVC (0.58)
Manual Labeling	TFIDF+SVC (0.33)	TFIDF+SVC(0.43)	**TFIDF+SVC(0.54)**	**GloVe+CNN (0.60)**

Figure 3: Accuracy of best model discovered by AutoAI for Text (together with the architecture of the model) for different denoising approaches and time periods. The baseline shows the accuracy that would be obtained if we assigned to all transcripts the same label of L: low, M: medium, or H: high volatility.

manually provided labels performs better for longer time periods (i.e., time periods of 15 and 30 days). This is an interesting result that we plan to explore and analyze further as part of our future work.

Which model architectures perform best? Finally, leveraging AutoAI for Text, we want to identify which model architectures perform best for the stock volatility prediction task. To aid in answering this question, Figure 3 includes the description of the best model discovered by AutoAI for Text. Each model is shown as $F + E$, where F is the featurizer and E is the estimator/transformer. For instance, GloVe+CNN is a model combining a GloVe featurizer with a convolutional neural network. As described above, in our experiments AutoAI for Text explored the GloVe and TFIDF featurizers. Similarly it searched among the following estimators/transformers: SVC, CNN, LSTM, and BERT.

By comparing the models reported in Figure 3, we can make the following observations: In all cases the models that perform best are based either on SVC and CNN combined with either GloVe or TFIDF featurizers. We cannot observe any systematic difference between SVC and CNN, leading us to believe that both work equally well for the studied problem. However, an important observation is that LSTM and BERT never appear among the best models.[6] However, both this as well as the performance of LSTM in this case our important results that we think are worth investigating further.

[6]All the experiments were done on a CPU-only machine. As such, we instructed AutoAI for Text to explore only CPU-friendly types of models. These are types of models that can be trained fast with CPU-only resources and include classical ones like SVC as well as faster deep-learning based models (CNN, LSTM). We left out BERT from the exploration space, since BERT works better when given GPU resources.

7 Conclusion and Future Work

Compared to existing work in the area, our work makes three main contributions: First, it models the problem as a text classification task (in contrast to the regression task considered before) and explores how one can leverage text classification models. Second, instead of just utilizing the long earnings call transcripts as-is, it explores the use of denoising approaches to distill the information found in the input documents and improve the performance of the learned models. We propose and explore an entire spectrum of denoising approaches, ranging from domain-agnostic techniques (such as general-purpose summarization models) to domain-specific techniques and compare their performance. Third, we leverage AutoML approaches to explore a range of NLP models and understand which model architectures perform best for the stock price volatility prediction task.

Our preliminary findings lead to several important insights. Denoising is shown to improve model performance with domain-specific denoising leading to bigger gains than domain-agnostic denoising approaches. Moreover, the use of AutoML leads to interesting insights on which model architectures perform best for the stock volatility task. We believe that these insights point to new interesting research directions both in developing better domain-specific denoising approaches, as well as further investigating which model architectures work best for long financial documents, which are some of the directions we plan to further explore in our future work.

References

Werner Antweiler and Murray Z Frank. 2004. Is all that talk just noise? the information content of internet stock message boards. *The Journal of finance*, 59(3):1259–1294.

Ray Ball and Philip Brown. 1968. An empirical evaluation of accounting income numbers. *Journal of accounting research*, pages 159–178.

Ursel Baumann, Erlend Nier, et al. 2004. Disclosure, volatility, and transparency: an empirical investigation into the value of bank disclosure. *Economic Policy Review*, 10(2):31–45.

Victor L Bernard and Jacob K Thomas. 1989. Post-earnings-announcement drift: delayed price response or risk premium? *Journal of Accounting research*, 27:1–36.

Hendrik Bessembinder and Paul J Seguin. 1992. Futures-trading activity and stock price volatility. *the Journal of Finance*, 47(5):2015–2034.

Ekaba Bisong. 2019. Google automl: Cloud natural language processing. In *Building Machine Learning and Deep Learning Models on Google Cloud Platform*, pages 599–612. Springer.

Matthias Blohm, Marc Hanussek, and Maximilien Kintz. 2020. Leveraging automated machine learning for text classification: Evaluation of automl tools and comparison with human performance. *arXiv preprint arXiv:2012.03575*.

Johan Bollen, Huina Mao, and Xiaojun Zeng. 2011. Twitter mood predicts the stock market. *Journal of computational science*, 2(1):1–8.

Robert M Bowen, Angela K Davis, and Dawn A Matsumoto. 2002. Do conference calls affect analysts' forecasts? *The Accounting Review*, 77(2):285–316.

Arunima Chaudhary, Alayt Issak, Kiran Kate, Yannis Katsis, Abel Valente, Dakuo Wang, Alexandre Evfimievski, Sairam Gurajada, Ban Kawas, Cristiano Malossi, Lucian Popa, Tejaswini Pedapati, Horst Samulowitz, Martin Wistuba, and Yunyao Li. 2021. Autotext: An end-to-end autoai framework for text. *Proceedings of the AAAI Conference on Artificial Intelligence*, 35(18):16001–16003.

Peter K Clark. 1973. A subordinated stochastic process model with finite variance for speculative prices. *Econometrica: journal of the Econometric Society*, pages 135–155.

Lauren Cohen and Dong Lou. 2012. Complicated firms. *Journal of financial economics*, 104(2):383–400.

Xiao Ding, Yue Zhang, Ting Liu, and Junwen Duan. 2014. Using structured events to predict stock price movement: An empirical investigation. In *Proceedings of the 2014 Conference on Empirical Methods in Natural Language Processing (EMNLP)*, pages 1415–1425, Doha, Qatar. Association for Computational Linguistics.

Suilan Estevez-Velarde, Yoan Gutiérrez, Andrés Montoyo, and Yudivián Almeida Cruz. 2019. Automl strategy based on grammatical evolution: A case study about knowledge discovery from text. In *Proceedings of the 57th Annual Meeting of the Association for Computational Linguistics*, pages 4356–4365.

Eugene F Fama. 1998. Market efficiency, long-term returns, and behavioral finance. *Journal of financial economics*, 49(3):283–306.

Josef Fink. 2021. A review of the post-earnings-announcement drift. *Journal of Behavioral and Experimental Finance*, 29:100446.

Richard Frankel, Marilyn Johnson, and Douglas J Skinner. 1999. An empirical examination of conference calls as a voluntary disclosure medium. *Journal of Accounting Research*, 37(1):133–150.

Kenneth R French and Richard Roll. 1986. Stock return variances: The arrival of information and the reaction of traders. *Journal of financial economics*, 17(1):5–26.

Sanford J Grossman and Joseph E Stiglitz. 1980. On the impossibility of informationally efficient markets. *The American economic review*, 70(3):393–408.

Xin He, Kaiyong Zhao, and Xiaowen Chu. 2021. Automl: A survey of the state-of-the-art. *Knowledge-Based Systems*, 212:106622.

Frank Hutter, Lars Kotthoff, and Joaquin Vanschoren. 2019. *Automated machine learning: methods, systems, challenges*. Springer Nature.

Katherine A Keith and Amanda Stent. 2019. Modeling financial analysts' decision making via the pragmatics and semantics of earnings calls. *arXiv preprint arXiv:1906.02868*.

Shimon Kogan, Dimitry Levin, Bryan R. Routledge, Jacob S. Sagi, and Noah A. Smith. 2009. Predicting risk from financial reports with regression. In *Proceedings of Human Language Technologies: The 2009 Annual Conference of the North American Chapter of the Association for Computational Linguistics*, pages 272–280, Boulder, Colorado. Association for Computational Linguistics.

Mark Lang and Russell Lundholm. 1993. Cross-sectional determinants of analyst ratings of corporate disclosures. *Journal of accounting research*, 31(2):246–271.

Jiazheng Li, Linyi Yang, Barry Smyth, and Ruihai Dong. 2020. MAEC: A multimodal aligned earnings conference call dataset for financial risk prediction. In *Proceedings of the 29th ACM International Conference on Information and Knowledge Management*, CIKM '20, page 3063–3070, New York, NY, USA. Association for Computing Machinery.

Ming-Yuan Leon Li and Hsiou-Wei William Lin. 2003. Examining the volatility of taiwan stock index returns via a three-volatility-regime markov-switching arch model. *Review of Quantitative Finance and Accounting*, 21(2):123–139.

Tim Loughran and Bill McDonald. 2011. When is a liability not a liability? textual analysis, dictionaries, and 10-ks. *The Journal of finance*, 66(1):35–65.

Dawn Matsumoto, Maarten Pronk, and Erik Roelofsen. 2011. What makes conference calls useful? the information content of managers' presentations and analysts' discussion sessions. *The Accounting Review*, 86(4):1383–1414.

Yu Qin and Yi Yang. 2019. What you say and how you say it matters: Predicting stock volatility using verbal and vocal cues. In *Proceedings of the 57th Annual Meeting of the Association for Computational Linguistics*, pages 390–401, Florence, Italy. Association for Computational Linguistics.

Colin Raffel, Noam Shazeer, Adam Roberts, Katherine Lee, Sharan Narang, Michael Matena, Yanqi Zhou, Wei Li, and Peter J. Liu. 2019. Exploring the limits of transfer learning with a unified text-to-text transformer. *CoRR*, abs/1910.10683.

Navid Rekabsaz, Mihai Lupu, Artem Baklanov, Allan Hanbury, Alexander Dür, and Linda Anderson. 2017. Volatility prediction using financial disclosures sentiments with word embedding-based ir models. *arXiv preprint arXiv:1702.01978*.

George E Tauchen and Mark Pitts. 1983. The price variability-volume relationship on speculative markets. *Econometrica: Journal of the Econometric Society*, pages 485–505.

Paul C Tetlock. 2007. Giving content to investor sentiment: The role of media in the stock market. *The Journal of finance*, 62(3):1139–1168.

Nikolaos Vlastakis and Raphael N Markellos. 2012. Information demand and stock market volatility. *Journal of Banking & Finance*, 36(6):1808–1821.

Dakuo Wang, Parikshit Ram, Daniel Karl I Weidele, Sijia Liu, Michael Muller, Justin D Weisz, Abel Valente, Arunima Chaudhary, Dustin Torres, Horst Samulowitz, et al. 2020. Autoai: Automating the end-to-end ai lifecycle with humans-in-the-loop. In *Proceedings of the 25th International Conference on Intelligent User Interfaces Companion*, pages 77–78.

Daniel Karl I Weidele, Justin D Weisz, Erick Oduor, Michael Muller, Josh Andres, Alexander Gray, and Dakuo Wang. 2020. Autoaiviz: opening the blackbox of automated artificial intelligence with conditional parallel coordinates. In *Proceedings of the 25th International Conference on Intelligent User Interfaces*, pages 308–312.

DigiCall: A Benchmark for Measuring the Maturity of Digital Strategy through Company Earning Calls

Hilal Pataci
Rensselaer Polytechnic Institute, USA
patach@rpi.edu

Kexuan Sun
University of Southern California, USA
kexuansu@usc.edu

T. Ravichandran
Rensselaer Polytechnic Institute, USA
ravit@rpi.edu

Abstract

Digital transformation reinvents companies, their vision and strategy, organizational structure, processes, capabilities, culture, and enables the development of new or enhanced products and services delivered to customers more efficiently. By formalizing their digital strategy, organizations attempt to plan for their digital transformations and accelerate their company growth. Understanding how successful a company is in its digital transformation starts with accurately measuring its digital maturity levels. However, existing approaches to measuring organizations' digital strategy have inconsistent results, and also do not provide resources (data) for future research to improve. In order to measure the digital strategy maturity of companies and provide a benchmark, we leverage the state-of-the-art NLP models on unstructured data (earning call transcripts), and reach the state-of-the-art levels (94%) for this task. We release 3.691 earning call transcripts and also annotated data set labeled particularly for the digital strategy maturity by linguists.

1 Introduction

Digital transformation (DT) has emerged as an important phenomenon and is expected to preserve its prominence for companies. International Data Corporation (IDC, 2021) forecast that global spending on digital transformation will reach $2.8 trillion by 2025 and to exceed $10 trillion over a five-year period. DT redefines how companies operate and enhances connectivity, and inclusion worldwide. According to United Nations(Nations, 2019), AI-enabled frontier technologies are helping to save lives, diagnose diseases and increase life expectancy, while AI-enabled education by enabling virtual learning environments, opens up programs to students who would otherwise be excluded. DT, at a high level, encompasses the profound changes taking place in society and industries due to the adaptation of digital technologies, while at the organizational level, organizations by practicing strategies that do not only embrace the implications of digital transformation but also reach better operational performance (Vial, 2019).

Vial(Vial, 2019) explores 282 works on digital transformation in the Information Systems literature and develops a conceptual definition of DT as *'a process that aims to improve an entity by triggering significant changes to its properties through combinations of information, computation, communication, and connectivity technologies* (p.118). Organizations, by formalizing their digital strategy and leveraging their digital resources, plan for their DT (Bharadwaj et al., 2013; Al-Ali et al., 2020; Jackson, 2015; Freitas Junior et al., 2016). In order to measure and evaluate the digital strategy of firms, the status quo of a company's digital transformation, and the digital maturity level are measured(Thordsen et al., 2020; Kane et al., 2017).

In this research, our conceptual interest is centered on measuring the digital strategy maturity of firms. By considering this as a text classification task of earnings call transcripts, we leverage several transformer-based architectures for text classification, in addition to rule-based approaches. In the end we present our measure and release two data sets for future research[1].

2 Related Work

Digital transformation research is one of the most growing areas and has been studied by management scientists(Gurbaxani and Dunkle, 2019; Vial, 2019; Kane et al., 2017; Bharadwaj et al., 2013; Sebastian et al., 2020), economists (Acemoglu and Restrepo, 2019; Nagaraj and Reimers, 2021), engineers(Issa et al., 2018), computer scientists (Al-Ali et al., 2020), and social scientists (Hilbert, 2022; Shibuya, 2020) in the literature. Despite there are many studies investigating the implications or drivers of DT

[1] https://github.com/hpataci/DigiCall

Proceedings of the Fourth Workshop on Financial Technology and Natural Language Processing (FinNLP), pages 58 - 67
December 8, 2022 ©2022 Association for Computational Linguistics

in different fields, our focus is limited to studies in management science, computer science, and their intersection.

In this research, we predict the maturity of the digital strategy of S&P 500 companies by leveraging transformer-based models with domain knowledge. The most similar work to ours (Al-Ali et al., 2020)'s that uses earning call transcripts but does not release any data. Therefore, we do not have chance to test our approach on their data. However, available earning calls data sets (Li et al., 2020; Qin and Yang, 2019) have limitations that make it infeasible to measure the digital strategy maturity of companies. Moreover, there is no task-specific annotated data set available in the area particularly to measure the digital strategy maturity of companies.

Every quarter the executive leadership of a public company holds an earnings call meeting with investors and analysts to inform them about the status of the company, including their major digital initiatives. An earning calls transcript has mainly three parts, the first part consists of the names of company call participants, the second part consists of the presentation session of company executives, and the third part consists of a question-and-answer session. Existing earning call transcripts data sets do not provide both sessions, but only provide the answers of the most spoken company executive in the Q&A session(Li et al., 2020). The executives might share more information during the first session than during the Q&A session. One of the other major issues with the existing data-sets is that they only share one company executive's sentences by discarding other company representatives' comments (Qin and Yang, 2019). Therefore, this would also yield inaccurate results leading to biased analysis when we attempt to learn about how companies are performing in their digital transformation. In this research, we release all sections of the earning call transcripts without any section removal.

Any public company has 4 (Q1, Q2, Q3, Q4) earning conference call meetings annually in the USA. However, existing data sets in the literature have missing transcripts for some of these meetings. Measuring digital strategy maturity with missing earning conference call transcripts would yield inaccurate results. Such that if we obtain Apple's digital maturity in Q1 and Q2 of 2018, any digital strategy maturity analysis of Apple would be biased given that Apple might have disclosed several accomplishments in Q3 and Q4 of 2018. Moreover,

Dataset	DigiCall	MAEC	Keith	Qin
Duration	2018/19	2015/18	2010/17	2017
Companies	469	1,213	642	280
Instances	3,691	3.443	12,285	576
Data Av.	Yes	Yes	No	Yes

Table 1: Comparisons of our earnings calls dataset and the existing public earnings call datasets

available data sets in the literature have missing data points for some companies and this might also lead to inconsistent results to measure digital strategy initiatives. Such that (Li et al., 2020) discloses 3443 earning call transcripts of 1213 companies (average 3 transcripts per company), while (Qin and Yang, 2019) discloses 576 earning call transcripts of 280 companies (average 2 transcripts per company). Therefore, to our knowledge, our data set has one of the longest time windows for earning conference call transcripts with the lowest number of missing transcripts (average 7 transcripts per company).

3 Problem Definition and Our Hypotheses

There are several research studies attempting to measure digital maturity in management science literature (Thordsen et al., 2020; Gurbaxani and Dunkle, 2019; Kane et al., 2017). However, among these studies, the only study that leverages transformer-based models is (Al-Ali et al., 2020)'s work, and therefore it is the most similar to ours. In their work (Al-Ali et al., 2020), that they identify two tasks; first, the prediction of the aspect of the digital strategy, and second, the prediction of the maturity of the digital strategy. For the first task, they disclose a dictionary of 350 terms in 17 topics to be used with the prediction task [2]. Any sentence *s1* contains a term for the aspect of digital strategy, they combine it with the preceding *s0* and subsequent *s2* sentence from the transcripts and feed the appended sentences *s0+s1+s2* into the model. *We hypothesize that appending s0 and s2 with s1* might increase the noise in the data. Therefore, we only process sentences containing aspect maturity terms *s1*, and drop *s0* and *s2*. In the second stage, they predict the maturity stage. If the digital initiative is being planned, it is labeled as *plan*, if the digital initiative is being developed or piloted, it is labeled as *pilot*, if the digital initiative is launched

[2]The list of these terms and topics is available in The Appendix

and making an active contribution to the business, it is labeled as *release*, if the digital initiative is being pioneered and making a significant business impact, it is labeled as *pioneer*. *We hypothesize that a digital initiative released or pioneered completed in the past.* Hence, these two labels are combined under the past label by considering the temporal orientation (Hasanuzzaman et al., 2016; Keith and Stent, 2019) (grammatical tenses); Plan as Future, Pilot as Present, and Release and Pioneer as Past.

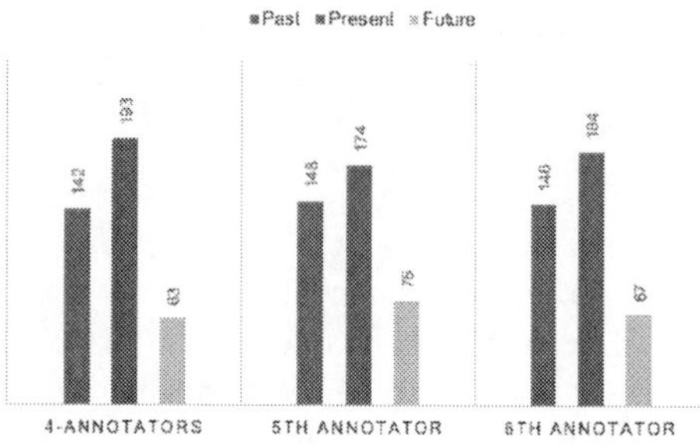

Figure 1: The Distribution of Annotations

4 Data Set Creation

4.1 Pre-Processing

Earning conference calls transcripts are recorded and shared as text and audio files by the company and third-party companies after each meeting. We collect earning conference call transcripts to measure the digital strategy maturity of the S&P 500 companies in 2018 and 2019 from Seeking Alpha. Each call document has mainly three parts, the first part consists of the names of company call participants, the second part consists of the presentation of company executives, and the third part consists of a question-and-answer section. We discarded the first section given that company executives' names have no impact on our task. [3] Despite the data was collected at the document level, we used Stanza (Qi et al., 2020)'s sentence tokenization to convert these documents into sentences and (Qi et al., 2020)'s Named-entity- recognition to remove questions, person's names, and this resulted with sentences of company executives. The baseline study in the area(Al-Ali et al., 2020) identifies two tasks; prediction of the aspect of the digital strategy, and prediction of the maturity of the digital strategy. They disclose a dictionary of 350 terms in 17 topics for the first task to be used with the prediction task. However, instead of considering the first task as a prediction task, we dropped the sentences that do not have matching terms with (Al-Ali et al., 2020)'s dictionary but kept if there is a match. In the second stage, we used the annotated data to fine-tune language models to predict the digital strategy maturity.

4.2 Annotation and Ethics

In order to annotate the pre-processed data, we instructed 4 freelancer linguists (2 Female, and 2 Male) from Upwork [4]. Each linguist at least had a bachelor's degree in linguistics, is a native-level English speaker, and at least has 95% positive feedback on Upwork. We randomly selected 400 sentences from 2018 data, distributed 100 sentences to each annotator, and compensated $40 to each annotator for this task and allocated one week. In the next stage, we instructed another linguist (5th person, Female), hired through Upwork with the same benchmarks and conditions, to agree or disagree with the annotated data by four people. The Cohen's kappa between the first 4-annotators and the 5th annotator is 84%. Finally, we instructed a 6th person (Male) with industry and domain experience, to agree or disagree with the annotated data by four people. The Cohen's kappa between the first 4-annotators and the 6th annotator is 95%, and between the 5th and 6th annotator is 88%.

5 Approaches

In this section, we provide details of different approaches applied for our task. For each following approach, the input is a textual string, i.e. a sentence from an earning call document, and the output is a label indicating the status of a company/a project. We consider three labels: *past*, *present* and *future*.

5.1 Part of Speech

The first approach is based on part-of-speech (POS). Given a sentence, POS tags provide grammatical information for individual words in the sentence. We use off-the-shelf tools to analyze each given sentence and use the output POS tags to determine the status of the sentence.

[3] We obtained the consent of Seeking Alpha to share the earning calls transcripts data on April 28, 2022. We thank them for their consent and acknowledgment. www.seekingalpha.com

[4] www.upwork.com

5.2 Language Models

Pre-trained language models have shown the state-of-the-art performance on various NLP tasks. We also fine-tune the pre-trained models for our task [5].

5.2.1 Domain-Agnostic

We first consider following models pre-trained on general corpus. **BERT**(Devlin et al., 2018): One of the commonly used models that is pre-trained with different novel tasks such as masked language modeling, and next sentence prediction. Similar to other fine-tuning tasks, we simply use the BERT tokenizer to tokenize the sentence and use the pre-trained model to encode the tokenized sentences. **ALBERT**(Lan et al., 2019): A model based on BERT but has different architectures that save more parameters. **RoBERTa**(Liu et al., 2019): It is also a variant of BERT. The main difference between RoBERTa and BERT is that RoBERTa uses different masking strategies during pre-training and provides more robust performance.

5.2.2 Domain-Specific

Different from previous models, we also consider models that are pre-trained on financial data as our task is based on financial documents. More specifically, we use another BERT-based model FinBERT(Araci, 2019). Based on the pre-trained BERT, FinBERT is further pre-trained on financial documents which demonstrates better performance on financial tasks. [6]

6 Experimental Evaluation and Findings

By building on previous work (Al-Ali et al., 2020) and several transformer-based models, we considered predicting the aspect maturity of the organizations' digital strategy as a text classification task with *past*, *present*, and *future* as labels. Consistent with the baseline study in the area (Al-Ali et al., 2020), we trained several domain-agnostic transformer-based models by applying fine-tuning with domain-specific data annotated by 4 different linguists. Despite RoBERTa provides the highest F-1 weighted at (Al-Ali et al., 2020)'s work, our findings show that BERT*base-uncased* provides the highest F1-weighted level (94%) while (Al-Ali et al., 2020) (58.2%). Given that we have different number of labels, and did not experiment with (Al-Ali et al., 2020)'s data, we are extending and adding to the literature by addressing some of the potential data issues in prior work. Different than previous work(Al-Ali et al., 2020), we experimented with a domain-specific model FinBERT (Araci, 2019). However, despite FinBERT being pre-trained and fine-tuned with finance domain-specific corpus it results lower F1-weighted. The rule-based approach, POS, provides the highest accuracy to predict the *Past* label.

Model	**F1**	**Past Acc**	**Present Acc**	**Future Acc**
Rule-based				
POS	0.91	0.92	0.88	0.88
Domain-agnostic				
BERT *base-cased*	0.91	0.87	0.88	0.92
BERT *base-uncased*	**0.94**	**0.88**	**0.98**	**0.92**
ALBERT *base-v2*	0.89	0.84	0.87	0.92
RoBERTa *base*	0.79	0.79	0.86	0.75
Domain-specific				
FinBERT	0.90	**0.91**	0.91	0.83

Table 2: Performance of the Proposed Models

7 Conclusions and Future Work

Predicting the maturity of the digital strategy of firms accurately might help researchers to explore organizations' digital transformation while providing insights on how to plan for digital transformation for organizations.

In our supplementary analysis, we find that industrial trends with respect to the maturity of the digital strategy also change with time, such that organizations disclose more past and future digital strategies in Q4 than in any other quarter. Future research might consider the time-variant factors that influence companies' digital strategy maturity. Such as, exogenous shocks, competitors' product releases might impact organizations' digital transformation. With the new proposed approach, it might be possible to predict which future digital strategy plans of organizations were suspended or accelerated by also considering the competitive behavior of organizations.

[5]In all transformer-based models, we randomly split the data as train, validation, test into 75%*75%, 75%*25%, and 25% respectively. All experiments were conducted at Google Colab Pro and randomly assigned to NVIDIA Tesla P100-PCIE (16GB) for GPU, and had the following settings: the learning rate 1e-5 (AdamW), epochs 6, batch size 3. We used the HuggingFace library https://huggingface.co/ for all models.

[6]https://huggingface.co/yiyanghkust/finbert-tone

References

Daron Acemoglu and Pascual Restrepo. 2019. Automation and new tasks: How technology displaces and reinstates labor. *Journal of Economic Perspectives*, 33(2):3–30.

Ahmed Ghanim Al-Ali, Robert Phaal, and Donald Sull. 2020. Deep learning framework for measuring the digital strategy of companies from earnings calls. *arXiv preprint arXiv:2010.12418*.

Dogu Araci. 2019. Finbert: Financial sentiment analysis with pre-trained language models. *arXiv preprint arXiv:1908.10063*.

Anandhi Bharadwaj, Omar A El Sawy, Paul A Pavlou, and N v Venkatraman. 2013. Digital business strategy: toward a next generation of insights. *MIS quarterly*, pages 471–482.

Jacob Devlin, Ming-Wei Chang, Kenton Lee, and Kristina Toutanova. 2018. Bert: Pre-training of deep bidirectional transformers for language understanding. *arXiv preprint arXiv:1810.04805*.

José Carlos Freitas Junior, Antonio Carlos Maçada, Rafael Brinkhues, and Gustavo Montesdioca. 2016. Digital capabilities as driver to digital business performance.

Vijay Gurbaxani and Debora Dunkle. 2019. Gearing up for successful digital transformation. *MIS Quarterly Executive*, 18(3).

Mohammed Hasanuzzaman, Wai Leung Sze, Mahammad Parvez Salim, and Gaël Dias. 2016. Collective future orientation and stock markets. In *ECAI 2016*, pages 1616–1617. IOS Press.

Martin Hilbert. 2022. Digital technology and social change: the digital transformation of society from a historical perspective. *Dialogues in clinical neuroscience*.

IDC. 2021. New idc spending guide shows continued growth for digital transformation as organizations focus on strategic priorities. `https://www.idc.com/getdoc.jsp?containerId=prUS48372321`.

Ahmad Issa, Bumin Hatiboglu, Andreas Bildstein, and Thomas Bauernhansl. 2018. Industrie 4.0 roadmap: Framework for digital transformation based on the concepts of capability maturity and alignment. *Procedia Cirp*, 72:973–978.

Paul J Jackson. 2015. Networks in a digital world: A cybernetics perspective.

GC Kane, D Palmer, AN Phillips, D Kiron, and N Buckley. 2017. Achieving digital maturity: Adapting your company to a changing world. findings from the 2017 digital business global executive study and research project. *MIT Sloan Management Review and Deloitte University Press*.

Katherine A Keith and Amanda Stent. 2019. Modeling financial analysts' decision making via the pragmatics and semantics of earnings calls. *arXiv preprint arXiv:1906.02868*.

Zhenzhong Lan, Mingda Chen, Sebastian Goodman, Kevin Gimpel, Piyush Sharma, and Radu Soricut. 2019. Albert: A lite bert for self-supervised learning of language representations. *arXiv preprint arXiv:1909.11942*.

Jiazheng Li, Linyi Yang, Barry Smyth, and Ruihai Dong. 2020. Maec: A multimodal aligned earnings conference call dataset for financial risk prediction. In *Proceedings of the 29th ACM International Conference on Information & Knowledge Management*, pages 3063–3070.

Yinhan Liu, Myle Ott, Naman Goyal, Jingfei Du, Mandar Joshi, Danqi Chen, Omer Levy, Mike Lewis, Luke Zettlemoyer, and Veselin Stoyanov. 2019. Roberta: A robustly optimized bert pretraining approach. *arXiv preprint arXiv:1907.11692*.

Abhishek Nagaraj and Imke Reimers. 2021. Digitization and the demand for physical works: Evidence from the google books project. *Available at SSRN 3339524*.

United Nations. 2019. The age of digital interdependence. `https://www.un.org/en/un75/impact-digital-technologies`.

Peng Qi, Yuhao Zhang, Yuhui Zhang, Jason Bolton, and Christopher D Manning. 2020. Stanza: A python natural language processing toolkit for many human languages. *arXiv preprint arXiv:2003.07082*.

Yu Qin and Yi Yang. 2019. What you say and how you say it matters: Predicting stock volatility using verbal and vocal cues. In *Proceedings of the 57th Annual Meeting of the Association for Computational Linguistics*, pages 390–401, Florence, Italy. Association for Computational Linguistics.

Ina M Sebastian, Jeanne W Ross, Cynthia Beath, Martin Mocker, Kate G Moloney, and Nils O Fonstad. 2020. How big old companies navigate digital transformation. In *Strategic information management*, pages 133–150. Routledge.

Kazuhiko Shibuya. 2020. *Digital Transformation of Identity in the Age of Artificial Intelligence*. Springer.

Tristan Thordsen, Matthias Murawski, and Markus Bick. 2020. How to measure digitalization? a critical evaluation of digital maturity models. In *Conference on e-Business, e-Services and e-Society*, pages 358–369. Springer.

Gregory Vial. 2019. Understanding digital transformation: A review and a research agenda. *The journal of strategic information systems*, 28(2):118–144.

Appendix

Digital Strategy Aspect

This list presents 17 topics of interest detailed by 350 definitional terms obtained from (Al-Ali et al., 2020)

Topic	Keyword	Keyword terms
Digital Technology	AI	\bAI\b, artificial intelligence, NLP, natural language processing, natural language understanding, NLU, natural language generation, NLG, speech recognition, sentiment analysis, speech to text, text to speech, deep learning, machine learning, \bML\b, neural network, algorithm, generative adversarial network, GANs, supervised learning, unsupervised learning, reinforcement learning, semi-supervised learning, active learning, self learning, transfer learning, back propogation, tensorflow, Salesforce Einstein, IBM Watson, kaggle, AI as a service, Microsoft azure ML, AutoML, autonomous vehicles, computer vision, image recognition, pattern recognition, cognitive computing, predictive analytics, predictive maintenance, algorithmic trading, clustering, dimensionality reduction, t-sne, PCA, principal component analysis, chatbot, \bbot\b, RPA, robotic process automation, matrix factorization, collaborative filtering, recommender system, recommendation engine, graph mining, graph theory, cortana, alexa, google assistant
	Cloud computing	cloud computing, cloud native, cloudless, distributed cloud, distributed computing, clustered computing, hybrid cloud, platform as a service, edge computing, cloud api, google cloud, azure cloud, aws cloud, software as a service, cloud applications, cloud, GPU, HPC management, cloud storage, elasticity, elastic computing, the cloud, data platform
	IoT	Internet of things, \bIoT\b, industrial internet, IIoT, embedded device, embedded sensor, digital twin, digital thread, building information modelling, BIM, connected devices, connected sensors, IoE, internet of everything, smart machines, connected machines, wearable, cyber physical systems, machine to machine, connected factory, model based definition
	Virtual reality	\bVR\b, virtual reality, immersive technologies, mixed reality
	Augmented reality	\bAR\b, augmented reality, immersive technologies, mixed reality
	Robotics	robots, humanoid, drone, drones, smart robots, smart warehouse, smart spaces, Lidar, computer vision, UAV, autonomous vehicles, swarm robots, industrial robot, robotics, automation
	Analytics	analytics, business intelligence, optimization, exploratory data analysis, data science, augmented analytics, descriptive analytics, descriptive statistics, prescriptive analytics, predictive, inference, inferential, customer segmentation, correlation, data visualization, data storytelling, text analytics, data lake, data warehouse, big data, social analytics, , network analytics, network mining, network analysis
	Mobile	mobile, smart phone, mobile app, mobile application, mobile platform, mobile solution, mobile technology
	Social	social media, social network, content marketing
	3D printing	3D print[a-z]*, additive manufacturing, 3D scan, material jetting, stereolithography, bioprint, bioprinted organ, Fused deposition modeling, Digital Light Processing, Selective Laser Sintering, Selective laser melting, Laminated object manufacturing, Digital Beam Melting
	Blockchain	blockchain, distributed ledger, decentralized, smart contracts, cryptocurrency, \bICO\b, initial coin offering, asset tokenization

Figure 2: Digital Strategy as Aspect: obtained from (Al-Ali et al., 2020)

Topic	Keyword	Keyword terms
Business Value	Digital Product	smart product*, connected product*, software as a service, Saas, platform as a service, Paas, platform, product as a service
	Digital Customer Experience	digital experience, customer experience, CX, user experience, UX, user journey, customer journey, digital engagement, customer engagement, personalization, personalisation, digital marketing, recommendation, market place, marketplace, e-commerce platform, digital service, digital services, e-service, online chat, chatbot, \bapp\b, digital chnnel, omnichannel
	Digital Operations	process automation, process mining, process analytics, process optimization, efficiency, cost saving, cost reduction, reduce cost, reducing cost, automation, predictive maintenance, ERP, supply chain, logistics, operations
	Digital Business Model	business model, new market, new segment, monitization, Saas, software as a service, on-demand, product as a service, value proposition, freemium, subscription, marketplace, ad-revenue, ads, peer-to-peer, two-sided, double-sided
Strategy Management	Enablers	digital strategy, digital business strategy, digital transformation strategy, governance, priositization, prioritization, digital vision, digital leadership, leadership support, leadership buy-in, communication, digital goals, data scientist, data analyst machine learning engineer, developer, coder, programmer, chief digital officer, CDO, head of digital transformation, head of digital, product manager, product owner, cross-functional, scrum master, agile coach, innovation manager, Data lake, data warehouse, middle ware, enterprise architecture, digital tools, digital workplace, digital integration, chat, video call, CRM, ERP, service oriented architecture, \bSOA\b
	Practices	Agile, scrum, MVP, minimum viable product, sprint, design thinking, business experiment, DevOps, \bepic\b, feature, user story, product owner, product manager, collaboration, cross functional, cross-functional, A/B testing, exploratory data analysis, data analysis, decision support system, dashboard, hypothesis testing, experimental design, product metrics, user metrics, usage metrics, click through rate, conversion rate, click stream, digital marketing, customer segmentation, risk modelling, simulation, decision analytics, decision support system, project management, digital skills, digital leadership, transformation, data analysis, social media management, social listening, user research, UX research, UX design, UI design, programming, coding, lean startup, experimentation, incubator, accelerator, innovation lab, digital lab, digital transformation, open innovation, design thinking, design sprint, digitalization, digitalisation, digitization, digital technolog[a-z]*

Figure 3: Digital Strategy as Aspect: obtained from (Al-Ali et al., 2020): *continued*

DigiCall's Contribution

1. **DigiCall's contribution as a dataset**

	Number of Sentences with Digital Strategy Related Words based on Al-Ali et al., 2020'work	
	DigiCall Data set	**MAEC (Li et al., 2020)**
Twitter 2016 Q4	#Past Digital: 8 #Present Digital: 18 #Future Digital:0	#Past Digital: 1 #Present Digital: 8 #Future Digital: 0

We first extracted Twitter's Q4 2016 transcript document from the MAEC paper. We also obtained Twitter Q4 2016 transcript in a way that each earning call transcript is collected at the DigiCall Data set. We used our proposed approach to extract digital strategy-related keywords based on Al-Ali et al., 2020's dictionary, from both transcripts (MAEC and DigiCall's). Later, we used the pre-trained model to predict the maturity label for each sentence.

	MAEC	DigiCall	Sentence	Technology	Categories	Label
1	YES	YES	The other thing that we're investing a lot in is making sure that we apply machine learning more broadly around our entire experience.	['machine learning']	['AI']	Present
2	YES	YES	We recently hired to consolidate all of our science efforts, all of our deep learning, all of our machine learning and artificial intelligence, so that we can get a lot smarter and provide more magical experiences for people around showing them what's breaking in real time and giving them a sense of what's going on without having to do as much work as they currently have to do on the platform.	['machine learning']	['AI']	Past
3	NO	YES	It's more what you have seen in the platform in sports, news, and entertainment and more globally.	['platform']	['Digital Product']	Present
4	NO	YES	One of the things that we've been very critical of Twitter on over the last several years is that it's been more of a passive platform where people have just been kind of reading almost RSS like, and my sense is over the course of the last couple of months or last six months, that you've seen an improvement in people actually engaging, whether that's actually tweeting themselves or liking or retweeting.	['platform']	['Digital Product']	Present
5	NO	YES	So to get double-digit growth for an entire quarter in impressions for three quarters in a row, it takes a fundamental change and that's being driven by machine learning in the timeline.	['machine learning']	['AI']	Present
6	YES	YES	And then the final point I'd make, which is somewhat tied to organizational decisions as opposed to execution or marketplace decisions, is that we are taking a step back and looking to simplify our product and putting our resources behind those products that we think have the greatest probability of success, that can deliver the best long-term growth potential, and that frankly leverage our competitive advantages in a unique way.	['marketplace']	['Digital Customer Experience', 'Digital Business Model']	Present
7	NO	YES	So hopefully that gives you perspective on the marketplace factors that are impacting our outlook.	['marketplace']	['Digital Customer Experience', 'Digital Business Model']	Present
8	NO	YES	We obviously want to build on that in 2017, and it's one part of our broader strategy to drive greater engagement of those that are already on our platform and to attract new users to the platforms.	['platform']	['Digital Product']	Present

Figure 4: Sentences Containing Digital Strategy Initiatives DigiCall vs MAEC

9	NO	**YES**	The percentage of the audience that was less than 25 years old was 50%, in addition to the fact that a majority of the people that consumed the product were not in front of televisions and they only consumed it on mobile applications.	['mobile']	['Mobile']	Past
10	NO	**YES**	And then finally for our partners CBS and NBC and our advertising partners, we're able to leverage our innovation on mid-roll advertising that used dynamic ad insertion to mobile devices, to over-the-top applications and to the desktop web, which is a great innovation and allowed us to deliver specific ads to specific individuals from specific advertisers all at the same time.	['ads', 'mobile']	['Mobile', 'Digital Business Model']	Present
11	NO	**YES**	Those ads had 95% completion rates with sound on which is very attractive for advertising partners and obviously can result in high CPMs.	['ads']	['Digital Business Model']	Past
12	NO	**YES**	The first products that we developed on the platform were really organic products.	['platform']	['Digital Product']	Past
13	NO	**YES**	We had 600 hours of live video content programming on the platform in Q4, and it was pretty diverse: about 50% in sports, about 40% in news and politics and 10% in live.	['programming', 'platform']	['Practices', 'Digital Product']	Past
14	NO	**YES**	And then we've been consolidating organizations to build our strength, most notably in our machine learning and artificial intelligence efforts, which is critical to us being able to move much faster.	['machine learning', 'artificial intelligence']	['AI']	Present
15	NO	**YES**	Now just doing the work to get everyone on the same page and make sure that we have a platform internally that every team can use to provide better and more magical experiences on Twitter through machine learning and artificial intelligence.	['machine learning', 'platform']	['Digital Product', 'AI']	Past
16	**YES**	**YES**	And this focus and this team allows me and gives me a lot of confidence that I can continue to focus on the most meaningful things at both companies and we have the right prioritization in front of us.	['prioritization']	['Enablers']	Present
17	NO	**YES**	On your first question what I would say is that the President's use of Twitter has broadened the awareness of how the platform can be used and it shows the power of Twitter.	['platform']	['Digital Product']	Present
19	**YES**	**YES**	So at a macro level discussion on the platform really helps us be the best at showing what's happening in the world and more discussions strengthens our key differentiators in comprehensive and fast.	['platform']	['Digital Product']	Present
19	**YES**	**YES**	As it relates to impressions growth, which is another area we look at, as I mentioned earlier, the magnitude of the impressions of the platform is so large, it'd be very hard for an event or a single person to drive sustained growth in impressions growth.	['platform']	['Digital Product']	Present
20	NO	**YES**	February is a time period that historically has been up 35% to 40% versus January, and that ramp really starts in mid-January through February and that's when we saw more marketplace challenges in our ability to attract demand from advertisers.	['marketplace']	['Digital Customer Experience', 'Digital Business Model']	Present
21	NO	**YES**	And then kind of more of a philosophical partnership question, in the early days of Twitter you worked aggressively to extend the tweet footprint through partnerships with media companies, and I guess from a perspective of distributing tweet content, and I'm just wondering in light of the election and 's use of Twitter, do you look back at that strategy and then just wonder if maybe that you provide a disincentive for users to actually explore the platform if they feel like they are consuming a lot of those tweet content through media partners instead.	['platform']	['Digital Product']	Past

Figure 5: Sentences Containing Digital Strategy Initiatives DigiCall vs MAEC

22	NO	**YES**	And so we really want to find these products that have multiple benefits, not just revenue but also content, and then also driving virality on the platform and faster distribution.	['platform']	['Digital Product']	Present
23	**YES**	**YES**	And we've now moved into a product area where we have a marketplace where content owners can put the content into the marketplace and advertisers can pick that content and not only put an ad in front of it but promote it.	['marketplace']	['Digital Customer Experience', 'Digital Business Model']	Present
24	NO	**YES**	They showed a real commitment post transaction to the developer community, and that was a really important element in our decision on where the product went in addition to maximizing shareholder value.	['developer']	['Enablers']	Past
25	**YES**	**YES**	So everything that we're doing around live streaming premium video within the app and also with individual-created, live-streaming video in Periscope has been the majority of our focus and we wanted to cut everything that did not go against that and did not matter.	['app']	['Digital Customer Experience']	Present
26	**YES**	**YES**	And that's why I am excited about really making sure that we apply artificial intelligence and machine learning in the right ways and that we really meet that superpower of being that little bird that told you something that you couldn't find anywhere else.	['machine learning', 'artificial intelligence']	['AI']	Present

2. DigiCall's Contribution as an Approach

	Example: Twitter 2016 Q4			
	Sentence with its original sequence	**Technology**	**Category**	**Maturity**
S0	So we're looking at all the patterns that we've seen for the past 10 years on how people use Twitter and to create experiences around that that make it easier to share what's happening, to talk about what's happening and to see it much faster.	[]	[]	Present
S1	The other thing that we're investing a lot in is making sure that we apply machine learning more broadly around our entire experience.	['machine learning']	['AI']	Present
S2	We recently hired to consolidate all of our science efforts, all of our deep learning, all of our machine learning and artificial intelligence, so that we can get a lot smarter and provide more magical experiences for people around showing them what's breaking in real time and giving them a sense of what's going on without having to do as much work as they currently have to do on the platform.	['machine learning']	['AI']	Past
S3	So we're looking at a lot of opportunities to organize all the tweets around relevance but also around the topics and the interest and the passions that people care about.	[]	[]	Present

<table>
<tr><th></th><th>Al- Ali et al. (2020)'s approach</th><th>DigiCall's approach</th></tr>
<tr><td>Approach</td><td>For any given sentence containing information about Digital Strategy initiatives (s1), combined with the previous (s0) and subsequent (s2) sentences.
So: s0+s1+s2 are processed to predict the maturity of the digital strategy.</td><td>Only considers the sentence (s1) with information about Digital Strategy.
So: s1 is processed to predict the maturity of the digital strategy.</td></tr>
<tr><td>Applied at Twitter 2016 Q4</td><td>S0(Present) + S1 (Present) +S2(Past)
Despite these three sentences containing different maturity levels, Al-Ali et al. (2020)'s approach would append these, and label them as Present (S1).</td><td>S0: would be discarded because no technology was disclosed.
S1: Present,
S2: Past.</td></tr>
<tr><td rowspan="2">Maturity Prediction: F-1 Weighted</td><td>BERT $_{(base)}$: 55.7 %</td><td>BERT $_{(base)}$: 94 %</td></tr>
<tr><td>RoBERTa $_{(base)}$: 58.2 %</td><td>RoBERTa $_{(base)}$: 79%</td></tr>
<tr><td>Label Level F-1 Weighted</td><td>Not Available</td><td>BERT $_{(base)}$: Past: 88% | Present: 98% | Future: 92%
RoBERTa $_{(base)}$: Past: 79% | Present: 86% | Future:75%</td></tr>
</table>

Figure 6: DigiCall's Contribution as An Approach

Learning Better Intent Representations for Financial Open Intent Classification

Xianzhi Li[1,2], **Will Aitken**[1,2], **Xiaodan Zhu**[1,2] **and Stephen W. Thomas**[3]

[1]Department of Electrical and Computer Engineering, Queen's University
[2]Ingenuity Labs Research Institute, Queen's University
[3]Smith School of Business, Queen's University
{21xl17, 16wca, xiaodan.zhu, stephen.thomas}@queensu.ca

Abstract

With the recent surge of NLP technologies in the financial domain, banks and other financial entities have adopted virtual agents (VA) to assist customers. A challenging problem for VAs in this domain is determining a user's reason or intent for contacting the VA, especially when the intent was unseen or *open* during the VA's training. One method for handling open intents is adaptive decision boundary (ADB) post-processing, which learns tight decision boundaries from intent representations to separate known and open intents. We propose incorporating two methods for supervised pre-training of intent representations: prefix-tuning and fine-tuning just the last layer of a large language model (LLM). With this proposal, our accuracy is 1.63% - 2.07% higher than the prior state-of-the-art ADB method for open intent classification on the banking77 benchmark amongst others. Notably, we only supplement the original ADB model with 0.1% additional trainable parameters. Ablation studies also determine that our method yields better results than full fine-tuning the entire model. We hypothesize that our findings could stimulate a new optimal method of downstream tuning that combines parameter efficient tuning modules with fine-tuning a subset of the base model's layers.

1 Introduction

As the popularity of virtual agent (VA) dialogue systems increases and their application in the finance domain is explored, the problem of intent classification demands greater attention. Several recent finance-specific VAs leverage technical advancements to respond to natural language queries (Galitsky and Ilvovsky, 2019; Khan and Rabbani, 2020). Determining the user's intent ensures that the VA can appropriately tailor its responses and/or perform relevant actions. Initial works in intent classification limited the task to classifying utterances as one of N known intents and achieved high accuracy (Weld et al., 2021). However, as depicted in Table 1, real-world applications often encounter intents unseen in training data that can be considered as *open* in the current context. Accounting for the open class establishes an $(N+1)$-class classification task (Shu et al., 2017), where the open class is used as a label for any unidentified intent.

Utterance	Label
When will I get my card?	Card Arrival
What exchange rates do you offer?	Exchange Rate
My card hasn't arrived yet.	Card Arrival
Is it a good time to exchange?	Exchange Rates
...	...
Is it possible to get a refund?	**Open**
Why has my withdrawal not posted?	**Open**

Table 1: Example user utterances and associated intent labels from banking77 dataset (Casanueva et al., 2020). In this example, only Card Arrival and Exchange Rate intents were known in training and thus refund and withdrawal related requests are Open intents in this context.

An optimal classifier for this problem must balance correctly labelling known-class utterances while avoiding mistakenly classifying open utterances as one of the known classes. (Zhang et al., 2021a) addresses this problem by proposing a novel loss function to learn an adaptive decision boundary (ADB) for each known intent. At inference, samples that do not fall within any ADB are classified as open. Compact intent representations are required as input for the ADB post-processing learning step and in the case of (Zhang et al., 2021a) the representations are learnt by fine-tuning the last layer of BERT (Devlin et al., 2019). Since most intent classification methods require post-processing on intent representations, our work focuses on deriving richer representations by leveraging large language models (LLM) in an efficacious manner while still minimizing

Proceedings of the Fourth Workshop on Financial Technology and Natural Language Processing (FinNLP), pages 68 - 77
December 8, 2022

trainable parameters.

Following the introduction of the transformer in (Vaswani et al., 2017a), an influx of LLM architectures have continually progressed state-of-the-art (SOTA) performance on many natural language processing (NLP) tasks (Otter et al., 2021). Usually these models are pre-trained on a general self-supervised learning task, after which they are fine-tuned for a specific task. Fine-tuning such a model can be computationally prohibitive due to the immense number of trainable parameters. Furthermore, (Kaplan et al., 2020) found that the most important factor for LLM performance is likely model size, indicating that development of even larger models is probable. Inspired by in-context prompting, (Li and Liang, 2021) proposed prefix tuning as a parameter efficient alternative to fine-tuning for natural language generation (NLG). The LLM's parameters are frozen and trainable prefix tokens are prepended to the input sequence. Prefix-tuning has been adapted to natural language understanding (NLU) and performs comparably to full fine-tuning across scales and tasks (Liu et al., 2022).

We achieve SOTA results by augmenting the pre-training architecture of ADB open intent classification (Zhang et al., 2021a) with prefix-tuning. The combination of prefix-tuning with fine-tuning only the last transformer layer was motivated by (Kumar et al., 2022), which discovered that fine-tuning the entire model can distort pre-trained features. We find that alone, both prefix-tuning or fine-tuning the last layer under-performs fine-tuning all of BERT but when trained in tandem, exceeds full fine-tuning.

The rest of this paper is structured as follows: Section 2 summarizes prior works in both intent classification and parameter efficient tuning (PET). Our methodology and model architecture are defined in Section 3. In Sections 4 and 5 respectively, we provide our experimentation structure and corresponding results as well as several ablations. We finish with a conclusion and brief discussion regarding limitations and ethics.

2 Related Works

2.1 Financial Virtual Agents

The effectiveness of VAs has led to their adoption in the financial domain. (Galitsky and Ilvovsky, 2019) demonstrated an exemplary session with a financial VA where the user queried for investment advice. CalFE leverages commercial chatbot frameworks to train a finance-specific VA (Khan and Rabbani, 2020). (Ng et al., 2020) evaluates the impact of a VA's social presence on usage intention in VAs for finance. All of these works require extracting intent from user utterances.

2.2 Intent Detection

Intent classification is a well-established NLU task but most research limits the problem to known classes (Zhang et al., 2019; E et al., 2019; Qin et al., 2019; Zhang et al., 2021b). While having prior knowledge of all expected intents is ideal, this is rarely possible in a production environment, especially for new dialogue systems. More realistically, a subset of intents are anticipated and new intents are discovered after deployment. (Brychcín and Král, 2017) recognized the challenge of identifying intents prior to training and proposed an unsupervised method to group intents, but by doing so, likely ignored information available in the already identified intents. (Xia et al., 2018) employed zero-shot learning to identify emerging intents but used an LSTM which is hindered by non-parallelized learning and challenges in propagating long-range dependencies. The same issue is present in DeepUnk, a BiLSTM-based intent classification method using margin loss (Lin and Xu, 2019). (Zhan et al., 2021) shared our open intent classification problem formulation but synthetically generated out-of-domain samples for training which may not be as realistic as a fine-grained open class representation.

Our work directly extends the ADB approach to establishing an open class representation (Zhang et al., 2021a). The novelty of our adaptation is in leveraging prefix tuning in combination with partial fine-tuning to improve the pre-training of known intent representations without drastically increasing the number of trainable parameters. In parallel with our work, (Zhang et al., 2022) extended their ADB approach to learn distance-aware intent representations. Doing so resulted in comparable performance to our modification of their original approach. However, our tuning method is model-agnostic and can easily be incorporated with their distance-aware representation learning, likely improving the SOTA further.

2.3 Parameter Efficient Tuning

The desire for PET quickly emerged following the introduction of LLMs. Adapter modules insert task-specific parameters sequentially between transformer layers while the rest of the model remains frozen (Houlsby et al., 2019). (Li and Liang, 2021) and (Lester et al., 2021) simultaneously substantiated the efficacy of prepending tokens to attention mechanisms as a means of efficient tuning. In (Li and Liang, 2021), the prefixes are applied at each layer of the transformer while (Lester et al., 2021) only prepends to the input sequence. (Liu et al., 2022) applied the same method to NLU tasks using deep prefixes with optional reparameterization. Without reparameterization, simple embeddings are learnt for the prefixes. Reparameterization inserts a multi-layer perceptron (MLP) between the embeddings and prefix tokens which allows for more complex embeddings.

Recently, (He et al., 2022) determined the theoretical impact of various PET methods and deduced that they are all modifications of a similar function. Allocating additional parameters to other PET modules as suggested by (He et al., 2022) could optimize intent representation beyond what is possible with prefixes alone. For now we limit our work to the most efficient method for low resource settings, prefix-tuning. To the best of our knowledge, this is the first PET work to combine partial fine-tuning with prefix-tuning.

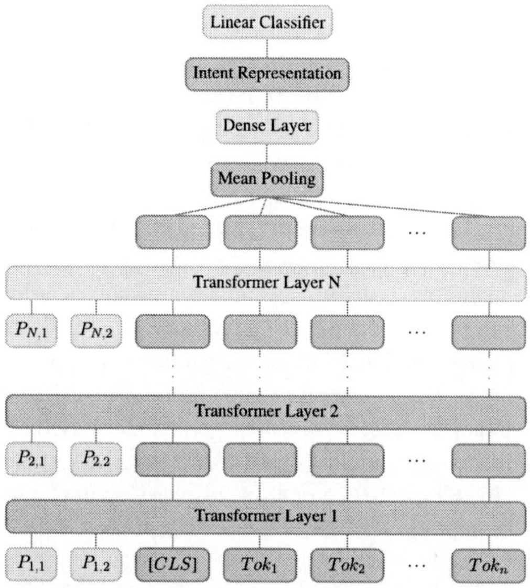

Figure 1: Pre-training architecture for learning intent representations. Orange blocks denote trainable parameters while blue are fixed. For this concrete example, the prefix length has been set to two, but this value is a tunable hyperparameter.

3 Methodology

In this section we explain our procedure for open intent classification. Section 3.1 describes prefix-tuning, the method we supplement partial fine-tuning with. Section 3.2 provides a brief summary of training the original ADB method that we have extended (Zhang et al., 2021a).

3.1 Prefix-Tuning

Prefix-tuning prepends trainable prefix tokens P_k,P_v in front of Key and Value vectors of multi-head attention in each transformer layer. The attention mechanism is applied to the concatenation of prefix and original tokens. Equation 1 details the computation.

$$head = Softmax(Q * Concat(P_k, K)^T) * Concat(P_v, V) \tag{1}$$

Where Q, K, and V are the Query, Key and Value matrices from the original transformer (Vaswani et al., 2017b). P_k and P_v are the additional prefix tokens and are prepended to the Key and Value matrices.

Often, prefix-tuning methods use a MLP to reparameterize the prefix since directly embedding can lead to unstable training and performance decrease (Li and Liang, 2021). However, (Liu et al., 2022) found that for NLU tasks, the efficacy of reparameterization is dependent on the task. From our experiments, we determine that reparameterizing the prefixes is crucial for intent classification. Following training, the MLP weights and biases from reparameterization are dropped and only prefixes are kept.

3.2 Training

Figure 1 illustrates our pre-training architecture of prefix-tuning plus tuning the last transformer layer to extract intent representations. The orange components of the diagram are trainable and the blue are frozen. This example shows a prefix length of two, but the length is a flexible hyperparameter. We detail our entire hyperparameter settings in Section 4.2. The outputs of BERT are first fed into a mean-pooling function to aggregate the sequence into a single vector x_i as described by Equation 2:

KIR	Method	BANKING		OOS		StackOverflow	
		Accuracy	F1-Score	Accuracy	F1-Score	Accuracy	F1-Score
25%	DeepUnk	64.21	61.36	81.43	71.16	47.84	52.05
	$(K+1)$-way	74.11	69.93	/	/	68.74	65.64
	ADB	78.85	71.62	87.59	77.19	86.72	**80.83**
	PFT-ADB	**80.14**	**72.86**	**88.03**	**78.85**	**87.60**	80.78
50%	DeepUnk	72.73	77.53	83.35	82.16	58.98	68.01
	$(K+1)$-way	72.69	79.21	/	/	75.08	78.55
	ADB	78.86	80.90	86.54	85.05	86.40	85.83
	PFT-ADB	**80.40**	**82.44**	**87.60**	**86.87**	**87.06**	**86.22**
75%	DeepUnk	78.52	84.31	83.71	86.23	72.33	78.28
	$(K+1)$-way	81.07	86.98	/	/	81.71	85.85
	ADB	81.08	85.96	86.32	88.53	82.78	85.99
	PFT-ADB	**82.76**	**87.35**	**88.94**	**90.93**	**83.46**	**86.61**

Table 2: Main results for known intent ratios (KIR) 25%, 50%, and 75% on BANKING, OOS, and StackOverflow datasets. Average accuracy and macro F1-Score are reported over all classes.

$$x_i = mp([CLS], Tok_1, Tok_2, ..., Tok_M) \quad (2)$$

where i refers to the current training sample. A dense layer transforms the vector to the intent representation feature space and the resultant vector is finally passed to a linear classifier. We pre-train on known intents and their labels with softmax as the loss function to optimize both the prefix tokens and the last transformer layer. Equation 3 is the softmax loss:

$$Loss = -\frac{1}{n}\sum_{c=1}^{n}\log(\frac{e^{z_i}}{\sum_{j=1}^{K} e^{z_j}}) \quad (3)$$

where n is the batch size and z_j refers to the output logits of j_{th} class.

Following pre-training, the intent representations are extracted from our model for ADB post-processing. ADB learns a tight spherical decision boundary for each known intent. At inference, intent representations that fall outside of all decision boundaries are classified as open. For clarification, the only alteration to the ADB method we employ is the addition of prefix tokens in Figure 1. See (Zhang et al., 2021a) for more information regarding decision boundaries and other training details.

4 Experiments

4.1 Datasets

BANKING: A dataset of 77 banking intents with samples summing to 13,083 banking-specific customer service queries (Casanueva et al., 2020). It is also commonly referred to as "banking77" but (Zhang et al., 2021a) uses "BANKING" and since we are comparing our results primarily with them, we conform to their choice.

OOS: A subset of CLINC50 specifically designed for out-of-scope intent prediction (Larson et al., 2019) with 22,500 and 1,200 in and out of domain samples respectively over 150 different intents spanning 10 domains.

StackOverflow: The processed version of the StackOverflow dataset (Xu et al., 2015), which has 20 different intents and 1,000 samples for each.

4.2 Experiment Settings

In accordance with previous methods, we sample 25%, 50%, and 75% of intent classes randomly during training as the "known" classes. The remaining are set aside as open classes and removed from training sets. We use BERT (bert-base-uncased) provided by Hugging Face (Wolf et al., 2020) to extract intent representations from utterances. The learning rate for prefixes and transformer parameters is set to 2e-5 since experimenting with setting different learning rates for prefixes and last layer of transformer did not consistently lead to a performance increase. All experiments are conducted on a NVIDIA 2080TI GPU. To fairly compare our method, we keep other hyperparameters the same as (Zhang et al., 2021a). For all results we average performance over ten random seeds.

KIR	Method	BANKING Open	BANKING Known	OOS Open	OOS Known	StackOverflow Open	StackOverflow Known
25%	DeepUnk	70.44	60.88	87.33	70.73	49.29	52.60
	$(K+1)$-way	80.12	69.39	/	/	74.86	63.80
	ADB	84.56	70.94	91.84	76.80	90.88	**78.82**
	PFT-ADB	**85.65**	**72.19**	**92.11**	**78.50**	**91.58**	78.62
50%	DeepUnk	69.53	77.74	85.85	82.11	43.01	70.51
	$(K+1)$-way	67.26	79.52	/	/	71.88	79.22
	ADB	78.44	80.96	88.65	85.00	87.34	85.68
	PFT-ADB	**80.02**	**82.51**	**89.34**	**86.83**	**88.17**	**86.02**
75%	DeepUnk	58.54	84.75	81.15	86.27	37.59	81.00
	$(K+1)$-way	60.71	87.47	/	/	65.44	87.22
	ADB	66.47	86.29	83.92	88.58	73.86	86.80
	PFT-ADB	**69.18**	**87.66**	**86.80**	**90.96**	**74.78**	**87.40**

Table 3: Open and known comparison of main results for known intent ratios 25%, 50%, and 75% on BANKING, OOS, and StackOverflow datasets. F1-Score and macro F1-Score are reported for open class and known classes respectively.

Regarding prefix-specific settings, we use reparameterization with a hidden size of 512 unless otherwise specified. The overall parameter size is determined by the prefix length. In this task, we found that enlarging the prefix length did not lead to a consistent performance increase due to its low-rank bottleneck. (He et al., 2022) also discusses that allocating additional parameter in self-attention is only worthwhile if they make up less than 0.1% of the parameter budget. Therefore, we choose our default prefix length as 10, which equates to roughly 0.1% of BERT's trainable parameters.

4.3 Baselines

We compare our results to the most competitive open intent classification methods: DeepUnk (Lin and Xu, 2019), $(K+1)$-way (Zhan et al., 2021), and the ADB method we directly extend (Zhang et al., 2021a). The DeepUnk results are taken from (Zhang et al., 2021a) which replaced the BiLSTM with BERT to generate intent representations for fair comparison. (Zhan et al., 2021) also uses BERT as its encoder but keeps just the CLS token's final hidden state instead of pooling the entire sequence. (Zhan et al., 2021) did not test on the same OOS split and cells corresponding to that configuration are left blank for tables in Section 5.

5 Results

Our main results and respective baseline comparisons are presented in Tables 2 and 3. Table 2 is limited to accuracy averaged over all classes, including the open class and macro F1 over the same set of classes. For a fine-grained analysis of open intent performance, Table 3 contrasts the F1 score of the open class with the macro F1 over the remaining known classes. *PFT-ADB* denotes our method of adding prefix tuning to ADB and the best result for each section is in boldface.

For each dataset we tested, PFT-ADB improves performance on all prior methods with the minor exception of StackOverflow F1-Score and known score. Specifically, as shown in Table 2, we achieve accuracy improvements of (1.63%, 1.95%, 2.07%) on BANKING, (0.50%, 1.22%, 3.03%) on OOS, and (1.01%, 0.76%, 0.82%) on StackOverflow for known intent ratios (25%, 50%, 75%). The consistency of our results across configurations suggests that paying closer attention to pre-training intent representations can enhance the distinction of decision boundaries in the post-processing step. Additionally, we do not add a significant number of trainable parameters to existing methods (only 0.1%), successfully avoiding trading substantial costs for performance increase. Note that our results are comparable to that of the most recently released DA-ADB (Zhang et al., 2022) model. We believe that due to their orthogonal nature, DA-ADB and our approach could be combined together for further performance improvements.

We note that the dataset with the lowest performance gain is StackOverflow. (Zhang et al., 2021a) found that their novel post-processing method, ADB, was most effective on this dataset

Method	Accuracy	F1-score	Open	Known
Emb	64.40	68.56	66.62	68.38
MLP	81.56	85.89	75.98	85.97
Emb+12th L	86.40	88.15	84.44	88.19
MLP+12th L	**90.07**	**91.52**	**88.48**	**91.54**
FFT-NoPT	87.56	89.20	85.71	89.24
ADB	86.32	88.53	83.92	88.58

Table 4: Experiments on the impact of different prefix encoding approaches with and without fine-tuning the last layer of transformer. We use OOS dataset with 75% known Intent Ratio. "Emb" refers to embedding-only method. "MLP" refers to method that uses 2 layers of MLP to encode prefix. "+12th L" means we unfreeze the last layer of transformer. "FFT-NoPT" denotes full fine-tuning without any prefixes.

Method	Length	Accuracy	F1-score	Open	Known
Emb+12th L	10	87.60	89.08	85.82	89.11
	20	**88.25**	**89.49**	**86.80**	**89.52**
	30	87.88	89.44	86.13	89.47
	50	85.70	87.49	83.72	87.53
	80	85.93	87.75	83.87	87.78
	100	87.95	89.45	86.16	89.48
MLP+12th L	10	**90.16**	91.57	**88.57**	91.60
	20	89.67	91.27	87.96	91.30
	30	90.05	**91.59**	88.35	**91.62**
	50	88.65	90.34	86.82	90.37
	80	89.49	91.27	87.51	91.30
	100	89.84	91.51	88.09	91.54

Table 5: Results of tuning with different prefix lengths. We use OOS dataset with 75% known intent ratio.

compared to prior methods. They hypothesized that this was due to being able to form tighter decision boundaries for the technical jargon more prevalent in StackOverflow. Following this reasoning, it could be that for this dataset the post-processing method is paramount and enriching the intent representations alone is not enough to yield a substantial performance improvement.

It is important that an open intent classification method balances the performance on known classes while still identifying open intents. Table 3 verifies that despite changing pre-training tuning methods, ADB post-processing still adequately addresses this issue. The performance increase is consistent between both the open class and known classes for each dataset indicating that prefix-tuning does not interfere with optimizing both aspects of the open intent problem. Again, we anticipate that combining PFT-ADB with the newer DA-ADB could result in even better performance.

The following ablations focus on the OOS dataset since it covers multiple domains and we wanted to generalize beyond just the financial domain.

5.1 Effect of Reparameterization and Tuning Variations

In Table 4 we show that under the same dataset and known intent ratio, performance varies considerably when adopting MLP as prefix encoder. In the first row, the embedding-only method leads to poor results of 64.40% accuracy. Contrarily, introducing a 2 layer MLP to encode prefixes increases the performance by around 15%. More importantly, the result is stable and reproducible. It indicates that using MLP to reparameterize prefixes is crucial in obtaining a consistent performance.

Results using prefix tuning alone (rows 1 and 2) in this task are slightly worse than ADB's fine-tuning results. In particular, the performance gap in identifying open intent is more salient, revealing prefix-tuning's lower capacity for out-of-scope classification. However, when we incorporate prefix tuning along with tuning the last layer of transformer, we find a surprisingly large performance increase. For embedding and MLP methods, tuning the last layer of transformer gives a performance boost to 86.40% and 90.07%, respectively, with only additional 0.1% of ADB's parameters. Since the latter transformer layer captures high-level feature of utterances, we believe that this small amount of parameter steer the higher layers to learn more task-oriented information as well as fit intents into a better-distributed latent space.

We also try the common method of fully fine-tuning, i.e., unfreezing all of BERT's parameters which was not done in (Zhang et al., 2021a). The performance is still 1% lower than our method while we use only 8.1% of parameters.

5.2 Impact of Prefix Lengths

We experimented with the prefix length to determine its effect on performance. From Table 5, we observe that with the increase of the prefix length from 10 to 100 (parameter size from .1% to 1.6%), the results do not follow the same ascending pattern. We argue that simply adding more prefix tokens would not lead to a consistent performance boost due to its bottleneck. (He et al., 2022) determined that prefix tuning is another form of low-rank update, which cannot make use of more than

x	Just x		x and Rest	
	Accuracy	F1-Score	Accuracy	F1-Score
No-FT	81.56	85.89	81.56	85.89
12	**90.07**	**91.62**	90.07	91.62
11	89.18	91.19	**90.21**	**91.81**
10	89.81	91.80	89.42	91.42
9	88.81	90.89	88.93	91.18
7	87.07	89.79	88.42	90.93
4	85.23	88.21	87.00	89.90
1	84.77	87.73	87.58	90.24

Table 6: Fine-tuning various groupings of transformer layers on OOS with known intent ratio 75%. "No-FT" is prefix-tuning without any fine-tuning. Prefix-tuning configuration was kept constant throughout runs.

0.1% of additional parameters.

5.3 Fine-Tuning Different Groupings of Layers

Combining prefix-tuning with fine-tuning a subset of transformer layers is, to the best of our knowledge, a novel approach. Fine-tuning the last layer alone is ideal for minimizing trainable parameters. We aim to determine whether varying which layer or group of several layers is unfrozen can achieve better results than the last layer alone. Table 6 summarizes our findings. The layer of interest is specified with the variable x. "Just x" is fine-tuning layer x alone and "x and Rest" is fine-tuning the layer x and all subsequent layers. Using this notation, "Layer *1* and Rest" is akin to fine-tuning all of BERT. "No-FT" refers to prefix-tuning without any additional fine-tuning. For this row and when x is 12, the results between the two main columns are of course the same.

Several interesting observations are evident in Table 6. Firstly, the fine-tuning of at least one layer in addition to prefix-tuning is strictly necessary for optimal performance. Under the constraint of tuning just a single layer, the last performs the best. The latter layers of the model are where higher-level details of natural language are processed. We hypothesize that tuning this layer best incorporates the propagation of prior prefixes with the base model. Tuning prior layers may have a similar effect, but if the subsequent layers are frozen, the understanding of prompts is obfuscated since the latter frozen layers have no experience attending to prefixes.

Another notable finding is that if performance is to be prioritized, fine-tuning the final two layers together is better than the last layer alone.

Method	Accuracy	F1-Score	Open	Known
Attention	87.49	89.69	85.19	89.73
Feed Forward	86.47	88.92	83.81	88.96
Layer Normalization	86.61	88.81	84.21	88.85
Keys and Values	85.67	88.58	82.39	88.64
Entire Layer	**90.07**	**91.52**	**88.48**	**91.54**

Table 7: Fine-tuning components of final transformer layer on OOS with known intent ratio 75%. Only the parameters of the component(s) are tuned and the rest of the layer is frozen.

This suggests that the prefixes are complex enough such that their value is maximized when the final two layers tune in tandem. However, the trade off of minor performance increase at the cost of doubling the trainable parameters may not be worth it depending on the application.

Lastly, we note that as layers beyond two are trained in the "x and Rest" column, performance begins to degrade. This supports the observation made by (Kumar et al., 2022) that fine-tuning disturbs pre-trained features in the base model. Training only the final layer(s) avoids perturbing low-level semantics learnt in earlier layers of the base model, but still adds sufficient capacity to attend to the prefixes.

5.4 Fine-Tuning Various Components in Last Layer

While fine-tuning only the last transformer layer reduces the trainable parameter count to 8%, this is still a large value compared to the 0.1% parameter count of the prefixes alone. We isolate various components of the last transformer layer to determine if some could be frozen to further reduce parameter count. The results are presented in Table 7. Tuning the entire layer significantly outperformed any other variation, alluding that there is an important relationship between the prefixes and every component of the final transformer layer. Tuning each of the components in the last layer is essential to procure maximum prefix performance.

6 Conclusion

We have shown that incorporating prefix-tuning with the ADB intent representation pre-training method achieves SOTA results in the financial domain on the banking77 benchmark dataset and others. Furthermore, our tuning method does not sacrifice excessive parameters count for the performance gain. The combination of prefix-tuning with fine-tuning only the last layer of transformer is simple yet novel to the best of our knowledge and surfaces interesting questions regarding the mechanisms they use to interact. We intend to address the limitations presented hereafter in the near future.

Limitations

Despite achieving SOTA results on open intent classification tasks, our work has several facets that could be furnished further. Firstly, we tune the last layer of transformer along with the prefixes, making our method less parameter efficient than prefixes alone. Other approaches to fine-tuning the last layer of the transformer during pre-training should be investigated. Moreover, this work does not include any other PET method such as adapter tuning (He et al., 2021) or LoRA (Hu et al., 2021). We anticipate that using other PET methods will reveal new observations regarding their interaction with partial fine-tuning. We restrict our study to simple single intent dialogues while industry-deployed models would likely encounter noise as well as multiple intents. Testing the robustness of our method under these conditions could be valuable. Lastly, we plan to research whether our success with prefix-tuning in combination with partial fine-tuning generalizes to other NLU and financial tasks.

Ethics Statement

Recent impressive achievements in NLP thanks to the advent of LLMs do not come without cost. Most relevant to our paper is the environmental impact and inequitable distribution of such technologies (Strubell et al., 2019). The resources required to train a LLM are large which from the environmental perspective increases our contribution to climate change and from an equity perspective limits who can access, research, and use the model.

While the self-supervised pre-training step often has the greatest resource requirements, fine-tuning LLMs is undertaken by many more parties following a model's public release. The numerous task-specific deployments of popular models likely have greater net CO_2 emissions than the initial pre-training. Our work directly combats this concern by promoting parameter efficient tuning as an efficacious alternative to relatively expensive fine-tuning. The fraction of trainable parameters reduces tuning memory requirements, in turn reducing power consumption and environmental impact. Additionally, the reduction of required memory enables the adoption of LLMs by those who do not have access to expensive high-quality hardware or cloud platforms. Finally, storing copies of the model for each task is efficient. Only a single copy of the frozen LLM is needed along with the smaller prefixes and in our case, trained last layer of transformer, resulting in similar benefits as the reduction of memory.

References

Tomáš Brychcín and Pavel Král. 2017. Unsupervised dialogue act induction using Gaussian mixtures. In *Proceedings of the 15th Conference of the European Chapter of the Association for Computational Linguistics: Volume 2, Short Papers*, pages 485–490, Valencia, Spain. Association for Computational Linguistics.

Iñigo Casanueva, Tadas Temcinas, Daniela Gerz, Matthew Henderson, and Ivan Vulic. 2020. Efficient intent detection with dual sentence encoders. In *Proceedings of the 2nd Workshop on NLP for ConvAI - ACL 2020*. Data available at https://github.com/PolyAI-LDN/task-specific-datasets.

Jacob Devlin, Ming-Wei Chang, Kenton Lee, and Kristina Toutanova. 2019. BERT: Pre-training of deep bidirectional transformers for language understanding. In *Proceedings of the 2019 Conference of the North American Chapter of the Association for Computational Linguistics: Human Language Technologies, Volume 1 (Long and Short Papers)*, pages 4171–4186, Minneapolis, Minnesota. Association for Computational Linguistics.

Haihong E, Peiqing Niu, Zhongfu Chen, and Meina Song. 2019. A novel bi-directional interrelated model for joint intent detection and slot filling. In *Proceedings of the 57th Annual Meeting of the Association for Computational Linguistics*, pages 5467–5471, Florence, Italy. Association for Computational Linguistics.

Boris Galitsky and Dmitry Ilvovsky. 2019. On a chatbot conducting a virtual dialogue in financial domain. In *Proceedings of the First Workshop on Financial Technology and Natural Language Processing*, pages 99–101, Macao, China.

Junxian He, Chunting Zhou, Xuezhe Ma, Taylor Berg-Kirkpatrick, and Graham Neubig. 2022. Towards a unified view of parameter-efficient transfer learning. In *International Conference on Learning Representations*.

Ruidan He, Linlin Liu, Hai Ye, Qingyu Tan, Bosheng Ding, Liying Cheng, Jia-Wei Low, Lidong Bing, and

Luo Si. 2021. On the effectiveness of adapter-based tuning for pretrained language model adaptation.

Neil Houlsby, Andrei Giurgiu, Stanislaw Jastrzebski, Bruna Morrone, Quentin de Laroussilhe, Andrea Gesmundo, Mona Attariyan, and Sylvain Gelly. 2019. Parameter-efficient transfer learning for nlp. In *ICML*, pages 2790–2799.

Edward J. Hu, Yelong Shen, Phillip Wallis, Zeyuan Allen-Zhu, Yuanzhi Li, Shean Wang, Lu Wang, and Weizhu Chen. 2021. Lora: Low-rank adaptation of large language models.

Jared Kaplan, Sam McCandlish, Tom Henighan, Tom B. Brown, Benjamin Chess, Rewon Child, Scott Gray, Alec Radford, Jeffrey Wu, and Dario Amodei. 2020. Scaling laws for neural language models.

Shahnawaz Khan and Mustafa Raza Rabbani. 2020. Chatbot as islamic finance expert (caife): When finance meets artificial intelligence. In *Proceedings of the 2020 4th International Symposium on Computer Science and Intelligent Control*, ISCSIC 2020, New York, NY, USA. Association for Computing Machinery.

Ananya Kumar, Aditi Raghunathan, Robbie Jones, Tengyu Ma, and Percy Liang. 2022. Fine-tuning can distort pretrained features and underperform out-of-distribution.

Stefan Larson, Anish Mahendran, Joseph J. Peper, Christopher Clarke, Andrew Lee, Parker Hill, Jonathan K. Kummerfeld, Kevin Leach, Michael A. Laurenzano, Lingjia Tang, and Jason Mars. 2019. An evaluation dataset for intent classification and out-of-scope prediction. In *Proceedings of the 2019 Conference on Empirical Methods in Natural Language Processing and the 9th International Joint Conference on Natural Language Processing (EMNLP-IJCNLP)*, pages 1311–1316, Hong Kong, China. Association for Computational Linguistics.

Brian Lester, Rami Al-Rfou, and Noah Constant. 2021. The power of scale for parameter-efficient prompt tuning. In *Proceedings of the 2021 Conference on Empirical Methods in Natural Language Processing*, pages 3045–3059, Online and Punta Cana, Dominican Republic. Association for Computational Linguistics.

Xiang Lisa Li and Percy Liang. 2021. Prefix-tuning: Optimizing continuous prompts for generation. In *Proceedings of the 59th Annual Meeting of the Association for Computational Linguistics and the 11th International Joint Conference on Natural Language Processing (Volume 1: Long Papers)*, pages 4582–4597, Online. Association for Computational Linguistics.

Ting-En Lin and Hua Xu. 2019. Deep unknown intent detection with margin loss. In *Proceedings of the 57th Annual Meeting of the Association for Computational Linguistics*, pages 5491–5496, Florence, Italy. Association for Computational Linguistics.

Xiao Liu, Kaixuan Ji, Yicheng Fu, Weng Tam, Zhengxiao Du, Zhilin Yang, and Jie Tang. 2022. P-tuning: Prompt tuning can be comparable to fine-tuning across scales and tasks. In *Proceedings of the 60th Annual Meeting of the Association for Computational Linguistics (Volume 2: Short Papers)*, pages 61–68, Dublin, Ireland. Association for Computational Linguistics.

Magdalene Ng, Kovila P.L. Coopamootoo, Ehsan Toreini, Mhairi Aitken, Karen Elliot, and Aad van Moorsel. 2020. Simulating the effects of social presence on trust, privacy concerns & usage intentions in automated bots for finance. In *2020 IEEE European Symposium on Security and Privacy Workshops (EuroS&PW)*, pages 190–199.

Daniel W. Otter, Julian R. Medina, and Jugal K. Kalita. 2021. A survey of the usages of deep learning for natural language processing. *IEEE Transactions on Neural Networks and Learning Systems*, 32(2):604–624.

Libo Qin, Wanxiang Che, Yangming Li, Haoyang Wen, and Ting Liu. 2019. A stack-propagation framework with token-level intent detection for spoken language understanding. In *Proceedings of the 2019 Conference on Empirical Methods in Natural Language Processing and the 9th International Joint Conference on Natural Language Processing (EMNLP-IJCNLP)*, pages 2078–2087, Hong Kong, China. Association for Computational Linguistics.

Lei Shu, Hu Xu, and Bing Liu. 2017. DOC: Deep open classification of text documents. In *Proceedings of the 2017 Conference on Empirical Methods in Natural Language Processing*, pages 2911–2916, Copenhagen, Denmark. Association for Computational Linguistics.

Emma Strubell, Ananya Ganesh, and Andrew McCallum. 2019. Energy and policy considerations for deep learning in NLP. In *Proceedings of the 57th Annual Meeting of the Association for Computational Linguistics*, pages 3645–3650, Florence, Italy. Association for Computational Linguistics.

Ashish Vaswani, Noam Shazeer, Niki Parmar, Jakob Uszkoreit, Llion Jones, Aidan N Gomez, Ł ukasz Kaiser, and Illia Polosukhin. 2017a. Attention is all you need. In *Advances in Neural Information Processing Systems*, volume 30. Curran Associates, Inc.

Ashish Vaswani, Noam Shazeer, Niki Parmar, Jakob Uszkoreit, Llion Jones, Aidan N. Gomez, Lukasz Kaiser, and Illia Polosukhin. 2017b. Attention is all you need.

H. Weld, X. Huang, S. Long, J. Poon, and S. C. Han. 2021. A survey of joint intent detection and slot-filling models in natural language understanding.

Thomas Wolf, Lysandre Debut, Victor Sanh, Julien Chaumond, Clement Delangue, Anthony Moi, Pierric Cistac, Tim Rault, Remi Louf, Morgan Funtowicz, Joe Davison, Sam Shleifer, Patrick von Platen, Clara Ma, Yacine Jernite, Julien Plu, Canwen Xu, Teven Le Scao, Sylvain Gugger, Mariama Drame, Quentin Lhoest, and Alexander Rush. 2020. Transformers: State-of-the-art natural language processing. In *Proceedings of the 2020 Conference on Empirical Methods in Natural Language Processing: System Demonstrations*, pages 38–45, Online. Association for Computational Linguistics.

Congying Xia, Chenwei Zhang, Xiaohui Yan, Yi Chang, and Philip Yu. 2018. Zero-shot user intent detection via capsule neural networks. In *Proceedings of the 2018 Conference on Empirical Methods in Natural Language Processing*, pages 3090–3099, Brussels, Belgium. Association for Computational Linguistics.

Jiaming Xu, Peng Wang, Guanhua Tian, Bo Xu, Jun Zhao, Fangyuan Wang, and Hongwei Hao. 2015. Short text clustering via convolutional neural networks. In *Proceedings of the 1st Workshop on Vector Space Modeling for Natural Language Processing*, pages 62–69, Denver, Colorado. Association for Computational Linguistics.

Li-Ming Zhan, Haowen Liang, Bo Liu, Lu Fan, Xiao-Ming Wu, and Albert Y.S. Lam. 2021. Out-of-scope intent detection with self-supervision and discriminative training. In *Proceedings of the 59th Annual Meeting of the Association for Computational Linguistics and the 11th International Joint Conference on Natural Language Processing (Volume 1: Long Papers)*, pages 3521–3532, Online. Association for Computational Linguistics.

Chenwei Zhang, Yaliang Li, Nan Du, Wei Fan, and Philip Yu. 2019. Joint slot filling and intent detection via capsule neural networks. In *Proceedings of the 57th Annual Meeting of the Association for Computational Linguistics*, pages 5259–5267, Florence, Italy. Association for Computational Linguistics.

Hanlei Zhang, Hua Xu, and Ting-En Lin. 2021a. Deep open intent classification with adaptive decision boundary. *Proceedings of the AAAI Conference on Artificial Intelligence*, 35(16):14374–14382.

Hanlei Zhang, Hua Xu, Shaojie Zhao, and Qianrui Zhou. 2022. Learning discriminative representations and decision boundaries for open intent detection.

Jianguo Zhang, Trung Bui, Seunghyun Yoon, Xiang Chen, Zhiwei Liu, Congying Xia, Quan Hung Tran, Walter Chang, and Philip Yu. 2021b. Few-shot intent detection via contrastive pre-training and finetuning. In *Proceedings of the 2021 Conference on Empirical Methods in Natural Language Processing*, pages 1906–1912, Online and Punta Cana, Dominican Republic. Association for Computational Linguistics.

Exploring Robustness of Prefix Tuning in Noisy Data: A Case Study in Financial Sentiment Analysis

Sudhandar Balakrishnan and **Yihao Fang** and **Xiaodan Zhu**
Department of Electrical and Computer Engineering & Ingenuity Labs Research Institute
Queen's University
{sudhandar.balakrishnan, yihao.fang, xiaodan.zhu}@queensu.ca

Abstract

The invention of transformer-based models such as BERT, GPT, and RoBERTa has enabled researchers and financial companies to finetune these powerful models and use them in different downstream tasks to achieve state-of-the-art performance. Recently, a lightweight alternative (approximately 0.1% - 3% of the original model parameters) to fine-tuning, known as prefix tuning has been introduced. This method freezes the model parameters and only updates the prefix to achieve performance comparable to full fine-tuning. Prefix tuning enables researchers and financial practitioners to achieve similar results with much fewer parameters. In this paper, we explore the robustness of prefix tuning when facing noisy data. Our experiments demonstrate that fine-tuning is more robust to noise than prefix tuning—the latter method faces a significant decrease in performance on most corrupted data sets with increasing noise levels. Furthermore, prefix tuning has high variances on the F1 scores compared to fine-tuning in many corruption methods. We strongly advocate that caution should be carefully taken when applying the state-of-the-art prefix tuning method to noisy data.

1 Introduction

The transformer architecture (Vaswani et al., 2017) has given rise to several powerful language models such as BERT (Devlin et al., 2018) and GPT (Radford et al., 2018). These models are trained on large text corpora and the pre-trained models can be used on different downstream tasks by finetuning these models, which refers to the process of updating the weights of the pre-trained model to adapt to the downstream task and the associated dataset. This approach is critical in achieving state-of-the-art results in many downstream tasks. However, these fine-tuned language models are large in size and the deployment of these models in production to solve real-world problems becomes difficult due to the memory requirement, constraining the deployment of models in many real-life financial applications. Given that it is anticipated that model sizes will continue to rise, this will become more serious.

Li and Liang (2021) introduced a lightweight alternative to finetuning known as prefix tuning. The authors freeze the model parameters of GPT-2 (Radford et al., 2019) and use a task-specific vector to tune the model for natural language generation. This method achieves comparable performance with finetuning and uses approximately 0.1% - 3% of the original model parameters. This method will enable the use of pre-trained language models for many industrial applications.

In the financial sector, natural language processing has a wide variety of applications ranging from building a chatbot to interact with customers (Yu et al., 2020), predicting stock movements based on sentiments from financial news headlines and tweets (Sousa et al., 2019), to summarizing financial reports (La Quatra and Cagliero, 2020). Prefix tuning can be applied to many tasks with fewer parameters and much less memory consumption.

However, in the real world, the data might be noisy, especially in the case of chatbots and social media data where misspellings, typographical errors, and out-of-vocabulary words occur frequently. Recent studies have investigated the robustness of finetuning language models such as Rychalska et al. (2019), Jin et al. (2020), Aspillaga et al. (2020), Sun et al. (2020) and Srivastava et al. (2020), and found that finetuning is not robust to noisy texts.

To the best of our knowledge, there have been no studies that explore the robustness of prefix tuning that reflect real-life scenarios and compare it with finetuning to identify the more robust method. Our work corrupts the financial phrasebank dataset (Malo et al., 2014), using various text corruption methods such as keyboard errors (typos), inserting random characters, deleting random words, replacing characters with OCR alternatives and replacing

Proceedings of the Fourth Workshop on Financial Technology and Natural Language Processing (FinNLP), pages 78 - 88
December 8, 2022

words with antonyms by varying percentages in each sentence. The corrupted dataset is used with two widely used pre-trained models, BERT-base (Devlin et al., 2018) and RoBERTa-large (Liu et al., 2019), under both prefix tuning and fine-tuning, to compare their performance at different noise levels. In addition, we evaluate the performance on a Kaggle Stock Market Tweets dataset (Chaudhary, 2020), which is a real-life noisy dataset. With our experiments, we show that fine-tuning is more robust than prefix tuning in most setups. Fine-tuning updates the weights based on the downstream task and the dataset, and because of this, it can adapt to the noise, whereas prefix tuning uses the pre-trained model without updating the weights which limits the model from learning task-oriented information when facing noisy data. In summary, the contributions of this paper are three-fold.

- To the best of our knowledge, this is among the first efforts in exploring the robustness of prefix tuning when facing noisy data, particularly noisy financial data.
- We use a comprehensive set of corrupted data and show that fine-tuning is more robust to noise compared to prefix tuning. The latter has also shown to have high variances in F1 scores.
- We provide detailed results at different levels of noise. With that, we advocate that caution should be carefully taken when practitioners apply state-of-the-art prefix tuning methods to noisy data. We hope our work will set baselines for further studies along this line.

2 Related Work

2.1 Sentiment Analysis in Financial Text

Sentiment analysis is the process of understanding the sentiments from textual data (Liu, 2012). Sentiment analysis in finance tries to achieve a different objective when compared to general sentiment analysis. Financial sentiment analysis aims to predict the stock movement or impact on stock price based on the sentiments of news headlines and news articles (Li et al., 2014). Loughran and McDonald (2016) provide a survey of the machine learning approaches used to predict the sentiments in financial data. With the introduction of transformer-based language models like BERT (Devlin et al., 2018), several attempts have been made to predict the sentiments using the pre-trained BERT models trained on large text corpora. Araci (2019) introduced FinBERT, where the BERT model was pre-trained on a large financial corpus and it achieved state-of-the-art results in financial sentiment analysis. Zhao et al. (2021) use RoBERTa (Liu et al., 2019), an optimized version of BERT to predict the sentiment of online financial texts generated on social media.

2.2 Robustness of Pretrained Language Models

Several attempts have been made to test the robustness of popular transformer-based language models. Rychalska et al. (2019) test the robustness of ULMFiT (Howard and Ruder, 2018) on various NLP tasks like QA, NLI, NER and Sentiment Analysis. The authors found that the high-performing language models are not robust to various corruption methods like removing articles, removing characters from words, misspellings, etc. Jin et al. (2020) introduced a technique called TEXTFOOLER to generate adversarial texts. The authors successfully attacked BERT and significantly reduced the accuracy of BERT on text classification tasks. Aspillaga et al. (2020) compared the robustness of RoBERTa, BERT and XLNET (Yang et al., 2019) with recurrent neural network models and found that RoBERTa, BERT and XLNET are more robust than recurrent neural networks but they are still not fully immune to the attacks and their robustness can be improved. Sun et al. (2020) performed a detailed study on the robustness of BERT, especially concerning mistyped words (keyboard typos) and found that typos in informative words affect the performance of the BERT to a greater extent than typos in other words. Srivastava et al. (2020) analyzed the robustness of BERT to noise (spelling mistakes and typos) on sentiment analysis and textual similarity. The authors discovered that BERT's performance had significantly declined in the presence of noise in the text.

Prefix tuning freezes the parameters of the language model and updates the prefix vector for downstream tasks. Yang and Liu (2022) used the GPT-2 (Radford et al., 2019) model to evaluate the robustness of prefix tuning to various textual adversarial attacks, but the attacks do not resemble the noise presented in real-world data. The authors did not compare the robustness of prefix tuning and fine-tuning and did not study which training methodology is more robust.

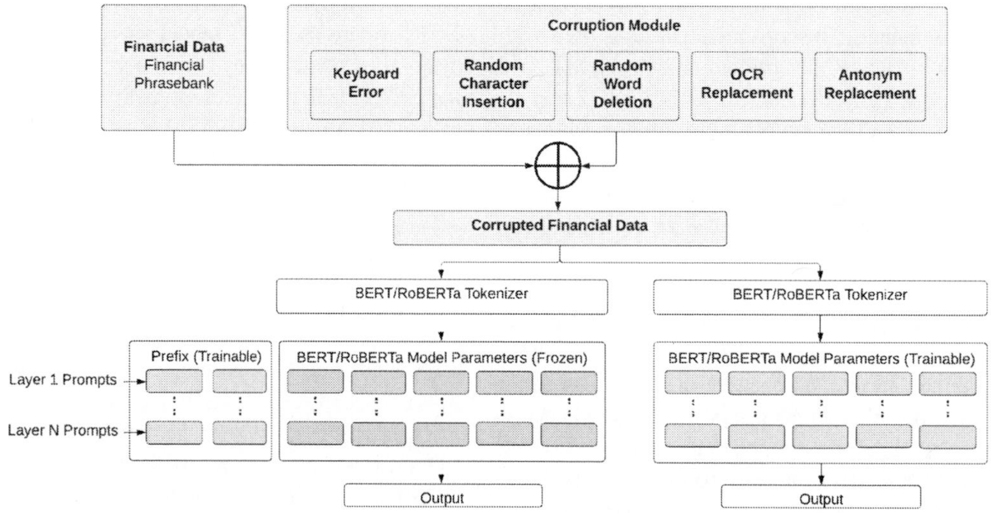

Figure 1: Overview of prefix tuning and fine-tuning methodologies. Green boxes represent trainable parameters and blue boxes represent frozen parameters.

Table 1: Train-validation-test split for the financial phrasebank 50% agreement level dataset

Label	Train Set	Validation Set	Test Set
Neutral	2011	431	431
Positive	954	204	205
Negative	423	91	90
Total	3388	726	726

Table 2: Train-validation-test split for the financial phrasebank 100% agreement level dataset

Label	Train Set	Validation Set	Test Set
Neutral	973	209	209
Positive	399	85	86
Negative	212	46	45
Total	1584	340	340

Table 3: Train-validation-test split for the Kaggle Stock Market Tweets dataset

Label	Train Set	Validation Set	Test Set
Positive	2577	553	552
Negative	1470	315	315
Total	4047	868	867

3 Approach

Figure 1 shows the overview of the approach used in this paper. The clean financial dataset is corrupted using the corruption module represented by yellow boxes in Figure 1, containing various corruption methods. The corruption module is explained in section 3.1. The corrupted financial dataset is fed into two state-of-the-art pre-trained models, BERT-base and RoBERTa-large (refer to section 3.2) using both prefix tuning and fine-tuning. Figure 1 also shows the difference between the traditional fine-tuning method and prefix tuning respectively, where blue boxes represent the frozen parameters and green boxes represent the trainable parameters.

3.1 Corruption Module

The corruption module consists of 5 text corruption methods which closely replicate the noise found in real-world data. This module is used to corrupt the clean financial dataset and the corrupted dataset is used to evaluate the performance of the models. The following are the various text corruption methods used in the corruption module. Table 4 shows an example for each corruption method. The nlpaug (Ma, 2019) library is used for generating the various corruption methods.

Keyboard Error (QWERTY) Simulates typing mistakes made while using a QWERTY-type keyboard.

Table 4: Corruption methods with an example

Corruption Method	Example
Original Sentence	In Finland's Hobby Hall's sales decreased by 10% , and international sales fell by 19% .
Keyboard Error	In cinland' s Hubby Hall' s sales decreased by 10% , and international saleW fell by 19%.
Random Character Insertion	In FrinDIa*nd' s HZobJb#y Hall's sales decreased by 10% , and international sales fell by 19% .
Random Word Deletion	In Finland' s Hobby Hall' s decreased 10% , and international fell by 19%.
OCR Replacement	In Finland' s H066y Ha1 l's sa1es decreased by 10% , and national sales decreased by 19%.
Antonym Replacement	In Finland' s Hobby Hall' s sales increase by 10% , and national sales increase by 19%.

Random Character Insertion (ChIns) Inserts random characters into a word in a sentence.

Random Word Deletion (WdDel) Randomly deletes a word from the sentence.

OCR Replacement (OCR) Replaces the characters in the word with their OCR equivalents, e.g., stock can be replaced as st0ck (here an alphabet, o, is replaced with the number zero, 0)

Antonym Replacement (AntRep) Replaces the words with their antonyms (opposite meaning) in the sentence.

3.2 Prefix Tuning and Fine Tuning in Noisy Data

Noisy Data Analysis When the models BERT and RoBERTa encounter a word that is not in their vocabulary, the models try to break down the word to see whether any of its subwords are present in their vocabulary. For example, if BERT has the word 'play' in its vocabulary and when it encounters 'playing' it will tokenize the word as "'play' + '#ing"'. If any word is not present in the vocabulary even after breaking it down, BERT assigns the unknown token (<UNK>) to that word. Table 5 shows how BERT and RoBERTa tokenize the normal and the corrupted word. From Table 5 we can understand how the corrupted word affects the BERT tokenizer and prevents it from learning the word's original meaning resulting in a drop in performance.

The process of prefix tuning and fine-tuning updating the weights is based on the downstream task and the dataset. In prefix tuning, most of the weights are not updated based on the downstream task. Since both the training and the validation sets are corrupted, in fine-tuning, the weights of the model have been updated based on the noisy datasets and contain more dataset-specific information than the prefix-tuned model. This enables the fine-tuned model to adjust to the noisy scenarios better than the prefix-tuned models. Evaluations of our intuition for prefix tuning and fine-tuning in noisy data can be found in Section 4.

4 Experiments

4.1 Financial Tasks

Two financial tasks are used to evaluate the performance of prefix tuning. The first task is the sentiment analysis of the Financial Phrasebank dataset (Malo et al., 2014), which is the main dataset used to compare the performance and evaluate the robustness of both prefix tuning and fine-tuning. The second task is the sentiment analysis of the Twitter Stockmarket dataset from Kaggle, Chaudhary (2020), which is also used to evaluate the performance of prefix tuning and fine-tuning.

Financial Phrasebank The Financial Phrasebank dataset (Malo et al., 2014), consists of 4840 sentences from financial news articles and the sentences were manually labelled as positive, negative or neutral by 16 annotators with backgrounds in finance and business. The annotators labelled the sentences depending on whether the information from the sentence had a positive, negative or no impact on the stock prices of the company mentioned in the sentence. It is an imbalanced dataset with 1363 positive sentences, 604 negative sentences and 2873 neutral sentences. In addition to it, depending

Table 5: Tokenization of corruption variants for the word 'stock'

Corruption Method	Corrupted Word	Tokenized Word BERT	Tokenized Word RoBERTa
No Corruption	'stock'	['stock']	['stock']
Keyboard error	'srosk'	['s', '##ros', '##k']	['s', 'ros', 'k']
Random character insertion	'sto*rck'	['s', '##to', '*', 'r', '##ck']	['st', 'o', '*', 'r', 'ck']
OCR replacement	'st0ck'	['s', '##t', '##0', '##ck']	['st', '0', 'ck']

on the agreement level among the annotators on the polarity of the sentence, the dataset was classified into 50%, 66%, 75% and 100% agreement levels. For example, 50% annotator agreement means more than 50% of the annotators agreed and selected the same polarity for a particular sentence. This paper uses the financial phrasebank dataset with 50% annotator agreement level (4840 sentences) to run the experiments on estimating the robustness of prefix tuning and the 100% agreement level (2262 sentences) to compare the performance. The dataset was split into the train, validation and test sets for the experiments with a 70-15-15 split (stratified split) giving rise to 3388 training sentences, 726 validation sentences and 726 test sentences in the 50% agreement level and 1582 training sentences, 340 validation sentences and 340 test sentences in the 100% agreement level dataset. Table 1 shows the split up of the 50% agreement level dataset and Table 2 shows the split up of the 100% agreement level dataset.

Kaggle Stock Market Tweets The Stock Market tweets dataset is from Kaggle, Chaudhary (2020). The reason for selecting this dataset is to evaluate the performance of prefix tuning and fine-tuning on a real-world noisy data. This dataset contains tweets from Twitter consisting of information about the stocks of multiple companies and the tweets are labelled as either positive or negative based on the sentiment associated with each tweet. This dataset is from Kaggle and it is not from a renowned journal and the authenticity cannot be validated. The dataset consists of 2106 negative tweets and 3685 positive tweets. The dataset was split into the train, validation and test sets with a 70-15-15 split giving rise to 4047 training sentences, 868 validation sentences and 867 test sentences. Table 3 shows the split up of the Kaggle Stock Market dataset.

4.2 Setup

Corruption Strategy The clean versions of the financial phrasebank dataset, 100% agreement level and 50% agreement level, are used to evaluate the performance of prefix tuning and fine-tuning on both BERT-base and RoBERTa-large models to establish the baseline performance levels. To test the robustness of prefix tuning and find out which one between prefix tuning and fine-tuning is more robust to the noisy text, the train and validation sets of the financial phrasebank dataset (50% agreement level) are corrupted by various text corruption methods. The reason for corrupting the train and validation sets is that it is difficult to find large-scale high-quality training data, especially with respect to chatbots and social media texts in an industrial setting. In general, test data is smaller in size compared to the training data and can be manually cleaned before feeding into the model. Due to this, the training and validation sets have been corrupted. For each corruption method, the sentences are corrupted by 10%, 20%, 30%, 40% and 50% corruption levels. Each corruption level represents the percentage of corrupted words in a sentence. For example, 10% corruption level means 10% of the words in the sentence are corrupted. For antonym replacement, all the words which have antonyms in the nlpaug (Ma, 2019) library are replaced with antonyms and there are no varying corruption levels for this particular corruption method.

Implementation Details After corrupting the dataset using the above-mentioned corruption strategy, we conduct the experiments on two models, BERT base and RoBERTa large. The BERT base fine-tuned model has 108,312,579 trainable parameters while the prefix-tuned model has 370,947 trainable parameters for 30 epochs for the financial phrasebank dataset. Similarly, the RoBERTa large fine-tuned model has 355,362,819 trainable parameters while the prefix-tuned model has 986,115 trainable parameters for 30 epochs for the financial phrasebank dataset. More information about the implementation details can be found in Appendix A.1 for replication.

Table 6: Results for the uncorrupted version of the datasets for the BERT-base model

Dataset	Prefix Tuning Acc.(%)	Prefix Tuning F1(%)	Fine Tuning Acc.(%)	Fine Tuning F1(%)
Financial Phrasebank - All agree	97.35	97.01	96.17	96.80
Financial Phrasebank - More than 50% agree	86.91	85.55	86.09	85.48
Kaggle Stock Market Tweets	79.60	77.74	80.41	78.96

Table 7: Results for the uncorrupted version of the datasets for the RoBERTa-large model

Dataset	Prefix Tuning Acc.(%)	Prefix Tuning F1(%)	Fine Tuning Acc.(%)	Fine Tuning F1(%)
Financial Phrasebank - All agree	98.24	98.09	98.53	98.35
Financial Phrasebank - More than 50% agree	87.60	87.25	88.15	87.45
Kaggle Stock Market Tweets	81.79	79.61	82.71	80.61

Table 8: Financial Phrasebank results for various text corruption methods for both the BERT-base and the RoBERTa-large model

		BERT-base				RoBERTa-large			
	Cor.	Prefix Tuning		Fine Tuning		Prefix Tuning		Fine Tuning	
Method	(%)	Acc.	F1	Acc.	F1	Acc.	F1	Acc.	F1
None	-	86.91	85.55	86.09	85.48	87.60	87.25	88.15	87.45
Qwerty	10	0.47	-0.47	-0.16	-0.5	-0.78	-1.60	-0.94	-1.63
	20	-0.96	-0.44	-0.01	-0.43	-1.40	-1.43	-1.08	-0.82
	30	-0.16	-0.68	0.15	-1.09	-4.37	-5.50	-3.26	-4.64
	40	-1.58	-2.50	-0.81	-1.12	-6.21	-8.85	-3.56	-4.55
	50	-6.34	-8.87	-3.04	-5.11	-6.21	-9.04	-3.57	-4.80
ChIns	10	-1.10	-1.27	-0.65	-1.31	-0.46	-1.58	-0.46	-1.84
	20	-3.01	-3.53	-0.96	-1.37	-2.80	-3.30	-1.86	-3.09
	30	-3.33	-4.57	-0.96	-2.40	-2.78	-3.81	-3.73	-5.15
	40	-3.01	-4.63	-3.68	-4.22	-2.64	-4.41	-4.04	-4.24
	50	-5.38	-6.63	-2.89	-4.73	-5.56	-8.31	-5.13	-7.40
WdDel	10	-0.63	-0.04	0.15	-1.42	-0.94	-1.45	-1.40	-1.26
	20	-0.96	-0.98	-0.82	-1.70	-1.70	-2.48	-1.56	-2.27
	30	-1.90	-2.49	-1.29	-2.06	-4.04	-3.75	-2.80	-3.69
	40	-3.01	-4.63	-0.80	-2.29	-1.70	-2.05	-0.94	-1.74
	50	-5.38	-6.63	-3.21	-3.11	-2.02	-2.86	-2.02	-2.29
OCR	10	-0.63	-0.28	-1.13	-1.04	-0.78	-1.31	-0.78	-1.89
	20	-0.79	-1.30	-0.01	-0.27	-0.94	-1.42	-0.78	-1.67
	30	-2.53	-2.93	-2.73	-2.69	-2.48	-3.01	-3.57	-4.04
	40	-2.53	-2.93	-2.73	-2.69	-4.66	-5.08	-2.80	-4.34
	50	-7.44	-11.30	-10.73	-10.45	-5.13	-8.59	-4.19	-6.62
AntRep	-	-12.36	-25.55	-14.25	-27.41	-14.13	-28.20	-16.78	-30.05

Evaluation Metrics The F1 score and accuracy are selected as the metrics for the evaluation of the experiments. The F1 score is used as the main metric for comparison since the financial phrasebank is an imbalanced dataset with 3 classes, positive, negative and neutral.

4.3 Results

Clean Baselines Table 6 and Table 7 show the performance of both models on the clean versions of the financial phrasebank dataset and the noisy Kaggle stock market tweets dataset (uncorrupted). Both prefix tuning and fine-tuning achieve comparable performance in both clean versions of the financial phrasebank dataset (all agree and more than 50% agree). In the noisy tweets dataset, fine-tuning performs better than prefix tuning in both models. The Bert-base finetuning method achieves an F1 score of 78.96% which is greater than prefix tuning (77.74%) by 1.22 point F1 score. Similarly, RoBERTa fine-tuning method achieves an F1 score of 80.61% which is greater than prefix tuning (79.61%) by 1 point F1 score.

Corruption Results Table 8 shows the change in the baseline scores of prefix tuning and fine-tuning on different corruption methods for BERT-base and RoBERTa-large respectively. The performance of both fine-tuning and prefix tuning drops as the noise level increases. Overall, finetuning performs better than prefix tuning in all the corruption methods except for antonym replacement. Even though the difference in F1 scores is very minimal for the lower percentage of noise like 10% and 20%, the difference becomes more predominant when the noise percentage in each sentence increases. This trend can be observed in both BERT-base and RoBERTa-large models.

To further evaluate the validity of the results, the variance (how the F1 scores vary from mean F1 scores across various iterations) for 50% noise level for all the corruption methods is measured. The experiments were repeated 5 times with reshuffled data for all the corruption methods to measure the mean and variance of F1 scores. Table 9 shows the mean and variance of F1 scores for the BERT-base model. It can be observed that the variance for prefix tuning is very high in two corruption methods, keyboard (qwerty) error and OCR replacement error.

There is a significant drop in performance (more than 25%) for antonym replacement. Fine tuning achieves an F1 score of 62.05% whereas prefix tuning achieves an F1 score of 63.69%. When compared to prefix tuning, the fine-tuned model achieves lower performance and it could be due to the following reason. The weights of the fine-tuned model are updated with the corrupted dataset containing antonyms instead of the original words. Since the model is trained to predict the opposite sentiment (sentences with antonyms), the performance drops significantly when evaluated on the test dataset. This results in the fine-tuned model being more adapted to the corrupted dataset and achieving lower performance when exposed to a clean test dataset whereas prefix tuning performs comparatively better.

Table 10 shows the predicted labels for BERT-base OCR replacement 50% corruption level where fine-tuning predicted the correct labels and prefix tuning predicted the wrong labels. In most of the cases, the positive labels were incorrectly predicted as neutral, the neutral labels were incorrectly predicted as positive and the negative labels were incorrectly predicted as neutral.

Another interesting observation is the minimal performance drop seen in the random word deletion corruption method even when 50% of the words are deleted from the sentences. The performance drop in the F1 score for the BERT base model was 6.63% for prefix tuning and 3.11% for fine-tuning. Similarly, the performance drop in the F1 score for the RoBERTa large model was 2.86% for prefix tuning and 2.29% for fine-tuning. The main reason behind this could be the way BERT is trained. BERT uses masked language modelling where it masks the words at random by varying percentages and tries to predict the masked word based on the context. This might be the reason why there is no significant drop in performance even when deleting 50% of the words since both BERT and RoBERTa are trained to handle the missing words in a sentence.

5 Conclusion

With the sizes of pre-trained models continuing to be significantly larger, lightweight models have become more important for many financial applications. However, the robustness of such models has not been well understood yet. In this paper, we explored the robustness of prefix tuning by corrupting the financial phrasebank dataset with various corruption methods, including keyboard (qwerty) er-

Table 9: Mean and Variance of F1 scores for the BERT-base model for 50% noise level

	Prefix Tuning		Fine Tuning	
Corruption Method	**Mean (F1%)**	**Variance**	**Mean (F1%)**	**Variance**
No Corruption	85.48	0.16	85.48	0.13
Keyboard error	80.57	5.66	82.00	1.15
Random character insertion	80.84	0.72	81.97	0.86
Random word deletion	81.98	0.10	82.50	0.13
OCR replacement	75.77	3.64	77.49	0.86
Antonym replacement	64.05	1.94	62.23	0.06

Table 10: Predicted labels for BERT-base OCR replacement 50% corruption level in cases where fine-tuning predicted the correct labels and prefix tuning predicted the wrong labels

Sentence	**True Label**	**Predicted Label**	
		Prefix Tuning	**Fine Tuning**
The amending of the proposal simplifies the proposed plan and increases the incentive for key employees to stay in the Company	Positive	Neutral	Positive
The company 's net sales in 2009 totalled MEUR 307.8 with an operating margin of 13.5 per cent	Neutral	Positive	Neutral
The move was triggered by weak demand for forestry equipment and the uncertain market situation	Negative	Neutral	Negative

ror, random character insertion, OCR replacement, random word deletion and antonym replacement under varying noise levels at 10%, 20%, 30%, 40% and 50%, as well as on the Kaggle stock market tweets, which is a real-world noisy dataset. We show that fine-tuning is more robust to noise than prefix tuning in most of the corruption methods. As the impact of noise is more significant along with increasing noise levels, prefix tuning shows a more significant decrease in performance compared to full fine-tuning. The variance of performance of prefix tuning is higher than that of fine-tuning for most corruption setups. Our study suggests that caution should be taken by practitioners when applying prefix tuning to noisy data. A solution to improving the robustness to reduce the impact of noise is desired and is our immediate future work.

6 Limitations

The words were randomly corrupted in a sentence with no emphasis on the word's context and no experiments were carried out to find out the importance of the corrupted word in the context of predicting the sentiment. Corrupting an important word may result in an increased drop in performance than corrupting a word which has minimal impact on the sentiment of a sentence. Sun et al. (2020) have found that typos on informative words affect the performance of the BERT to a greater extent than typos in other words. Furthermore, the robustness was evaluated on the sentiment analysis task and it was not evaluated on other natural language processing tasks like question answering, named entity recognition and text summarization.

References

Dogu Araci. 2019. Finbert: Financial sentiment analysis with pre-trained language models. *arXiv preprint arXiv:1908.10063.*

Carlos Aspillaga, Andrés Carvallo, and Vladimir Araujo. 2020. Stress test evaluation of transformer-based models in natural language understanding tasks. *arXiv preprint arXiv:2002.06261.*

Yash Chaudhary. 2020. Stock-market sentiment dataset. https://www.kaggle.com/datasets/yash612/stockmarket-sentiment-dataset.

Jacob Devlin, Ming-Wei Chang, Kenton Lee, and Kristina Toutanova. 2018. Bert: Pre-training of deep bidirectional transformers for language understanding. *arXiv preprint arXiv:1810.04805.*

Jeremy Howard and Sebastian Ruder. 2018. Universal

language model fine-tuning for text classification. *arXiv preprint arXiv:1801.06146*.

Di Jin, Zhijing Jin, Joey Tianyi Zhou, and Peter Szolovits. 2020. Is bert really robust? a strong baseline for natural language attack on text classification and entailment. In *Proceedings of the AAAI conference on artificial intelligence*, volume 34, pages 8018–8025.

Moreno La Quatra and Luca Cagliero. 2020. End-to-end training for financial report summarization. In *Proceedings of the 1st Joint Workshop on Financial Narrative Processing and MultiLing Financial Summarisation*, pages 118–123.

Xiang Lisa Li and Percy Liang. 2021. Prefix-tuning: Optimizing continuous prompts for generation. *arXiv preprint arXiv:2101.00190*.

Xiaodong Li, Haoran Xie, Li Chen, Jianping Wang, and Xiaotie Deng. 2014. News impact on stock price return via sentiment analysis. *Knowledge-Based Systems*, 69:14–23.

Bing Liu. 2012. Sentiment analysis and opinion mining. *Synthesis lectures on human language technologies*, 5(1):1–167.

Xiao Liu, Kaixuan Ji, Yicheng Fu, Zhengxiao Du, Zhilin Yang, and Jie Tang. 2021. P-tuning v2: Prompt tuning can be comparable to fine-tuning universally across scales and tasks. *arXiv preprint arXiv:2110.07602*.

Yinhan Liu, Myle Ott, Naman Goyal, Jingfei Du, Mandar Joshi, Danqi Chen, Omer Levy, Mike Lewis, Luke Zettlemoyer, and Veselin Stoyanov. 2019. Roberta: A robustly optimized bert pretraining approach. *arXiv preprint arXiv:1907.11692*.

Tim Loughran and Bill McDonald. 2016. Textual analysis in accounting and finance: A survey. *Journal of Accounting Research*, 54(4):1187–1230.

Edward Ma. 2019. Nlp augmentation. https://github.com/makcedward/nlpaug.

Pekka Malo, Ankur Sinha, Pekka Korhonen, Jyrki Wallenius, and Pyry Takala. 2014. Good debt or bad debt: Detecting semantic orientations in economic texts. *Journal of the Association for Information Science and Technology*, 65(4):782–796.

Alec Radford, Karthik Narasimhan, Tim Salimans, Ilya Sutskever, et al. 2018. Improving language understanding by generative pre-training.

Alec Radford, Jeffrey Wu, Rewon Child, David Luan, Dario Amodei, Ilya Sutskever, et al. 2019. Language models are unsupervised multitask learners. *OpenAI blog*, 1(8):9.

Barbara Rychalska, Dominika Basaj, Alicja Gosiewska, and Przemysław Biecek. 2019. Models in the wild: On corruption robustness of neural nlp systems. In *International Conference on Neural Information Processing*, pages 235–247. Springer.

Matheus Gomes Sousa, Kenzo Sakiyama, Lucas de Souza Rodrigues, Pedro Henrique Moraes, Eraldo Rezende Fernandes, and Edson Takashi Matsubara. 2019. Bert for stock market sentiment analysis. In *2019 IEEE 31st International Conference on Tools with Artificial Intelligence (ICTAI)*, pages 1597–1601. IEEE.

Ankit Srivastava, Piyush Makhija, and Anuj Gupta. 2020. Noisy text data: Achilles' heel of bert. In *Proceedings of the Sixth Workshop on Noisy User-generated Text (W-NUT 2020)*, pages 16–21.

Lichao Sun, Kazuma Hashimoto, Wenpeng Yin, Akari Asai, Jia Li, Philip Yu, and Caiming Xiong. 2020. Adv-bert: Bert is not robust on misspellings! generating nature adversarial samples on bert. *arXiv preprint arXiv:2003.04985*.

Ashish Vaswani, Noam Shazeer, Niki Parmar, Jakob Uszkoreit, Llion Jones, Aidan N Gomez, Łukasz Kaiser, and Illia Polosukhin. 2017. Attention is all you need. *Advances in neural information processing systems*, 30.

Zhilin Yang, Zihang Dai, Yiming Yang, Jaime Carbonell, Russ R Salakhutdinov, and Quoc V Le. 2019. Xlnet: Generalized autoregressive pretraining for language understanding. *Advances in neural information processing systems*, 32.

Zonghan Yang and Yang Liu. 2022. On robust prefix-tuning for text classification. *arXiv preprint arXiv:2203.10378*.

Shi Yu, Yuxin Chen, and Hussain Zaidi. 2020. A financial service chatbot based on deep bidirectional transformers. *arXiv preprint arXiv:2003.04987*.

Lingyun Zhao, Lin Li, Xinhao Zheng, and Jianwei Zhang. 2021. A bert based sentiment analysis and key entity detection approach for online financial texts. In *2021 IEEE 24th International Conference on Computer Supported Cooperative Work in Design (CSCWD)*, pages 1233–1238. IEEE.

A Appendix

A.1 Implementation Details

The experiments were carried out on four Nvidia GeForce RTX 2080 GPU's for 30 epochs. The length of the prefix plays a significant role in prefix tuning. In (Liu et al., 2021), the authors have suggested that Natural Language Understanding (NLU) tasks prefer shorter prefix lengths and they have used a prefix length of 20 for sentiment classification to obtain the best performance. We have also used a prefix length of 20 to evaluate the performance of the models. The learning rate differs for each model and method. For prefix tuning, both BERT-base and RoBERTa-large models use a learning rate of 1e-2. For fine-tuning, BERT-base uses a learning rate of 2e-5 and RoBERTa-large used a learning rate of 2e-6. Furthermore, the 50% noise level is selected for all the corruption methods and the variance is measured for both prefix tuning and fine-tuning for the BERT base model. The Kaggle Stock Market tweets dataset is also used to evaluate the performance of prefix tuning and fine-tuning on real-world noisy data (tweets) with the same set of hyperparameters as the financial phrasebank dataset.

A.2 Experimental Results - Visualizations

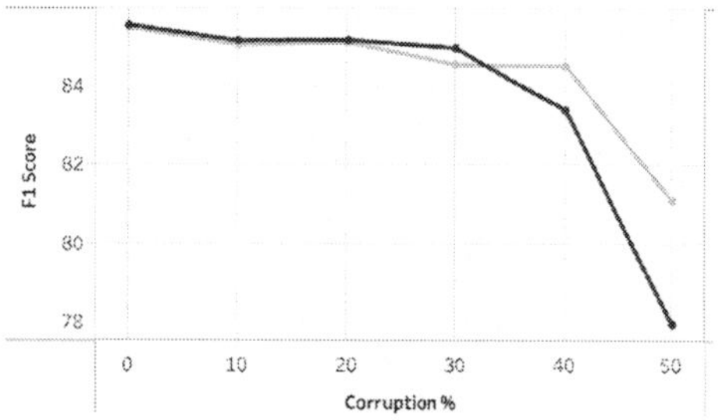

(a) Keyboard Error

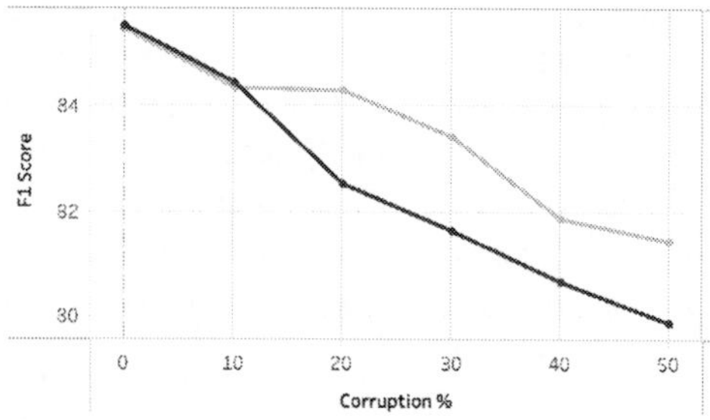

(b) Random Char. Insertion

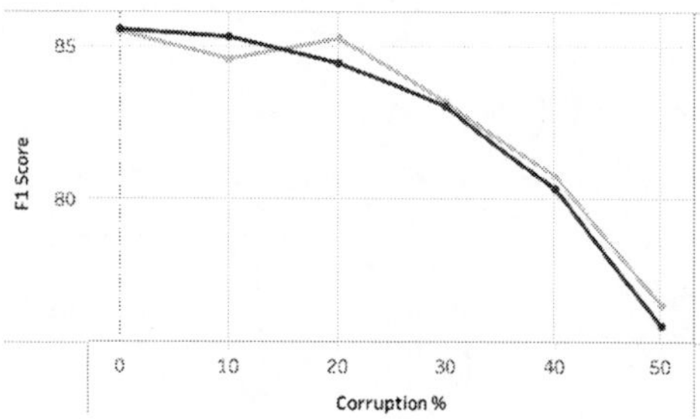

(c) OCR Replacement

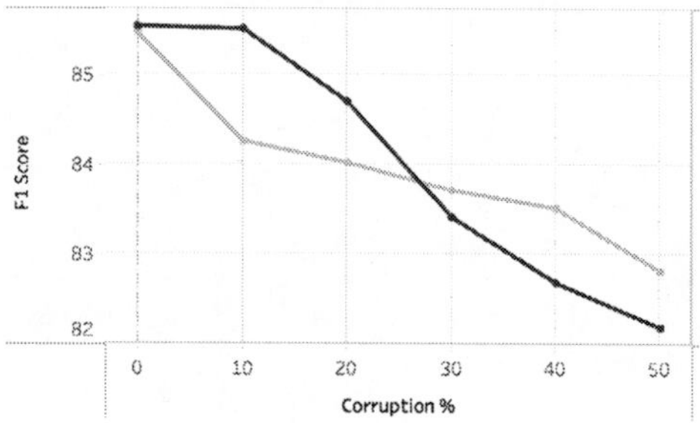

(d) Random word Deletion

Figure 2: Plot of F1 scores of BERT-base model for various corruption methods. Red line represents prefix tuning and yellow line represents fine-tuning.

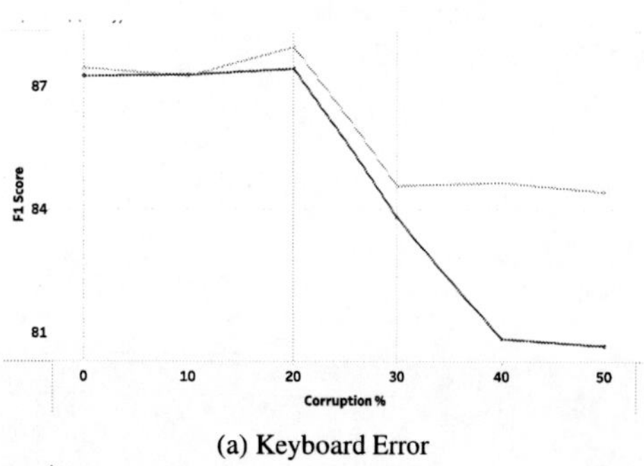

(a) Keyboard Error

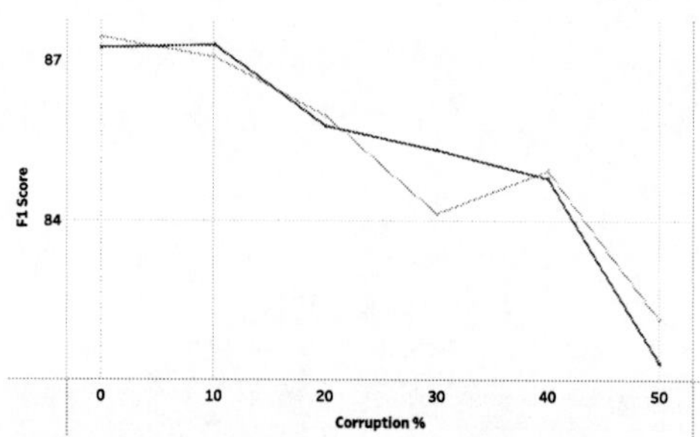

(b) Random Char. Insertion

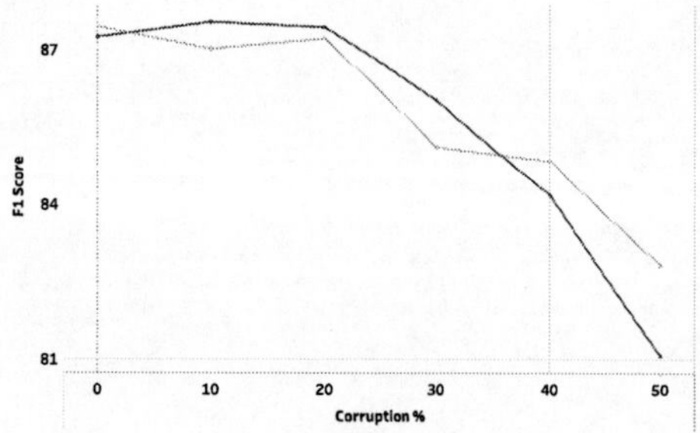

(c) OCR Replacement

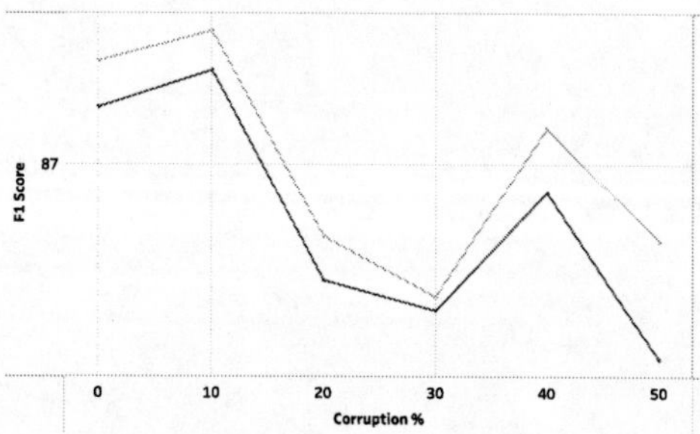

(d) Random word Deletion

Figure 3: Plot of F1 scores of RoBERTa-large model for various corruption methods. Red line represents prefix tuning and yellow line represents fine-tuning.

A Taxonomical NLP Blueprint to Support Financial Decision Making through Information-Centred Interactions

Siavash Kazemian† and **Cosmin Munteanu**‡ and **Gerald Penn**†
†Department of Computer Science
‡Institute of Communication, Culture, Information and Technology
University of Toronto
{kazemian,mcosmin,gpenn}@cs.toronto.edu

Abstract

Investment management professionals (IMPs) often make decisions after manual analysis of text transcripts of central banks' conferences or companies' earning calls. Their current software tools, while interactive, largely leave users unassisted in using these transcripts. A key component to designing speech and NLP techniques for this community is to qualitatively characterize their perceptions of AI as well as their legitimate needs so as to (1) better apply existing NLP methods, (2) direct future research and (3) correct IMPs' perceptions of what AI is capable of. This paper presents such a study, through a contextual inquiry with eleven IMPs, uncovering their information practices when using such transcripts. We then propose a taxonomy of user requirements and usability criteria to support IMP decision making, and validate the taxonomy through participatory design workshops with four IMPs. Our investigation suggests that: (1) IMPs view visualization methods and natural language processing algorithms primarily as time-saving tools that are incapable of enhancing either discovery or interpretation and (2) their existing software falls well short of the state of the art in both visualization and NLP.

1 Introduction

There are many stakeholders and agents that interact within the space of financial markets. *Investment management professionals* (IMPs) play the most prominent role here. On a macro scale, IMPs are responsible for the long-term strategies of institutions such as mutual funds, pension funds, sovereign wealth funds, etc. At the core of their activities lies information seeking - staying well informed by understanding market trends through reading external reports and developing their own predictive models based on thorough statistical analysis of large and varied sources of data.

Within the technological space of tools that support such information-seeking activities, natural language processing (NLP) research is already tackling tasks that IMPs perform, e.g., trading securities based on sources such as newswire, company quarterly reports, financial blog posts, and social media text (Bollen et al., 2011; Kazemian et al., 2016; Zhang and Skiena, 2010). Our study has revealed that textual and spoken documents are highly valued by experienced analysts, because they yield nuanced insights not available in aggregated, numerical data.[1]

Our critical survey of major financial-analysis software (e.g., Bloomberg Terminal, FactSet) reveals, however, that while this software is ubiquitous, its use of tools that could amplify understanding or enable discovery within natural-language sources is extremely conservative. This is particularly noticeable against the backdrop of a general trend in the financial sector towards automation of information processes, and an abstract awareness that ever-expanding NL datasets can facilitate more nuanced decision making (Flood et al., 2016).

Nevertheless, as we elaborate upon below, we have found that the "boots on the ground," the IMPs themselves, seem to assess the value of visualization and NLP techniques, as applied to their own use of unstructured natural language artifacts, exclusively in terms of *faster* analysis, with no prospect of *better* analysis — a world of "little data," mostly disconnected from the "big data" that they have read about in the popular press, in which computers can be relied upon to fetch and render natural language content but are largely superfluous to the analysis and interpretation of that content as IMPs require. This view persists because of a commodified view of NLP in which the literal under-

[1] As one of our participants bluntly explained: *"The thing about having a job in the market is at all times you're trying to not lose money and hopefully gain money. At any point when relevant information comes out, you need to know. For example, what Yellen said, everyone needs to know, if there is a loser who doesn't know, he is going to lose money at the expense of his ignorance"* (P1).

Proceedings of the Fourth Workshop on Financial Technology and Natural Language Processing (FinNLP), pages 89 - 98
December 8, 2022

standing of speech and language is viewed as either trivial or at least a mostly solved problem, through the lens of commercial successes such as Siri, IBM Watson, and Google Now (Milanesi, 2016). In other words, zealous misrepresentations of what NLP research has already accomplished have tragically impaired IMPs' awareness of the goals and capabilities of contemporary NLP, and have been perhaps *the* major obstacle to a more pragmatic utilization of NLP within this community.

As will shortly become apparent, this is not an NLP research paper, nor have we attempted to reform the perceptions of IMPs. But because a central goal of the financial NLP community is to design intelligent interfaces and software that will better support the information practices of these IMPs, the ethnographic HCI research presented here is important to the financial NLP community, as it identifies critical aspects of the information practices of IMPs that are not being supported. The good news is that the problems being addressed by past offerings of this workshop series are well positioned to address many of these aspects.

Below, we first describe our investigation of the information practices and processes of IMPs from an Information-Seeking Process (ISP) perspective (Marchionini, 1995). We conducted a Contextual Inquiry (CI), from which we infer a taxonomy of information seeking tasks related to analyzing natural language documents (Study 1). We then conducted a series of Participatory Design (PD) workshops to validate the taxonomy and explore how revisions to the current software interfaces can better support the ISPs captured in our proposed taxonomy (Study 2). After presenting the insights from Study 2, anchored in the proposed taxonomy, we suggest design approaches for using visualization and NLP tools to support the ISPs of IMPs.

2 Background

Central banks such as the US Federal Reserve (Fed) or the European Central Bank (ECB) play a prominent role in deciding the monetary policy of a jurisdiction (Bernanke and Kuttner, 2005). The leaders of central banks hold several press conferences a year to inform the public about their activities, and to give guidance on how they might act going forward. Similarly, publicly traded companies play a significant role in the capital markets by providing investment and risk mitigation opportunities to financial organizations. Public companies are required to hold regular earning calls to update the public on their activities. To IMPs, such events are critical to their risk mitigation efforts; the transcripts of these calls or conferences are thus valuable.

IMPs (often referred to as *financial analysts*) make investment decisions on behalf of their employers (*buy-side analysts*) or provide advice to large investment banks (*sell-side analysts*). The scale and complexity of their decision making sets them apart from retail analysts who advise individuals or small businesses on their investments.

In our first study, we examine how IMPs make use of spoken records of central bank news conferences and earning calls in their professional activities. In the second study, we will use their input from this first study to investigate better design approaches for software that supports the use of such records in their information seeking practices.

3 Related Work

Observational studies have investigated the workflow and information practices of IMPs, producing taxonomies of the information transfer process from sell-side to buy-side analysts (Ramnath et al., 2008) or details of accounting practices (Bouwman et al., 1995). However, these do not capture the IMPs' information-seeking needs themselves. They also do not describe how IMPs interact with information systems to satisfy their information needs.

Under the banner of Interaction Capture and Retrieval or ICR (Whittaker et al., 2008), however, there have been observational studies of somewhat related information practices that use spoken records of events. Whittaker et al. (1998), for example, investigated how recorded voicemail was used in a corporate setting, and incorporated their findings in the design of an improved voicemail indexing and retrieval system (Whittaker et al., 2002). Jaimes et al. (2004) studied why and how users review meeting records in order to guide their development of a cue-based meeting retrieval system. Whittaker et al. (2008) conducted another field study in which they observed how people were using records of meetings, and showed that although technology such as Speech Excision (Nenkova and Passonneau, 2004) is effective, it was not incorporated into state-of-the-art meeting browsers.

These prior studies, along with other research in the meeting domain (Bertini and Lalanne, 2007;

Jaimes et al., 2004; Lalanne and Popescu-Belis, 2012), have confirmed the relatively limited utility of more traditional meeting artifacts such as minutes, personal notes, and raw audio-visual recordings, and point to software-enabled tools as more effective. These include speech recognition and speech excision for voicemail and meetings (Whittaker et al., 2002, 2008), but there are many other promising candidate technologies: speech alignment (Goldman, 2011), disfluency detection (Liu et al., 2006), speaker segmentation (Budnik et al., 2016), information extraction (McCallum et al., 2000), answer selection, an important step in question answering (QA) systems (e.g., Jauhar et al., 2016; Rao et al., 2016), machine comprehension (Rajpurkar et al., 2016), and sentiment analysis (e.g., Rosenthal et al., 2017; Socher et al., 2013).

These technologies, furthermore, as well as the remarkable pace of their advancement, are known to software developers who support IMPs, despite the lack of a design investigation that explicitly connects these advancements to IMPs' needs and practices. The remarkable performance boost in answer selection between 2004 to 2016 on datasets containing financial news (from a mean reciprocal rank of 0.4939 (Wang et al., 2007) to 0.877 (Rao et al., 2016)), for example, was well publicized among these vendors, as were the significant improvements to machine comprehension, which extracts exact answer phrases to questions from raw text, in the space of a single year — from 50.5% (Rajpurkar et al., 2016) to 78.6% (Rajpurkar et al., 2018) (3.6% shy of human performance). Sentiment analysis of financial news was understood to have improved automatic trading from roughly 30% to 70.1% annualized returns (Kazemian et al., 2016), and the use of sentiment analysis in market analysis tools has been commonplace now for almost 10 years (Cambria et al., 2013).

With the exception of sentiment analysis, however, the absence of any serious, contemporary NLP functionality is notable. This paper takes a first step towards an explicit design investigation of the potential of this functionality by proposing (Study 1) and validating (Study 2) a design-minded taxonomy of information practices within the financial analysis domain.

The information-seeking process has been characterized as a highly variable process shaped by information seeking factors such as the task and information domain (Marchionini, 1995). For different tasks and information seeking factors, different types of support are needed by information seekers (Toms et al., 2003; Vakkari, 2003). Methods such as Contextual Inquiry (CI) are effective in uncovering such information seeking factors (Beyer and Holtzblatt, 1999), while approaches such as Participatory Design (PD) (Schuler and Namioka, 1993) are useful not only for engaging users in the design process but for refining the functional requirements of information support tools (Lalanne and Popescu-Belis, 2012).

4 Study 1: Observing Spoken Document Use

Spoken documents contain unique and critical information for IMPs. They are rich with both factual and affective data, and yet this medium is not adequately supported by existing financial analysis software such as Bloomberg or FactSet. Moreover, these spoken documents contain both content authored by the institutions holding the events (e.g. Federal Reserve), as well as Q&A from journalists and analysts that, as will be discussed, give transcript readers clues about their future publications, and thus about the markets' reaction to the events. Hence, the focus of our taxonomy is on IMPs' use of spoken documents such as transcripts from the Federal Reserve. In particular, we focus on overall information and decision-making practices, instead of users' interaction, or the use of specific elements of the text, a topic extensively studied in linguistics.

We conducted a contextual inquiry, observing how IMPs utilized spoken records. Eleven analysts (4 female, 7 male) who actively use transcripts responded to our participation call, which had been distributed through our professional network and word of mouth. All participants had more than 5 years of experience in their field, and were currently working at Wall Street (New York, USA) hedge funds, asset management firms, central banks, and large multinational investment banks. The study was conducted at participant offices. Participants were instructed to choose spoken records they would be interested in reading as part of their professional activities. The documents that they chose were transcripts of earning calls of publicly traded companies or of news conferences given by leaders of central banks.

A researcher observed them during reading; after they read, he later conducted a semi-structured interview with the participants to gain insights into the 6 information-seeking factors defined by Marchionini (1995) that characterize their ISP, the lens through which we view their interactions with information systems. These are: *setting, information seeker, domain, task, search systems,* and *outcomes.* The interviews were recorded and transcribed. The study's data consist of these transcripts as well as the observation notes. An Inductive Thematic Analysis was used to extract the major themes in the dataset (Braun and Clarke, 2006), conducted under an essentialist epistemological approach, in which language is seen as a reflection of intended meaning and individual experience (versus a constructional perspective, in which meaning and experience are viewed as socially constructed). In this paradigm, one can theorise about individual motivations. No theoretical framework was used, however, as our goal was not to measure fit with a particular theory.

The participants/readers all work for organizations that are market participants, entities that buy and/or sell assets in the investment markets. When describing their professional duties, the participants noted that they exclusively made decisions in a group, highlighting the collaborative nature of their ISPs. 8 of the 11 participants noted that they usually updated their team about what they learned after reading transcripts. Their task can therefore be formulated as extracting from the content of these spoken records key takeaway points that could be referenced later or shared with colleagues.

They furthermore noted that in this industry, time is of the essence. Even minor delays in investment decisions could be very costly. This is the major reason that IMPs tolerate working with error-laden transcripts, so long as they are available sooner. It also explains their expert proficiency in skimming and skipping over information they already know or find irrelevant.

The meta-goal of participants is to increase institutional returns. For this, participants need to develop insights about future actions (e.g., whether the Fed would raise rates) and outcomes (e.g., whether a company's total revenue would appreciate over the next year) of the organizations they study (e.g. a company or a central bank). Just as important, the users also need to develop a good understanding of the markets' expectations of those actions and outcomes. The success of an IMP hinges not just upon a more accurate grasp of the organizations' futures actions and outcomes, but of a differentially better understanding than the general market consensus.

Table 1 summarizes the information our participants tried to extract: the *Essential Predictive Knowledge (EPK).* In order to assess the future actions and outcomes of an institution and the markets' reactions to them, readers mined information related to the organization, the speakers in the recordings, and external factors (T1 in Figure 1).

4.1 Taxonomy of ISP Subtasks

Our interviews reveal that none of what is communicated by the speakers is viewed by our participants as ground truth. Instead, the content is interpreted by comparing it to previous communications from the same organization and speakers, and in the context of their activities and market perceptions. The speakers representing the institution know about this complexity. Their aim is to send carefully drafted messages to their audience (T2a), which may or may not be supported by all of the facts available. From these messages, and by considering contextual information, our participants aim to extract "the truth" about the organizations. To do so, they performed several sub-tasks, which we summarize as a taxonomy in Figure 1. First, all participants interpreted facts about EPK from transcript content (the what). This starts with forming a solid understanding of the company's past actions and outcomes, as well as the "dialogue" about the company. Next, readers take notes on disclosed information as well as referencing related information not shared in the transcript. For instance, in his analysis of a company's unusually large reported loss in revenues, P7 had to consider market rumors that the company was losing its largest institutional client, concluding that the rumors could be true, and that they would negatively impact the company's long-term profitability.

In addition, the users assessed the communication acts themselves in the transcript (the how). Special attention was paid to tone or sentiment of communication (P1, P3-5, P7-10), which was described as "bullish" (or "bearish"), "unabashed" (or "reserved"), "positive" (or "less positive"), "gung ho" (or "defensive"), and "hawkish" (or "dovish"). According to these participants, the expressed sentiments were not only a good clue about the organizations' future actions, but also have an effect on the short-term market reaction to the communicated content. Communications tactics used by the speakers were also discussed (P1, P4-5, P7,

	Past	Present	Future
External Factors	Market / A&O of other institutions	Analysts' Q&A	*Market reactions*
Speakers	Professional history, previous remarks	Cognitive and affective state	*Leading actions*
Studied Institutions	A&O, Guidance	A&O, Guidance	*A&O*

Table 1: The sought-after knowledge for predicting future actions and outcomes (A&O).

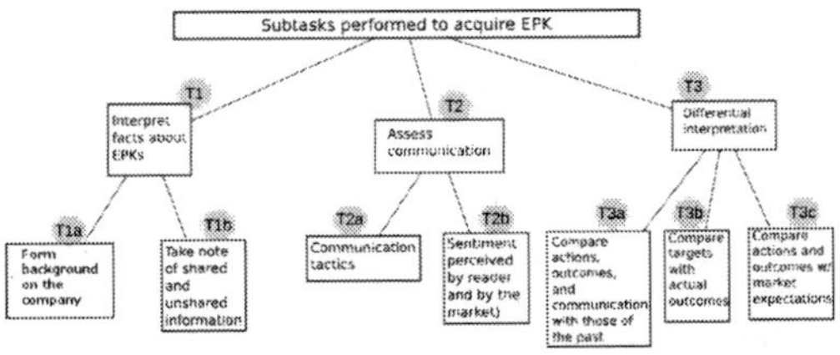

Figure 1: Tasks performed by IMPs to predict future action and outcomes of the studied organization and the market's reaction.

P10-11), such as side-stepping questions, providing "evasive" responses, repeating important content to signal salience, or providing more details about key subjects during Q&A.

Finally, as our participants integrated their newly gained EPK and made higher-level assessments, they compared it with past actions, outcomes, past communications, market expectation, and (differentially) the organization's past guidance.

5 Study 2: Participatory Design

The competitive nature of the financial markets has made this user group largely unavailable to participation in user studies. We were fortunate to be able to recruit four professionals to participate in Participatory Design (PD) workshops (3 males, 1 female, identified as D1 to D4). D1 and D2 had also participated in Study 1. All had more than six years of experience. D3 and D4 were sell-side analysts for investment banks and equity firms, while D1 and D2 were buy-side analysts for large global asset management firms and hedge funds.

5.1 Methodology

The four PD workshops were attended by a facilitator, a participant, and a visual artist. The visual artist's role was to assist participants with sketching their proposed ideas and to help facilitate the visual conversation, mitigating participants' potential lack of sketching or drawing expertise. In the design workshops, the participants started with a warm-up by reading a transcript as they normally would in their work routine. They were subsequently asked questions about how and why they read transcripts. The participants were then introduced to a scenario similar to the first study. The scenario involved examining the content of a transcript relevant to an investment decision that the participant's hypothetical employer was considering. The participant then wrote five takeaways from the transcript, potentially including an investment recommendation, for the purpose of sharing it with their team members.

After presenting the scenario, the participants were provided with drawing tools, large sheets of paper, and a new transcript of their choosing. The participants were told that 'the sky is the limit' for technologies they can incorporate into their designs: visualization, navigation, and artificial intelligence. We deliberately described the available technologies vaguely, to avoid priming participants toward specific technologies. They were also asked to think about tools that would provide appropriate assistance for their ISPs given the ecosystem of platforms they regularly use (e.g. Bloomberg Terminal or FactSet).

5.2 Data Collected

Each workshop (1.5 to 2.5 hours), was video recorded, and produced one design sketch. The components of the designed systems (UI features, labelled as Fi in our analysis) were identified by examining the produced sketches alongside the sessions' video recordings. Affinity diagramming was used to categorize the elements into themes that were present in all of the designs.

5.3 Analysis

5.3.1 Content Themes Presented in Design Components

Functionally speaking, the components could be categorized into three groups, with many components providing functionality from multiple categories. In support of our hypothesis, each of the functional categories in fact did assist in the performance of one sub-task depicted in Study 1's task taxonomy (Figure 1): (1) Elements showing useful shared and unshared information about EPK ("the what"), (2) Elements assessing communication acts ("the how"), and (3) Tools for differential interpretation.

5.3.2 Showing Useful Shared & Unshared Information about EPK

Some components in this category presented important qualitative data such as management outlook, past and current guidance, and the organization's performed strategic and corporate actions, in a bullet list to make them easier to access (D1, D3).

Other features augmented disclosed information with additional data to enhance their interpretability (D1, D3). A Cashflow Overview feature visualized components of key performance figures such as cashflow (D3). The visualization showed a graph of the historic and forecasted values of key figures and their components, allowing the user to rapidly uncover the causes of change.[2]

This feature also facilitated the rapid comparison of quantifiable outcomes across companies, which are often calculated differently within or between industries. Although much of the information presented in D3's tools exists in products such as Bloomberg Terminal, they could not all be accessed simultaneously, forcing IMPs to often collect the information into a spreadsheet for analysis.

Another component in this category provided additional detail about the company's productions facilities, enabling the user to better interpret the consequences of production stoppages on the company's future profitability (D1). The component visualized different production facilities on a zoomable map, annotating each facility with its production capacity as well as production costs per unit, and highlighting the facilities that were affected by a production stoppage (F1a in Figure 4). D1's design allows users to rapidly assess the extent to which the company's profits would be affected. Although information about production stoppages also exists in products such as Bloomberg Terminal, it is typically dispersed amongst multiple text documents. Extraction techniques are required to populate such visualizations, which are now becoming possible given machine comprehension's success under similar scenarios (Wang et al., 2017a,b) (F1b).

Yet another designed component, named "Sensitivity Analysis" (see Appendix, Figure 2), augmented the organization's guidance about future outcomes (D1). Each predicted outcome (e.g., revenue), is based on assumptions made by the company (e.g. oil prices, exchange rates), which may not be reasonable from the reader's perspective. To alleviate this, the "Sensitivity Analysis" tool extrapolates the provided guidance to a range of alternative values, enabling readers to inspect the sensitivity of guidance to the company's key assumptions (F2a).

Sensitivity analysis is currently performed manually by junior analysts on Wall Street (D1). To automate this, one needs to build a model of the company's outcomes (e.g., revenues) as a function of one or more assumed variables (e.g. oil prices, exchange rates). Such models are currently built using spreadsheets. As participants in both studies have indicated, the information needed to build these models can be found verbatim in earnings call transcripts as well as the company's filings. This is also true of the map widget discussed above. What is missing in current tools is the effective visualization designed by D1, which requires the use of machine comprehension techniques (F2b) to be fully automated. All four of the participants stressed time pressure as the motivation for automation, but not accuracy of the resulting computations, nor recall rates of important information from source material.

5.3.3 Elements Assessing Communication

Visualizing sentiment in transcripts was envisioned as one of the tools for assessing communication (D1, D5). D1 designed widgets to visualize the sentiment score of the transcripts along with the distribution of sentiment scores from the company's previous communications using a box chart (F3a). The widgets also facilitated the comparison of sentiment information across companies in the same industry (see Appendix, Figure 3). Moreover, the widget allowed users to track the evolution of sentiment over time using a popup line chart (F3a), allowing them to account for "sentiment inflation" in companies exhibiting the common habit of finding the "silver lining in the cloud" (D1). The IMP can use the widget to determine whether the studied company beats its competitors or peers in positive sentiment. Interestingly, D1's sentiment visualization included two copies of the described widget, one representing sentiment in the prepared remarks and another for the Q&A content.

The central feature of D4's prototype compared expressed sentiment across time on a hawkish-

[2]*"this quarter EBITDA went down, why was it? was it because your revenue went down... was management taking out some money um what was it..."* (D3).

dovish scale (F3a). Depending on the value of sentiment, the system would also recommend a set of trades to the end user. D4's prototype contained four tables: a table containing hawkish terms in the transcript along with their frequencies, a table containing dovish terms along with their frequencies, as well as two similar tables representing frequencies in only the most recent transcript (F3a). The component showing the change in sentiment on a scale would be used most often, with the term tables being used only when an explanation was needed about how the system arrived at the computed sentiment. This would work naturally for current sentiment analysis algorithms, which assign sentiment based on frequencies of sentiment-bearing words (e.g., Pennebaker et al., 2007). Since IMPs often access sentiment to appraise short-term investment opportunities, successful sentiment analysis technology used in automatic trading algorithms (e.g., Bollen et al., 2011; Kazemian et al., 2016; Zhang and Skiena, 2010) is an excellent candidate to provide the accurate sentiment scores needed to populate these widgets (F3b).

Participants also designed tools to support mining information from the Q&A sections. D3's design allowed for more rapid access to Q&A content by initially hiding the answers in order to quickly scan all the questions at once before choosing which answer(s) to view. D1's designs aimed to characterize how speakers responded to questions, by measuring: the amount of time taken by speakers before formulating a response,[3] the average length of answers relative to with the company's peers,[4] and the percentage of responses that resulted in the disclosure of specific facts or quantifiable information.[5] Companies that have direct and quantifiable responses are viewed by the market as more certain investment opportunities (D1). The goal of these widgets, using similar visualizations to D1's sentiment widgets (F4a), is to convert qualitatively expressed metadata about a speaker's communication tactics into a quantitative score depicting the investment attractiveness of the company.

Although D3's design does not require the use of NLP, D1's three widgets do. For these widgets, using established tools such as speaker segmentation (Budnik et al., 2016) and speech alignment (Goldman, 2011), each transcript portion can be aligned with its underlying audio signal, and to also calculate average duration of responses. Disfluency detection (Liu et al., 2006) can help find the time taken by disfluencies before a coherent response is produced. Thus, current NLP technology can be used to populate D1's first two widgets (F4b). However, to the best of our knowledge, state-of-the-art NLP tools such as answer selection (Rao et al., 2016) or fact extraction (Pasca et al., 2006) have not yet been evaluated in scenarios similar to the third widget.

An important observation can be made about the tools designed so far. With the aid of visualization and NLP techniques, these tools extract information from examined transcripts, augment it with information from other sources, and present it to users visually. All users noted the time savings accrued in comparison to manually reading and producing similar visualizations with current software. No user noted that such tools may also help them because they are more accurate or methodical in their detection of implicit information such as sentiment or communication tactics into the analysis. Participants, when questioned, saw no particular advantage to cognitively offloading to a computer the interpretative or analytic activity that followed upon the information gathering sub-tasks because: 1) they themselves were highly effective at doing it, whereas 2) a computer might make mistakes.

Although all users enlisted the aid of NLP to populate their visualizations, in one case, the use of NLP even here was doubted. D2 reluctantly considered automatic highlighting to mark a transcript's salient parts, but indicated that this amounts to the system thinking on her behalf. There are areas of NLP such as summarization and information extraction that could indeed be used to highlight text, but this falls within the purview of interpretation, whereas parsing complex syntactic constructions in free-flowing text to identify objective quantities was considered more reliable. D2 remarked that she was only willing to use automated highlighting when extreme time pressure prevented her from reading the entire transcript. Observations such as this suggest that IMPs do not embrace NLP when it removes their own decision-making agency.

[3]"*did the candidate... dilly-dally a lot or was he very forthcoming ... [with] answers*"

[4]"*what was the average length ... usually they give longer answers when they don't have an answer*"

[5]"*what percentage of the time was he BS-ing and what percentage of the time was he giving a clear direct answer*"

This, together with the prior important observation, highlights a key theme running through all the features Fi mentioned: our participants view such designs and the possible underlying NLP technology simply as time-saving tools, and not tools that may enhance discovery or interpretation. This suggests the need to preserve decision making agency when using software that provides assistance during information-seeking tasks - software that must be transparent in the use of the NLP tools.

5.3.4 Tools for Differential Interpretation

Most tools designed by participants compared actions and outcomes to those of the past, to those of the institutions' peers, and to published projections. Although the described comparisons are not supported for natural language data in current analysis software, comparing curated, quantitative data to historic values or projections is well-supported in current products such as Bloomberg Terminal or FactSet.

Similarly, many components in the sketched prototypes included easy-to-access links to related research reports that complement users' analysis of market perception and anticipate market reaction to transcript content. Again, links to research reports are available in software such as Bloomberg Terminal and FactSet, but are not integrated with tools for the qualitative analysis of transcripts.

6 Conclusion: HCI-NLP Co-Design

Our studies have revealed many information practices of IMPs. Several are not well supported by existing software marketed to IMPs, partly due to the complexity of the processes that IMPs typically carry out (Figure 3). Our studies suggest that IMPs need more and more detailed visualizations than what currently exists in their software. They also suggest that NLP technology will be most enthusiastically received when it is bundled with visualization techniques as an extraction mechanism that populates visualizations in such a way that preserves the IMPs' sense of agency over decision making proper.

An extensive taxonomy (see Appendix, Figure 4) synthesizes our findings, capturing the requisite high-level information practices, the software functionality that would serve the typical cases envisioned by analysts, the available NLP tools to support this, and the common UI elements in which these tools can be encapsulated (as drawn or described by the PD workshop participants). Note that the "desired" functionality here consists mainly of very close variants of problems that have already received considerable attention from the NLP community, such as aspect-based sentiment analysis, but recast as more vertical tasks that IMPs will assign value to. Without that domain-specific context, the more abstract tasks that NLP researchers generally ascribe to their own work are more likely to be construed by IMPs as a combination of trite and insufficiently nuanced, because their own vocational expertise is more highly prized by them than the general cognitive mechanisms that the AI community focus on in popular representations of their accomplishments.

Finally, this investigation has shown the importance of conducting user studies to assess the usefulness of technology (in this case, for supporting ISPs) alongside the development of the technology. Blindly pursuing a "deep-learning" crusade for general intelligence is unlikely to result in widespread adoption of black boxes, even at the level of speech recognition and sentiment analysis, by IMPs. To some extent, this is a Catch-22. Their current software does not incorporate advanced NLP, and so IMPs are unaware of its potential specific to their needs, and thus they are resigned to reserving agency over even the minutest of their decision-making tasks, which software vendors capitulate to in the design of their products. For their real potential to be embraced by IMPs, NLP tools need to be embedded in designs and visualizations in a manner that emphasizes superior extractive accuracy and generative quality over the time value of using the tools, while maintaining a sense of ISP agency.

References

B.S. Bernanke and K.N. Kuttner. 2005. What explains the stock market's reaction to Federal Reserve policy? *Journal of Finance*, 60(3):1221–1257.

E. Bertini and D. Lalanne. 2007. Total recall survey report. Technical report, University of Fribourg, Department of Computer Science.

H. Beyer and K. Holtzblatt. 1999. Contextual design. *Interactions*, 6(1):32–42.

J. Bollen, H. Mao, and X. Zeng. 2011. Twitter mood predicts the stock market. *Journal of Computational Science*, 2(1):1–8.

M.J. Bouwman, P. Frishkoff, and P.A. Frishkoff. 1995. The relevance of gaap-based information: a case study exploring some uses and limitations. *Accounting Horizons*, 9(4):22.

V. Braun and V. Clarke. 2006. Using thematic analysis in psychology. *Qualitative Research in Psychology*, 3(2):77–101.

M. Budnik, L. Besacier, A. Khodabakhsh, and C. Demiroglu. 2016. Deep complementary features for speaker identification in tv broadcast data. In *Proceedings of ODYSSEY*, pages 146–151.

E. Cambria, B. Schuller, Y. Xia, and C. Havasi. 2013. New avenues in opinion mining and sentiment analysis. *IEEE Intelligent Systems*, 28(2):15–21.

M. Flood, H.V. Jagadish, and L. Raschid. 2016. Big data challenges and opportunities in financial stability monitoring. *Financial Stability Review*, 20:129–142.

J.-P. Goldman. 2011. Easyalign: an automatic phonetic alignment tool under praat. In *Proceedings of INTERSPEECH*, pages 3233–3236.

A. Jaimes, K. Omura, T. Nagamine, and K. Hirata. 2004. Memory cues for meeting video retrieval. In *Proceedings of the the 1st ACM workshop on Continuous archival and retrieval of personal experiences*, pages 74–85.

S.K. Jauhar, P.D. Turney, and E. Hovy. 2016. Tables as semi-structured knowledge for question answering. In *Proceedings of ACL*, pages 474–483.

S. Kazemian, S. Zhao, and G. Penn. 2016. Evaluating sentiment analysis in the context of securities trading. In *Proceedings of ACL*, pages 2094–2103.

D. Lalanne and A. Popescu-Belis. 2012. *User requirements for meeting support technology*. Cambridge University Press.

Y. Liu, E. Shriberg, A. Stolcke, D. Hillard, M. Ostendorf, and M. Harper. 2006. Enriching speech recognition with automatic detection of sentence boundaries and disfluencies. *IEEE Transactions on Audio, Speech, and Language Processing*, 14(5):1526–1540.

G. Marchionini. 1995. *Information Seeking In Electronic Environments*. Cambridge University Press.

A. McCallum, D. Freitag, and F.C.N. Pereira. 2000. Maximum entropy markov models for information extraction and segmentation. In *Proceedings of ICML*, pages 591–598.

C. Milanesi. 2016. Voice assistant anyone? yes please, but not in public! Technical report, Creative Strategies, Inc.

A. Nenkova and R.J. Passonneau. 2004. Evaluating content selection in summarization: The pyramid method. In *Proceedings of HLT-NAACL*, pages 145–152.

M. Pasca, D. Lin, J. Bigham, A. Lifchits, and A. Jain. 2006. Organizing and searching the World Wide Web of facts-step one: the one-million fact extraction challenge. In *Proceedings of AAAI*, pages 1400–1405.

J.W. Pennebaker, C.K. Chung, M. Ireland, A. Gonzales, and R.J. Booth. 2007. *The development and psychometric properties of LIWC2007*. UT Austin.

P. Rajpurkar, R. Jia, and P. Liang. 2018. Know what you don't know: Unanswerable questions for SQuAD. In *Proceedings of ACL*, pages 784–789.

P. Rajpurkar, J. Zhang, K. Lopyrev, and P. Liang. 2016. Squad: 100,000+ questions for machine comprehension of text. In *Proceedings of EMNLP*, pages 2383–2392.

S. Ramnath, S. Rock, and P. Shane. 2008. The imp forecasting literature: A taxonomy with suggestions for further research. *International Journal of Forecasting*, 24(1):34–75.

J. Rao, H. He, and J. Lin. 2016. Noise-contrastive estimation for answer selection with deep neural networks. In *Proceedings of ACM CIKM*, pages 1913–1916.

S. Rosenthal, N. Farra, and P. Nakov. 2017. Semeval-2017 task 4: Sentiment analysis in twitter. In *Proceedings of SemEval*, pages 502–518.

D. Schuler and A. Namioka. 1993. *Participatory design: Principles and practices*. CRC Press.

R. Socher, A. Perelygin, J.Y. Wu, J. Chuang, C.D. Manning, A.Y. Ng, and C. Potts. 2013. Recursive deep models for semantic compositionality over a sentiment treebank. In *Proceedings of EMNLP*, pages 1631–1642.

E.G. Toms, L. Freund, R. Kopak, and J.C. Bartlett. 2003. The effect of task domain on search. In *Proceedings of CASCON*, pages 303–312.

P. Vakkari. 2003. Task-based information searching. *Annual Review of Information Science and Technology*, 37(1):413–464.

M. Wang, N.A. Smith, and T. Mitamura. 2007. What is the jeopardy model? a quasi-synchronous grammar for qa. In *Proceedings of EMNLP/CoNLL*, pages 22–32.

T. Wang, X. Yuan, and A. Trischler. 2017a. A joint model for question answering and question generation. In *ICML Workshop on Learning to Generate Natural Language*, page 7 pages.

W. Wang, N. Yang, F. Wei, B. Chang, and M. Zhou. 2017b. Gated self-matching networks for reading comprehension and question answering. In *Proceedings of ACL*, pages 189–198.

S. Whittaker, J. Hirschberg, B. Amento, L. Stark, M. Bacchiani, P. Isenhour, L. Stead, G. Zamchick, and A. Rosenberg. 2002. Scanmail: a voicemail interface that makes speech browsable, readable and searchable. In *Proceedings of CHI*, pages 275–282.

S. Whittaker, J. Hirschberg, and C.H. Nakatani. 1998. All talk and all action: strategies for managing voicemail messages. In *CHI-98 Conference Summary*, pages 249–250.

S. Whittaker, S. Tucker, K. Swampillai, and R. Laban. 2008. Design and evaluation of systems to support interaction capture and retrieval. *Personal Ubiquitous Computing*, 12(3):197–221.

W. Zhang and S. Skiena. 2010. Trading strategies to exploit blog and news sentiment. *Proceedings of the International AAAI Conference on Weblogs and Social Media*, 4(1):375–378.

Appendix: Design Artefacts

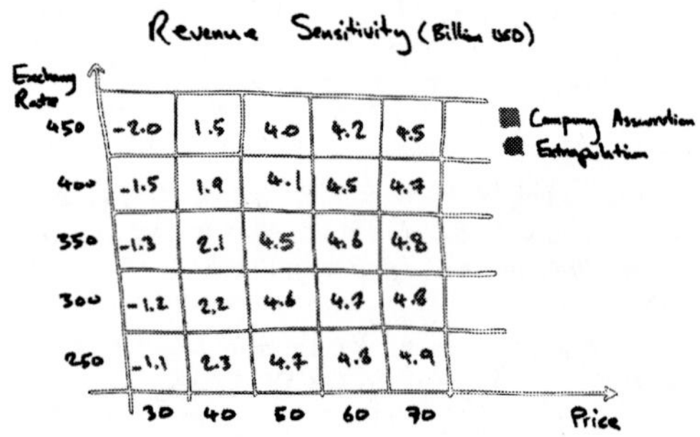

Figure 2: Sensitivity Analysis extrapolating the value of a company's important outcomes (e.g., revenue) under different assumptions about key performance factors.

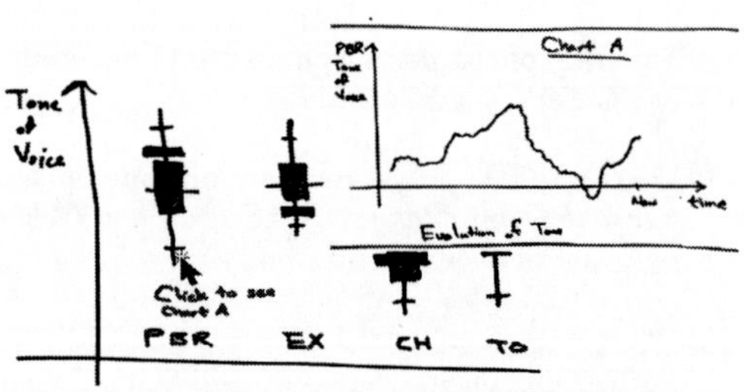

Figure 3: Components comparing the document's sentiment with the company's previous communication (using box chart and line graph), and with competitors' communications.

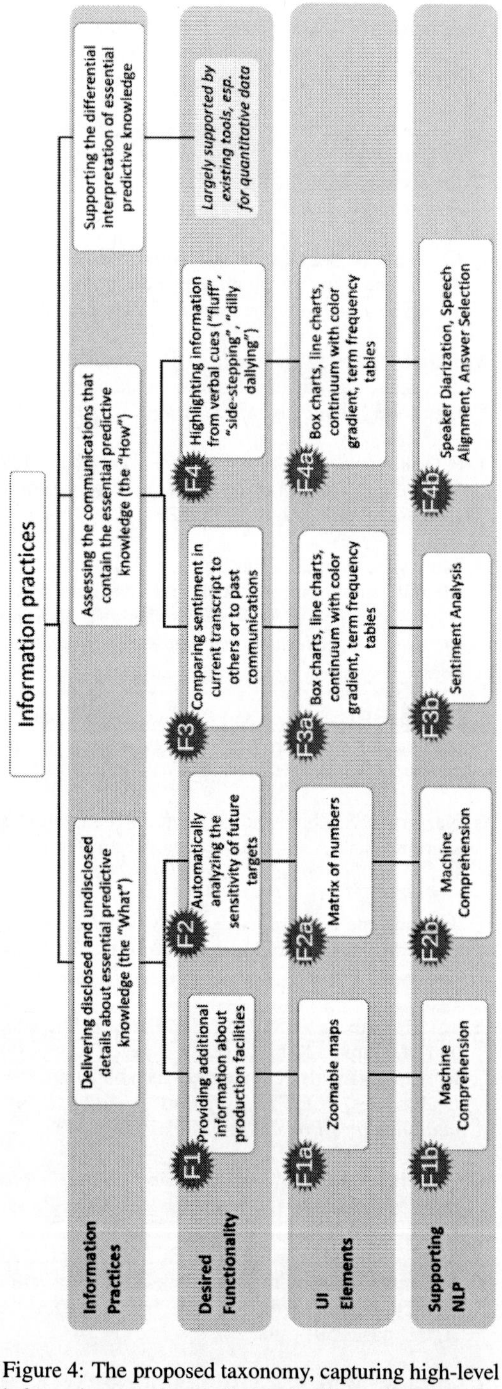

Figure 4: The proposed taxonomy, capturing high-level information practices and related software functionality, along with available NLP technology and common UI elements that can implement the functionality to support information practices.

Overview of the FinNLP-2022 ERAI Task: Evaluating the Rationales of Amateur Investors

Chung-Chi Chen,[1] Hen-Hsen Huang,[2] Hiroya Takamura,[1] Hsin-Hsi Chen[3]
[1] AIST, Japan
[2] Institute of Information Science, Academia Sinica, Taiwan
[3] Department of Computer Science and Information Engineering
National Taiwan University, Taiwan
c.c.chen@acm.org, hhhuang@iis.sinica.edu.tw,
takamura.hiroya@aist.go.jp, hhchen@ntu.edu.tw

Abstract

This paper provides an overview of the shared task, Evaluating the Rationales of Amateur Investors (ERAI), in FinNLP-2022 at EMNLP-2022. This shared task aims to sort out investment opinions that would lead to higher profit from social platforms. We obtained 19 registered teams; 9 teams submitted their results for final evaluation, and 8 teams submitted papers to share their methods. The discussed directions are various: prompting, fine-tuning, translation system comparison, and tailor-made neural network architectures. We provide details of the task settings, data statistics, participants' results, and fine-grained analysis.

1 Introduction

In the financial market, people have different reasons to make trading/investment decisions. Thanks to the development of social media platforms, people can share these reasons and discuss them with others rapidly. However, there are hundreds of thousands of posts on social media platforms every day. Selecting the posts (opinions) that have the potential to help investors make profitable investment decisions becomes a challenge. Inspired by the ideas of persuasive essay scoring (Ghosh et al., 2016) and argument quality assessment (Skitalinskaya et al., 2021; Hasan et al., 2021), we proposed a new task: evaluating investment opinions based on the rationales in the post (Chen et al., 2021).

There are some steps when reading and evaluating investment opinions. First, as in most sentiment analysis studies (Chen et al., 2020; Xing et al., 2020), investors need to identify the sentiment of the opinion (bullish/bearish/neutral). Second, investors will read the reasons that are provided to support the sentiment. Third, investors will evaluate whether these reasons are rational, and further decide whether to follow the suggestions in the opinion. When we attempt to select useful investment opinions automatically, we think that systems also need to follow the above steps. However, in many cases, it is hard to decide the ground truth for the opinion quality because it is somehow subjective and varies due to the viewpoints. In the debate scenario, we can use the voting records as a proxy for evaluation. In the financial market, we can use historical information as a proxy to assess forecasting skills (Zong et al., 2020). Therefore, we propose to use maximum possible profit (MPP) and maximum loss (ML) as evaluation metrics to measure the quality of investment opinions (Chen et al., 2021).

In this shared task, we propose two kinds of settings, pairwise comparison and unsupervised ranking. The findings under these settings not only can be used in investment recommendations in the future, but also can be used in evaluating the generated reports and investor education. Additionally, we also expect that we can improve models' performances in market information forecasting tasks by sorting out high-quality opinions and filtering out low-quality opinions in the first step when selecting input data. Participants explore various directions for solving these challenges. There are several interesting discussions for a better understanding of where we are in the financial opinion scoring. We summarize the details of their methods in Section 3.

2 Tasks and Datasets

2.1 Task Setting

In ERAI shared task, we use MPP and ML to label opinions. Below are the definitions of MPP and ML in our previous work (Chen et al., 2021):

$$MPP_{bullish} = (\max(H_{(t+1,T)}) - O_{t+1})/O_{t+1} \quad (1)$$

$$ML_{bullish} = (\min(L_{(t+1,T)}) - O_{t+1})/O_{t+1} \quad (2)$$

Proceedings of the Fourth Workshop on Financial Technology and Natural Language Processing (FinNLP), pages 99 - 103
December 8, 2022 ©2022 Association for Computational Linguistics

Team	Language Model	Method & Features & Lexicon
PromptShots (Wiriyathammabhum, 2022)	T5-Small (Raffel et al., 2020) Instruct-GPT (Ouyang et al., 2022) text-davinci-002 FinBERT-tone (Yang et al., 2020)	Part of Speech FinProLex (Chen et al., 2021) NTUSD-Fin (Chen et al., 2018) Bayesian lexicons (Eisenstein, 2017) Loughran-McDonald lexicon (Loughran and McDonald, 2011)
LIPI (Ghosh and Naskar, 2022)	sbert-chinese-qmc-finance[1] FinBERT (Araci, 2019)	Linear regression MLP
DCU_ML (Lyu et al., 2022)	BERT-Chinese (Devlin et al., 2019)	BERT-Senti (Proposed)
UOA (Zou et al., 2022b)	Bert-Base-Chinese (Devlin et al., 2019) RoBERTa-wwm-ext (Cui et al., 2021)	Astock (Zou et al., 2022a)
aiML (Qin et al., 2022)	FinBERT-tone (Yang et al., 2020)	Sec-Bert-Shape (Loukas et al., 2022) Astock (Zou et al., 2022a)
Yet (Zhuang and Ren, 2022)	FinBERT-Chinese [2] Mengzi-Fin (Zhang et al., 2021) RoBERTa-large-pair (Xu et al., 2020) RoBERTa-wwm (Cui et al., 2021)	Stochastic Weight Averaging MADGRAD Optimizer multi-sample dropout Modified-RoBERTa-wwm (Proposed)
UCCNLP (Trust et al., 2022)	SBERT (Reimers and Gurevych, 2019)	DPP-VAE (Proposed)
Jetsons (Gon et al., 2022)	Chinese-BERT (Devlin et al., 2019) xlm-roberta-large (Conneau et al., 2020)	Part of Speech

Table 1: Methods

$$MPP_{bearish} = (O_{t+1} - \min(L_{(t+1,T)}))/O_{t+1} \tag{3}$$

$$ML_{bearish} = (O_{t+1} - \max(H_{(t+1,T)}))/O_{t+1}, \tag{4}$$

where O_t and $H_{(t,T)}$ denote the opening price of day t and a list of the highest prices of day t to day T, respectively, and $L_{(t,T)}$ denotes a list of the lowest prices of day t to day T.

Based on the above labels, there are two task settings in ERAI shared task:

1. **Pairwise Comparison**: In the pairwise setting, there are two given opinions with MPP and ML labels. Models are asked to determine (i) whether the given opinion 1 will lead to higher MPP than the given opinion 2 and (ii) whether the given opinion 1 will lead to more loss than the given opinion 2. Thus, both would be binary classification tasks. We will use accuracy to evaluate the performances.

2. **Unsupervised Ranking**: In the unsupervised ranking setting, a pool of investors' opinions will be given, and the participants need to rank them with unsupervised methods. The goal is to find out the top 10% of posts that will lead to higher MPP. We will use the average MPP of the selected posts as the evaluation metrics.

2.2 Dataset Construction and Statistics

The dataset for the pairwise comparison setting is collected from Mobile01.[3] We manually checked the sentiment (bullish/bearish) in each opinion, and calculated MPP and ML based on the above equations. We labeled 574 posts (287 pairs), and further used 200 pairs as the training set and 87 pairs as the test set. The dataset for the unsupervised ranking setting is collected from PTT.[4] We also checked the sentiment (bullish/bearish) in each opinion manually and further obtained the MPP and ML labels. It is worth noting that, there are some posts that do not provide investment suggestions, but also follow the same template and are posted on the same platform as those that contain suggestions. We remain these posts in the pool to keep the dataset close to the real-world scenario. Thus, the posts that do not contain investment suggestions will get "nan" when annotating MPP and ML. Finally, a total of 210 posts are left in this set.

The original data for both tasks are written in Chinese. We use Google Translate API to prepare the English version. Participants can explore these tasks with the original data, translated data, or both.

3 Participants' Methods

Table 1 summarizes the methods used in this shared task. Both generation and classification language models are explored. Different kinds of domain-specific language models are also probed. Several lexicons are used for enhancing the performances, and some state-of-the-art architectures are used in the experiments. Tailor-made architectures and methods are also proposed by some teams.

[3] https://www.mobile01.com/

[4] https://www.ptt.cc/bbs/Stock/index.html

Team	MPP	Team	ML
Jetsons_1	62.07%	DCU-ML_1	59.77%
Yet_1	57.47%	DCU-ML_3	59.77%
Yet_2	57.47%	PromptShots_2	54.02%
Yet_3	57.47%	uoa_1	54.02%
LIPI_2	57.47%	aimi_1	52.87%
LIPI_1	54.02%	LIPI_2	50.57%
fiona	54.02%	fiona	48.28%
DCU-ML_1	52.87%	LIPI_3	48.28%
DCU-ML_3	52.87%	DCU-ML_2	45.98%
uoa_1	51.72%	PromptShots_1	45.98%
DCU-ML_2	51.72%	LIPI_1	44.83%
Jetsons_3	49.43%	Jetsons_2	41.38%
aimi_1	48.28%	PromptShots_3	41.38%
PromptShots_2	48.28%	Yet_1	40.23%
Jetsons_2	47.13%	Yet_2	40.23%
PromptShots_3	47.13%	Yet_3	40.23%
PromptShots_1	47.13%	Jetsons_1	37.93%
LIPI_3	44.83%	Jetsons_3	36.78%

Table 2: Pairwise Results (Accuracy).

Wiriyathammabhum (2022) prompt models for answering the instances in pair-wise setting, and aggregate lexicons' scores for unsupervised setting. Ghosh and Naskar (2022) ensemble the output of five models for both subtasks. Lyu et al. (2022) propose BERT-Senti, which is based on the notion that posts with more positive (negative) sentiment would lead to higher (lower) MPP. Both Zou et al. (2022b) and Qin et al. (2022) show that the method, AStock, talior-made for stock movement prediction cannot outperform vanilla pretrained language models in pairwise dataset. However, in unsupervised dataset, AStock outperforms vanilla pretrained language models. Zhuang and Ren (2022) explore different techniques such as the strategies of optimizer and drop out. Trust et al. (2022) propose DPP-VAE, and take the diversity and representation of the given opinion into consideration. Gon et al. (2022) provide a comparison of using various cross-lingual combination in training and testing.

4 Participants' Results

Table 2 and Table 3 show the results of participants' methods. It is worth noting that general language models perform better than domain-specific language models. For example, BERT-Chinese performs the best (Jetsons_1) in MPP comparison task, and Modified-RoBERTa-wwm (Yet_1,2,3) also performs well. However, both of them perform worse in ML comparison task. Additionally, positive/negative sentiment seems more related to ML instead of MPP (DCU-ML_1). In the unsupervised setting, sentiment lexicons still play important roles (PromptShots_1,2,3). Most supervised results with the model trained with pair-wise setting dataset cannot outperform lexicon-based method and the baseline (Chen et al., 2021), which count the expert-like sentences in the post. On the other hand, the ML results in unsupervised setting imply that expert-like sentences matters in sorting out the opinions containing lower risk.

Team	Top 10% MPP	Team	Top 10% ML
PromptShots_2	24.39%	Baseline (Chen et al., 2021)	-2.46%
PromptShots_3	23.76%	Yet_3	-3.24%
PromptShots_1	22.53%	LIPI_1	-4.11%
LIPI_2	18.27%	aimi_1	-4.17%
Baseline (Chen et al., 2021)	17.61%	Yet_1	-4.35%
LIPI_1	17.46%	LIPI_3	-5.56%
UCCNLP_3	14.81%	Yet_2	-5.77%
Yet_3	14.61%	UCCNLP_3	-5.85%
aimi_1	14.02%	UCCNLP_1	-6.22%
DCU-ML_1	13.97%	UCCNLP_2	-6.77%
UoA_1	12.35%	PromptShots_1	-7.80%
Yet_2	12.10%	LIPI_2	-7.81%
LIPI_3	11.83%	DCU-ML_1	-8.25%
UCCNLP_2	11.34%	UoA_1	-9.39%
UCCNLP_1	11.10%	PromptShots_3	-12.33%
Yet_1	8.52%	PromptShots_2	-13.04%

Table 3: Unsupervised Results.

5 Future Directions

We want to highlight that before we try to sort opinions, we may need to first filter out those posts that do not contain trading ideas. For example, there are 57 of these kinds of posts in the unsupervised set. These posts follow the same format but may just ask questions. There are two reasons why we need to remove such posts. Firstly, in most cases, the models' input length is limited. Under this limitation, ideally, we should only use those considered important. Secondly, since this kind of posts does not contain opinion, putting them into a model may lead to incorrect claims and increase the noise. Following this line of thought, one of the future directions is to filter out both irrelevant and low MPP posts in the preprocessing process. On the other hand, the proposed idea can also use in a recommendation system for investors. Instead of only suggesting the relevant opinions as previous work (Liou et al., 2021), we think that recommending high potential suggestions would be more preferred in the investment scenario.

6 Conclusion

This paper introduces the methods explored in the ERAI shared task, and summarizes the performances of these methods. We think this is a pilot exploration for evaluating the rationales of investors, and plan to dig into this direction more deeply in the future. The first step is exploring the role of argument in these tasks. We will present several datasets for extracting argument features from financial opinions, and we think that it will be useful in scoring investors' opinions. The enlarged dataset for evaluating investors' opinions will also be proposed. Please refer to the FinArg@NTCIR for more details.[5]

Acknowledgments

This paper is based on results obtained from a project JPNP20006, commissioned by the New Energy and Industrial Technology Development Organization (NEDO). This research was also partially supported by National Science and Technology Council, Taiwan, under grants MOST 110-2221-E-002-128-MY3 and MOST 110-2634-F-002-050-.

References

Dogu Araci. 2019. Finbert: Financial sentiment analysis with pre-trained language models. *arXiv preprint arXiv:1908.10063.*

Chung-Chi Chen, Hen-Hsen Huang, and Hsin-Hsi Chen. 2018. Ntusd-fin: a market sentiment dictionary for financial social media data applications. In *Proceedings of the 1st Financial Narrative Processing Workshop (FNP 2018)*, pages 37–43.

Chung-Chi Chen, Hen-Hsen Huang, and Hsin-Hsi Chen. 2020. Issues and perspectives from 10,000 annotated financial social media data. In *Proceedings of The 12th language resources and evaluation conference*, pages 6106–6110.

Chung-Chi Chen, Hen-Hsen Huang, and Hsin-Hsi Chen. 2021. Evaluating the rationales of amateur investors. In *Proceedings of the Web Conference 2021*, pages 3987–3998.

Alexis Conneau, Kartikay Khandelwal, Naman Goyal, Vishrav Chaudhary, Guillaume Wenzek, Francisco Guzmán, Edouard Grave, Myle Ott, Luke Zettlemoyer, and Veselin Stoyanov. 2020. Unsupervised cross-lingual representation learning at scale. In *Proceedings of the 58th Annual Meeting of the Association for Computational Linguistics*, pages 8440–8451, Online. Association for Computational Linguistics.

Yiming Cui, Wanxiang Che, Ting Liu, Bing Qin, and Ziqing Yang. 2021. Pre-training with whole word masking for chinese bert. *IEEE/ACM Transactions on Audio, Speech, and Language Processing*, 29:3504–3514.

[5]http://finarg.nlpfin.com/

Jacob Devlin, Ming-Wei Chang, Kenton Lee, and Kristina Toutanova. 2019. BERT: Pre-training of deep bidirectional transformers for language understanding. In *Proceedings of the 2019 Conference of the North American Chapter of the Association for Computational Linguistics: Human Language Technologies, Volume 1 (Long and Short Papers)*, pages 4171–4186, Minneapolis, Minnesota. Association for Computational Linguistics.

Jacob Eisenstein. 2017. Unsupervised learning for lexicon-based classification. In *Proceedings of the AAAI Conference on Artificial Intelligence*, volume 31.

Debanjan Ghosh, Aquila Khanam, Yubo Han, and Smaranda Muresan. 2016. Coarse-grained argumentation features for scoring persuasive essays. In *Proceedings of the 54th Annual Meeting of the Association for Computational Linguistics (Volume 2: Short Papers)*, pages 549–554, Berlin, Germany. Association for Computational Linguistics.

Sohom Ghosh and Kumar Sudip Naskar. 2022. Lipi at the FinNLP-2022 erai task: Ensembling sentence transformers for assessing maximum possible profit and loss from online financial posts. In *Proceedings of the Fourth Workshop on Financial Technology and Natural Language Processing*, Abu Dhabi, United Arab Emirates. Association for Computational Linguistics.

Alolika Gon, Sihan Zha, Sai Krishna Rallabandi, Parag Pravin Dakle, and Preethi Raghavan. 2022. Jetsons at the FinNLP-2022 erai task: Bert-chinese for mining high mpp posts. In *Proceedings of the Fourth Workshop on Financial Technology and Natural Language Processing*, Abu Dhabi, United Arab Emirates. Association for Computational Linguistics.

Md Kamrul Hasan, James Spann, Masum Hasan, Md Saiful Islam, Kurtis Haut, Rada Mihalcea, and Ehsan Hoque. 2021. Hitting your MARQ: Multimodal ARgument quality assessment in long debate video. In *Proceedings of the 2021 Conference on Empirical Methods in Natural Language Processing*, pages 6387–6397, Online and Punta Cana, Dominican Republic. Association for Computational Linguistics.

Yi-Ting Liou, Chung-Chi Chen, Tsun-Hsien Tang, Hen-Hsen Huang, and Hsin-Hsi Chen. 2021. Finsense: an assistant system for financial journalists and investors. In *Proceedings of the 14th ACM International Conference on Web Search and Data Mining*, pages 882–885.

Tim Loughran and Bill McDonald. 2011. When is a liability not a liability? textual analysis, dictionaries, and 10-ks. *The Journal of finance*, 66(1):35–65.

Lefteris Loukas, Manos Fergadiotis, Ilias Chalkidis, Eirini Spyropoulou, Prodromos Malakasiotis, Ion Androutsopoulos, and Georgios Paliouras. 2022. FiNER: Financial numeric entity recognition for

XBRL tagging. In *Proceedings of the 60th Annual Meeting of the Association for Computational Linguistics (Volume 1: Long Papers)*, pages 4419–4431, Dublin, Ireland. Association for Computational Linguistics.

Chenyang Lyu, Tianbo Ji, and Liting Zhou. 2022. Dcuml at the FinNLP-2022 erai task: Investigating the transferability of sentiment analysis data for evaluating rationales of investors. In *Proceedings of the Fourth Workshop on Financial Technology and Natural Language Processing*, Abu Dhabi, United Arab Emirates. Association for Computational Linguistics.

Long Ouyang, Jeff Wu, Xu Jiang, Diogo Almeida, Carroll L Wainwright, Pamela Mishkin, Chong Zhang, Sandhini Agarwal, Katarina Slama, Alex Ray, et al. 2022. Training language models to follow instructions with human feedback. *arXiv preprint arXiv:2203.02155*.

Zhaoxuan Qin, Jinan Zou, Qiaoyang Luo, Haiyao Cao, and Yang Jiao. 2022. aiML at the FinNLP-2022 erai task: Combining classification and regression tasks for financial opinion mining. In *Proceedings of the Fourth Workshop on Financial Technology and Natural Language Processing*, Abu Dhabi, United Arab Emirates. Association for Computational Linguistics.

Colin Raffel, Noam Shazeer, Adam Roberts, Katherine Lee, Sharan Narang, Michael Matena, Yanqi Zhou, Wei Li, Peter J Liu, et al. 2020. Exploring the limits of transfer learning with a unified text-to-text transformer. *J. Mach. Learn. Res.*, 21(140):1–67.

Nils Reimers and Iryna Gurevych. 2019. Sentence-BERT: Sentence embeddings using Siamese BERT-networks. In *Proceedings of the 2019 Conference on Empirical Methods in Natural Language Processing and the 9th International Joint Conference on Natural Language Processing (EMNLP-IJCNLP)*, pages 3982–3992, Hong Kong, China. Association for Computational Linguistics.

Gabriella Skitalinskaya, Jonas Klaff, and Henning Wachsmuth. 2021. Learning from revisions: Quality assessment of claims in argumentation at scale. In *Proceedings of the 16th Conference of the European Chapter of the Association for Computational Linguistics: Main Volume*, pages 1718–1729, Online. Association for Computational Linguistics.

Paul Trust, Rosane Minghim, Ahmed Zahran, and Evangelos Milos. 2022. Uccnlp at the FinNLP-2022 erai task: Determinantal point processes and variational auto-encoders for identifying high-quality opinions from a pool of social media posts. In *Proceedings of the Fourth Workshop on Financial Technology and Natural Language Processing*, Abu Dhabi, United Arab Emirates. Association for Computational Linguistics.

Peratham Wiriyathammabhum. 2022. Promptshots at FinNLP-2022 erai task: Pairwise comparison and unsupervised ranking. In *Proceedings of the Fourth Workshop on Financial Technology and Natural Language Processing*, Abu Dhabi, United Arab Emirates. Association for Computational Linguistics.

Frank Xing, Lorenzo Malandri, Yue Zhang, and Erik Cambria. 2020. Financial sentiment analysis: An investigation into common mistakes and silver bullets. In *Proceedings of the 28th International Conference on Computational Linguistics*, pages 978–987, Barcelona, Spain (Online). International Committee on Computational Linguistics.

Liang Xu, Xuanwei Zhang, and Qianqian Dong. 2020. Cluecorpus2020: A large-scale chinese corpus for pre-training language model. *arXiv preprint arXiv:2003.01355*.

Yi Yang, Mark Christopher Siy Uy, and Allen Huang. 2020. Finbert: A pretrained language model for financial communications. *arXiv preprint arXiv:2006.08097*.

Zhuosheng Zhang, Hanqing Zhang, Keming Chen, Yuhang Guo, Jingyun Hua, Yulong Wang, and Ming Zhou. 2021. Mengzi: Towards lightweight yet ingenious pre-trained models for chinese. *arXiv preprint arXiv:2110.06696*.

Yan Zhuang and Fuji Ren. 2022. Yet at the FinNLP-2022 erai task: Modified models for evaluating the rationales of amateur investors. In *Proceedings of the Fourth Workshop on Financial Technology and Natural Language Processing*, Abu Dhabi, United Arab Emirates. Association for Computational Linguistics.

Shi Zong, Alan Ritter, and Eduard Hovy. 2020. Measuring forecasting skill from text. In *Proceedings of the 58th Annual Meeting of the Association for Computational Linguistics*, pages 5317–5331, Online. Association for Computational Linguistics.

Jinan Zou, Haiyao Cao, Lingqiao Liu, Yuhao Lin, Ehsan Abbasnejad, and Javen Qinfeng Shi. 2022a. Astock: A new dataset and automated stock trading based on stock-specific news analyzing model. In *Proceedings of the Fourth Workshop on Financial Technology and Natural Language Processing*.

Jinan Zou, Haiyao Cao, Yanxi Liu, Lingqiao Liu, Ehsan Abbasnejad, and Javen Qinfeng Shi. 2022b. Uoa at the FinNLP-2022 erai task: Leveraging the label information for financial opinion mining. In *Proceedings of the Fourth Workshop on Financial Technology and Natural Language Processing*, Abu Dhabi, United Arab Emirates. Association for Computational Linguistics.

PromptShots at the FinNLP-2022 ERAI Tasks: Pairwise Comparison and Unsupervised Ranking

Peratham Wiriyathammabhum
peratham.bkk@gmail.com

Abstract

This report describes our PromptShots submissions to a shared task on Evaluating the Rationales of Amateur Investors (ERAI). We participated in both pairwise comparison and unsupervised ranking tasks. For pairwise comparison, we employed instruction-based models based on T5-small and OpenAI InstructGPT language models. Surprisingly, we observed OpenAI InstructGPT language model few-shot trained on Chinese data works best in our submissions, ranking 3rd on the maximal loss (ML) pairwise accuracy. This model works better than training on the Google translated English data by a large margin, where the English few-shot trained InstructGPT model even performs worse than an instruction-based T5-small model finetuned on the English data. However, all instruction-based submissions do not perform well on the maximal potential profit (MPP) pairwise accuracy where there are more data and learning signals. The Chinese few-shot trained InstructGPT model still performs best in our setting. For unsupervised ranking, we utilized many language models, including many financial-specific ones, and Bayesian lexicons unsupervised-learned on both Chinese and English words using a method-of-moments estimator. All our submissions rank best in the MPP ranking, from 1st to 3rd. However, they all do not perform well for ML scoring. Therefore, both MPP and ML scores need different treatments since we treated MPP and ML using the same formula. Our only difference is the treatment of market sentiment lexicons.

1 Introduction

Evaluating the rationals of amateur investors (ERAI) (Chen et al., 2021a,b) is a shared task on evaluating social media opinions on the topic of investments and whether they are going to be useful or not. Mining high-quality opinions by inspecting their supporting rationales might utilize the wisdom of the crowd on social media. Previous work (Chen et al., 2021a) proposes stylistic and semantic features to filter out noisy crowd opinions which may not be high-quality and profitable. There are two settings in this ERAI shared task, pairwise comparison and unsupervised ranking. These settings sort out the opinions based on two metrics, higher maximal potential profit (MPP) and lower maximal loss (ML). In pairwise comparison, two posts are given with a binary label whether the MPP and ML of the first post are more or less than the second post. In unsupervised ranking, the goal is to filter and keep the top 10% posts based on MPP and ML given a set of unranked posts.

For pairwise comparison, our best submission ranks 3rd on the maximal loss (ML) pairwise accuracy on the leaderboard[1]. For unsupervised ranking, our best submission ranks 1st on the maximal potential profit (MPP) ranking. The codes for our systems are open-sourced and available at our GitHub repository[2].

2 Models

2.1 Pairwise Comparison

For pairwise comparison, we utilized instruction-based models based on T5-small (Raffel et al., 2020) and OpenAI InstructGPT language models (Ouyang et al., 2022) in a few-shot prompt-based setting (Brown et al., 2020b).

2.1.1 T5

T5 is an encoder-decoder language model which was trained by treating every text processing problem as a "text-to-text" problem to unify NLP tasks using only a single model, loss function, hyperparameter set, etc. The input texts will be encoded and the T5 decoder will decode them. Specifically, T5 was unsupervised-pretrained by denois-

[1] https://sites.google.com/nlg.csie.ntu.edu.tw/finnlp-2022-emnlp/erai-shared-task

[2] https://github.com/perathambkk/finnlp_erai_shared_task_emnlp2022

Proceedings of the Fourth Workshop on Financial Technology and Natural Language Processing (FinNLP), pages 104 - 110
December 8, 2022 ©2022 Association for Computational Linguistics

ing masked inputs on the "Colossal Clean Crawled Corpus" (C4) dataset, Common Crawled from web scraping. Then, T5 can be further supervised fine-tuned using the "text-to-text" format and T5's decoder will be in the teacher forcing mode where the decoder will be trained using input and a right-shifted target sequence. T5 architecture is pretty much the same as the vanilla transformer (Vaswani et al., 2017) except removing the LayerNorm bias term, placing the LayerNorm outside the residual path, and using a relative position embedding (Shaw et al., 2018).

In the T5 paper, the authors state that T5 can be specified which task it should perform by adding a task-specific textual prefix to the original input sequence before feeding into the model. Therefore, we take T5-small as an instruction-based model using the input prompt template, 'post1 : %s post2 : %s </s>', where the %s contains texts from the corresponding post, and the output prompt, 'maximal potential profit (MPP) : %s maximal loss (ML) : %s </s>', where the %s contains the MPP and the ML corresponding labels accordingly. This is similar to the baseline system in the FLUTE figurative language understanding dataset paper (Chakrabarty et al., 2022), however, in our case, the T5-small is expected to jointly predict both MPP and ML in one forward pass of preparing the probability tensor. We use top-p sampling for text generation (Holtzman et al., 2019).

2.1.2 OpenAI's InstructGPT

The OpenAI API has many variants of InstructGPT language models based on the GPT-3 autoregressive language model to conveniently perform various NLP tasks with the prompt library. The InstructGPT was trained with a human-in-the-loop style and is claimed to be better at following instructions, more truthful, and less toxic than the GPT-3. In this shared task, we engineered the prompts for InstructGPT using a few-shot learning setting, as in the GPT-3 paper (Brown et al., 2020a), where few data instances were given from the target task/domain. Each data instance will become a prompt as 'post1 : d['post1'] post2: d['post2'] > maximal potential profit (MPP)| %s# maximal loss (ML)| %s.', where d['post1'] and d['post2'] are texts from the corresponding post. Then, we append the query we want to predict MPP and ML as just a truncated template, 'post1 : d['post1'] post2: d['post2'] >', and let the language model generate the rest.

We use the 'text-davinci-002' model and randomly construct those few-shot prompts where each prompt will be a length of around $4,000$ because of the API token length limit. We use the same setting and the model pipeline for both of our submissions 2 and 3 where we use the Chinese posts as d['post1'] and d['post2'] for our submission 2 and the Google-translated English posts for our submission 3. By this we mean, for example, we use the same tokenizer for Chinese and English. Therefore, these systems are very simple and to-go prompt-based systems. We had done very minimal parameter tuning to the model, only prompt engineering. For a survey in prompt-based systems, please consider (Liu et al., 2021).

2.2 Unsupervised Ranking

For unsupervised ranking, we utilized many financial and general language models and Bayesian lexicons in both Chinese and English.

2.2.1 Base Model

Our first submission, our base model, consists of a stylistic length feature (Zong et al., 2020) derived from the opinion (sub)word lengths segmented using the 'hfl/chinese-bert-wwm-ext' tokenizer (Cui et al., 2021), prediction scores from FinBERT-FLS (Huang et al., 2020), a professional lexicon count from FinProLex (Chen et al., 2021a), and a market sentiment lexicon count from NTUSD-Fin (Chen et al., 2018).

In the measuring forecasting skill from text paper (Zong et al., 2020), the authors observe various linguistics phenomena indicating that skilled forecasters tend to write significantly longer justifications because of more rationale. For example, skilled forecasters also provide less readability, because of the usage of more complex languages, and less emotion, because of the usage of less emotional languages as neutral sentiments. Moreover, skilled forecasters tend to use more cardinal numbers, prepositions, and nouns. They tend to use fewer verbs and pronouns. Therefore, in this base model, we just stick with the lengths of justifications as our simplest skill indicator.

FinBERT (Huang et al., 2020) is essentially BERT (Devlin et al., 2019) customized for financial texts, pretrained on corporate filings, analyst reports, and earnings conference call transcripts, which differ from normal texts in both vocabulary and writing style. In the FinBERT paper, FinBERT outperforms all other methods, Loughran McDonald lexicon, and machine learning algorithms, especially in negative financial sentiment prediction, when finetuned for financial sentiment analysis (FinBERT-tone). FinBERT was finetuned in two additional tasks, labeling environment, social, and governance (ESG) discussions and labeling forward-looking statements (FLS), from firms' corporate social responsibility (CSR) reports and management discussion and analyses (MD&As) textual sentences. For this base model, we sum and normalize the prediction logit outputs from FinBERT-FLS classes, $\{FLS, NON\_FLS, NOT\_FLS\}$ on each sentence of the textual inputs as our scores.

FinProLex (Chen et al., 2021a) is a Chinese financial lexicon derived from Bloomberg Terminal and PTT Stock Taiwanese social media platform, containing $5,162$ tokens from professional analysts' reports and social media posts paired with expertise scores. FinProLex uses Point-wise Mutual Information (PMI), as in (Turney, 2002; Li and Shah, 2017), to measure the association strengths between a word and either the positive or negative lexicon. The formula of the expert-like score (ELScore) of a given word w is as follows:

$$ELScore_w = PMI(w, analyst) - PMI(w, amateur), \quad (1)$$

$$ELScore_w = \log_2 \frac{p(w, analyst)}{p(w)p(analyst)} - \log_2 \frac{p(w, amateur)}{p(w)p(amateur)}, \quad (2)$$

where $analyst$ and $amateur$ are labels of whether a given word is from an analyst report or an amateur post. This is the difference value between the PMI scores measuring how much a term is associated with either analyst or amateur documents. This is similar to the term's sentiment score (S_{PMI}) (Li and Shah, 2017) which is

$$S_{PMI} = PMI(w, bullish) - PMI(w, bearish). \quad (3)$$

FinProLex tends to include hard words, complex semantics, noun phrase modifiers, content words, transition words, personal pronouns, and negative words as experts tend to use most of them, except personal pronouns and negative words which are used more by amateurs, based on the paper findings that can be summarized as experts tend to evaluate pricing and valuations while amateurs tend to predict the stock movements.

NTUSD-Fin is an English lexicon for market sentiment analysis from StockTwits, containing $8,331$ words, 112 hashtags, and 115 emojis. We used their market sentiment scores which are also computed essentially from equation (3).

We aggregated the scores to predict MPP and ML using these heuristic functions (base-1),

$$MPP = len + FinProLex + |FinWord > 0| + (FLS + 0.5\,\text{NON\_FLS} - \text{NOT\_FLS}), \quad (4)$$

$$ML = len + FinProLex + |FinWord < 0| + (FLS + 0.5\,\text{NON\_FLS} - \text{NOT\_FLS}). \quad (5)$$

We simply used a weighted sum as our heuristic function. We grouped similar scores together. $len + FinProLex$ are stylistic features where we put an equal weight of 1 for each of them. We used $FinWord$ as a switch feature for either MPP or ML that would behave differently because of the market sentiment based on our belief. MPP posts should be from a bullish market while ML posts should instead be from a bearish market. FLS has 3 different class scores so we weighted 1 for a positive class, 0.5 for a less positive one, and -1 for a negative class. The weights are just our rule-of-thumb (make-up numbers that we felt they made sense solely from our intuitions).

It is like trying to intuitively come up with a good feature weighting number for a Maximum Entropy (MaxEnt) model. From our heuristic functions, we just down-weighted some scores and specify some negative interactions. We did not normalize the weighting into probabilities but the ranking should be the same anyway. Most weightings are uniformly the same number.

- If a score should positively correlate with the target, we should give a high weight.
- If a score should weakly correlate with the target, we should give a low weight.
- If a score should negatively correlate with the target, we should give a high negative weight.
- For the rest that we are not certain of, they should retain a maximum entropy (uniformity).
- These heuristics can be estimated with intuitions and give an intuitive unsupervised aggregated scoring function.

However, we submitted the same function for MPP and ML to get a sense of using the same strategy for both bullish and bearish markets.

2.2.2 Bayesian Lexicons

Next, we added Bayesian lexicons (Eisenstein, 2017) (by fitting FinProLex and NTUSD-Fin), FinBERT-tone (Huang et al., 2020), (fitted) Loughran-McDonald financial sentiment lexicon (LM) (Loughran and McDonald, 2011) and Part-of-Speech (POS) features (Zong et al., 2020) into the score aggregators. We would like to note that these lexicons are not multi-word (only unigrams) so they are not expected to be able to handle negations except the creators of those lexicons had made them handle some kind of negations, like in the LM lexicon Fin-Pos list. The authors use bigram to quadgrams counts when that bigram to quadgram follows some negation patterns. Our second and third submissions differ in the normalization of scores and Bayesian lexicon variants.

Loughran-McDonald financial sentiment lexicon (LM) (Loughran and McDonald, 2011) was created because the Harvard Psychosociological Dictionary, specifically, the Harvard-IV-4 TagNeg (H4N) file, does not perform well in financial and accounting domains. Lots of Harvard dictionary negative words are not negative in finance.

Bayesian lexicon learns predictive weights for each word in a lexicon using a method-of-moments estimator from co-occurrence statistics without any labels as a special case of multinomial Naïve Bayes. For the second submission, we use the Dirichlet Compound Multinomial likelihood to reduce effective counts for repetitive words. For the third submission, we use the multinomial likelihood model. For example, when we fitted the LM lexicon using the pairwise comparison data, we gave 0.02626 to 'good', 0.00501 to 'optimistic', and 0.00278 to 'highest'. For LM negative words, we gave 0.00243 to 'decline', 0.00234 to sharply, and 0.00186 to 'difficult'.

Our POS features are motivated by the measuring forecasting skill from text paper. We simply counted cardinal numbers, nouns, and verbs from Chinese jieba segmented texts. Then, these counts were normalized into the range of $[0, 1]$.

For these submissions, we sum and normalize the prediction logit outputs from FinBERT-tone classes, $\{pos\_tone, neg\_tone\}$ on each sentence of the textual inputs as our scores.

For the second submission, we aggregated the scores to predict MPP and ML using these heuristic functions (bayesdcm-2),

$$\begin{aligned} MPP = len + FinProLex + |FinWord > 0| \\ + (FLS + 0.5\,\text{NON\_FLS} - \text{NOT\_FLS}) \\ + (pos\_tone - neg\_tone + LM) \\ + (nouns + cards - verbs), \end{aligned} \quad (6)$$

$$\begin{aligned} ML = len + FinProLex + |FinWord < 0| \\ + (FLS + 0.5\,\text{NON\_FLS} - \text{NOT\_FLS}) \\ + (pos\_tone - neg\_tone + LM) \\ + (nouns + cards - verbs). \end{aligned} \quad (7)$$

For the third submission, we aggregated the scores to predict MPP and ML using these heuristic functions (multinomial-3),

$$\begin{aligned} MPP = 0.5(len + FinProLex) \\ + 0.33(FLS + 0.5\,\text{NON\_FLS} - \text{NOT\_FLS}) \\ + 0.33(pos\_tone - neg\_tone + LM) \\ + 0.33(nouns + cards - verbs) \\ + |FinWord > 0|, \end{aligned} \quad (8)$$

$$\begin{aligned} ML = 0.5(len + FinProLex) \\ + 0.33(FLS + 0.5\,\text{NON\_FLS} - \text{NOT\_FLS}) \\ + 0.33(pos\_tone - neg\_tone + LM) \\ + 0.33(nouns + cards - verbs) \\ + |FinWord < 0|. \end{aligned} \quad (9)$$

In these functions, we tried to group and reweigh the scores as normalization. If two or more scores mean the same thing, we might double count.

3 Experimental Results

In our experiments, most of our submissions (except T5-small) are intuition-based heuristics, and we did not even measure neither their training nor validation performance at all during the competition. We did not use any data augmentation techniques.

3.1 Pairwise Comparison

The experimental results in Table.1 show that the OpenAI InstructGPT language model few-shot trained on Chinese data works best in our submissions, ranking 3rd on the maximal loss (ML) pairwise accuracy, even better than instead training on the Google translated English data by a

Table 1: MPP and ML accuracies of our models in pairwise comparison test data. (The numbers in subscript are submission rankings on the leaderboard. The symbol † denotes a top-3 performance.)

Model	MPP acc.	ML acc.
T5-small	47.13_{16}	45.98_{10}
InstructGPT-zh	$\mathbf{48.28_{14}}$	$\mathbf{54.02_{3}}$†
InstructGPT-en	47.13_{16}	41.38_{13}
FinNLP-22 best	62.07	59.77

Table 2: Average MPP and ML from top 10% posts of our models in unsupervised ranking test data. (The numbers in subscript are submission rankings on the leaderboard. The symbol † denotes a top-3 performance and the symbol ‡ denotes the score beats the baseline.)

Model	avg. MPP	avg. ML
Stylistic baseline	17.61%	−2.46%
base-1	$22.53\%_{3}$ † ‡	$\mathbf{-7.80\%_{11}}$
bayesdcm-2	$\mathbf{24.39\%_{1}}$ † ‡	$-13.04\%_{16}$
multinomial-3	$23.76\%_{2}$ † ‡	$-12.33\%_{15}$
FinNLP-22 best	24.39% (ours)	−2.46%

large margin, where the English few-shot trained InstructGPT model even performs worse than an instruction-based T5-small model finetuned on the English data. However, all instruction-based submissions do not perform well on the maximal potential profit (MPP) pairwise accuracy where there are more data and learning signals, nonetheless, the Chinese few-shot trained InstructGPT model still performs best in our setting.

We additionally split the training data into a held-out train/val split and evaluated our methods on the val split in Table 3. The results are a bit different since the English version of the InstructGPT works better. However, we did not hope for an accurate cross-validation estimation given a small amount of data. Using leave-one-out validation (LOOCV) or k-fold cross-validation with a high value of k can produce a better estimation but they are costly. We might be able to generate more data pairs, but we decided to keep the same setting.

3.2 Unsupervised Ranking

For the unsupervised ranking task, we utilized many language models, including many financial-specific ones, and Bayesian lexicons unsupervisely learned on both Chinese and English words. All of our submissions rank best in the MPP ranking, from 1st to 3rd in this task. However, they all do not perform well for the ML scoring. Therefore, both MPP and ML scores need different treatments

Table 3: Additional experiments on using our pairwise comparison methods on a held-out train/val split (ratio=0.3). The evaluation metric is accuracy.

Model	MPP acc.	ML acc.
T5-small	0.4833	**0.6000**
InstructGPT-zh	0.4667	0.4167
InstructGPT-en	**0.6167**	0.4667

Table 4: Additional experiments on using our unsupervised ranking methods to rank all posts of the pairwise data. The evaluation metrics are average MPP and average ML of the top 10% posts.

Model	avg. MPP	avg. ML
base-1	0.2083	-0.2108
bayesdcm-2	**0.2085**	**-0.2104**
multinomial-3	**0.2085**	**-0.2104**

substantially since we treated MPP and ML using the same formula. Our only difference is the treatment of market sentiment lexicons. We feel that the sentiment features, or mostly semantic features, might be negatively correlated, weakly correlated, or even uncorrelated with ML because the stylistic baseline performs best, and our base submission performs better than our Bayesian lexicon submissions.

We conducted additional experiments on unsupervised ranking by using the whole training set of the pairwise comparison data. We compared all posts using our scoring functions in Table 4. The results show not much difference among our methods. When we tried to evaluate using the pairwise comparison accuracy, the results show no difference (0.545 MPP comparison acc. and 0.525 ML comparison acc.) as our methods were not designed for that.

4 Conclusion

This report describes our systems for a shared task of evaluating the rationales of amateur investors at FinNLP-2022. From the experimental results in pairwise comparison, we conclude that few-shot prompted instruction-based language models can work reasonably well in low resource settings with minimal training efforts but might need quite accurate data from sources since using translated data seems not to perform well. From the experimental results in unsupervised ranking, financial language models perform well and Bayesian-fitting the lexicons helps improve the performance. Also, the heuristic function design needs to differ between MPP and ML.

Limitations

We only sampled a relatively small portion of models and draw conclusions. We also conducted experiments only on one dataset for evaluating the rationales of amateur investors. Besides, the dataset is in Chinese with English translation using Google Translate. Lots of our methods rely on the translated data.

Because we are limited to only three submissions, we don't know how each feature set contributes to the score. There were no ablations. However, the shared task organizers released the test data with ground truths in private.

The authors are self-affiliated and do not represent any entities. The authors also participated in the shared task under many severe unattended local personal criminal events in their home countries. There might be some unintentional errors and physical limitations based on these unlawful interruptions. Even at the time of drafting this report, the authors suffer from unknown toxin flumes spraying into their places. We want to participate in the shared task because it is fun and educational. We apologize for any errors in this report. We tried our best.

Ethics Statement

Scientific work published at EMNLP 2022 must comply with the ACL Ethics Policy. We, the authors, hope the intended uses of our systems are for peace, well-being, and social good only. No harm.

Acknowledgments

We would like to thank anonymous reviewers for their constructive feedback and additional experiment suggestions.

References

Tom Brown, Benjamin Mann, Nick Ryder, Melanie Subbiah, Jared D Kaplan, Prafulla Dhariwal, Arvind Neelakantan, Pranav Shyam, Girish Sastry, Amanda Askell, Sandhini Agarwal, Ariel Herbert-Voss, Gretchen Krueger, Tom Henighan, Rewon Child, Aditya Ramesh, Daniel Ziegler, Jeffrey Wu, Clemens Winter, Chris Hesse, Mark Chen, Eric Sigler, Mateusz Litwin, Scott Gray, Benjamin Chess, Jack Clark, Christopher Berner, Sam McCandlish, Alec Radford, Ilya Sutskever, and Dario Amodei. 2020a. Language models are few-shot learners. In *Advances in Neural Information Processing Systems*, volume 33, pages 1877–1901. Curran Associates, Inc.

Tom Brown, Benjamin Mann, Nick Ryder, Melanie Subbiah, Jared D Kaplan, Prafulla Dhariwal, Arvind Neelakantan, Pranav Shyam, Girish Sastry, Amanda Askell, et al. 2020b. Language models are few-shot learners. *Advances in neural information processing systems*, 33:1877–1901.

Tuhin Chakrabarty, Arkadiy Saakyan, Debanjan Ghosh, and Smaranda Muresan. 2022. Flute: Figurative language understanding and textual explanations. *arXiv preprint arXiv:2205.12404*.

Chung-Chi Chen, Hen-Hsen Huang, and Hsin-Hsi Chen. 2018. Ntusd-fin: a market sentiment dictionary for financial social media data applications. In *Proceedings of the 1st Financial Narrative Processing Workshop (FNP 2018)*, pages 37–43.

Chung-Chi Chen, Hen-Hsen Huang, and Hsin-Hsi Chen. 2021a. Evaluating the rationales of amateur investors. In *Proceedings of the Web Conference 2021*, pages 3987–3998.

Chung-Chi Chen, Hen-Hsen Huang, and Hsin-Hsi Chen. 2021b. *From opinion mining to financial argument mining*. Springer Nature.

Yiming Cui, Wanxiang Che, Ting Liu, Bing Qin, and Ziqing Yang. 2021. Pre-training with whole word masking for chinese bert. *IEEE/ACM Transactions on Audio, Speech, and Language Processing*, 29:3504–3514.

Jacob Devlin, Ming-Wei Chang, Kenton Lee, and Kristina Toutanova. 2019. BERT: Pre-training of deep bidirectional transformers for language understanding. In *Proceedings of the 2019 Conference of the North American Chapter of the Association for Computational Linguistics: Human Language Technologies, Volume 1 (Long and Short Papers)*, pages 4171–4186, Minneapolis, Minnesota. Association for Computational Linguistics.

Jacob Eisenstein. 2017. Unsupervised learning for lexicon-based classification. In *Proceedings of the AAAI Conference on Artificial Intelligence*, volume 31.

Ari Holtzman, Jan Buys, Li Du, Maxwell Forbes, and Yejin Choi. 2019. The curious case of neural text degeneration. In *International Conference on Learning Representations*.

Allen Huang, Hui Wang, and Yi Yang. 2020. Finbert—a deep learning approach to extracting textual information. *Available at SSRN 3910214*.

Quanzhi Li and Sameena Shah. 2017. Learning stock market sentiment lexicon and sentiment-oriented word vector from StockTwits. In *Proceedings of the 21st Conference on Computational Natural Language Learning (CoNLL 2017)*, pages 301–310, Vancouver, Canada. Association for Computational Linguistics.

Pengfei Liu, Weizhe Yuan, Jinlan Fu, Zhengbao Jiang, Hiroaki Hayashi, and Graham Neubig. 2021. Pre-train, prompt, and predict: A systematic survey of prompting methods in natural language processing. *arXiv preprint arXiv:2107.13586*.

Tim Loughran and Bill McDonald. 2011. When is a liability not a liability? textual analysis, dictionaries, and 10-ks. *The Journal of finance*, 66(1):35–65.

Long Ouyang, Jeff Wu, Xu Jiang, Diogo Almeida, Carroll L Wainwright, Pamela Mishkin, Chong Zhang, Sandhini Agarwal, Katarina Slama, Alex Ray, et al. 2022. Training language models to follow instructions with human feedback. *arXiv preprint arXiv:2203.02155*.

Colin Raffel, Noam Shazeer, Adam Roberts, Katherine Lee, Sharan Narang, Michael Matena, Yanqi Zhou, Wei Li, Peter J Liu, et al. 2020. Exploring the limits of transfer learning with a unified text-to-text transformer. *J. Mach. Learn. Res.*, 21(140):1–67.

Peter Shaw, Jakob Uszkoreit, and Ashish Vaswani. 2018. Self-attention with relative position representations. In *Proceedings of the 2018 Conference of the North American Chapter of the Association for Computational Linguistics: Human Language Technologies, Volume 2 (Short Papers)*, pages 464–468, New Orleans, Louisiana. Association for Computational Linguistics.

Peter Turney. 2002. Thumbs up or thumbs down? semantic orientation applied to unsupervised classification of reviews. In *Proceedings of the 40th Annual Meeting of the Association for Computational Linguistics*, pages 417–424, Philadelphia, Pennsylvania, USA. Association for Computational Linguistics.

Ashish Vaswani, Noam Shazeer, Niki Parmar, Jakob Uszkoreit, Llion Jones, Aidan N Gomez, Łukasz Kaiser, and Illia Polosukhin. 2017. Attention is all you need. *Advances in neural information processing systems*, 30.

Shi Zong, Alan Ritter, and Eduard Hovy. 2020. Measuring forecasting skill from text. In *Proceedings of the 58th Annual Meeting of the Association for Computational Linguistics*, pages 5317–5331, Online. Association for Computational Linguistics.

LIPI at the FinNLP-2022 ERAI Task: Ensembling Sentence Transformers for Assessing Maximum Possible Profit and Loss from Online Financial Posts

Sohom Ghosh[1,2] and **Sudip Kumar Naskar**[2]
[1]Fidelity Investments, Bengaluru, India
[2]Jadavpur University, Kolkata, India
{sohom1ghosh, sudip.naskar}@gmail.com

Abstract

Using insights from social media for making investment decisions has become mainstream. However, in the current era of information explosion, it is essential to mine high-quality social media posts. The FinNLP-2022 ERAI task deals with assessing Maximum Possible Profit (**MPP**) and Maximum Loss (**ML**) from social media posts relating to finance. In this paper, we present our team LIPI's approach. We ensembled a range of Sentence Transformers to quantify these posts. Unlike other teams with varying performances across different metrics, our system performs consistently well. Our code is available here[1].

1 Introduction

Over the last few years, financial opinion mining has emerged to be an interesting area of research (Chen et al., 2021b). Several research (Mao et al. (2012), Sprenger et al. (2014), Lee et al. (2015), Pagolu et al. (2016), Asur and Huberman (2010), Elliott et al. (2018), Crowley et al. (2021)) highlight the importance of social media posts for predicting stock markets. Although the wisdom of the crowd matters, it is still necessary to mine quality posts from the rest. Quantifying social media posts in terms of the expected profitability is an open area for research. Chen et al. (2021a) proposed two metrics: Maximum Possible Profit (**MPP**) and Maximum Loss (**ML**) for evaluating such posts. They recently hosted the FinNLP-2022 ERAI Task[2] (in conjunction with EMNLP-2022[3]). It comprises pairwise comparison (Task-1) and unsupervised ranking (Task-2) of financial social media posts with respect to **MPP** and **ML**. In this paper, we describe our best-performing systems (Task-1 $\rightarrow$ **MPP**: 57.47% & **ML**: 59.77%; Task-2 $\rightarrow$ **MPP**:18.27% & **ML**: -3.90%).

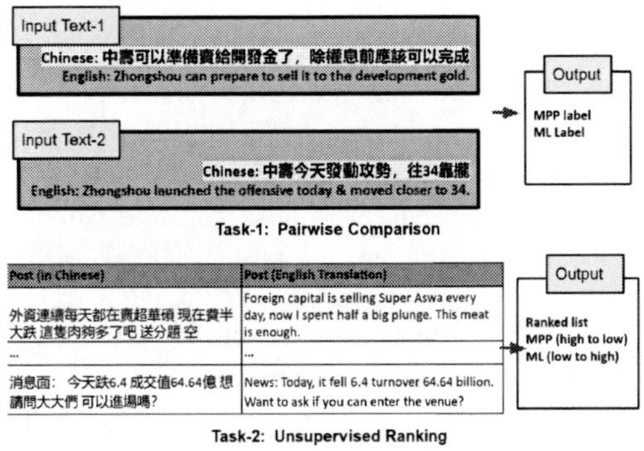

Figure 1: ERAI FinNLP-2022 Tasks

2 Problem Statement

For Task-1, given two posts, the task is to develop a system for evaluating which of them will lead to greater **MPP** and lower **ML**.
For Task-2, given a set of posts, the task is to develop a system for ranking these posts in terms of higher **MPP** and lower **ML** values.
Results of Task-1 were evaluated using accuracy. For Task-2, average **MPP** and **ML** values of top 10% posts were considered for evaluation.

3 Datasets

The organizers initially provided the participants with two datasets. The first dataset (corresponding to Task-1) had 200 instances out of which 2 were null. We dropped the null instances from our experiments. Each instance consists of two posts (in Chinese as well as in English), their **MPP** and **ML** values, and labels corresponding to each post. In the dataset, the **ML** label is set to '1' for an instance (i.e., a pair of posts) when the **ML** value of the first post is less than that of the second post, otherwise the ML label is set to '0'. On the contrary, the **MPP**

[1]https://github.com/sohomghosh/LIPI_ERAI_FinNLP_EMNLP-2022/

[2]https://sites.google.com/nlg.csie.ntu.edu.tw/finnlp-2022-emnlp/erai-shared-task

[3]https://2022.emnlp.org/

Proceedings of the Fourth Workshop on Financial Technology and Natural Language Processing (FinNLP), pages 111 - 115
December 8, 2022 ©2022 Association for Computational Linguistics

is set to '0' for an instance (i.e., a pair of posts) when the **ML** value of the first post is less than that of the second post, otherwise the **MPP** label is set to '1'. The posts in the dataset were collected from social media platforms like PTT[4] and Mobile01[5]. We refer to this as **D1**. For Task-2, a dataset consisting of 210 unlabelled posts (in Chinese as well as in English) were provided. This dataset is referred to as **D2**. **D2** serves as the test set for Task-2. Subsequently, the organizers released a test set consisting of 87 pairs of unlabelled posts (in Chinese and English) for pairwise comparison. We refer to this as **D3**.

Data Preparation

We created training and validation sets from **D1** maintaining a split ratio of 80:20. We extended **D1** in two ways.

Firstly, we treat each post from the pair individually, i.e.,tuple (post-1, post-2, MPP-1, MPP-2, ML-1, ML-2) is converted into 2 tuples – (post-1, MPP-1, ML-1) and (post-2, MPP-2, ML-2). This gave us 320 instances for training and 80 for validation. We refer to this training set as **D4**. For sub-systems SB-1 (§4.1), SB-2 (§4.2) and SB-4 (§4.4), we used this set.

Secondly, we expanded **D4** by comparing each post to every other post after removing the null instances. It resulted in 97,032 instances of training. This is referred to as **D5**. The validation set was kept as it is. We use this in sub-systems SB-3 (§4.3) and SB-5 (§4.5).

Chen et al. (2022) narrates the dataset and problem statement in more detail. The formulas for calculating **MPP** and **ML** are mentioned in (Chen et al., 2021a). In Figure 1, we present the problem statement and a sample dataset.

4 Sub-systems

Since our submitted systems are ensemble of multiple sub-systems, we explain each of the sub-systems here. More details regarding the hyper-parameters of each sub-system are reported in the shared codebase.

4.1 Sub-System 1 (SB-1)

For all the Chinese posts in **D4**, we extracted the corresponding embeddings using sbert-chinese-qmc-finance.[6] We trained a linear regression model using the embedding as input to learn either **MPP** values or **ML** values based on requirements. We chose linear regression to start with as we did not have much data to train.

4.2 Sub-System 2 (SB-2)

This sub-system is similar to SB-1 (§4.1). The only difference is that we trained a neural network (multi-layer perceptron model) for 50 iterations instead of linear regression.

4.3 Sub-System 3 (SB-3)

For this sub-system, we used the **D5** dataset. For each pair of Chinese posts present in **D5**, we concatenated the embeddings for each of the posts obtained using sbert-chinese-qmc-finance[7]. We trained a linear regression mode to learn the difference of either **MPP** values or **ML** values between each post present in a given pair.

4.4 Sub-System 4 (SB-4)

We customised the BERT model's architecture (Devlin et al., 2019) for the task of regression such that its last layer learns to predict either the **MPP** values or the **ML** values. This was done by passing the representation of the [CLS] token through a fully connected linear layer having 128 neurons followed by a layer with $tanh$ activation. We initialised it with the weights from the FinBERT model (Araci, 2019). We used only the English posts present in **D4** for this.

4.5 Sub-System 5 (SB-5)

We extracted FinBERT (Araci, 2019) embeddings corresponding to all the English posts present in **D5**. We trained a multi-layer perceptron model for 500 iterations which takes this embedding as input and predicts the difference between either **MPP** values or **ML** values corresponding to each post present in a given pair.

5 Best Performing Systems

In this section, we narrate the systems corresponding to our best-performing submissions.

[4]https://www.ptt.cc/index.html accessed on 09/17/2022

[5]https://www.mobile01.com/ accessed on 09/17/2022

[6]https://huggingface.co/DMetaSoul/sbert-chinese-qmc-finance-v1 accessed on 09/17/2022

[7]https://huggingface.co/DMetaSoul/sbert-chinese-qmc-finance-v1 accessed on 09/17/2022

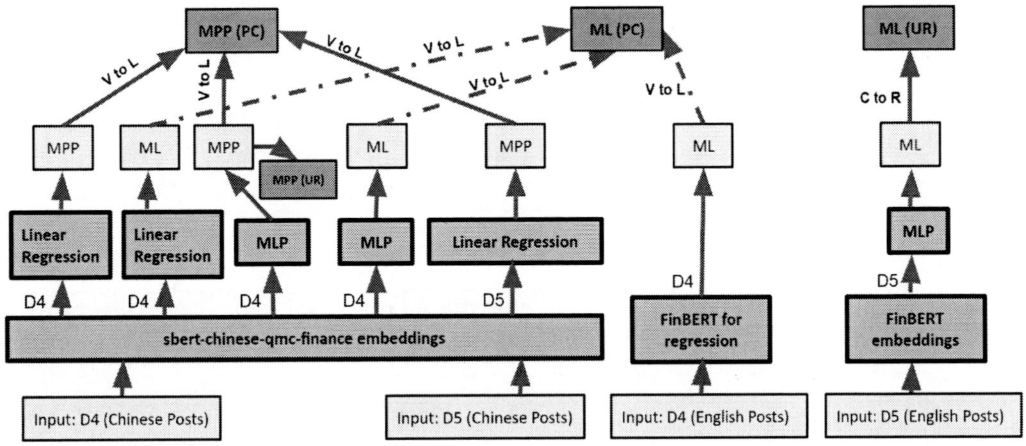

Figure 2: Ensemble Architecture. PC: Pairwise comparison, UR: Unsupervised Rankings, V to L: values to labels by comparison, C to R: comparison to rankings.

5.1 MPP calculation for Pairwise Comparison

This is an ensemble of three subsystems SB-1 (§4.1), SB-2 (§4.2) and SB-3 (§4.3). While SB-1 and SB-2 were trained with the objective of learning the **MPP** values, SB-3 was trained with the objective of learning the difference in **MPP** values for a given pair of posts. For SB-1 and SB-2, to obtain labels from raw **MPP** values, we computed and compared the **MPP** values of the posts constituting each pair in the test set. When **MPP** value of the first post was greater than **MPP** value of the second post, we assigned label '1', otherwise we assigned label '0'. For SB-3, we assigned label '1' when the predicted difference in **MPP** is greater than 0, otherwise we assigned label '0'. The final decision for the **D3** is made based on majority voting.

5.2 ML calculation for Pairwise Comparison

This system consists of selecting the final output from the predictions made by SB-1 (§4.1), SB-2 (§4.2) and SB-4 (§4.4) based on majority voting. Each of these constituent sub-systems were trained with the objective to learn the **ML** values. We scored each of these sub-systems on every post present in **D3**. Subsequently, we compared the raw **ML** values of posts constituting each pair in the test set. Label '1' was assigned when **ML** value of the first post was lesser than that of the second post, otherwise label '0' was assigned.

5.3 MPP calculation for Unsupervised Ranking

SB-2 (§4.2) was trained to predict the **MPP** value for a given post. We scored **D2** using SB-2 and ranked the posts in decreasing order of predicted **MPP** values.

5.4 ML calculation for Unsupervised Ranking

We trained SB-5 (§4.5) to learn the difference in **ML** values for a given pair of posts. We used this system to compare and sort the instances in **D2** in increasing order of predicted **ML** values.

Figure 2 gives a pictorial representation of all the ensemble models.

6 Experiments and Results

This section states various experiments we performed and their results. We started with SB-1 which is a linear regression model trained over sentence embeddings. We tried financial sentence embeddings available for Chinese as well as the English language. Subsequently, we replaced the linear regression model with a multi-layer perceptron model. We further experimented by transforming the original training set **D1** to **D4** and **D5**. We also tried altering the last layer of the BERT (Devlin et al., 2019) model for the task of regression. For the pairwise classification task, we used the regression models to get the **MPP/ML** values for each post in a pair. We then assigned a label to the pair by comparing these values as mentioned in §3. The results are presented in Tables 1 and 2. In this paper we focus on the best-performing systems among

		Train/Valid.		MPP (Pairwise Comparison)			MPP (Unsupervised Ranking)		
Sl.#	Model	Data	Language	Train	Valid.	Test (D3)	Train	Valid.	Test (D2)
1.1	SB-1	D4	Chinese	100.00%	70.00%	54.02%	8.04%	2.98%	11.83%
1.2	SB-2	D4	Chinese	62.18%	67.50%	48.28%	3.89%	2.45%	**18.27%**
1.3	SB-3	D5	Chinese	99.63%	60.00%	41.38%	-	-	17.46%
1.4	SB-4	D4	English	51.92%	47.50%	50.57%	2.11%	3.94%	4.17%
1.5	SB-5	D5	English	99.59%	45.00%	55.17%	-	-	16.63%
1.6	Ensemble (§5.1)	-	-	-	72.50%	**57.47%**	-	-	-

Table 1: MPP Results

		Train/Valid.		ML (Pairwise Comparison)			ML (Unsupervised Ranking)		
Sl.#	Model	Data	Language	Train	Valid.	Test (D3)	Train	Valid.	Test (D2)
2.1	SB-1	D4	Chinese	97.44%	52.50%	50.57%	-10.26%	-2.16%	-7.81%
2.2	SB-2	D4	Chinese	57.69%	55.00%	50.57%	-5.55%	-8.01%	-5.56%
2.3	SB-3	D5	Chinese	99.65%	52.50%	47.12%	-	-	**-3.90%**
2.4	SB-4	D4	English	58.00%	50.00%	**59.77%**	-1.87%	-1.35%	-6.29%
2.5	SB-5	D5	English	91.24%	55.00%	44.83%	-	-	-4.11%
2.6	Ensemble (§5.2)	-	-	82.05%	57.50%	50.57%	-	-	-

Table 2: ML Results

all our submissions due to page constraints. The other approaches we tried include classification of posts separated by *[SEP]* token using various variants of BERT (Devlin et al., 2019). Since the **D4** dataset consists of single posts, we use the same training and validation set for both the tasks. As the **D5** dataset comprises only of pairs of posts, we are unable to provide its performance in the unsupervised ranking task corresponding to the training and validation set. We ensembled models with varying lengths of the training set, therefore we do not report the performance of the model mentioned in §5.1 for the training set. Similarly, for the unsupervised ranking task, we do not report the performances of the models describe in §5.1 and §5.2 as these models were suitable for pairwise comparison task only. The performance of the participating teams has been reported here(Chen et al., 2022).We used labelled instances from **D4** to assess the performance of the unsupervised ranking models as well. This helped us in choosing the best performing models. As **D5** was suitable for pairwise comparison task only, we could not use it to evaluate the models which were developed for the unsupervised ranking task. It is interesting to observe that our ensemble system's performance (Sl.# 1.6) is next only to that of team *Jetsons* in the pairwise comparison task using **MPP**. Moreover, in the same task using **ML** our subsystem SB-4 (Sl.# 2.4) performs as good as that of the best performing team *DCU-ML* (accuracy: 59.77%). However, we did not submit this sub-system separately as it did not perform well on the validation set and submitted the results of the ensemble model (Sl.# 2.6) instead. In the unsupervised ranking using **MPP** task, only team *PromptShots*'s system performed better than that of ours (Sl.# 1.2). However, in the unsupervised ranking using **ML** task, the performance of the system developed by team *Yet* and the baseline solution were better than that of our systems (Sl.# 2.3 and 2.5). In this case as well we did not submit the result corresponding to SB-3 (Sl.# 2.3) where **ML** of top 10% post is -3.90% on the test set because the underlying system could not be evaluated on the validation set obtained from **D5**. We submitted results of SB-5 (Sl.# 2.5) instead.

7 Conclusion

Comparing the performance of our models with that of the other participants, we conclude that our models performed consistently well. We also observe that in most cases we achieve better performances using the Chinese texts than the translated version in English. This is because we are losing out on the nuances during translation. We further observe that ensembling helps in improving the overall performance.

Collecting more financial posts in a resource-rich language like English and incorporating prices of the stock whose **MPP** and **ML** are being discussed as input to the model are interesting directions for future work.

8 Limitations

The training dataset is very small in size and does not assure how the system will perform in real life. Fine-tuning large language models like BERT on `D5` is compute intensive. Moreover as the **MPP** and **ML** calculation differs for bullish and bearish market, it would be nice to take market conditions into consideration.

Ethics Statement

This research has been done for academic purposes. The authors declare that there are no underlying commercial interests. Investment in stock markets is risky and may lead to monetary losses. Investors are advised to use their discretion instead of blindly relying on these models' output.

Disclaimer

The opinions expressed in this paper are of the authors. They do not reflect the opinions of their affiliations.

References

Dogu Araci. 2019. Finbert: Financial sentiment analysis with pre-trained language models.

Sitaram Asur and Bernardo A. Huberman. 2010. Predicting the future with social media. In *2010 IEEE/WIC/ACM International Conference on Web Intelligence and Intelligent Agent Technology*, volume 1, pages 492–499.

Chung-Chi Chen, Hen-Hsen Huang, and Hsin-Hsi Chen. 2021a. Evaluating the rationales of amateur investors. In *Proceedings of the Web Conference 2021*, WWW '21, page 3987–3998, New York, NY, USA. Association for Computing Machinery.

Chung-Chi Chen, Hen-Hsen Huang, and Hsin-Hsi Chen. 2021b. Financial opinion mining. In *Proceedings of the 2021 Conference on Empirical Methods in Natural Language Processing: Tutorial Abstracts*, pages 7–10, Punta Cana, Dominican Republic & Online. Association for Computational Linguistics.

Chung-Chi Chen, Hen-Hsen Huang, Hiroya Takamura, and Hsin-Hsi Chen. 2022. Overview of the finnlp-2022 erai task: Evaluating the rationales of amateur investors. In *Proceedings of the Fourth Workshop on Financial Technology and Natural Language Processing*, Abu Dhabi, United Arab Emirates. Association for Computational Linguistics.

Richard M Crowley, Wenli Huang, and Hai Lu. 2021. Executive tweets. *Available at SSRN 3975995*.

Jacob Devlin, Ming-Wei Chang, Kenton Lee, and Kristina Toutanova. 2019. BERT: Pre-training of deep bidirectional transformers for language understanding. In *Proceedings of the 2019 Conference of the North American Chapter of the Association for Computational Linguistics: Human Language Technologies, Volume 1 (Long and Short Papers)*, pages 4171–4186, Minneapolis, Minnesota. Association for Computational Linguistics.

W Brooke Elliott, Stephanie M Grant, and Frank D Hodge. 2018. Negative news and investor trust: The role of $ firm and # ceo twitter use. *Journal of Accounting Research*, 56(5):1483–1519.

Lian Fen Lee, Amy P Hutton, and Susan Shu. 2015. The role of social media in the capital market: Evidence from consumer product recalls. *Journal of Accounting Research*, 53(2):367–404.

Yuexin Mao, Wei Wei, Bing Wang, and Benyuan Liu. 2012. Correlating s&p 500 stocks with twitter data. In *Proceedings of the First ACM International Workshop on Hot Topics on Interdisciplinary Social Networks Research*, HotSocial '12, page 69–72, New York, NY, USA. Association for Computing Machinery.

Venkata Sasank Pagolu, Kamal Nayan Reddy, Ganapati Panda, and Babita Majhi. 2016. Sentiment analysis of twitter data for predicting stock market movements. In *2016 International Conference on Signal Processing, Communication, Power and Embedded System (SCOPES)*, pages 1345–1350.

Timm O Sprenger, Andranik Tumasjan, Philipp G Sandner, and Isabell M Welpe. 2014. Tweets and trades: The information content of stock microblogs. *European Financial Management*, 20(5):926–957.

DCU-ML at the FinNLP-2022 ERAI Task: Investigating the Transferability of Sentiment Analysis Data for Evaluating Rationales of Investors

Chenyang Lyu
School of Computing
Dublin City University
Dublin, Ireland
chenyang.lyu2@mail.dcu.ie

Tianbo Ji
School of Computing
Dublin City University
Dublin, Ireland
tianbo.ji2@mail.dcu.ie

Liting Zhou
School of Computing
Dublin City University
Dublin, Ireland
liting.zhou@dcu.ie

Abstract

In this paper, we describe our system for the FinNLP-2022 shared task: Evaluating the Rationales of Amateur Investors (ERAI). The ERAI shared tasks focuses on mining profitable information from financial texts by predicting the possible Maximal Potential Profit (MPP) and Maximal Loss (ML) based on the posts from amateur investors. There are two subtasks in ERAI: Pairwise Comparison and Unsupervised Rank, both target on the prediction of MPP and ML. To tackle the two tasks, we frame this task as a text-pair classification task where the input consists of two documents and the output is the label of whether the first document will lead to higher MPP or lower ML. Specifically, we propose to take advantage of the transferability of Sentiment Analysis data with an assumption that a more positive text will lead to higher MPP or higher ML to facilitate the prediction of MPP and ML. In experiment on the ERAI blind test set, our systems trained on Sentiment Analysis data and ERAI training data ranked 1st and 8th in ML and MPP pairwise comparison respectively. Code available in this link.

1 Introduction

Financial Opinion Mining (Chen et al., 2021b,a), the focus of the FinNLP-2022 shared task ERAI, has attracted the attention of the Natural Language Processing (NLP) community in recent years (El-Haj et al., 2021; Mariko et al., 2022; Lyu et al., 2022) for its potential use in financial analytic such as stock movement and volatility prediction (Chen, 2021). The FinNLP-2022 shared task ERAI (Chen et al., 2022) targets at extracting profitable information from financial documents particularly the posts from amateur investors. In the shared task, ERAI aims to predict the Maximal Potential Profit (MPP) and Maximal Loss (ML) conveyed by the posts from amateur investors as such mined opinions could be possibly used to analyse the financial market.

To tackle this task, we firstly frame it as a text-pair classification task where the input consists of two documents from different amateur investors. And the output is the label of whether the first document will lead to higher MPP or lower ML. Second, we take advantage of Sentiment Analysis data that have been shown to be useful in financial NLP (Chen, 2021; Wan et al., 2021; Valle-Cruz et al., 2022). Moreover, sentiment data are rich-resource and can be easily obtained (Liu, 2012) and the ERAI data that is in relatively small scale could benefit from it. Specifically, we use sentiment analysis data with an assumption that more positive text would give a higher profitable outcome. Practically, we build the ERAI-like dataset based on sentiment analysis data via iteratively sample two documents from sentiment analysis corpus, if the sentiment polarity of the first document is more positive than the second document then we think the first document would lead to higher MPP as well as higher ML (as a more positive document could mean a more aggressive action which could lead to higher MPP but also with high risk resulting in higher ML). Then we use the ERAI-like sentiment data to pre-train our model, of which the basic architecture is a text-pair classification model, and further fine-tune it with the ERAI training data.

In experiment, we employ BERT-Chinese (Devlin et al., 2019) as our base model since ERAI data is in Chinese. We experimented with three different strategies for training our model: 1) BERT-Senti: only use sentiment data thus fully relying on the transferability of sentiment data; 2) BERT-ERAI: only use ERAI training data; 3) BERT-Senti+ERAI: fine-tune our model after training it using sentiment data. We submit the three systems trained based on the above strategies to ERAI Pairwise Comparison blind test set. We submit the first system for ERAI Unsupervised Ranking evaluation as it is only trained on sentiment data thus it's an unsupervised system. The experimental results on ERAI

Proceedings of the Fourth Workshop on Financial Technology and Natural Language Processing (FinNLP), pages 116 - 121
December 8, 2022 ©2022 Association for Computational Linguistics

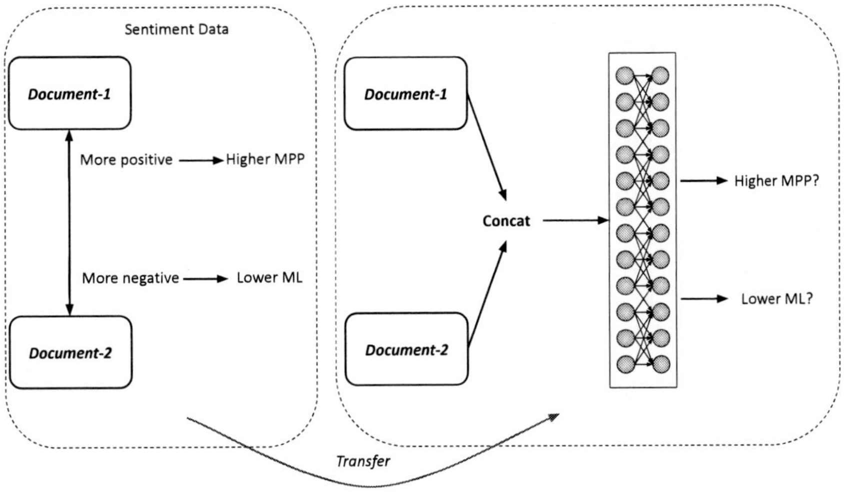

Figure 1: The main architecture of our model. We transfer the sentiment data to the ERAI text-pair classification task.

blind test set show that our BERT-Senti achieves 1st and 8th in ML and MPP pairwise comparison with accuracy of 59.77% and 52.87% respectively. Our BERT-Senti achieves average MPP and ML of 13.97% and -8.25% for Unsupervised Ranking, which ranked at 10th and 13th respectively.

2 Methodology

The main architecture of our proposed approach is shown in Figure 1, where we take advantage of the sentiment data to construct a ERAI-like dataset based on an assumption that a more positive document would lead to higher MPP and a more negative document would lead to higher ML. We pre-train our model based on the ERAI-like sentiment data followed by fine-tuning with the ERAI training data. The resulting systems are submitted to ERAI Pairwise Comparison and Unsupervised Ranking for evaluation.

2.1 Transferring Sentiment Data

We propose to utilize sentiment data as it has been shown that sentiment polarity information can be useful for Financial Opinion Mining (Chen, 2021; Valle-Cruz et al., 2022). Specifically, we assume that a more positive document would lead to higher MPP and a more negative document would lead to lower ML. Based on this assumption, we build our ERAI-like data via iteratively sampling two documents from sentiment corpus, if the first document has more positive sentiment polarity then we assign the document-pair with higher MPP label and higher ML label. The detailed process is shown in Algorithm 1.

Algorithm 1: The process of constructing ERAI-like based on sentiment corpus

```
S: Sentiment Corpus
examples = []
for i in iteration do
    Sample d1 from S
    Sample d2 from S - d1
    if d1.sentiment > d2.sentiment then
        d.text1 = d1
        d.text2 = d2
        d.MPP = 1
        d.ML = 0
    end
    if d1.sentiment < d2.sentiment then
        d.text1 = d1
        d.text2 = d2
        d.MPP = 0
        d.ML = 1
    end
    examples.append(d)
end
```

2.2 Pairwise Comparison

Based on the ERAI-like dataset built in Section 2.1 and ERAI training data, we adopt three strategies to train our BERT model: 1) only use ERAI-like sentiment data built in Section 2.1 and therefore produce an unsupervised system; 2) only use ERAI training data; 3) firstly pre-train using ERAI-like sentiment data followed by fine-tuning with ERAI training data. These three strategies result three corresponding systems: BERT-Senti, BERT-ERAI and BERT-Senti+ERAI. We train the BERT model using our data as a text-pair classification task in which two documents are concatenated and assigned with different segment ID. The prediction head consists of two layers: one for predicting whether the first document would lead to higher MPP (1), the other one for predicting whether the first document would lead to higher ML (0).

2.3 Unsupervised Ranking

For unsupervised ranking, we employ our BERT-Senti system since it is only trained on our ERAI-like sentiment data thus BERT-Senti is an unsupervised system. However, the output of our systems in Section2.2 only indicate whether the first document would lead to higher MPP or ML (boolean value) with a real-valued number. To address such a gap, we reshape the Unsupervised Ranking task as a text-pair classification task where we compare the MPP and ML prediction of each document to all other documents in Unsupervised Ranking dataset. The document with more predictions of higher MPP and lower ML with obtain a higher rank. The process is shown in Algorithm 2.

Algorithm 2: Unsupervised Ranking based on pairwise comparison

```
U: Unsupervised Ranking Corpus
for d in U do
    for d' in U − d do
        if d.MPP > d'.MPP then
            d.MPP+ = 1
        end
        if d.ML < d'.ML then
            d.ML+ = 1
        end
    end
end
sort(U, key = MPP)
sort(U, key = ML)
```

3 Experiment

3.1 Data

The training set and test set of ERAI Pairwise Comparison task contain 200 and 87 examples respectively, the test set of the Unsupervised Ranking task contains 210 examples. We shown some examples from ERAI Pairwise Comparison training set with corresponding English translation in Table 3. The sentiment analysis data we used is from (Zhang and LeCun, 2017), which is a fine-grained sentiment classification dataset based on news in Chinese [1] that has 5 classes (Very Negative, Negative, Neutral, Positive, Very Positive).

[1] lfeng in https://github.com/zhangxiangxiao/glyph#download

Systems	MPP	Systems	ML
Jetsons_1	62.07%	**DCU-ML_1**	59.77%
Yet_1	57.47%	**DCU-ML_3**	59.77%
Yet_2	57.47%	PromptShots_2	54.02%
Yet_3	57.47%	uoa_1	54.02%
LIPI_2	57.47%	aimi_1	52.87%
LIPI_1	54.02%	LIPI_2	50.57%
fiona	54.02%	fiona	48.28%
DCU-ML_1	52.87%	LIPI_3	48.28%
DCU-ML_3	52.87%	**DCU-ML_2**	45.98%
uoa_1	51.72%	PromptShots_1	45.98%
DCU-ML_2	51.72%	LIPI_1	44.83%
Jetsons_3	49.43%	Jetsons_2	41.38%
aimi_1	48.28%	PromptShots_3	41.38%
PromptShots_2	48.28%	Yet_1	40.23%
Jetsons_2	47.13%	Yet_2	40.23%
PromptShots_3	47.13%	Yet_3	40.23%
PromptShots_1	47.13%	Jetsons_1	37.93%
LIPI_3	44.83%	Jetsons_3	36.78%

Table 1: The evaluation results for ERAI Pairwise Comparison task, where our systems are **DCU-ML_1, DCU-ML_2, DCU-ML_3**, which correspond to BERT-Senti, BERT-ERAI and BERT-Senti+ERAI respectively

3.2 Training Setup

We employ BERT (Devlin et al., 2019) which has shown superior performance across many NLP tasks (Zhang et al., 2020; Bommasani et al., 2021)as our base model. Our implementation is based on BERT-Chinese (Devlin et al., 2019; Cui et al., 2020) from Huggingface (Wolf et al., 2020). We train our system with a learning rate of 2×10^{-5} for 2 epochs for BERT-Senti and 20 epochs for BERT-ERAI and BERT-Senti+ERAI, the batch size is set to 64 for BERT-Senti and 4 for the other systems. We use a maximum gradient norm of 1. The optimizer we used is AdamW (Loshchilov and Hutter, 2019), for which the ϵ is set to 1×10^{-8}. We perform early stopping when the performance on validation set degrades.

3.3 Results

The evaluation results on the blind test sets for ERAI Pairwise Comparison and Unsupervised Ranking are shown in Table 1 and Table 2. The results in Table 1 show that our BERT-Senti and BERT-Senti+ERAI outperform BERT-ERAI, which show the effectiveness of the transferability of sentiment data. Moreover, our BERT-Senti and BERT-Senti+ERAI outperform all other systems in

Systems	Average MPP of Top 10% Posts	Systems	Average ML of Top 10% Posts
PromptShots_2	24.39%	Baseline	-2.46%
PromptShots_3	23.76%	Yet_3	-3.24%
PromptShots_1	22.53%	LIPI_1	-4.11%
LIPI_2	18.27%	aimi_1	-4.17%
Baseline	17.61%	Yet_1	-4.35%
LIPI_1	17.46%	LIPI_3	-5.56%
UCCNLP_3	14.81%	Yet_2	-5.77%
Yet_3	14.61%	UCCNLP_3	-5.85%
aimi_1	14.02%	UCCNLP_1	-6.22%
DCU-ML_1	13.97%	UCCNLP_2	-6.77%
UoA_1	12.35%	PromptShots_1	-7.80%
Yet_2	12.10%	LIPI_2	-7.81%
LIPI_3	11.83%	**DCU-ML_1**	-8.25%
UCCNLP_2	11.34%	UoA_1	-9.39%
UCCNLP_1	11.10%	PromptShots_3	-12.33%
Yet_1	8.52%	PromptShots_2	-13.04%

Table 2: The evaluation results for ERAI Unsupervised Ranking task, where our submitted is **DCU-ML_1**, which corresponds to BERT-Senti.

Document-1	Document-2	MPP Label	ML Label
中壽可以準備賣給開發金了，除權息前應該可以完成 *(Zhongshou can prepare to sell it to the development gold.)*	中 壽 今 天 發 動 攻 勢 ， 往*34*靠攏 *(Zhongshou launched the offensive today and moved closer to 34.)*	0	0
有在往上動的感覺了 各位覺的呢 *(I feel like moving up What do you think about it?)*	永豐金融卷減少了*1000*多張,會不會停損在最高點啊 *(The Yongfeng Financial Volume has been reduced by more than 1,000 pieces. Will it stop at the highest point?)*	0	0
低接買盤開始浮現,不過近期也應該是盤整(除非有新的進度消息) *(Low buying the market has begun to emerge, but it should also be consolidated recently (unless there is new progress news))*	宏和一開盤,一路往上衝,漲的有點太高,希望能穩穩漲就好 *(As soon as Honghe opened, rushing up all the way, the rise was a bit too high, I hope to rise steadily)*	1	1

Table 3: Examples from ERAI Pairwise Comparison training set with English translation, where 0 represents *lower* MPP and *lower* ML for Document-1.

ML prediction with an accuracy of 59.77%. The results of BERT-Senti and BERT-Senti+ERAI are the same, we think the possible reason could be that the relatively small scale of test set (87 examples) introduces little variance on performance. In Unsupervised Ranking task, our submitted system BERT-Senti achieves an average MPP and ML of 13.97% and -8.25 respectively, which indicates the need for further improvement. We think the possible reason for that BERT-Senti fails to select documents with higher MPP and lower ML could be that sentiment data only provides a binary estimation for which document leads to higher MPP or lower ML, which is not precise. Besides, the noises in the prediction of Pairwise Comparison also makes it more difficult for accurately identifying the MPP and ML for documents.

4 Conclusion

In this paper, we proposed to use sentiment analysis data to enhance the ERAI shared task, results show that our proposed approach achieves superior performance in Pairwise Comparison, showing the effectiveness of our method. The results on Unsupervised Ranking task indicate there is still room for further improvement.

Limitations

Our method relies on a strong assumption that a more positive document would lead to higher MPP and a more negative document would lead to lower ML. However, this is an empirical assumption which needs more careful investigation before further using.

Acknowledgements

This work was funded by Science Foundation Ireland through the SFI Centre for Research Training in Machine Learning (18/CRT/6183).

References

Rishi Bommasani, Drew A. Hudson, Ehsan Adeli, Russ Altman, Simran Arora, Sydney von Arx, Michael S. Bernstein, Jeannette Bohg, Antoine Bosselut, Emma Brunskill, Erik Brynjolfsson, Shyamal Buch, Dallas Card, Rodrigo Castellon, Niladri Chatterji, Annie Chen, Kathleen Creel, Jared Quincy Davis, Dora Demszky, Chris Donahue, Moussa Doumbouya, Esin Durmus, Stefano Ermon, John Etchemendy, Kawin Ethayarajh, Li Fei-Fei, Chelsea Finn, Trevor Gale, Lauren Gillespie, Karan Goel, Noah Goodman, Shelby Grossman, Neel Guha, Tatsunori Hashimoto, Peter Henderson, John Hewitt, Daniel E. Ho, Jenny Hong, Kyle Hsu, Jing Huang, Thomas Icard, Saahil Jain, Dan Jurafsky, Pratyusha Kalluri, Siddharth Karamcheti, Geoff Keeling, Fereshte Khani, Omar Khattab, Pang Wei Koh, Mark Krass, Ranjay Krishna, Rohith Kuditipudi, Ananya Kumar, Faisal Ladhak, Mina Lee, Tony Lee, Jure Leskovec, Isabelle Levent, Xiang Lisa Li, Xuechen Li, Tengyu Ma, Ali Malik, Christopher D. Manning, Suvir Mirchandani, Eric Mitchell, Zanele Munyikwa, Suraj Nair, Avanika Narayan, Deepak Narayanan, Ben Newman, Allen Nie, Juan Carlos Niebles, Hamed Nilforoshan, Julian Nyarko, Giray Ogut, Laurel Orr, Isabel Papadimitriou, Joon Sung Park, Chris Piech, Eva Portelance, Christopher Potts, Aditi Raghunathan, Rob Reich, Hongyu Ren, Frieda Rong, Yusuf Roohani, Camilo Ruiz, Jack Ryan, Christopher Ré, Dorsa Sadigh, Shiori Sagawa, Keshav Santhanam, Andy Shih, Krishnan Srinivasan, Alex Tamkin, Rohan Taori, Armin W. Thomas, Florian Tramèr, Rose E. Wang, William Wang, Bohan Wu, Jiajun Wu, Yuhuai Wu, Sang Michael Xie, Michihiro Yasunaga, Jiaxuan You, Matei Zaharia, Michael Zhang, Tianyi Zhang, Xikun Zhang, Yuhui Zhang, Lucia Zheng, Kaitlyn Zhou, and Percy Liang. 2021. On the opportunities and risks of foundation models.

Chung-Chi Chen, Hen-Hsen Huang, and Hsin-Hsi Chen. 2021a. Financial opinion mining. In *Proceedings of the 2021 Conference on Empirical Methods in Natural Language Processing: Tutorial Abstracts*, pages 7–10.

Chung-Chi Chen, Hen-Hsen Huang, and Hsin-Hsi Chen. 2021b. *From Opinion Mining to Financial Argument Mining*. Springer Briefs in Computer Science. Springer.

Chung-Chi Chen, Hen-Hsen Huang, Hiroya Takamura, and Hsin-Hsi Chen. 2022. Overview of the finnlp-2022 erai task: Evaluating the rationales of amateur investors. In *Proceedings of the Fourth Workshop on Financial Technology and Natural Language Processing*, Abu Dhabi, United Arab Emirates. Association for Computational Linguistics.

Qinkai Chen. 2021. Stock movement prediction with financial news using contextualized embedding from bert. *arXiv preprint arXiv:2107.08721*.

Yiming Cui, Wanxiang Che, Ting Liu, Bing Qin, Shijin Wang, and Guoping Hu. 2020. Revisiting pre-trained models for Chinese natural language processing. In *Proceedings of the 2020 Conference on Empirical Methods in Natural Language Processing: Findings*, pages 657–668, Online. Association for Computational Linguistics.

Jacob Devlin, Ming-Wei Chang, Kenton Lee, and Kristina Toutanova. 2019. BERT: Pre-training of deep bidirectional transformers for language understanding. In *Proceedings of the 2019 Conference of the North American Chapter of the Association for Computational Linguistics: Human Language Technologies, Volume 1 (Long and Short Papers)*, pages 4171–4186, Minneapolis, Minnesota. Association for Computational Linguistics.

Mahmoud El-Haj, Paul Rayson, and Nadhem Zmandar, editors. 2021. *Proceedings of the 3rd Financial Narrative Processing Workshop*. Association for Computational Linguistics, Lancaster, United Kingdom.

Bing Liu. 2012. Sentiment analysis and opinion mining. *Synthesis lectures on human language technologies*, 5(1):1–167.

Ilya Loshchilov and Frank Hutter. 2019. Decoupled weight decay regularization. In *International Conference on Learning Representations*.

Chenyang Lyu, Tianbo Ji, Quanwei Sun, and Liting Zhou. 2022. Dcu-lorcan at fincausal 2022: Span-based causality extraction from financial documents using pre-trained language models. In *Proceedings of the The 4th Financial Narrative Processing Workshop in the Thirteenth Language Resources and Evaluation Conference*, pages 116–120, Marseille, France. European Language Resources Association.

Dominique Mariko, Hanna Abi-Akl, Kim Trottier, and Mahmoud El-Haj. 2022. The financial causality extraction shared task (fincausal 2022). In *Proceedings of the The 4th Financial Narrative Processing Workshop @LREC2022*, pages 105–107, Marseille, France. European Language Resources Association.

David Valle-Cruz, Vanessa Fernandez-Cortez, Asdrúbal López-Chau, and Rodrigo Sandoval-Almazán. 2022. Does twitter affect stock market decisions? financial sentiment analysis during pandemics: A comparative study of the h1n1 and the covid-19 periods. *Cognitive computation*, 14(1):372–387.

Xingchen Wan, Jie Yang, Slavi Marinov, Jan-Peter Calliess, Stefan Zohren, and Xiaowen Dong. 2021. Sentiment correlation in financial news networks and associated market movements. *Scientific reports*, 11(1):1–12.

Thomas Wolf, Lysandre Debut, Victor Sanh, Julien Chaumond, Clement Delangue, Anthony Moi, Pierric Cistac, Tim Rault, Remi Louf, Morgan Funtowicz, Joe Davison, Sam Shleifer, Patrick von Platen, Clara Ma, Yacine Jernite, Julien Plu, Canwen Xu, Teven Le Scao, Sylvain Gugger, Mariama Drame, Quentin Lhoest, and Alexander Rush. 2020. Transformers: State-of-the-art natural language processing. In *Proceedings of the 2020 Conference on Empirical Methods in Natural Language Processing: System Demonstrations*, pages 38–45, Online. Association for Computational Linguistics.

Xiang Zhang and Yann LeCun. 2017. Which encoding is the best for text classification in chinese, english, japanese and korean? *arXiv preprint arXiv:1708.02657*.

Zhuosheng Zhang, Hai Zhao, and Rui Wang. 2020. Machine reading comprehension: The role of contextualized language models and beyond.

UOA at the FinNLP-2022 ERAI Task: Leveraging the Class Label Description for Financial Opinion Mining

Jinan Zou, Haiyao Cao, Yanxi Liu, Lingqiao Liu, Ehsan Abbasnejad, Javen Qinfeng Shi
Australian Institute for Machine Learning, The University of Adelaide
jinan.zou, haiyao.cao, yanxi.liu@adelaide.edu.au
lingqiao.liu, ehsan.abbasnejad, javen.shi@adelaide.edu.au

Abstract

Evaluating the Rationales of Amateur Investors (ERAI) is a task about mining expert-like viewpoints from social media. This paper summarizes our solutions to the ERAI shared task, which is co-located with the FinNLP workshop at EMNLP 2022. There are 2 sub-tasks in ERAI. Sub-task 1 is a pair-wised comparison task, where we propose a BERT-based pre-trained model projecting opinion pairs in a common space for classification. Sub-task 2 is an unsupervised learning task ranking the opinions' maximal potential profit (MPP) and maximal loss (ML), where our model leverages the regression method and multi-layer perceptron to rank the MPP and ML values. The proposed approaches achieve competitive accuracy of 54.02% on ML Accuracy and 51.72% on MPP Accuracy for pairwise tasks, also 12.35% and -9.39% regression unsupervised ranking task for MPP and ML.

1 Introduction

Using textual information to guide investment decisions is not a novel topic in either financial or fintech settings. Many researchers have devoted endeavors to social media posts and tried to dig out the rationale underlying the standpoints. However, these works struggle to cope with a considerable amount of data in the information explosion era, which brings an unnecessary expense to computation efficiency. Moreover, posts with high rationality have more probability of leading to profitable outcomes than those less rational. Thus, selecting high-quality analytical opinions can be a meaningful first step in investment opinion mining.

The ERAI shared task (Chen et al., 2022) proposes the rationale evaluation challenge with the goal of mining opinions leading to higher maximal potential profit (MPP) and lower maximal loss (ML). This challenge uses forecasting skills as a proxy and focuses on amateur investors' viewpoints. Two settings are involved in this challenge, including 1) Pairwise Comparison, which aims to find posts with more rationality; 2) Unsupervised Ranking, which aims to sort out the posts leading to the highest MPP and lowest ML. Several related works have launched good pilots for high-quality mining reviews. The BERT model proposed by Devlin et al. (2019) has been proven efficient in many NLP tasks since it was published. Chen et al. (2021c) presented and summarized the opinion mining methods. Chen et al. (2021a) provides methods to measure forecasting skills from the text. Chen et al. (2021b) creatively introduces the MPP and ML values to support digging into the review quality. Moreover, their proposed dataset, which is utilized in this paper, is the first dataset focusing on revealing text rationals.

Our model is based on a pre-trained language model, and for the binary classification task, we propose a method that utilizes the class-label information, and then we fine-tuned BERT for the regression task. The official results show that our models achieve competitive performance on both tasks, indicating our approaches' effectiveness. We introduce the tasks and present our work as follows. Section 2 elaborates on the shared task ERAI and the datasets for sub-tasks Pairwise Comparison and Unsupervised Ranking. We introduce our methodology and models in Section 3 and present the experimental setup and official results in Section 4. Finally, we conclude our work in Section 5.

2 Shared tasks

The ERAI shared tasks aim to spark interest from NLP and financial communities and to launch a novel pilot with the perspective of text rationality evaluation. The shared tasks have two sub-tasks focusing on digging into investors' posts and sorting out those with higher possibilities leading to MPP and ML.

Proceedings of the Fourth Workshop on Financial Technology and Natural Language Processing (FinNLP), pages 122 - 126
December 8, 2022

2.1 Sub-task 1: ERAI-pairwise

In the pairwise comparison setting, models are asked to determine rational-amateur post pairs' MPP and ML labels. Each pair gives two opinion posts together with their MPP and ML values. Also, the model is asked to predict: 1) the MPP label based on whether post1 has higher MPP than post2; 2) the ML label based on whether post1 has lower ML than post2. According to the findings of Chen et al. (2021b), a rational post may lead to higher MPP and lower ML values.

2.2 Sub-task 2: ERAI-unsupervised

In the unsupervised ranking setting, models are asked to rank the investors' posts within an opinion pool by the MPP and ML values. Unsupervised models would be utilized in this sub-task where the given data only contains the posts without any other supplementary information. The ranked top 10% posts should be the group having the highest average MPP value or lowest average ML value.

3 Methodology

3.1 Sub-task 1: Binary Classification

Label information is essential for humans to accurately interpret the meaning of a limited number of training samples. We proposed a method that utilized the class-label information for the two given opinions. We use BERT (Devlin et al., 2019) as the Pre-trained Language Model(PLM) unless specified otherwise. Specifically, we consider the following process to project two opinions in a common space in order to classify the class using [CLS] token. We append the corresponding class name and a [SEP] token after each training opinion to implement the binary classification tasks (i.e.[CLS] opinion1 [SEP] opinion2 [SEP] MPP Label Info [SEP] ML Label Info [SEP], where MPP Label Info could be 'higher maximum possible profit' or 'lower maximum possible profit', and ML Label Info could be 'higher maximum loss' or 'lower maximum loss'). We took the representation of [CLS] token at the model's last layer and added a linear layer for outputting MPP and ML binary classification results in Figure 1. In this binary classification task, we use Binary Cross Entropy Loss (BCE loss) as the loss function, which reflects the distributions divergence between labels and predictions. The smaller the value of cross-entropy is, the closer the two probability distributions are. BCE

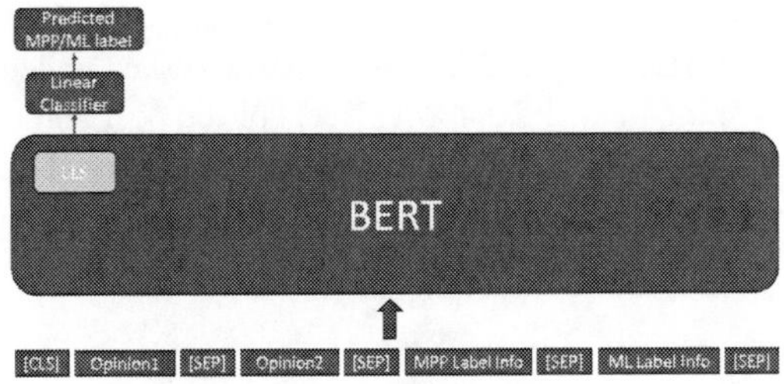

Figure 1: Overview of binary classification for sub-task 1 by leveraging the label information

loss can be described as equation (1):

$$\ell_{BCE} = -(y_i \cdot \log(\hat{y}_i) + (1 - y_i) \cdot \log(1 - \hat{y}_i)) \quad (1)$$

where $\hat{y}_i$ represents the predictions and y_i represents the labels.

3.2 Sub-task 2: Regression for the Unsupervised Ranking

In sub-task 2, the results are the ordered posts by the descending MPP and ascending ML, respectively. We fine-tuned a BERT model to adjust the regression task, whose outputs are ML and MPP values. We apply a dense pooling layer with dropout on the [CLS] embedding for the regression in sub-task 2 rather than just a dense linear layer in sub-task 1.

Mean squared error (MSE) loss is used to reflect the true error of the model in sub-task 2. The gradient of MSE loss increases as the loss increases and decreases as the loss tends to zero. The advantage of MSE in this task is that it converges effectively even with a fixed learning rate. MSE loss is as shown in the following equation (2):

$$\ell_{MSE} = \frac{1}{N}\sum_{i=1}^{N}(y_i - \hat{y}_i)^2 \quad (2)$$

4 Experimental Setup and Evaluation

4.1 Dataset

The shared ERAI tasks aim to sort out the posts leading to higher MPP and lower ML. Regarding sub-task 1, the labeled and unlabeled datasets contain 200 and 87 pairs of posts, respectively. Each piece of the data consists of two posts, two MPP values with the MPP label, and two ML values with the ML label. The MPP label is determined by **Label "1": "MPP1" > "MPP2"; Label "0": "MPP1" < "MPP2"**. While the ML label relies on **Label "1": "ML1" < "ML2"; Label "0": "ML1" > "ML2"**. This sub-task is asked to determine the MPP and ML labels of the post pairs in the unlabeled dataset. As Figure 2 shows, the labeled dataset containing 200 posts has a relatively even data distribution (i.e. MPP label 1/ label 0 is 109/91 and ML label 1/ label 0 is 105/95). We use the same labeled dataset in both sub-task 1 and sub-task 2.

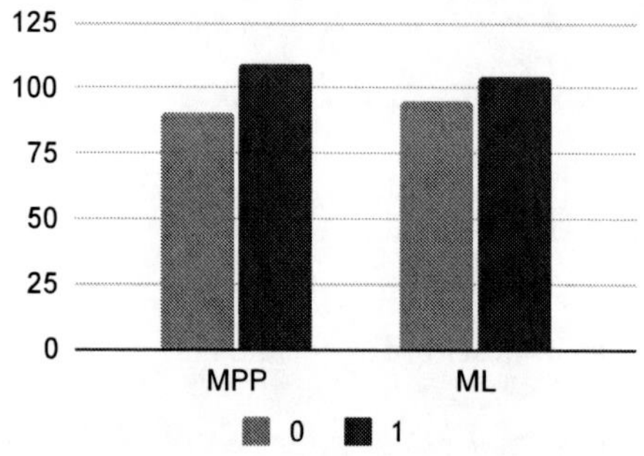

Figure 2: Distribution of MPP and ML label in labeled dataset

In terms of sub-task 2, the dataset contains 210 pieces of posts. This sub-task calls for an unsupervised model to dig into the posts' rationality and sort out the top 10% posts by the MPP and ML values, respectively.

4.2 Evaluation Metrics

According to the criteria of the ERAI challenge (Chen et al., 2021a), we use different evaluation methods for the two sub-tasks. We split 70% of the labeled dataset as training set and 30% as the validation set. In terms of sub-task 1, we use the accuracy to evaluate the model where the result indicates the model performance on two binary classifications (i.e., MPP label and ML label). We show the evaluation metric as the formula (3) (Linhares Pontes et al., 2022):

$$Accuracy = \frac{1}{n_{pair}} \sum_{i=1}^{n_{pair}} 1(\hat{y_i} = y_i) \quad (3)$$

where $\hat{y_i}$ is the predicted label with the ground truth label y_i.

In sub-task 2, we use the average MPP value of the sorted top 10% to evaluate the model where a higher average MPP refers to better model performance. The evaluation metric shows the following formula (4):

$$Average = \frac{1}{n_{top}} \sum_{i=1}^{n_{top}} MPP_i \quad (4)$$

where MPP_i represents the MPP value of the i_{th} post in the final rank list.

4.3 Hyperparameter setting

The models were trained on one Nvidia 2080Ti. The models were trained for 30 epochs with runtime ranging from 35 minutes to 1 hours. We used AdamW (Kingma and Ba, 2014) to optimize our model, and a learning rate of $2e - 5$. The batch size is 8.

4.4 Experimental Evaluation

For optimizing purposes, we compared three pretrained models, including BERT-Base-Chinese (Wolf et al., 2020), a Chinese RoBERTa model named RoBERTa-wwm-ext (Cui et al., 2021), and a Chinese BERT-based model named Astock (Zou et al., 2022) that has been performed domain adaption by training the model with Masked-Language Model (MLM) loss on financial news articles.

Sub-task 1 MPP and ML Accuracy Value		
PLMs	MPP	ML
RoBERTa-wwm-ext (Cui et al., 2021)	**62.50%**	**57.50%**
Astock (Zou et al., 2022)	55.00%	52.50%
BERT-base-Chinese (Wolf et al., 2020)	60.00%	52.50%

Table 1: Experimental results for pairwise comparison in our split evaluation dataset

Sub-task 2 Average MPP and ML Value				
PLMs	Golden MPP	Golden ML	Pred MPP	Pred ML
RoBERTa-wwm-ext (Cui et al., 2021)	6.51%	-10.92%	3.2%	-3.21%
Astock (Zou et al., 2022)	**9.36%**	**-10.58%**	**4.23%**	**-3.11%**
BERT-base-Chinese (Wolf et al., 2020)	6.51%	-10.92%	2.86%	-3.85%

Table 2: Experimental results for the unsupervised ranking task in our split evaluation dataset, 'Golden' represents the real value and 'Pred' represents the predicted value

RoBERTa-wwm-ext achieved the best performance in MPP and ML accuracy on sub-task 1 as shown in Table 1. In sub-task 2, as shown in Table 2, the predicted MPP values and ML values of Astock are closer to the real values than other models, Golden MPP values are also approximately 3%

higher than others. Astock achieved outstanding performance than other PLM models on sub-task 2 in our split evaluation dataset. Therefore, we employed RoBERTa-wwm-ext for sub-task 1 and Astock for sub-task 2 due to the excellent performance as our final submission.

4.5 Official Released Results

The official results of each model across all teams are shown in Table 3. The listed MPP and ML results range from 62.07% to 44.83%, and 59.77% to 36.78%, respectively. Our result with 52.87% is ranked 2nd position (in Table 4) when taking the average of MPP and ML accuracy, which shows our model's high robustness and effectiveness. Specifically, UOA_1 yields an outstanding performance in MPP with an accuracy of 51.72%, and the accuracy of ML is 54.02%. Average MPP value and

Accuracy			
Model Name	MPP	Model Name	ML
Jetsons_1	62.07%	DCU-ML_1	59.77%
Yet_1	57.47%	DCU-ML_3	59.77%
Yet_2	57.47%	PromptShots_2	54.02%
Yet_3	57.47%	**UOA_1**	**54.02%**
LIPI_2	57.47%	aimi_1	52.87%
LIPI_1	54.02%	LIPI_2	50.57%
fiona	54.02%	fiona	48.28%
DCU-ML_1	52.87%	LIPI_3	48.28%
DCU-ML_3	52.87%	DCU-ML_2	45.98%
UOA_1	**51.72%**	PromptShots_1	45.98%
DCU-ML_2	51.72%	LIPI_1	44.83%
Jetsons_3	49.43%	Jetsons_2	41.38%
aimi_1	48.28%	PromptShots_3	41.38%
PromptShots_2	48.28%	Yet_1	40.23%
Jetsons_2	47.13%	Yet_2	40.23%
PromptShots_3	47.13%	Yet_3	40.23%
PromptShots_1	47.13%	Jetsons_1	37.93%
LIPI_3	44.83%	Jetsons_3	36.78%

Table 3: Official results for pairwise comparison task

Average Accuracy	
Team Name	MPP+ML
DCU-ML	56.32%
UOA	**52.87%**
fiona	51.15%
PromptShots	51.15%
aimi	50.58%
Jetsons	50%
LIPI	49.43
Yet	48.85

Table 4: Best average accuracy on MPP and ML for each group

average ML values are used to evaluate the model performance in sub-task 2. Following the task instruction, a higher average MPP and a lower ML

Pairwise sub-task 2 Averaged Value		
	MPP	ML
Baseline	17.61%	-2.46%
UOA-1	12.35%	-9.39%

Table 5: Official results for the unsupervised ranking task

value suggest a better performance. Compared to the baseline (Table 5), UOA_1 provides an average MPP value of 12.35%, which is 5.26% lower than the baseline result. Regarding the average ML, the average value provided by UOA_1 is -9.39% lower than the baseline by 6.93%.

In terms of model improvement, there are two directions we can move on. 1) Different layers of BERT capture different levels of semantic and syntactic information. The current UOA_1 model only uses the extracted features from the last layer, which loses much information. Future work can address this by fine-tuning the output features of each layer of the BERT model and invoking methods such as ablation strategies to extract more useful information from these features (Wang and Neumann, 2018). 2) A more considerable amount of data is preferred as BERT usually requires large quantities of data in regression tasks for a better result. Utilizing data augmentation techniques such as GPT-3 (Brown et al., 2020) could be a promising method.

5 Conclusion

This work presents the UOA team with how to tackle the ERAI shared tasks. For sub-task 1, we proposed a model by appending the class-label description from a pre-trained language model to accomplish the classification task. This suggests that our model is able to learn more discriminative features. Specifically, in sub-task 1, our proposed system achieved the second position considering the average of MPP and ML accuracy by statistical manually. For sub-task 2, we leveraged a regression framework to rank ML and MPP values. The official results show that our approaches could effectively solve the two tasks. Our models are simple but effective, and we achieved competitive performance on the shared tasks.

6 Limitations

Since our framework relies on a pre-trained model based on BERT, we have not considered other pre-trained models like GPT-3 (Brown et al., 2020), and will be explored in the future.

References

Tom Brown, Benjamin Mann, Nick Ryder, Melanie Subbiah, Jared D Kaplan, Prafulla Dhariwal, Arvind Neelakantan, Pranav Shyam, Girish Sastry, Amanda Askell, Sandhini Agarwal, Ariel Herbert-Voss, Gretchen Krueger, Tom Henighan, Rewon Child, Aditya Ramesh, Daniel Ziegler, Jeffrey Wu, Clemens Winter, Chris Hesse, Mark Chen, Eric Sigler, Mateusz Litwin, Scott Gray, Benjamin Chess, Jack Clark, Christopher Berner, Sam McCandlish, Alec Radford, Ilya Sutskever, and Dario Amodei. 2020. Language models are few-shot learners. In *Advances in Neural Information Processing Systems*, volume 33, pages 1877–1901. Curran Associates, Inc.

Chung-Chi Chen, Hen-Hsen Huang, and Hsin-Hsi Chen. 2021a. Evaluating the rationales of amateur investors. In *Proceedings of the Web Conference 2021*, WWW '21, page 3987–3998, New York, NY, USA. Association for Computing Machinery.

Chung-Chi Chen, Hen-Hsen Huang, and Hsin-Hsi Chen. 2021b. Evaluating the rationales of amateur investors. In *Proceedings of the Web Conference 2021*, pages 3987–3998.

Chung-Chi Chen, Hen-Hsen Huang, and Hsin-Hsi Chen. 2021c. *From opinion mining to financial argument mining*. Springer Nature.

Chung-Chi Chen, Hen-Hsen Huang, Hiroya Takamura, and Hsin-Hsi Chen. 2022. Overview of the finnlp-2022 erai task: Evaluating the rationales of amateur investors. In *Proceedings of the Fourth Workshop on Financial Technology and Natural Language Processing*, Abu Dhabi, United Arab Emirates. Association for Computational Linguistics.

Yiming Cui, Wanxiang Che, Ting Liu, Bing Qin, and Ziqing Yang. 2021. Pre-training with whole word masking for chinese bert. *IEEE/ACM Transactions on Audio, Speech, and Language Processing*, 29:3504–3514.

Jacob Devlin, Ming-Wei Chang, Kenton Lee, and Kristina Toutanova. 2019. BERT: Pre-training of deep bidirectional transformers for language understanding. In *Proceedings of the 2019 Conference of the North American Chapter of the Association for Computational Linguistics: Human Language Technologies, Volume 1 (Long and Short Papers)*, pages 4171–4186, Minneapolis, Minnesota. Association for Computational Linguistics.

Diederik Kingma and Jimmy Ba. 2014. Adam: A method for stochastic optimization. *International Conference on Learning Representations*.

Elvys Linhares Pontes, Mohamed Benjannet, Jose G Moreno, and Antoine Doucet. 2022. Using contextual sentence analysis models to recognize esg concepts. *arXiv e-prints*, pages arXiv–2207.

Weiyue Wang and Ulrich Neumann. 2018. Depth-aware cnn for rgb-d segmentation. In *Proceedings of the European Conference on Computer Vision (ECCV)*, pages 135–150.

Thomas Wolf, Lysandre Debut, Victor Sanh, Julien Chaumond, Clement Delangue, Anthony Moi, Pierric Cistac, Tim Rault, Remi Louf, Morgan Funtowicz, Joe Davison, Sam Shleifer, Patrick von Platen, Clara Ma, Yacine Jernite, Julien Plu, Canwen Xu, Teven Le Scao, Sylvain Gugger, Mariama Drame, Quentin Lhoest, and Alexander Rush. 2020. Transformers: State-of-the-art natural language processing. In *Proceedings of the 2020 Conference on Empirical Methods in Natural Language Processing: System Demonstrations*, pages 38–45, Online. Association for Computational Linguistics.

Jinan Zou, Haiyao Cao, Lingqiao Liu, Yuhao Lin, Ehsan Abbasnejad, and Javen Qinfeng Shi. 2022. Astock: A New Dataset and Automated Stock Trading based on Stock-specific News Analyzing Model. *arXiv e-prints*, page arXiv:2206.06606.

aiML at the FinNLP-2022 ERAI Task: Combining Classification and Regression Tasks for Financial Opinion Mining

Zhaoxuan Qin, Jinan Zou, Qiaoyang Luo, Haiyao Cao, Yang Jiao
The University of Adelaide
zhaoxuan.qin, jinan.zou, qiaoyang.luo@adelaide.edu.au
haiyao.cao, yang.jiao@adelaide.edu.au

Abstract

Identifying posts of high financial quality from opinions is of extraordinary significance for investors. Hence, this paper focuses on evaluating the rationales of amateur investors (ERAI) in a shared task, and we present our solutions. The pairwise comparison task aims at extracting the post that will trigger higher MPP and ML values from pairs of posts. The goal of the unsupervised ranking task is to find the top 10% of posts with higher MPP and ML values. We initially model the shared task as text classification and regression problems. We then propose a multi-learning approach applied by financial domain pre-trained models and multiple linear classifiers for factor combinations to integrate better relationships and information between training data. The official results have proved that our method achieves 48.28% and 52.87% for MPP and ML accuracy on pairwise tasks, 14.02% and -4.17% regarding unsupervised ranking tasks for MPP and ML. Our source code is available[1].

1 Introduction

The fast-growing financial social media has become a mainstream information source for investors. They prefer to follow high quality viewpoints with persuasive rationales. However, browsing numerous and noisy posts is time-consuming and inefficient. Therefore, automatically identifying high quality posts in the financial field is vital. FinNLP workshop of EMNLP-2022 (Chen et al., 2022) publishes a shared task regarding the above problem focusing on evaluating the rationales of amateur investors. There are two sub-tasks: pairwise comparison and unsupervised ranking for online posts. The posts are all from the financial social platforms of Chinese. Regarding sub-task1, we are asked to select high financial quality posts from pairs of posts. Regarding sub-task2, all given posts are required to rank by their potential financial quality. As evaluation, it is difficult to assess the quality of a post directly. Therefore, we propose and utilize the maximum possible profit (MPP) and the maximum loss (ML) in a certain period (Chen et al., 2021a) as the evaluation metric of opinion quality.

Several recent findings evaluate user-generated social media content, such as posts, tweets, and blogs, by NLP technology. Chen et al. (2021b) explores using AI models for detecting financial fine-grained sentiment tendencies. They proved the importance of mining the premises and evaluating the rationales of a financial opinion. Moreover, Patel and Ezeife (2021) investigated that Bidirectional Encoder Representations from Transformers (Bert) (Devlin et al., 2018) is an advanced deep learning model for fine-grained aspect-based opinion mining on social media posts. Besides, many natural language processing (NLP) technologies have been widely used to analyze financial-related domain information, for instance, stock price prediction (Mehtab and Sen, 2019) and financial sentiment analysis (Sohangir et al., 2018).

In our work, we leverage several pre-trained language models (PLM) for two tasks, roughly described as (1) Posts classification: Comparing financial quality for two given posts. (2) Posts ranking: Ranking all the test posts by the financial quality and selecting the top 10% of posts. We propose two strategies which are financial domain pre-training and multi-task learning. We are mainly concerned with shared word embedding learning through extracting financial semantic information on a large financial corpus for the pre-training process. Financial embedding would give precise and helpful semantic information for models in order to settle downstream financial tasks. Also, we introduce a multi-task learning approach that combines regression and classification tasks. In addition, multi-task learning can make good use of

[1]Source code: https://github.com/Zhaoxuanqin/EMNLP-competition

Proceedings of the Fourth Workshop on Financial Technology and Natural Language Processing (FinNLP), pages 127 - 131
December 8, 2022

the relationship between tasks. Specifically, we combine our models with multiple linear classifiers regarding both tasks and optimize the models by joint weighted loss calculation.

At last, we introduce our methodology and solve the task as follows. Section 2 elaborates on the ERAI shared task and the datasets for sub-tasks Pairwise Comparison and Unsupervised Ranking. We introduce our methodology and models in Section 3 and present the experimental setup and official results in Section 4. Finally, We conclude our work in the final Section 5.

2 Datasets

We conduct experiments on two different datasets corresponding to two sub-tasks.

2.1 ERAI-Dataset-Pairwise

ERAI-Dataset-pairwise train dataset comprises 200 pairs of Chinese posts and their English translation version. Each piece of data includes 10 rows: Chinese post1 text, Chinese post2 text, English post1 text, English post2 text, post1 MPP value, post2 MPP value, post1 ML value, post2 ML value, MPP label, and ML label. MPP and ML labels represent the comparison result of MPP and ML values. For the MPP and ML values comparison settings, MPP Label "1" : "MPP1" < "MPP2"; MPP Label "0": "MPP1" > "MPP2" , on the other hand, ML Label "1": "ML1" < "ML2"; ML Label "0": "ML1" > "ML2". (Chen et al., 2021a). ERAI-Dataset-pairwise test dataset has 87 pieces data and identical settings with the train dataset except without the MPP and ML labels.

2.2 ERAI-Dataset-Unsupervised

The ERAI-Dataset-unsupervised dataset contains 210 Chinese rational posts and their English translation version without actual MPP and ML values. Our target is to rank all the posts by their potential MPP values and ML values, then select the top 10% of posts that will lead to higher MPP and lower ML.

MPP	labels 1	labels 0
	109	97
ML	**labels 1**	**labels 0**
	105	91

Table 1: ERAI-Dataset-pairwise labels distribution

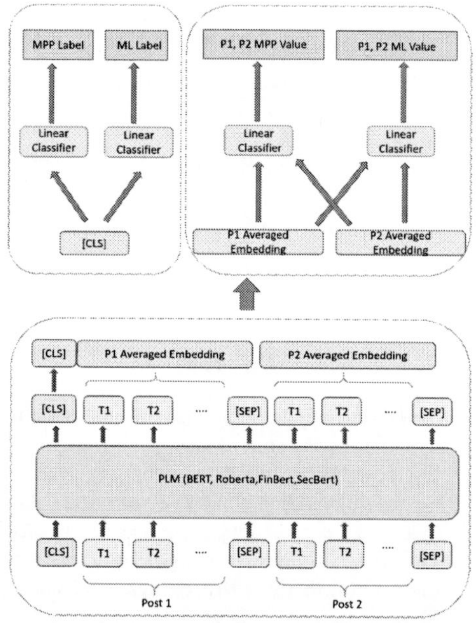

Figure 1: Our multi-learning process is composed of two modules. (a) text classification by the output of linear classifiers after [CLS] token from PLM. (b) text regression by the output of shared linear classifiers from the input post1 and post2 averaged sentence embedding. Two modules are trained together in the PLM, while they do not share the same linear classifiers in different tasks.

3 Method

3.1 In-domain Pre-training

In recent works, the pre-training of language models on specialized domains has been illustrated to have advantages for NLP downstream tasks. (Alsentzer et al., 2019; Yang et al., 2020). We compare three financial domain pre-training models to extract financial features that can improve the performance of the deep learning model.

Fin-Bert: We utilize Fin-Bert model (Yang et al., 2020), which is pre-trained on massive financial domain communication corpora including 4.9 billion tokens.

Sec-Bert-Shape: We also fin-tune Sec-Bert-Shape model (Loukas et al., 2022), which pre-trained on financial domain corpus on both tasks of our original dataset. The Sec-Bert-Shape model also trained word embedding by '[SHAPE]' pseudo-tokens. The English version datasets are applied to the models for extracting a financial representation

Astock: For Chinese models, We apply the Chinese financial domain adapted pre-trained RoBERTa model called Astock from Zou et al. (2022) on the Chinese financial news corpus .

3.2 Sub-task 1: ERAI Pairwise Comparison

Multi-task learning is explored for the task because the original dataset contains not only MPP and ML labels for text classification but specific MPP and ML values for text regression. Our proposed multi-task learning method is to classify the given post1 and post2 over MPP and ML labels. We consider this process a combination of text classification and a text regression task. Figure 1 illustrates the overall architecture of our multi-learning models. We add linear classifiers to process the [CLS] token embedding output from PLM, and shared linear classifiers to process the averaged post1 and post2 sentence embedding output from PLM. Specifically, the model is jointly optimized by the binary cross entropy loss and mean squared error text classification and regression. Furthermore, losses are weighted from those double tasks because there is a significant numerical difference, and it is essential to balance the losses. The formula 1 and formula 2 show how MSE loss and BCE loss are calculated where $\hat{y_i}$ represents the predicted labels and y_i represents the ground truth labels.

$$\ell_{mse} = \frac{1}{N}\sum_{i=1}^{N}(y_i - \hat{y_i})^2 \quad (1)$$

$$\ell_{bce} = -(y_i \cdot \log(\hat{y_i}) + (1 - y_i) \cdot \log(1 - \hat{y_i})) \quad (2)$$

The final loss we apply is composed of the weighted MSE loss and BCE loss, shown in the formula 3 below.

$$\ell_{total} = (1 - \omega) \cdot \ell_{bce} + \omega \cdot (\ell_{mse}^{mpp} + \ell_{mse}^{ml}) \quad (3)$$

As the total loss function (ℓ_{total}) defined, the learning loss function is modeled as the summation of weighted BCE loss (ℓ_{bce}) of classification and weighted MSE loss (ℓ_{mse}) for MPP and ML of regression. Specifically, The modeled MSE loss function consists of MPP and ML because the model can output MPP and ML values together in regression tasks. On the other hand, BCE loss is calculated by MPP and ML label together, so there is no need to sum the sub-BCE loss of MPP and ML.

3.3 ERAI Unsupervised Ranking

As sub-task2, there is no ground truth label for the posts in ERAI unsupervised dataset, so we use ERAI-Dataset-pairwise as the train and validation dataset on which we perform our experiment. This task requires a text regression task, and the model receives one sentence as input. Therefore, we separately trained the models which can output a single MPP or ML value. The PLM last hidden layer [CLS] token embedding is taken as the input of a one-dimension linear classifier to obtain predicted labels.

4 Experimental Setup and Evaluation

4.1 Evaluation Metric

All our experiments for both tasks use different evaluation metrics, where accuracy for the sub-task1 and averaged top 10% ranked values for the sub-task2 (Chen et al., 2021a). Accuracy determines how close the predicted labels are to their true labels:

$$Accuracy = \frac{1}{n_{sample}} \sum_{i=1}^{n_{sample}} 1(\hat{y_i} = y_i) \quad (4)$$

where $\hat{y_i}$ is the predicted values in our samples with their true labels y_i.
In sub-task2, we use the average MPP value of the sorted top 10% to evaluate the model where a higher average MPP or a lower ML refers to better model performance. The evaluation metric is shown in the formula 5:

$$Averaged\ Rank = \frac{1}{n_{top}}\sum_{i=1}^{n_{top}} y_i \quad (5)$$

where y_i represents i_{th} sample in the final MPP or ML rank list.

4.2 Experimental Details

We implement our approach with PyTorch 1.12.1 . We train all models for 30 epochs and choose the best model with the validation set. We use a batch size of 16, a maximum sequence length of 256, and a dropout probability of 0.1. For the optimizers, we utilize AdamW (Loshchilov and Hutter, 2017) with a learning rate of 2e-6.

4.3 Experimental Evaluation

We split the original ERAI pairwise train dataset into 80% for the new train dataset and 20% for the validation dataset. For both task1 and task2, we select four models which are Chinese base Bert (Devlin et al., 2018), Astock (Zou et al., 2022), Fin-Bert (Yang et al., 2020), and Sec-Bert-Shape (Loukas et al., 2022) respectively.

4.4 Experimental and Official results

We report the accuracy and mean rank based on five runs with different seeds for the above method. The averaged results of those 5 runs are shown in Table 2 and Table 3. As sub-task1, Table 2 has shown all the experimental performances on our validation dataset, which can be seen that Chinese Bert reaches a relatively high accuracy compared with the other three pre-trained models, which are 63.75% and 63% for MPP and ML prediction respectively. Astock and Sec-Bert-Shape perform best on MPP and ML values rank, respectively, with predicted averaged top 10% MPP 5.08% against true averaged top 10% MPP 9.04%, and predicted averaged top 10% ML -11.30% against true averaged top 10% ML -7.5%. We apply Chinese Bert, Astock, and Sec-Bert-Shape to the official test datasets.

Models	MPP	ML
Chinese-Bert	63.75%	63%
Fin-Bert	61%	54.20%
Sec-Bert-Shape	52.75%	59.30%
Astock	59.3%	60.25%

Table 2: MPP and ML accuracy

Models	MPP	ML
Chinese-Bert	3.94%	-12.05%
Fin-Bert	3.48%	-12.63%
Sec-Bert-Shape	3.30%	-11.30%
Astock	5.08%	-11.57%

Table 3: Average MPP and ML of Top 10% Posts

Our official results of submitted files are shown in Table 4. Our team achieves 48.28% and 52.87% regarding MPP accuracy and ML accuracy. As sub-task2, we report 14.02% and -4.17% over averaged top 10% MPP and ML values.

pairwise sub-task 1 accuracy		
team name	MPP	ML
aimi-1	48.28%	52.87%
pairwise sub-task 2 averaged values		
team name	MPP	ML
aimi-1	14.02%	-4.17%

Table 4: Official results

5 Conclusion

This paper describes a multi-task learning approach based on financial domain PLM for dealing with pairwise comparison and unsupervised ranking derived from rationales of amateur investors dataset. We demonstrate that joint loss optimization based on PLM can achieve competitive results. We also observed that Chinese-based PLM performs better than English-based PLM because the English translation cannot accurately express the exact meaning represented by the original Chinese version. For the results regarding both tasks, our models obtain an accuracy of 48.28% and 52.87% for MPP and ML labels in the first task. Besides, our second task achieves 14.02% and -4.17% for MPP and ML in the second task.

6 Limitations

There exist additional limitations in the current methods based on our method. Firstly, the Pre-trained Sec-Bert-Shape model tends to capture advanced representations of numerical tokens, while numerical token rarely appears in original datasets based on our observation. Secondly, we can not provide an efficient data augmentation method for a limited original dataset. The limitation of data may bring an overfitting problem for leading to an inferior result.

References

Emily Alsentzer, John Murphy, William Boag, Wei-Hung Weng, Di Jindi, Tristan Naumann, and Matthew McDermott. 2019. Publicly available clinical BERT embeddings. In *Proceedings of the 2nd Clinical Natural Language Processing Workshop*, pages 72–78, Minneapolis, Minnesota, USA. Association for Computational Linguistics.

Chung-Chi Chen, Hen-Hsen Huang, and Hsin-Hsi Chen. 2021a. Evaluating the rationales of amateur investors. In *Proceedings of the Web Conference 2021*, pages 3987–3998.

Chung-Chi Chen, Hen-Hsen Huang, and Hsin-Hsi Chen. 2021b. A research agenda for financial opinion mining. *ICWSM*, pages 1059–1063.

Chung-Chi Chen, Hen-Hsen Huang, Hiroya Takamura, and Hsin-Hsi Chen. 2022. Overview of the finnlp-2022 erai task: Evaluating the rationales of amateur investors. In *Proceedings of the Fourth Workshop on Financial Technology and Natural Language Processing*, Abu Dhabi, United Arab Emirates. Association for Computational Linguistics.

Jacob Devlin, Ming-Wei Chang, Kenton Lee, and Kristina Toutanova. 2018. Bert: Pre-training of deep bidirectional transformers for language understanding. *arXiv preprint arXiv:1810.04805*.

Ilya Loshchilov and Frank Hutter. 2017. Decoupled weight decay regularization. *arXiv preprint arXiv:1711.05101*.

Lefteris Loukas, Manos Fergadiotis, Ilias Chalkidis, Eirini Spyropoulou, Prodromos Malakasiotis, Ion Androutsopoulos, and Georgios Paliouras. 2022. Finer: Financial numeric entity recognition for xbrl tagging. *arXiv preprint arXiv:2203.06482*.

Sidra Mehtab and Jaydip Sen. 2019. A robust predictive model for stock price prediction using deep learning and natural language processing. *arXiv preprint arXiv:1912.07700*.

Manil Patel and Christie I Ezeife. 2021. Bert-based multi-task learning for aspect-based opinion mining. In *International Conference on Database and Expert Systems Applications*, pages 192–204. Springer.

Sahar Sohangir, Dingding Wang, Anna Pomeranets, and Taghi M Khoshgoftaar. 2018. Big data: Deep learning for financial sentiment analysis. *Journal of Big Data*, 5(1):1–25.

Yi Yang, Mark Christopher Siy Uy, and Allen Huang. 2020. Finbert: A pretrained language model for financial communications. *arXiv preprint arXiv:2006.08097*.

Jinan Zou, Haiyao Cao, Lingqiao Liu, Yuhao Lin, Ehsan Abbasnejad, and Javen Qinfeng Shi. 2022. Astock: A new dataset and automated stock trading based on stock-specific news analyzing model. *arXiv preprint arXiv:2206.06606*.

Yet at the FinNLP-2022 ERAI Task: Modified models for evaluating the Rationales of Amateur Investors

Yan Zhuang
University Of Electronic Science And Technology Of China
delecisz@gmail.com

Fuji Ren*
University Of Electronic Science And Technology Of China
renfuji@uestc.edu.cn

Abstract

The financial reports usually reveal the recent development of the company and often cause the volatility in the company's share price. The opinions causing higher maximal potential profit and lower maximal loss can help the amateur investors choose rational strategies. FinNLP-2022 ERAI task aims to quantify the opinions' potentials of leading higher maximal potential profit and lower maximal loss. In this paper, different strategies were applied to solve the ERAI tasks. Valinna 'RoBERTa-wwm' showed excellent performance and helped us rank second in 'MPP' label prediction task. After integrating some tricks, the modified 'RoBERTa-wwm' outperformed all other models in 'ML' ranking task.

1 INTRODUCTION

With the development of data mining and natural language processing techniques, more and more people are looking at textual information in various fields. One such area is finance. Based on the financial corpora, researchers have pre-trained several models, like Mengzi-Fin (Zhang et al., 2021) and various versions of FinBERT (Liu et al., 2021; Yang et al., 2020; Araci, 2019), which help better learn the semantic layer of financial domain knowledge and more comprehensively learn the feature distribution of financial domain words and phrases. Besides, there are a number of researchers who predict future events with texts (Zong et al., 2020), like mining the sentiment of financial posts to predict which stock has better returns (Chen et al., 2021b). Chen et al. (2021a) compares the rationales of experts and those of the crowd from stylistic and semantic perspectives to find the top-ranked opinions, and find they can increase potential returns and reduce downside risk.

In addition, FinNLP teams holds a series of workshops to help collect the research related to AI in FinTech (Chen et al., 2019, 2018; Zong et al., 2020; Chen et al., 2020), and to handle some frontier financial problems. This year they have partnered with EMNLP and hold ERAI shared task to evaluate the rationales of amateur investors by predicting the maximal potential profit (MPP) and maximal loss (ML) of the given analytical opinions (Chen et al., 2022). We participated it and came up with several solutions like changing the optimizer, using 'Stochastic Weight Averaging' method, which helped us rank 2nd in the 'MPP' classification subtask and 1st in the 'ML' ranking subtask.

2 TASK SETTING AND DATASETS

There are two subtasks in the Evaluating the Rationales of Amateur Investors (ERAI) shared task (Chen et al., 2022), namely 'Pairwise Comparison' and 'Unsupervised Ranking'. The former one includes two binary classification tasks. One aims to determine, given the opinion pairs, whether the given opinion 1 will lead to higher maximal potential profit (MPP) than the given opinion 2, while another requires to determine whether the opinion 1 will to higher maximal loss (ML) than the given opinion 2. 'Unsupervised Ranking' task requires to find out the top 10% of the given posts that will lead to higher MPP. The datasets are collected from one of the largest financial social media platforms in Taiwan, PTT Stock [1] and MObile01 (Chen et al., 2022). And the posts are available in both English and Chinese. There are 200 post pairs and their corresponding 'MPP' values and 'ML' values in the training phase, while 87 post pairs in testing phase of 'Pairwise Comparison' task and 210 posts in testing phase of 'Unsupervised Ranking' task.

*Corresponding author

[1] https://www.ptt.cc/bbs/Stock/index.html

Proceedings of the Fourth Workshop on Financial Technology and Natural Language Processing (FinNLP), pages 132 - 135
December 8, 2022 ©2022 Association for Computational Linguistics

3 METHOD

We applied different strategies to handle the ERAI tasks. In both subtasks, we used a BERT-type pre-trained model (Devlin et al., 2018), but we treated 'Pairwise Comparison' subtask as a sentence pair classification task and 'Unsupervised Ranking' subtask as a regression task.

We processed Chinese posts in one more step than English posts, i.e. turning Traditional Chinese into Simplified Chinese using 'zhconv' library [2] for that many models were pre-trained on simplified Chinese corpus (Cui et al., 2021). Then we removed the '\n' characters, urls, and Emoticons in the posts. Finally, we used a max length of 128 truncation of the posts and fed the cleaned posts into the models.

3.1 Models for Pairwise Comparison Subtask

We used only the original pre-trained model in this task, in both Chinese and English, and applied three-fold cross validation for model fusion. Models include but are not limited to:

FinBERT [3] incorporated knowledge from the financial domain, introduced phrase and semantic level tasks, extracted proper nouns or phrases from the domain, and was pre-trained using a full word mask and two types of supervised tasks on Chinses corpora in the BERT pre-training procedure (Devlin et al., 2018).

Mengzi-Fin (Zhang et al., 2021) was pre-trained on financial news, announcements, research reports crawled from the web following RoBERTa pre-training procedure (Liu et al., 2019).

RoBERTa-large-pair (Xu et al., 2020) was prt-trained on CLUECorpus2020 using a semantic similarity model. It has a high probability of working better than using a direct pre-trained model in semantic similarity or sentence pair problems.

RoBERTa-wwm (Cui et al., 2021) was pre-trained on Chinese corpora using whole word masking (WWM). Points to note that the model is not the original RoBERTa model, but only a BERT model trained in a similar way to RoBERTa training, i.e. RoBERTa-like BERT.

3.2 Models for Unsupervised Ranking Subtask

We used the values of the 'MPP' and 'ML' columns corresponding to the two posts in 'Pairwise Comparison' subtask as targets to train the regression model. Three strategies were applied.

BERT-LR fed the features of [CLS] token from the BERT-base model into a regression layer, which consists of a dropout layer and linear layer. The model updated the weights of BERT-model and the regression layer.

BERT-lightGBM selected BERT-base model as the feature extractor, and put the selected features from the [CLS] token into lightGBM regressor. It is important to note that the model only updated the weights of lightGBM and not the weights of BERT.

Modified-RoBERTa-wwm chose RoBERTa-wwm as the backbone and modified it with 'Stochastic Weight Averaging' (SWA) (Izmailov et al., 2018), 'MADGRAD Optimizer' (Defazio and Jelassi, 2022) and multi-sample dropout (Inoue, 2019). Specifically, SWA generates an aggregate by combining the weights of the same network at different training stages, and then uses this model with the combined weights to make predictions. Here we trained the first 7 out of 10 epochs with learning rate 2e-5, and trained the left 3 epochs with learning rate 1e-4. Besides, we replaced the Adaw optimizer with MADGRAD optimizer for that the latter one showed excellent performance on deep learning optimization. Then the [CLS] token of all hidden states were averaged for multi-sample dropout, and the output were averaged for the final predicting.

4 EXPERIMENTS AND RESULTS

Seven models were adapted in 'Pairwise Comparison' task and accuracy was selected as the evaluation metric, while three strategies were applied in 'Unsupervised Ranking' task and average MPP and ML are used as the evaluation metric, just as table 1 and table 2 show. The definition and the calculation method of MPP and ML can be found in Chen et al. (2021a).

4.1 Experiments and Results on Pairwise Comparison Subtask

To better compare the effectiveness of each model, we first split the data into three folds and then trained the three models accordingly. The offline evaluation metric was the average accuracy of the three models. All the seven models we used in 'Pairwise Comparison' task shared a fixed training config. They were all trained for 3 epochs with

[2] https://pypi.org/project/zhconv/

[3] https://github.com/valuesimplex/FinBERT

Models	MPP Offline	MPP Online	ML Offline	ML Online
FinBERT	55.48	-	**59.01**	40.23
Mengzi-Fin	61.48	-	**59.01**	40.23
BERT-en	62.98	57.47	58.05	40.23
RoBERTa-en	60.48	-	58.47	-
RoBERTa-large-pair	63.00	57.47	-	-
RoBERTa-wwm	**63.98**	57.47	58.47	-
RoBERTa-large	57.53	-	-	-

Table 1: The evaluation metric is accuracy. '-' denotes that we don't test the corresponding model. The figures in 'MPP Offline' and 'MPP Online' columns are the averaged validation accuracy and test accuracy of the three-fold models in 'MPP' label prediction task repectively, and the highest accuracy is highlighted in boldface.

Models	Average MPP of Top 10% Posts	Average ML of Top 10% Posts
BERT-LR	8.52%	-4.35%
BERT-lightGBM	12.10%	-5.77%
Modified-RoBERTa-wwm	**14.61%**	**-3.24%**
Baseline	17.61%	-2.46%

Table 2: The evaluation metric was the average MPP and ML of the top 10% posts. Values in 'Average ML of Top 10% Posts' column are all negative may because the given golden label values are all negative. The best performance is highlighted in boldface and the baseline scores are underlined.

learning rate 4e-5, max input length 128, weight decay rate 0.01 and the Adam parameter 1e-8. Table 1 shows the offline and online performance different models. 'FinBERT', 'Mengzi-Fin', 'RoBERTa-large-pair' and 'RoBERTa-wwm' were trained on the Chinese posts, while the others were all trained on the English opinions. Although 'FinBERT' and 'Mengzi-Fin' were pre-trained on financial domain texts, they still performed worse than the models pre-trained on general domain corpora like 'BERT-en'. And the models pre-trained on Chinese corpora showed better performance than the ones pre-trained on English corpora. This may be because the English posts were translated and the translation can lead to errors, in addition to the fact that there are inherent differences between different languages. 'RoBERTa-wwm' achieved the best accuracy, which ranked 2nd in the MPP prediction task. However, all three models we submitted showed same accuracy on the test set, which may imply we should not split the dataset into three folds, or there is gap between the training and test dataset and our model don't learn anything.

4.2 Experiments and Results on Unsupervised Ranking Subtask

The training config of the models in 'Unsupervised Ranking' task were not the same. 'BERT-LR' was trained for 5 epochs with learning rate 4e-5 and max input length 300 while 'Modified-RoBERTa-wwm' was trained for 10 epochs with max input length 256. Besides, the first 7 epochs were trained with learning rate 2e-5 and the last 3 epochs with learning rate 1e-4. The [CLS] token of all hidden states were averaged and then put softmax layer, normalization layer, regressor with multi-sample dropout sequentially. Finally, the average output were used to make predictions. The baseline only used stylistic and semantic features of the posts, which can be found in Chen et al. (2021a).

The performance of the three models could be seen in table 2. The performance of all our models don't exceed the baseline. 'Modified-RoBERTa-wwm' outperformed the left two models in both tasks, while 'BERT-LR' performed worst in 'MPP ' rank subtask and second worse in 'ML' subtask. It is important to notice that 'Modified-RoBERTa-wwm' ranked first in all competition teams in 'ML' rank subtask. Due to time constraints, we did not apply either the ablation study or the model from the 'unsupervised ranking' task to the 'pairwise comparison' task, which may also be a good solution.

5 CONCLUSION

In this work, we introduced our system models in FinNLP-2022 ERAI task. In 'Pairwise Comparison' task, seven models were discussed and 'RoBERTa-wwm' outperformed other models and helped us rank 2nd in the 'MPP' classification among all submissions. While in 'Unsupervised Ranking' task, we tried three strategies and 'Modified-RoBERTa-wwm', which incorporated 'Stochastic Weight Averaging' (SWA), 'MADGRAD Optimizer' and multi-sample dropout, showed best performance and ranked 1st in the 'ML' ranking subtask.

In the future, we want to apply the models in 'Unsupervised Ranking' task to 'Pairwise Comparison' task through predicting the 'MPP' and 'ML' values of the posts. Besides, we found that the values of 'MPP' and 'ML' showed a negative correlation in both 'Pairwise Comparison' task and 'Unsupervised Ranking' task. This may be because the 'MPP' values are all positive and the 'ML' values are all negative, and we are trying to figure out if this is the reason or not.

References

Dogu Araci. 2019. Finbert: Financial sentiment analysis with pre-trained language models. *arXiv preprint arXiv:1908.10063*.

Chung-Chi Chen, Hen-Hsen Huang, and Hsin-Hsi Chen. 2018. Ntusd-fin: a market sentiment dictionary for financial social media data applications. In *Proceedings of the 1st Financial Narrative Processing Workshop (FNP 2018)*, pages 37–43.

Chung-Chi Chen, Hen-Hsen Huang, and Hsin-Hsi Chen. 2020. Issues and perspectives from 10,000 annotated financial social media data. In *Proceedings of The 12th language resources and evaluation conference*, pages 6106–6110.

Chung-Chi Chen, Hen-Hsen Huang, and Hsin-Hsi Chen. 2021a. Evaluating the rationales of amateur investors. In *Proceedings of the Web Conference 2021*, WWW '21, page 3987–3998, New York, NY, USA. Association for Computing Machinery.

Chung-Chi Chen, Hen-Hsen Huang, and Hsin-Hsi Chen. 2021b. *From opinion mining to financial argument mining*. Springer Nature.

Chung-Chi Chen, Hen-Hsen Huang, Hiroya Takamura, and Hsin-Hsi Chen. 2019. Proceedings of the first workshop on financial technology and natural language processing. In *Proceedings of the First Workshop on Financial Technology and Natural Language Processing*.

Chung-Chi Chen, Hen-Hsen Huang, Hiroya Takamura, and Hsin-Hsi Chen. 2022. Overview of the finnlp-2022 erai task: Evaluating the rationales of amateur investors. In *Proceedings of the Fourth Workshop on Financial Technology and Natural Language Processing*, Abu Dhabi, United Arab Emirates. Association for Computational Linguistics.

Yiming Cui, Wanxiang Che, Ting Liu, Bing Qin, and Ziqing Yang. 2021. Pre-training with whole word masking for chinese bert. *IEEE/ACM Transactions on Audio, Speech, and Language Processing*, 29:3504–3514.

Aaron Defazio and Samy Jelassi. 2022. Adaptivity without compromise: a momentumized, adaptive, dual averaged gradient method for stochastic optimization. *Journal of Machine Learning Research*, 23:1–34.

Jacob Devlin, Ming-Wei Chang, Kenton Lee, and Kristina Toutanova. 2018. Bert: Pre-training of deep bidirectional transformers for language understanding. *arXiv preprint arXiv:1810.04805*.

Hiroshi Inoue. 2019. Multi-sample dropout for accelerated training and better generalization. *arXiv preprint arXiv:1905.09788*.

Pavel Izmailov, Dmitrii Podoprikhin, Timur Garipov, Dmitry Vetrov, and Andrew Gordon Wilson. 2018. Averaging weights leads to wider optima and better generalization. *arXiv preprint arXiv:1803.05407*.

Yinhan Liu, Myle Ott, Naman Goyal, Jingfei Du, Mandar Joshi, Danqi Chen, Omer Levy, Mike Lewis, Luke Zettlemoyer, and Veselin Stoyanov. 2019. Roberta: A robustly optimized bert pretraining approach. *arXiv preprint arXiv:1907.11692*.

Zhuang Liu, Degen Huang, Kaiyu Huang, Zhuang Li, and Jun Zhao. 2021. Finbert: A pre-trained financial language representation model for financial text mining. In *Proceedings of the Twenty-Ninth International Conference on International Joint Conferences on Artificial Intelligence*, pages 4513–4519.

Liang Xu, Xuanwei Zhang, and Qianqian Dong. 2020. Cluecorpus2020: A large-scale chinese corpus for pre-training language model. *arXiv preprint arXiv:2003.01355*.

Yi Yang, Mark Christopher Siy Uy, and Allen Huang. 2020. Finbert: A pretrained language model for financial communications. *arXiv preprint arXiv:2006.08097*.

Zhuosheng Zhang, Hanqing Zhang, Keming Chen, Yuhang Guo, Jingyun Hua, Yulong Wang, and Ming Zhou. 2021. Mengzi: Towards lightweight yet ingenious pre-trained models for chinese. *arXiv preprint arXiv:2110.06696*.

Shi Zong, Alan Ritter, and Eduard Hovy. 2020. Measuring forecasting skill from text. In *Proceedings of the 58th Annual Meeting of the Association for Computational Linguistics*, pages 5317–5331, Online. Association for Computational Linguistics.

LDPP at the FinNLP-2022 ERAI Task: Determinantal Point Processes and Variational Auto-encoders for Identifying High-Quality Opinions from a pool of Social Media Posts

Paul Trust
University College Cork
Cork, Ireland

Rosane Minghim
University College Cork
Cork, Ireland

Abstract

Social media and online forums have made it easier for people to share their views and opinions on various topics in society. In this paper, we focus on posts discussing investment related topics. When it comes to investment , people can now easily share their opinions about online traded items and also provide rationales to support their arguments on social media. However, there are millions of posts to read with potential of having some posts from amateur investors or completely unrelated posts. Identifying the most important posts that could lead to higher maximal potential profit (MPP) and lower maximal loss for investment is not a trivial task. In this paper, propose to use determinantal point processes and variational autoencoders to identify high quality posts from the given rationales. Experimental results suggest that our method mines quality posts compared to random selection and also latent variable modeling improves improves the quality of selected posts.

1 Introduction

The internet revolution and the social media era has made it easy for the public to create and share information including their opinions about certain aspects in society like politics (Chambers et al., 2015), economy (Pekar and Binner, 2017), finance (Chen et al., 2021b) and investment (Wang et al., 2020). When it comes to investment, it is now so simple for people to share their opinions about online traded items in online platforms, stock investment websites in real time. These numerous public comments are of great value in reflecting market conditions and making trading decisions.

The open nature of most of these online platforms means that anyone can share any information whether they are experts on the topic being discussed or not. This presents a serious challenge in identifying high quality opinions especially for critical purposes like investment from such a large crowd of mined results. When people are giving their investments opinions, they provide supporting augments which we define as rationales supporting their reasoning. In the paper, we use the rationales behind the view points by sorting out the opinions that would to higher maximal potential profit (MPP) and lower maximal loss (ML) (Chen et al., 2021a).

The majority of the previous studies have lied on the idea of large numbers using average results obtained from popular tasks for example opinion mining and sentiment analysis. The most recent and competitive approach by (Chen et al., 2021a) identifies posts of high quality by making an assumption that these posts will have similar characteristics as those written by experts.

In this work, we present an approach based on idea that high quality opinions are those that are less redundant but at the same time highly valuable. Unlike the previous approaches, we do not use any documents written by experts since they may not be available but rather only base on contextualized representations from the provided rationales using sentence transformers (Reimers and Gurevych, 2019). We select begin by identifying groups of similar opinions by performing joint dimensionality reduction and deep clustering on the embedding space of the opinions using variational autoencoders (Märtens and Yau, 2020). Determinantal point process (Kulesza and Taskar, 2010) are then used to select a set of representative opinions from the groups identified by variational autoencoders while maintaining high diversity among them.

2 Related Work

Social media and online data have exponentially grown in the last few years and many domains are trying it to leverage to their advantage. Some previous works have focused on utilizing user-generated data from social media (Ghosh Chowdhury et al.,

Proceedings of the Fourth Workshop on Financial Technology and Natural Language Processing (FinNLP), pages 136 - 140
December 8, 2022 ©2022 Association for Computational Linguistics

2019; Rouhizadeh et al., 2018), online forums (Wang et al., 2010), and e-commerce platforms (Backus et al., 2020). Most existing works aims to find clusters, topics, classes or categories from social media data (Jiang et al., 2019; Preoţiuc-Pietro et al., 2019). These approaches usually take into account the law of large numbers and simply average the results extracted from tasks such as opinion mining and sentiment analysis.

Few of the previous works have focused on evaluating opinion quality. Zhongyu and Yang used feature-based methods using textual information in the comments and social interaction related features (Wei et al., 2016). Ying and Duboue provided an annotated pilot dataset and used a vanilla neural network with semantic information to classification (Ying and Duboue, 2019). The most recent work is then one by (Chen et al., 2021a) that leverages high-accuracy models trained on documents written by experts and the crowd to mine high quality opinions from the crowd. In contract, to the existing work, we take a purely unsupervised approach using determinantal point processes and variational autoencoders without assuming access to documents written by experts.

3 Methodology

This section describes our proposed methodology to identify the most import important opinions from a pool of opinions provided by amateur investors. Our methodology is based on the assumption that the most important articles should not be redundant but at the same time should contain the most valuable information that could lead to higher MPP and lower ML.

3.1 Text Representation

We obtain embeddings for all the input sentences using a pre-trained SBERT (Sentence Bidirectional Encoder Representations from Transformers) (Reimers and Gurevych, 2019). SBERT is a modification of the pre-trained BERT networks using Siamese and triplet networks, which make it able to derive semantically meaningful sentence embeddings. This model was trained using Stanford Natural Language Inference(SNLI) and Multi-Genre Natural Language Inference (MNLI) datasets. SNLI contained $570,000$ annotated sentence pairs and MNLI contained 430000 annotated sentence pairs.

3.2 Latent Variable Modeling

In this section, we use a variational autoencoder (a likelihood based deep generative model) for identifying the most interesting groups from a large collection of online posts. Deep generative models define a joint probability distribution over a set of random variables composed of multiple layers of hierarchies. Our methodology is based on an assumption that online posts belong to a certain unobserved latent space, and it is only sufficient to read through only representative posts from the same group.

More formally, let $x = \{x^{(i)}\}_{i=1}^{N}$ be a dataset consisting of N Independent and identically distributed ($i.i.d$) samples of a variable x in a potentially high-dimensional space. We make an assumption that data is generated by some random process involving an unobserved continuous random variable z in a much lower dimensional space. Suppose that z has a normal prior distribution $z \sim \mathcal{N}(0, 1)$ and that $f^{\theta}(z)$ is a family of deterministic functions given by deep neural networks. The process of latent variable modeling involves of two steps: (1) Latent variables z are generated from some prior distribution $p(z)$. (2) Observed variables x are generated from some conditional distribution $p(x|z)$.

The goal here is to learn the model distribution $p(x)$ to fit parameters of the true data distribution as well as possible. This is achieved by minimizing the Kullback-Leibler (KL) divergence between the two distribution equivalent to maximum likelihood objective. Our focus is on latent variable models, which define the marginal log-likelihood via a latent variable z

$$\log p(x) = \log \int p(x|z)p(z)dz \quad (1)$$

Assuming that conditional likelihood is described by the Gaussian likelihood just like the prior distribution; $x_i|z_i, \theta \sim \mathcal{N}(f^{\theta}(z_i), \sigma^2)$.

Estimating $\log p_{\theta}(x)$ involves an intractable integral, VAE instead optimizes maximizing a variational lower bound $\mathcal{L}_{VAE}(x)$ on the log-likelihood $\log p(x) \geq \mathcal{L}_{VAE}(x)$ where:

$$\mathcal{L}_{VAE} = E_{q(z|x)}[\log p(x|z)] - KL(q(z|x)||p(z)) \quad (2)$$

In a standard VAE, the variational approximation $q(z|x)$ is known as the encoder and the latent variable z is known as the decoder. Since our interest lies in identifying the groups of similar articles from where we can sample from, we use a decoder that has a mixture prior during the decoding process as proposed by Martens and Yau (2020).

The mixture prior is introduces a set of basis functions $f_{basis}^{(k)}$ parameterized by neural networks. The decoder in the standard VAE is replaced with a basis decoder network $f_{basis} : \mathcal{R}^{\mathcal{Q}} \rightarrow \mathcal{R}^{\mathcal{P}}$ with output mapped to the data via a categorical random variable, that is for every data dimension $m \in \{1, .., M\}$

$$f_{decoder}^{(m)}(z) = \sum_{k=1}^{K} w^{m,k}.f_{basis}^{(k)}(z) \quad (3)$$

where $\{w^{j,1}, ...w^{j,K}\} \sim Categorical(\lambda_1, ..., \lambda_K)$ (Märtens and Yau, 2020).

We identify the high quality opinions by selecting from the categorical distributions $Categorical(\lambda_1, ..., \lambda_K)$ using determinantal point process (DPP).

3.3 Determinantal Point Process

Let $\mathcal{S} = \{1, .., n\}$ denote a finite ground set containing n items corresponding to all sentences from one of the K groups identified by the variational autoencoder. Our goal is to find subsets of sentences $s \subseteq \mathcal{S}$ from all the K group that are most likely to lead to higher maximal potential profit (MPP) and lower maximal loss (ML).

A point process $\mathcal{P}$ on a discrete set $\mathcal{S}$ is a probability measure on $2^{\mathcal{S}}$ (the set of all possible subsets of $\mathcal{S}$). $\mathcal{P}$ is called a determinantal point process if there exists a positive semi-definite matrix L indexed by elements of $\mathcal{S}$ such that if $S \sim \mathcal{P}$, we have

$$\begin{aligned} \mathcal{P}(Y; L) &= \frac{det(L_s)}{det(L + I)} \\ \sum_{s \subseteq \mathcal{S}} det(L_s) &= det(L + I) \end{aligned} \quad (4)$$

where $det(.)$ is the determinant of a matrix; I is the identity matrix; $L \in \mathcal{R}^{n \times n}$ is a positive semi-definite matrix known as $L-$ensemble. L_{ij} is a measure of the correlation between sentences i and j, L_s is a sub matrix of L containing only entries indexed by elements of $s \subseteq \mathcal{S}$.

We decompose the kernel matrix $L-$ensemble matrix assuming L is Gram matrix adopted from (Kulesza and Taskar, 2010): $L_{ij} = q_i.Z_{ij}.q_j$ where $q_i \in \mathcal{R}^+$ is a positive real number indicating the quality of a sentence and Z_{ij} is a measure of similarity between sentences i and j. Let $s = \{i, j\}$ be a summary containing only two sentences i and j, its probability $\mathcal{P}(Y; L)$ can be computed as:

$$\begin{aligned} \mathcal{P}(Y = \{i, j\}; L) &\propto det(L_Y) \\ &= \begin{vmatrix} q_i Z_{ii} q_i & q_i Z_{ij} q_j \\ q_j Z_{ji} q_i & q_j Z_{jj} q_j \end{vmatrix} \\ &= q_i^2.q_j^2.(1 - Z_{ij}^2) \end{aligned} \quad (5)$$

If two sentences i and j are similar to each other, denoted by Z_{ij}, then any subset containing both sentences will have low probability of inclusion. The selected subset S achieving the highest probability thus should contain a set of high-quality sentences while maintaining high diversity among the selected sentences via pairwise repulsion.

4 Experimental Results

4.1 Evaluation

The quality of the top retrieved opinions are evaluated using maximal potential profit (MPP) and lower maximal loss (ML). To calculate MPP and ML, we follow the opinion of the post on day t when entering the market at opening price on day $t + 1$. The maximum possible profit and the maximum loss are traced during the backtesting period to find the unrealized return of the trading based on the opinions of amateur investors. For bullish opinions posted on day t, MPP and ML are calculated as shown in Equation 6 (Chen et al., 2021a):

$$\begin{aligned} MPP_{bullish} &= (max(H_{(t+1,T)}) - O_{t+1})/O_{t+1} \\ ML_{bullish} &= (min(L_{(t+1,T)}) - O_{t+1})/O_{t+1} \end{aligned} \quad (6)$$

where O_t represents the opening price of the day t, $H_{t,T}$ denotes a list of the highest price of the day t to day T, $L_{t,T}$ denotes a list of the lowest prices of day t to day T, and T is the last day of the back testing period.

For bearish opinions posted on day t, the MPP and the ML are calculated as follows in Equation 7 (Chen et al., 2021a):

$$\begin{aligned} MPP_{bearish} &= (O_{t+1} - min(L_{(t+1,T)}))/O_{t+1} \\ ML_{bearish} &= (O_{t+1} - max(H_{(t+1,T)}))/O_{t+1} \end{aligned} \quad (7)$$

4.2 Data

The dataset used for experiments in this paper was provided by the organizers of the shared task on

Model	Average MPP	Average ML
Random	11.94%	-17.28%
DPP	11.34%	-6.77%
DPP-VAE	**14.81%**	**-5.85%**

Table 1: Experimental results showing average Maximal potential profit (MPP) and Maximal Loss (ML) of the the top 10% of the posts identified by proposed method (DPP-VAE) and the comparison methods

Evaluating the Rationales of Amateur Investors (ERAI) organized at FinNLP: The Fourth Workshop on Financial Technology and Natural Language Processing at EMNLP 2022. The dataset consists of of social media posts from 2019/05/13 to 2019/06/13 consisting of 210 texts of investors' opinions written in text (Chen et al., 2021a).

4.3 Experimental Setup

We used sentence transformers library (Reimers and Gurevych, 2019) to obtain sentence representations of opinions. BasicVAE(Märtens and Yau, 2020) was used for latent variable modeling and implementing translation invariant variational autoencoder. Determinantal Point Processes (DPP) were implemented using submodlib library (Kaushal et al., 2022).

4.4 Discussion

In this section, we discuss the results obtained with our model (DPP-VAE) and other comparison methods in terms of average maximal potential profit (MPP) and lower maximal loss (ML). Table 1 summarizes the average results of the top 10% of the posts on the ERAI dataset. For interpretation purposes, the higher the MPP and the lower the average absolute ML, the better the model performance.

Our results demonstrate that selecting the most important and diverse opinions from the a pool of investor opinions can lead to a lower average ML (-6.77% against -17.28%). Contrary to our expectations, a naive random selection for our case can sometimes be better than a careful selection in terms of average MPP (11.94% versus 11.34%). The difference in average lower maximal loss (ML) between random selection and DPP could be possibly be attributed to the fact that DPP select the most diverse opinions. This can be seen as a more risk-averse strategy of investment which would lead to lower maximal loss but not necessary higher profits.

Our proposed methodology (DPP-VAE) which combines latent variable modeling and DPP registers a significant performance gain in terms of average MPP over naive random selection (14.81% against 11.94%) and average ML (-5.85% versus -17.28%). These performance differences reenforces that careful selection rather random selection of opinions or articles to read is very key to achieve optimal results.

Our experimental results as demonstrated in Table 1 also demonstrate the importance of latent variable modeling in reducing redundancy over selected opinions from the crowd. The performance difference can be attributed to the fact that the marginal benefit of reading two important articles from the same groups (assumed to be similar) is much less than reading two important articles from different groups.

However, the proposed method (DPP-VAE) is still out-performed by the top method proposed in (Chen et al., 2021a) in terms of average ML (-2.46% versus -5.77%) and average MPP (17.61% versus 14.81%). The difference in performance can be attributed that methods leverages high accuracy models trained on documents written by experts to mine top of opinions. Much as their method is unsupervised but stylistic and semantic features learned from expert documents contributes significantly to their performance. Our method assumes no access to any documents written by experts which in most cases may not be available and thus takes a completely unsupervised approach.

5 Conclusion

In this paper, we propose an approach that identifies the most diverse and important opinions a large pool of opinions as high quality opinions. The proposed approach approach (DPP-VAE) combines variational auto-encoders and determinantal point process (DPP) to mine top quality opinions. The rationale behind our methods is that looking at diverse and well-represented opinions from a large crowd is more likely to lead to average maximal potential profit (MPP) and lower maximal loss (ML). Experimental results reveal that our proposed method improves over baseline determinantal point process (DPP) and also achieves significant performance gains over random selection.

Results further reveal that the gain obtained from our method (DPP-VAE) on average ML is much more than that obtained on average MPP. We attribute this to the fact that reading diverse opinions from different investors may be seen as a more risk averse strategy. As future work, it is important to experiment how guiding a determinantal point process selection with a few opinions written by experts would boost its performance and also extending the methodology beyond the ERAI dataset.

References

Matthew Backus, Thomas Blake, Jett Pettus, and Steven Tadelis. 2020. Communication and bargaining breakdown: An empirical analysis. Technical report, National Bureau of Economic Research.

Nathanael Chambers, Victor Bowen, Ethan Genco, Xisen Tian, Eric Young, Ganesh Harihara, and Eugene Yang. 2015. Identifying political sentiment between nation states with social media. In *Proceedings of the 2015 Conference on Empirical Methods in Natural Language Processing*, pages 65–75, Lisbon, Portugal. Association for Computational Linguistics.

Chung-Chi Chen, Hen-Hsen Huang, and Hsin-Hsi Chen. 2021a. Evaluating the rationales of amateur investors. In *Proceedings of the Web Conference 2021*, WWW '21, page 3987–3998, New York, NY, USA. Association for Computing Machinery.

Chung-Chi Chen, Hen-Hsen Huang, Hiroya Takamura, and Hsin-Hsi Chen, editors. 2021b. *Proceedings of the Third Workshop on Financial Technology and Natural Language Processing*. -, Online.

Arijit Ghosh Chowdhury, Ramit Sawhney, Rajiv Ratn Shah, and Debanjan Mahata. 2019. #YouToo? detection of personal recollections of sexual harassment on social media. In *Proceedings of the 57th Annual Meeting of the Association for Computational Linguistics*, pages 2527–2537, Florence, Italy. Association for Computational Linguistics.

Jyun-Yu Jiang, Xue Sun, Wei Wang, and Sean Young. 2019. Enhancing air quality prediction with social media and natural language processing. In *Proceedings of the 57th Annual Meeting of the Association for Computational Linguistics*, pages 2627–2632, Florence, Italy. Association for Computational Linguistics.

Vishal Kaushal, Ganesh Ramakrishnan, and Rishabh Iyer. 2022. Submodlib: A submodular optimization library. *arXiv preprint arXiv:2202.10680*.

Alex Kulesza and Ben Taskar. 2010. Structured determinantal point processes. *Advances in neural information processing systems*, 23.

Kaspar Märtens and Christopher Yau. 2020. Basisvae: Translation-invariant feature-level clustering with variational autoencoders. In *International Conference on Artificial Intelligence and Statistics*, pages 2928–2937. PMLR.

Viktor Pekar and Jane Binner. 2017. Forecasting consumer spending from purchase intentions expressed on social media. In *Proceedings of the 8th Workshop on Computational Approaches to Subjectivity, Sentiment and Social Media Analysis*, pages 92–101, Copenhagen, Denmark. Association for Computational Linguistics.

Daniel Preoţiuc-Pietro, Mihaela Gaman, and Nikolaos Aletras. 2019. Automatically identifying complaints in social media. In *Proceedings of the 57th Annual Meeting of the Association for Computational Linguistics*, pages 5008–5019, Florence, Italy. Association for Computational Linguistics.

Nils Reimers and Iryna Gurevych. 2019. Sentence-bert: Sentence embeddings using siamese bert-networks. *arXiv preprint arXiv:1908.10084*.

Masoud Rouhizadeh, Kokil Jaidka, Laura Smith, H. Andrew Schwartz, Anneke Buffone, and Lyle Ungar. 2018. Identifying locus of control in social media language. In *Proceedings of the 2018 Conference on Empirical Methods in Natural Language Processing*, pages 1146–1152, Brussels, Belgium. Association for Computational Linguistics.

Heyuan Wang, Tengjiao Wang, and Yi Li. 2020. Incorporating expert-based investment opinion signals in stock prediction: A deep learning framework. In *Proceedings of the AAAI Conference on Artificial Intelligence*, volume 34, pages 971–978.

Jia Wang, Qing Li, Yuanzhu Peter Chen, and Zhangxi Lin. 2010. Recommendation in Internet forums and blogs. In *Proceedings of the 48th Annual Meeting of the Association for Computational Linguistics*, pages 257–265, Uppsala, Sweden. Association for Computational Linguistics.

Zhongyu Wei, Yang Liu, and Yi Li. 2016. Is this post persuasive? ranking argumentative comments in online forum. In *Proceedings of the 54th Annual Meeting of the Association for Computational Linguistics (Volume 2: Short Papers)*, pages 195–200, Berlin, Germany. Association for Computational Linguistics.

Annie Ying and Pablo Duboue. 2019. Rationale classification for educational trading platforms. In *Proceedings of the First Workshop on Financial Technology and Natural Language Processing*, pages 14–20, Macao, China.

Jetsons at the FinNLP-2022 ERAI Task: BERT-Chinese for mining high MPP posts

Alolika Gon*, **Sihan Zha***, **SaiKrishna Rallabandi***, **Parag Pravin Dakle***, **Preethi Raghavan**
Fidelity Investments, AICoE, Boston
{alolika.gon, sihan.zha, saikrishna.rallabandi, paragpravin.dakle, preethi.raghavan}@fmr.com

Abstract

In this paper, we discuss the various approaches by the *Jetsons* team for the "Pairwise Comparison" sub-task of the ERAI shared task to compare financial opinions for profitability and loss. Our BERT-Chinese model considers a pair of opinions and predicts the one with a higher maximum potential profit (MPP) with 62.07% accuracy. We analyze the performance of our approaches on both the MPP and maximal loss (ML) problems and deeply dive into why BERT-Chinese outperforms other models.

1 Introduction

Natural language processing (NLP) has the potential to uncover meaningful insights from the vast amounts of unstructured data and impact the financial services industry. The use cases for financial NLP range from quantitative trading, portfolio selection, and risk assessment to speech recognition and customer chatbots on various unstructured sources, including transcripts of quarterly earnings calls, research reports, company filings, and social media chatter. People frequently express opinions about financial products, services, investments, and the stock market on social media. Such financial opinions can be effectively mined to provide recommendations and influence user/enterprise perception.

The Evaluating the Rationales of Amateur Investors (ERAI) shared task (Chen et al., 2022) focuses on opinions that would lead to profitable outcomes by using forecasting skills as a proxy. It is formulated as follows: given two opinions about a company extracted from Chinese social forums by amateur investors, predict the opinion that would lead to a higher profitable outcome or higher loss. We approach this problem using several strategies to represent and classify opinions, including: (1) using BERT-Chinese[1] on the original Chinese posts, (2) using RoBERTa (Liu et al., 2019) and other BERT (Devlin et al., 2018) variants on the English translated opinions, (3) using (2) in conjunction with POS tag features and (4) an ensemble of some of these approaches. Our approach using BERT-Chinese topped the test leaderboard for the MPP task.

We present the results of all these approaches and analyze how these models perform for the MPP task. We also examine what we may have lost in translation between Chinese and English and why the BERT-Chinese model outperforms the English-language BERT models.

2 Related Work

2.1 NLP on User generated content

The world of NLP has started focusing on user-generated content on the internet. There have been several works (Yadav et al., 2018; Wang et al., 2010) targeted at blogs, online forums (Yates et al., 2017), e-commerce platforms, and social media. Most of these works are oriented towards mining data from these sources, while of late, work targeted towards evaluating the opinion quality has garnered the community's interest. In (Diaz and Ng, 2018), authors present a survey in the context of e-commerce platforms. Chen et al. (2019) propose numeral attachment highlighting the relationship between cashtags and numerals in financial content. Lin et al. (2019) use sentiment on social media platforms to predict company sales while Xu and Cohen (2018) adopt tweets to predict stock movement. Basile et al. (2019) find that the style information of restaurant reviews can provide information about the authors. Zhang et al. (2019) show that authorship styles can predict the trafficker. Our current work follows the ideology of employing user-generated content online. Specifically, we are interested in comparing a pair of opinions presented by amateur investors and identifying the profitable

*These authors contributed equally to this work
[1] https://huggingface.co/bert-base-chinese

Proceedings of the Fourth Workshop on Financial Technology and Natural Language Processing (FinNLP), pages 141 - 146
December 8, 2022 ©2022 Association for Computational Linguistics

one among them.

2.2 Ranking Opinions

Feature-based approaches have been developed to rank argumentative comments (Wei et al., 2016) and product reviews (Eirinaki et al., 2012). In Ying and Duboue (2019), authors annotate a pilot dataset and classify rationales into four levels for educational purposes. In Chambers and Jurafsky (2008); Chambers et al. (2007), authors demonstrate how action words impact the narrative chain. In our work, we apply a similar strategy to opinions by grounding the model on action words in the opinion.

2.3 NLP based on Machine Translation

Several works have documented the advantages of employing a machine translation model to perform NLP tasks in a target language. Back translation has been a very useful part of several tasks such as sentence simplification (Vo et al., 2022), style transfer (Prabhumoye et al., 2018), semantic role labeling (Wu et al., 2022), etc. However, translation has been shown to cause confounding errors due to the errors in the translated content. In our current work, we highlight this by comparing the performance of models trained directly on Chinese and the models trained on the translated English version of the data. We identify two categories of translation errors and highlight them in our analysis.

3 Dataset and Methods

The training dataset contains 200 instances of opinion pairs in Chinese, their English translations, along with an MPP (maximum potential profit) label and an ML (maximum loss) label (Chen et al., 2021). In every instance, the pair of opinion posts have associated MPP_i and ML_i values where $i \in \{1, 2\}$, $\text{MPP}_i \in [0.0, 0.16)$ and $\text{ML}_i \in (-0.24, 0.0]$. If opinion 1 leads to higher MPP than opinion 2 i.e., $\text{MPP}_1 \geq \text{MPP}_2$, the MPP label is 1, otherwise 0. Similarly, if opinion 1 leads to higher loss than opinion 2 i.e. $\text{ML}_1 \leq \text{ML}_2$, the ML label is 1, otherwise 0. Out of the 200, there are only seven instances where the absolute difference between ML values of opinion 1 and 2 is greater than 0.1. Similarly, for MPP values, there are only six instances where the absolute difference between opinions 1 and 2 is greater than 0.1. The dataset distribution of ML and MPP labels as shown in Table 1. The test dataset contains 87 pairs of Chinese opinion posts and their English translations.

Dataset	Labels	**ML**	**MPP**
Training	1	105	109
	0	95	91
Testing	1	63	44
	0	24	43

Table 1: Distribution of labels

For the "Pairwise Comparison" subtask, given pairs of opinions in Chinese and their English translations as input, we train two separate classification models to predict the MPP label and ML label, respectively. We describe some of our approaches in the following subsections.

3.1 BERT-Chinese (BBC)

Since Chinese is the original language of the posts, we consider using a language model to process the information embedded in Chinese. We choose the 'bert-base-chinese' model (BBC), a pre-trained Chinese model based on the 'bert-base-uncased' model. We finetune a classification model based on the pre-trained BBC model by adding a binary classification layer on top of the pre-trained model. We tokenize and append the opinion pairs separated by a *[SEP]* token and feed it to our models as input. The learning rate is set to $1e-5$, and the model is trained for 20 epochs.

3.2 Using POS Tags and Named Entities

Given the small size of the training set, we consider hand-crafted features to train our classification models. We fine-tune 'xlm-roberta-large' (Conneau et al., 2019) on verbs (XRL-VERBS in table 2) and named entities (XRL-ENTITIES in table 2) extracted from the opinions using the 'spacy' python library [2]. Instead of feeding the entire posts as input to the models, we use space-separated verbs or named entities. The tokenization, input sequence, and final classification layer for both models are generated as described in subsection 3.1. The learning rate is set to $8e-6$, and the models are trained for ten epochs.

3.3 Ensemble

We also develop an ensemble model combining the Chinese posts and the corresponding English translations. We feed the Chinese posts into the

[2]https://spacy.io/usage/linguistic-features

Model	MPP-test	ML-test
BBC	**62.07**	37.93
XRL-VERBS	49.43	36.78
XRL-ENTITIES	53.49	59.30
ENSEMBLE	47.13	41.38

Table 2: Results of the experiments on the test set.

BBC model and the English posts into the 'xlm-roberta-large' model, respectively. We concatenate the final hidden states from the two models and add a linear layer on the combined hidden states to generate the binary classification results. Considering the complexity of the model, a dropout layer is added with a dropout ratio set to 0.3, and weighted cross-entropy loss is used as the loss function. The learning rate is set to $1e - 5$, and the model is trained for 15 epochs.

4 Experimental Results

All models are trained using 10-fold cross-validation on the training set. The model corresponding to the best fold accuracy is used to obtain predictions on the test set. Table 2 shows the accuracy scores on the test set. The table shows that the *BBC* model performs the best on the test set for the MPP task with an accuracy of 62.07%. The *XRL-ENTITIES* model performs the best for the ML task with an accuracy of 59.30%.

5 Analysis

This section focuses on analyzing the impact of using the original Chinese posts for classification. The analysis is carried out in two ways - understanding the translation errors and probing the BBC model. All analysis presented in this section is for the MPP classification task.

5.1 Translation Errors

Out of the 87 test instances, the BBC model incorrectly classifies 33 instances. We further filter these instances using three steps. First, train an equivalent English model, M_e, for the MPP classification task. Second, Let S_e be the set of instances where the model M_e makes an incorrect classification. Lastly, filter S_e to obtain S_{e-c} by keeping instances that BBC correctly classified.

The BBC model is the 'bert-base-uncased' model further pre-trained on the Chinese Wikipedia data. Therefore, for M_e we use the 'bert-base-uncased' model and obtain S_{e-c} containing 17 instances. One annotator fluent in both languages manually analyzed the English translations of these 17 posts. The observed errors are divided into two categories:

1. **Literal translation of idioms** - In some cases, the Chinese text span that represents an idiom is translated literally and not contextually. For example, '盤中給賣掉，現在給我漲起~~氣死人' in the provided dataset is translated to 'Sold it on the plate, and now give me up ~~ Furious people' where the span '盤中給賣掉' literally translates to 'Sold it on the plate'. However, contextually, the span means 'sold it in the middle of the day'.
2. **Missing words/insertion of new words** - In some cases, the translation of a span of Chinese text does not match the actual meaning or inserts new words. For example, in the provided dataset, '發哥每天的利多還是比利空多 但股價磨人阿 三不五時還會破底 支撐都不是支撐 能抱的住真的很厲害' is translated to 'Big Brother's daily Lido is still Billy, But the stock price is grinding It will break the bottom of three or five o'clock Support is not support It's really amazing to hold it.' However, the span '每天的利多還是比利空多' actually translates to 'is more bullish than bearish every day.'

5.2 BBC Model Probing

The BBC model has been pre-trained first on English text, followed by Chinese text. Since the model has been trained in both languages, we evaluate the model using posts in different training and test languages. In addition to using the original English-translated posts, we also generate training and test datasets using Google Translate[3] to evaluate the effect of using another translation system. Table 3 shows the results of these experiments. The table reports the average test set accuracy across the ten folds and the best test set accuracy.

The results show that using Chinese as the training language and English as the testing language results in the highest accuracy and average accuracy. Additionally, we see an increase in the test set accuracy when the English posts generated using Google Translate are used, showing the impact of the translation errors. These observations lead to two questions - (1) if the BBC model vocabulary

[3]https://translate.google.com/

Train language	Test language	Avg. accuracy	Best accuracy
zh	zh	59.8	64
zh	en-old	63.9	66
zh	en-cor	**66.3**	**67**
en-cor	en-cor	62.3	66
en-cor	zh	47.6	52
zh	es	63.7	64

Table 3: Results of experiments using different languages for train and test set with the BBC model on the MPP label classification task. zh - Chinese, en - English, en-old - the original English posts, en-cor - the corrected English posts, es - Spanish.

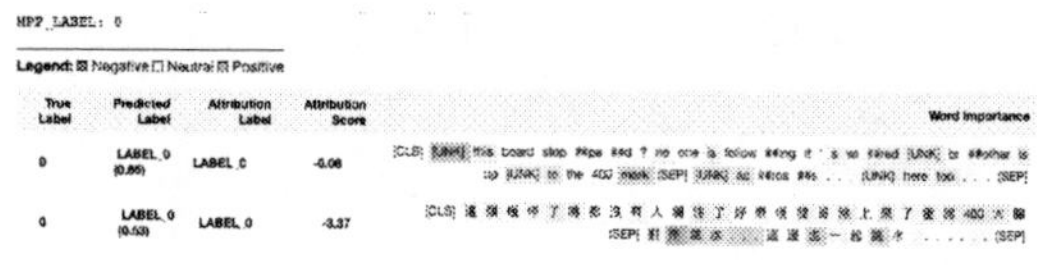

Figure 1: Test example showing the BBC model with token attentions for English and Chinese language with correct predictions for both languages

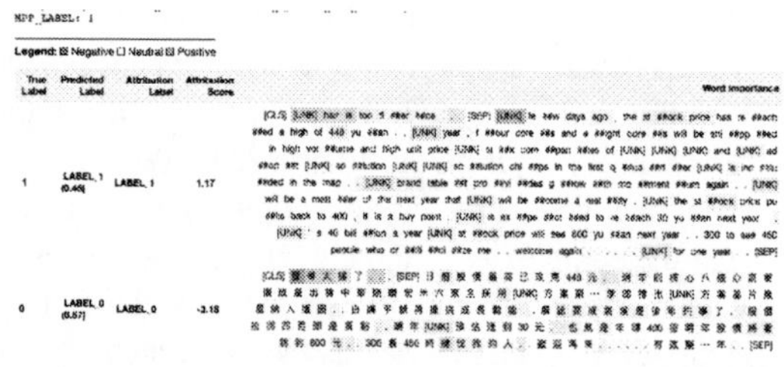

Figure 2: Test example showing the BBC model with token attentions for English and Chinese language with correct predictions for English

is in Chinese, what information is the model extracting from English tokens to classify the posts correctly? and (2) what happens when a third language is used for the test set?

To answer the first question, we use the *transformers-interpret*[4] package to visualize the token level attentions to understand which tokens helped the model in correctly classifying the posts. For this experiment, we use two models - the BBC model trained on Chinese posts but tested on the corrected English posts (BBC_{CE}), and a BBC model trained on Chinese posts and tested on the Chinese posts (BBC_{CC}). We look at two examples: both models make a correct prediction, and only BBC_{CE} makes a correct prediction. Figures 1 and 2 show two examples, first, where the model makes a correct prediction for both languages, and second, where the model predicts correctly only for the English language. The attention weights (in green) in Figure 1 show that the models mostly attend to the same tokens when making the prediction. However, this is not the case for the second example in Figure 2, where the model attends to different tokens when given the Chinese posts as input. The attention scores also show that the model significantly attends to *UNK* tokens. We intend to investigate this observation as part of our future work.

In the final set of analyses, we experiment by using Spanish for the test set to evaluate if the model can transfer the learning to another language owing to its impressive performance when using English for testing. Table 3 shows that using Spanish results in the best test set accuracy of 64%. Empirically, this seems to match the accuracy obtained when using Chinese for the test set. However, when analyzed, we observe that the model predicts class label 1 for all test samples resulting in high accuracy. This experiment yields two key observations - (1) the BBC model exhibits impressive performance on the English test set as it is pre-trained on the language, and (2) the accuracy metric cannot be used to evaluate models for this task owing to its class imbalance. Another metric, like Macro F1, can alleviate the class imbalance and help in better model comparison.

6 Conclusion

This paper discusses the models submitted for the ERAI Pairwise Comparison subtask organized at FinNLP 2022. Of the submitted models, the BERT-Chinese model trained on the Chinese posts ranks first on the MPP label leaderboard. We investigate why using Chinese posts over translated English posts results in higher accuracy and attribute the behavior to errors in translation. Additionally, we probe the BERT-Chinese model using different training and testing language combinations to evaluate the impact of two language pre-training. We show that the model did better when trained on Chinese posts and tested on English translations. Lastly, we show that the accuracy metric is not suited for the task owing to its inability to handle class imbalance.

[4]https://github.com/cdpierse/transformers-interpret

References

Angelo Basile, Albert Gatt, and Malvina Nissim. 2019. You write like you eat: Stylistic variation as a predictor of social stratification. *arXiv preprint arXiv:1907.07265*.

Nathanael Chambers and Dan Jurafsky. 2008. Unsupervised learning of narrative event chains. In *Proceedings of ACL-08: HLT*, pages 789–797.

Nathanael Chambers, Shan Wang, and Dan Jurafsky. 2007. Classifying temporal relations between events. In *Proceedings of the 45th annual meeting of the association for computational linguistics companion volume proceedings of the demo and poster sessions*, pages 173–176.

Chung-Chi Chen, Hen-Hsen Huang, and Hsin-Hsi Chen. 2019. Numeral attachment with auxiliary tasks. In *Proceedings of the 42nd International ACM SIGIR Conference on Research and Development in Information Retrieval*, pages 1161–1164.

Chung-Chi Chen, Hen-Hsen Huang, and Hsin-Hsi Chen. 2021. Evaluating the rationales of amateur investors. In *Proceedings of the Web Conference 2021*, WWW '21, page 3987–3998, New York, NY, USA. Association for Computing Machinery.

Chung-Chi Chen, Hen-Hsen Huang, Hiroya Takamura, and Hsin-Hsi Chen. 2022. Overview of the finnlp-2022 erai task: Evaluating the rationales of amateur investors. In *Proceedings of the Fourth Workshop on Financial Technology and Natural Language Processing*, Abu Dhabi, United Arab Emirates. Association for Computational Linguistics.

Alexis Conneau, Kartikay Khandelwal, Naman Goyal, Vishrav Chaudhary, Guillaume Wenzek, Francisco Guzmán, Edouard Grave, Myle Ott, Luke Zettlemoyer, and Veselin Stoyanov. 2019. Unsupervised cross-lingual representation learning at scale. *CoRR*, abs/1911.02116.

Jacob Devlin, Ming-Wei Chang, Kenton Lee, and Kristina Toutanova. 2018. BERT: pre-training of deep bidirectional transformers for language understanding. *CoRR*, abs/1810.04805.

Gerardo Ocampo Diaz and Vincent Ng. 2018. Modeling and prediction of online product review helpfulness: a survey. In *Proceedings of the 56th Annual Meeting of the Association for Computational Linguistics (Volume 1: Long Papers)*, pages 698–708.

Magdalini Eirinaki, Shamita Pisal, and Japinder Singh. 2012. Feature-based opinion mining and ranking. *Journal of Computer and System Sciences*, 78(4):1175–1184.

Zhaojiang Lin, Andrea Madotto, Genta Indra Winata, Zihan Liu, Yan Xu, Cong Gao, and Pascale Fung. 2019. Learning to learn sales prediction with social media sentiment. In *Proceedings of the First Workshop on Financial Technology and Natural Language Processing*, pages 47–53.

Yinhan Liu, Myle Ott, Naman Goyal, Jingfei Du, Mandar Joshi, Danqi Chen, Omer Levy, Mike Lewis, Luke Zettlemoyer, and Veselin Stoyanov. 2019. Roberta: A robustly optimized bert pretraining approach. *arXiv preprint arXiv:1907.11692*.

Shrimai Prabhumoye, Yulia Tsvetkov, Ruslan Salakhutdinov, and Alan W Black. 2018. Style transfer through back-translation. *arXiv preprint arXiv:1804.09000*.

Vy Vo, Weiqing Wang, and Wray Buntine. 2022. Unsupervised sentence simplification via dependency parsing. *arXiv preprint arXiv:2206.12261*.

Jia Wang, Qing Li, Yuanzhu Peter Chen, and Zhangxi Lin. 2010. Recommendation in internet forums and blogs. In *Proceedings of the 48th Annual Meeting of the Association for Computational Linguistics*, pages 257–265.

Zhongyu Wei, Yang Liu, and Yi Li. 2016. Is this post persuasive? ranking argumentative comments in online forum. In *Proceedings of the 54th Annual Meeting of the Association for Computational Linguistics (Volume 2: Short Papers)*, pages 195–200.

Han Wu, Haochen Tan, Kun Xu, Shuqi Liu, Lianwei Wu, and Linqi Song. 2022. Zero-shot cross-lingual conversational semantic role labeling. *arXiv preprint arXiv:2204.04914*.

Yumo Xu and Shay B Cohen. 2018. Stock movement prediction from tweets and historical prices. In *Proceedings of the 56th Annual Meeting of the Association for Computational Linguistics (Volume 1: Long Papers)*, pages 1970–1979.

Shweta Yadav, Asif Ekbal, Sriparna Saha, Pushpak Bhattacharyya, and Amit Sheth. 2018. Multi-task learning framework for mining crowd intelligence towards clinical treatment.

Andrew Yates, Arman Cohan, and Nazli Goharian. 2017. Depression and self-harm risk assessment in online forums. *arXiv preprint arXiv:1709.01848*.

Annie Ying and Pablo Duboue. 2019. Rationale classification for educational trading platforms. In *Proceedings of the First Workshop on Financial Technology and Natural Language Processing*, pages 14–20.

Yiming Zhang, Yujie Fan, Wei Song, Shifu Hou, Yanfang Ye, Xin Li, Liang Zhao, Chuan Shi, Jiabin Wang, and Qi Xiong. 2019. Your style your identity: Leveraging writing and photography styles for drug trafficker identification in darknet markets over attributed heterogeneous information network. In *The World Wide Web Conference*, pages 3448–3454.

A Appendix

Table 4 shows the 10 fold cross validation accuracy scores for our best models in the MPP and ML subtask. The high variance in the scores is due to the dataset's small size.

k	MPP-test	ML-test
0	45	60
1	80	60
2	55	55
3	80	60
4	65	80
5	35	60
6	50	50
7	50	60
8	55	65
9	60	20

Table 4: Ten-fold cross validation accuracy scores of the *BBC* model for the MPP task and the *XRL-ENTITIES* model for ML task.

No Stock is an Island: Learning Internal and Relational Attributes of Stocks with Contrastive Learning

Shicheng Li[1*], **Wei Li**[2*], **Zhiyuan Zhang**[1], **Ruihan Bao**[3†], **Keiko Harimoto**[3] and **Xu Sun**[1]
[1]MOE Key Lab of Computational Linguistics, School of Computer Science, Peking University
[2]Institute of Information Science, Beijing Language and Culture Univeristy
[3]Mizuho Securities Co., Ltd.
lisc99@pku.edu.cn, liweitj47@blcu.edu.cn, zzy1210@pku.edu.cn {ruihan.bao, keiko.harimoto}@mizuho-sc.com, xusun@pku.edu.cn

Abstract

Previous work has demonstrated the viability of applying deep learning techniques in the financial area. Recently, the task of stock embedding learning has been drawing attention from the research community, which aims to represent the characteristics of stocks with distributed vectors that can be used in various financial analysis scenarios. Existing approaches for learning stock embeddings either require expert knowledge, or mainly focus on the textual part of information corresponding to individual temporal movements. In this paper, we propose to model stock properties as the combination of internal attributes and relational attributes, which takes into consideration both the time-invariant properties of individual stocks and their movement patterns in relation to the market. To learn the two types of attributes from financial news and transaction data, we design several training objectives based on contrastive learning to extract and separate the long-term and temporary information in the data that are able to counter the inherent randomness of the stock market. Experiments and further analyses on portfolio optimization reveal the effectiveness of our method in extracting comprehensive stock information from various data sources.

1 Introduction

With the prosperity of machine learning, a whole new range of powerful data analysis tools has been introduced to applied fields such as health and economics. One of the areas that benefit most from this revolution is the area of financial technologies, where machine learning has been widely used in tasks including stock trend prediction [Li *et al.*, 2020; Zhao *et al.*, 2021] and optimal execution [Ning *et al.*, 2018].

In this work, we focus on the task of stock embedding learning. Similar to the well-studied task of word embeddings, stock embedding learning aims to represent the characteristics of a stock with a densely distributed vector. Stock embeddings that capture the comprehensive properties of stocks accurately can provide valuable stock information for downstream financial analysis.

Previous methods for learning stock embeddings broadly fall into two categories. Methods in the first category propose to combine stock representation learning with traditional technical analysis and learn the intrinsic properties or indicators based on the investment behavior of fund managers [Li *et al.*, 2019; Chen *et al.*, 2019]. However, the professional knowledge of human experts is usually difficult to access for the public, limiting the scope of application. Also, due to the vast amount of data in the stock market, even experts cannot take a comprehensive view of all available information.

The second category consists of methods that are more focused on data-driven deep learning techniques and bear more resemblance to our approach [Du and Tanaka-Ishii, 2020]. These methods make use of financial news and stock price data by employing learnable stock embeddings in the stock movement prediction or classification task. The main drawback of these approaches is that they only focus on the textual part of information corresponding to the movement of stock. Consequently, they either neglect the intrinsic properties of a stock or fail to explicitly model the relations between stocks, both of which carry valuable information for the process of financial analysis.

In view of the downsides of existing work, we propose a method to extract comprehensive stock information solely from news and price data. To be specific, we model the characteristics of a stock from two aspects: the internal attributes and the relational attributes. For example, consider the following excerpt from a financial news article:

> ...Carmakers Toyota [7203.T] and Nissan [7201.T], for instance, have both underperformed the Nikkei's 5.6 percent gain this year, posting losses of 11 percent and 6.6 percent respectively. ...

Here, "*Carmakers*" conveys information about the internal attributes of Toyota (7203.T) and Nissan (7201.T), i.e., both are in the industrial sector of "Transportation Equipment". On the other hand, "*both underperformed*" reflects the resemblance in the market performance of these two stocks, an example of what we define as the relational attributes .

However, information regarding the two types of attributes is implicit, largely blended in the data and subject to the ran-

*These authors contributed equally to this work.
†Contact Author.

Proceedings of the Fourth Workshop on Financial Technology and Natural Language Processing (FinNLP), pages 147 - 153
December 8, 2022

domness of the market. To address these issues, we propose to disentangle the long-term information and the temporary information in the data for mining the stable properties of individual stocks and stock relations. Inspired by the success of contrastive learning, we design several contrastive training objectives that extract long-term and temporary information from data to learn internal and relational attributes, respectively. Compared to previous methods, our stock embeddings are able to capture more comprehensive information contained in the text and price data, thus modeling the inherent properties and relations of stocks more accurately.

To testify the effectiveness of our approach, we apply our learned stock embeddings to the task of portfolio optimization. The portfolio yielded by our method achieves the highest return and the lowest risk of all tested approaches, demonstrating the superiority of our approach.

Our contributions can be summarized as follows:

- We propose to model stock properties as the combination of internal attributes and relational attributes and to learn these attributes from the long-term information and temporary information in the data.
- We design several contrastive objectives to counter the effect of randomness in the market and extract long-term and temporary information into stock embeddings.
- Experiments on portfolio optimization and further analyses show the effectiveness of our method in learning internal and relational attributes of the stocks.

2 Method

In this section, we describe the model architecture and the designed contrastive objectives to capture the internal and relational attributes of stocks from textual news and transaction data in our embeddings, as shown in Figure 1.

2.1 Overview

We argue that the stock embeddings should contain the intrinsic attributes of stocks from two aspects, internal and relational. **Internal attributes** refer to the attributes that are inherent in a stock and remain stable over time, such as the sector of the stock, while **relational attributes** encode the relationship between stocks in the market. Whereas internal attributes contain information about individual stocks, relational attributes can tell us about their positions in the stock market and allow us to infer knowledge of one stock from other stocks. Our goal is to capture these two types of attributes into stock embeddings from textual financial news and time series transaction data.

However, learning these attributes is non-trivial as they are not explicitly available in the data. To make matters worse, we observe that both news articles and price history are subject to large temporal variations rooted in the randomness of the market. To solve these problems, we propose to view the relevant information in the data as the combination of two independent parts: long-term information and temporary information. **Long-term information** is the time-invariant part of stock information that usually encodes the internal attributes of a stock. **Temporary information** corresponds to the temporal variations specific to a short time period. Despite its randomness with respect to individual stocks, patterns exist in the relative fluctuation between different stocks and are informative of their relationship. By treating the two types of information separately and focusing on the stable, invariant elements, we are able to alleviate the negative effect of random market fluctuations and capture the attributes of the stocks.

2.2 Preliminaries: Contrastive Learning

The key idea behind contrastive learning is that the representations of similar inputs should be close to each other, while the representations of dissimilar inputs should lie far apart. To be more specific, the representation of each input example is treated as an anchor point. Several positive examples and negative examples are constructed using heuristic rules. Then the model tries to reduce the distance between the anchor and the positive examples while enlarging the distance between the anchor and the negative examples by minimizing a contrastive loss such as InfoNCE [van den Oord *et al.*, 2018] or the triplet loss [Schroff *et al.*, 2015].

Previous work on contrastive learning has explored various ways to construct positive and negative examples. Methods to construct positive examples include applying different data augmentations or transformation to the input [Ye *et al.*, 2019] and using different views of the same object such as different channels of the image [Tian *et al.*, 2020]. Negative examples are usually randomly sampled from the dataset, within the same mini-batch or from a memory bank of previously computed representations [He *et al.*, 2020].

In our work, we regard the stock embedding and data from different sources on different days as multiple views of the same piece of information. We use the triplet loss which encourages the anchor to be at least closer to the positive example than the negative examples by a distance $\mathcal{D}(\cdot, \cdot)$ of 1, i.e.,

$$\mathcal{L}_{\text{cont}} = \frac{1}{N} \sum_{i=1}^{N} \max(1 + \mathcal{D}(x, x^+) - \mathcal{D}(x, x_i^-), 0) \quad (1)$$

where x is the anchor, x^+ is the positive example, and $\{x_i^-\}_{i=1}^N$ are the negative examples.

2.3 Notations

In this work, we assume access to two types of data: the financial news of a given set of stocks over a certain time period, and the numerical transaction data of these stocks over the same period. We also assume each news article is annotated with the stock codes it concerns. Datasets that satisfy these requirements are readily available as they are provided by news organizations such as Reuters.

We denote the set of stocks as $\mathcal{S}$ and the trading days as $\mathcal{T} = \{1, 2, \ldots, T\}$. Let e_s be the embedding of stock $s \in \mathcal{S}$. For each stock $s \in \mathcal{S}$ and each trading day $\tau \in \mathcal{T}$, we aim to extract information from two data sources: the news article concerning stock s on day τ denoted by $n_{s,\tau}$, and the sequence of transaction data of stock s leading up to day τ denote by $p_{s,\tau}$. We use h to denote the vector representing the information in the data. Superscripts $^{\text{l}}/^{\text{t}}$ indicate whether the

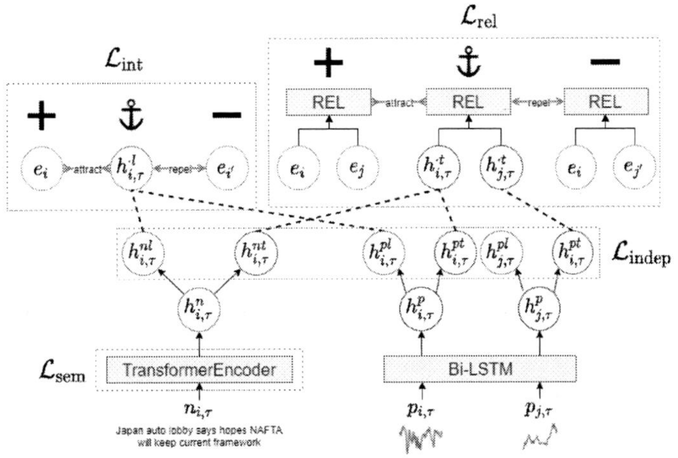

Figure 1: The model architecture and training objectives of our stock embedding learning method.

representation corresponds to long-term or temporary information and $^{\mathrm{n}}/^{\mathrm{p}}$ indicate whether the information comes from the news article or the price time series, while subscripts $_{s,\tau}$ indicate the stock and trading date associated with the data.

2.4 Encoder Architecture

We use a transformer [Vaswani *et al.*, 2017] encoder and a bidirectional LSTM to encode the textual news and transaction time series, respectively. After obtaining the news representation $h^{\mathrm{n}}_{s,\tau}$ and price representation $h^{\mathrm{p}}_{s,\tau}$, we apply separate linear transformations for $h^{\mathrm{n}}_{s,\tau}$ (or $h^{\mathrm{p}}_{s,\tau}$) to extract the long-term representations $h^{\mathrm{nl}}_{s,\tau}$ (or $h^{\mathrm{pl}}_{s,\tau}$) and temporary representations $h^{\mathrm{nt}}_{s,\tau}$ (or $h^{\mathrm{pt}}_{s,\tau}$) with different transformation weights. These long-term and temporary representations serve as the basis of our contrastive learning objectives.

2.5 Training Objectives

We design the following training objectives to guide the training of stock embeddings: the internal contrastive loss $\mathcal{L}_{\mathrm{int}}$, the relational contrastive loss $\mathcal{L}_{\mathrm{rel}}$, the semantic loss $\mathcal{L}_{\mathrm{sem}}$ and the independence loss $\mathcal{L}_{\mathrm{indep}}$.

Internal Contrastive Loss $\mathcal{L}_{\mathrm{int}}$

The internal contrastive loss is designed to capture the internal attributes of the stocks. In most cases, the internal attributes of a stock should remain invariant over different time periods despite the temporal fluctuations of the market. Therefore, information concerning such attributes should appear consistently in the financial news and transaction data associated with the same stock on different days, which we define as long-term information.

Based on this observation, our internal contrastive loss aims at reducing the distance between the long-term representation and the embedding of its associated stock while enlarging the distance between the long-term representation and other stock embeddings. We choose the long-term representation vector as the anchor and stock embeddings as positive and negative examples:

$$\begin{aligned}\mathcal{L}_{\mathrm{int}} &= \mathcal{L}_{\mathrm{cont}}(x_{\mathrm{int}}, x^{+}_{\mathrm{int}}, \{x^{-}_{\mathrm{int},i}\}_{i=1}^{N}),\\ x_{\mathrm{int}} &= h^{\cdot\mathrm{l}}_{s,\tau}, \quad x^{+}_{\mathrm{int}} = e_{s}, \quad x^{-}_{\mathrm{int},i} = e_{s'_i}\end{aligned} \tag{2}$$

where $\{s'_i\}_{i=1}^{N}$ are N randomly sampled stocks.

By minimizing the internal contrastive loss of these representations with respect to the same positive example (i.e., the corresponding stock embedding), the encoders are encouraged to extract from the data the long-term information that is consistent over time. Furthermore, since all these long-term representation vectors are encouraged to be close to their corresponding stock embeddings, we implicitly tell the model to capture the information concerning internal attributes in the stock embeddings.

Relational Contrastive Loss $\mathcal{L}_{\mathrm{rel}}$

Besides regarding each stock as an individual entity, it is also crucial to consider its position in the market and its relation to other stocks. One rationale behind this is that the stocks in a stock market are inter-correlated and information about one stock may reveal some information about other stocks. Also, some financial analytic methods such as portfolio optimization explicitly call for the modeling of stock correlation. This motivates us to design the relational contrastive loss.

Whereas the computation of internal contrastive loss only concerns a single stock, for the relational contrastive loss we need to represent the relationship between two stocks or the temporary information with a vector. Inspired by Socher *et al.* [2013], we design the following REL module which produces a relational vector for any two d-dimensional vectors h_1 and h_2 as follows,

$$\mathrm{REL}(h_1, h_2) = \tanh(h_1^T W^{[1:k]} h_2 + V \begin{bmatrix} h_1 \\ h_2 \end{bmatrix} + b) \tag{3}$$

where $W^{[1:k]} \in \mathbb{R}^{d\times d\times k}$ is a tensor, and the result of $h_1^T W^{[1:k]} h_2$ is a k-dimensional vector with the i-th dimension being $h_1^T W^{[i]} h_2$. $W^{[1:k]} \in \mathbb{R}^{d \times d \times k}$, $V \in \mathbb{R}^{k \times 2d}$, $b \in \mathbb{R}^k$ are all learnable parameters.

For simplicity, we view the relation between any stock pair as a stable quantity that remains unchanged throughout despite the temporal fluctuations of the market. Reflected in the data, this means that for the temporary information of the two stocks on the same day τ, their relational vector is consistent over different τs. Our relational contrastive loss strives to mine this stable pattern by comparing the relational vector computed using the temporary information of different stocks and the relational vector of their stock embeddings,

$$\begin{aligned} \mathcal{L}_{\text{rel}} &= \mathcal{L}_{\text{cont}}(x_{\text{rel}}, x_{\text{rel}}^+, \{x_{\text{rel},i}^-\}_{i=1}^N) \\ x_{\text{rel}} &= \text{REL}(h_{s,\tau}^{\cdot t}, h_{\bar{s},\tau}^{\cdot t}) \\ x_{\text{rel}}^+ &= \text{REL}(e_s, e_{\bar{s}}), \quad x_{\text{rel},i}^- = \text{REL}(e_s, e_{s_i'}) \end{aligned} \tag{4}$$

where $\{s_i'\}_{i=1}^N$ are N randomly sampled stocks.

Similar to the internal contrastive loss, the relational contrastive loss tries to push the temporary information relational vector towards the stock embedding relational vector of the corresponding stock pair, while pushing it away from that of other pairs. By assigning the same positive example (i.e., the relational vector of the corresponding stock embeddings) to the temporary information of the same stock pair, the model is encouraged to extract the stable relational attributes implied in the data and capture them in the stock embeddings.

Semantic Loss $\mathcal{L}_{\text{sem}}$

The contrastive losses serve the purpose of guiding the model to filter out relevant information that benefits stock embedding learning from the deluge of extracted information. However, due to the complexity of natural language, such high-level guidance alone is insufficient for the extraction of useful information from the news. Inspired by the success of masked language modeling (MLM) in pretrained language models, we incorporate an MLM-based semantic loss to inject our training objective with low-level supervision signals that endow the text encoder with the capability of understanding natural language and extracting semantic information from news articles. In this way, the text encoder not only learns the semantics of textual data, but also aligns the stock embeddings with the embeddings of natural language, providing extra supervision signals for capturing long-term information into the internal attributes of the stocks.

Independence Loss $\mathcal{L}_{\text{indep}}$

Ideally, the relational contrastive loss should only capture the attributes that are not inherent to a stock and extract the temporary information that is only invariant when considered in relation to the temporary information of another stock. In reality, however, since the long-term information and temporary information are intertwined with each other in the data, it is difficult for the model to tell them apart from each other, leading to the degeneration of representations. To alleviate this problem, we incorporate an independence loss to encourage statistical independence between the long-term representations and temporary representations by training the model to minimize the mutual information (MI) between them.

As calculating the MI between continuous random vectors is intractable, following Belghazi *et al.* [2018], we leverage a neural network T_θ to estimate the MI between the long-term representation random vector $H^{\cdot l}$ and the temporary representation random vector $H^{\cdot t}$ by maximizing

$$\hat{I}(H^{\cdot l}, H^{\cdot t}) = \mathbb{E}_{\mathbb{P}_{H^{\cdot l}H^{\cdot t}}}[T_\theta] - \log(\mathbb{E}_{\mathbb{P}_{H^{\cdot l}} \otimes \mathbb{P}_{H^{\cdot t}}}[e^{T_\theta}]) \tag{5}$$

where $\mathbb{P}_{H^{\cdot l}H^{\cdot t}}$ denotes the joint distribution of $H^{\cdot l}$ and $H^{\cdot t}$, and $\mathbb{P}_{H^{\cdot l}} \otimes \mathbb{P}_{H^{\cdot t}}$ denotes the product of marginal distributions.

In the meantime, our encoder serves as an adversary for the estimator T_θ, trained to minimize the MI between $H^{\cdot l}$ and $H^{\cdot t}$. To allow the entire model to be trained in an end-to-end manner, a gradient reversal layer [Ganin and Lempitsky, 2015] is inserted between the representations and the estimator T_θ. Through the independence loss, we are able to separate the long-term and temporary information in the data and prevent potential representation degeneration.

Final Objective Our final training objective is a linear combination of all the aforementioned losses,

$$\mathcal{L} = \lambda_{\text{int}}\mathcal{L}_{\text{int}} + \lambda_{\text{rel}}\mathcal{L}_{\text{rel}} + \lambda_{\text{sem}}\mathcal{L}_{\text{sem}} + \lambda_{\text{indep}}\mathcal{L}_{\text{indep}} \tag{6}$$

where the λs are manually chosen hyper-parameters to balance the effect of different objectives.

3 Experiments

3.1 Dataset

We carry out our experiments on the 500 largest stocks of Tokyo Stock Exchange known as TOPIX 500. Our data is composed of hourly transaction data (open, high, low, close, volume) and Reuters news articles of these stocks from *2013-01-01* to *2018-09-30*. We use the data from *2017-10-01* to *2018-03-31* as the validation set and the data from *2018-04-01* to *2018-09-30* as the test set.

3.2 Model

We set the dimension of the stock embeddings to 512. Our price encoder is a 2-layer bidirectional LSTM with a hidden size of 512. The news encoder is a randomly initialized 6-layer transformer encoder with a vocabulary size of 50000.

We use the Adam [Kingma and Ba, 2015] optimizer with a batch size of 64 and a weight decay of 1e-4. The learning rate is warmed up linearly to 1e-4 for the first 10,000 steps and then decays on a cosine annealing schedule. For stability, the model is trained only with the semantic loss during the warmup stage before we add other objectives into the training process.

3.3 Portfolio Optimization

To demonstrate that the information captured in our stock embeddings is useful in real-world financial analysis, we follow Du and Tanaka-Ishii [2020] and evaluate the quality of our stock embeddings on the task of portfolio optimization.

The goal of portfolio optimization is to decide the proportion of capital to invest in each stock within a stock list to maximize the expected return or minimize the risk. Based on the intuition that risk can be reduced by investing money in uncorrelated or negatively correlated stocks, the problem is formulated by Markowitz [1959] as

$$\begin{aligned} \min_{w_j \in [0,1], 1 \le j \le J} \quad & w^T \Sigma w \\ \text{s.t.} \quad & w^T r = E, \quad w^T \mathbf{1} = 1 \end{aligned} \tag{7}$$

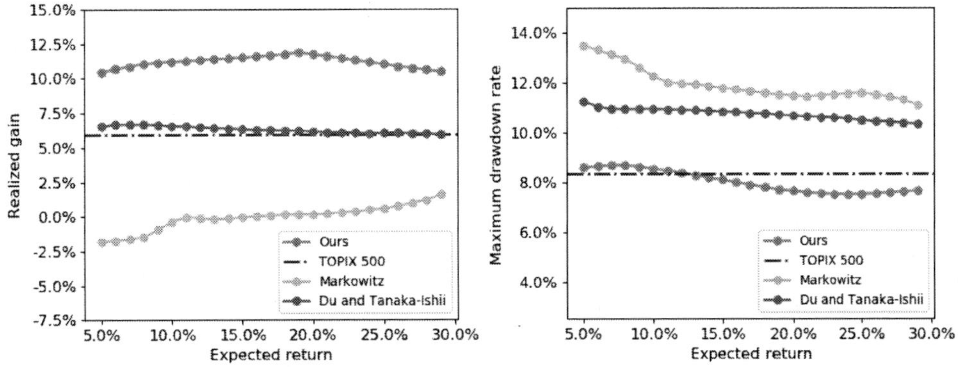

Figure 2: Results on portfolio optimization. Our model achieves higher gain (income) and lower drawdown rate (risk) than baseliness.

where $\Sigma \in \mathbb{R}^{J \times J}$ is the risk matrix measuring the correlation between each two stocks; w is a weight vector that sums to 1 denoting how much capital to invest in each stock; r is the vector indicating the historical returns for each stock; and E is a parameter set by the investor denoting the expected portfolio return. In other words, the goal is to minimize the correlation between invested stocks contingent on a given amount of expected return.

Following Du and Tanaka-Ishii [2020], we define the correlation between two stocks i and j as the cosine similarity between their stock embeddings, i.e.

$$\Sigma_{i,j} = \cos(e_i, e_j) \tag{8}$$

The expected return is set to different values in $\{0.05, 0.06, \dots, 0.29\}$. The optimization problem is then solved using quadratic programming.

We measure the quality of our stock embeddings primarily based on the realized gain of the portfolio, which is the profit rate over the test period. To assess the risk of the portfolio induced by our embeddings, we also compute the maximum drawdown rate, i.e., the maximum loss rate from a historical peak at any time point over the period.

We compare our method against three baselines that restrict available external data to news articles and transaction data:

- **TOPIX 500 Market Index:** The captalization-weighted portfolio of all TOPIX 500 stocks;
- **Markowitz:** The portfolio computed by the original Markowitz model where the risk matrix is the covariance matrix of stock returns;
- **Du and Tanaka-Ishii:** Our re-implementation of the stock embedding-based portfolio propose by Du and Tanaka-Ishii [2020].

The results are presented in Figure 2. As can be seen, our method achieves higher realized gain (higher income) and lower maximum drawdown rate (lower risk) compared to all the baselines. The original Markowitz model constructs the risk matrix only from the correlation between stock price series. This approach neither utilizes information from textual data, nor takes the randomness of the market into account, and therefore performs considerably worse even compared to the market baseline of the TOPIX 500 Index. On the other hand, although taking advantage of both price and news data, Du and Tanaka-Ishii [2020] only focuses the textual information concerning stock movements and therefore performs only slightly over the TOPIX 500 Index. In contrast, our method is able to make use of the comprehensive information regarding both internal and relational attributes in the data, thus modeling the relationship between different stocks more accurately and obtaining the best-performing portfolio out of all considered approaches.

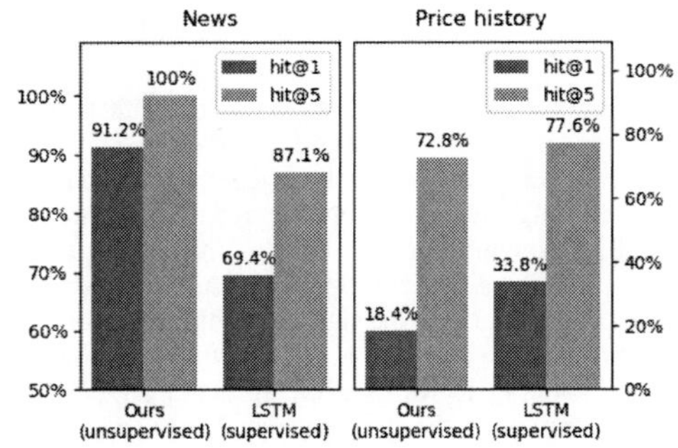

Figure 3: Results on news/price history classification

3.4 News and Price History Classification

To verify that our stock embeddings can capture the internal attributes of a stock by extracting stock-specific long-term information from data, we apply our model and stock embeddings to the task of news and price history series classification, where the model is asked to predict which stock corresponds to a given news article or price time series.

We directly encode the news article or price history with our model and make predictions based on the distances between the stock embeddings and the long-term representation of the input data. Note that no further training or fine-tuning is required for our model, which means that our model works in a purely unsupervised way. For simplicity, we only consider the 30 stocks from TOPIX Core 30 Index. We compare our results with two LSTMs trained on the news article or price history from the training data and report hit@1 and hit@5 on the test set. As shown in Figure 3, although not trained on the classification task, our model achieves comparable or even better results than the baseline methods. This demonstrates that our method is able to encode the long-term information in the data and capture stock attributes in its embedding.

3.5 Clustering

To examine whether our stock embeddings indeed encode internal attributes of the stocks, we perform spectral clustering [Shi and Malik, 1997] on the learned representations of the stocks. Two examples of the resulting clusters are shown in Table 1. Cluster 1 is primarily composed of stocks from the industrial sector of "Electric Power & Gas", while the second cluster contains several of Japan's largest carmakers. This result lends credence to our statement that our stock embeddings manage to capture internal attributes of the stocks such as the industrial area of the company.

3.6 Ablation Study

We conduct ablation studies to verify the effect of the designed objectives on portfolio optimization.

For simplicity, we average the realized gains and maximum drawdown rates over different expected returns. As shown in Table 2, although using long-term information or temporary information alone leads to positive results compared to the baselines, their performance lags far behind our whole model. This supports our motivation of jointly learning the internal and relational attributes by utilizing the two types of information. Removing the independence loss also causes slight performance degradation, which may be the consequence of representation degeneration.

We further remove all training objectives related to one of the data sources. Unsurprisingly, the removal of information from either financial news or transaction data leads to a significant drop in the realized gain. This substantiates the importance to leverage information from both data sources.

Cluster 1	
Hokuriku Electric Power	Electric Power & Gas
Osaka Gas	Electric Power & Gas
Daiwa House Industry	Construction
Tokyo Gas	Electric Power & Gas
Sumitomo Forestry	Construction
Chugoku Electric Power	Electric Power & Gas
Chubu Electric Power	Electric Power & Gas
Shikoku Electric Power	Electric Power & Gas
Cluster 2	
Hino Motors	Transportation Equipment
Honda Motor	Transportation Equipment
Subaru Corporation	Transportation Equipment
Toyota Motor Corporation	Transportation Equipment
Tohoku Electric Power	Electric Power & Gas
Skylark Holdings	Retail Trade
Kawasaki Heavy Industries	Transportation Equipment
Mitsubishi Gas Chemical	Chemicals
Suzuki Motor Corporation	Transportation Equipment
JGC Holdings Corporation	Construction
Japan Tobacco	Foods
Daicel Corporation	Chemicals

Table 1: Examples of the clusters acquired from our embeddings.

Method	Gain(+)	Drawdown(-)
Ours	**11.20%**	8.02%
w/o $\mathcal{L}_{\text{indep}}$	10.01%	**7.65%**
w/o $\mathcal{L}_{\text{int}}$	7.16%	9.11%
w/o $\mathcal{L}_{\text{rel}}$	7.10%	9.50%
w/o price	9.42%	8.27%
w/o news	7.27%	9.53%

Table 2: Ablation study. (+): the higher the better; (-): the opposite.

4 Related Work

4.1 Distributed Representations

Representing the semantic meaning of tokens with distributed vectors has been studied for a long time. Mikolov *et al.* [2013a; 2013b] first propose to learn the semantic meaning of words from their context. Apart from natural language, efforts have also been made to represent the entities and relations in knowledge bases [Bordes *et al.*, 2013; Wang *et al.*, 2014; Lin *et al.*, 2015] or the nodes and edges in graphs [Perozzi *et al.*, 2014; Tang *et al.*, 2015; Grover and Leskovec, 2016]. In this work, we focus on the topic of learning stock embeddings where we introduce both textual financial news and time series transaction data to learn both internal and relational attributes of stocks.

4.2 Contrastive Learning

Contrastive learning is a promising approach in unsupervised representation learning. Early attempts in this area include Mikolov *et al.* [2013b] which designs a negative sampling method based on noise-contrastive estimation [Gutmann and Hyvärinen, 2010] to learn word embeddings. Recent years have witnessed a flourishing of literature concerning contrastive learning. CPC [van den Oord *et al.*, 2018; Hénaff, 2020] proposes to predict subsequent inputs based on previous inputs to learn representations for any data that is serializable on the dimension of time or space. MoCo [He *et al.*, 2020] formulates contrastive learning as a dictionary lookup task and propose to use a momentum encoder to improve the consistency between the key-value pairs. In this work, we first introduce contrastive learning into stock representation learning to help extract information from news and price data and learn expressive stock embeddings.

5 Conclusion

In this paper, we propose to model the properties of a stock from two aspects: its internal attributes as an individual stock, and its relational attributes relative to other stocks. We propose to extract long-term information and temporary information from financial news and transaction data to learn these two types of attributes. To capture these attributes in the stock embeddings, we design several training objectives based on contrastive learning that are able to counter the randomness of the stock market. Comprehensive empirical evidence demonstrates that our stock embeddings are able to model stock properties and relations more accurately.

References

[Belghazi *et al.*, 2018] Mohamed Ishmael Belghazi, Aristide Baratin, Sai Rajeswar, Sherjil Ozair, Yoshua Bengio, R. Devon Hjelm, and Aaron C. Courville. Mutual information neural estimation. In *ICML*, volume 80 of *Proceedings of Machine Learning Research*, pages 530–539. PMLR, 2018.

[Bordes *et al.*, 2013] Antoine Bordes, Nicolas Usunier, Alberto García-Durán, Jason Weston, and Oksana Yakhnenko. Translating embeddings for modeling multi-relational data. In *NIPS*, pages 2787–2795, 2013.

[Chen *et al.*, 2019] Chi Chen, Li Zhao, Jiang Bian, Chunxiao Xing, and Tie-Yan Liu. Investment behaviors can tell what inside: Exploring stock intrinsic properties for stock trend prediction. In *KDD*, pages 2376–2384. ACM, 2019.

[Du and Tanaka-Ishii, 2020] Xin Du and Kumiko Tanaka-Ishii. Stock embeddings acquired from news articles and price history, and an application to portfolio optimization. In *ACL*, pages 3353–3363. Association for Computational Linguistics, 2020.

[Ganin and Lempitsky, 2015] Yaroslav Ganin and Victor S. Lempitsky. Unsupervised domain adaptation by backpropagation. In *ICML*, volume 37 of *JMLR Workshop and Conference Proceedings*, pages 1180–1189. JMLR.org, 2015.

[Grover and Leskovec, 2016] Aditya Grover and Jure Leskovec. node2vec: Scalable feature learning for networks. In *KDD*, pages 855–864. ACM, 2016.

[Gutmann and Hyvärinen, 2010] Michael Gutmann and Aapo Hyvärinen. Noise-contrastive estimation: A new estimation principle for unnormalized statistical models. In *AISTATS*, volume 9 of *JMLR Proceedings*, pages 297–304. JMLR.org, 2010.

[He *et al.*, 2020] Kaiming He, Haoqi Fan, Yuxin Wu, Saining Xie, and Ross B. Girshick. Momentum contrast for unsupervised visual representation learning. In *CVPR*, pages 9726–9735. IEEE, 2020.

[Hénaff, 2020] Olivier J. Hénaff. Data-efficient image recognition with contrastive predictive coding. In *ICML*, volume 119 of *Proceedings of Machine Learning Research*, pages 4182–4192. PMLR, 2020.

[Kingma and Ba, 2015] Diederik P. Kingma and Jimmy Ba. Adam: A method for stochastic optimization. In *ICLR (Poster)*, 2015.

[Li *et al.*, 2019] Zhige Li, Derek Yang, Li Zhao, Jiang Bian, Tao Qin, and Tie-Yan Liu. Individualized indicator for all: Stock-wise technical indicator optimization with stock embedding. In *KDD*, pages 894–902. ACM, 2019.

[Li *et al.*, 2020] Wei Li, Ruihan Bao, Keiko Harimoto, Deli Chen, Jingjing Xu, and Qi Su. Modeling the stock relation with graph network for overnight stock movement prediction. In *IJCAI*, pages 4541–4547. ijcai.org, 2020.

[Lin *et al.*, 2015] Yankai Lin, Zhiyuan Liu, Maosong Sun, Yang Liu, and Xuan Zhu. Learning entity and relation embeddings for knowledge graph completion. In *AAAI*, pages 2181–2187. AAAI Press, 2015.

[Markowitz, 1959] Harry Markowitz. Portfolio selection, 1959.

[Mikolov *et al.*, 2013a] Tomás Mikolov, Kai Chen, Greg Corrado, and Jeffrey Dean. Efficient estimation of word representations in vector space. In *ICLR (Workshop Poster)*, 2013.

[Mikolov *et al.*, 2013b] Tomás Mikolov, Ilya Sutskever, Kai Chen, Gregory S. Corrado, and Jeffrey Dean. Distributed representations of words and phrases and their compositionality. In *NIPS*, pages 3111–3119, 2013.

[Ning *et al.*, 2018] Brian Ning, Franco Ho Ting Ling, and Sebastian Jaimungal. Double deep q-learning for optimal execution. *CoRR*, abs/1812.06600, 2018.

[Perozzi *et al.*, 2014] Bryan Perozzi, Rami Al-Rfou, and Steven Skiena. Deepwalk: online learning of social representations. In *KDD*, pages 701–710. ACM, 2014.

[Schroff *et al.*, 2015] Florian Schroff, Dmitry Kalenichenko, and James Philbin. Facenet: A unified embedding for face recognition and clustering. In *CVPR*, pages 815–823. IEEE Computer Society, 2015.

[Shi and Malik, 1997] Jianbo Shi and Jitendra Malik. Normalized cuts and image segmentation. In *CVPR*, pages 731–737. IEEE Computer Society, 1997.

[Socher *et al.*, 2013] Richard Socher, Danqi Chen, Christopher D. Manning, and Andrew Y. Ng. Reasoning with neural tensor networks for knowledge base completion. In *NIPS*, pages 926–934, 2013.

[Tang *et al.*, 2015] Jian Tang, Meng Qu, Mingzhe Wang, Ming Zhang, Jun Yan, and Qiaozhu Mei. LINE: large-scale information network embedding. In *WWW*, pages 1067–1077. ACM, 2015.

[Tian *et al.*, 2020] Yonglong Tian, Dilip Krishnan, and Phillip Isola. Contrastive multiview coding. In *ECCV (11)*, volume 12356 of *Lecture Notes in Computer Science*, pages 776–794. Springer, 2020.

[van den Oord *et al.*, 2018] Aäron van den Oord, Yazhe Li, and Oriol Vinyals. Representation learning with contrastive predictive coding. *CoRR*, abs/1807.03748, 2018.

[Vaswani *et al.*, 2017] Ashish Vaswani, Noam Shazeer, Niki Parmar, Jakob Uszkoreit, Llion Jones, Aidan N. Gomez, Lukasz Kaiser, and Illia Polosukhin. Attention is all you need. In *NIPS*, pages 5998–6008, 2017.

[Wang *et al.*, 2014] Zhen Wang, Jianwen Zhang, Jianlin Feng, and Zheng Chen. Knowledge graph embedding by translating on hyperplanes. In *AAAI*, pages 1112–1119. AAAI Press, 2014.

[Ye *et al.*, 2019] Mang Ye, Xu Zhang, Pong C. Yuen, and Shih-Fu Chang. Unsupervised embedding learning via invariant and spreading instance feature. In *CVPR*, pages 6210–6219. Computer Vision Foundation / IEEE, 2019.

[Zhao *et al.*, 2021] Liang Zhao, Wei Li, Ruihan Bao, Keiko Harimoto, Yunfang Wu, and Xu Sun. Long-term, short-term and sudden event: Trading volume movement prediction with graph-based multi-view modeling. In *IJCAI*, pages 3764–3770. ijcai.org, 2021.

Prospectus Language and IPO Performance

Jared Sharpe
Institute for Financial Services Analytics
University of Delaware
Newark, Delaware, USA
jaredws@udel.edu

Keith Decker
Department of Computer &
Information Sciences
University of Delaware
Newark, Delaware, USA
decker@udel.edu

Abstract

Pricing a firm's Initial Public Offering (IPO) has historically been very difficult, with high average returns on the first-day of trading. Furthermore, IPO withdrawal, the event in which companies who file to go public ultimately rescind the application before the offering, is an equally challenging prediction problem. This research utilizes word embedding techniques to evaluate existing theories concerning firm sentiment on first-day trading performance and the probability of withdrawal, which has not yet been explored empirically. The results suggest that firms attempting to go public experience a decreased probability of withdrawal with the increased presence of positive, litigious, and uncertain language in their initial prospectus, while the increased presence of strong modular language leads to an increased probability of withdrawal. The results also suggest that frequent or large adjustments in the strong modular language of subsequent filings leads to smaller first-day returns.

1 Introduction

Underpricing, the high average return over a stock's Initial Public Offering (IPO) price on the first-day of trading, is a subject of great financial research (Ritter and Welch, 2002; Huibers, 2020). While the price of the offering is believed to be the best efforts of the underwriter, the individual or firm who assigns the final price, the average first-day return tends to be between 10–14% (Ritter and Welch, 2002). The difference between the first-day closing price and the IPO price, magnified by the number of shares sold, is referred to as 'money left on the table' since it would seem that the firm whose stock is being sold at a premium was undervalued by the underwriter (Ritter and Welch, 2002). A great wealth of literature has attempted explanations using industry, year, momentum, and an assortment of variables and incentive theories (Sherman and Titman, 2000; Lowry and Schwert, 2004; Loughran and Ritter, 2004; Quintana et al., 2005; King and Banderet, 2014; Tao et al., 2018; Seth et al., 2019; Moran and Pandes, 2019), to name a few.

The Efficient Market Hypothesis (EMH) (Fama, 1970) theorizes that current stock prices incorporate all present market information, including the previous price for which a stock traded. IPOs do not have this luxury; market information that would be contained in its price must be discovered through other means, such as within the documents that must be filed with the SEC in order to conduct the IPO: the prospectus filings. Incorporating information from text sources, such as news articles and financial documents, has become exceedingly popular in stock pricing and market valuation, (Hanley and Hoberg, 2012; Loughran and McDonald, 2013; Bajo and Raimondo, 2017; Sehrawat, 2019; Yan et al., 2019; Araci, 2019; Desola et al., 2019; Ly and Nguyen, 2020).

The sentiment construction described below is a strong middle-ground between percentage-of-words in a user defined list techniques common in the finance literature, (Loughran and McDonald, 2013; Hanley and Hoberg, 2012; Loughran and McDonald, 2020), and the effective techniques of word embedding (Araci, 2019; Sehrawat, 2019; Picasso et al., 2019; Peng and Jiang, 2016). In place of counting the number of times sentiment specific words occur in a document, the results utilize the cosine similarity between the embeddings of all words[1] and all words in each of the sentiment word lists of Loughran and McDonald (2011). Four pre-trained embeddings are compared with standard percentage-of-words.

Therefore, the contribution of this work is three-fold. Firstly, the analysis of initial prospectus sentiment in withdrawal prediction. The second con-

[1]All non-English words, symbols, and common stop words ('a','an','the', etc.) are purged from the document using the python package *ntlk.corpus* and are not included in the analysis.

Proceedings of the Fourth Workshop on Financial Technology and Natural Language Processing (FinNLP), pages 154 - 162
December 8, 2022 ©2022 Association for Computational Linguistics

tribution of this work is the expansion of existing sentiment scoring techniques to utilize a stronger, more modern tool: word embeddings. The third contribution of this work is the incorporation of all prospectus amendment document sentiments published before issuing, contributing to the growing literature studying the information revealed during the IPO filing process and how it relates to IPO valuation.

2 Literature Review

2.1 IPO Pricing

Many IPO intrinsic variables have been shown to be correlated with first-day returns; Ritter and Welch (2002) offer a review of IPO pricing factors. A recent investigation into the influence venture capitalist (VC) support has on IPOs shows that such firms are less susceptible to financial distress (Megginson et al., 2016) supporting the screening hypothesis, wherein VCs conduct their own screening analysis so only those firms that will perform well will receive VC backing, contrary to the treatment hypothesis in which VC backed firms do well because of the influence the VC has on the firm.

The litigation risk theory, as extended by Hanley and Hoberg (2010) and Hanley and Hoberg (2012), hypothesizes that underpricing exists to decrease the chance of a lawsuit for misleading investors on the positive quality of a firm (overpricing). In both papers, the authors use the number of root words (i.e if 'will' and 'willing' occurred in the section of text, the root word 'will' would only be counted once), as the total amount of information in each of section of the prospectus filing. Surprisingly, their findings suggest that firms whose filings contain more standard content experience higher first-day returns. Recently, McGuinness (2019) examines how IPO disclosures contained in the Risk Factors and Use of Proceeds sections affect returns and trading volume. Unsurprisingly, firms who deploy more of their proceeds to pay down debt (reduce risk factors) experience less IPO subscriptions and lower first-day and following returns; however, this has little affect on trading volume, compared to those firms that apportion more proceeds to internal investments.

2.2 IPO Withdrawals

Helbing (2019) offer a comprehensive review of the withdrawal literature, calling for more attention from NLP techniques. Busaba et al. (2001) hypothesize that the ability to withdraw from an IPO grants additional power to the issuing firm, since the underwriter can make no profits from underpricing if the offering never happens. Their study focuses on 113 firms that withdraw between 1990 and 1992 identified by the Securities Data Company (SDC) database and employs a probit model for the probability of withdrawal. They find a negative correlation between underpricing and probability of withdrawal, suggesting that underpricing is compensation for *information revelation* rather than *information production*, contradicting theories relating positive information to increased underpricing. Their findings also support the claim that IPO withdrawals are more common in periods of poor market performance. Importantly, the authors suggest that higher uncertainty about the firms value on the part of the underwriter creates a higher chance to receive negative news, increasing the possibility of withdrawal.

Benveniste et al. (2002) theorize that underwriters (investment banks) are responsible for the clustering of IPO timings by industry to overcome the coordination problem of pioneering firms taking the bulk of the cost, through underpricing, in newly developing industries; the authors take the example of Internet based firms following the highly successful Netscape IPO of 1995. Their research includes the 'option-to-abandon' by firms and withdraw their offering if a more favorable option, such as private funding, is available. Their study finds that despite the strong/poor performance of pioneer offerings, follower firms often withdraw/complete their IPO, contrary to original beliefs.

2.3 ML and NLP in Finance

Loughran and McDonald (2020) and Ke et al. (2019) offer recent reviews of natural language processing in finance.

Most famously, Loughran and McDonald (2013), examine the influence of initial prospectus sentiment, final prospectus sentiment, and the time between initial and final prospectus filings on IPO return and post IPO return volatility. Using a percent-of-words approach and regressing the percentage of words within each of a 6-sentiment corpus (Loughran and McDonald, 2011), their results are mixed, leaving more questions about how to quantify and evaluate the sentiment of these crucial documents, though they do find a strong correlation between prospectus uncertainty and high first-day returns. This follows the theory that underpricing is a reward to the underwriter for their assumed risk. McGuinness (2019) amend Hanley and Hoberg (2012) and suggest that each section of the prospectus may have different sentiment for different reasons, such as having different audiences. Thng (2019) examine the differences in tone between firms with and without VC backing, using only the Management Discussion and Analysis section of the prospectus filing, and they conclude that VC-backed firms tend to be less optimistic. Similarly, González et al. (2019) use the Loughran McDonald approach to investigate the impact of tone in IPO prospectus filings in Latin America and find a significant positive relationship between board size and underpricing and a negative relationship between board independence and underpricing when controlling for uncertain tone.

Araci (2019) compare the performance of publicly available BERT, (Devlin et al., 2018), which is trained on a corpus of Wikipedia articles and books, to the performance of the BERT model trained solely on 10-k's from 1998-1999 and 2017-2019, which they call 'FinBERT,' on the task of sentiment classification for financial documents. There are several other published 'FinBERT' models including Desola et al. (2019), Yang et al. (2020), and (Liu et al., 2020)[2]. Their results show a clear improvement on language comprehension by the models on masked language model accuracy (MLM) and next sentence accuracy (NS) on new 10-Q data. Thus, as expected, domain knowledge and verbiage differ greatly from ordinary language, but for Earnings Calls, the models trained on financial documents are over-training, suggesting another language barrier. Araci (2019) compares the average in-list similarity of each Loughran McDonald sentiment using the publicly available pre-trained BERT embeddings and BERT embeddings trained on a corpus of financial documents; the results indicate that there is a significant difference between the resultant word embeddings, suggesting that the language of financial documents is unique to the field.

Tao et al. (2018) deploy deep learning techniques to extract 'forward looking statements' (FLS) from the final prospectus filing for successful IPOs between 2003 and 2013 to train a custom word2vec embedding. FLS are statements concerning the firms future projects, works-in-progress, and goals. Latent Dirichlet allocation (LDA) (Blei et al., 2003) is used to determine the common topics to which the FLS are addressing across all firms. The FLS features, including their Loughran McDonald sentiment and topics are combined with common IPO features (underwriter rank, industry, etc.) in several ML algorithms (Decision Tree, Bayes Classifier, Neural Network, etc.) and feature importance algorithms for the prediction tasks. With all of the machinery in place, the authors best report a 0.76 area under the curve (AUC) in predicting if the IPO will have a positive first-day return from an ensemble ML model and a 0.68 AUC if the IPO will have a positive up-revision. While this work is extensive and well-documented, the authors only review the final prospectus document and ignore the probability of withdrawal by only focusing on successful IPOs.

Recently, Ly and Nguyen (2020) apply several machine learning algorithms to prospectus sentiment factors as calculated using percent-of-words modeling and Loughran McDonald word lists to predict if the third, fifth, tenth, twentieth, and thirtieth day closing price is higher than the IPO offer price. Despite the expected strength of ML models, the logistic regression model performed the best and above 50% accuracy at all event horizons, without any market controls – the only data uses were text derivatives from the prospects filing such as total number of non-stop words, total characters in the document, and the Loughran McDonald word counts.

3 Data Collection

Following the method used by Lowry et al. (2017) and their published R code, IPO data is first collected from Thomson Financial Securities Data New Issues database (SDC) for firms who issue or withdraw between 2004 and 2020. Using the given SEC File Number, the correct CIK numbers are identified and all prospectus related forms, the initial prospectus (S-1), prospectus amendments (S-1/A, 424A, all 424B[3] variants), are collected using Loughran and McDonald (2013). Only those CIKs who filed an S-1 between 2004 and 2020 and issued or withdrew in that time are considered. Firms that have a non-missing *Withdrawn Date* field from SDC are considered to have withdrawn. While the

[2]Araci (2019) is used in the results as it was easily available at the start of this project Python FinBERT.

[3]Form 424B has variants 424B1-424B8, although Tao et al. (2018) only cite '424B' as the final prospectus.

withdrawn firms seldom publish after the S-1, the initial prospectus and final prospectus are fractions of the final picture for those that issue. The information revealed in the amendments must be taken into consideration when forecasting the final offer price and first-day return as it was likely disclosed strategically, (Hanley and Hoberg, 2012; Dambra et al., 2021); this is especially true considering that the final prospectus is often published **after** the issue date, (Loughran and McDonald, 2013). A total of 2201 unique CIK firms are found with sufficient, non-missing control variables following the method of (Lowry et al., 2017) with a total of 10,683 forms to evaluate, after the removal of common stop words (a, an, the, etc.) and all non-English characters[4].Of these, a remaining 1908 CIK firms have qualifying forms to be processed and analyzed in this model.

Index and first-day returns are collected from the Center for Research in Security Prices (CRSP) database accessed through the Wharton Research Data Services (WRDS). The collection of additional firm identifiers was attempted, but the best results were obtained by uniquely identifying all PERMNOs[5] on their first day of record, taking their CUSIP6[6] matches with the firms and taking the sample with the least missing data following Lowry et al. (2017). Carter and Manaster (1990) continue to publish a ranking on underwriters. While this ranking is standard in the underpricing literature, (Loughran and Ritter, 2004; Hanley and Hoberg, 2012; Loughran and McDonald, 2013), it only supplies a ranking in 1984, 1991, 2000, 2004, 2007, 2009, 2011, and 2015; therefore an underwriter ranked 8 in 2000 is still considered to be rank 8 in 2003, but if their rank is missing in 2004, it will also be missing in 2005. The most recent ranking is from 2015. The up-to-date 7-sentiment Loughran McDonald word lists are downloaded from their website.

[4]As Lowry et al. (2017) mention, there is nevertheless room for some errors of firm identification and form acquisition. Only those forms with more than 16 'clean words' are evaluated, as 16 was the 10th percentile of all documents and the 10.1th percentile was 35. This is to account for errors in form acquisition and noisy data.

[5]All publicly traded stocks are assigned a PERMNO (permanant number) by WRDS that follows them through Merger and Acquisition (M&A) activity, re-branding, corporate restructuring, etc. Some firms may have more than one PERMNO if they have multiple classes of stock traded.

[6]CUSIP is a 9-character identifier issued by CUSIP Global Services and uniquely identifies financial instruments and their issuers; CUSIP6 uses the first 6 characters of the CUSIP, which identify only the issuer.

4 Methodology

For these results, instead of using a percentage of words to represent each sentiment, the cosine similarity between every word in a document and every word in each Loughran McDonald sentiment list is calculated using the publicly available GloVe (Pennington et al., 2014) embeddings trained on Wikipedia, Sehrawat's GloVe embeddings (Sehrawat, 2019) trained on 10-K filings, BERT (Devlin et al., 2018) embeddings trained on BookCorpus and Wikipedia, and the FinBERT model from Araci (2019).

Algorithm 1 Sentiment Score Matrix: T

Inputs:
Embedding Matrix: M
Loughran McDonald Word List: LM
Vocabulary: V
Output:
Sentiment Score Matrix: T
for all $w \in V$ **do**
  $score = zeros(7)$
  if $w \in$ any $LM_{category}$ **then**
    $score_{category} = 1$
  else
    $v^w = M_w$
    $v^{lm} = M_{lm}$
    $score_i = max_i(cossim(v^w, v^{lm}))$
  end if
  $T_w = score$
end for

Algorithm 2 Document Scoring

Inputs:
Score Matrix: T
Document: D
Output:
Document Score: $score$
for all $w \in D$ **do**
  $score += T_w$
end for
$score = \frac{1}{||score||_2} score$

All seven Loughran McDonald categories are used (Positive, Negative, Constraining, Litigious, Uncertain, Strong Modal, and Weak Modal), giving every word a sentiment vector of dimension seven. Each word in the Loughran McDonald list receives a score of '1' for its category, and zero in all other categories; words not in an Loughran McDonald list receive a score equal to its maximum similarity to any word in the Loughran McDonald lists for the category of that word, and zero else[7]. See Algorithm 1 for the construction of the word sentiment score matrix T. The formulas are the same for the standard GloVe, Sehrawat, BERT, and FinBERT embeddings[8]. For an entire document, the similarity vectors of all words are vector-summed into the document's total vector, which is normalized by dividing by the 2-norm to be the document's score vector; see Algorithm 2. This process is very similar to the one used by Araque et al. (2019). All documents are scored for each sentiment category by each embedding model; the percentage of words metric is also calculated for comparison. Additionally, for every document after the initial prospectus of each firm, the difference between its sentiment score over the previous document is recorded; these sentiment differences are then summarized by an expanding average leaving the final prospectus with an average difference in the changing published sentiment. This metric will capture large spikes in new sentiments that had not yet been revealed; a similar metric that takes the average in absolute differences between the documents was tested, but the results were insignificant. The following predictions are made: use the initial prospectus sentiment, present market average return, and underwriter ranking to predict if a firm will withdraw, for those firms that issue, use the sentiment of the final prospectus to predict the first-day return, for those firms that issue,use the sentiment of the final prospectus and the average sentiment update difference to predict the first-day return.

Supplementary materials for reproducibility are available upon request; however, the complete data set will take over a week of machine time due to the inclusion of four embedding models and the number of forms to process. Moreover, WRDS and SDC are proprietary, restricting the ability to publicize the entire data set. As noted in (Ritter and Welch, 2002), the years being evaluated often have measurable effects on the final results and thus a large volume of data is preferable.

[7]A few words appear in more than 1 list; these words are given a 1 in each category they appear.

[8]Both GloVe and Sehrawat embedding vocabularies were missing several words in each Loughran McDonald list but never more than 10%

5 Results

5.1 Probability of Withdrawal

Table 1 shows logistic regression coefficients and p-values of the left column regressors with withdrawal as the dependent variable[9]. While the pseudo R-squared is unimpressive, the p-values show significant relationships between the regressors and withdrawal. All of the sentiment scoring methods agree on the general form of the results, but the Sehrawat model achieves the highest pseudo R-squared with a significant positive relationship between negative, strong modal, and constraining language at a 0.05% level and a significant negative relationship between positive and weak modal language at a 0.05% level. The more positive language a firm includes in its filing, the less likely it will withdraw; this can be read as the firm has good intentions or good prospects within the offer, rather than needing to cover debts. Strong modal language is likely taking the role of commitments to future projects or ventures that firms are but eventually either drop or find cheaper capital.

While the percentage model only finds strong significance for the litigious and strong modal coefficients, the embedding methods capture a significantly positive coefficient on constraining language, suggesting that the embedding methods are better at disentangling the presence of constraining language from litigious. Additionally, the positive coefficient suggests that firms are more likely to withdraw given more obligations, and likely debt, acknowledged in their prospectus, all else equal. The change in significance of the litigious language factor between the percent and the proposed methods is likely due to the overlap between Loughran McDonald word lists and the concentration of legal-language words in the S-1 filing, being it is a registration statement; this confusion is better handled by the embedding methods as seen by the increased significance of negative, constraining, and weak modal language in the Sehrawat construction. Uncertain language in the context of new firms that are conducting their IPO is likely to be closely tied with projects whose possible outcomes upon are still under review, works-in-progress, and the FLS of Tao et al. (2018); thus, firms who have docu-

[9]Year fixed effects, the average market return at the time of S-1 filing, top tier, and log sales were included, but are not displayed for brevity. Additionally, the inclusion of the VC factor resulted in a singular matrix as did the separate inclusion of industry fixed effects.

	Percent Coef.	Percent p	GloVe Coef.	Glove p	Sehrawat Coef.	Sehrawat p	BERT Coef	BERT p	FinBERT Coef	FinBERT p
Positive	-51.572	0.0041	-62.7989	0.0004	-66.6374	0.0002	-49.3533	0.0011	-49.4866	0.001
Negative	7.1987	0.5731	32.8713	0.014	33.8713	0.0126	31.5083	0.0218	31.0429	0.0234
Uncertainty	-9.008	0.694	1.4227	0.9495	19.517	0.3971	10.4519	0.6568	11.1548	0.6349
Litigious	60.167	0	18.4975	0.1427	18.9262	0.1187	20.9076	0.0838	21.1957	0.0804
StrongModal	67.3125	0	89.6144	0	90.6276	0	93.2129	0	93.6087	0
WeakModal	-31.1342	0.2533	-45.7306	0.0843	-65.6305	0.017	-56.0963	0.0454	-56.2674	0.0441
Constraining	-21.3634	0.5155	63.4077	0.0127	51.4216	0.0374	68.447	0.0219	66.3964	0.0289
Pseudo R2		0.0961		0.1065		0.1073		0.1065		0.1067

Table 1: Probit regression coefficients and p-values for predicting the probability of withdrawal at time of S-1 filing.

mented an abundance of future projects are less likely to withdraw. While this insignificant result does not support existing theories that uncertainly should increase the probability of withdrawal, (Helbing, 2019), it opens the door for the potential of a more in-depth analysis as to why.

5.2 Amendment and Final Prospectus Sentiment on Underpricing

Since the initial and final prospectus sentiments are well studied (Hanley and Hoberg, 2010; Loughran and McDonald, 2013; Bajo and Raimondo, 2017; Tao et al., 2018), the tables are available upon request[10]. In Table 2, sentiment factors from the final filing and the average difference as described above bring all models significant coefficients on litigious and uncertainty at a 10% level. However, the Sehrawat, BERT, and FinBERT methods strong modal coefficient to significance at a 10% level and the strong modal average difference to be significant at nearly a 5% level. This result suggests that a sudden increase in the committal language during the filing process decreases first-day returns, all else equal. Given the significant coefficient on strong modal, this decrease is lessened if it is maintained in the final filing. The percentage based method appears to be unable to capture this in-process information spike. As stated previously, the current status of this technology is has a difficult time disentangling strong modal and uncertain language particularly with respect to opportunity, though they have different key words. Inclusion of more methods inspired by Tao et al. (2018), Bajo and Raimondo (2017), and Araque et al. (2019) may provide the answer.

5.3 Amendment and Final Prospectus Sentiment on IPO Price

As before, the analysis of the initial and final filings alone on IPO price is well documented, but the associated tables are available upon request. For all factors, the Sehrawat and FinBERT methods capture as many or more significant factors than their general counterparts. The Sehrawat embeddings capture a significant value for the probability of withdrawal derived from the initial prospectus, unlike the other metrics. Although it is debated whether or not the probability of withdrawal should increase the offer price, to entice the issuer to carry out the offer or be lower to hedge the underwriter against a bad investment, (Helbing, 2019), the results are unable to capture any significant relationship, all else equal.

Table 3 reinforces the conclusions on strong modal language from the underpricing regression; the joint conclusion is that it causes a belief between the underwriter and investors that firm is less valuable or a lower quality investment. All methods significantly suggest that average increases in the litigious language of filings over time increase the offer price over time while the degree to which it is present in the final filing decreases the offer price. This result is likely an escalation effect or a bi-product of the filing process itself, but a greater analysis could reveal more acute reasoning, such as appropriate compliance or inappropriate deviation from the law that causes improved or disproved evaluations. The GloVe method shows significant positive affects from the average difference in uncertainty with strong collaboration, save the Sehrawat model. While uncertain language appeared to have no relationship to underpricing from the market, it has a strong negative relationship to price of the IPO itself; however, if this language changed during the filing process, it was strongly positive. Coupled with the effects of constraining and modal language, this suggests that the uncertainty factor is better capturing growth opportunities rather than pitfalls for those that ultimately issue, being as those that do encounter unexpected hardship during the filing process have the option to withdraw.

Perhaps most interesting of all is that the change

[10]Controls for year, industry, market return, sales, positive earnings per share, number of shares, VC backing, mid-point price, top tier, share overhang, and a constant are employed in both Table 3 and Table 2 but not shown for brevity.

	Percent Coef.	Percent p	GloVe Coef.	Glove p	Sehrawat Coef.	Sehrawat p	BERT Coef	BERT p	FinBERT Coef	FinBERT p
Positive	1.9765	0.3259	1.257	0.5356	1.5567	0.4448	1.2468	0.4715	1.0749	0.5343
Negative	2.0639	0.16	2.6669	0.088	2.463	0.1192	2.65	0.0958	2.7093	0.0878
Uncertainty	-5.0807	0.0684	-5.0429	0.0616	-4.8004	0.0842	-5.1086	0.065	-5.1058	0.0653
Litigious	-1.3484	0.0665	-1.4648	0.0869	-1.4729	0.0851	-1.5364	0.0613	-1.5559	0.0584
StrongModal	3.1631	0.1288	3.6144	0.1284	3.899	0.0989	3.9006	0.0992	3.8934	0.0994
WeakModal	3.8294	0.2569	3.1572	0.3409	2.901	0.4047	3.107	0.3662	3.0628	0.3716
Constraining	-3.6886	0.3373	-4.0297	0.1962	-2.5583	0.3755	-3.1642	0.3745	-3.3668	0.3512
Positive_diff_av	-9.5925	0.3854	-6.0314	0.5721	-8.2718	0.4416	-7.4402	0.411	-6.3503	0.4833
Negative_diff_av	1.0585	0.912	-3.4888	0.7117	-2.7914	0.7717	-3.2401	0.7388	-3.7394	0.6995
Uncertainty_diff_av	16.8429	0.3593	17.1491	0.3427	19.3985	0.2707	18.2553	0.3189	19.0574	0.2971
Litigious_diff_av	5.5487	0.1983	8.5279	0.0771	9.0347	0.0585	8.1941	0.0758	8.4348	0.0679
StrongModal_diff_av	-19.3434	0.1745	-28.911	0.0721	-33.0815	0.0408	-32.9693	0.0429	-32.6582	0.0426
WeakModal_diff_av	-21.7586	0.312	-19.7252	0.3361	-22.2543	0.2909	-22.0189	0.3013	-22.3597	0.2903
Constraining_diff_av	35.2237	0.1005	18.9233	0.2967	9.9023	0.5515	16.8016	0.4076	18.7874	0.3625
Prob. Withdraw	-0.0132	0.8734	-0.0413	0.6314	-0.0443	0.6038	-0.0543	0.5231	-0.056	0.5103
Adj. R2		0.2347		0.2362		0.2363		0.2364		0.2364

Table 2: OLS regression coefficients and p-values for predicting the first-day return at time of last prospectus filing before the issue date and average sentiment difference factors.

	Percent Coef.	Percent p	GloVe Coef.	Glove p	Sehrawat Coef.	Sehrawat p	BERT Coef	BERT p	FinBERT Coef	FinBERT p
Positive	-6.1661	0.8453	5.2554	0.8694	19.521	0.5439	23.72	0.3851	18.9184	0.4878
Negative	-7.6335	0.741	-14.1084	0.5666	-21.1526	0.3965	-14.5755	0.5611	-12.723	0.6109
Uncertainty	-108.394	0.0132	-110.549	0.0091	-101.639	0.0202	-102.34	0.0188	-103.334	0.0177
Litigious	-20.5922	0.0745	-22.2152	0.099	-19.556	0.1472	-19.298	0.1356	-20.3935	0.1152
StrongModal	100.47	0.0022	100.85	0.0072	106.814	0.0042	106.684	0.0043	107.174	0.0041
WeakModal	140.97	0.0078	146.841	0.0048	136.551	0.0128	137.419	0.011	137.896	0.0105
Constraining	-209.425	0.0005	-144.483	0.0033	-99.3955	0.0293	-131.574	0.0192	-142.266	0.0125
Positive_diff_av	-35.6215	0.8375	-131.485	0.4345	-204.96	0.2272	-219.687	0.1239	-196.378	0.1693
Negative_diff_av	-75.4334	0.616	-11.5933	0.9378	29.436	0.8462	-15.7184	0.9182	-22.5583	0.8825
Uncertainty_diff_av	579.447	0.0446	662.025	0.0198	434.901	0.1173	546.091	0.0582	555.273	0.0536
Litigious_diff_av	162.524	0.0166	163.973	0.0309	133.752	0.0759	142.764	0.0497	146.61	0.044
StrongModal_diff_av	-429.83	0.0552	-517.888	0.041	-510.633	0.0455	-517.604	0.0438	-529.138	0.0371
WeakModal_diff_av	-424.648	0.2089	-592.593	0.0659	-368.377	0.2675	-458.019	0.172	-463.063	0.164
Constraining_diff_av	967.254	0.0041	592.201	0.0382	333.329	0.2042	506.593	0.1133	558.24	0.0861
Prob. Withdraw	-1.6947	0.1929	-1.4496	0.285	-1.1776	0.3823	-1.4537	0.2782	-1.4774	0.2703
Adj. R2		0.7338		0.7333		0.7324		0.7331		0.7332

Table 3: OLS regression coefficients and p-values for predicting the IPO price at time of last prospectus filing before the issue date and average sentiment difference factors.

in language is opposite in relationship to price to its level in the final filing. This implies that the the act of revealing this information during the IPO process has a measurable affect on the IPO price beyond the effect it has by being present in the final filing. This is especially true for the uncertain and litigious language that were themselves insignificant before the inclusion of their change factors in the final filing.

6 Contributions and Continuing Future Research

This work contributes to the ever growing literature on NLP in finance by first evaluating prospectus sentiment on the likelihood of withdrawal, second by expanding the sentiment evaluation to the use of word embedding methods, which does significantly better at disentangling uncertainty and constraining language from that of strong and weak modality, and thirdly by incorporating a measurement for the change in sentiment throughout the filing process, rather than just at the beginning and end. The BERT embedding method has additional strength beyond the embeddings themselves, which would imply that training a model on this data directly would likely improve the significance of the BERT factors by better capturing the context of prospectus filings. While the inclusion of a probability of withdrawal factor was statistically insignificant, its insignificance raises more questions. The method presented is able to disentangle the effects of uncertain and litigious language throughout the filing process, but more work needs to be done to better evaluate the factors behind the IPO price and first-day returns. Moreover, the ability of the embedding-based methods to first replicate and second out-perform that of the basic percentage-of-words method is a necessary bridge to advance the existing financial literature to more modern techniques.

Acknowledgements

Jared Sharpe's research is supported by the graduate fellowship from the Institute for Financial Services Analytics at University of Delaware.

References

Dogu Araci. 2019. Finbert: Financial sentiment analysis with pre-trained language models.

Oscar Araque, Ganggao Zhu, and Carlos A. Iglesias. 2019. A semantic similarity-based perspective of affect lexicons for sentiment analysis. *Knowledge-Based Systems*, 165:346 – 359.

Emanuele Bajo and Carlo Raimondo. 2017. Media sentiment and ipo underpricing. *Journal of Corporate Finance*, 46:139 – 153.

Lawrence M. Benveniste, Walid Y. Busaba, and William J. Wilhelm. 2002. Information externalities and the role of underwriters in primary equity markets. *Journal of Financial Intermediation*, 11(1):61 – 86.

David M Blei, Andrew Y Ng, and Michael I Jordan. 2003. Latent dirichlet allocation. *the Journal of machine Learning research*, 3:993–1022.

Walid Y. Busaba, Lawrence M. Benveniste, and Re-Jin Guo. 2001. The option to withdraw ipos during the premarket: empirical analysis. *Journal of Financial Economics*, 60(1):73 – 102.

Richard Carter and Steven Manaster. 1990. Initial public offerings and underwriter reputation. *The Journal of Finance*, 45(4):1045–1067.

Michael Dambra, Bryce Schonberger, and Charles E Wasley. 2021. Creating visibility: Voluntary disclosure by private firms pursuing an initial public offering. *Available at SSRN 3213482*.

Vinicio Desola, Kevin Hanna, and Pri Nonis. 2019. Finbert: pre-trained model on sec filings for financial natural language tasks.

Jacob Devlin, Ming-Wei Chang, Kenton Lee, and Kristina Toutanova. 2018. BERT: pre-training of deep bidirectional transformers for language understanding. *CoRR*, abs/1810.04805.

Eugene F. Fama. 1970. Efficient capital markets: A review of theory and empirical work. *The Journal of Finance*, 25(2):383–417.

Maximiliano González, Diego Téllez, María Andrea Trujillo, et al. 2019. Governance, sentiment analysis, and initial public offering underpricing. *Corporate Governance: An International Review*, 27(3):226–244.

Kathleen Weiss Hanley and Gerard Hoberg. 2010. The information content of ipo prospectuses. *The Review of Financial Studies*, 23(7):2821–2864.

Kathleen Weiss Hanley and Gerard Hoberg. 2012. Litigation risk, strategic disclosure and the underpricing of initial public offerings. *Journal of Financial Economics*, 103(2):235 – 254.

Pia Helbing. 2019. A review on ipo withdrawal. *International Review of Financial Analysis*, 62(C):200–208.

Fred E. Huibers. 2020. Towards an optimal ipo mechanism. *Journal of Risk and Financial Management*, 13(6):115.

Shikun Ke, José Luis Montiel Olea, and James Nesbit. 2019. A robust machine learning algorithm for text analysis. Technical report, Working paper.

Emmet King and Luca Banderet. 2014. Ipo stock performance and the financial crisis. *Econometric Modeling: Capital Markets - Asset Pricing eJournal*.

Zhuang Liu, Degen Huang, Kaiyu Huang, Zhuang Li, and Jun Zhao. 2020. Finbert: A pre-trained financial language representation model for financial text mining. In *Proceedings of the Twenty-Ninth International Joint Conference on Artificial Intelligence, IJCAI*, pages 5–10.

Tim Loughran and Bill McDonald. 2011. When is a liability not a liability? textual analysis, dictionaries, and 10-ks. *The Journal of Finance*, 66(1):35–65.

Tim Loughran and Bill McDonald. 2013. Ipo first-day returns, offer price revisions, volatility, and form s-1 language. *Journal of Financial Economics*, 109(2):307–326.

Tim Loughran and Bill McDonald. 2020. Textual analysis in finance. *Annual Review of Financial Economics*, 12:357–375.

Tim Loughran and Jay Ritter. 2004. Why has ipo underpricing changed over time? *Financial Management*, 33(3):5–37.

Michelle Lowry, Roni Michaely, and Ekaterina Volkova. 2017. Initial public offerings: A synthesis of the literature and directions for future research. *Forthcoming Foundations and Trends in Finance*.

Michelle Lowry and G. Schwert. 2004. Is the ipo pricing process efficient? *Journal of Financial Economics*, 71(1):3–26.

T. H. Ly and K. Nguyen. 2020. Do words matter: Predicting ipo performance from prospectus sentiment. In *2020 IEEE 14th International Conference on Semantic Computing (ICSC)*, pages 307–310.

Paul B. McGuinness. 2019. Risk factor and use of proceeds declarations and their effects on ipo subscription, price 'fixings', liquidity and after-market returns. *The European Journal of Finance*, 25(12):1122–1146.

William Megginson, Antonio Meles, Gabriele Sampagnaro, and Vincenzo Verdoliva. 2016. Financial distress risk in initial public offerings: How much do venture capitalists matter?*. *Journal of Corporate Finance*.

Pablo Moran and J. Ari Pandes. 2019. Elite law firms in the ipo market. *Journal of Banking & Finance*, 107:105612.

Yangtuo Peng and Hui Jiang. 2016. Leverage financial news to predict stock price movements using word embeddings and deep neural networks. In *Proceedings of the 2016 Conference of the North American Chapter of the Association for Computational Linguistics: Human Language Technologies*, pages 374–379, San Diego, California. Association for Computational Linguistics.

Jeffrey Pennington, Richard Socher, and Christopher D. Manning. 2014. Glove: Global vectors for word representation. In *Empirical Methods in Natural Language Processing (EMNLP)*, pages 1532–1543.

Andrea Picasso, Simone Merello, Yukun Ma, Luca Oneto, and Erik Cambria. 2019. Technical analysis and sentiment embeddings for market trend prediction. *Expert Systems with Applications*, 135:60 – 70.

David Quintana, Cristóbal Arco-Calderón, and Pedro Isasi. 2005. Evolutionary rule-based system for ipo underpricing prediction. pages 983–989.

Jay R Ritter and Ivo Welch. 2002. A review of ipo activity, pricing, and allocations. *The journal of Finance*, 57(4):1795–1828.

Saurabh Sehrawat. 2019. Learning word embeddings from 10-k filings using pytorch. *Available at SSRN 3480902*.

Rama Seth, S. R. Vishwanatha, and Durga Prasad. 2019. Allocation to anchor investors, underpricing, and the after-market performance of ipos. *Financial Management*, 48(1):159–186.

Ann E. Sherman and S. Titman. 2000. Building the ipo order book: Underpricing and participation limits with costly information. *Capital Markets: Market Efficiency*.

Jie Tao, Amit V Deokar, and Ashutosh Deshmukh. 2018. Analysing forward-looking statements in initial public offering prospectuses: a text analytics approach. *Journal of Business Analytics*, 1(1):54–70.

Tiffany Thng. 2019. Do vc-backed ipos manage tone? *The European Journal of Finance*, 25(17):1655–1682.

Yumeng Yan, Xiong Xiong, J Ginger Meng, and Gaofeng Zou. 2019. Uncertainty and ipo initial returns: evidence from the tone analysis of china's ipo prospectuses. *Pacific-Basin Finance Journal*, 57:101075.

Yi Yang, Mark Christopher Siy UY, and Allen Huang. 2020. Finbert: A pretrained language model for financial communications.

It's Time to Reason: Annotating Argumentation Structures in Financial Earnings Calls: The FinArg Dataset

Alaa Alhamzeh[1,2*], **Romain Fonck**[1,2+], **Erwan Versmée**[1,2+], **Előd Egyed-Zsigmond**[1], **Harald Kosch**[2] and **Lionel Brunie**[1]

[1]INSA de Lyon, France

[2]Universität Passau, Germany

{firstname.secondname}@uni-passau.de, {firstname.secondname}@insa-lyon.fr

Abstract

With the goal of reasoning on the financial textual data, we present in this paper, a novel approach for annotating arguments, their components and relations in the transcripts of earnings conference calls (ECCs). The proposed scheme is driven from the argumentation theory at the micro-structure level of discourse. We further conduct a manual annotation study with four annotators on 136 documents. By that, we obtained inter-annotator agreement of α_U = 0.70 for argument components and α = 0.81 for argument relations. The final created corpus, with the size of 804 documents, as well as the annotation guidelines are publicly available for researchers in the domains of computational argumentation, finance and FinNLP.

1 Introduction

The rise of data and the development of machine learning have led to the interdisciplinary financial technology (FinTech) that aims at supporting the financial industry with digital innovations and technology-enabled business models [Philippon, 2016]. Different applications have been explored such as fraud detection, digital payment, blockchain and trading systems. In terms of the latter, several factors impact its movement and it is hard, in reality, to get a very accurate prediction of the future stock prices. The *efficient market hypothesis* theory [Fama, 1970] states that it is impossible to "beat the market" consistently since current prices incorporate all available information and expectations. Nevertheless, the current view of the market comes from behavioural economics which see humans as irrational beings who are influenced by biases and experience when making investment decisions. In our previous work [Alhamzeh *et al.*, 2021b], we analysed the impact of stockTwits [1] and online news using a hybrid approach which consists of sentiment and event-based features as well as the price information for different observation and prediction time windows. [Chen *et al.*, 2021a] aimed at capturing expert-like rationales from social media platforms without the requirement of the annotated data. Similarly, [Zong *et al.*, 2020] hit the question: what makes some forecasters better than others? By exploring connections between the language people use to describe their predictions and their forecasting skills. On the other hand, [Keith and Stent, 2019] targeted the prediction of professional analysts recommendations who influence the decisions of many investors towards buying or selling in particular markets. Their findings confirm that earnings calls are moderately predictive of analysts' decisions even though theses decisions are function of different parameters including private communication with company executives and market conditions.

Moreover, while different works considered the sentiment and semantic analysis of text, we are looking towards a deeper understanding and interpretation of the language by the means of argument mining. According to [Chen *et al.*, 2021b], argument mining can be applied to understand the public's expectations for the market, providing valuable information for investment and other close applications. While they mostly studied the investors' posts on social platforms, we aim to particularly study the impact of arguments on the professional analysts themselves during the earnings conference calls (ECCs). Therefore, we present in this paper the first step of that methodology by discovering and annotating argumentation structures in ECCs.

ECCs are generally held in every fiscal quarter and consist of three main parts: a safe harbor statement, a presentation and the question answering (Q&A) session. In the presentation, executives give the statements about the performance of company in the last quarter and exhibit their expectations for the next one. During the Q&A session, professional analysts ask their questions and demand clarifications from the company's representatives. Different studies found that the discussion during the question answering session is the most informative and influencing part on the market [Matsumoto *et al.*, 2011; Price *et al.*, 2012]. Therefore, we focus in our study on these sessions, and more specially on annotating the arguments, their components and relations in the given answers of the company executives, where they try to justify their opinions and convince the other party to believe in them, which is indeed the essence of argumentation [Alhamzeh *et al.*, 2021a].

To the best of our knowledge, no prior work has been carried out to annotate arguments in earnings calls transcripts.

*Contact Author, + Equal Contribution

[1]https://stocktwits.com/

Proceedings of the Fourth Workshop on Financial Technology and Natural Language Processing (FinNLP), pages 163 - 169
December 8, 2022 ©2022 Association for Computational Linguistics

Therefore, the contributions of this paper are the following:

- First, we introduce a novel annotation scheme for modeling arguments in the answers of Q&A sections of earnings calls conferences.
- Second, we present our annotation study and the reliability of data by the inter-annotator agreement with four annotators.
- Third, we evaluate our data on using a fine-tuned DistilBERT model [Sanh *et al.*, 2019] for the argument identification task.
- Fourth, we provide our annotated FinArg corpus freely to encourage future research [2].

This paper is organized as follows: in Section 2, we explore a conceptual background of argumentation modeling, and we highlight related works on argumentation in finance and on ECCs in particular. In Section 3, we present our proposed annotation scheme to model the argument components and relations in the executives' answers stated during the earning call. We further illustrate in Section 4 the whole process of corpus creation. We move to DistilBERT results on our dataset in Section 5. We finally move back to the big picture of the financial application and discuss the future directions in Section 6.

2 Related Work

2.1 Argumentation Models: Background

Argumentation is a fundamental aspect of human communication, thinking, and decision making [Alhamzeh *et al.*, 2021a]. The simplest form of argument consists of one premise (also known as evidence or reason) supporting one claim (also known as a conclusion). Therefore, recognizing arguments in text includes several subtasks [Stab and Gurevych, 2014]: (1) argument identification by separating argumentative from non-argumentative text units. (2) argument unit classification by further identifying premises and claims in the argumentative units, and (3) argument structure identification to associate relations between argument components.

Since the study of argumentation involves philosophy, logic, communication science, and more recently computer science, the literature reports a diverse range of proposals to model argumentation based on the text genre and the task at hand. [Bentahar *et al.*, 2010] organized arguments models into three categories:

- Monological models: focus on the internal structure of an argument (micro-structure).
- Dialogical models: focus on the relations between arguments in a discussion, debate or similar (macro-structure).
- Rhetorical models: focus on the rhetorical patterns of arguments (neither micro nor macro-structure).

[2]https://github.com/Alaa-Ah/The-FinArg-Dataset-Argument-Mining-in-Financial-Earnings-Calls

Those three perspectives on the study of argumentation are closely related [Walton and Reed, 2003]. In our study, we focus on the monological perspective, which is more relevant to our data type and well-suited for developing computational method [Peldszus and Stede, 2013]. Toulmin's model [Toulmin, 2003] is a well known argument model that formalize the internal micro-structure of an argument optimally by means of six parts: claim, data, warrant, backing, qualifier and rebuttal. [Chen *et al.*, 2021a] proposed to use this model to structure argumentation in analysts' opinions (in analysts' reports). However, this model has several drawbacks to model the daily life argumentation [Habernal and Gurevych, 2017a; Palau and Moens, 2009], mainly due to the fuzzy distinction between the defined argument components. For instance, the distinction between data, warrant and backing is often vague in practice [Freeman, 2011]. Therefore, we do not follow this model and instead we design a simpler annotation scheme which we will discuss in details in Section 3.

2.2 Earnings Conference Calls (ECCs)

The analysis of financial textual data has been studied from multiple aspects and types of documents in the state of the art. In terms of earning calls, one inspiring work is the study of [Keith and Stent, 2019] who identified a set of 20 pragmatic features of analysts' questions (e.g., hedging, concreteness and sentiment) during the earning conference calls which they correlate with analysts' pre-call investor recommendations. They also analyze the degree to which semantic and pragmatic features from an earnings call complement market data in predicting analysts' post-call changes in price targets. [Matsumoto *et al.*, 2011; Price *et al.*, 2012] found that the question-answer portions of earnings calls to be most informative. Moreover, given that executives cannot predict analysts' questions with complete certainty, executives' responses tend to be more unscripted than in the presentation section. Therefore, in our work, we focus only on Q&A sessions especially that it implies also the interaction with the analysts who we seek to understand their persuasion and decision making process via argumentation at the first place. In other words, we investigate only on the arguments stated in the answers of company representatives to the questions of professional analysts.

2.3 Argumentation in Finance

Argumentation in financial domain has been addressed mainly in communication studies in the literature [Palmieri, 2017; Hursti, 2011; Estrada and others, 2010]. Recently, [Pazienza *et al.*, 2019] introduced an abstract argumentation approach for the prediction of analysts' recommendations following earnings conference calls. They actually did not apply any argument mining method. Instead, they abstractly considered each question and answer as an argument, and they applied sentiment analysis between them to be considered as the relation itself.

On the other hand, there are huge efforts in the FinNLP domain, presented by Chen et al. [Chen *et al.*, 2021b]. However, most of their work efforts are towards the Chinese language (and market) while we consider mainly the English language with respect to S&P 500. Furthermore, they have also organized a series of FinNum tasks that consider the numerical understanding with respect to the financial text properties. The challenge of 2021, namely, FinNum-3 [3] considers the classification of *in-claim* and *out-of-claim* numerals in the manager's speech during the earning call [Chen *et al.*, 2022]. However, this data answers only if a numeral is playing a role in a claim or not, without any extra information about premises or non-argumentative sentences. Moreover, sine one sentence may have two different labels of numerals (in and out of claim), we cannot know if this sentence represents a claim or not. In other words, the data is not about argument units, rather the focus is on the numeral understanding itself [Alhamzeh *et al.*, 2022].

Based on those studies and on our own experiments on different types of text, we found that ECCs are the best candidate for an argument-based solution. This could be justified by different reasons like the fact that social media posts are restricted with a maximum character count, and people tend to express their opinions and views more that structuring them in sort of premises and claims. For example, according to our analysis on stockTwits, different posts are only claims with no premises. Therefore, we build henceforth on the ECCs and we present the annotation study in the following sections.

3 Argumentation Structure in Earnings Calls

In this section, we discuss our proposed annotation scheme to model the argument components as well as the argumentative relations that constitute the argumentative discourse structure of earnings calls. We have first to point that the answers do not exhibit any common structure among all of them, to be hence structured as a connected tree or graph with circular relations. Rather, the answers are full of arguments that may or may not be directly related. This could be justified by the fact that those answers are part of an oral argumentation limited by time. Therefore, the company representatives tend to basically enumerate their evidences (premises) that support their claims. They may make the link between different claims and reasons they mentioned (or reformulate the same claim as well), whereas in most cases, they move to the next question. Hence and to simplify the task enough, we did not ask the annotators to define the relations between the arguments (macro-structure level) or to follow more fine-grained annotation scheme that will differentiate the major claim from other claims as in [Stab and Gurevych, 2014]. Instead, we are interested in detecting the arguments themselves as independent units. In particular, we model the structure of *each argument* using *one-claim-approach* proposed by [Cohen, 1987]. This approach considers only the root node of an argument as a claim and the remaining nodes in the structure as premises. The arrow from the premise to the claim composites the relation which can be either a support or an attack relation. Figure 1 represents a sample of our annotation scheme which implies that we can have different types of micro-structure arguments (e.g., basic, convergent and serial) in one answer.

[3]https://sites.google.com/nlg.csie.ntu.edu.tw/finnum3/task-definition?authuser=0

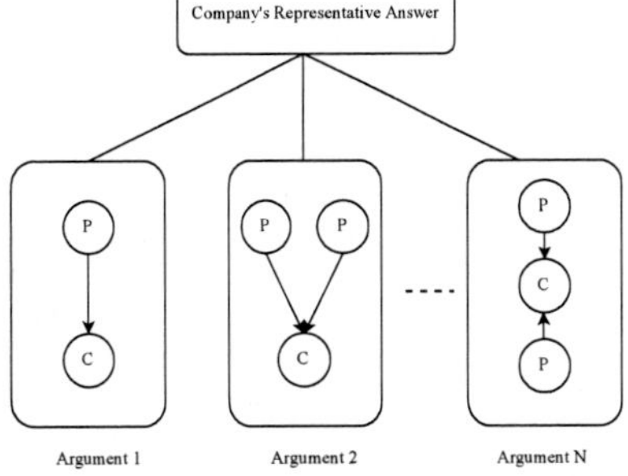

Figure 1: Argument annotation scheme (a sample) including argument components and argumentative relations (support/attack) indicated by arrows

Moreover, you can see a real example of the data in Figure 2. As we have mentioned, we are in particular interested in annotating the arguments stated by the company representatives. Therefore, in the answer of *Luca Maestri*, we see first some general information that is not argumentative (stated in Italic face), then the speaker start to argue about his claim (C_1) by stating different premises. The annotator marked every sentence (P_1 to P_4) as a premise since they all emphasize the stance of the speaker. In this example, all those premises belong to the same claim and they are all marked with a support relation type.

4 Corpus Creation

The motivation for creating a new corpus is threefold:

- First, we believe that it's time to reason the financial data and to move from shallow linguistic features and opinion mining to the reasons behind it, the analysis of persuading and decision making process via argument mining.
- Second, the lack of publicly available datasets is one of the big issues for the researchers who focus on both NLP and finance [Chen *et al.*, 2020].
- Third, the same challenge applies for argumentation field, where available datasets are often of small size and very domain and task dependent [Habernal and Gurevych, 2017b]. Therefore, our dataset can serve the computational argumentation scholars as well.

4.1 Data

We downloaded our data using the Financial Modeling Prep API [4]. We used Label Studio [5] as an annotation tool.

Our annotated data concerns the quarterly earnings calls of four companies: Amazon, Apple and Microsoft and Facebook for the period of 2015-2019 (i.e., we have 80 earning call transcripts). For each transcript, we created the list of all the speakers. After having determined the role of each of them (Analyst, Representative or an Operator), we were able

[4]https://site.financialmodelingprep.com/developer

[5]https://labelstud.io/

to split the whole text into different documents. Each document contains one or two questions asked by a single analyst and the corresponding response(s) by the company's representatives. We formulated these documents following Label Studio guidelines, and imported them to be further labeled with the argument units and relations.

In other words, we have a set of documents equal to the number of questions for each earning call, as far as every analyst asks only one question. In most cases, the same analyst will have two questions and two (or more) answers in the same document. Therefore, we observe a difference between the number of documents, number of questions, and the number of answers in our final corpus (cf. Table 1).

4.2 Argument Unit Segmentation

In the basic case, an argument component would be one complete sentence. However, in some cases, a sentence may contain several argument components. Accordingly, we annotated argument components at the clause-level (at minimum) and at the sentence level (at maximum). In other words, if we have complete statements in the same sentence we only consider them as different argument components if there is an inference relation between them. Particularly, neither statements connected with conjunctions like "and" or "or " nor conditional sentences (if, then) imply an inference relation. On the contrary, inference could appear in the following forms:

*"**claim** because of **premise**"*
*"Since **premise** then **claim**."*
*"In view of the fact **premise** that it follows that **claim**"*

However, since there is no punctuation in spoken language, segmentation is more challenging and it must be based on breaks, pitch, etc. In our case, we let the annotators segment each sentence based on the context with respect to the splitting roles we defined earlier.

4.3 Annotation Study

Our annotation study consists of three stages:

1. Annotation guidelines: We conduct a preliminary study to define the annotation guidelines with one of our annotators.
2. Pilot annotations: The goal of this stage was to test the annotation guidelines before a complete corpus is annotated. This was done by training sessions and discussions with the annotators. We got feedback from them to update the guidelines and solve unclear situations. We observed at this step that the annotation is more complicated in practice and even with our simple annotation scheme, one quarter takes between 2 to 3 hours to be completely annotated. This confirms our choice of annotation at the micro-structure level of argument and with the one-claim-approach.
3. Inter annotator agreement: To compute how homogeneous and thus reliable the annotations are.

4.4 Inter-Annotator Agreement (IAA)

To evaluate the reliability of our data, we determine a group of 12 earnings calls that represent about 20% of the whole data and covering all four companies to be annotated by a permutation of two annotators (out of four) separately. Those individual versions of the annotations are used later to compute the inter annotator agreement. To this end, we used Krippendorff's α_U [Krippendorff, 2004] and Krippendorff's α [Krippendorff, 1980] for the argument components and argument relations annotations respectively. That's because the former considers the differences in the markable boundaries of the two annotators and thus allows for assessing the reliability of argument units annotations. However, in terms of the relation annotation, the markables are the set of premise-claim pairs. We obtained a degree of α_U =0.70 for argument components and α=0.81 for argument relations. Hence, we conclude that the annotation of arguments in earnings calls is reliably possible. However, it can be tricky to get identical annotations given that the argument component types are strongly related (i.e., the annotation of a claim depends on its connected premises). Therefore, every permutation of two annotators had to meet and discuss their disagreement cases to produce the last validated document *(gold annotations)*. As a result, we discovered that the primary source of uncertainty is due to the missing of sentence boundaries and the connected context that covers multiple sentences. Therefore, we asked the annotators to read the entire question to identify the controversial topic before starting with the actual annotation task on the answer paragraph. Despite the fact that this approach is more time-consuming than a direct identification of argument components and relations, it yields to a more reliable annotated data. Furthermore, the understanding of the question will help to assess the quality of the arguments which we will address in our future work.

4.5 Creation of the Final Corpus: the FinArg Dataset

Once we extracted our data annotated using LabelStudio, the output file is a very long document in JSON format. However, before using this data, we ran some scripts to detect annotations that did not follow the guidelines. In most of the cases, a document was classified wrong because it contained at least one of these three issues: the answer part of the document was not fully annotated, the same piece of text was annotated twice or a relation was misdirected. When it is possible, the issue was corrected by code. Otherwise, we ask the corresponding document's annotator to correct that mistake. Thereafter and to increase the usability and reproducibility of our FinArg dataset, we structured the important information of arguments in a similar way to the student essays dataset [Stab and Gurevych, 2014] since it is simply understandable and almost the most used one in computational argumentation.

Hence, the annotation document includes for every premise, claim or Non-argument text:

"Id, label, start index, end index, text"

and for every argument component relation:

"Id, label, ARG1: source component id, ARG2: target component id"

Moreover, we provide an additional JSON file including the following labels:

Operator (Intro): From JPMorgan, Rod Hall.
Rod Hall (Question): Hi, guys. Thanks for taking my questions. I wanted to start off just going back to the 165 million subscriptions and ask Tim or Luca if you could comment on the unique number of users there. And I think you had made a comment, Tim, in your prepared remarks that the average revenue per user was up, or maybe that was you, Luca. But if you guys could just talk about any more color around that average revenue per user, it would be interesting to us. And then I have one follow-up to that. Thanks.
Luca Maestri (Answer): *Yes, I'll take it, Rod. We don't disclose into the number of subscriptions. Of course, we're just giving you the total count of subscriptions that are out there. Of course, there are several customers that subscribe to more than one of our services.* [There is some level of overlap, but the total number of subscribers is very, very large, obviously less than 165 million]$\mathbf{P}_1$. [But it's very good for us to see the breadth of subscriptions that we offer and that customers are interested in]$\mathbf{C}_1$. *It is very large.*[And if you remember, we quoted the same number a quarter ago and we talked about 150 million]$\mathbf{P}_2$ [So when you think about a sequential increase of 15 million subscriptions from the December quarter to the March quarter, it really gives you a sense for the momentum that we have on our content stores]$\mathbf{P}_3$.
[It's quite impressive to add 15 million subscriptions in 90 days.]$\mathbf{P}_4$. [.....]

Figure 2: An example of the Apple Q2 2017- the annotation covers the answer where the Italic text is for *Non-argument*, Claim is marked as $\mathbf{C}_1$ and Premises are marked with $\mathbf{P}_{count}$

Operator, Analyst, Representative, Intro, Question, Answer

This latter annotations could be useful especially for a financial application scenario.

4.6 Corpus Statistics

Table 1 shows statistics about our annotated data distributions. The number of documents represents the number of different analysts. However, usually an analyst asks two different questions. Also, for some questions, two of the company representatives will answer separately. Therefore, the number of annotated answers can be (and it is) more than number of questions and about twice the number of documents. The found proportion between claims and premises is also common in argumentation and confirms the findings of [Mochales and Moens, 2011; Stab and Gurevych, 2014] that claims are usually supported by several premises for ensuring a complete and stable standpoint. Additionally, the proportion between support and attack relations is normal, since discussing the opposite point of view (as a strategy to prevent any future criticism) is less commonly used in argumentation comparing to the direct supporting premises. There is also a couple of unlinked premises or claims in the data, mostly for "reformulated" claims since we ask our annotators not to link them again to the same premises as the original stated claim. In other words, we want to avoid counting them as new arguments. Furthermore, Table 2 shows a detailed version of the classes distributions per different companies.

Type	Count	%
Documents	804	-
Questions	1553	-
Answers	1777	-
Premises	4894	35.856%
Claims	4478	32.808%
Non-argument	4277	31.336%
Support	4604	98.355%
Attack	77	1.645%
Unlinked	1778	18.971%

Table 1: Corpus statistics and class distribution

5 Evaluation

As a base-line model, we fine-tuned DistilBERT [Sanh *et al.*, 2019] with our dataset on the argument identification task (i.e., argument/ non-argument classification) at the sentence-level. Table 3 shows that we got an accuracy of 0.84 and F1-score of 0.80, which are comparable to DistilBERT outcomes on the well known argumentation corpora: *Student essays* [Stab and Gurevych, 2014] and *User-generated web discourse* [Habernal and Gurevych, 2017a] presented in [Alhamzeh *et al.*, 2021a] and the BERT-based results presented in [Wambsganss *et al.*, 2020].

Hence, our primary findings suggest that we can automatically export further earnings conference calls annotations with a good degree of reliability using a supervised machine learning algorithm trained on our corpus. Based on that, we can reach the granularity of data needed for future work on the prediction of analysts' post-call recommendations.

6 Conclusions and Future Work

Recently, different cutting-edge technologies have been addressed in FinTech domain, including numeracy understanding, opinion mining and financial document processing. In this paper, we contribute to the (1) theory, (2) data and (3) evaluation aspect of argumentation structure in the financial domain by (1) proposing a micro-structure argumentation scheme for modeling arguments presented in analysts' responses during the earnings conference calls, (2) work-

Type	FB	AAPL	AMZN	MSFT
Documents	264	140	213	187
Questions	421	431	330	371
Answers	489	431	330	527
Premises	1722	1035	1010	1127
Claims	1423	1103	969	983
Non-argument	1332	1183	924	838
Support	1638	949	924	1093
Attack	20	35	6	16
Unlinked	385	499	457	437

Table 2: Distribution per company where FB: Facebook, AAPL: Apple, AMZN: Amazon, MSFT: Microsoft

Model	Accuracy	Precision	Recall	F1-score
DistilBERT	0.84	0.83	0.78	0.80

Table 3: Evaluations of the DistilBERT fine-tuned model on the **FinArg** dataset

ing on the related annotation covering a period of five years (2015-2019) on four companies (FB, AMZN, MSFT, AAPL) to produce the FinArg dataset with a size 804 documents, and (3) evaluating this data using DistilBERT as a baseline model.

We aim in the future work to employ this data and train models to the end of prediction of analysts' post-call recommendations. This opens up different research questions like the required granularity of the data, the emission time of the recommendation's announcement, the analyst's questions (topic and sentiment) during the earning call (if applicable) and others. However, we believe that it's time to reason on financial textual data and to move from basic linguistic features, semantics and sentiment analysis to the reasons behind it and the quality of it with the help of argument mining and argument quality assessment which we will address in our future work as well. As a conclusion, we claim that our dataset presented in this paper will foster the research in FinTech domain in parallel with computational argumentation as an NLP task itself.

References

[Alhamzeh *et al.*, 2021a] Alaa Alhamzeh, Bouhaouel Mohamed, Előd Egyed-Zsigmond, Jelena Mitrović, Lionel Brunie, and Harald Kosch. A stacking approach for cross-domain argument identification. In *International Conference on Database and Expert Systems Applications*, pages 361–373. Springer, 2021.

[Alhamzeh *et al.*, 2021b] Alaa Alhamzeh, Saptarshi Mukhopadhaya, Salim Hafid, Alexandre Bremard, Előd Egyed-Zsigmond, Harald Kosch, and Lionel Brunie. A hybrid approach for stock market prediction using financial news and stocktwits. In *International Conference of the Cross-Language Evaluation Forum for European Languages*, pages 15–26. Springer, 2021.

[Alhamzeh *et al.*, 2022] Alaa Alhamzeh, M. Kürsad Lacin, and Előd Egyed-Zsigmond. Passau21 at the ntcir-16 finnum-3 task: Prediction of numerical claims in the earnings calls with transfer learning. In *Proceedings of the 16th NTCIR Conference on Evaluation of Information Access Technologies, pp. 121-125, 2022. Tokyo, Japan*, 2022.

[Bentahar *et al.*, 2010] Jamal Bentahar, Bernard Moulin, and Micheline Bélanger. A taxonomy of argumentation models used for knowledge representation. *Artificial Intelligence Review*, 33(3):211–259, 2010.

[Chen *et al.*, 2020] Chung-Chi Chen, Hen-Hsen Huang, and Hsin-Hsi Chen. Nlp in fintech applications: past, present and future. *arXiv preprint arXiv:2005.01320*, 2020.

[Chen *et al.*, 2021a] Chung-Chi Chen, Hen-Hsen Huang, and Hsin-Hsi Chen. Evaluating the rationales of amateur investors. In *Proceedings of the Web Conference 2021*, pages 3987–3998, 2021.

[Chen *et al.*, 2021b] Chung-Chi Chen, Hen-Hsen Huang, and Hsin-Hsi Chen. *From Opinion Mining to Financial Argument Mining*. Springer Nature, 2021.

[Chen *et al.*, 2022] Chung-Chi Chen, Hen-Hsen Huang, Yu-Lieh Huang, Hiroya Takamura, and Hsin-Hsi Chen. Overview of the ntcir-16 finnum-3 task: Investor's and manager's fine-grained claim detection. In *Proceedings of the 16th NTCIR Conference on Evaluation of Information Access Technologies, Tokyo, Japan*, 2022.

[Cohen, 1987] Robin Cohen. Analyzing the structure of argumentative discourse. *Computational linguistics*, 13:11–24, 1987.

[Estrada and others, 2010] Fernando Estrada et al. Theory of argumentation in financial markets. *Journal of Advanced Studies in Finance (JASF)*, 1(01):18–22, 2010.

[Fama, 1970] Eugene F Fama. Efficient capital markets: A review of theory and empirical work. *The journal of Finance*, 25(2):383–417, 1970.

[Freeman, 2011] James B. Freeman. *Dialectics and the Macrostructure of Arguments: A Theory of Argument Structure*. De Gruyter Mouton, 2011.

[Habernal and Gurevych, 2017a] Ivan Habernal and Iryna Gurevych. Argumentation mining in user-generated web discourse. *Computational Linguistics*, 43(1):125–179, 2017.

[Habernal and Gurevych, 2017b] Ivan Habernal and Iryna Gurevych. Argumentation mining in user-generated web discourse. *Computational Linguistics*, 43(1):125–179, April 2017.

[Hursti, 2011] Kristian Hursti. Management earnings forecasts: Could an investor reliably detect an unduly positive bias on the basis of the strength of the argumentation? *The Journal of Business Communication (1973)*, 48(4):393–408, 2011.

[Keith and Stent, 2019] Katherine A Keith and Amanda Stent. Modeling financial analysts' decision making via the pragmatics and semantics of earnings calls. *arXiv preprint arXiv:1906.02868*, 2019.

[Krippendorff, 1980] Klaus Krippendorff. Content analysis: An introduction to its methodology. *Sage*, 1980.

[Krippendorff, 2004] Klaus Krippendorff. Measuring the reliability of qualitative text analysis data. *Quality and quantity*, 38:787–800, 2004.

[Matsumoto *et al.*, 2011] Dawn Matsumoto, Maarten Pronk, and Erik Roelofsen. What makes conference calls useful? the information content of managers' presentations and analysts' discussion sessions. *The Accounting Review*, 86(4):1383–1414, 2011.

[Mochales and Moens, 2011] Raquel Mochales and Marie-Francine Moens. Argumentation mining. *Artificial Intelligence and Law*, 19(1):1–22, 2011.

[Palau and Moens, 2009] Raquel Mochales Palau and Marie-Francine Moens. Argumentation mining: the detection, classification and structure of arguments in text. In *Proceedings of the 12th international conference on artificial intelligence and law*, pages 98–107, 2009.

[Palmieri, 2017] Rudi Palmieri. The role of argumentation in financial communication and investor relations. *Handbook of financial communication and investor relations*, pages 45–60, 2017.

[Pazienza *et al.*, 2019] Andrea Pazienza, Davide Grossi, Floriana Grasso, Rudi Palmieri, Michele Zito, and Stefano Ferilli. An abstract argumentation approach for the prediction of analysts' recommendations following earnings conference calls. *Intelligenza Artificiale*, 13(2):173–188, 2019.

[Peldszus and Stede, 2013] Andreas Peldszus and Manfred Stede. From argument diagrams to argumentation mining in texts: A survey. *International Journal of Cognitive Informatics and Natural Intelligence (IJCINI)*, 7(1):1–31, 2013.

[Philippon, 2016] Thomas Philippon. The fintech opportunity. Technical report, National Bureau of Economic Research, 2016.

[Price *et al.*, 2012] S McKay Price, James S Doran, David R Peterson, and Barbara A Bliss. Earnings conference calls and stock returns: The incremental informativeness of textual tone. *Journal of Banking & Finance*, 36(4):992–1011, 2012.

[Sanh *et al.*, 2019] Victor Sanh, Lysandre Debut, Julien Chaumond, and Thomas Wolf. Distilbert, a distilled version of bert: smaller, faster, cheaper and lighter. *arXiv preprint arXiv:1910.01108*, 2019.

[Stab and Gurevych, 2014] Christian Stab and Iryna Gurevych. Annotating argument components and relations in persuasive essays. In *Proceedings of COLING 2014, the 25th international conference on computational linguistics: Technical papers*, pages 1501–1510, 2014.

[Toulmin, 2003] Stephen E Toulmin. *The uses of argument*. Cambridge university press, 2003.

[Walton and Reed, 2003] Douglas Walton and Chris Reed. Diagramming, argumentation schemes and critical questions. In *Anyone Who Has a View*, pages 195–211. Springer, 2003.

[Wambsganss *et al.*, 2020] Thiemo Wambsganss, Nikolaos Molyndris, and Matthias Söllner. Unlocking transfer learning in argumentation mining: A domain-independent modelling approach. In *15th International Conference on Wirtschaftsinformatik*, 2020.

[Zong *et al.*, 2020] Shi Zong, Alan Ritter, and Eduard Hovy. Measuring forecasting skill from text. *arXiv preprint arXiv:2006.07425*, 2020.

How Can a Teacher Make Learning From Sparse Data Softer? Application to Business Relation Extraction

Hadjer Khaldi[1,2] and **Camille Pradel**[1]
and **Farah Benamara** [2] and **Nathalie Aussenac-Gilles** [2]
[1]Geotrend , [2]IRIT, Université de Toulouse, CNRS, Toulouse INP, UT3, Toulouse, France
{hadjer,camille}@geotrend.fr
{hadjer.khaldi,farah.benamara,nathalie.aussenac-gilles}@irit.fr

Abstract

Business Relation Extraction between market entities is a challenging information extraction task that suffers from data imbalance due to the over-representation of negative relations (also known as *No-relation* or *Others*) compared to positive relations that corresponds to the taxonomy of relations of interest. This paper proposes a novel solution to tackle this problem, relying on *binary soft-labels supervision* generated by an approach based on knowledge distillation. When evaluated on a business relation extraction dataset, the results suggest that the proposed approach improves the overall performances, beating state-of-the art solutions for data imbalance. In particular, it improves the extraction of under-represented relations as well as the detection of false negatives.

1 Introduction

Nowadays, the web is considered as an important source of business and financial information that can be used to analyze business interactions between market entities. These interactions enable financial institutions to take well-informed decisions (Oberlechner and Hocking, 2004), as well as business professionals to sustain and innovate in a rapidly changing business world. However, structuring this information remains a challenging task, given the volume and velocity of the textual data generated online. Hence, the availability of systems that automatically extract business interactions between organizations (e.g., *startups*, *companies*, *non-profit organizations*, etc.) from textual content becomes crucial.

Business Relation Extraction (BRE) is an NLP task that aims at discovering relations involving different companies (e.g. company-customer, company-partner) at the sentence level (Zhao et al., 2010). For example, from the sentence in (1), extracted from BIZREL dataset (Khaldi et al., 2021), a relation extraction system can infer that the company *Airbus* is a supplier for the company *Inmarsat*.

Dataset	# Sent.	#Rel.	% NR
TACRED	106,264	42	79.5
BioRel	533,560	125	50
BizRel	10,034	6	63

Table 1: NR in existing generic and domain specific datasets.

Example 1 *The [**Airbus**]$_{E_1}$ group has signed a contract with [**Inmarsat**]$_{E_2}$ for the delivery of three reconfigurable geostationary satellites in orbit.*

Recent works for BRE rely on supervised approaches, where neural models are trained on annotated datasets for business relations (Collovini et al., 2020; De Los Reyes et al., 2021; Reyes et al., 2021; Khaldi et al., 2021). In general, supervised approaches consider relation extraction (RE) as a multi-class classification problem where each class corresponds to a predefined relation type (Zhang et al., 2017; Wu, 2019). In addition to the set of *positive relations* (henceforth PR) which corresponds to the taxonomy of relations of interest (like hypernymy, meronymy, and cause-effect relationships), most popular datasets manually annotated either for generic (e.g., SemEval-2010 Task 8 (Hendrickx et al., 2010), TACRED (Zhang et al., 2017)) or domain specific relations (e.g., ChemProt (Krallinger et al., 2017), BizRel (Khaldi et al., 2021)) include a *negative relation* (henceforth NR) to account either for the absence of a relation between two target entities (see NO-RELATION in TACRED), or any other types of relations not present in the annotation scheme (see OTHERS in SemEval-2010 and BizRel). NRs share two main characteristics: (C1) they have irregular and unstable linguistic realizations and (C2) are often over-represented making PR hard to predict due to the highly imbalanced nature of the problem (see the ratio of NR in Table 1).

Several solutions have been proposed to address NR: discard them during training (Doddington et al., 2004), ignore them at the evaluation stage

Proceedings of the Fourth Workshop on Financial Technology and Natural Language Processing (FinNLP), pages 170 - 177
December 8, 2022 ©2022 Association for Computational Linguistics

focusing only on the performances of PR as done in most RE shared tasks (Zhang et al., 2017; Hendrickx et al., 2010), or include them during training by treating all relations equally (Wu, 2019; Zhou and Chen, 2021). These strategies however fail to deal with the sparseness of PR and the characteristics of NR in a real world scenario. To overcome the data imbalance problem, four main solutions have been proposed in the literature:

(1) *Data augmentation* where different strategies based on lexical variations are used to generate new instances for minority classes (Su et al., 2021; Papanikolaou and Pierleoni, 2020).

(2) *Cost-sensitive learning* by assigning higher wrong classification costs to classes with small proportion (Lin et al., 2018; Zhang et al., 2017) .

(3) *Multitask learning* where auxiliary tasks help the main task to improve performances of under-represented classes (Khaldi et al., 2021; Wang and Hu, 2020).

(4) *Knowledge distillation* (henceforth KD) that aims to transfer knowledge from a complex teacher model to a small student model, where the outputs of the teacher network, called soft labels, are used to train a student network (Hinton et al., 2015; Zhang et al., 2020; Song et al., 2021). The basic idea behind KD is that the teacher's soft probabilities have more knowledge about classes than the one hot-encoded labels used usually to train the student.

The first three solutions rely on hard labels supervision, where the ground truth labels are represented using one-hot encoded vectors that are not able to represent the semantic information among relations. Indeed, NR can have unstable patterns, and can share similar linguistic realizations with PR. For example, the SemEval 2010 Task 8 dataset (Hendrickx et al., 2010) includes the OTHERS relations for near misses of PR as NR instances, while in the BIZREL dataset (Khaldi et al., 2021) sentences expressing PR and NR at the same time between different pair of entities are one of the main sources of false negatives. While hard label supervision successes to counter the class imbalance problem (i.e. (C2)), it does not however fully capture the dissimilarities between PR and NR, making the optimization of model's output probabilities hard. Recent studies show that soft labels generated via KD by a teacher model are more adequate to efficiently handle the inherent characteristics of NR (C1) (Song et al., 2021). In this paper, we aim to continue these efforts by proposing a new knowledge distillation approach based on *binary soft labels supervision (BSLS)*. The soft outputs generated by the teacher model trained for binary classification (PR vs. NR), are used to supervise the student model to perform multi-class RE. Our contributions are three folds:

- A new knowledge distillation approach to account for NR characteristics in imbalanced RE problem based on *binary soft labels supervision*. As far as we know, KD has never been used for business RE.

- A comparison of our approach against several state of the art hard labels (data augmentation, cost-sensitive learning, multitask) and soft labels approaches.

- An evaluation of the performances of our model on a business relation extraction dataset. Our results show that our approach improves the extraction of under-represented relations as well as the detection of false negatives, addressing therefore both (C1) and (C2).

This paper is organized as follows: We first present the related work, then describe our KD architecture. We finally detail the carried experiments and give our results.

2 Related Work

2.1 Knowledge Distillation for RE

The main idea behind KD is to design a simple student model that mimics the behavior of a complex, more informed, or a large teacher model in order to achieve comparable results in performing a specific task. It has first been proposed for model compression task (Hinton et al., 2015).

KD has been recently proposed for RE. Zhang (2020) incorporates knowledge about type constraints between entities and relations into the teacher model then use knowledge distillation to generate well informed soft labels used to supervise a student model that is able to inherit this knowledge from its teacher. Song et al. (2021) integrate ground truth sentence-level identification information into the teacher network during training then transfer it to the student by sharing the classification layer to counter data imbalance problem. KD has also been used to alleviate the interference of noise from relation annotations in distant supervision via label softening (Li et al., 2022).

Our work is close to (Song et al., 2021) but instead of adding more features to the teacher model, we rather train the teacher and student models on two different complementary tasks: binary relation identification (PR vs. NR) and multi-class relation extraction. We assume that training a teacher model on binary relation identification helps to learn discriminative features that differentiate PR from NR, on a less imbalanced dataset, since all PR are merged into one class. The student model can therefore inherit from the teacher's produced binary soft labels the salient learnt features about PR and NR, to mitigate NR irregular patterns problem. We also experiment with different data-imbalance sensitive loss functions in the student model in order to alleviate the (PR vs. NR) imbalance problem.

2.2 Business Relation Extraction

Most existing works for BRE have used semi-supervised approaches relying either on lexico-syntactic patterns generated from dependency trees (Braun et al., 2018), or lexical patterns based on a list of keywords which are specific to each predefined relation type (Lau and Zhang, 2011). Recent works rely on supervised approaches, where neural models are trained on annotated datasets for business relations. For example, Collovini et al. (2020) extract relations between Fintech companies from news text using Bi-directional Gated Recurrent Units. Recently, De Los Reyes et al. (2021), Reyes et al. (2021), and Khaldi et al. (2021) relied on BERT pretrained language model (Devlin et al., 2019) fine-tuned on annotated datasets to classify relations between financial and economic entities. Most works focus either on business relations classification (Braun et al., 2018; Lau and Zhang, 2011) where NR is not considered, or on business relation identification where all relations are merged into one PR type (Reyes et al., 2021; Collovini et al., 2020). Only few works handles both business relation identification (PR vs. NR) and business relation classification by including a NR in the set of relations to extract (Khaldi et al., 2021; De Los Reyes et al., 2021). Our work continues these efforts by proposing a supervised model for BRE based on BERT, to perform both business relation identification and classification, while handling for the first time, as far as we know, business PR sparsity through knowledge distillation.

3 A Binary Soft-labels Supervision for Multi-class RE (BSLS)

Our *binary soft label supervision* approach for multi-class relation extraction is based on knowledge distillation where binary soft labels generated by a teacher model noted T are used to supervise the training of a student model noted S (cf. Figure 1). Following (Zhou and Chen, 2021), both S and T have the same architecture based on an improvement of R-BERT (Wu, 2019), a transformer model specifically designed to handle RE tasks. This architecture has two main components: **a)** *a sentence encoder* noted $Encoder_i$ with $i \in \{S, T\}$ based on the pre-trained BERT model (Devlin et al., 2019) while using entity markers as sentence representation vectors, **b)** *a relation classifier* noted $Classifier_i$ composed of two linear layers followed by dropout layer then a softmax activation function.

An input sentence is first fed into $Encoder_i$, to get its contextual representations that are injected into $Classifier_i$ to predict the relation type. Let $P_i = (P_{i0}, ..., P_{in})$ the prediction probabilities generated by $Classifier_i$, with n being the number of relations to predict. Let P_{SoftT} the *soft labels*, i.e., the prediction probabilities generated by a pre-trained teacher binary classifier $Classifier_T$ whose weights are frozen and shared with S. Finally, let Y_b and Y_m be respectively the binary and multi-class *hard labels* that encode the ground-truth labels as one hot vectors. These soft and hard labels are used by two different losses in order to optimize the models parameters through back-propagation: $\mathcal{L}_{cT}$ (resp. $\mathcal{L}_{cS}$) , the classification loss that minimizes the errors between P_T and Y_b (resp. P_S and Y_m). and $\mathcal{L}_D$, the distillation loss calculated between a binarised form of P_S and P_{SoftT}.

The distillation algorithm consists in the following steps:

(1) First, train T on binary relation identification (PR Vs. NR), while optimizing the teacher classification loss $\mathcal{L}_{cT}$.

(2) Then $Classifier_T$'s weights are frozen and shared with S.

(3) S is trained on multi-class RE and supervised by both Y_m and P_{SoftT}, while optimizing

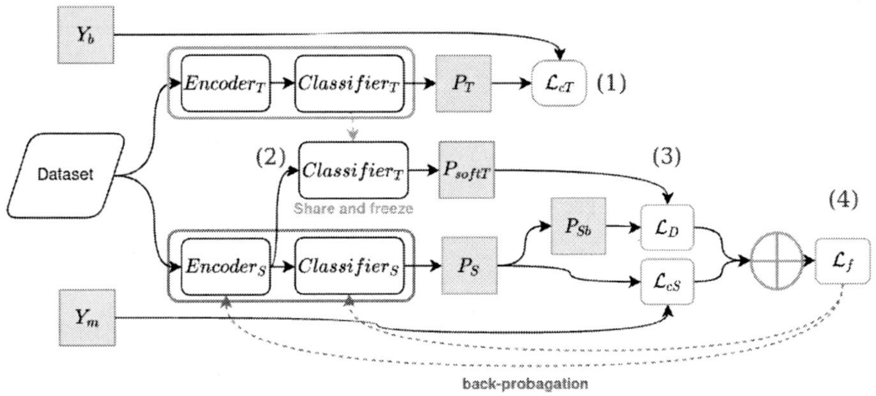

Figure 1: Binary soft-labels supervision architecture for Business Relation Extraction. (1) Teacher training, (2) Teacher classifier freezing and sharing, (3) Student training through knowledge distillation, (4) Final loss to train the student.

both the student classification loss $\mathcal{L}_{cS}$ and the distillation loss $\mathcal{L}_D$. To this end, P_S are first binarised into P_{Sb} following the equation (1) where P_{S_0} refers to the prediction probability of NR as given by $Classifier_S$.

$$(1) \quad P_{Sb} = (P_{S0}, max(P_{S1}, ..., P_{Sn}))$$

(4) The weighted sum of $\mathcal{L}_{cS}$ and $\mathcal{L}_D$ is the final loss $\mathcal{L}_f$ optimized to train the student model, α =0.6 , β = 0.4, being loss weights.

$$(2) \quad \mathcal{L}_f = \alpha.\mathcal{L}_{cS} + \beta.\mathcal{L}_D$$

4 Data and Experiments

4.1 Baselines

We compare our model against four baseline models used to tackle data imbalance in RE: augmentation of the training data (DA), multitask architecture (MLT), optimizing using an adapted loss (ALS), and knowledge distillation (KD) via soft labels. We describe below each of these configurations.

1- Shortest dependency path data augmentation (DA_{SDP}) (Su et al., 2021): The main idea of data augmentation is to generate new instances that express the same relation. As the shortest dependency path is assumed to capture the required information to express a relation between two target entities (Bunescu and Mooney, 2005), the augmentation consists in extracting tokens located in this path, fixing them, then the rest of tokens are randomly transformed by: synonyms replacement, random swapping, and random deletion. In our experiment, this method augments the positive instances by 300%.

2- Multitask architecture (MLT_{bin}) (Khaldi et al., 2021): This is a multitask RE model that performs both relation identification (PR vs. NR) and relation extraction (multi-class classification). The relation identification task is an auxiliary task designed to help the main task of multi-class relation classification learn more features about PR vs. NR distinction. We use here a simplified version of MLT without considering any additional semantic features.

3- Adapted loss (ALS) : We rely on four adapted losses as follows:

– Weighted Cross Entropy loss (ALS_{WCE}) : A variant of cross-entropy loss that assigns to each class a pre-computed weight that corresponds to the penalty of miss-classifying its instances.

– Focal loss (ALS_{FC}) (Lin et al., 2017): This loss has shown to be very effective for object detection from highly imbalanced datasets since it down-weights easy examples and thus focus the training on hard negatives by adding a modulating factor to the cross-entropy loss.

–Adaptive scaling (ALS_{AD}) (Lin et al., 2018): It is a dynamic cost-sensitive learning algorithm that optimizes the F-score rather than the accuracy and adaptively scales costs of instances of different classes with a marginal utility that quantify the importance of positive/negative instances during training.

– Dice loss (ALS_{DC}) (Li et al., 2020): The Dice

function is a widely used metric for evaluating image segmentation accuracy. It is the harmonic mean of precision and recall. It attaches equal importance to false positives and false negatives. We use here the weighted version of Dice loss to control the trade-off between precision and recall and down-weight easy examples. As far as we know, dice loss has never been used for RE.

4- Soft label supervision using knowledge distillation (KD_{SLS}): Soft labels generated by a teacher model trained on multi-class RE task are use to supervise a student model performing the same task. We use the focal loss to train the teacher model in order to handle class-imbalance when generating soft labels. This is the standard KD following (Hinton et al., 2015), where the teacher and the student models perform the same task, while only the teacher classifier is distilled as in (Song et al., 2021). Note that our teacher model is simpler as it does not include any additional features.

4.2 Data

We run experiments on the BIZREL dataset, (Khaldi et al., 2021) a business relation extraction corpus freely available for research purposes.[1] The dataset has 10k relation instances between named entities of type *Organization*. It is composed of 5 positive relations (INVESTMENT, COMPETITION, COOPERATION, LEGAL-PROCEEDING, and SALE-PURCHASE) and one negative relation named OTHERS.

Data distribution per relation type and dataset type (train, test) are presented in Table 2. We can observe that the NR is over-represented compared to the other PR, representing 66.2% of the training data and 66.2% of the test. When looking at NR instances, we can notice that the patterns used to express this relation are irregular (see Examples 2 and 3), since a negative relation can be assigned to any other non-business relation such as: *list of sponsors*, *list of innovative companies*, or *employee's transfer from company A to company B*.

Example 2 *Shira Goodman, the former CEO of Framingham office supply retailer* ***[Staples]$_{E1}$****, has been elected to the board of directors of Los Angeles real estate giant* ***[CBRE Group]$_{E2}$***.

Example 3 *Ten French entities were among the world's 100 most innovative organizations in 2016: three research centers (CNRS, CEA, IFP Energies Nouvelles) and seven companies (Alstom,* ***[Arkema]$_{E1}$****,* ***[Safran]$_{E2}$*** *, Saint-Gobain, Thales, Total, and Valeo).*

[1]Link to BizRel dataset

Data	Inv.	Com.	Coo.	Leg.	Sal.	Oth.	**#Tot.**
Train	281	1,675	627	50	248	5,647	8,528
Test	50	296	111	8	44	997	1,506

Table 2: BIZREL dataset distribution per relation type and per dataset type (train, test).

	Inv.	Com.	Coo.	Leg.	Sal.	Oth.
Avg. w_per_s	32	44	35	29	32	40
Avg. e_per_s	4	8	5	3	4	7
Avg. v_per_s	3	2	3	3	2	2

Table 3: BIZREL dataset complexity per relation type.

In addition, these patterns can be very close to the ones used to express PR. In Example 4, a NR is annotated between E_1 and E_3 while a PR of type COOPERATION exists between E_1 and E_2. We can notice that for both entity pairs, the pattern form E_1 *partners with* E_2 exists.

Example 4 *While* ***[Airbus]$_{E1}$*** *partners with* ***[Audi]$_{E2}$****, Boeing is cozying to* ***[Adient]$_{E3}$****, Mercedes-Benz, and even General Motors.*

To measure the complexity of business relations in BIZREL dataset and their syntactic richness, we compute the average count of words, verbs, and entities per relation type (*Avg. w_per_s*, *Avg. v_per_s*, and *Avg. e_per_s* respectively). Table 3 shows the results. We observe that sentences contain on average from 3 to 8 named entities of type *organization*, therefore, potentially a maximum of 6 to 28 relations could occur in a single sentence between different entity pairs. In addition, sentences are complex containing in average from 2 to 3 verbs and the context surrounding a given relation instance varies from 29 to 44 tokens on average. Overall, these measures confirm the diversity and complexity of business relations expressed in BIZREL. This is more salient for OTHERS and COMPETITION where the average number of entities per sentence is 7 and 8 respectively, while the context (i.e., number of words per sentence) is respectively of 40 and 44.

5 Main Results

Results of the baselines and BSLS experiments are reported in Table 4, in terms of macro precision, recall, and F-score. [2]

[2]All models are based on `bert-base-cased`. Using FinBERT (Araci, 2019) did not improve the overall performances,

Model	P	R	F1
ALS_{CE}	62.5	72.5	66.7
ALS_{WCE}	63.1	**75.1**	68.1
ALS_{FC} (Lin et al., 2017)	65.9	71.7	68.5
ALS_{DC} (Li et al., 2020)	66.9	65.4	65.7
ALS_{AD} (Lin et al., 2018)	62.6	70.9	66.0
MLT_{bin} (Khaldi et al., 2021)	62.8	73.2	67.2
DA_{SDP} (Su et al., 2021)	**69.7**	67.8	68.2
KD_{SLS} (Song et al., 2021)	63.9	70.9	67.0
$BSLS_{CE}$	65.4	71.7	68.2
$BSLS_{WCE}$	63.0	73.2	67.1
$BSLS_{FC}$	66.1	75.0	**69.9**
$BSLS_{DC}$	66.7	69.8	68.1
$BSLS_{AD}$	66.6	69.8	67.6

Table 4: Experimental results on the BIZREL dataset. Best results are in bold.

Overall, we can observe that the proposed model based on *binary soft labels supervision* (BSLS) optimized using a focal loss (FC) is the best, achieving an F-score of 69.9%, outperforming therefore all the baselines (+1.4% over the best one). *Shortest dependency path* (AD_{SDP}) data augmentation obtains the best precision (69.7%) while the *weighted cross entropy loss* (ALS_{WCE}) the best recall (75.1%).

When comparing between knowledge distillation models, we can observe that our *binary soft labels* (BSLS) are more efficient than KD_{SLS}, the *multi-class soft labels* state-of-the art (+2.9% F-score).

When experimenting BSLS with different loss functions, we notice that, for most of the experiments, BSLS optimized using $loss_i$ outperforms the baseline model optimized using the same $loss_i$. For example, $BSLS_{CE}$ scores higher than ALS_{CE} (+1.5 % F-score), $BSLS_{DC}$ is better than ALS_{DC} (+2.4 % F-score), $BSLS_{AD}$ outperforms ALS_{AD} (+1.6 % F-score), and finally $BSLS_{FC}$ outperforms ALS_{FC} (+1.4 % F-score).

6 Discussion and Analysis

We further compare the performances of the best baseline (ALS_{FC}) with our best performing model ($BSLS_{FC}$). Figure 2 gives a confusion matrix that shows the number of false/true positives/negatives between PR and NR. We can see that $BSLS_{FC}$ was able to reduce the number of false negative

where $BSLS_{FC}$ achieves the best F1 (68.9%), followed by ALS_{FC} (68.7%).

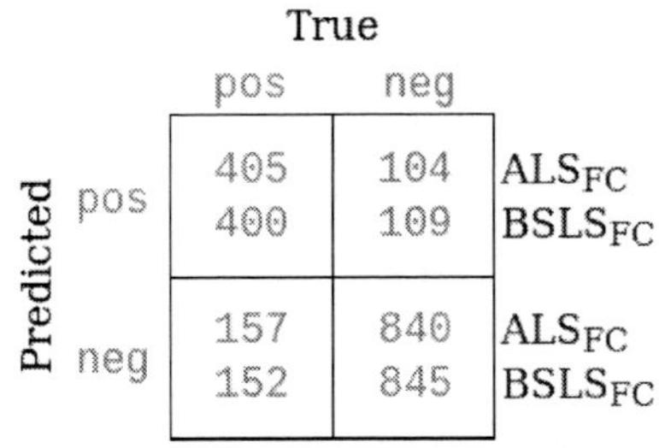

Figure 2: Confusion matrix to compare between business and non-business instance classification in our best model ($BSLS_{FC}$) and the best baseline (ALS_{FC})

	Inv.	Com.	Coo.	Leg.	Sal.	Oth.
ALS_{FC}	61.0	**78.8**	65.0	**77.8**	41.9	**86.6**
$BSLS_{FC}$	**68.9**	77.2	**66.7**	73.7	**46.2**	**86.6**

Table 5: Best baseline (ALS_{FC}) and our best model ($BSLS_{FC}$) F1-score per relation type. Best results of each relation are in bold.

instances (from 157 to 152), and increase the true negative (from 840 to 845). We can also observe the impact of these changes on the recall where our model achieve one of the best score. It was however not able to reduce misclassifications due to false positive, leading therefore to a decrease in the precision when compared to the best precision.

A closer look into the results per class for the best baseline and best performing model (cf. Table 5) shows that our model is able to improve the performances of most under-represented positive relations, namely: INVESTMENT, COOPERATION and SALE-PURCHASE that represent 3.3%, 7.3% and 2.9% of test set. NR results remain stable and this was expected as our approach was specifically designed to handle under-represented PR. A final interesting finding is that PR with less frequencies are the one that benefits the most from *binary soft labels*. For example, an improvement of +7.9 % (resp. +4.3 %) in terms of F1 is observed for under-represented relation INVESTMENT (resp. SALE-PURCHASE) over the best baseline.

In order to gain insights into the main strengths of the current approach when compared to the best baseline, we analyse well classified instances by $BSLS_{FC}$, that ALS_{FC} fails to classify correctly. We notice that our approach is able to identify the NR OTHERS in some cases where many relations are expressed between different target entities, unlike ALS_{FC} (See example 5).

Example 5 *While there were few mega acquisi-*

*tions/ mergers primarily Chinese players acquiring European and US robotics/ automation companies (Kuka AG by **[Midea Group]**$_{E_1}$, Dematic by **[Kion Group]**$_{E_2}$ and KraussMaffei Automation by ChemChina) and few others by US industry giants (Affeymetrix by ThermoFisher and Intelligrated by Honeywel), most acquisitions were in the sub $ 500 M range .*

BSLS$_{FC}$'s correct label : OTHERS, **ALS$_{FC}$'s wrong label:** INVESTMENT

In addition, our model is also able to distinguish between semantically close PR such as INVESTMENT, SALE-PURCHASE, and COOPERATION, that uses the same lexical cues to be expressed such as *signing agreement, entering into a contract.* In example 6, the expression *entering into a contract* refers to *service-selling* contract rather than a COOPERATION relation.

Example 6 *[**General Electric Corporation**]$_{E_1}$ has entered into a five - year, $ 128,500 million contract with **[Electronic Data Systems]**$_{E_2}$ (EDS) to handle the corporation's desktop computer procurement, service, and maintenance activities.*

BSLS$_{FC}$'s correct label : SALE-PURCHASE, **ALS$_{FC}$'s wrong label:** COOPERATION

7 Conclusion

In this paper, we propose a novel solution to tackle PR vs. NR imbalance and NR irregular patterns problems, relying on *binary soft-labels supervision* generated by knowledge distillation. When evaluated on a business relation dataset, our approach improves the overall performances by enhancing the detection of under-represented relations and reducing false negative misclassification rates. As future work, we plan to evaluate our method to other generic and domain specific RE datasets in order to assess its adaptability to other domains.

References

Dogu Araci. 2019. Finbert: Financial sentiment analysis with pre-trained language models.

D. Braun, A. Faber, A. Hernandez-Mendez, and F. Matthes. 2018. Automatic relation extraction for building smart city ecosystems using dependency parsing. In *Proceedings of the 2nd Workshop on Natural Language for Artificial Intelligence*, pages 29–39.

R. Bunescu and R. Mooney. 2005. A shortest path dependency kernel for relation extraction. In *Proceedings of HLT and EMNLP*, pages 724–731.

S. Collovini, P. N. Gonçalves, G. Cavalheiro, J. Santos, and R. Vieira. 2020. Relation extraction for competitive intelligence. In *International Conference on Computational Processing of the Portuguese Language*, pages 249–258. Springer.

D. De Los Reyes, A. Barcelos, R. Vieira, and I. Manssour. 2021. Related named entities classification in the economic-financial context. In *Proceedings of the EACL Hackashop on News Media Content Analysis and Automated Report Generation*, pages 8–15.

J. Devlin, MW. Chang, K. Lee, and K. Toutanova. 2019. BERT: Pre-training of deep bidirectional transformers for language understanding. In *Proceedings of NAACL*, pages 4171–4186.

G. R Doddington, A. Mitchell, M. A Przybocki, L. A Ramshaw, S. M Strassel, and R. M Weischedel. 2004. The automatic content extraction (ace) program-tasks, data, and evaluation. In *Lrec*, pages 837–840.

I. Hendrickx, S. N. Kim, Z. Kozareva, P. Nakov, D. Séaghdha, S. Padó, M. Pennacchiotti, L. Romano, and S. Szpakowicz. 2010. Semeval-2010 task 8: Multi-way classification of semantic relations between pairs of nominals. In *Proceedings of the 5th International Workshop on Semantic Evaluation*, pages 33–38.

G. Hinton, O. Vinyals, and J. Dean. 2015. Distilling the knowledge in a neural network. In *In Proc. of NeurIPS*.

H. Khaldi, F. Benamara, A. Abdaoui, N. Aussenac-Gilles, and E. Kang. 2021. Multilevel entity-informed business relation extraction. In *International Conference on Applications of Natural Language to Information Systems*, pages 105–118. Springer.

M. Krallinger, O. Rabal, S. A Akhondi, M. P. Pérez, J. Santamaría, G. P. Rodríguez, G. Tsatsaronis, and A. Intxaurrondo. 2017. Overview of the biocreative vi chemical-protein interaction track. In *Proceedings of the sixth BioCreative challenge evaluation workshop*, volume 1, pages 141–146.

R. Lau and W. Zhang. 2011. Semi-supervised statistical inference for business entities extraction and business relations discovery. In *SIGIR 2011 workshop*, pages 41–46.

R. Li, C. Yang, T. Li, and S. Su. 2022. Midtd: A simple and effective distillation framework for distantly supervised relation extraction. *ACM Transactions on Information Systems (TOIS)*, (4):1–32.

X. Li, X. Sun, Y. Meng, J. Liang, F. Wu, and J. Li. 2020. Dice loss for data-imbalanced nlp tasks. In *Proceedings of the 58th ACL*, pages 465–476.

H. Lin, Y. Lu, X. Han, and L. Sun. 2018. Adaptive scaling for sparse detection in information extraction. *arXiv preprint arXiv:1805.00250*.

T.-Y. Lin, P. Goyal, R.s Girshick, K. He, and P. Dollár. 2017. Focal loss for dense object detection. In *Proceedings of the IEEE international conference on computer vision*, pages 2980–2988.

T. Oberlechner and S. Hocking. 2004. Information sources, news, and rumors in financial markets: Insights into the foreign exchange market. *Journal of economic psychology*, pages 407–424.

Y. Papanikolaou and A. Pierleoni. 2020. Dare: Data augmented relation extraction with gpt-2. *arXiv preprint arXiv:2004.13845*.

D.D.L. Reyes, D. Trajano, I. Manssour, R. Vieira, and R. Bordini. 2021. Entity relation extraction from news articles in portuguese for competitive intelligence based on bert. In *Brazilian Conference on Intelligent Systems*, pages 449–464. Springer.

D. Song, J. Xu, J. Pang, and H. Huang. 2021. Classifier-adaptation knowledge distillation framework for relation extraction and event detection with imbalanced data. *Information Sciences*, 573:222–238.

Peng Su, Yifan Peng, and K. Vijay-Shanker. 2021. Improving BERT model using contrastive learning for biomedical relation extraction. In *Proceedings of the 20th Workshop BioNLP*, pages 1–10. ACL.

W. Wang and W. Hu. 2020. Improving relation extraction by multi-task learning. In *Proceedings of HPCCT'20 BDAI'20*, pages 152–157.

Y. Wu, S.and He. 2019. Enriching pre-trained language model with entity information for relation classification. In *Proceedings of the CIKM'19*, pages 2361–2364.

Y. Zhang, V. Zhong, D. Chen, G. Angeli, and C. D. Manning. 2017. Position-aware attention and supervised data improve slot filling. In *Proceedings of the 2017 Conference on EMNLP*, pages 35–45. ACL.

Z. Zhang, X. Shu, B. Yu, T. Liu, J. Zhao, Q. Li, and L. Guo. 2020. Distilling knowledge from well-informed soft labels for neural relation extraction. In *Proceedings of the AAAI Conference*, pages 9620–9627.

J. Zhao, P. Jin, and Y. Liu. 2010. Business relations in the web: Semantics and a case study. *Journal of Software*, (8):826–833.

W. Zhou and M. Chen. 2021. An improved baseline for sentence-level relation extraction.

Astock: A New Dataset and Automated Stock Trading based on Stock-specific News Analyzing Model

Jinan Zou *, Haiyao Cao *, Lingqiao Liu, Yuhao Lin, Ehsan Abbasnejad, Javen Qinfeng Shi †
Australian Institute for Machine Learning, The University of Adelaide, Australia
jinan.zou, haiyao.cao, lingqiao.liu@adelaide.edu.au
yuhao.lin01, ehsan.abbasnejad, javen.shi@adelaide.edu.au

Abstract

Natural Language Processing(NLP) demo strates a great potential to support financi decision-making by analyzing the text fro social media or news outlets. In this work, w build a platform to study the NLP-aided stoc auto-trading algorithms systematically. In co trast to the previous work, our platform is cha acterized by three features: (1) We provide f nancial news for each specific stock. (2) W provide various stock factors for each stock. (We evaluate performance from more financia relevant metrics. Such a design allows us t develop and evaluate NLP-aided stock auto-trading algorithms in a more realistic setting. In addition to designing an evaluation platform and dataset collection, we also made a technical contribution by proposing a system to automatically learn a good feature representation from various input information. The key to our algorithm is a method called semantic role labeling Pooling (SRLP), which leverages Semantic Role Labeling (SRL) to create a compact representation of each news paragraph. Based on SRLP, we further incorporate other stock factors to make the stock movement prediction. In addition, we propose a self-supervised learning strategy based on SRLP to enhance the out-of-distribution generalization performance of our system. Through our experimental study, we show that the proposed method achieves better performance and outperforms all the baselines' annualized rate of return as well as the maximum drawdown of the CSI300 index and XIN9 index on real trading. Our Astock dataset and code are available at https://github.com/JinanZou/Astock.

1 Introduction

The stock prediction has been an attractive task for a long time, and it is still challenging since the stochasticity of the market and behavior patterns

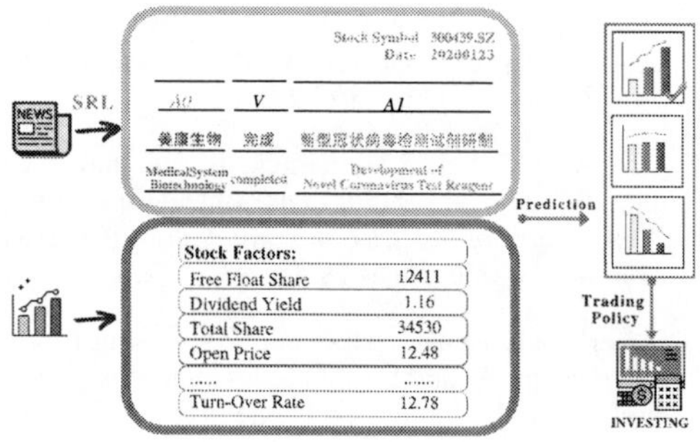

Figure 1: Overview of the automated stock trading system.

of participators are fluctuating and elusive. Stock forecasting based on Natural Language Processing (NLP) techniques is a promising solution since text information, e.g., tweets, financial news etc., is strongly correlated with the stock prices. However, the NLP-based stock forecasting research is still scattered without unified definitions, benchmark datasets, clear articulations of the tasks, which severaly hinders progress of this field.

Existing approaches are usually based on market sentiment analysis (Xu and Cohen, 2018; Cheng and Li, 2021) and use news to predict the related securities' price on the following trading day(s) (Zhang et al., 2017; Li et al., 2020). Despite the limited success in those studies, the existing works are still far from realistic for two reasons: Firstly, previous methods ignore the financial factors, which plays a key role in practical trading. Secondly, these models are evaluated only on intermediate performance metric, e.g., stock movement prediction accuracy. It is unclear how well they can support a practical trading system to make sufficient profit.

To address the problems above, we construct a China A-shares market dataset with news and stock factors called Astock. Specifically, we an-

*Both authors contributed equally
†Corresponding Author

Proceedings of the Fourth Workshop on Financial Technology and Natural Language Processing (FinNLP), pages 178 - 186
December 8, 2022 ©2022 Association for Computational Linguistics

notate all occurrences of the three trading actions (long, preserve, short) in 40,963 news originated from Tushare [1] with a valid official license, which describes the major financial events. The dataset also includes various stock factors to build a realistic system. Based on Astock, we establish a semantic role labeling pooling (SRLP) to build a compact representation for stock-specific news and predict the stock movement. This work also explores how to leverage a self-supervised method better to upgrade the SRLP method, which achieves better performance for classification and high domain generalization ability.

In experiments, we further propose a realistic trading platform that outperforms the state-of-the-art text classification baseline's average returns and Sharpe Ratios over the CSI300 index and XIN9 index of testing period from January 2021 to November 2021. Specifically, we analyze the profitability of the proposed strategy based on stock movement prediction result for real trading as shown in Figure 1. The primary contributions of this work can be summarized as follows:

- We construct a brand new Chinese stock movement prediction task dataset with stock-specific news and stock factors.
- Our SRLP characterizes the key attributes of financial events, which is convenient for incorporating other stock factors and further creating a self-supervised module on top of the SRLP method. Our self-supervised SRLP method obtains competitive stock movement prediction and out-of-distribution (OOD) generalization results.
- We further evaluate algorithm performance on real-world trading from more financial-relevant metrics. By conducting extensive experimental studies, we show that our self-supervised SRLP achieves remarkable performance on these metrics. Furthermore, we observe that the proposed trading strategies work well in practice.

2 Related Work

2.1 Text-based Stock Movement Prediction

In recent years, the use of text-based information, especially news and social media, has significantly improved the performance of stock movement prediction tasks and these methods usually rely on text-based features and sentiment analysis to forecast stock movements (Xu and Cohen, 2018; Hu et al., 2018; Ding et al., 2015). However, These approaches assume that the real-trading distribution was the same as the training distribution, which is not realistic as it is difficult to generalize to future trading. By contrast, our self-supervised SRL approach pays closer attention to the quality and comprehensiveness of the news, which could help with out-of-distribution generalization on the realistic trading.

2.2 Semantic Role Labeling and Self-Supervised Learning Approach

Semantic role labeling (SRL) aims to disclose the predicate-argument structure of a given sentence, which could provide a clear overlay that uncovers the underlying semantics of text (Conia et al., 2021). However, previous stock movement prediction methods (Xu and Cohen, 2018; Hu et al., 2018; Ding et al., 2015) adopted the word or sentence level representation to predict the stock movement. Due to the lack of abstract information of the news, these approaches can overfit the training data and fail to distinguish the key features of news. To deal with this problem, we used the SRL's characteristics for extracting a clear overlay that uncovers the underlying semantics of news.

Recently, self-supervised learning has become a very popular technique in the training stage of NLP, which generates labels without any human intervention and learns common language representations. Some researches (Im et al., 2021; Zheng et al., 2021) have proven that self-supervised learning strengthens the generalization ability for models as it improves the performance in many tasks.

3 Dateset Creation

Table 1: The comparison between Astock and other existing widely-used stock movement prediction dataset.

Dataset	Num of Stock	Text Source	Price-level	Stock Factors
DMFT's dataset (Zhang et al., 2017) EMNLP 17'	50	✗	Daily	✗
StockNet's dataset (Xu and Cohen, 2018) ACL 18'	88	Twitter	✗	✗
Dingxia's dataset (Ding et al., 2014) EMNLP 14'	500	News	Daily	✗
Trade the event 's dataset (Zhou et al., 2021) ACL 21'	✗	News	✗	✗
Ours	3680	Stock News	Minute-level when news published Daily-level for all the stocks	✓

The stock movement prediction task aims to explore a realistic method to predict the stock move-

[1]http://tushare.org

ment with comprehensive and reasonable information in the China stock market. To this end, it is important to have minute-level price information in the dataset and we are motivated to collect one.

3.1 Standard of news and stock factors collection

There are two main components in our dataset: News and stock factors for the China stock market. In terms of news data, there are 40,963 pieces of listed company news, including company announcements and company-related news from July 2018 to November 2021. The news data are split into two parts: the In-distribution split and the out-of-distribution split. The in-distribution split is from July 2018 to December 2020 for training and testing where the training set occupies by 80%, and the validation set and test set occupy 10% respectively. The out-of-distribution split is selected from January 2021 to November 2021, which is used for OOD generalization testing. Every piece of news includes its published time and a corresponding news summary. Factor investing is an investment approach that involves targeting quantifiable firm characteristics or factors that can explain the differences in stock returns. Factor-based strategies may help investors meet particular investment objectives—such as potentially improving returns or reducing risk over the long term. Our Astock dataset covers the 24 stock factors on each stock of the China A-shares including Dividend yield, Total share, Circulated share, Free Float share, Market Capitalization, Price-earning ratio, PE for Trailing Twelve Months, Price/book value ratio, Price-to-sales Ratio, Price to Sales ratio, Circulate Market Capitalization, Open price, High price,Low price, Close price , Previous close price, Price change, Percentage of change, Volume, Amount, Turn over rate, Turn over rate for circulated Market Capitalization, Volume ratio. Furthermore, We compare Astock with several widely used stock movement prediction datasets in Table 1. The value is reflected in the following aspects: (1) Astock provides financial news for each specific stock over the entire China A-shares market. (2) Astock provides various stock factors for each stock. (3) Astock provides minute-level historical prices for the news.

3.2 Task Formulation

We divide the automated trading system into two tasks: stock movement classification and simulated trading.

3.2.1 Text-based stock movement classification

The goal of the stock movement classification task is to classify the effects of the input information. We measure the impact of each piece of company news by the stock return rate. In this paper, the news is annotated by the stock return rate r , and three cases are considered in our annotation: outperforming, neutral, and underperforming as shown in Equation 1. We further model the stock movement by classifying it into three categories. The ground truth for those categories can be derived from r. Specifically, we follow the following rules to categorize the data into three classes after ranking all the news by r, which aims to find the most strong signal of the stock movement, and to reduce the disturbance of noises comparing to dividing the data evenly. After the domain experts gave us the advice and the experiments with different thresholds was conducted, we set 20% as the threshold where the tunable parameters a, b, c, and d are 20, 40, 60, and 20, respectively.

$$\text{label=}\begin{cases}\text{outperforming,} & \text{if } r \text{ ranked top a\%}\\ \text{neutral,} & \text{if } r \text{ ranked top b\%-c\%}\\ \text{underperforming,} & \text{if } r \text{ ranked bottom d\%}\end{cases} \tag{1}$$

where r is the return rate of the news. We randomly select 80% of the in-distribution dataset as the training set, and the other 20% is split evenly into validation and test sets.

3.2.2 Simulated Trading

Stock movement prediction accuracy may not necessarily translate to a profitability of an auto-trading system. To further investigate how the stock movement prediction can benefit for the actual trading practice, we employ a practical trading strategy based on the stock movement prediction results and evaluate various metrics for the trading actions. The trading strategy details can be found at our github page.

4 Methodology

This section describes the technical contribution of this work: a novel system for stock movement prediction. Our system consists of two major components: semantic role labeling pooling method and a self-supervised learning based on SRLP, we will elaborate on those two parts.

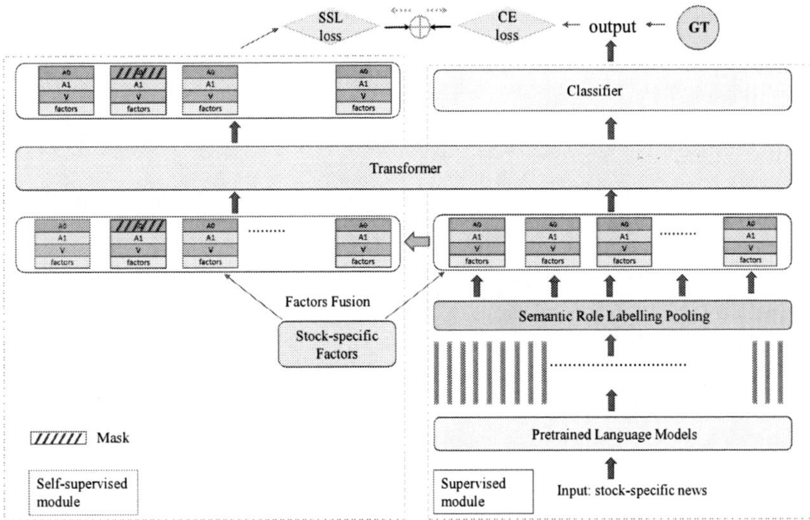

Figure 2: Overall framework of our approach, including a domain adapted pre-trained model (RoBERTa WWM Ext), Semantic Roles Pooling, transformer layer, self-supervised module (left part), and the supervised module (right part). The green arrow represents a duplicate for the SRLP. The final result is generated from the stock movement classifier, and the total loss is obtained from the self-supervised SRLP part and supervised stock movement classification part.

4.1 Semantic Role Labelling Pooling

In this work, we propose to leverage the off-the-shelf semantic role labeling, i.e., Propbank (Kingsbury and Palmer, 2003), to pool the output embeddings of a pre-trained language model to construct an alternative representation. The rationale is that the semantic roles in Propbank, i.e., verb (V), proto-agent (A0), and proto-patient (A1), are general-purposed and are also strongly associated with the event arguments. We show an example for semantic role labeling for financial news in Figure 3.

Original text: 科锐国际股东Career HK减持公司股份199万股,占公司总股本的1.103%。

Translation: Career HK, a shareholder of Kerui international, reduced 1.99 million shares of the company, accounting for 1.103% of the total share capital of the company

A0	V	A1
科锐国际股东Career HK	减持	公司股份199万股
Career HK, a shareholder of Kerui international	reduced	1.99 million shares

Figure 3: A Semantic role labeling example for a piece of news.

More specifically, we first use the Language Technology Platform (LTP) (Che et al., 2020) to automatically mark the semantic roles from the sentences of an entire piece of news and then select V, A0, and A1 to represent the roles for each sentence. Secondly, we process each sentence with a pretrained language model to obtain a sequence of output embeddings $\{\mathbf{s}_1, \mathbf{s}_2, \cdots, \mathbf{s}_n\}$. We use $\mathcal{V}$, $\mathcal{A}_0$ and $\mathcal{A}_1$ to denote the indices of tokens corresponding to the V, A0, A1 components. At last, we perform pooling for embeddings with their indices falling into $\mathcal{V}$, $\mathcal{A}_0$ and $\mathcal{A}_1$. We call this scheme Semantic Role Labelling Pooling SRLP in short. Taking A0 as an example, the SRLP feature for A0 is

$$\mathbf{e}_{A0} = \frac{1}{|\mathcal{A}_0|} \sum_{i \in \mathcal{A}_0} \mathbf{s}_i \tag{2}$$

For a sentence with N sets of V, A0 and A1, we concatenate $\mathbf{e}_{A0}$,$\mathbf{e}_{A1}$,$\mathbf{e}_V$ of each sentence and the financial factor $\mathbf{F}$ of the stock-of-interest into a data matrix:

$$\mathbf{E} = \begin{bmatrix} \mathbf{e}_V^1 & \dots & \mathbf{e}_V^t & \dots & \mathbf{e}_V^N \\ \mathbf{e}_{A0}^1 & \cdots & \mathbf{e}_{A0}^t & \cdots & \mathbf{e}_{A0}^N \\ \mathbf{e}_{A1}^1 & \cdots & \mathbf{e}_{A1}^t & \cdots & \mathbf{e}_{A1}^N \\ \mathbf{F} & \dots & \mathbf{F} & \dots & \mathbf{F}, \end{bmatrix} \tag{3}$$

where $\mathbf{E}$ is output of the above process. Each column of $\mathbf{E}$, denoted as $\mathbf{e}_j$, is the concatenation of $\mathbf{e}_V^j, \mathbf{e}_{A0}^j, \mathbf{e}_{A1}^j$ and $\mathbf{F}$. $\mathbf{E}$ is then processed by a Transformer encoder in the same way as the standard text classification to generate the stock movement prediction.

4.2 Self-Supervised Learning based on SRLP

Besides standard supervised training loss for stock movement classification, in this work, we further propose to use a self-supervised training task as an auxiliary task to train the network. For stock movement prediction, good generalization is highly desirable since the training data is usually sampled from a period different from the test period. A significant problem in practice is to ensure that our model generalizes to scenarios different from the training set. We further create a self-supervised learning method on top of the SRLP. Recent studies (Mohseni et al., 2020; Hendrycks et al., 2019) have shown that incorporating a self-supervised learning task along with the supervised training task could lead to better generalization. As shown in Figure 2, the self-supervised task is defined as predicting the position of one randomly masked SRL role from all the roles of SRL in a piece of news. Intuitively, the self-supervised learning task should be designed to encourage the favorable properties of features. In this work, we propose to randomly mask one pooled embedding, i.e., $\mathbf{e}_V^j$, $\mathbf{e}_{A0}^j$ or $\mathbf{e}_{A1}^j$, from a randomly selected sentence, and then ask the network to identify the masked embedding from a pool of candidate embeddings. Such a cloze-style task encourages the network to perform reasoning over other unmasked cues to work out the missing item. We hypothesize that such a reasoning capability is beneficial for understanding the financial news and thus helps stock movement prediction.

Formally, we randomly select a $\mathbf{e}_j$ from $\mathbf{E}$ and then select one element from $\mathbf{e}_j$ = { $\mathbf{e}_V^j$, $\mathbf{e}_{A0}^j$, $\mathbf{e}_{A1}^j$ }, after that we replace the selected element with an all-zero vector, indicating a "mask" operation. Taking masked V at the t-th sentence as an example, we denote the $\mathbf{E}$ after this mask operation as $\mathbf{E}'$.

$$\mathbf{E}' = \begin{bmatrix} \mathbf{e}_V^1 & \dots & \mathbf{M} & \dots & \mathbf{e}_V^N \\ \mathbf{e}_{A0}^1 & \dots & \mathbf{e}_{A0}^t & \dots & \mathbf{e}_{A0}^N \\ \mathbf{e}_{A1}^1 & \dots & \mathbf{e}_{A1}^t & \dots & \mathbf{e}_{A1}^N \\ \mathbf{F} & \dots & \mathbf{F} & \dots & \mathbf{F} \end{bmatrix}$$

Then we feed $\mathbf{E}'$ into the transformer to obtain a query vector sequence $\mathbf{q} \in \mathbb{R}^d$

$$\mathbf{q} = Transformer(\mathbf{E}')[:, t]$$

where $[:, t]$ means extract the t-th column of the vector sequences calculated by the transformer. The unmasked SRLP-V features (or SRLP-A0, SRLP-A1 features, depending on which type of SRLP feature is chosen) is also send to an encoder to calculate candidate key vectors: Formally, $\mathbf{K}$ is defined as:

$$\mathbf{K} = [f_V(\mathbf{e}_V^1), \cdots, f_v(\mathbf{e}_V^t), \cdots, f_V(\mathbf{e}_V^N)] \in \mathbf{R}^{d \times N}$$

where f_V is an encoder specified for encoding V-type SRLP feature. Then the query vector is compared against each column vector in $\mathbf{K}$ and is expected to have the highest matching score at the t-th location. This process could be implemented via matrix multiplication and the softmax operation:

$$P_{SSL} = \text{Softmax}(\mathbf{qK}) \quad (4)$$

and we hope the highest probability entry in Eq. 4 is at the t-th dimension. This requirement could be enforced via the cross-entropy loss. Finally, the training loss for the models is

$$\mathcal{L} = \alpha\mathcal{L}_{CLS} + (1-\alpha)\mathcal{L}_{SSL} \quad (5)$$

where $\mathcal{L}_{CLS}$ is the cross-entropy loss for the text classification and $\mathcal{L}_{SSL}$ is the cross-entropy loss on the self-supervised learning prediction P_{SSL}. α here is a trade-off parameter.

5 Experiments

In this section, we conduct experiments to evaluate the performance of the proposed model. We conduct experiments on two different splits of our dataset for each model: In-distribution split and out-of-distribution split. We also feed the prediction result of our method to the proposed trading strategy to analyze the profitability through back-testing on real-world stock data.

5.1 Evaluation metrics

We evaluated the stock movement prediction and simulated trading performance. For the Stock movement prediction, we applied the **Accuracy, F1 Score, Recall and Precision** as evaluation metrics. For simulated trading, we applied the **Annualized Rate of Return, Maximum Drawdown and Sharpe Ration** as evaluation metrics based on our simulated trading strategy.

5.2 Compared Methods

We re-implement the current state-of-art stock movement prediction models as baselines, including StockNet (Xu and Cohen, 2018), HAN Stock (Hu et al., 2018). **StockNet** (Xu and Cohen, 2018)

Table 2: The stock movement classification performance(%) of in-distribution evaluation on our scheme and others demonstrates the effectiveness of our self-supervised SRL method. ✔ indicates that the model adopted this Semantic role's pooling information. - indicates that the method does not adopt this semantic role's pooling. ✗ indicates that semantic role's pooling is masked.

Model	Resource	Semantic Role			Accuracy	F1 Score	Recall	Precision
		A0	V	A1				
StockNet (Xu and Cohen, 2018) ACL 18'	News	-	-	-	46.72	44.44	46.68	47.65
HAN Stock (Hu et al., 2018) ICWSDM 18'	News	-	-	-	57.35	56.61	57.20	58.41
Bert Chinese (Devlin et al., 2019)NAACL 19'	News	-	-	-	59.11	58.99	59.20	59.07
ERNIE-SKEP (Tian et al., 2020) ACL 20'	News	-	-	-	60.66	60.66	60.59	61.85
XLNET Chinese (Cui et al., 2020)EMNLP 20'	News	-	-	-	61.14	61.19	61.09	61.60
RoBERTa WWM Ext (Cui et al., 2020)EMNLP 20'	News	-	-	-	61.34	61.48	61.32	61.97
	News + Factors	-	-	-	62.49	62.54	62.51	62.59
Our SRLP	News	✔	✔	✔	61.76	61.69	61.62	61.87
	News + Factors	✔	✔	✔	64.79	64.85	64.79	65.26
Our Self-supervised SRLP	News	✗	✔	✗	61.07	61.11	61.11	61.11
	News	✗	✔	✔	62.36	62.32	62.43	62.64
	News	✔	✔	✗	62.42	62.46	62.44	62.62
	News	✗	✗	✔	62.15	62.15	62.15	62.59
	News	✔	✗	✗	61.34	61.23	61.46	61.30
	News	✔	✗	✔	62.97	63.05	62.93	63.47
Our Self-supervised SRLP with Factors	News + Factors	✗	✔	✗	64.59	64.62	64.63	64.65
	News + Factors	✗	✔	✔	66.82	66.81	66.90	66.82
	News + Factors	✔	✔	✗	65.54	65.53	65.62	65.50
	News + Factors	✗	✗	✔	65.34	65.21	65.43	65.43
	News + Factors	✔	✗	✗	65.27	65.35	65.24	65.77
	News + Factors	✔	✗	✔	**66.89**	**66.92**	**66.95**	**66.92**

is a stock temporally-dependent movement prediction model which also uses Twitter data and price information to predict two classes for stock movement. Hybrid Attention Networks **(HAN)** Stock (Hu et al., 2018) is a stock trend prediction model based on a sequence of recent related news to predict three classes for stock movement task, which are the same as ours. We also construct baselines by formulating the stock movement prediction problem as text classification and use four strong pre-trained Chinese language models as backbones such as **XLNet-base-Chinese**(Cui et al., 2020), Sentiment Knowledge Enhanced pre-trained language model(**SKEP**)(Tian et al., 2020), **Bert Chinese**(Devlin et al., 2019) and **RoBERTa WWM Ext**(Cui et al., 2020). For the above four pre-trained language models, we extract sentence embedding from the [CLS] token and attach a three-way classifier to predict the stock movements. In addition, we also compare the CSI300 index, XIN9 index[2] against the proposed method when analyzing the profitability of the proposed system. For our methods, we used RoBERTa WWM Ext as our backbone PLM since the remarkable performance.

[2]Equivalent to the Standard and Poor's 500 (S&P 500) or the Dow Jones Industrial Average (DJIA) in the US stock market

5.3 Stock Movement Evaluation

We first compare different methods on the task of stock movement prediction. We conduct experiments on two different splits of our dataset: In-distribution split and out-of-distribution split. In the in-distribution split, both training and testing data are sampled from the same period while the out-of-distribution split uses data from different periods to construct the training and testing data.

In-distribution evaluation

The results are shown in Table 2. From the results, we made the following two observations:

1. If only text information is used, the proposed SRLP approach achieves the state-of-the-art performance. Interestingly, we find that SRLP achieves superior performance when further combines the stock factors. It outperforms RoBERTa WWM Ext (News+Factors) by more than 2%. We postulate that this is because the compact representation in SRLP make incorporation of stock factors easier. Note that the proposed way of incorporating stock factors (see Section 3.1) does not only introduce extra modalities for the stock movement prediction but also could make the text analysis module

adaptive to the stock factors. This could be useful to model the scenario like the effect of a similar event could result in a different impact on the stock movement for a different type of company.

2. The proposed self-supervised SRLP can further boost the performance of SRLP. In the best setting of self-supervised SRLP, i.e., with V being masked, self-supervised SRLP achieves more than 1% improvement over SRLP. The improvement is even larger when the stock factors are provided, showing more than 2% improvement over SRLP (News+Factors), achieving 66.89% prediction accuracy. This validates the effectiveness of the proposed self-supervised learning approach. Interestingly, we observe that masking A0 and A1 usually will not bring improvement in contrast to the case of masking V. Note that V encodes the type of an event, and the argument is encoded by A0 or A1. It seems that predicting the type of events is a more effective self-supervised learning task than working on the argument.

Out-of-distribution evaluation

In the experiments above, the training data and testing data are sampled from the same period. Thus the distributions of training data and testing data are similar. For real-world applications, the stock movement prediction model is applied to future data unseen at the training time. Hence, it is critical to evaluate the model in such an out-of-distribution setting.

Table 3: The comparison (%) of the out-of-distribution evaluation on stock movement classification with StockNet, RoBERTa-WWM Ext, HAN Stock method and our method from 1/1/2021 to 12/11/2021.

Model	Accuracy	F1 Score	Recall	Precision
StockNet(Xu and Cohen, 2018)	44.35	42.52	45.42	45.82
HAN Stock(Hu et al., 2018)	53.41	53.33	53.69	54.53
RoBERTa WWM Ext(Cui et al., 2020)	60.15	60.08	59.89	60.78
Ours	**64.09**	**63.95**	**63.90**	**64.43**

To this end, we construct a new training/testing split by using the data from July 2018 to December 2020 as training data and the data from January 2021 to November 2021 for the testing data. We first conduct an evaluation on the stock movement prediction task, and the results are shown in Table 3. From the results, we can see that the proposed method is still comparably competitive over other baselines.

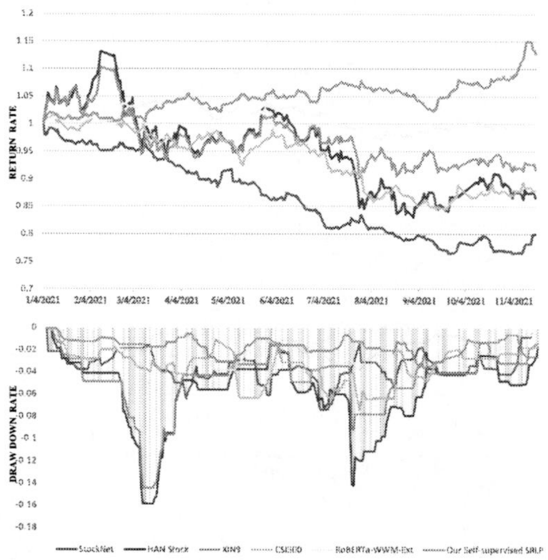

Figure 4: The comparison for the real trading performance on Return Rate, Draw Down Rate with CSI300 index, XIN9, Roberta WWM Ext, HAN Stock, StockNet and our proposed method from 1/1/2021 to 12/11/2021

5.4 Profitability Evaluation in Real-world

Table 4: The comparison of profitability test on Maximum Drawdown(%), Annualized Rate of Return(%), and Sharpe Ratio Rate(%) with strong baselines, XIN9, CSI300 and our proposed method from 1/1/2021 to 12/11/2021.

Model	Maximum Drawdown↓	Annualized Rate of Return↑	Sharpe Ratio↑
XIN9	-15.85	-15.38	-32.01
CSI300	-14.40	-9.34	-32.99
StockNet(Xu and Cohen, 2018)	-7.40	-22.42	-177.65
HAN Stock(Hu et al., 2018)	-7.38	-13.50	-55.84
RoBERTa WWM Ext(Cui et al., 2020)	-3.83	1.35	-16.31
Ours	**-3.60**	**13.85**	**40.93**

In this section, we discuss the possible profitability of the proposed strategy in real-world trading. We use our trading strategy to conduct trading simulation (backtesting) on stock data from January 2021 to November 2021 using the stock movement prediction result of our model trained from July 2018 to December 2020 as mentioned in Section 3.1. In Table 4, we show that our self-supervised SRLP model achieves a remarkable annualized rate of return of 13.85% , which surpasses the previous baselines and market index XIN9 and CSI300. The resulting baseline HAN Stock (Hu et al., 2018) and StockNet (Xu and Cohen, 2018) achieve an annualized rate of return of -13.5% and -22.42% respectively, and the market XIN9 index and CSI300 were overall declining in 2021, which obtains -15.38 % and -9.34% respectively. In addition, our self-supervised learning method also obtains the lowest Maximum Drawdown of -3.6% and the highest Sharpe Ratio of 40.93% , which significantly outperforms the previous methods and indicates that our self-supervised could successfully achieve higher expected returns while remaining relatively less risky as shown in Figure 4.

6 Conclusion

In this paper, we study the problem of NLP-based stock movement prediction and build a platform with a new dataset, AStock, featured by: (1) Large number of stocks, stock-relevant news. (2) Availability of various financial factors. (3) Financial-relevent metrics for Evaluation. The Platform is based on two novel techniques. One leverages Propbank-style semantic role labeling results to create compact news representation. Building on top of this representation, the other technique is a customized self-supervised learning training strategy for improving generalization performance. We demonstrate that the proposed method achieves superior performance over other baselines through extensive experiments in both in-distribution and out-of-distribution settings. Also, by feeding our prediction to a practical simulated trading, our method achieves better profitability in backtesting.

References

Wanxiang Che, Yunlong Feng, Libo Qin, and Ting Liu. 2020. N-ltp: A open-source neural chinese language technology platform with pretrained models. *arXiv preprint arXiv:2009.11616*.

Rui Cheng and Qing Li. 2021. Modeling the momentum spillover effect for stock prediction via attribute-driven graph attention networks. In *Proceedings of the AAAI Conference on Artificial Intelligence*, volume 35, pages 55–62.

Simone Conia, Riccardo Orlando, Fabrizio Brignone, Francesco Cecconi, and Roberto Navigli. 2021. Invero-xl: Making cross-lingual semantic role labeling accessible with intelligible verbs and roles. In *Proceedings of the 2021 Conference on Empirical Methods in Natural Language Processing (EMNLP), Punta Cana, Dominican Republic.*

Yiming Cui, Wanxiang Che, Ting Liu, Bing Qin, Shijin Wang, and Guoping Hu. 2020. Revisiting pre-trained models for Chinese natural language processing. In *Proceedings of the 2020 Conference on Empirical Methods in Natural Language Processing: Findings*, pages 657–668, Online. Association for Computational Linguistics.

Jacob Devlin, Ming-Wei Chang, Kenton Lee, and Kristina Toutanova. 2019. BERT: Pre-training of deep bidirectional transformers for language understanding. In *Proceedings of the 2019 Conference of the North American Chapter of the Association for Computational Linguistics: Human Language Technologies, Volume 1 (Long and Short Papers)*, pages 4171–4186, Minneapolis, Minnesota. Association for Computational Linguistics.

Xiao Ding, Yue Zhang, Ting Liu, and Junwen Duan. 2014. Using structured events to predict stock price movement: An empirical investigation. In *Proceedings of the 2014 Conference on Empirical Methods in Natural Language Processing (EMNLP)*, pages 1415–1425, Doha, Qatar. Association for Computational Linguistics.

Xiao Ding, Yue Zhang, Ting Liu, and Junwen Duan. 2015. Deep learning for event-driven stock prediction. In *Twenty-fourth international joint conference on artificial intelligence*.

Dan Hendrycks, Mantas Mazeika, Saurav Kadavath, and Dawn Song. 2019. Using self-supervised learning can improve model robustness and uncertainty. *Advances in Neural Information Processing Systems (NeurIPS)*.

Ziniu Hu, Weiqing Liu, Jiang Bian, Xuanzhe Liu, and Tie-Yan Liu. 2018. Listening to chaotic whispers: A deep learning framework for news-oriented stock trend prediction. In *Proceedings of the eleventh ACM international conference on web search and data mining*, pages 261–269.

Jinbae Im, Moonki Kim, Hoyeop Lee, Hyunsouk Cho, and Sehee Chung. 2021. Self-supervised multimodal opinion summarization. In *Proceedings of the 59th Annual Meeting of the Association for Computational Linguistics and the 11th International Joint Conference on Natural Language Processing (Volume 1: Long Papers)*, pages 388–403, Online. Association for Computational Linguistics.

Paul Kingsbury and Martha Palmer. 2003. Propbank: the next level of treebank. In *Proceedings of Treebanks and lexical Theories*, volume 3. Citeseer.

Yelin Li, Hui Bu, Jiahong Li, and Junjie Wu. 2020. The role of text-extracted investor sentiment in chinese stock price prediction with the enhancement of deep learning. *International Journal of Forecasting*, 36(4):1541–1562.

Sina Mohseni, Mandar Pitale, JBS Yadawa, and Zhangyang Wang. 2020. Self-supervised learning for generalizable out-of-distribution detection. In *Proceedings of the AAAI Conference on Artificial Intelligence*, volume 34, pages 5216–5223.

Hao Tian, Can Gao, Xinyan Xiao, Hao Liu, Bolei He, Hua Wu, Haifeng Wang, and feng wu. 2020. SKEP: Sentiment knowledge enhanced pre-training for sentiment analysis. In *Proceedings of the 58th Annual Meeting of the Association for Computational Linguistics*, pages 4067–4076, Online. Association for Computational Linguistics.

Yumo Xu and Shay B. Cohen. 2018. Stock movement prediction from tweets and historical prices. In *Proceedings of the 56th Annual Meeting of the Association for Computational Linguistics (Volume 1: Long Papers)*, pages 1970–1979, Melbourne, Australia. Association for Computational Linguistics.

Liheng Zhang, Charu Aggarwal, and Guo-Jun Qi. 2017. Stock price prediction via discovering multi-frequency trading patterns. In *Proceedings of the 23rd ACM SIGKDD international conference on knowledge discovery and data mining*, pages 2141–2149.

Yuanhang Zheng, Zhixing Tan, Meng Zhang, Mieradilijiang Maimaiti, Huanbo Luan, Maosong Sun, Qun Liu, and Yang Liu. 2021. Self-supervised quality estimation for machine translation. In *Proceedings of the 2021 Conference on Empirical Methods in Natural Language Processing*, pages 3322–3334.

Zhihan Zhou, Liqian Ma, and Han Liu. 2021. Trade the event: Corporate events detection for news-based event-driven trading. In *Findings of the Association for Computational Linguistics: ACL-IJCNLP 2021*, pages 2114–2124, Online. Association for Computational Linguistics.

A Appendix

A.1 Stock Financial Factors

The stock financial factors in our dataset include Fundamental factors: Dividend yield, Total share, Circulated share, Free circulated share, Market Capitalization, Price-earning ratio(PE), PE for Trailing Twelve Months(TTM), Price/book value ratio, Price-to-sales Ratio, Price to Sales ratio (TTM), Circulate Market Capitalization, Open price, High price,Low price, Close price , Previous close price, Price change, Percentage of change, Volume, Amount, Turn over rate, Turn over rate for circulated Market Capitalization, Volume ratio.

Next-Year Bankruptcy Prediction from Textual Data: Benchmark and Baselines

Henri Arno[1*] and **Klaas Mulier**[1] and **Joke Baeck**[1] and **Thomas Demeester**[2]
[1]Ghent University
[2]Ghent University - imec
first.last@UGent.be

Abstract

Models for bankruptcy prediction are useful in several real-world scenarios, and multiple research contributions have been devoted to the task, based on structured (numerical) as well as unstructured (textual) data. However, the lack of a common benchmark dataset and evaluation strategy impedes the objective comparison between models. This paper introduces such a benchmark for the unstructured data scenario, based on novel and established datasets, in order to stimulate further research into the task. We describe and evaluate several classical and neural baseline models, and discuss benefits and flaws of different strategies. In particular, we find that a lightweight bag-of-words model based on static in-domain word representations obtains surprisingly good results, especially when taking textual data from several years into account. These results are critically assessed, and discussed in light of particular aspects of the data and the task. All code to replicate the data and experimental results will be released.

1 Introduction

Since the seminal work of Beaver (1966), bankruptcy prediction has received considerable attention by both academics and practitioners. A sound prediction model has numerous applications. For instance, successful quantitative methods can help professionals, such as creditors and investors, in managing financial risk (Bielecki and Rutkowski, 2013). Furthermore, as Bernanke (1981) has shown that economy-wide levels of bankruptcy risk play a structural role in propagating recession, regulators can use bankruptcy prediction models to monitor the financial health of key economic actors and control systematic risk.

A large number of bankruptcy prediction models have been proposed in literature, such as the models from Beaver (1966), Ohlson (1980), Odom and Sharda (1990), Kim and Kang (2010) and Mai et al. (2019). However, it appears difficult to compare these studies and objectively assess progress in the field. We have identified the following three aspects that make comparison difficult: (1) the temporal nature and typical class imbalance of the bankruptcy prediction task leads to strongly deviating evaluation scenarios, (2) there is little consensus on the key evaluation metrics, and (3) there is no standard benchmark dataset. These issues are further discussed in section 2.2. In order to overcome these problems, we have designed and described our experimental setup with reproducibility on a common benchmark in mind. To that end, scripts to reconstruct the benchmark and reproduce the presented results are available at `https://github.com/henriarnoUG/BankruptcyBenchmarkBaselines`. Note that this paper investigates the potential to predict bankruptcy from textual disclosures only. Extending this benchmark to the hybrid case of combined textual and structured features will be part of our future work.

The contributions of this paper are as follows: (1) we introduce a reproducible benchmark for text-based bankruptcy prediction, based on novel and established economic datasets, (2) classical as well as neural baseline prediction models are provided, including results on next-year bankruptcy prediction from multiple years of textual data, and (3) insights into the results are given along with pointers to potential next steps in bankruptcy prediction.

2 Related Work

After a general overview of research on bankruptcy prediction (Section 2.1), we describe some key aspects that make contributions in literature hard to compare (Section 2.2).

* Corresponding author

Proceedings of the Fourth Workshop on Financial Technology and Natural Language Processing (FinNLP), pages 187 - 195
December 8, 2022 ©2022 Association for Computational Linguistics

Three years prior to bankruptcy	*"We are highly leveraged and a substantial portion of our liquidity needs arise from debt service requirements and from funding our costs of operations and capital expenditures, including acquisitions... we entered into a new asset-based revolving credit facility (ABL Facility)... secured by substantially all of our assets..."*
One year prior to bankruptcy	*"... we received a waiver of certain events of default under the TLA arising from the inclusion of a going concern qualification from our registered public accounting firm, breach of the EBITDA financial covenant, and cross-default arising from the default under our ABL Facility... In order to address our liquidity issues and provide for a restructuring of our indebtedness to improve our long-term capital structure, we have entered into a Restructuring Support Agreement ... pursuant to a prepackaged plan of reorganization to be filed in a case commenced under chapter 11 of the United States Bankruptcy Code..."*

Table 1: Extracts from the MD&A section of a distressed company in our dataset, one year and three years prior to bankruptcy. Underlined words correspond to the top 20 tokens most informative for imminent bankruptcy in our respective Binary Bag-of-Words models.

2.1 Bankruptcy Prediction Research

Beaver (1966) pioneered bankruptcy prediction literature with a discriminant model based on financial ratios. Subsequently, well-chosen structured financial variables were proposed to predict failure, along with increasingly advanced prediction models. Statistical models, such as discriminant analysis (Beaver, 1966; Altman, 1968), have been dominant in the past but rely on stringent assumptions about the data (Balcaen and Ooghe, 2006). Today, machine learning models are commonplace as they rely on fewer assumptions and learn directly from the data. Odom and Sharda (1990) used neural networks to predict bankruptcy, Kim and Kang (2010) have built an ensemble model and Hosaka (2019) generates predictions through a convolutional neural network with ratios presented as images. Keasey and Watson (1987) were the first to include non-financial variables in a corporate failure model, Shumway (2001) has shown that market-driven variables are strongly related to bankruptcy and Cecchini et al. (2010) found that textual disclosures can be used to discriminate between bankrupt and non-bankrupt firms. The information value of textual data was further established by Mayew et al. (2015) as they found that the opinion of management on the future of the company and the linguistic tone of the Management Discussion and Analysis has significant explanatory power for corporate failure. Mai et al. (2019) provide large-sample evidence of the predictive power of textual disclosures and show that deep learning models yield superior results when using textual data together with traditional accounting features. Furthermore, the authors compare two deep learning architectures based on skip-gram word representations (Mikolov et al., 2013) and conclude that an average embedding model leads to better results than a ConvNet architecture. Despite this promising work, bankruptcy prediction models using textual data are scarce.

2.2 Need for a Reproducible Benchmark

The following aspects prevent a straightforward comparison of research contributions, and may be avoided by a common benchmark along with the tools to reproduce experimental results, one of the goals of this work.

Temporal nature and class imbalance of bankruptcy data: Due to the temporal nature of the data and the typically much smaller fraction of positive cases (enterprises going bankrupt), many strategies have been proposed to construct training data and define evaluation sets. The data source that serves as a basis for the model typically contains annual (or more fine-grained) observations for each firm in the sampling period. In earlier work (Beaver, 1966; Altman, 1968) the explanatory variables were selected only once for each firm in the dataset. In the 'paired sampling' approach (Altman, 1968), the independent variables for failed firms were retained in the year before failure, together with those for a paired healthy firm in that same year, to induce a balanced dataset from which a random evaluation set is sampled. Shumway (2001) has shown that such an approach leads to poor out-of-sample prediction performance and incorrect statistical inference. As an alternative, hazard models can be estimated by treating each firm-year sample as an independent observation, with the bankruptcy status by the end of the following year as the prediction target. Typically, the observations prior to some date are used for model training, and observations after this date are used to estimate the out-of-period prediction performance (Shumway, 2001; Mai et al., 2019). Sometimes even a random split is used, independent of time (Mai et al., 2019). In the work of Volkov et al. (2017), the explanatory variables for a number of consecutive years are used as input, with company status as the prediction target in the year afterwards. The class imbalance is managed through undersampling of healthy companies. Evaluation is done on a held-out subset of companies, which is therefore artificially balanced as well. Undersampling, oversampling, and data augmentation techniques are investigated by Veganzones and Séverin (2018). Training and evaluation are done on a non-overlapping subset of firms, with a one-year shift in between, while also maintaining a predefined artificial ratio between the number of healthy and bankrupt firms (for both training and evaluation).

In our considered population (public companies in the US, see Section 3.1), all companies are known, as well as their yearly reports so far, and the goal is predicting bankruptcy for all of these firms in the near future (the coming year). This is simulated in our evaluation scenario, where we make predictions for *all* companies not (yet) bankrupt and observed through annual reports up to a given year, on their bankruptcy status the year afterwards (as further detailed in section 3.2).

Large variety of evaluation metrics: The choice of evaluation metrics is often linked to the experimental setup, e.g., depending on whether a balanced test set is used. The evaluation scenario also influences the choice of threshold used for metrics like accuracy, precision, or recall. For example, Volkov et al. (2017) select a threshold that maximises the F_2-measure. Alternatively, Veganzones and Séverin (2018) select the threshold that minimises the expected cost of misclassification with equal weights. Aggregated metrics that avoid the use of a threshold, such as area under the ROC curve (AUC), decile rank, and cumulative accuracy profile ratio (CAP) are regularly reported as well (Mai et al., 2019).

Use of private datasets: The final reason that makes model comparison hard is the lack of a standard benchmark dataset. Bankruptcy prediction literature either reports results on proprietary datasets (Matin et al., 2019) or on data obtained by manual collection or custom web scraping strategies (and kept private) (Cecchini et al., 2010; Wang et al., 2020). For a comprehensive overview of data sources used in recent corporate failure literature we refer the reader to the work of Mai et al. (2019). Our datasets are based on the combination of existing sources, i.e., the UCLA-LoPucki Bankruptcy Research Database (BRD)[1] and the public EDGAR-CORPUS (Loukas et al., 2021). This allows researchers to reconstruct the same train, validation and test data from these sources, even if we are not allowed to make the resulting datasets public directly.

3 Methodology

In the next sections, we describe the data sources (Section 3.1) and motivate our design choices for the benchmark (Section 3.2), document preprocessing (Section 3.3), and the selected evaluation metrics (Section 3.4).

3.1 Data Sources

Our study makes use of the EDGAR-CORPUS, a novel economic dataset containing 10-k reports from all publicly traded companies in the US, spanning 25 years (Loukas et al., 2021). As we need information on bankruptcies as prediction target, these reports were matched with the UCLA-LoPucki Bankruptcy Research Database (the BRD)[2], through the unique Central Index Key to identify companies. The BRD contains information on all Chapter 7 and Chapter 11 filings of the United States Bankruptcy Code since 1997 and is updated monthly.

Consistent with prior work (Cecchini et al., 2010; Mayew et al., 2015; Mai et al., 2019), we limit the 10-k reports to section 7: "Management Discussion and Analysis". According to the U.S. Securities and Exchange Commission[3], it *"... gives the company's perspective on the business results of the past financial year. This section, known as the MD&A for short, allows company management to tell its story in its own words."* It also contains the risks and uncertainties that could materially affect the company. As an example, consider the extracts from the MD&A's of a distressed firm in Table 1.

Public company bankruptcy is a rare event. Figure 1 shows that the number of 10-k reports filed by

[1]https://lopucki.law.ucla.edu/

[2]The BRD does require a paid annual subscription or a one-time purchase for academic single use.

[3]https://www.sec.gov/fast-answers/answersreada10khtm.html

non-bankrupt companies heavily exceeds the yearly number of Chapter 7 and Chapter 11 cases. Note how the influence of the Dot-com crisis (2000), the financial crisis (2007-2008), and the COVID crisis (2020) on our population can be observed. Table 2 provides additional statistics for the aligned data sources.

3.2 Task Definition and Setup

3.2.1 Determining the prediction time window

Prior work has not always been very transparent about the temporal aspect of the textual and numerical data in their models, but this requires special attention in order to arrive at a correct setup. A 10-k report is characterised by two dates, as schematically shown in Fig. 2: (1) the fiscal year-end t_{PR} of the one-year time window T_{PR} ('period of report') used to calculate the financial statements, and (2) the filing date t_{FD} on which the report is filed with the SEC. Since in practice $t_{FD} \geq t_{PR}$, there may be a period after t_{PR} yielding textual information in the MD&A (i.e., before t_{FD}), not present in the financial statements. It is therefore important to use the one-year period directly *after* t_{FD} as the prediction time window $T_{prediction}$ when the textual data is used as input to the model. In the extreme case of bankruptcy in between t_{PR} and t_{FD} ('potential bankruptcy' in Fig. 2), it would lead to leakage and artificially high prediction accuracies if the year directly after t_{PR} were used for prediction. It is possible, though, that information on an imminent bankruptcy shortly *after* t_{FD} is already included in the report, but this does not present a conceptual problem for the prediction setup.

3.2.2 Dealing with missing 10-k reports

The dataset contains yearly 10-k reports from the first time a company appears, starting from the year 2000, until 2021 or until bankruptcy. However, some reports are missing for a number of companies, and our analysis reveals the following three scenarios. First, some companies stop reporting from a certain point in time onwards, without filing for bankruptcy. This may be due to a merger or an acquisition, but that particular information is not present in the data. Second, there may be gaps in the sequence of yearly reports. This arises when a company either does not submit a 10-k report (due to unknown reasons) or because of data quality issues. Third, we observe that some companies headed towards bankruptcy tend to fail in their reporting in the year(s) leading up to the bankruptcy

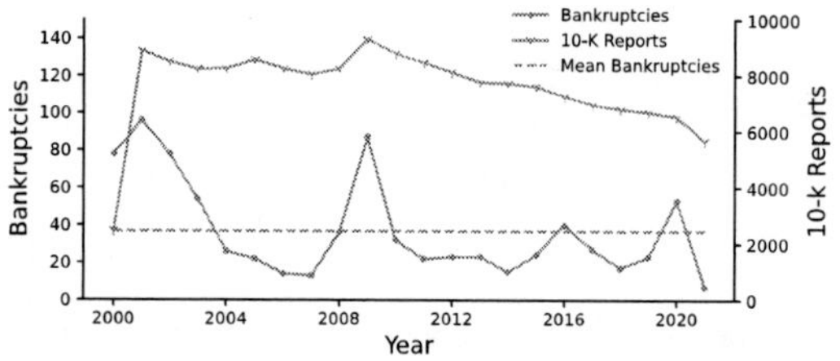

Figure 1: The number of bankruptcies (including the mean) (left y-axis) and the number of 10-k reports filed (right y-axis) per year.

period	2000-2021
avg. reports per year	7599 ± 1477
avg. bankruptcies per year	39 ± 26
avg. new enterprises per year	1467 ± 1376
avg. doc. length (# tokens)	6492 ± 1138

Table 2: Summary statistics of our aligned data sources.

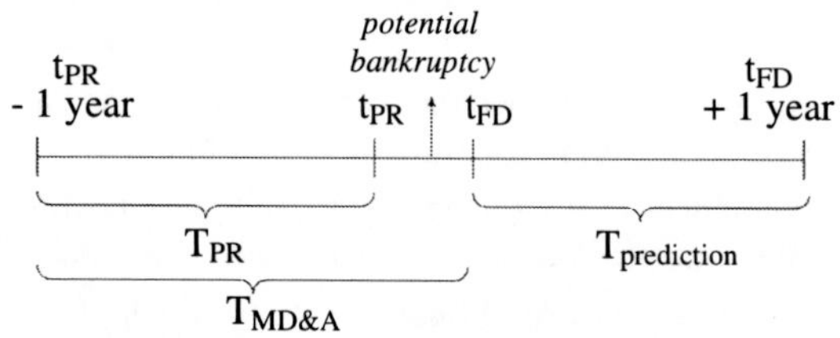

Figure 2: Timeline containing the characterising dates (t_{PR}, t_{FD}) of a 10-k report and corresponding periods (T_{PR}, $T_{MD\&A}$, $T_{prediction}$)

filing. A naive approach would be to simply discard all instances with missing reports. However, this would make the evaluation scenario biased, since missing reports are not distributed uniformly over the data, due to the different scenarios described above.

Consider our 2019 test set with a history of three years (discussed later in this section) as an example, of which close to 45% of companies have at least one missing report during the three-year history. The relative frequency of bankruptcy is 0.27% for the entire population, 0.00% for companies with only missing data (cf. an M&A event), 0.35% for companies with no missing data and 0.93% for companies where the data in only the year before prediction is missing. Therefore, we do not remove these companies and keep them in our dataset which results in a more realistic evaluation scenario.

3.2.3 Construction of input and target per firm-year

In order to create time-agnostic firm-year samples (following Shumway (2001)) during the construction of our train, validation and test sets (see further), we process a given year and company as follows:

1. **Determine $T_{prediction}$:** If a 10-k report was filed by the company in the considered year, $T_{prediction}$ is the period between t_{FD} and t_{FD} + 1 year (cf. Figure 2). Otherwise, we use the one-year period starting the same day as the latest available t_{FD}, but in the considered year.

2. **Assign target label:** If the company filed for bankruptcy during $T_{prediction}$, the label is 1, otherwise 0. Note that potential firm-year instances with a bankruptcy filing *before* t_{FD} are invalid for the considered year, as explained above.

3. **Collect textual data:** The MD&A text from the report filed at t_{FD} is used for the one-year history setting, as well as from the two previous years for the three-year scenario. For missing reports, the token 'missing' is used.

3.2.4 Train / validation / test segmentation

Training data: We construct two training sets in total. The first, using data up to 2015, is used for initial training while leaving sufficient data for validation during hyperparameter tuning. The second, with data up to 2017, is used to train the final models. They are constructed as follows:

1. We leave out all reports with a t_{FD} later than 2015 (2017), to ensure a proper temporal split between training and evaluation data.

2. For every firm and every year between the first year of the training data and 2015 (2017), we construct a firm-year instance as described above.

3. To reduce the impact on the training process of instances without any reports in their considered history (i.e., the one-year or three-year history, respectively), 95% of those are randomly removed.

Validation data: We construct two validation sets, one for 2017 and one for 2018, both to be used for hyperparameter tuning. First, we filter out companies that have not filed any reports during the 5 years leading up to and including 2017 (2018). For each of these companies, one firm-year sample is created according to the method described above for the year (and hence t_{FD}, even when the report is missing) 2017 (2018).

Test data: In the same way, we construct two test sets, one for 2019 and one for 2020 (denoting the calendar year containing t_{FD}), for the final evaluation of the trained models.

3.3 Pre-processing

When dealing with textual data it is common to perform document pre-processing in order to decrease the dimensionality of the problem and reduce the computational cost of encoding the documents. We perform four pre-processing steps for the Bag-of-Words models presented in sections 4.1-4.3. First, we lowercase all documents. Second, we remove stopwords and punctuation. Third, we lemmatize each word in the documents through the NLTK library (Loper and Bird, 2002). Inflicted word forms such as *paying* and *payed* are transformed into the root form *pay*. Finally, we replace uncommon words by the token '_UNK_' (for 'unknown'). A word is deemed uncommon when it does not appear in the 50,000 most frequent words in the training set. When dealing with transformer models (Vaswani et al., 2017), such as the Longformer (Beltagy et al., 2020), these steps are typically not required and might even lead to deteriorating performance. Preprocessing then consists of proper tokenization of the input text. We use the tokenization tools from Huggingface [4], which allow transforming the input text into a sequence of well-chosen word pieces.

3.4 Evaluation Metrics

Following Mai et al. (2019), we report the **Area Under the Receiver Operating Curve** (AUC) as main evaluation metric. The AUC is often used to quantify the overall prediction performance of binary decision models. It aggregates the information in the Receiver Operator Curve (ROC), which quantifies the trade-off between the true positive rate (or recall) and the false positive rate at various classification thresholds. However, in certain scenarios, a high true positive rate may be more relevant than a low false positive rate. Therefore, we

[4]https://huggingface.co/

	Single year history				Three year history			
	Binary	TF-IDF	W2V	Longformer	Binary	TF-IDF	W2V	Longformer
AUC	0.79 (0.84)	0.80 (0.85)	**0.88 (0.90)**	0.78 (0.79)	0.90 (0.92)	0.92 (0.96)	**0.95 (0.95)**	0.85 (0.84)
AP	0.07 (0.05)	**0.16 (0.16)**	0.08 (0.12)	0.01 (0.03)	0.03 (0.06)	**0.10 (0.10)**	0.04 (0.09)	0.02 (0.02)
rec@100	0.19 (0.18)	0.26 (0.31)	**0.37 (0.31)**	0.04 (0.07)	0.15 (0.22)	**0.37 (0.29)**	0.22 (0.24)	0.11 (0.02)
CAP	0.56 (0.68)	0.59 (0.72)	**0.75 (0.80)**	0.52 (0.58)	0.82 (0.84)	0.83 (0.92)	**0.89 (0.89)**	0.71 (0.68)
1	0.56 (0.67)	**0.74 (0.71)**	0.70 (0.73)	0.56 (0.51)	0.78 (0.73)	0.70 (0.91)	**0.85 (0.84)**	0.41 (0.40)
2	0.74 (0.78)	0.74 (0.84)	**0.78 (0.80)**	0.70 (0.71)	0.89 (0.87)	**0.93 (1)**	0.93 (0.93)	0.78 (0.80)
3	0.78 (0.84)	0.78 (0.87)	**0.85 (0.80)**	0.74 (0.76)	0.96 (0.93)	0.96 (1)	**1 (0.98)**	0.93 (0.91)
4	0.78 (0.87)	0.78 (0.87)	**0.96 (0.91)**	0.74 (0.82)	0.96 (1)	0.96 (1)	**1 (1)**	0.93 (0.93)
5	0.78 (0.87)	0.78 (0.87)	**0.96 (0.98)**	0.74 (0.87)	0.96 (1)	0.96 (1)	**1 (1)**	0.93 (0.96)

Table 3: Bankruptcy prediction results on the test sets: 2019 (2020), for several bag-of-words models: with binary one-hot vectors (Binary), TF-IDF, and mean word-to-vec (W2V) representations, as well as a Longformer classifier, and for single-year vs. three-year text inputs. Reported metrics are the area-under-the-ROC-curve (AUC), average precision (AP), recall@100 (rec@100), cumul. accuracy profile ratio (CAP), and cumul. decile rank (1-5).

also report the **Recall@100**. It quantifies the proportion of positive cases (bankrupt firms) present in the 100 highest ranked ones, out of all positive samples (all bankrupt firms in the considered year). In our context, this metric evaluates the models in their effectiveness to detect as many distressed enterprises as possible for a given budget (e.g., the manpower to investigate a hundred firms). The **Cumulative Accuracy Profile Ratio** (CAP) is a ranking based metric with a strong emphasis on recall of the positive class. It summarises the information in the CAP curve, which plots the cumulative proportion of positive samples against the percentage of the ranked data taken into account. The **Cumulative Decile Rank** is also a recall oriented metric. It gives the cumulative proportion of all positive samples (bankrupt firms) in each decile when ranking the samples according to the classifier score. Although we consider recall more important for the bankruptcy case from the perspective of the 'given budget' scenario outlined above, we report a precision oriented metric as well. The **Average Precision** (AP) is the weighted mean of the precision at each classification threshold with the increase in recall as weight.

4 Models

Sections 4.1-4.3 introduce our bag-of-words (BoW) models (which discard word order), followed by a neural sequence encoder model that does account for word order (Section 4.4), and some training details (Section 4.5).

4.1 Binary Bag-of-Words Model

As a trivial baseline (referred to as 'Binary') we represent our documents as vocabulary-sized binary vectors with '1' at a particular position indicating the presence of the corresponding word. As vocabulary, all occurring unigrams and bigrams are initially considered as features, and reduced to the 20 most informative ones through univariate feature selection, to be used in a logistic regression classifier. This baseline intends to quantify how well the occurrence of a small set of keywords allows predicting bankruptcy. The model for three-year history is obtained the same way, from the joint BoW over the considered years.

4.2 TF-IDF Bag-of-Words Model

The second model is similar to the Binary baseline, but considers *term frequency - inverse document frequency* (TF-IDF) features (Manning et al., 2008) rather than binary ones, combined with feature selection and an L2-regularized logistic regression classifier. The number of features to retain and the inverse regularisation strength are treated as hyperparameters. The three-year model is constructed the same way, after concatenating the texts per year.

4.3 Word2Vec Average Embedding Model

As a final bag-of-words model (W2V), we implement the best performing architecture proposed by Mai et al. (2019), based on the Word2Vec model of Mikolov et al. (2013). First, the pre-processed data is used to train skip-gram word representations of dimension 100 (consistent with Mai et al. (2019)). Documents are then represented by the mean word vector over all occurring words. These serve as input to a two-layer feed-forward neural network with ReLU activations (Glorot et al., 2011) and standard dropout (Srivastava et al., 2014), followed by a sigmoid output. During training, we minimize the binary cross entropy loss with an L2-penalty, using the Adam optimizer (Kingma and Ba, 2014). The learning rate, weight decay (L2-penalty), hidden layer width, and dropout rate are treated as hyperparameters. When performing classification based on a history of three years, the document representations of each year are concatenated, resulting in a 300-dimensional input to the first hidden layer of the neural network.

4.4 Longformer

For our most advanced neural model, we encode the documents through the Longformer of Beltagy et al. (2020). This transformer-based model is able to handle sequences up to 4096 tokens through its attention mechanism that scales linearly with the input text length (as opposed to the quadratic behavior in earlier Transformer models such as BERT (Devlin et al., 2018). Given the mean document length of over 6k words in our corpus (cf. Table 2), we considered the Longformer a plausible baseline. We process the first 4096 tokens of each document with the Longformer model and retain the 768-dimensional pooled output as the document representation that feeds the same feed-forward classification neural network as described above. For dealing with a history of three years, the individual representations per year are again concatenated, and the input size of the first hidden layer is adjusted accordingly. During training, these representations are kept static (i.e., the Longformer weights are not further fine-tuned on our classification task).

4.5 Training Details

The classical models (Sections 4.1 and 4.2) are implemented in scikit-learn[5] and the hyperparameters are optimised through a grid search procedure. As constructing the vocabulary of all tokens in the training data is expensive, we choose to undersample the majority class until a 90%-10% distribution was reached. The neural models (Sections 4.3 and 4.4) are implemented in PyTorch[5] while the Word2Vec model was trained with Gensim[5] and the forward pass through the Longformer was performed with Huggingface[4]. Since hyperparameter optimisation for deep learning models is expensive, we made use of the Tree-Structured Parzen Estimation algorithm to find the optimal hyperparameter settings (Bergstra et al., 2011) implemented in Optuna[5]. The hyperparameters are tuned to maximise the weighted AUC of the 2017 and 2018 validation data, and the obtained values are then used to train the final models using training data up to 2017, to be tested on the 2019 and 2020 test sets.[6]

Top 15 selected unigrams and bigrams
waiver (0.26), _UNK_ million (0.21), restructuring (0.21), severance (0.20), subordinated (0.20), financial covenant (0.15), indenture (0.14), lender (0.14), interest payment (0.14), senior secured (0.14), asset sale (0.12), senior (0.09), cross default (0.09), indebtedness (0.07), event default (0.05), credit facility (0.05)

Table 4: Top 15 tokens with largest logistic regression coefficients (shown in parentheses) of the Binary bag-of-words model with single year history.

5 Results and Discussion

Table 3 presents the out-of-period test performance metrics for our text-based bankruptcy prediction models, taking a single year or three years of history into account.

When taking a single year of history into account, the W2V model is superior in terms of AUC, recall@100 and CAP while the TF-IDF model achieves the best results in terms of AP. For the 2019 test set, the TF-IDF model contains a slightly higher proportion of positive samples in the first decile but the W2V model is superior from the second decile onwards. When taking three years of history into account, the W2V model achieves the best results for the AUC and CAP metrics while the TF-IDF model performs better with respect to AP and recall@100. When looking at decile rank, the W2V models performs best, having ranked all bankrupt companies in the top 30% of the samples for the 2019 test set.

For each model, AUC and CAP are better when taking three years of history into account compared to a single year of history. The same applies for the decile rank (except for the TF-IDF model and the Longformer model in the first decile). AP is generally worse when using a longer history, except for the Binary model with test set 2020 and the Longformer model with test set 2019. The recall@100 metric varies over the two setups.

We observe that the Binary models based on a mere 20 keywords perform surprisingly well, although not on par with the TF-IDF and W2V models. Note that the latter are based on many more

[5]Scikit-learn: https://scikit-learn.org/stable/
PyTorch: https://pytorch.org/
Optuna: https://optuna.org/
Gensim= https://radimrehurek.com/gensim/

[6]The considered hyperparameter ranges can be accessed through the GitHub repository.

features (in particular, hyperparameter tuning led for the TF-IDF model to 25.000 (10.000) features for single (three) year history). The relatively good performance of the Binary baseline suggests that the presence of few very informative words is a strong indicator for impending bankruptcy. As an illustration, we list the top 15 unigrams and bigrams selected by the single year Binary model in table 4 and underline these features in the extracts in table 1.

Furthermore, the Longformer model performs significantly worse than the other models. Since we do not finetune the generic pre-trained Longformer model on the our end task, the resulting generic document representations appear unable to capture those features in the text that are important for bankruptcy prediction.

The W2V model leads overall to the best results, in particular for AUC (on which model selection was performed over the validation set) and CAP, and better than the Longformer over the entire line. Even though it is based on the mean representation over all words, it appears the relevant information regarding bankruptcy prediction is still sufficiently present. As opposed to the Longformer, the W2V document representations come from in-domain data (i.e., pretrained on 10-k reports).

Finally, we critically evaluate the observed performance improvements for the three-year w.r.t. single-year history setting. The Binary and TF-IDF models are by construction unable to distinguish the different years, but in principle the W2V and Longformer models could learn to capture a deteriorating financial situation over three years of history. However, when evaluating our final W2V models on the test sets with only complete observations (i.e., discard test instances with missing reports), we get the following results. The single year of history AUC is 0.93 (0.94) and the recall@100 is 0.48 (0.36) while the three year history AUC is 0.93 (0.93) and recall@100 was 0.24 (0.28). These results imply that our models taking three years of history into account only lead to better performance metrics as they are able to generate meaningful predictions for companies with some missing reports. Building more expressive models that can leverage the changes in the documents over the years present an interesting avenue for future research.

6 Conclusion and Future Work

Bankruptcy prediction models are valuable in many real-world applications and have received considerable research attention. However, assessing actual progress in the field is not obvious due to the lack of a common benchmark. In this work, we introduce such a benchmark for bankruptcy prediction using textual data along with several baseline models that demonstrate the predictive value of the textual data. We give a detailed discussion on our benchmark and evaluation design choices and share our code to reproduce the experiments.

In future work, we will focus on more advanced models to take into account the temporal evolution of enterprises' financial situation and more advanced language representations (i.e., by finetuning transformer encoders). We also plan to extend the benchmark with structured financial data to build hybrid prediction models.

Acknowledgements

This work was supported by the Research Foundation - Flanders (Grant number G006421N).

References

Edward I Altman. 1968. Financial ratios, discriminant analysis and the prediction of corporate bankruptcy. *The journal of finance*, 23(4):589–609.

Sofie Balcaen and Hubert Ooghe. 2006. 35 years of studies on business failure: an overview of the classic statistical methodologies and their related problems. *The British Accounting Review*, 38(1):63–93.

William H Beaver. 1966. Financial ratios as predictors of failure. *Journal of accounting research*, pages 71–111.

Iz Beltagy, Matthew E. Peters, and Arman Cohan. 2020. Longformer: The long-document transformer.

James Bergstra, Rémi Bardenet, Yoshua Bengio, and Balázs Kégl. 2011. Algorithms for hyper-parameter optimization. *Advances in neural information processing systems*, 24.

Ben S Bernanke. 1981. Bankruptcy, liquidity, and recession. *The American Economic Review*, 71(2):155–159.

Tomasz R Bielecki and Marek Rutkowski. 2013. *Credit risk: modeling, valuation and hedging*. Springer Science & Business Media.

Mark Cecchini, Haldun Aytug, Gary J Koehler, and Praveen Pathak. 2010. Making words work: Using financial text as a predictor of financial events. *Decision Support Systems*, 50(1):164–175.

Jacob Devlin, Ming-Wei Chang, Kenton Lee, and Kristina Toutanova. 2018. Bert: Pre-training of deep bidirectional transformers for language understanding. *arXiv preprint arXiv:1810.04805*.

Xavier Glorot, Antoine Bordes, and Yoshua Bengio. 2011. Deep sparse rectifier neural networks. In *Proceedings of the fourteenth international conference on artificial intelligence and statistics*, pages 315–323. JMLR Workshop and Conference Proceedings.

Tadaaki Hosaka. 2019. Bankruptcy prediction using imaged financial ratios and convolutional neural networks. *Expert Systems with Applications*, 117:287–299.

Kevin Keasey and Robert Watson. 1987. Non-financial symptoms and the prediction of small company failure: A test of argenti's hypotheses. *Journal of Business Finance & Accounting*, 14(3):335–354.

Myoung-Jong Kim and Dae-Ki Kang. 2010. Ensemble with neural networks for bankruptcy prediction. *Expert Systems with Applications*, 37(4):3373–3379.

Diederik P Kingma and Jimmy Ba. 2014. Adam: A method for stochastic optimization. *arXiv preprint arXiv:1412.6980*.

Edward Loper and Steven Bird. 2002. Nltk: The natural language toolkit. *arXiv preprint cs/0205028*.

Lefteris Loukas, Manos Fergadiotis, Ion Androutsopoulos, and Prodromos Malakasiotis. 2021. Edgar-corpus: Billions of tokens make the world go round.

Feng Mai, Shaonan Tian, Chihoon Lee, and Ling Ma. 2019. Deep learning models for bankruptcy prediction using textual disclosures. *European journal of operational research*, 274(2):743–758.

Christopher D. Manning, Prabhakar Raghavan, and Hinrich Schütze. 2008. *Introduction to Information Retrieval*. Cambridge University Press, USA.

Rastin Matin, Casper Hansen, Christian Hansen, and Pia Mølgaard. 2019. Predicting distresses using deep learning of text segments in annual reports. *Expert Systems with Applications*, 132:199–208.

William J Mayew, Mani Sethuraman, and Mohan Venkatachalam. 2015. Md&a disclosure and the firm's ability to continue as a going concern. *The Accounting Review*, 90(4):1621–1651.

Tomas Mikolov, Kai Chen, Greg Corrado, and Jeffrey Dean. 2013. Efficient estimation of word representations in vector space.

Marcus D Odom and Ramesh Sharda. 1990. A neural network model for bankruptcy prediction. In *1990 IJCNN International Joint Conference on neural networks*, pages 163–168. IEEE.

James A Ohlson. 1980. Financial ratios and the probabilistic prediction of bankruptcy. *Journal of accounting research*, pages 109–131.

Tyler Shumway. 2001. Forecasting bankruptcy more accurately: A simple hazard model. *The journal of business*, 74(1):101–124.

Nitish Srivastava, Geoffrey Hinton, Alex Krizhevsky, Ilya Sutskever, and Ruslan Salakhutdinov. 2014. Dropout: a simple way to prevent neural networks from overfitting. *The journal of machine learning research*, 15(1):1929–1958.

Ashish Vaswani, Noam Shazeer, Niki Parmar, Jakob Uszkoreit, Llion Jones, Aidan N Gomez, Łukasz Kaiser, and Illia Polosukhin. 2017. Attention is all you need. *Advances in neural information processing systems*, 30.

David Veganzones and Eric Séverin. 2018. An investigation of bankruptcy prediction in imbalanced datasets. *Decision Support Systems*, 112:111–124.

Andrey Volkov, Dries F Benoit, and Dirk Van den Poel. 2017. Incorporating sequential information in bankruptcy prediction with predictors based on markov for discrimination. *Decision Support Systems*, 98:59–68.

Gang Wang, Jingling Ma, Gang Chen, and Ying Yang. 2020. Financial distress prediction: Regularized sparse-based random subspace with er aggregation rule incorporating textual disclosures. *Applied Soft Computing*, 90:106152.

AdaK-NER: An Adaptive Top-K Approach for Named Entity Recognition with Incomplete Annotations

Hongtao Ruan[1] , **Liying Zheng**[2] and **Peixian Hu**[3]
[1]Ant Group
[2]Ebay Inc.
[3]Huaneng Guicheng Trust Corp.,Ltd.
ruanhongtao.rht@antgroup.com

Abstract

State-of-the-art Named Entity Recognition (NER) models rely heavily on large amounts of fully annotated training data. However, accessible data are often incompletely annotated since the annotators usually lack comprehensive knowledge in the target domain. Normally the unannotated tokens are regarded as non-entities by default, while we underline that these tokens could either be non-entities or part of any entity. Here, we study NER modeling with incomplete annotated data where only a fraction of the named entities are labeled, and the unlabeled tokens are equivalently multi-labeled by every possible label. Taking multi-labeled tokens into account, the numerous possible paths can distract the training model from the gold path (ground truth label sequence), and thus hinders the learning ability. In this paper, we propose AdaK-NER, named the adaptive top-K approach, to help the model focus on a smaller feasible region where the gold path is more likely to be located. We demonstrate the superiority of our approach through extensive experiments on both English and Chinese datasets, averagely improving 2% in F-score on the CoNLL-2003 and over 10% on two Chinese datasets compared with the prior state-of-the-art works.

1 Introduction

Named Entity Recognition (NER) [Li *et al.*, 2020; Sang and De Meulder, 2003; Peng *et al.*, 2019] is a fundamental task in Natural Language Processing (NLP). NER task aims at recognizing the meaningful entities occurring in the text, which can benefit various downstream tasks, such as question answering [Cao *et al.*, 2019], event extraction [Wei *et al.*, 2020], and opinion mining [Poria *et al.*, 2016].

Strides in statistical models, such as Conditional Random Field (CRF) [Lafferty *et al.*, 2001] and pre-trained language models like BERT [Devlin *et al.*, 2018], have equipped NER with new learning principles [Li *et al.*, 2020]. Pre-trained model with rich representation ability can discover hidden features automatically while CRF can capture the dependencies between labels with the BIO or BIOES tagging scheme.

However, most existing methods rely on large amounts of fully annotated information for training NER models [Li *et al.*, 2020; Jia *et al.*, 2020]. Fulfilling such requirements is expensive and laborious in the industry. Annotators, are not likely to be fully equipped with comprehensive domain knowledge, only annotate the named entities they recognize and let the others off, resulting in incomplete annotations. They typically do not specify the non-entity [Surdeanu *et al.*, 2010], so that the recognized entities are the only available annotations. Figure 1(a) shows examples of both gold path[1] and incomplete path.

For corpus with incomplete annotations, each unannotated token can either be part of an entity or non-entity, making the token equivalently multi-labeled by every possible label. Since conventional CRF algorithms require fully annotated sentences, a strand of literature suggests assigning weights to possible labels [Shang *et al.*, 2018; Jie *et al.*, 2019]. Fuzzy CRF [Shang *et al.*, 2018] focused on filling the unannotated tokens by assigning equal probability to every possible path. Further, Jie [2019] introduced a weighted CRF method to seek a more reasonable distribution q for all possible paths, attempting to pay more attention to those paths with high potential to be gold path.

Ideally, through comprehensive learning on q distribution, the gold path can be correctly discovered. However, this perfect situation is difficult to achieve in practical applications. Intuitively, taking all possible paths into consideration will distract the model from the gold path, as the feasible region (the set of possible paths where we search for the gold path) grows exponentially with the length of the unannotated tokens increasing, which might cause failure to identify the gold path.

To address this issue, one promising direction is to prune the size of feasible region during training. We assume the unknown gold path is among or very close to the top-K paths with the highest possibilities. Specifically, we utilize a novel adaptive K-best loss to help the training model focus on a smaller feasible region where the gold path is likely to be located. Furthermore, once a path is identified as a disqualified sequence, it will be removed from the feasible region. This operation can thus drastically eliminate redundancy without undermining the effectiveness. For this purpose, a candidate

[1]A path is a label sequence for a given sentence.

Proceedings of the Fourth Workshop on Financial Technology and Natural Language Processing (FinNLP), pages 196 - 202
December 8, 2022 ©2022 Association for Computational Linguistics

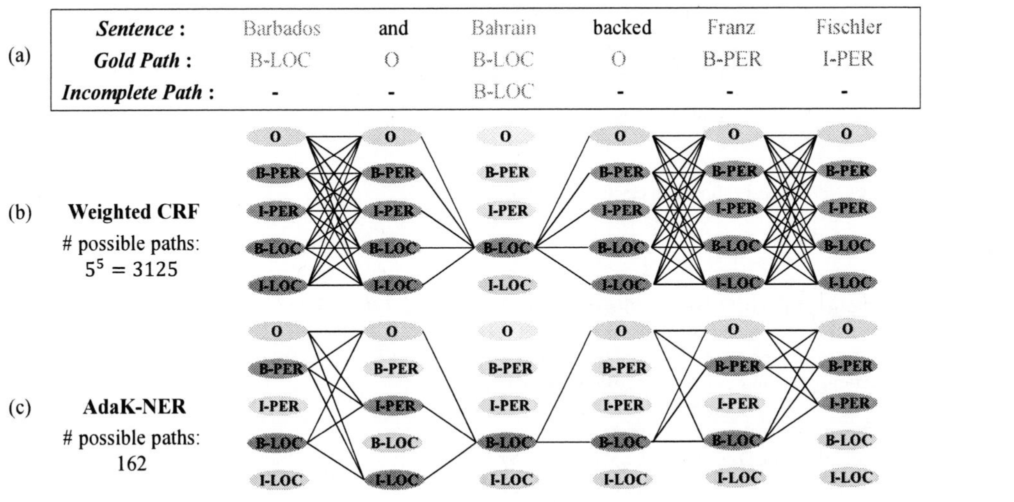

Figure 1: (a) The sentence is annotated with BIO tagging scheme. The entity types are person (PER) and location (LOC). Only the entity 'Bahrain' of LOC is recognized, while 'Barbados' of LOC and 'Franz Fischler' of PER are missing. (b) Weighted CRF model considers all the 3125 possible paths with 5 unannotated tokens for q estimation. (c) In our model, we build a candidate mask to filter out the less likely labels (labels in faded color). Therefore, the possible paths of our model is significantly less than weighted CRF.

mask is built to filter out the less likely paths, so as to restrict the size of the feasible region.

Trained in this way, our AdaK-NER overcomes the shortcomings of Fuzzy CRF and weighted CRF, resulting in a significant improvement on both precision and recall, and a higher F_1 score as well.

In summary, the contributions of this work are:

- We present a K-best mechanism for improving incomplete annotated NER, aiming to focus on the gold path effectively from the most possible candidates.
- We demonstrate both qualitatively and quantitatively that our approach achieves state-of-the-art performance compared to various baselines on both English and Chinese datasets.

2 Proposed Approach

Let $\boldsymbol{x} = (\boldsymbol{x}_1, \boldsymbol{x}_2, \cdots, \boldsymbol{x}_n)$ be a training sentence of length n, token $\boldsymbol{x}_i \in \boldsymbol{X}$. Correspondingly, $\boldsymbol{y} = (\boldsymbol{y}_1, \boldsymbol{y}_2, \cdots, \boldsymbol{y}_n)$ denotes the complete label sequence, $\boldsymbol{y}_i \in \boldsymbol{Y}$. The NER problem can be defined as inferring $\boldsymbol{y}$ based on $\boldsymbol{x}$.

Under the incomplete annotation framework, we introduce the following terminologies. A possible path refers to a possible complete label sequence consistent with the annotated tokens. For example, a possible incomplete annotated label sequence for $\boldsymbol{x}$ can be $\boldsymbol{y}_u = (-, \boldsymbol{y}_2, -, \cdots, -)$, where token $\boldsymbol{x}_2$ is annotated as $\boldsymbol{y}_2$ and other missing labels are labeled as $-$. $\boldsymbol{y}_c = (\boldsymbol{y}_{c_1}, \boldsymbol{y}_2, \cdots, \boldsymbol{y}_{c_n})$ with $\boldsymbol{y}_{c_i} \in \boldsymbol{Y}$, is a possible path for $\boldsymbol{x}$, where all the missing labels $-$ are replaced by some elements in $\boldsymbol{Y}$. Set $C(\boldsymbol{y}_u)$ denotes all possible complete paths for $\boldsymbol{x}$ with incomplete annotation $\boldsymbol{y}_u$. $D = \{(\boldsymbol{x}^i, \boldsymbol{y}_u^i)\}$ is the available incompletely annotated dataset.

For NER task, CRF [Lafferty *et al.*, 2001] is a traditional approach to capture the dependencies between the labels by modeling the conditional probability $p_{\boldsymbol{w}}(\boldsymbol{y}|\boldsymbol{x})$ of a label sequence $\boldsymbol{y}$ given an input sequence $\boldsymbol{x}$ of length n as:

$$p_{\boldsymbol{w}}(\boldsymbol{y}|\boldsymbol{x}) = \frac{\exp(\boldsymbol{w} \cdot \Phi(\boldsymbol{x}, \boldsymbol{y}))}{\sum_{\boldsymbol{y} \in \boldsymbol{Y}^n} \exp(\boldsymbol{w} \cdot \Phi(\boldsymbol{x}, \boldsymbol{y}))}. \tag{1}$$

$\Phi(\boldsymbol{x}, \boldsymbol{y})$ denotes the map from a pair of $\boldsymbol{x}$ and $\boldsymbol{y}$ to an arbitrary feature vector, $\boldsymbol{w}$ is the model parameter, $p_{\boldsymbol{w}}(\boldsymbol{y}|\boldsymbol{x})$ is the probability of $\boldsymbol{y}$ predicted by the model. Once $\boldsymbol{w}$ has been estimated via minimizing negative log-likelihood:

$$L(\boldsymbol{w}, \boldsymbol{x}) = -\log p_{\boldsymbol{w}}(\boldsymbol{y}|\boldsymbol{x}), \tag{2}$$

the label sequence can be inferred by:

$$\hat{\boldsymbol{y}} = \arg\max_{\boldsymbol{y} \in \boldsymbol{Y}^n} p_{\boldsymbol{w}}(\boldsymbol{y}|\boldsymbol{x}). \tag{3}$$

The original CRF learning algorithm requires a fully annotated sequence $\boldsymbol{y}$, thus the incompletely annotated data is not directly applicable to it. Jie [2019] modified the loss function as follows:

$$L(\boldsymbol{w}, \boldsymbol{x}) = -\log \sum_{\boldsymbol{y} \in C(\boldsymbol{y}_u)} q(\boldsymbol{y}|\boldsymbol{x}) p_{\boldsymbol{w}}(\boldsymbol{y}|\boldsymbol{x}), \tag{4}$$

where $q(\boldsymbol{y}|\boldsymbol{x})$ is an estimated distribution of all possible complete paths $\boldsymbol{y} \in C(\boldsymbol{y}_u)$ for $\boldsymbol{x}$.

We illustrate their model in (Figure 1b). Note that when q is a uniform distribution, the above CRF model is Fuzzy CRF [Shang *et al.*, 2018] which puts equal probability to all possible paths in $C(\boldsymbol{y}_u)$. Jie [2019] claimed that q should be highly skewed rather than uniformly distributed, therefore they presented a k-fold cross-validation stacking method to approximate distribution q.

Nonetheless, as Figure 1(b) shows, a sentence with only 6 words (1 annotated, 5 unannotated) have 3125 possible paths.

We argued that identifying the gold path from all possible paths is like looking for a needle in a haystack. This motivates us to reduce redundant paths during training. We propose two major strategies (adaptive K-best loss and candidate mask) to induce the model to focus on the gold path (Figure 1(c)), and two minor strategies (annealing technique and iterative sample selection) to further improve the model effectiveness in NER task. The workflow is summarized in Algorithm 1.

2.1 Adaptive K-best Loss

Viterbi decoding algorithm is a dynamic programming technique to find the most possible path with only linear complexity, thus it could be used to predict a path for an input based on the parameters provided by the NER model. K-best Viterbi decoding [Huang and Chiang, 2005] extends the original Viterbi decoding algorithm to extract the top-K paths with the highest probabilities. In the incomplete data, the gold path is unknown. We hypothesize it is very likely to be the same with or close to one of the top-K paths. This inspires us to introduce an auxiliary K-best loss component to help the model focus on a smaller yet promising region. Weight is added to balance the weighted CRF loss and the auxiliary loss, and thus we modify (4) into:

$$\begin{aligned} L_k(\boldsymbol{w}, \boldsymbol{x}) = &- (1-\lambda) \log \sum_{\boldsymbol{y} \in C(\boldsymbol{y}_u)} q(\boldsymbol{y}|\boldsymbol{x}) p_w(\boldsymbol{y}|\boldsymbol{x}) \\ &- \lambda \log \sum_{\boldsymbol{y} \in K_{\boldsymbol{w}}(\boldsymbol{x})} p_w(\boldsymbol{y}|\boldsymbol{x}), \end{aligned} \tag{5}$$

where $K_{\boldsymbol{w}}(\boldsymbol{x})$ represents the top-K paths decoded by constrained K-best Viterbi algorithm[2] with parameters $\boldsymbol{w}$, and λ is an adaptive weight coefficient.

2.2 Estimating q with Candidate Mask

We divide the training data into k folds and employ k-fold cross-validation stacking to estimate q for each hold-out fold [Jie *et al.*, 2019]. We propose an interpolation mode to adjust q by increasing the probabilities for paths with high confidence and decreasing for the others. The probability of each possible path is a temperature softmax of $\log p_{\boldsymbol{w}_i}$:

$$q_{\boldsymbol{w}_i}(\boldsymbol{y}|\boldsymbol{x}) = \frac{\exp\left(\log p_{\boldsymbol{w}_i}(\boldsymbol{y}|\boldsymbol{x})/T\right)}{\sum_{\boldsymbol{y}} \exp\left(\log p_{\boldsymbol{w}_i}(\boldsymbol{y}|\boldsymbol{x})/T\right)}, \tag{6}$$

where $T > 0$ denotes the temperature and $\boldsymbol{w}_i$ is the model trained by holding out the i-th fold. A higher temperature produces a softer probability distribution over the paths, resulting in more diversity and also more mistakes [Hinton *et al.*, 2015]. We iterate the cross-validation until q converges.

Jie [2019] estimated $q(\boldsymbol{y}|\boldsymbol{x})$ for each $\boldsymbol{y} \in C(\boldsymbol{y}_u)$ while the size of $C(\boldsymbol{y}_u)$ grows exponentially on the number of unannotated tokens in $\boldsymbol{x}$. To reduce the number of possible paths for q estimation, we build candidate mask based on the K-best candidates and the self-built candidates.

[2]The constrained decoding ensures the resulting complete paths are compatible with the incomplete annotations.

Algorithm 1 AdaK-NER

Data: $D = \{(\boldsymbol{x}^i, \boldsymbol{y}_u^i)\}$
Randomly divide D into k folds: $D_1, D_2, \cdots, D_k$
Entity Dictionary $\mathcal{H} \leftarrow \emptyset$
Initialize model M with parameters $\hat{\boldsymbol{w}}$
Initialize q distributions $\{q(\cdot|\boldsymbol{x}^i)\}$
Sample importance score $s_i \leftarrow 1$
hyper-parameters s and c
for *iteration* = $1, \cdots, N$ **do**
  % Sample Selection
  $D' \leftarrow D$
  for $j = 1, \cdots, k$ **do**
    $D'_j \leftarrow D_j$
    for $(\boldsymbol{x}^i, \boldsymbol{y}_u^i) \in D'_j$ **do**
      if $s_i < s$ **then**
        remove $(\boldsymbol{x}^i, \boldsymbol{y}_u^i)$ from D'_j and D'
      end
    end
  end
  % q Distribution Estimating
  for $j = 1, \cdots, k$ **do**
    Train $M(\boldsymbol{w}_j)$ on $D' \backslash D'_j$: Eq.(7)
    for $(\boldsymbol{x}^i, \boldsymbol{y}_u^i) \in D'_j$ **do**
      Predict $K_b(\boldsymbol{x}^i)$ by $M(\hat{\boldsymbol{w}})$
      Extract $H(\boldsymbol{x}^i)$ by $\mathcal{H}$
      Possible paths $S = S(\boldsymbol{y}_u^i, K_b(\boldsymbol{x}^i), H(\boldsymbol{x}^i))$
      Estimate $q(\boldsymbol{y}|\boldsymbol{x}^i)$ for $\boldsymbol{y} \in S$: Eq.(6)
      $s_i = \max_{\boldsymbol{y}} p_{\boldsymbol{w}_j}(\boldsymbol{y}|\boldsymbol{x}^i)$
      $e_i \leftarrow \{entities\}$ predicted by $M(\boldsymbol{w}_j)$
    end
  end
  % Dictionary $\mathcal{H}$ Updating
  $\mathcal{H} \leftarrow \emptyset$
  for $entity \in \cup e_i$ **do**
    if $entity \notin \mathcal{H}$ *and* $freq(entity) > c$ **then**
      $\mathcal{H} \leftarrow add\_entity(\mathcal{H}, entity)$
    end
  end
  Train $M(\boldsymbol{w}')$ on D with q: Eq.(7)
  if F_1 *of* $M(\boldsymbol{w}') > F_1$ *of* $M(\hat{\boldsymbol{w}})$ *on Dev* **then**
    $\hat{\boldsymbol{w}} \leftarrow \boldsymbol{w}'$
  end
end
Return the final NER model $M(\hat{\boldsymbol{w}})$

K-best Candidates. During the end of each iteration, we train a model $M(\hat{\boldsymbol{w}})$ on the whole training data D. In the next iteration, we use the trained model $M(\hat{\boldsymbol{w}})$ to identify K-best candidates set $K_b(\boldsymbol{x})$ for each sample $\boldsymbol{x}$ by constrained K-best Viterbi decoding. $K_b(\boldsymbol{x}) = \{\hat{K}_i(\boldsymbol{x})\}_{i=1,\cdots,K}$ contains top-K possible paths with the highest probabilities, where $\hat{K}_i(\boldsymbol{x}) = [\hat{K}_i(\boldsymbol{x}_1), \hat{K}_i(\boldsymbol{x}_2), \cdots, \hat{K}_i(\boldsymbol{x}_n)]$.

Self-built Candidates. In the current iteration, after training a model $M(\boldsymbol{w}_i)$ on $(k-1)$ folds, we use $M(\boldsymbol{w}_i)$ to predict a path for each sample in the hold-out fold, and extract entities from the predicted path. Then we merge all

Dataset	Train		Dev		Test	
	#entity	#sent	#entity	#sent	#entity	#sent
CoNLL-2003	23499	14041	5942	3250	5648	3453
Taobao	29397	6000	4941	998	4866	1000
Youku	12754	8001	1580	1000	1570	1001

Table 1: Data statistics for CoNLL-2003, Taobao and Youku. '#entity' represents the number of entities, and '#sent' is the number of sentences.

entities identified by k models $\{M(\boldsymbol{w}_i)\}_{i=1,\cdots,k}$, resulting an entity dictionary $\mathcal{H}$. For each sample $\boldsymbol{x}$ we conjecture that its named entities should lie in the dictionary $\mathcal{H}$. Consequently, in the next iteration we form a self-built candidate $H(\boldsymbol{x}) = [H(\boldsymbol{x}_1), H(\boldsymbol{x}_2), \cdots, H(\boldsymbol{x}_n)]$ for each $\boldsymbol{x}$ of length n. $H(\boldsymbol{x}_j)$ is the corresponding entity label if the token $\boldsymbol{x}_j$ is part of an entity in $\mathcal{H}$, otherwise $H(\boldsymbol{x}_j)$ is O label.

We utilize the above candidates (*i.e.*, the K-best candidates set $K_b(\boldsymbol{x})$ and the self-built candidate $H(\boldsymbol{x})$) to construct a candidate mask for $\boldsymbol{x}$. For each unannotated $\boldsymbol{x}_j$ in $\boldsymbol{x}$, the possible label set consists of (1) O label (2) $H(\boldsymbol{x}_j)$, (3) $\cup_{i=1}^{K} \hat{K}_i(\boldsymbol{x}_j)$.

For example, as Figure 1(c) shows, the unannotated token 'Barbados' is predicted as B-PER and B-LOC in the above candidate paths, we treat B-PER, B-LOC and O label as the possible labels of 'Barbados' and mask the other labels.

With this masking scheme, we can significantly narrow down the feasible region of $\boldsymbol{x}$ (Figure 1(c)) when estimating $q(\cdot|\boldsymbol{x})$. After estimating $q(\cdot|\boldsymbol{x})$, we can train a model through the modified loss:

$$L_m(\boldsymbol{w}, \boldsymbol{x}) = -(1-\lambda)\log \sum_{\boldsymbol{y}\in S} q(\boldsymbol{y}|\boldsymbol{x}) p_{\boldsymbol{w}}(\boldsymbol{y}|\boldsymbol{x}) - \lambda \log \sum_{\boldsymbol{y}\in K_{\boldsymbol{w}}(\boldsymbol{x})} p_{\boldsymbol{w}}(\boldsymbol{y}|\boldsymbol{x}), \quad (7)$$

where $S = S(\boldsymbol{y}_u, K_b(\boldsymbol{x}), H(\boldsymbol{x}))$ contains the possible paths restricted by the candidate mask.

2.3 Annealing Technique for λ

Intuitively, the top-K paths decoded by the algorithm could be of poor quality at the beginning of training, because the model's parameters used in decoding haven't been trained adequately. Therefore, we employ an annealing technique to adapt λ during training as:

$$\lambda(b) = \exp\left[\gamma\left(\frac{b}{B} - 1\right)\right],$$

where b is the current training step, B is the total number of training steps, and γ is the hyper-parameter used to control the accelerated speed of λ. The coefficient λ increases rapidly at the latter half of the training, enforcing the model to extracting more information from the top-K paths.

2.4 Iterative Sample Selection

Due to the incomplete annotation, there exist some samples whose q distributions are poorly estimated. We use an idea of sample selection to deal with these samples. In each iteration, after training a model $M(\boldsymbol{w}_i)$ on $(k-1)$ folds, we utilize $M(\boldsymbol{w}_i)$ to decode a most possible path $\hat{\boldsymbol{y}}$ for $\boldsymbol{x} \in D_i$, and assign a probability score $s = p_{\boldsymbol{w}_i}(\hat{\boldsymbol{y}}|\boldsymbol{x})$ to $\boldsymbol{x}$ at the meantime. Iterative sample selection is to select the samples with probability scores beyond a threshold to construct new training data, which are used in the training phase of k-fold cross-validation in the next iteration (more Algorithm details can be found in Algorithm 1). We use this strategy to help model identify the gold path effectively with high-quality samples.

3 Experiments

3.1 Dataset

To benchmark AdaK-NER against its SOTA alternatives in realistic settings, we consider one standard English dataset and two Chinese datasets from Financial Technology Industry: (*i*) *CoNLL-2003 English* [Sang and De Meulder, 2003]: annotated by person (PER), location (LOC) and organization (ORG) and miscellaneous (MISC). (*ii*) *Taobao*[3]: a Chinese e-commerce site. The model type (PATTERN), product type (PRODUCT), brand type (BRAND) and the other entities (MISC) are recognized in the dataset. (*iii*) *Youku*[4]: a Chinese video-streaming website with videos from various domains. Figure type (FIGURE), program type (PROGRAM) and the others (MISC) are annotated. Statistics for datasets are presented in Table 1.

We randomly remove a proportion of entities and all O labels to construct the incomplete annotation, with ρ representing the ratio of entities that keep annotated. We employ two schemes for removing entities:

- **Random-based Scheme** is simply removing entities by random [Jie *et al.*, 2019; Li *et al.*, 2021], which simulates the situation that a given entity is not recognized by an annotator.
- **Entity-based Scheme** is removing all occurrences of a randomly selected entity until the desired amount remains [Mayhew *et al.*, 2019; Effland and Collins, 2021; Wang *et al.*, 2019]. For example, if the entity 'Bahrain' is selected, then every occurrence of 'Bahrain' will be removed. This slightly complicated scheme matches the situation that some entities in a special domain could not be recognized by non-expert annotators.

According to the low recall of entities tagged by non-speaker annotators in Mayhew [2019], we set $\rho = 0.2$ and $\rho = 0.4$ in our experiments. Note that a smaller ρ means a larger proportion of missing annotation, $\rho = 1$ means complete annotation.

3.2 Experiment Setup

Evaluation Metrics. We consider the following performance metrics: Precision (P), Recall (R), and balanced F-score (F_1). These metrics are calculated based on the true entities and the recognized entities. F_1 score is the main metric to evaluate the NER models of baselines and our approach.

Baselines. We consider several strong baselines to compare with the proposed methods, including BERT with conventional CRF (or CRF for abbreviation) [Lafferty *et al.*, 2001], BERT with Fuzzy CRF [Shang *et al.*, 2018], and BERT with weighted CRF presented by Jie [2019]. CRF regards all unannotated tokens as O label to form complete paths, while Fuzzy

[3]http://www.taobao.com

[4]http://www.youku.com

Ratio	Model	CoNLL-2003			Taobao			Youku		
		P ↑	R ↑	F_1 ↑	P ↑	R ↑	F_1 ↑	P ↑	R ↑	F_1 ↑
$\rho = 0.2$	BERT CRF	81.42	15.05	25.40	**83.11**	24.06	37.32	64.85	20.45	31.09
	BERT Fuzzy CRF	17.94	**88.14**	29.81	41.48	**80.39**	54.72	22.74	**84.65**	35.85
	BERT weighted CRF	85.03	82.65	83.82	70.06	57.85	63.37	70.18	38.98	50.12
	AdaK-NER	**87.05**	86.74	**86.89**	74.24	78.89	**76.50**	**78.21**	79.96	**78.09**
$\rho = 0.4$	BERT CRF	80.07	51.25	62.49	84.76	47.68	61.03	78.89	50.70	61.73
	BERT Fuzzy CRF	14.89	86.61	25.41	43.51	85.02	57.56	30.88	84.01	45.16
	BERT weighted CRF	85.40	88.69	87.01	73.17	81.09	76.93	74.99	82.29	78.47
	AdaK-NER	87.47	88.70	**88.08**	74.08	80.13	**76.99**	78.38	81.53	**79.93**
$\rho = 1.0$	BERT CRF	91.34	92.36	91.85	86.01	88.20	87.09	83.20	84.52	83.85

Table 2: Performance comparison between different models on three datasets with Random-based Scheme.

Ratio	Model	CoNLL-2003			Taobao			Youku		
		P ↑	R ↑	F_1 ↑	P ↑	R ↑	F_1 ↑	P ↑	R ↑	F_1 ↑
$\rho = 0.2$	BERT CRF	**86.79**	18.36	30.31	39.62	10.58	16.70	69.10	15.67	25.55
	BERT Fuzzy CRF	15.99	**86.30**	26.98	42.49	**82.33**	56.05	27.79	**86.37**	42.05
	BERT weighted CRF	83.40	70.96	76.68	**73.49**	52.63	61.33	74.71	32.55	45.34
	AdaK-NER	86.32	71.72	**78.35**	73.24	76.59	**74.88**	**78.86**	75.54	**76.20**
$\rho = 0.4$	BERT CRF	**86.68**	34.26	49.11	**78.43**	39.68	52.70	62.16	35.16	44.91
	BERT Fuzzy CRF	13.84	**84.60**	23.79	42.24	81.07	55.54	32.10	82.87	46.27
	BERT weighted CRF	84.68	76.91	80.61	74.65	79.57	77.03	75.67	80.64	78.08
	AdaK-NER	85.48	77.85	**81.49**	74.58	**80.54**	**77.44**	**79.01**	81.02	**80.00**
$\rho = 1.0$	BERT CRF	91.34	92.36	91.85	86.01	88.20	87.09	83.20	84.52	83.85

Table 3: Performance comparison between different models on three datasets with Entity-based Scheme.

CRF treats all possible paths compatible with the incomplete path with equal probability. Weighted CRF assigns an estimated distribution to all possible paths derived from the incomplete path to train the model.

Training details. We employ BERT model [Devlin *et al.*, 2018] as the neural architecture for baselines and our AdaK-NER. Specifically, we use pretrained Chinese BERT with whole word masking [Cui *et al.*, 2019] for the Chinese datasets and pretrained BERT with case-preserving WordPiece [Devlin *et al.*, 2018] for CoNLL-2003 English dataset. Unless otherwise specified, we set the hyperparameter over [top K] as 5 by default for illustrative purposes. Based on the fact that a larger k-fold value has a negligible effect [Jie *et al.*, 2019], we choose to split the training data into 2 folds (*i.e.*, $k = 2$). We initialize q distribution by assign each unannotated token as O label to form complete paths, and iteratively updated q by k-fold cross-validation stacking. Empirically, we set the iteration number to 10, which is enough for our model to converge.

3.3 Experimental Results

To validate the utility of our model, we consider a wide range of real-world tasks experimentally with entity keeping ratio $\rho = 0.2$ and $\rho = 0.4$. We present the results with Random-based Scheme in Table 2 and Entity-based Scheme in Table 3. We compare the performance of our method to other competing solutions, with each baseline carefully tuned to ensure fairness. In all cases, CRF has high precision and low recall because it labels all the unannotated tokens as O label. In contrast, taking all possible paths into account yields the mismatch of the gold path, hence Fuzzy CRF recalls more entities. Weighted CRF outperforms CRF and Fuzzy CRF, indicating that distribution q should be highly skewed rather than uniformly distributed.

With adaptive K-best loss, candidate mask, annealing technique and iterative sample selection approach, our approach AdaK-NER performs strongly, exhibits high precision and high recall on all datasets and gives best results in F_1 score over the other three models. The improvement is especially remarkable on Chinese Taobao and Youku datesets for $\rho = 0.2$, as it delivers over 13% and 27% increase in F_1 score with Random-based Scheme, while over 13% and 30% increase with Entity-based Scheme.

Note that in CoNLL-2003 and Youku, the F_1 score of AdaK-NER with Random-based Scheme is only roughly 5% lower than that of CRF trained on complete data ($\rho = 1$), while we build AdaK-NER on the training data with only 20% entities available ($\rho = 0.2$). In the other Chinese dataset, our model also achieves encouraging improvement compared to the other methods and presents a step toward more accurate incomplete named entity recognition.

Entity-based Scheme is more restrictive, which is likely to happen in the industry like Financial Technology. However, our model still achieves best F_1 score compared with other methods. The overall results show AdaK-NER achieves state-of-the-art performance compared to various baselines on both English and Chinese datasets with incomplete annotations.

The Effect of K. As discussed in Section 2.1 and 2.2, the parameter K can affect the learning procedure from two aspects. We compare the performance of different K on Taobao dataset with Random-based Scheme and $\rho = 0.2$. The hyperparameter over [top K] is selected from $\{1, 3, 5, 7, 9\}$ on the validation set. As illustrated in Figure 2, a relatively large K delivers better empirical results, and the metrics (precision,

Model	CoNLL-2003			Taobao			Youku		
	P↑	R↑	F_1↑	P↑	R↑	F_1↑	P↑	R↑	F_1↑
w/o K-best loss	88.55	80.49	84.33	78.64	53.12	63.41	62.26	39.3	48.18
w/o weighted loss	83.79	82.84	83.32	47.85	66.15	55.53	73.46	71.59	72.52
w/o annealing	88.36	84.01	86.13	76.09	60.05	67.13	80.98	62.29	70.79
w/o K-best candidates	84.42	73.76	78.73	72.75	56.62	63.68	73.94	58.03	65.02
w/o self-built candidates	87.52	86.33	**86.92**	72.38	77.44	74.82	77.88	74.46	76.13
w/o candidate mask	84.97	86.51	85.73	68.29	79.16	73.32	73.40	79.81	76.47
w/o sample selection	86.64	86.03	86.33	72.88	79.59	76.09	78.48	79.43	**78.95**
AdaK-NER	87.05	86.74	**86.89**	74.24	78.89	**76.50**	78.21	79.96	78.09

Table 4: Ablation study for AdaK-NER on three datasets with Random-based Scheme for $\rho = 0.2$.

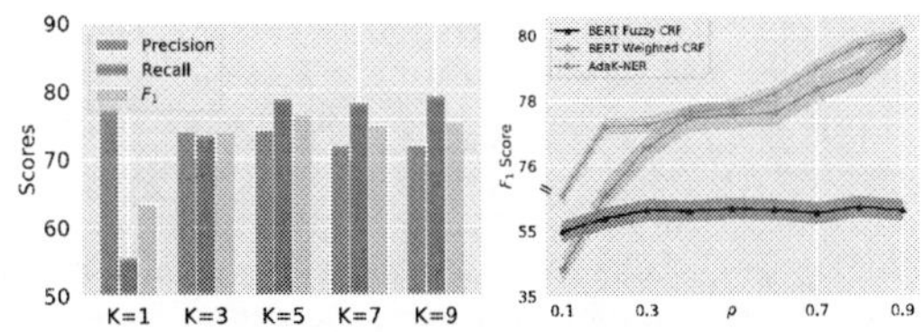

Figure 2: (left) Sensitivity analysis of top truncation K. A smaller K is more sensitive to the truncation. (right) F_1 score comparison between Fuzzy CRF, weighted CRF and our model on Taobao dataset across different ρ selection with Random-based Scheme

recall and F_1) are pretty close when $K = 5, 7, 9$. Meanwhile, a smaller K can narrow down the possible paths more effectively in theory. Hence we favor $K = 5$ which might be a balanced choice.

The Effect of ρ. We further examine annotation rate (ρ) interacts with learning. We plot F_1 score on Taobao dataset with Random-based Scheme across varying annotation rate in Figure 2. The annotation removed with large ρ inherits the annotation removed with the small ρ. All the performance deliver better results with the increase of ρ. Our model consistently outperforms weighted CRF and Fuzzy CRF, and the improvement is significant when ρ is relatively small, which indicates our model is especially powerful when the annotated tokens are fairly sparse.

3.4 Ablation Study

To investigate the effectiveness of the proposed strategies used in AdaK-NER, we conduct the following ablation with Random-based Scheme and $\rho = 0.2$. As shown in Table 4, the adaptive K-best loss contributes most to our model on the three datasets. It helps our model achieve higher recall while preserving acceptable precision. Especially on Youku dataset, removing it would cause a significant drop on recall by 40%. The weighted CRF loss is indispensable, and annealing method could help our model achieve better results. Candidate mask is attributed to promote precision while keeping high recall. Both K-best candidates and self-built candidates facilitate the model performance. Iterative sample selection makes a positive contribution to our model on CoNLL-2003 and Taobao, whereas it slightly hurts the performance on Youku. In general, incorporating these techniques enhances model performance on incomplete annotated data.

4 Related Works

Pre-trained Language Models has been an emerging direction in NLP since Google launched BERT [Devlin *et al.*, 2018] in 2018. With the powerful Transformer architecture, several pre-trained models, such as BERT and generative pretraining model (GPT), and their variants have achieved state-of-the-art performance in various NLP tasks including NER [Devlin *et al.*, 2018; Liu *et al.*, 2019]. Yang [2019] proposed a pre-trained permutation language model (XLNet) to overcome the limitations of denoising autoencoding based pretraining. Liu [2019] demonstrated that more data and more parameter tuning could benefit pre-trained language models, and released a new pre-trained model (RoBERTa). To follow the trend, we use BERT as our neural model in this work.

Statistical Modeling has been widely employed in sequence labeling. Classical models learn label sequences through graph-based representation, with prominent examples such as Hidden Markov Model (HMM), Maximum Entropy Markov Models (MEMM) and Conditional Random Fields (CRF) [Lafferty *et al.*, 2001]. Among them, CRF is an optimal model, since it resolves the labeling bias issue in MEMM and doesn't require the unreasonable independence assumptions in HMM. However, conventional CRF is not directly applicable to the incomplete annotation situation. Ni [2017] select the sentences with the highest confidence, and regarding missing labels as O. Another line of work is to replace CRF with Partial CRF [Nooralahzadeh *et al.*, 2019; Huang *et al.*, 2019] or Fuzzy CRF [Shang *et al.*, 2018], which assign unlabeled words with all possible labels and maximize the total probability [Yang *et al.*, 2018]. Although these works have led to many promising results, they still need external knowledge for high-quality performance. Jie [2019] presented a weighted CRF model which is most closely related to our work. They estimated a proper distribution for all possible paths derived from the incomplete annotations. Our work enhances Fuzzy CRF by reducing the possible paths by a large margin, aiming to better focus on the gold path.

5 Conclusion

In this paper, we explore how to build an effective NER model by only using incomplete annotations. We propose two major strategies including introducing a novel adaptive K-best loss and a mask based on K-best candidates and self-built candidates to help our model better focus on the gold path. The results show that our approaches can significantly improve the performance of NER model with incomplete annotations.

References

[Cao *et al.*, 2019] Yu Cao, Meng Fang, and Dacheng Tao. Bag: Bi-directional attention entity graph convolutional network for multi-hop reasoning question answering. *arXiv preprint arXiv:1904.04969*, 2019.

[Cui *et al.*, 2019] Yiming Cui, Wanxiang Che, Ting Liu, Bing Qin, Shijin Wang, and Guoping Hu. Cross-lingual machine reading comprehension. *arXiv preprint arXiv:1909.00361*, 2019.

[Devlin *et al.*, 2018] Jacob Devlin, Ming-Wei Chang, Kenton Lee, and Kristina Toutanova. Bert: Pre-training of deep bidirectional transformers for language understanding. *arXiv preprint arXiv:1810.04805*, 2018.

[Effland and Collins, 2021] Thomas Effland and Michael Collins. Partially supervised named entity recognition via the expected entity ratio loss. *arXiv preprint arXiv:2108.07216*, 2021.

[Hinton *et al.*, 2015] Geoffrey Hinton, Oriol Vinyals, and Jeff Dean. Distilling the knowledge in a neural network. *arXiv preprint arXiv:1503.02531*, 2015.

[Huang and Chiang, 2005] Liang Huang and David Chiang. Better k-best parsing. In *Proceedings of the Ninth International Workshop on Parsing Technology*, 2005.

[Huang *et al.*, 2019] Xiao Huang, Li Dong, Elizabeth Boschee, and Nanyun Peng. Learning a unified named entity tagger from multiple partially annotated corpora for efficient adaptation. *arXiv preprint arXiv:1909.11535*, 2019.

[Jia *et al.*, 2020] Chen Jia, Yuefeng Shi, Qinrong Yang, and Yue Zhang. Entity enhanced bert pre-training for chinese ner. In *Proceedings of the 2020 Conference on Empirical Methods in Natural Language Processing (EMNLP)*, pages 6384–6396, 2020.

[Jie *et al.*, 2019] Zhanming Jie, Pengjun Xie, Wei Lu, Ruixue Ding, and Linlin Li. Better modeling of incomplete annotations for named entity recognition. In *Proceedings of the 2019 Conference of the North American Chapter of the Association for Computational Linguistics: Human Language Technologies, Volume 1 (Long and Short Papers)*, pages 729–734, 2019.

[Lafferty *et al.*, 2001] John Lafferty, Andrew McCallum, and Fernando CN Pereira. Conditional random fields: Probabilistic models for segmenting and labeling sequence data. 2001.

[Li *et al.*, 2020] Xiaonan Li, Hang Yan, Xipeng Qiu, and Xuanjing Huang. Flat: Chinese ner using flat-lattice transformer. *arXiv preprint arXiv:2004.11795*, 2020.

[Li *et al.*, 2021] Yangming Li, lemao liu, and Shuming Shi. Empirical analysis of unlabeled entity problem in named entity recognition. In *International Conference on Learning Representations*, 2021.

[Liu *et al.*, 2019] Yinhan Liu, Myle Ott, Naman Goyal, Jingfei Du, Mandar Joshi, Danqi Chen, Omer Levy, Mike Lewis, Luke Zettlemoyer, and Veselin Stoyanov. Roberta: A robustly optimized bert pretraining approach. *arXiv preprint arXiv:1907.11692*, 2019.

[Mayhew *et al.*, 2019] Stephen Mayhew, Snigdha Chaturvedi, Chen-Tse Tsai, and Dan Roth. Named entity recognition with partially annotated training data. *arXiv preprint arXiv:1909.09270*, 2019.

[Ni *et al.*, 2017] Jian Ni, Georgiana Dinu, and Radu Florian. Weakly supervised cross-lingual named entity recognition via effective annotation and representation projection. *arXiv preprint arXiv:1707.02483*, 2017.

[Nooralahzadeh *et al.*, 2019] Farhad Nooralahzadeh, Jan Tore Lønning, and Lilja Øvrelid. Reinforcement-based denoising of distantly supervised ner with partial annotation. Association for Computational Linguistics, 2019.

[Peng *et al.*, 2019] Minlong Peng, Xiaoyu Xing, Qi Zhang, Jinlan Fu, and Xuanjing Huang. Distantly supervised named entity recognition using positive-unlabeled learning. *arXiv preprint arXiv:1906.01378*, 2019.

[Poria *et al.*, 2016] Soujanya Poria, Erik Cambria, and Alexander Gelbukh. Aspect extraction for opinion mining with a deep convolutional neural network. *Knowledge-Based Systems*, 108:42–49, 2016.

[Sang and De Meulder, 2003] Erik F Sang and Fien De Meulder. Introduction to the conll-2003 shared task: Language-independent named entity recognition. *arXiv preprint cs/0306050*, 2003.

[Shang *et al.*, 2018] Jingbo Shang, Liyuan Liu, Xiang Ren, Xiaotao Gu, Teng Ren, and Jiawei Han. Learning named entity tagger using domain-specific dictionary. *arXiv preprint arXiv:1809.03599*, 2018.

[Surdeanu *et al.*, 2010] Mihai Surdeanu, Ramesh Nallapati, and Christopher Manning. Legal claim identification: Information extraction with hierarchically labeled data. In *Workshop Programme*, page 22, 2010.

[Wang *et al.*, 2019] Zihan Wang, Jingbo Shang, Liyuan Liu, Lihao Lu, Jiacheng Liu, and Jiawei Han. Crossweigh: Training named entity tagger from imperfect annotations. *arXiv preprint arXiv:1909.01441*, 2019.

[Wei *et al.*, 2020] Qiang Wei, Zongcheng Ji, Zhiheng Li, Jingcheng Du, Jingqi Wang, Jun Xu, Yang Xiang, Firat Tiryaki, Stephen Wu, Yaoyun Zhang, et al. A study of deep learning approaches for medication and adverse drug event extraction from clinical text. *Journal of the American Medical Informatics Association*, 27(1):13–21, 2020.

[Yang *et al.*, 2018] Yaosheng Yang, Wenliang Chen, Zhenghua Li, Zhengqiu He, and Min Zhang. Distantly supervised ner with partial annotation learning and reinforcement learning. In *Proceedings of the 27th International Conference on Computational Linguistics*, pages 2159–2169, 2018.

[Yang *et al.*, 2019] Zhilin Yang, Zihang Dai, Yiming Yang, Jaime Carbonell, Russ R Salakhutdinov, and Quoc V Le. Xlnet: Generalized autoregressive pretraining for language understanding. In *Advances in neural information processing systems*, pages 5753–5763, 2019.

A Sentiment and Emotion Annotated Dataset for Bitcoin Price Forecasting Based on Reddit Posts

Pavlo Seroyizhko* and **Zhanel Zhexenova*** and **Muhammad Zohaib Shafiq***
Fabio Merizzi* and **Andrea Galassi** ✉ and **Federico Ruggeri** ✉
DISI, University of Bologna, Bologna, Italy
a.galassi@unibo.it
federico.ruggeri6@unibo.it

Abstract

Cryptocurrencies have gained enormous momentum in finance and are nowadays commonly adopted as a medium of exchange for online payments. After recent events during which GameStop's stocks were believed to be influenced by WallStreetBets subReddit, Reddit has become a very hot topic on the cryptocurrency market. The influence of public opinions on cryptocurrency price trends has inspired researchers on exploring solutions that integrate such information in crypto price change forecasting. A popular integration technique regards representing social media opinions via sentiment features. However, this research direction is still in its infancy, where a limited number of publicly available datasets with sentiment annotations exists. We propose a novel Bitcoin Reddit Sentiment Dataset, a ready-to-use dataset annotated with state-of-the-art sentiment and emotion recognition. The dataset contains pre-processed Reddit posts and comments about Bitcoin from several domain-related subReddits along with Bitcoin's financial data. We evaluate several widely adopted neural architectures for crypto price change forecasting. Our results show controversial benefits of sentiment and emotion features advocating for more sophisticated social media integration techniques. We make our dataset publicly available for research.

1 Introduction

Cryptocurrencies, often referred to as cryptocurrency or cryptos, are any type of currencies that exist virtually and are secured by encryption or cryptography to safeguard transactions. These currencies are decentralized and do not have any regulating or governing authorities to track them or to create new units. Bitcoin (BTC) is one of the most dominant cryptocurrencies that is driven by investor expectations, and its demand is becoming increasingly appealing (Foley et al., 2019), with investors adopting it to diversify their portfolios. Due to the similarity of its features with speculative stocks and its decentralized nature, the perception and sentiments of investors are likely to drive the price of bitcoin (Kraaijeveld and De Smedt, 2020).

Among the many challenges presented by economics and finance businesses, there is indeed the modeling of customers' sentiment, including their polarity and diversity, and the intentions that may be associated with them. For this purpose, social media constitute rich and useful sources of information that can be analyzed to obtain useful insights. Additionally, it is worth noting that social media may contain misinformation and biases that can potentially exacerbate the information extraction process, eventually making it unreliable (Cao, 2022).

Reddit is a social media platform that has recently gained a lot of attention due to its influence on cryptocurrencies trends. For instance, the subReddit *r/wallstreetbets* allegedly played a role in influencing GameStop's stocks in 2021.[1] Reddit is structured in communities, i.e., subReddits, with a user base of more than 50 million and more than 1.5 billion monthly visitors and has become one of the most popular social media in the US.[2] Recently, the gained momentum of cryptocurrencies has been observed and enhanced by the increasing number of dedicated subReddits. In particular, almost every influential cryptocurrency has its dedicated subReddit. The popularity of some of them, such as r/wallstreebets (12 million subscribers), r/CryptoCurrency (4.8 million subscribers), and r/Bitcoin (4.2 million subscribers), highlight the widespread interest in cryptocurrencies in social media.[3]

* Equal contribution

[1] https://edition.cnn.com/2021/01/27/investing/gamestop-reddit-stock/index.html

[2] https://www.statista.com/statistics/248074/most-popular-us-social-networking-apps-ranked-by-audience/

[3] https://frontpagemetrics.com/

Proceedings of the Fourth Workshop on Financial Technology and Natural Language Processing (FinNLP), pages 203 - 210
December 8, 2022

One peculiar aspect of cryptocurrencies is that they are not regulated by governments or other international institutions, but rather public opinions represent the main cause of crypto price changes. Thus, we commonly observe the rise and fall of popular cryptocurrencies due to their high dependence on people's opinions. In this perspective, the role of public communities and social media platforms like Reddit is highly influential in determining the trend of a cryptocurrency.

This phenomenon has inspired researchers to leverage publicly available social media information, i.e., people's opinions, to evaluate their effect on cryptocurrency price forecasting. To do so, as a common conveyor of people's opinions, researchers have extracted sentiment information from textual data to enrich the set of input features for a forecasting model (Wooley et al., 2019). In particular, the statistical analysis of recent work has shown that a correlation between extracted social media information and crypto price trends does exist (Kraaijeveld and De Smedt, 2020). It is worth noting that the integration of public opinion is not new in the field of finance. Other similar domains like stock market forecasting have shown promising results when integrating heterogeneous information from social media (Kearney and Liu, 2014). Nonetheless, the existing work on this matter is still preliminary from several perspectives. First, few available datasets providing scraped social media data exist nowadays and the number decreases drastically when considering the subset with sentiment annotations (Loginova et al., 2021). Second, the integration of social media information is carried out by a limited subset of sentiment features (Carmezim, 2018; SocialGrep, 2021), while a wide variety of sentiment and emotion tools for efficient and accurate extraction can be leveraged on this matter.

In this work, we propose a novel dataset for Bitcoin price forecasting, called Bitcoin Reddit Sentiment Dataset (BRSD). We create this dataset by pre-processing and integrating an existing dataset of Reddit posts and comments with crypto price values. We employ a wide suite of sentiment and emotion recognition techniques to automatically annotate Reddit textual data in addition to the existing comment-level sentiment annotations. We formulate the task of crypto price forecasting with both prices, sentiment, and emotion features with different widely adopted architectures. In particular, we carry out an ablation study to evaluate the impact of extracted social media information by considering three different input configurations: (i) price data only, (ii) sentiment and emotion data only, and (iii) all available data. We make our dataset publicly available for research.[4] Our experimental setting shows controversial results on the impact of sentiment and emotion data. In particular, the best-performing models' performance deteriorates when adding social media features. In contrast, the less-performing model shows trend learning capabilities only when considering the full set of features.

In Section 2 we analyze similar datasets in the field of crypto currency forecasting. Section 3 describes the dataset creation process. In Section 4, we introduce our experimental setting. Section 5 concludes.

2 Related Work

The automatic forecasting of the stock market and cryptocurrency prices has gained a lot of interest in the past years (Yenidoğan et al., 2018; Lahmiri and Bekiros, 2019; Pang et al., 2020). Indeed, cryptocurrencies are currently widely adopted in finance due to their popularity (Foley et al., 2019). Nonetheless, they are subject to public influence since they rely on decentralization and are not managed or regularized by government institutions. In particular, public opinion and crypto prices are strongly related (Wooley et al., 2019; Phillips and Gorse, 2018a). Recent works on this topic have shown that social media can affect price changes and stand as reasonable indicators of the current economic trends (Kraaijeveld and De Smedt, 2020; Phillips and Gorse, 2018b).

Such a characteristic allowed the introduction of datasets for crypto price forecasting with users opinions extracted from online social media like Reddit (Loginova et al., 2021; Prajapati, 2020; Leukipp, 2022) and Twitter (Pant et al., 2018). However, there are few available datasets regarding Reddit posts and comments with sentiment information (Loginova et al., 2021; SocialGrep, 2021). Loginova et al. introduced a large dataset collected over 768 days (from February 2017 to April 2019) regarding several social media like Reddit, Bitcointalk, and CryptoCompare. Social media

[4]https://www.kaggle.com/datasets/paulsero/bitcoin-reddit-sentiment-dataset

data is collected by leveraging Pushshift APIs,[5] a widely adopted tool for extracting such information (Leukipp, 2022; SocialGrep, 2021; Reinerink, 2022), and later merged with financial data of five popular cryptocurrencies, namely BTC, ETH, LTC, XPR, and XMR, from the website *coinmarketcap.com*.

In contrast, our dataset leverages multiple state-of-the-art sentiment and emotion recognition tools like lexicons, rule-based, and contextual techniques rather than employing aspect-based sentiment analysis. For what concern the period, our dataset covers only one month (August 2021) and focuses only on the BTC cryptocurrency. Nonetheless, its size is comparable to previous works and it is publicly available. Another difference with (Loginova et al., 2021) is the time range on which we base our predictions. Due to the length of our dataset, we predict the price in 15 minutes based on the last hour, whereas, they predict the price in 1 day based on features collected in 7 days averaged with a rolling window of 1 day.

Table 1 provides a summary of existing datasets highlighting their characteristics.

3 Dataset Creation

We rely on a publicly available dataset of Reddit content and on a well-known finance platform to build our dataset. We firstly collect and process data for each of the two datasets. Subsequently, we derive our dataset by merging the information extracted from these two datasets and reporting statistics.

3.1 Kaggle Dataset

We selected a publicly available dataset of Reddit posts and comments from Kaggle (SocialGrep, 2021). The dataset contains 250,569 posts and 3,756,097 comments collected from Reddit in August 2021. In particular, the following subReddits were considered during data collection:

- /r/cryptocurrency
- /r/cryptocurrencyclassic
- /r/cryptocurrencyico
- /r/cryptomars
- /r/cryptomoon
- /r/cryptomoonshots
- /r/satoshistreetbets

The Kaggle dataset does not come with additional pre-processing steps concerning posts filtering and text cleaning. To this end, we devised a preliminary pre-processing phase to only select posts and comments that could potentially correlate with crypto price changes. We removed posts that were tagged as *'deleted'* or *'removed'* since they do not have any relevant textual content. In particular, these posts constituted around 49% of the Kaggle dataset. This is a known phenomena of popular and controversial subReddits like the ones related to cryptocurrencies. Additionally, we remove every comment that contained blacklisted words regarding scam/phishing or advertisements (e.g. *'giveaway'* or *'pump join'*. We use the custom blacklist suggested by (Kraaijeveld and De Smedt, 2020).

Subsequently, we applied a series of traditional text normalization operations for the remaining posts. These operations included (i) merging the title and the body of a post; (ii) cleaning URLs and special symbols and (iii) removing stopwords. This preliminary pre-processing phase reduced the number of posts to 121,593 and the number of comments to 2,755,329.

Lastly, on Reddit the presence of bots is common. We detected and removed spam or bots sentences from Reddit posts by relying on the set of heuristics proposed by (Kraaijeveld and De Smedt, 2020). This approach assumes that bot and spam sentences are short-length sentences that are frequently repeated throughout a document. The spam and bot filtering procedure further reduced the number of posts to 55,002. Table 2 summarizes the described pre-processing process.

3.2 Extracting Sentiment and Emotion from Reddit texts

The use of Reddit posts and comments for crypto price forecasting relies on the extraction of sentiment features that could potentially act as indicators for price changes. The Kaggle dataset comes with comment-level sentiment annotations, which we refer to as **Kaggle-Sentiment**. Nonetheless, no information about how these annotations have been produced is reported.

We have therefore decided to enrich our data through additional unsupervised labels. Indeed, a

[5] `https://github.com/pushshift/api`

Name	Date	Social media	Data	Source	Sentiments	Sentiment type
(Carmezim, 2018)	2018	Twitter	1,578,627 tweets	unspecified, general	Yes	Word polarity
(Leukipp, 2022)	Jan 2022- May 2022	Reddit	518,610 posts	51 subreddit	No	
(Loginova et al., 2021)	Feb 2017- Apr 2019	CryptoCompare, Reddit, Bitcointalk	Respectively, 78,902, 2,635,046, and 1,643,705 texts	r\cryptocurrency, news headlines	Yes	Vader, TextBlob, JST, and TS-LDA
(Reinerink, 2022)	Nov 2017- Mar 2018	Reddit	2,161,000 comments	r\cryptocurrency	No	
Kaggle dateset (SocialGrep, 2021)	August 2021	Reddit	3,756,097 comments and 250,569 posts	7 subreddits	Yes	Kaggle-Sentiment
(Pano and Kashef, 2020)	May 2022 - Jun 2022	Twitter	4,169,709 tweets	BTC related tweets	No	
BRSD (our dataset)	August 2021	Reddit	2,755,329 comments and 55,002 posts	7 subreddits (BTC only)	Yes	Vader, TextBlob, BERT, RoBERTa, Flair, Kaggle-Sentiment

Table 1: A comparison between the Bitcoin Reddit Sentiment Dataset and similar cryptocurrency datasets that integrate social media information.

Dataset → Property ↓	Original	Deleted	Bots/Ads	Cleaned
Posts	250,569	127,891	67,676	55,002
Avg Posts/Hour	336.96	171.99	89.68	73.95
Avg Posts/Minute	5.71	2.9	1.52	1.25
Comments	3,756,097	998,568	2,200	2,755,329
Avg Comments/Hour	3,708.91	1,109.90	2.96	3,705.89
Avg Comments/Minute	62.84	20.13	0.05	62.75

Table 2: Kaggle Reddit dataset statistics throughout our preliminary pre-processing pipeline. We report information about filtered posts and comments after each pre-processing phase.

wide suite of off-of-the-shelf tools for accurate and efficient sentiment extraction can be found in the literature. In this work, we consider multiple state-of-the-art tools to extract sentiment and emotion features from Reddit posts and comments. We employed the following tools:

- **Flair** (Akbik et al., 2018): A multilingual library that comprises of several state-of-the-art contextual text embedding methods like BERT. Flair methods are pre-trained on the well-known IMDB movie review dataset. We adopted the English embedding models of this library. In particular, each method extract sentiments scores in the $[0, 1]$ range and polarity scores as either being `negative` or `positive`. In particular, the two scores are combined to provide a single sentiment score.

- **TextBlob** (Loria, 2018): A high-level library built on top of NLTK (Bird et al., 2009). TextBlob extracts sentiment scores in the $[-1, 1]$ range. Additionally, the library extracts subjectivity scores ($[0, 1]$ range) and related subjectivity intensity scores. Subjectivity determines if a text is subjective or factual, whereas the intensity score of a word quantifies to what extent the word modifies the meaning of the next word. We use the extracted sentiment, subjectivity, and intensity scores as features.

- **VADER** (Hutto and Gilbert, 2014): A rule-based model based on a fixed list of lexical features. VADER does not take into account the contextual information of a word, unlike Flair. VADER extracts classifies the sentiment of a text as `positive`, `negative` or `neutral` and return their probabilities which we use a features.

- **BERT** (Devlin et al., 2019): We employ a BERT model pre-trained on multilingual product reviews for sentiment analysis.[6] In particular, the extracted sentiment of a text ranges from 1 (negative) to 5 (positive).

- **RoBERTA** (Liu et al., 2019): We employ a RoBERTa model pre-trained on the TweetEval benchmark (Barbieri et al., 2020) for the emotion recognition task.[7] The model is trained on English tweets and identifies the following emotion categories: *anger*, *joy*, *optimism*, *sadness*. We use the prediction probabilities of emotion classes as features.

Where not explicitly stated, we consider raw probability scores for categorical variables (e.g. VADER, BERT and RoBERTA). The features extracted using each tool are first transformed to obtain a uniform set of value ranges (e.g. Flair and TextBlob sentiment scores) and later normalized.

[6] `https://huggingface.co/nlptown/bert-base-multilingual-uncased-sentiment`

[7] `https://huggingface.co/cardiffnlp/twitter-roberta-base-sentiment`

Tool	Feature	Range
TextBlob	Polarity	[-1, 1]
	Subjectivity	[-1, 1]
Kaggle	Kaggle-Sentiment	[-1, 1]
RoBERTA	Anger	[0, 1]
	Joy	[0, 1]
	Optimism	[0, 1]
	Sadness	[0, 1]
VADER	Positive	[0, 1]
	Negative	[0, 1]
	Neutral	[0, 1]
	Compound	[-1, 1]
Flair	Flair-Sentiment	[-1, 1]
BERT	BERT-Sentiment	[1, 5]

Table 3: Score ranges of sentiment analysis tools

In total, we extract a set of 12 sentiment and emotion features for each input Reddit post or comment.

The described suite of sentiment and emotion features is employed to encode each Reddit post and comment. In particular, we aggregate individual comments sentiment and emotion feature set by summing them. This information is added to the provided sentiment annotations of the original Kaggle dataset. Table 3 provides a summary.

3.3 Finance Bitstamp Dataset

We extracted raw crypto price values from the exchanger Bitstamp platform.[8] We considered the time period of the posts and comments in the Reddit Finance dataset to extract time-aligned raw crypto price values. We observed that the Reddit Finance dataset covered the period of August 2021 and downloaded corresponding finance data from Bitstamp. We denote this dataset as the Finance Bitstamp dataset. The collected dataset contains crypto price values on a minute base and has 530,324 entries. Each entry contains metadata (*id*, *date*, *crypto currency*, *open*), trend-related values (*high*, *low*, *close*) and price information (*Volume BTC*, *Volume USD*).

3.4 BTC Reddit Sentiment Dataset

We integrate the extracted sentiment features from Reddit posts and comments into the Finance Bitstamp dataset. To do that, Reddit posts and comments are first temporally aligned with crypto price values. We leverage the reported timestamp metadata of both datasets to perform this operation. The alignment of Reddit posts and comments with crypto price values is done at minute-level. We opted for a minute-based alignment motivated by two main observations. First, it is the granularity used in the Reddit Finance dataset. Thus, the integration of crypto price values based on this granularity is straightforward. Second, this dataset contains information extracted from August 2021. A more coarse-grained granularity would significantly reduce the number of samples for forecasting. Note that it is still possible to operate with more coarse-grained granularities (e.g. hours) to further evaluate the impact of social media information. Indeed, the influence of social media opinions works at higher scales (e.g. hours, days) and cause-effect delays have to be considered as well.

We collect Reddit posts published each minute and aggregate them by summing the set of sentiment features, obtaining a new layer of sentiment and emotion annotations. The built dataset, which we denote as the BTC Reddit Sentiment Dataset, contains 44.639 entries on a minute base with 19 features concerning sentiment, emotion, and price values.

4 Experiments

We address the task of crypto value forecasting by jointly leveraging price and sentiment features of domain-related Reddit posts. Formally, a forecasting model receives a sequence of price values $\{v_1, v_2, \ldots, v_T\}$ regarding a time-window of size T and a sequence of sentiment features $\{s_1, s_2, \ldots, s_T\}$. Each sentiment feature s_t is a collection of sentiment values as described in Section 3The two sequences are concatenated temporally-wise and fed as input to a model. The forecasting model then outputs a price value v_{T+W} where W is the forecasting window size.

Our main objective is to study the impact of social media data on crypto price changes. Therefore, we define an ablation study by considering three experimental input configurations for a forecasting model: **(P)** only price values $\{v_1, v_2, \ldots, v_T\}$ are considered; **(S)** only sentiment features $\{s_1, s_2, \ldots, s_T\}$ are considered; **(P + S)** both sentiment and price information are considered.

We generally consider the forecasting task of predicting a time window of future crypto price values given a past time window of price, sentiment, and emotion features. In this work, we set $T = 60$

[8]https://www.bitstamp.net/

minutes and $W = 15$ minutes.

To quantitatively evaluate the selected set of forecasting models, we split our dataset into train (25,025), validation (10,698), and test (8,916) splits. Splits follow the sequential flow of crypto price time-series and, thus, no data shuffling is involved. We devise a preliminary hyper-parameter calibration phase based on the validation set. Models are trained to minimize the mean squared error loss on the train set and are later evaluated on the test set. We apply a L^2 regularization to all the described models. Furthermore, we consider early stopping regularization with patience set to 10 epochs. Models are trained with Adam optimizer (Kingma and Ba, 2015).

4.1 Models

We select several widely adopted architectures for price forecasting to evaluate our dataset. In particular, we consider two recurrent neural network models which have been proven to achieve state-of-the-art performance for the stock price prediction task (Gao et al., 2021). Additionally, we consider a transformer model due to its widespread popularity (Vaswani et al., 2017). More precisely, the multi-head attention (Galassi et al., 2021) of the transformer is used to capture high-level interactions between the heterogeneous set of features.

- **RNN**: A 2-layer recurrent neural network with a linear regression layer on top. The first recurrent layer is a simple RNN with 64 units followed by a GRU layer with 64 units.

- **LSTM-GRU**: A 2-layer recurrent neural network with a linear regression layer on top. The first recurrent layer is an LSTM with 64 units followed by a GRU layer with 64 units and L2 regularization.

- **Transformer**: A 6 heads attention model with 4 transformer-encoder blocks followed by a linear layer on top with 256 units.

4.2 Results

We evaluate the selected set of forecasting models on our dataset by computing the Root Mean Squared Error (RMSE) and the Mean Absolute Error (MAE) metrics. Table 4 reports the achieved performance on our dataset. Additionally, we report each model forecast on the test set in Figure 1. We distinguish between each input configuration for forecasting. We observe that RNN-GRU is the best performing model in terms of regression metrics with an RMSE of 468, and an MAE of 445,98. Additionally, the LSTM-GRU model achieves comparable performance while the transformer model falls behind. We notice that sentiment features have controversial effects on selected models. In particular, recurrent models performance is significantly deteriorated when considering the (P + S) input configuration compared to the (P) one (Figures 1a and 1b). In contrast, the transformer model achieves higher regression performance in the (P + S) setting while it fails to learn the trend of crypto price changes when relying on price values only (P) (Figure 1c). We speculate that this result could be motivated by the limited period considered in our dataset.

As expected, the (S) setting leads to the worst-performing results for all models. This is mainly motivated by the fact that social media information captures trend changes and provides general opinions on the cryptocurrency status rather than discussing exact crypto price forecasts.

The proposed method for social media information integration has shown promising results in similar settings (Prajapati, 2020). Nonetheless, our experimental results suggest that more sophisticated methodologies for social media information integration could be explored. In particular, we identify two major challenges. First, textual information encoding should scale to large sets of sources For instance, in our experimental setup, 3,705 comments and about 74 posts are reported hourly (Table 2). Properly encoding and aggregating such a large amount of textual data still remains an open research direction. We show that summing sentiment and emotion scores for aggregating Reddit posts and comments are not sufficient to achieve satisfying results.

5 Conclusions

We have introduced Bitcoin Reddit Sentiment, a novel dataset for crypto price values forecasting. Our dataset is built upon an existing Kaggle dataset with Reddit posts and comments taken from a wide set of domain-related subReddits. We enrich such a dataset by leveraging several state-of-the-art sentiment and emotion extraction tools to encode textual data. This approach is motivated by the assumption that public platforms like social media can affect the current trend of cryptocurrencies. Thus, sentiment and emotion features stand as valuable

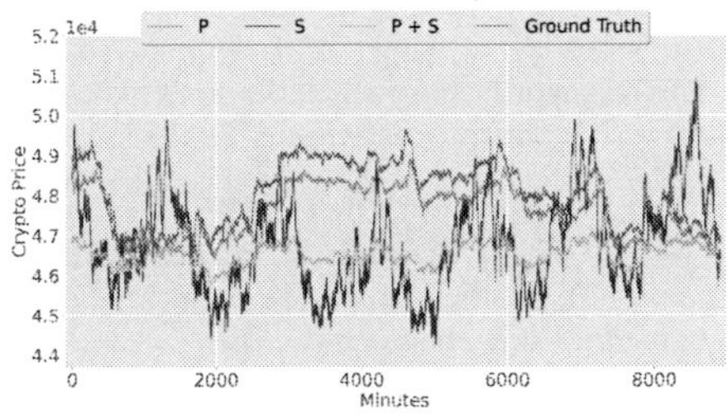

(a) RNN.

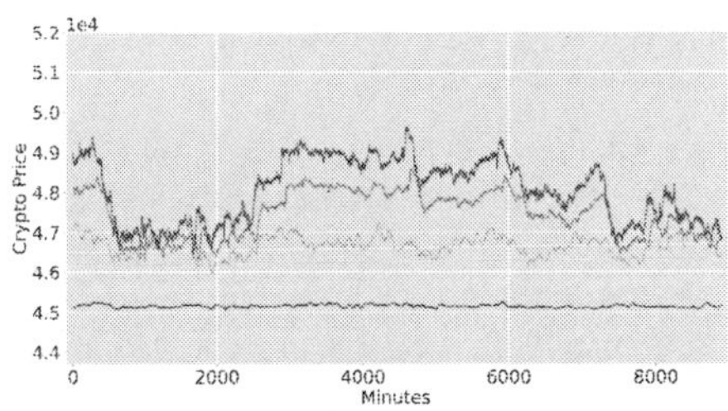

(b) LSTM-GRU.

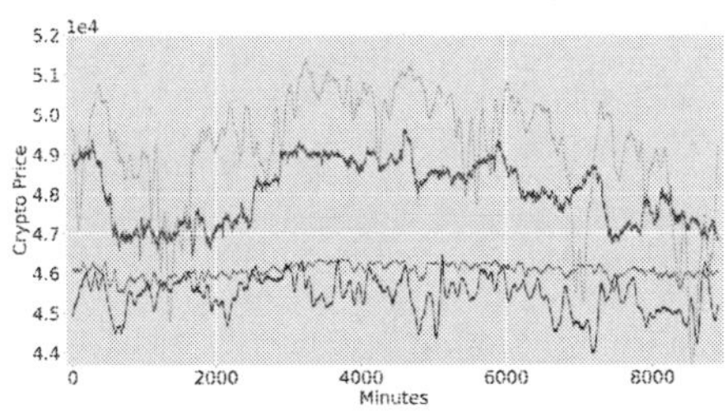

(c) Transformer.

Figure 1: Minute-based models forecasting performance with different input configurations.

Model	RMSE ↓	Δ RMSE	MAE ↓	Δ MAE
RNN (P)	**468,39**	-	**445,98**	-
RNN (S)	1961,30	-1492,91	1634,07	-1188,09
RNN (P + S)	1685,18	-1216,79	1518,82	-1072,84
LSTM-GRU (P)	623,70	-	589,75	-
LSTM-GRU (S)	2984,22	-2360,52	2883,50	-2293,75
LSTM-GRU (P + S)	1532,76	-909,06	1365,96	-776,21
Transformer (P)	2099,18	-	1992,60	-
Transformer (S)	2708,79	-609,61	2592,62	-600,02
Transformer (P + S)	1693,90	**405,28**	1515,48	**477,12**

Table 4: Model forecasting regression performance on our dataset. We report performance for each model input configuration. Additionally, we report the performance delta (Δ columns) between the (P) configuration and the remaining ones for each model.

indicators of the opinions reported on those platforms. The collected dataset is challenging due to the high number of textual data that has to be digested. Our experimental results show that well-known neural architectures like recurrent neural models and transformers can reach satisfying to modest forecasting performance when using price information only. In contrast, the high amount of encoded textual data deteriorates their successful integration by leveraging sentiment and emotion features, and no significant benefit is shown regarding the task. Our results suggest that the integration of social media information is still an open research direction. We advocate for novel techniques that adapt easily to large and heterogeneous sources of information like Reddit, Twitter, Facebook, and Google News. In future works, a critical investigation perspective would be the evaluation of the contribution of each set of sentiment features. Another possible research direction would be to analyze the argumentative content of the social media (Lytos et al., 2019) to obtain a score that can be used as a feature (Lippi et al., 2022).

Acknowledgements

We would like to thank Paolo Torroni for his help and supervision. This work was partially funded by EU Horizon 2020 project StairwAI, grant agreement number 101017142.

References

Alan Akbik, Duncan Blythe, and Roland Vollgraf. 2018. Contextual string embeddings for sequence labeling. In *COLING*, pages 1638–1649. Association for Computational Linguistics.

Francesco Barbieri, José Camacho-Collados, Luis Espinosa Anke, and Leonardo Neves. 2020. Tweeteval: Unified benchmark and comparative evaluation for tweet classification. In *EMNLP (Findings)*, volume EMNLP 2020 of *Findings of ACL*, pages 1644–1650. Association for Computational Linguistics.

Steven Bird, Ewan Klein, and Edward Loper. 2009. *Natural language processing with Python: analyzing text with the natural language toolkit.* O'Reilly Media, Inc.

Longbing Cao. 2022. Ai in finance: Challenges, techniques, and opportunities. *ACM Comput. Surv.*, 55(3).

Adriano Carmezim. 2018. Sentiment analysis on crypto tweets. https://github.com/Carmezim/crypto-twitter-sentiment-analysis.

Jacob Devlin, Ming-Wei Chang, Kenton Lee, and Kristina Toutanova. 2019. BERT: pre-training of deep bidirectional transformers for language understanding. In *NAACL-HLT (1)*, pages 4171–4186. Association for Computational Linguistics.

Sean Foley, Jonathan R Karlsen, and Tālis J Putniņš. 2019. Sex, drugs, and bitcoin: How much illegal activity is financed through cryptocurrencies? *The Review of Financial Studies*, 32(5):1798–1853.

Andrea Galassi, Marco Lippi, and Paolo Torroni. 2021. Attention in natural language processing. *IEEE Transactions on Neural Networks and Learning Systems*, 32(10):4291–4308.

Ya Gao, Rong Wang, and Enmin Zhou. 2021. Stock prediction based on optimized LSTM and GRU models. *Sci. Program.*, 2021:4055281:1–4055281:8.

Clayton J. Hutto and Eric Gilbert. 2014. VADER: A parsimonious rule-based model for sentiment analysis of social media text. In *ICWSM*. The AAAI Press.

Colm Kearney and Sha Liu. 2014. Textual sentiment in finance: A survey of methods and models. *International Review of Financial Analysis*, 33:171–185.

Diederik P. Kingma and Jimmy Ba. 2015. Adam: A method for stochastic optimization. In *ICLR*.

Olivier Kraaijeveld and Johannes De Smedt. 2020. The predictive power of public twitter sentiment for forecasting cryptocurrency prices. *Journal of International Financial Markets, Institutions and Money*, 65:101188.

Salim Lahmiri and Stelios Bekiros. 2019. Cryptocurrency forecasting with deep learning chaotic neural networks. *Chaos, Solitons & Fractals*, 118:35–40.

Leukipp. 2022. Reddit - crypto posts (r/cryptocurrency, r/eth...). https://www.kaggle.com/datasets/leukipp/reddit-crypto-data.

Marco Lippi, Francesco Antici, Gianfranco Brambilla, Evaristo Cisbani, Andrea Galassi, Daniele Giansanti, Fabio Magurano, Antonella Rosi, Federico Ruggeri, and Paolo Torroni. 2022. AMICA: an argumentative search engine for COVID-19 literature. In *IJCAI*, pages 5932–5935. ijcai.org.

Yinhan Liu, Myle Ott, Naman Goyal, Jingfei Du, Mandar Joshi, Danqi Chen, Omer Levy, Mike Lewis, Luke Zettlemoyer, and Veselin Stoyanov. 2019. Roberta: A robustly optimized bert pretraining approach. *arXiv preprint arXiv:1907.11692*.

Ekaterina Loginova, Wai Kit Tsang, Guus van Heijningen, Louis-Philippe Kerkhove, and Dries F Benoit. 2021. Forecasting directional bitcoin price returns using aspect-based sentiment analysis on online text data. *Machine Learning*, pages 1–24.

Steven Loria. 2018. Textblob documentation.

Anastasios Lytos, Thomas Lagkas, Panagiotis G. Sarigiannidis, and Kalina Bontcheva. 2019. The evolution of argumentation mining: From models to social media and emerging tools. *Inf. Process. Manag.*, 56(6).

Xiongwen Pang, Yanqiang Zhou, Pan Wang, Weiwei Lin, and Victor Chang. 2020. An innovative neural network approach for stock market prediction. *The Journal of Supercomputing*, 76(3):2098–2118.

Toni Pano and Rasha Kashef. 2020. A corpus of btc tweets in the era of covid-19. In *2020 IEEE International IOT, Electronics and Mechatronics Conference (IEMTRONICS)*, pages 1–4. IEEE.

Dibakar Raj Pant, Prasanga Neupane, Anuj Poudel, Anup Kumar Pokhrel, and Bishnu Kumar Lama. 2018. Recurrent neural network based bitcoin price prediction by twitter sentiment analysis. In *ICCCS*, pages 128–132. IEEE.

Ross C. Phillips and Denise Gorse. 2018a. Cryptocurrency price drivers: Wavelet coherence analysis revisited. *PLOS ONE*, 13(4):1–21.

Ross C. Phillips and Denise Gorse. 2018b. Mutual-excitation of cryptocurrency market returns and social media topics. In *ICFET*, page 80–86, New York, NY, USA. Association for Computing Machinery.

Pratikkumar Prajapati. 2020. Predictive analysis of bitcoin price considering social sentiments. *CoRR*, abs/2001.10343.

Nick Reinerink. 2022. Reddit /r/cryptocurrency. https://www.kaggle.com/datasets/nickreinerink/reddit-rcryptocurrency.

SocialGrep. 2021. Reddit cryptocurrency data for august 2021. https://www.kaggle.com/pavellexyr/Reddit-cryptocurrency-data-for-august-2021.

Ashish Vaswani, Noam Shazeer, Niki Parmar, Jakob Uszkoreit, Llion Jones, Aidan N. Gomez, Lukasz Kaiser, and Illia Polosukhin. 2017. Attention is all you need. In *NeurIPS*, pages 5998–6008.

Stephen Wooley, Andrew Edmonds, Arunkumar Bagavathi, and Siddharth Krishnan. 2019. Extracting cryptocurrency price movements from the reddit network sentiment. In *ICMLA*, pages 500–505. IEEE.

Işil Yenidoğan, Aykut Çayir, Ozan Kozan, Tuğçe Dağ, and Çiğdem Arslan. 2018. Bitcoin forecasting using arima and prophet. In *UBMK*, pages 621–624. IEEE.

FinSim4-ESG Shared Task: Learning Semantic Similarities for the Financial Domain. Extended edition to ESG insights

Juyeon Kang[1] , **Mehdi Kchouk**[1] , **Sandra Bellato**[1] and **Mei Gan**[1] and **Ismail El Maarouf**[2]
[1]Fortia Financial Solutions
[2]Imprevisible
{juyeon.kang, mehdi.kchouk, sandra.bellato, mei.gan}@fortia.fr, ismail.elmaarouf@imprevisible.com

Abstract

This paper describes *FinSim4-ESG*[1] shared task organized in the 4th FinNLP workshopwhich is held in conjunction with the IJCAI-ECAI-2022 conferenceThis year, the FinSim4 is extended to the Environment, Social and Government (ESG) insights and proposes two subtasks, one for ESG Taxonomy Enrichment and the other for Sustainable Sentence Prediction. Among the 28 teams registered to the shared task, a total of 8 teams submitted their systems results and 6 teams also submitted a paper to describe their method. The winner of each subtask shows good performance results of 0.85% and 0.95% in terms of accuracy, respectively.

1 Introduction

The FinSim shared task aims to spark interest from communities in NLP, ML/AI, Knowledge Engineering and Financial document processing. Going beyond the mere representation of words is a key step to industrial applications that make use of Natural Language Processing (NLP). This is typically addressed using either 1) Unsupervised corpus-derived representations like word embeddings, which are typically opaque to human understanding but very useful in NLP applications or 2) Supervised approach to semantic representations learning, which typically requires an important volume of labeled data, but has high coverage for the target domain or 3) Manually labeled resources such as corpora, lexica, taxonomies and ontologies, which typically have low coverage and contain inconsistencies, but provide a deeper understanding of the target domain.

These approaches form a different spectrum which a number of them have attempted to combine, particularly in tasks aiming at expanding the coverage of manual resources using automatic methods.

- The Semeval community has organized several evaluation campaigns to stimulate the development of methods which extract semantic/lexical relations between concepts/words ([Bordea *et al.*, 2015], [Bordea *et al.*, 2016], [Jurgens and Pilehvar, 2016], [Camacho-Collados *et al.*, 2018]).
- A large number of datasets and challenges specifically look at how to automatically populate knowledge bases such as DBpedia or Wikidata (e.g. KBP challenges, https://tac.nist.gov/2020/KBP/SM-KBP/).
- There are also a number of studies on the supervised and unsupervised approaches to the extraction of semantic relations between concepts and terms ([Fauconnier and Kamel, 2015], [Shwartz *et al.*, 2016], [Wang *et al.*, 2017], [Sarkar *et al.*, 2018], [Martel and Zouaq, 2021]).

This new edition of FinSim4-ESG is extended to the "Environment, Social and Governance (ESG)" related issues based on the sustainability reports, ESG reports, Environment report and annual reports periodically published by financial companies. The ESG criteria is a set of standards for a company's behavior used by socially conscious investors to screen potential investments. Environmental criteria consider how a company safeguards the environment, including corporate policies addressing climate change, for example. Social criteria examine how it manages relationships with employees, suppliers, customers, and the communities where it operates. Governance deals with a company's leadership, executive pay, audits, internal controls, and shareholder rights. For example, in financial domain, the ESG criteria are applied to assess the companies risk on these ESG aspects, so that help investors supporting business aligned with green initiatives.

According to the European Commission, from the end of 2022, companies providing investment products that make sustainability or environmental claims will be required to disclose how their portfolios align with the EU taxonomy[2] and ESG regulations for sustainable activities. The objective of this shared task is to elaborate an ESG taxonomy, ESG concepts representations, based on the data like companies' sustainability reports, annual reports, environment reports, etc. and make use of them to analyze how an economic activity complies with the taxonomy. Consequently, it allows us to know how an investment product aligns with ESG regulations.

[1]https://sites.google.com/nlg.csie.ntu.edu.tw/finnlp-2022/shared-task-finsim4-esg

[2]https://ec.europa.eu/info/business-economy-euro/banking-and-finance/sustainable-finance/eu-taxonomy-sustainable-activities_en

Proceedings of the Fourth Workshop on Financial Technology and Natural Language Processing (FinNLP), pages 211 - 217
December 8, 2022 ©2022 Association for Computational Linguistics

2 Related works

The FinSim4-ESG proposes two subtasks: ESG Taxonomy Enrichment and Sustainability Prediction. The subtask1 is similar to the previous tasks of FinSim shared tasks, given a training set of terms and a fixed set of concepts, participants are asked to propose systems allowing to categorize new terms to their most likely concepts. A term-concept pair has a hierarchical and semantic relation if one of them can be conceived as a more generic term (e.g. *Emissions - Greenhouse gas emissions*). And the subtask2 proposes to solve a sentence classification problem in order to classify each sentence extracted from the ESG related reports into sustainable or unsustainable.

A taxonomy represents a semantic relation of term pairs, which is "*isa*" pairs, largely used in NLP and IE tasks. The taxonomy extraction task from a domain specific corpora as a competition is first proposed by the shared task TExEval [Bordea *et al.*, 2015] and TExEval-2 [Bordea *et al.*, 2016] as part of SemEval-2015 and 2016. Several works introduced methods to learn hypernymy from the corpora and showed how to induce taxonomies from "*isa*" pairs. While those systems largely exploit semantic lexical resources like WordNet, BabelNet, YAGO, Wiki, DBPedia, distributional approach was not meaningfully adopted.
More recently, as part of SemEval 2020, the shared task on Predicting Multilingual and Cross-Lingual (Graded) Lexical Entailment [Glavaš *et al.*, 2020] proposed a challenge for detecting semantic hierarchical relation, hypernym-hyponym, from multilingual and cross-lingual datasets. The Distributional track was newly added in order to evaluate distributional systems. The participating systems make use of rule-based approach by exploiting Wiktionary definitions of concepts [Kovács *et al.*, 2020] or distributional approach combining distributional word vectors, multilingual lexical resources and translated parallel corpora to obtain cross lingual synonyms, then to extract a set of terms which are semantically most similar to a seed term [Hauer *et al.*, 2020] [Wang *et al.*, 2020]. Also, in the previous FinSim shared tasks [Maarouf *et al.*, 2020] [Kang *et al.*, 2021], the authors proposed various approaches for the hypernyms and synonyms ranking of financial terms by using the state-of-art models like BERT and its variants (e.g. FinBERT) with good performance results.

The distributional semantic models are widely explored in different NLP based financial data analysis. A lot of studies make use of the fine-tuned models from various extensions of BERT model like Sentence-BERT [Reimers and Gurevych, 2019], RoBERTa [Liu *et al.*, 2019], DistilBERT [Sanh *et al.*, 2019]. For example, the fine-tuned model on the financial data, FinBERT [Yang *et al.*, 2020], is largely used and ESG-BERT [Mukherjee, 2020] is also trained on sustainability corpus with the growing interest in the ESG data analysis. Recently, we observe that the ESG related data like 10K report, 10Q filling or annual reports has been studied for automating the ESG ratings of the companies. [Balakrishnan *et al.*, 2010] proposes a linear SVM classifier to predict market performance based on narrative disclosures of 10K reports while [Mehra *et al.*, 2022] and [Armbrust *et al.*, 2020] investigate the effect of the environmental performance of a company on the relationship between the company's disclosures and financial performance. [Sokolov *et al.*, 2021] also proposes an approach to automatically convert unstructured data into ESG scores using a pre-trained BERT model. [Matthew Purver and Pollak, 2022] proposes a diachronic analysis of ESG terms in UK annual reports at the First Computing Social Responsibility Workshop-NLP Approaches to Corporate Social Responsibilities (CSR-NLP[3]). [Luccioni *et al.*, 2020] proposes NLP based methods for the analysis of financial reports in order to identify climate-relevant sections based on a question answering approach and [Guo *et al.*, 2020] develops a pipeline of ESG news extraction, news representations, and Bayesian inference of deep learning models.

3 Task Description

The new edition proposes two subtasks: ESG taxonomy enrichment and Sustainability prediction.

3.1 ESG Taxonomy Enrichment

We have created an in-house sustainable finance taxonomy called "Fortia ESG taxonomy". It is based on different financial data provider's taxonomies as well as several sustainability and annual reports where we looked for ESG related criteria. Given a subset of "Fortia ESG taxonomy", participants will be asked to enrich this training set to cover the rest of the terms of the original "Fortia ESG taxonomy". For this purpose, participants are given a set of ESG related reports of financial companies from which they can develop a model allowing to induce semantically related terms to the concepts defined in the training set. For example, given a set of terms related to the concept *Waste management* (e.g. *Hazardous Waste, Waste Reduction Initiatives*), the participating systems need to find the missing ones by the way that you predict a corresponding concept to unlabeled terms.

3.2 Sustainability Prediction

Participants are asked to design a system which can automatically classify sentences into sustainable or unsustainable sentences making use of the enriched taxonomy. For this purpose, participants are given a list of carefully selected labeled sentences from the sustainability reports and other documents. In this shared task, we consider a sentence as sustainable if a sentence semantically mentions the Environmental or Social or Governance related factors as defined in our ESG taxonomy.

Performance is measured according to the accuracy with which label is assigned, and according to recall (based on the total number of predictions).

This year, we propose a subset of our in-house ESG taxonomy and a dataset composed of financial and non-financial reports. And we are interested in systems which make use of contextual word embeddings such as BERT ([Devlin *et al.*, 2019]), as well as systems which make use of resources related to the ESG (Environmental, Social and Governance) and sustainability including EU taxonomy.

[3]https://csr-nlp.github.io/CSR-NLP-2022/

3.3 ESG Dataset

ESG related Reports Corpus The main topic of FinSim4 is the ESG taxonomy based sustainable activities analysis of the financial companies. For this purpose, we built a corpus composed of 190 sustainability reports, environment reports, annual reports and ESG reports, where the companies periodically publish the results of their activities showing its social or environmental impact.

ESG Taxonomy and Concepts-Terms Data Preparation We elaborated a first version of ESG taxonomy where the Environment, Social and Government topics are organized into groups of concepts and each concept is composed of semantically related terms. The Environment topic contains 9 concepts: Carbon factor, Emissions, Energy efficiency and renewable energy, Waste management, Water & waste-water management, Biodiversity, Sustainable Transport, Sustainable Food & Agriculture and Circular economy while the Social topic has 9 concepts: Employee development, Recruiting and retaining employees (incl. work-life balance), Future of work, Employee engagement, Injury frequency rate, Injury frequency rate for subcontracted labour, Community, Human rights and Product Responsibility, the Government topic with 6 concepts: Board Independence, Board Make-Up, Audit Oversight, Shareholder rights, Executive compensation and Share Capital. And we carefully selected the terms for each of these concepts as described in Table 1 taking into account the principals of EU taxonomy for sustainable activitiesand manually validated them based on the criteria used by ESG data providers[4].

Sustainable and Unsustainable Sentences Annotation For the subtask2, we first collected the candidate sentences using the dataset elaborated for the subtask1, a total of 792 terms. These terms based sentences extraction allowed creating a dataset of 2265 sustainable and unsustainable sentences from the corpus composed of the ESG related reports as above mentioned (See Table 2). Then, we manually annotated them reading the whole context from where the candidate sentence is extracted, otherwise, this information was not included in the dataset provided by the shared task. For this task, two experienced annotators cross-validated the annotated sentences.

Concepts	Training	Test
Energy efficiency and renewable energy	59	12
Sustainable Food & Agriculture	54	10
Product Responsibility	51	10
Circular economy	47	8
Sustainable Transport	46	7
Emissions	39	9
Shareholder rights	38	10
Board Make-Up	37	6
Injury frequency rate for subcontracted labour	35	5
Executive compensation	32	7
Biodiversity	29	10
Community	27	7
Employee engagement	23	5
Employee development	22	5
Water & waste-water management	21	4
Carbon factor	19	6
Future of work	18	5
Waste management	16	4
Recruiting and retaining employees	11	4
Human Rights	10	4
Audit Oversight	7	3
Share Capital	2	1
Board Independence	2	2
Injury frequency rate	2	1
Total	647	145

Table 1: ESG terms-concepts data for the subtask1

Label	Training	Test
Sustainable	1223	103
Unsustainable	1042	102
Total	2265	205

Table 2: Sustainability sentences data for the subtask2

4 Evaluation Setup

4.1 Baselines

We prepared two simple baselines in order to help the participants get started. Both baselines are based on a custom Word2Vec model that was trained on a corpus composed of ESG reports, Sustainability reports, environment reports and annual reports. The vector representation for each term is computed as the average of the word embeddings of their tokens. In the case of the subtask1, for each test sample, the first baseline ranks all the possible hypernyms using the hyponym-hypernym similarity in the embedding space. The second baseline trains a logistic regression model that classifies each test sample into different classes where each class represents one possible hypernym. In the case of the subtask2, for each test sample, the first baseline classifies a list of sentences into sustainable or unsustainable based on the sentence similarity and the second trains a classic classifier, both using the custom Word2Vec trained on the ESG dataset.

4.2 Evaluation metrics

We use the same metrics as the previous edition of FinSim, Accuracy for the subtasks 1 and 2, and Mean Rank for the subtask1. For each term x_i with a label y_i, the expected prediction is a top 3 list of labels ranked from most to least likely to be equal to the ground truth by the predictive system $\hat{y}_i^l$. We note by $rank_i$ the rank of the correct label in the top-3 prediction list, if the ground truth does not appear in the top-3 then $rank_i$ is equal to 4. Given those notation the accuracy can be expressed as:

$$Accuracy = \frac{1}{n} * \sum_{i=1}^{n} I(y_i = \hat{y}_i^l[0])$$

And the Mean Rank as:

$$Mean\_Rank = \frac{1}{n} * \sum_{i=1}^{n} rank_i$$

[4] Among others, we can refer to https://numeum.fr/societe/vigeo-eiris and https://www.refinitiv.com/fr/sustainable-finance/esg-scores

4.3 Submissions

Among 28 teams registered to the shared task, a total of 8 teams submitted their systems results and 6 teams also submitted a paper to describe their method. The extended version of the shared task to ESG has gained more attention from private institutions including Rakuten, Trading Central, Tata Consultancy Services, Fidelity Investments, Fidelity Brokerage Services LLC. (See Table 3 for more details).

Team name	Institutions
FORMICA	Jozef Stefan Institute & Queen Mary University of London
JETSONS	Fidelity Brokerage Services LLC.
KAKA	Rakuten Group
LIPI	Fidelity Investments
TCSTWIM	Tata Consultancy Services
Trading Central Labs	Trading Central Labs - La Rochelle

Table 3: Participant teams

FORMICA The FORMICA team proposes a system for the subtask2. The authors make use of knowledge background approach for the prediction of sustainable sentences, especially the embeddings model based on the knowledge derived from taxonomies, Tax2Vec, and an extended BERT model introducing the background knowledge, LinkBERT, to capture dependencies and knowledge that span across documents. The authors led experiments, first, using contextual or non contextual word features on BERT representations and LSA representations, second, using knowledge graph or taxonomy based features on Tax2Vec, TransE, DisMult and RotatE representations, finally using the joint representations of all the generated representations. The two submitted runs were generated based on the joint latent representations (first run) and using the result of the ensemble modeling methods from multiple models, LinkBERT, FinBERT and the joint SVD (second run). The second run slightly outperforms the first with 0.89% of accuracy in the testset while the fine-tuned LinkBERT achieved 0.96% of F1-score on the internal data split.

JETSONS The JETSONS team tackles both of the subtasks proposed by FinSim4-ESG. For the first subtask, the final submission was generated from the approach using the fine-tuned Sentence-BERT representations as encoder and the logistic regression classifier as decoder. We observe that the result of the classification varies from 0.89% to 0.61% on the ten-fold cross validation on the train set and on the testset, respectively. Their experiments show that the submitted approach outperforms the results of the similarity measuring either based on the pre-trained DistilBERT without fine-tuning or fine-tuned DistilBERT on the financial reports or the pre-trained Sentence-BERT without fine-tuning. For the second subtask, the fine-tuned RoBERTa shows the best performance with 93% of accuracy comparing to the results from BERT and T5[Raffel *et al.*, 2020] (Text-to-Text Transfer Transformer) models.

KAKA team The KAKA team tackles two subtasks leading several experiments based on the state-of-the art algorithms. For the subtask1, the authors propose two approaches: one with a classical Machine Learning model as our first baseline proposes but combining the tf-idf vectors with the custom Word2Vec and the other with a deep attention model using the custom Word2Vec model. They trained the word embeddings on an augmented data by adding the term-definition pair in the provided corpus by the organizer and also in the training and test data. The second approach slightly outperforms the classical approach on the test data while the first outperforms the deep learning approach on the validation data. For the subtask2, the authors led experiments based on different pre-trained Language models like BERT, RoBERTa, ALBERT, DistillBert and XLNet by fine-tuning them for the sustainable sentence classification. The fine-tuned RoBERTa model outperforms all the submitted systems with 94.63% of accuracy.

LIPI The LIPI team proposes the solutions to both of the subtasks. For the subtask1, the authors first propose an augmented terms dataset by adding definitions of each concept to make use of more contextual information. Then the pre-trained Sentence-BERT model was fine-tuned on the United Nations (UN)'s sustainable development goals[5] for the first run and the RoBERTa model for the second run while the Sentence-BERT fine-tuned on UN reports results the best performing score with 0.76% of accuracy. For the subtask2, the pre-trained FinBERT was fine-tuned for the first run and the pre-trained RoBERTa for the second run. We observe that the latter outperforms for the sentence classification task too on the testset with 0.93% of accuracy.

TCSWITM The TCSWITM team submitted the results for both of the subtasks. For the subtask1, the authors explore semantic similarity features inside BERT architecture by the way that they augment the obtained embeddings from the fine-tuned BERT model on the ESG related reports with Word2Vec, Cosine and Jaccard similarity features. Then they trained a logistic regression classifier on top of these representations also using PCA to handle the dimensionality issue. The experiments show that it improves the ESG terms prediction results with 0.82% of accuracy comparing to the result of the generic BERT model (0.76%) on their internal data split. For the subtask2, they introduce various lexical features for the sustainable sentence classification task like sentiment polarity, POS tags, NER tags, etc. Then they led various experiments based on different word and sentence embeddings including Word2Vec, GloVe, FastText, ELMo, InferSent, BERT, and ESG BERT and also trained several widely used classification methods including Logistic Regression, Gradient Boosting and XGBoost Classifier, gradually augmenting the models by adding the features one by one. The results show that the logistic regression classifier trained on top of the ESG BERT along with all the NLP features performs better than other setups with 0.87% of accuracy.

Trading Central Labs-LaRochelle The Trading Central Labs team tackles two subtasks of the shared task FinSim4-ESG. For the first one, the authors use a pre-trained Sentence-

[5]https://www.undp.org/sustainable-development-goals

BERT to embed the terms and then train a classifier on the train set to reach the top 1 of the subtask1 with 0.85% of accuracy. The authors consider all the terms of a same concept as paraphrases having similar semantic information so the trained model returns a high score in terms of similarity on two paraphrases. They propose a simple but effective way to combine Sentence-BERT and a logistic regression to classify terms without concepts. In the second subtask, for the final submission, based on the results of experiments on DistillBERT, BERT and RoBERTa, they use a pre-trained RoBERTa model with a feed forward layer to classify the sentences to reach the fourth best performing system with 0.93% of accuracy on the testset.

5 Results and Analysis

In Table 4, we ranked the results of the 12 system runs submitted by 6 teams and in Table 5 the results of the 14 system runs by 8 teams according to the metric described in the section 4.2, both including those of our baselines. The overall results of the subtask1 were obtained by combining those of Mean Rank and Accuracy and the Trading Central Labs-La Rochelle team's runs won first and second places for both metrics. For the subtask2, the KAKA team's second run won first place and CompLx team came second with the accuracy of 0.95 and 0.94%, respectively.

Team	Accuracy (%)	Mean Rank
Baseline_1	0.46	2.28
Baseline_2	0.74	1.52
JETSONS_1	0.61	1.97
KAKA_1	0.74	1.44
KAKA_2	0.75	1.54
LIPI_1	0.71	1.52
LIPI_2	0.70	1.67
TCSWITM_1	0.77	1.46
TCSWITM_2	0.78	1.45
TradingCentralLabs_1	0.83	1.26
TradingCentralLabs_2	**0.85**	**1.26**
vishleshak_1	0.68	1.61

Table 4: Mean Rank and Accuracy (listed alphabetically) for the subtask1: ESG Taxonomy Enrichment

All the participating teams commonly explored BERT models along with its variants to measure the semantic relatedness between terms and concepts. The fine-tuned models on the ESG corpus on a basis of BERT [Devlin *et al.*, 2019], Sentence-BERT [Reimers and Gurevych, 2019], DistilBERT [Sanh *et al.*, 2019], RoBERTa [Liu *et al.*, 2019], LinkBERT [Yasunaga *et al.*, 2022], FinBERT [Yang *et al.*, 2020], ALBERT [Lan *et al.*, 2019] are proposed by most of the participating systems either for the word representations in vector space or for the term/sentence classification task and the classical logistic regression model is trained for the classification task giving the most performing results.

5.1 Subtask1: ESG Taxonomy Enrichment

For the ESG taxonomy enrichment task, the data augmentation methods was introduced by KAKA and LIPI teams not only to enrich the data size but also to add more contextual information for each term using the definition related to the term and its concept. The LIPI team also used the ESG related UN's reports data, in addition to the data provided by the shared task, which is not yet widely explored by showing that it helps improve the result of ESG terms prediction. The fine-tuned Sentence-BERT model representations and a classical linear classification model like logistic regression commonly shows a high performance to predict the ESG term-concept.

Team name	Accuracy (%)
Baseline_1	0.50
Baseline_2	0.82
CompLx_1	0.94
FORMICA_1	0.88
FORMICA_2	0.89
JETSONS_1	0.93
KAKA_1	0.93
KAKA_2	**0.95**
LIPI_1	0.92
LIPI_2	0.93
TCSTWIM_1	0.87
TradingCentralLabs-LaRochelle_1	0.91
TradingCentralLabs-LaRochelle_2	0.93
vishleshak_1	0.91

Table 5: Accuracy (listed alphabetically) for the subtask2: Sustainability Prediction

5.2 Subtask2: Sustainability Prediction

The teams JETSONS, KAKA, LIPI and Trading Central show that the fine-tuned RoBERTa outperforms other models like the fine-tuned Sentence-BERT or FinBERT on the sustainable sentence classification task.

We observe that the evaluation results on the training set by the participant's internal data split tend to show an important gap comparing to the results on the testset even though the training and test sets have a high level of similarity. We also observe this between the sustainable and unsustainable sentences:

- Unsustainable: ***By transitioning*** *the gas network to bring hydrogen (and other gases such as biomethane) to homes and industries, it* ***can reduce*** *its carbon footprint.*
- Sustainable: *Together, these initiatives further* ***reduced*** *the carbon footprint of the Autolease portfolio.*

Some sentences in both classes require more contexts for a clear understanding in terms of sustainability. This issue was already taken into account at the sustainability data preparation, consequently, the sentences were selected by the way that it can be easily classifiable for the participants but the results analysis show that there still remain difficulties to classify into sustainable or unsustainable even by human.

6 Conclusions and Perspectives

The FinSim4-ESG proposed two subtasks: ESG Taxonomy Enrichment and Sustainability Prediction. Among the 8 participating teams, 6 teams submitted the systems runs to the subtask1 and all submitted to the subtask2. All of the system runs showed very promising results using state-of-art NLP and ML techniques and features. As the first edition about ESG Taxonomy and Sustainability prediction, the systems with the best performance achieved a good accuracy of 83%∼85% for the subtask1 and a high accuracy of 94%∼95% for the subtask2. All the participating systems largely exploited distributional methods for the similarity measures between terms and sentences, and for the classification task, and the results showed that using distributed and contextual features improve the performance of their systems. Especially, several experiments from the participating systems show that the fine-tuned RoBERTa on the ESG data outperforms other models like BERT, Sentence-BERT, FinBERT, LinkBERT and the linear classifier performs better than non linear classifiers for both subtasks. And the results confirm that the data augmentation helps improve the overall results as also shown in the results of the previous editions of the FinSim shared task.

The impact of AI technologies grows more and more in ESG related domains like ESG ratings for analyzing the sustainable activities of the companies, Green investments supporting activities aligned with environmentally friendly business and helping investors to hold green bonds, green ETFs, green funds or stock of the companies supporting green initiatives, ESG risk assessment, ESG databases, etc. and this requires a study on how to exploit a large scale of ESG related concepts and build a knowledge representation of those concepts. The EU Taxonomy was already released in the objectives of European Green Deal[6] but they needs to extend the scope of the concepts toward Social and Government topics. In this shared task, we elaborated and provided a first version of ESG Taxonomy taking into account the EU taxonomy along with the ESG criteria proposed by the well known ESG data providers like Refinitiv and Moody's. It will be possible to improve FinSim-ESG task by proposing to increase the coverage of ESG concepts and its terms as the proposed concepts are still limited to those observed in the corpus composed of a limited number of reports. Also, the current task is focused on a monolingual data processing. Knowing that ESG data analysis is gaining increasing global attention and has become an increasingly important part of the investment, every year, more companies publish their activities related to ESG topics in non financial reports in different languages from different countries. The majority of the ESG concepts are language-independent, so it will be interesting to extend the task to a multilingual data processing.

Acknowledgments

This shared task is fully supported by Fortia Financial Solutions. We thank all the participants for their motivations and constructive exchange.

References

[Armbrust *et al.*, 2020] Felix Armbrust, Henry Schäfer, and Roman Klinger. A computational analysis of financial and environmental narratives within financial reports and its value for investors. In *Proceedings of the 1st Joint Workshop on Financial Narrative Processing and MultiLing Financial Summarisation*, pages 181–194, Barcelona, Spain (Online), December 2020. COLING.

[Balakrishnan *et al.*, 2010] Ramji Balakrishnan, Xin Ying Qiu, and Padmini Srinivasan. On the predictive ability of narrative disclosures in annual reports. *European Journal of Operational Research*, 202(3):789–801, 2010.

[Bordea *et al.*, 2015] Georgeta Bordea, Paul Buitelaar, Stefano Faralli, and Roberto Navigli. SemEval-2015 task 17: Taxonomy extraction evaluation (TExEval). In *Proceedings of the 9th International Workshop on Semantic Evaluation (SemEval 2015)*, pages 902–910, Denver, Colorado, June 2015. Association for Computational Linguistics.

[Bordea *et al.*, 2016] Georgeta Bordea, Els Lefever, and Paul Buitelaar. SemEval-2016 task 13: Taxonomy extraction evaluation (TExEval-2). In *Proceedings of the 10th International Workshop on Semantic Evaluation (SemEval-2016)*, pages 1081–1091, San Diego, California, June 2016. Association for Computational Linguistics.

[Camacho-Collados *et al.*, 2018] Jose Camacho-Collados, Claudio Delli Bovi, Luis Espinosa-Anke, Sergio Oramas, Tommaso Pasini, Enrico Santus, Vered Shwartz, Roberto Navigli, , and Horacio Saggion. Semeval-2018 task 9: Hypernym discovery. In *Proceedings of the 12th International Workshop on Semantic Evaluation (SemEval-2018)*, New Orleans, LA, United States, 2018.

[Devlin *et al.*, 2019] Jacob Devlin, Ming-Wei Chang, Kenton Lee, and Kristina Toutanova. BERT: Pre-training of deep bidirectional transformers for language understanding. In *Proceedings of the 2019 Conference of the North American Chapter of the Association for Computational Linguistics: Human Language Technologies, Volume 1 (Long and Short Papers)*, pages 4171–4186, Minneapolis, Minnesota, June 2019. Association for Computational Linguistics.

[Fauconnier and Kamel, 2015] Jean-Philippe Fauconnier and Mouna Kamel. Discovering hypernymy relations using text layout. In *Proceedings of the Fourth Joint Conference on Lexical and Computational Semantics*, pages 249–258, Denver, Colorado, June 2015. Association for Computational Linguistics.

[Glavaš *et al.*, 2020] Goran Glavaš, Ivan Vulić, Anna Korhonen, and Simone Paolo Ponzetto. SemEval-2020 task 2: Predicting multilingual and cross-lingual (graded) lexical entailment. In *Proceedings of the Fourteenth Workshop on Semantic Evaluation*, Barcelona (online), December 2020.

[Guo *et al.*, 2020] Tian Guo, Nicolas Jamet, Valentin Betrix, Louis-Alexandre Piquet, and Emmanuel Hauptmann. Esg2risk: A deep learning framework from esg news to stock volatility prediction, 2020.

[Hauer *et al.*, 2020] Bradley Hauer, Amir Ahmad Habibi, Yixing Luan, Arnob Mallik, and Grzegorz Kondrak. UAlberta at SemEval-2020 task 2: Using translations to predict cross-lingual entailment. In *Proceedings of the Four-*

[6]https://ec.europa.eu/info/strategy/priorities-2019-2024/european-green-deal_en

teenth Workshop on Semantic Evaluation, pages 263–269, Barcelona (online), December 2020. International Committee for Computational Linguistics.

[Jurgens and Pilehvar, 2016] David Jurgens and Mohammad Taher Pilehvar. SemEval-2016 task 14: Semantic taxonomy enrichment. In *Proceedings of the 10th International Workshop on Semantic Evaluation (SemEval-2016)*, pages 1092–1102, San Diego, California, June 2016. Association for Computational Linguistics.

[Kang *et al.*, 2021] Juyeon Kang, Ismail El Maarouf, Sandra Bellato, and Mei Gan. FinSim-3: The 3rd shared task on learning semantic similarities for the financial domain. In *Proceedings of the Third Workshop on Financial Technology and Natural Language Processing*, pages 31–35, Online, 19 August 2021.

[Kovács *et al.*, 2020] Ádám Kovács, Kinga Gémes, Andras Kornai, and Gábor Recski. BMEAUT at SemEval-2020 task 2: Lexical entailment with semantic graphs. In *Proceedings of the Fourteenth Workshop on Semantic Evaluation*, pages 135–141, Barcelona (online), December 2020. International Committee for Computational Linguistics.

[Lan *et al.*, 2019] Zhenzhong Lan, Mingda Chen, Sebastian Goodman, Kevin Gimpel, Piyush Sharma, and Radu Soricut. Albert: A lite bert for self-supervised learning of language representations, 2019.

[Liu *et al.*, 2019] Yinhan Liu, Myle Ott, Naman Goyal, Jingfei Du, Mandar Joshi, Danqi Chen, Omer Levy, Mike Lewis, Luke Zettlemoyer, and Veselin Stoyanov. Roberta: A robustly optimized bert pretraining approach, 2019.

[Luccioni *et al.*, 2020] Alexandra Luccioni, Emily Baylor, and Nicolas Duchene. Analyzing sustainability reports using natural language processing. *CoRR*, abs/2011.08073, 2020.

[Maarouf *et al.*, 2020] Ismail El Maarouf, Youness Mansar, Virginie Mouilleron, and Dialekti Valsamou-Stanislawski. The FinSim 2020 shared task: Learning semantic representations for the financial domain. In *Proceedings of the Second Workshop on Financial Technology and Natural Language Processing*, pages 81–86, Kyoto, Japan, 5 January 2020.

[Martel and Zouaq, 2021] Félix Martel and Amal Zouaq. Taxonomy extraction using knowledge graph embeddings and hierarchical clustering. In *Proceedings of the 36th Annual ACM Symposium on Applied Computing*, SAC '21, page 836–844, New York, NY, USA, 2021. Association for Computing Machinery.

[Matthew Purver and Pollak, 2022] Riste Ichev Igor Lončarski Katarina Sitar Šuštar Aljoša Valentinčič Matthew Purver, Matej Martinc and Senja Pollak. Tracking changes in esg representation: Initial investigations in uk annual reports. In *Proceedings of the LREC Workshop on Corporate Social Responsibility*, 2022.

[Mehra *et al.*, 2022] Srishti Mehra, Robert Louka, and Yixun Zhang. ESGBERT: Language model to help with classification tasks related to companies' environmental, social, and governance practices. In *Embedded Systems and Applications*. Academy and Industry Research Collaboration Center (AIRCC), mar 2022.

[Mukherjee, 2020] Mukut Mukherjee. Esg-bert: Nlp meets sustainable investing. https://towardsdatascience.com/nlp-meets-sustainable-investing-d0542b3c264b, 2020.

[Raffel *et al.*, 2020] Colin Raffel, Noam Shazeer, Adam Roberts, Katherine Lee, Sharan Narang, Michael Matena, Yanqi Zhou, Wei Li, and Peter J. Liu. Exploring the limits of transfer learning with a unified text-to-text transformer. *Journal of Machine Learning Research*, 21(140):1–67, 2020.

[Reimers and Gurevych, 2019] Nils Reimers and Iryna Gurevych. Sentence-bert: Sentence embeddings using siamese bert-networks, 2019.

[Sanh *et al.*, 2019] Victor Sanh, Lysandre Debut, Julien Chaumond, and Thomas Wolf. Distilbert, a distilled version of bert: smaller, faster, cheaper and lighter, 2019.

[Sarkar *et al.*, 2018] Rajdeep Sarkar, John P. McCrae, and Paul Buitelaar. A supervised approach to taxonomy extraction using word embeddings. In *Proceedings of the Eleventh International Conference on Language Resources and Evaluation (LREC 2018)*, Miyazaki, Japan, May 2018. European Language Resources Association (ELRA).

[Shwartz *et al.*, 2016] Vered Shwartz, Yoav Goldberg, and Ido Dagan. Improving hypernymy detection with an integrated path-based and distributional method. In *Proceedings of the 54th Annual Meeting of the Association for Computational Linguistics (Volume 1: Long Papers)*, pages 2389–2398, Berlin, Germany, August 2016. Association for Computational Linguistics.

[Sokolov *et al.*, 2021] Alik Sokolov, Jonathan Mostovoy, Jack Jie Ding, and Luis A. Seco. Building machine learning systems for automated esg scoring. 2021.

[Wang *et al.*, 2017] Chengyu Wang, Xiaofeng He, and Aoying Zhou. A short survey on taxonomy learning from text corpora: Issues, resources and recent advances. In *Proceedings of the 2017 Conference on Empirical Methods in Natural Language Processing*, pages 1190–1203, Copenhagen, Denmark, September 2017. Association for Computational Linguistics.

[Wang *et al.*, 2020] Shike Wang, Yuchen Fan, Xiangying Luo, and Dong Yu. SHIKEBLCU at SemEval-2020 task 2: An external knowledge-enhanced matrix for multilingual and cross-lingual lexical entailment. In *Proceedings of the Fourteenth Workshop on Semantic Evaluation*, pages 255–262, Barcelona (online), December 2020. International Committee for Computational Linguistics.

[Yang *et al.*, 2020] Yi Yang, Mark Christopher Siy UY, and Allen Huang. FinBERT: A Pretrained Language Model for Financial Communications. *arXiv e-prints*, page arXiv:2006.08097, June 2020.

[Yasunaga *et al.*, 2022] Michihiro Yasunaga, Jure Leskovec, and Percy Liang. Linkbert: Pretraining language models with document links, 2022.

Using contextual sentence analysis models to recognize ESG concepts

Elvys Linhares Pontes and **Mohamed Benjannet**
Trading Central Labs, Trading Central, Paris, France
{elvys.linharespontes,mohamed.benjannet}@tradingcentral.com

Jose G. Moreno
IRIT, UMR 5505 CNRS, University of Toulouse
Toulouse, France
jose.moreno@irit.fr

Antoine Doucet
L3i, La Rochelle Université
La Rochelle, France
antoine.doucet@univ-lr.fr

Abstract

This paper summarizes the joint participation of the Trading Central Labs and the L3i laboratory of the University of La Rochelle on both sub-tasks of the *Shared Task FinSim-4* evaluation campaign. The first sub-task aims to enrich the 'Fortia ESG taxonomy' with new lexicon entries while the second one aims to classify sentences to either 'sustainable' or 'unsustainable' with respect to ESG (Environment, Social and Governance) related factors. For the first sub-task, we proposed a model based on pre-trained Sentence-BERT models to project sentences and concepts in a common space in order to better represent ESG concepts. The official task results show that our system yields a significant performance improvement compared to the baseline and outperforms all other submissions on the first sub-task. For the second sub-task, we combine the RoBERTa model with a feed-forward multi-layer perceptron in order to extract the context of sentences and classify them. Our model achieved high accuracy scores (over 92%) and was ranked among the top 5 systems.

1 Introduction

Financial markets and investors can support the transition to a more sustainable economy by promoting investments in companies complying to ESG (Environment, Social and Governance) rules. Today there is growing interest among investors in the performances of firms in terms of sustainability. Therefore, the automatic identification and extraction of relevant information regarding companies' strategy in terms of ESG is important. The use of NLP (Natural Language Processing) methods adapted to the field of finance and ESG could help identify and process related information.

Taxonomies are important NLP resources, especially for semantic analysis tasks and similarity measures(Vijaymeena and Kavitha, 2016; Bordea et al., 2016). In this context, the FinSim4-ESG Shared Task proposed the tasks of enrichment of ESG taxonomy and sentences classification. FinSim-4 is the fourth edition of a set of evaluation campaigns that aggregate efforts on text-based needs for the Financial domain (Maarouf et al., 2020; Mansar et al., 2021; Kang et al., 2021). This latest edition is particularly challenging due to the continuously evolving nature of terminology in the domain-specific language of the ESG which leads to a poor generalization of pre-trained word and sentence embeddings.

Several studies addressed the problem of taxonomy generation for different domains (Shen et al., 2020a; Karamanolakis et al., 2020). Deep learning based embedding networks, such as BERT (Devlin et al., 2018) have proven to be efficient for many NLP tasks. Malaviya *et al.* (2020) used BERT for knowledge base completion and showed that BERT performs well for this task. Liu *et al.* (2020) used BERT to complete an ontology by inserting a new concept with the right relation. Kalyan and Sangeetha (2021) used sentence BERT (Reimers and Gurevych, 2019) to measure semantic relatedness in biomedical concepts and showed that sentence BERT outperforms corresponding BERT models. Shen *et al.* (2020b) used sentence BERT to build a knowledge graph for the biomedical domain and showed that it obtains the best results.

For the Shared Task FinSim-4, we proposed several strategies based on BERT language models. For the first sub-task, we proposed a model based on pre-trained Sentence-BERT models to project sentences and concepts in a common space in order to better represent ESG concepts. For the second sub-task, we combined the RoBERTa model with a feed-forward multi-layer perceptron to extract the context of sentences and classify them. Official results of our participation show the effectiveness of our models over the Shared Task FinSim-4 benchmark. In terms of accuracy, our best runs respectively ranked 1st and 4th for the sub-tasks 1 and 2

Proceedings of the Fourth Workshop on Financial Technology and Natural Language Processing (FinNLP), pages 218 - 223
December 8, 2022

with scores 0.848 and 0.927, respectively.

The remainder of this paper is organized as follows. In Section 2, we present the shared task FinSim-4 and the datasets for both sub-tasks. Our proposed models are detailed in Section 3. The setup and official results are described in Section 4. Finally, Section 5 concludes this paper.

2 Shared Task FinSim-4

The FinSim 2022 shared task aims to spark interest from communities in NLP, ML/AI, Knowledge Engineering and Financial document processing. Going beyond the mere representation of words is a key step to industrial applications that make use of natural language processing. The 2022 edition proposes two sub-tasks.

2.1 Sub-task 1: ESG taxonomy extension

The first sub-task aims to extend the 'Fortia ESG taxonomy' provided by the organizers. This taxonomy was built based on different financial data providers' taxonomies as well as several sustainability and annual reports. It has twenty five different ESG concepts that belong to the ESG, split as: environment, social or governance. The organizers provide a training set which consists of terms belonging to each concept. This training set is unbalanced as one can observe in Table 1 where one can find the number of terms for each concept in the train set.

Participants were asked to complete this taxonomy to cover the rest of the terms of the original 'Fortia ESG taxonomy'. For example, given a set of terms related to the concept 'Waste management' (e.g. Hazardous Waste, Waste Reduction Initiatives), participating systems had to automatically assign to it all other adequate terms.

Concepts	#terms
Audit Oversight	7
Biodiversity	29
Board Independence	2
Board Make-Up	37
Carbon factor	19
circular economy	47
Community	27
Emissions	39
Employee development	22
Employee engagement	23
Energy efficiency and renewable energy	59
Executive compensation	32
Future of work	18
Human Rights	10
Injury frequency rate	2
Injury frequency rate for subcontracted labour	35
Product Responsibility	51
Recruiting and retaining employees (incl. work-life balance)	11
Share capital	2
Shareholder rights	38
Sustainable Food & Agriculture	54
Sustainable Transport	46
Waste management	16
Water & waste-water management	21

Table 1: Dataset description for the ESG taxonomy extension sub-task.

2.2 Sub-task 2: Sustainability classification

The second sub-task aims to automatically classify sentences into sustainable or unsustainable sentences. A sentence is considered as sustainable if it semantically mentions the Environmental or Social or Governance related factors as defined in the Fortia ESG taxonomy. Table 2 summarizes the training data provided by the organizers.

Classes	#sentences
Sustainable	1223
Unsustainable	1042

Table 2: Dataset description for the sustainability sub-task.

3 Proposed strategies

3.1 Sub-task 1: ESG taxonomy extension

Semantic text similarity is an important task in natural language processing applications such as information retrieval, classification, extraction, question answering and plagiarism detection. This task consists in measuring the degree of similarity between two texts and to determine whether how semantically close they are (from completely independent to fully equivalent). In our case, the terms of a same concept are considered semantically equivalent. Siamese models have been shown to be effective on the semantic analysis of sentences (Linhares Pontes et al., 2018; Reimers and Gurevych, 2019).

Our model is based on Sentence-BERT (SBERT) (Reimers and Gurevych, 2019), a modifi-

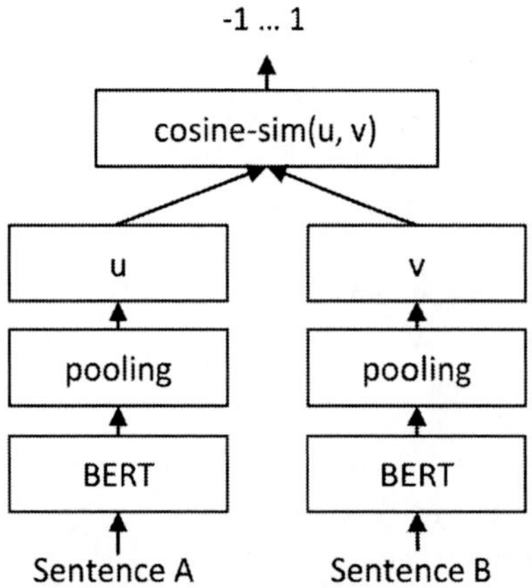

Figure 1: Sentence transformer architecture at inference to compute semantic similarity scores between two sentences.

cation of the pre-trained BERT network that uses siamese and triplet network structures to derive semantically meaningful sentence embeddings that can be compared using cosine-similarity (Figure 1). This model is trained on a parallel dataset where two paraphrases or similar semantic sentences have high cosine similarity.

We consider all terms about a concept as paraphrases because they share the same semantic information. For instance, the terms 'carbon footprint' and 'carbon data' should have similar sentence representation because they share the same concept 'carbon factor'; meanwhile, the terms 'Water Risk Assessment' and 'Transition to a circular economy' do not share the same concept and, consequently, their representations should have different sentence representation.

With the SBERT model, we project all terms on the same dimensional space and then, we train our logistic regression model[1] to analyze and classify them to their corresponding concept classes.

3.2 Sub-task 2: Sustainability classification

For this sub-task, we combine a BERT-based language model (Liu et al., 2019) with a feed-forward multi-layer perceptron to extract the context of sentences and classify them into 'sustainable' or 'unsustainable'. The architecture of our model is described in Figure 2.

We took the representation of the [CLS] token at the last layer of these models and we added a feed-forward layer to classify a input sentence as '*sustainable*' or '*unsustainable*'.

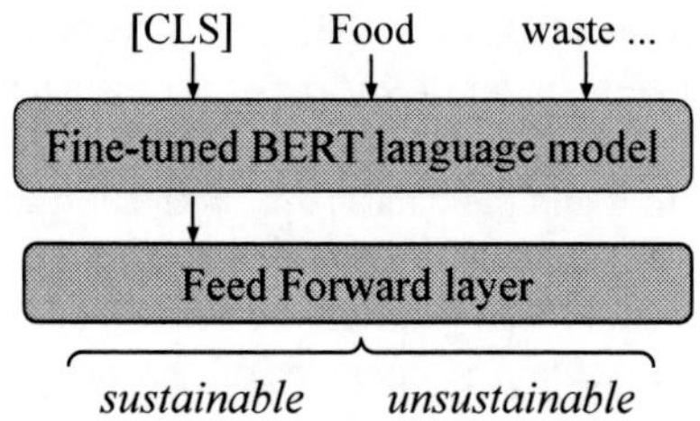

Figure 2: Architecture model for the sustainability classification task.

Sub-task	#Training	#Dev
ESG taxonomy extension	452	195
Sustainability classification	1585	680

Table 3: Details of the split of the 'Fortia ESG taxonomy' dataset to set our meta-parameters.

4 Experimental setup and evaluation

4.1 Evaluation metrics

All runs were ranked based on mean rank and accuracy for the first sub-task and only accuracy for the second sub-task. The mean rank is the average of the ranks for all observations within each sample.

Accuracy determines how close the candidates' predictions are to their true labels:

$$accuracy = \frac{1}{n_{samples}} \sum_{i=1}^{n_{samples}} 1(\hat{y}_i = y_i), \quad (1)$$

where $\hat{y}_i$ is the predicted value of the i-th sample and y_i is the corresponding true value.

4.2 Experimental evaluation

In order to select the best pre-trained models for each sub-task, we split the training datasets into 70% training and 30% for development. Table 3 shows the number of examples in the resulting training and development split for our analysis.

For the first sub-task, we selected the sentence BERT models: '*bert-base-nli-mean-tokens*'[2], '*all-roberta-large-v1*'[3], and '*paraphrase-mpnet-base-v2*'[4]. The first and second pre-trained SBERT

[1] https://scikit-learn.org/stable/modules/generated/sklearn.linear_model.LogisticRegression.html

[2] https://huggingface.co/sentence-transformers/bert-base-nli-mean-tokens

[3] https://huggingface.co/sentence-transformers/all-roberta-large-v1

[4] https://huggingface.co/sentence-transformers/paraphrase-mpnet-base-v2

SBERT model	Mean rank	Accuracy
bert-base-nli-mean-tokens	1.502	0.764
all-roberta-large-v1	1.461	0.779
paraphrase-mpnet-base-v2	**1.349**	**0.810**

Table 4: Results of our approach (Section 3.1) using different SBERT models for the first sub-task.

BERT model	Accuracy
distilbert-base-uncased	0.906
bert-base-uncased	0.921
roberta-base	**0.922**

Table 5: Results of our approach (Section 3.2) using different BERT-based language models for the second sub-task.

models are based on the well-know BERT-based language models (BERT and RoBERTa language models, respectively). The third pre-trained model was trained on the paraphrase dataset where two paraphrases have close representation. Table 4 shows the results for each pre-trained model. The '*paraphrase-mpnet-base-v2*' achieved the best results for both metrics. We assume that the analysis of paraphrases is similar to the analysis of terms that share the same concept, which allowed this model to outperform the other models.

For the second sub-task, we selected the BERT language models: DistilBERT (Sanh et al., 2019), BERT, and RoBERTa. RoBERTa (Robustly Optimized BERT Pre-training Approach) is an extension of BERT with changes to the pre-training procedure (Liu et al., 2019). They trained their model with bigger batches and over more data with long sentences. They also removed the next sentence prediction objective and dynamically changed the masking pattern applied to the training data. In this case, the RoBERTa language model outperformed the other models (Table 5).

4.3 Official results

We submitted two runs for ESG taxonomy extension. The first run used the approach described in Section 3.1 to train our model on the training data (Fortia ESG taxonomy). For the second run, we extended the Fortia ESG taxonomy with our in-house ESG taxonomy[5] and we used the same procedure to train the model. Our ESG taxonomy consists of a total of 65 terms spread across 22 concepts. For both runs, we used the pre-trained SBERT model '*paraphrase-mpnet-base-v2*'.

[5]No terms from our ESG taxonomy appear in the test data set published by the organizers.

Team name	Mean rank	Accuracy
kaka_1	1.441	0.745
kaka_2	1.670	0.662
kaka_3	1.545	0.752
JETSONS_1	1.972	0.607
LIPI_subtask1_1	1.517	0.710
LIPI_subtask1_2	1.669	0.703
TCSWITM_1	1.462	0.772
TCSWITM_2	1.448	0.779
vishleshak_task1	1.614	0.683
Baseline1	2.276	0.462
Baseline2	1.524	0.745
ours_wo_extended_data	1.262	0.834
ours_with_extended_data	**1.255**	**0.848**

Table 6: Official results for the first sub-task. Our approaches are listed at the bottom of the table. The best results are in bold. Our model *ours_wo_extended_data* was trained on the original training data provided by the organizers and the version *ours_with_extended_data* was trained on the original data set combined with our taxonomy.

Official results for the first sub-task are listed in Table 6. Both of our runs achieved the best results for mean rank and accuracy. In fact, our siamese model provided a better semantic representation of terms and outperformed the other approaches. The extension of the training data with our taxonomy enabled our model to better analyze the context of terms and their corresponding concepts and, consequently, improved the accuracy of 0.014 points.

We also submitted two runs for the second sub-task. The first run follows the same idea described in Section 3.1 to represent the sentences by using SBERT. Then, the logistic regression classifies these sentence representations into only two classes: '*sustainable*' and '*unsustainable*'. The second run uses the deep-learning model described in Section 3.2. Our model uses the pre-trained RoBERTa language model and two feed-forward layers to classify a sentence into '*sustainable*' or '*unsustainable*'.

Official results for the second sub-task are listed in Table 7. Our runs achieved the fourth best result. The combination of fine-tuned RoBERTa language model and feed-forward layers outperformed both baselines as well as our run with SBERT and logis-

Team name	Accuracy
kaka_4	0.927
kaka_2	**0.946**
CompLx_1	0.936
FORMICA2_1	0.883
FORMICA2_2	0.888
LIPI_1	0.922
LIPI_2	0.932
TCSWITM_1	0.873
vishleshak_task2	0.912
JETSONS_1	0.927
Baseline1	0.497
Baseline2	0.819
ours_sbert_logistic_regression	0.907
ours_roberta_with_ffnn	0.927

Table 7: Official results for the second sub-task. Our approaches are listed at the bottom of the table. The best results are in bold.

tic regression. Our models performed well (over 92% accuracy) and was ranked among the top 5 systems (0.19 points below the best-performing system).

5 Conclusion

This paper described the joint effort of the L3i laboratory of the University of La Rochelle and the Trading Central Labs in the *Shared Task FinSim-4* evaluation campaign for the task of ESG in financial documents. For this task, we developed BERT-based models. Our model based on siamese sentence analysis achieved the best results for the first sub-task. For the second sub-task, our approach based on the RoBERTa model got the fourth position.

Acknowledgments

This work has been partially supported by the TERMITRAD (2020-2019-8510010) project funded by the Nouvelle-Aquitaine Region, France.

References

Georgeta Bordea, Els Lefever, and Paul Buitelaar. 2016. Semeval-2016 task 13: Taxonomy extraction evaluation (texeval-2). In *Proceedings of the 10th international workshop on semantic evaluation (semeval-2016)*, pages 1081–1091.

Jacob Devlin, Ming-Wei Chang, Kenton Lee, and Kristina Toutanova. 2018. Bert: Pre-training of deep bidirectional transformers for language understanding. *arXiv preprint arXiv:1810.04805*.

Katikapalli Subramanyam Kalyan and Sivanesan Sangeetha. 2021. A hybrid approach to measure semantic relatedness in biomedical concepts. *arXiv preprint arXiv:2101.10196*.

Juyeon Kang, Ismail El Maarouf, Sandra Bellato, and Mei Gan. 2021. FinSim-3: The 3rd shared task on learning semantic similarities for the financial domain. In *Proceedings of the Third Workshop on Financial Technology and Natural Language Processing*, pages 31–35, Online. -.

Giannis Karamanolakis, Jun Ma, and Xin Luna Dong. 2020. Txtract: Taxonomy-aware knowledge extraction for thousands of product categories. *arXiv preprint arXiv:2004.13852*.

Elvys Linhares Pontes, Stéphane Huet, Andréa Carneiro Linhares, and Juan-Manuel Torres-Moreno. 2018. Predicting the semantic textual similarity with Siamese CNN and LSTM. In *Actes de la Conférence TALN. Volume 1 - Articles longs, articles courts de TALN*, pages 311–320, Rennes, France. ATALA.

Hao Liu, Yehoshua Perl, and James Geller. 2020. Concept placement using bert trained by transforming and summarizing biomedical ontology structure. *Journal of Biomedical Informatics*, 112:103607.

Yinhan Liu, Myle Ott, Naman Goyal, Jingfei Du, Mandar Joshi, Danqi Chen, Omer Levy, Mike Lewis, Luke Zettlemoyer, and Veselin Stoyanov. 2019. Roberta: A robustly optimized bert pretraining approach. Cite arxiv:1907.11692.

Ismail El Maarouf, Youness Mansar, Virginie Mouilleron, and Dialekti Valsamou-Stanislawski. 2020. The FinSim 2020 shared task: Learning semantic representations for the financial domain. In *Proceedings of the Second Workshop on Financial Technology and Natural Language Processing*, pages 81–86, Kyoto, Japan. -.

Chaitanya Malaviya, Chandra Bhagavatula, Antoine Bosselut, and Yejin Choi. 2020. Commonsense knowledge base completion with structural and semantic context. In *Proceedings of the AAAI conference on artificial intelligence*, volume 34, pages 2925–2933.

Youness Mansar, Juyeon Kang, and Ismail El Maarouf. 2021. The finsim-2 2021 shared task: Learning semantic similarities for the financial domain. WWW '21, page 288–292, New York, NY, USA. Association for Computing Machinery.

Nils Reimers and Iryna Gurevych. 2019. Sentence-bert: Sentence embeddings using siamese bert-networks. In *Proceedings of the 2019 Conference on Empirical Methods in Natural Language Processing*. Association for Computational Linguistics.

Victor Sanh, Lysandre Debut, Julien Chaumond, and Thomas Wolf. 2019. Distilbert, a distilled version of bert: smaller, faster, cheaper and lighter.

Jiaming Shen, Zhihong Shen, Chenyan Xiong, Chi Wang, Kuansan Wang, and Jiawei Han. 2020a. Taxoexpan: Self-supervised taxonomy expansion with position-enhanced graph neural network. In *Proceedings of The Web Conference 2020*, pages 486–497.

Si Shen, Xiao Liu, Hao Sun, and Dongbbo Wang. 2020b. Biomedical knowledge discovery based on sentence-bert. *Proceedings of the Association for Information Science and Technology*, 57(1):e362.

MK Vijaymeena and K Kavitha. 2016. A survey on similarity measures in text mining. *Machine Learning and Applications: An International Journal*, 3(2):19–28.

Automatic Term and Sentence Classification Via Augmented Term and Pre-trained Language Model in ESG Taxonomy texts

Ke, Tian[1] , **ZePeng, Zhang**[2] , **Hua, Chen**[2]
[1]Rakuten Group, Inc, Japan
[2]School of Computer and Information Engineering, Jiangxi Normal University, China
tianke0711@gmail.com, gottenzzp@jxnu.edu.cn, hua.chen@jxnu.edu.cn

Abstract

In this paper, we present our solutions to the FinSim4 shared task which is co-located with the FinNLP workshop at IJCAI-2022. This new edition of FinSim4-ESG is extended to the "Environment, Social and Governance (ESG)" related issues in the financial domain. There are two sub-tasks in the FinSim4 shared task. The goal of sub-task1 is to develop a model to classify correctly a list of given terms from ESG taxonomy domain into the most relevant concepts. The aim of sub-task2 is to design a system that can automatically classify the ESG Taxonomy text sentences into sustainable or unsustainable class. We have developed several classifiers to automatically predict the concepts of terms with augmented terms and word vectors and classify sentences into sustainable or unsustainable label with pre-trained language models. The final result leaderboard shows that our proposed methods yield a significant performance improvement compared to the baseline which ranked 1st in the sub-task2 and 2rd (Mean Rank) in the sub-task1.

1 Introduction

Natural Language Processing (NLP) is a kind of computational techniques which processes and analyzes large volume of natural language data, such as document text. In the last decade, term frequency-inverse document frequency (tf-idf) [wikipedia,] word vector and word embedding such as word2vec [Mikolov *et al.*, 2013] and Glove [Jeffrey Pennington and Manning, 2014] are widely used in the NLP tasks which became the default standard features in many NLP tasks, such as text classification. Recently, transformer model which utilizes the mechanism of self-attention is considered as a breakthrough for NLP [Vaswani *et al.*, 2017] and computer vision field [Dosovitskiy *et al.*, 2020]. The transformers model has caused the paradigm shift in NLP domain such that pre-trained language models which are applied widely in NLP tasks. Pre-trained language model has been gained wide attention after BERT achieved state-of-the-art results on a variety of NLP tasks [Devlin *et al.*, 2018]. OpenAI GPT [Radford and Narasimhan, 2018], BERT [Devlin *et al.*, 2018], DistilBERT [Sanh *et al.*, 2019], RoBERTa [Liu *et al.*, 2019], XLNet [Yang *et al.*, 2019] and XLM [Lample and Conneau, 2019] are examples of pre-trained language model (PLM) that could be applied to a wide range of NLP tasks. In the finance domain, there is a large volume of document texts to be processed for analysing financial markets, investment support, trading and so on. One of tasks is to classify these document text sentences into proper classification. The word vectors and PLMs are implemented widely for text classification in the finance text field [Araci, 2019] [Tian and Peng, 2019b] [Tian and Peng, 2019a] [Tian and Chen, 2021]. Recently "Environment, Social and Governance (ESG)" related issues in the financial domain are gained more and more attention with the goal of building sustainable environment. The aim of the FinSim4 shared task [Organizer,]is to elaborate an ESG taxonomy (ESG related concepts representations) based on the document data like companies' annual reports, sustainability reports, environment reports, etc. and utilizes them to analyse how the economic activity complies with the taxonomy. There are two sub-tasks in the FinSim4 task. Regarding the sub-task1, there is a number of terms which are selected from ESG taxonomy texts. For example, the given terms: "low-carbon", "carbon footprint" et al., These terms are related to the "Carbon factor" concept. The goal of sub-task1 is to develop a model to classify correctly a list of given terms from ESG taxonomy domain into the most relevant concepts. Regarding the sub-task2, there are selected sentences texts from the sustainability reports and other documents about sustainable or unsustainable activities. The aim of sub-task2 is to design a system that can automatically classify the ESG Taxonomy text sentence into sustainable or unsustainable class.

As sub-task1, we make use of on-line data such as Wikipedia data to augment the financial terms with terms' definition to be term sentence. Moreover, we combine the given dataset composed of financial and non-financial reporting documents files with augmented terms' sentences to train word2vec with the context-free Word2vec model. The Logistic Regression and Deep Attention Model [Tian and Chen, 2021] by inputting word2vec and tf-idf vectors are implemented to predict the concepts of the test terms. As sub-task2, the Bert, Albert, Distil BERT, Roberta, XLNet are applied to this task. Based on the results of the experiments, the proposed models have achieved good performance for each task.

Section 2 describes the task data and the term augmenta-

Proceedings of the Fourth Workshop on Financial Technology and Natural Language Processing (FinNLP), pages 224 - 227
December 8, 2022 ©2022 Association for Computational Linguistics

Label	Num	Label	Num
Sustainable Transport	46	Biodiversity	29
Board Independence	27	Waste management	16
Energy efficiency and renewable energy	59	Community	27
Sustainable Food & Agriculture	54	Human Rights	10
circular economy	47	Carbon factor	19
Injury frequency rate for subcontracted labor	59	Share Capital	2
Injury frequency rate	35	Audit Oversight	7
Employee engagement	37	Board Make-Up	23
Employee development	22	Emissions	39
Product Responsibility	51	Future of work	18
Recruiting and retaining employees	11	Human Rights	10
Executive compensation	32	Shareholder rights	38

Table 1: The numbers of each label in training data

tion method. Section 3 describes our proposed methods for two tasks. Section 4 shows experimental configurations and discusses the results. Then, we conclude this paper in Section 5.

2 Data Description and Augmented Terms

As the sub-task1, the number of training and test set data are 647 and 145 respectively. There are 24 categories of concepts in the training data. The number of each concept in training data is listed as Table 1.

Based on the above table, the concept of "Energy efficiency and renewable energy" has the largest number of label data. Some concepts like the "Injury frequency rate"," SHARE CAPITAL" and "Board Independence" have just 2 label data. We found that some concepts are very similar, such as the "Injury frequency rate for subcontracted labor" and "Injury frequency rate" concepts, "Waste management and Water" and "waste-water management" concepts which have common words. Moreover, some terms are composed of a single word like "Strikes", "Contraceptives" terms which are not easy to understand the meaning of terms. We augment the terms with terms' definition in the training and test set data. The Wikipedia terms' definitions are utilized to describe the meaning of the terms. We take the "Recycle" as an example to describe how we augment the term with term's definition. The definition of "Recycling" in the Wikipedia is "Recycling is the process of converting waste materials into new materials and objects". We merge the term word "Recycle" and definition of "Recycling" with a space as a new sentence: "Recycle Recycling is the process of converting waste materials into new materials and objects". Some terms like "Tobacco 5% Revenues" which have intuitive meaning, we keep the term words as sentence without adding additional definition. Since the number of provided training and test

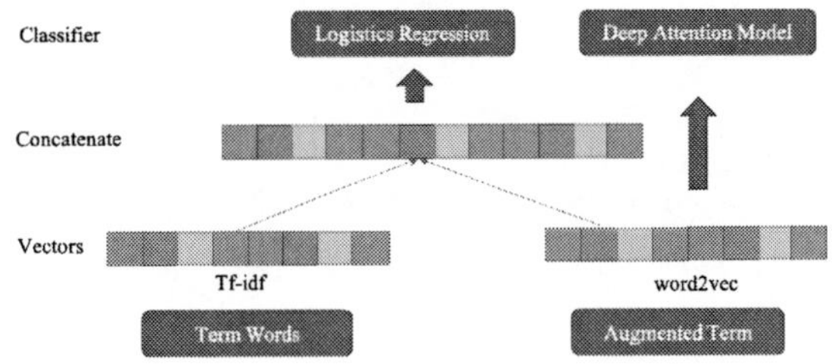

Figure 1: Structure of proposed method for sub-task1.

data is still limited for training a good word embedding. We combine the given dataset composed of financial and non-financial reporting documents files with augmented term sentences to train the word embedding. There are a total of about 196615 sentences for training word2vec. As the task 2, there are 2265 rows in the training data and 205 rows in the test data. The number of sustainable and unstainable sentences are 1223 and 1042 respectively.

3 Methods

3.1 TF-IDF Vector, Word Embedding for Sub-task1

As the task1, we mainly use the tf-idf vector and work2vec for creating features. The Logistics Regression and Deep Attention Model are applied for classifier. The overall structure of proposed method is shown in Figure 1.

We observed that some key words in term words are strongly related to concept category, for example, the "low-carbon", "carbon footprint" terms have "carbon" word which indicates the concept is "Carbon factor". The tf-idf is a kind of numerical statistics that could reflect how important a word is to a document in a collection or corpus [wikipedia,]. We extracted key word features for term words using the tf-idf vector. We trained the tf-idf vector with the scikit-learn library's TfidfVectorizer class, we set the 300 dimensions features for the tf-idf vector. We trained the 100 dimensions word2vec using the genism library with augmented term sentence and given financial and non-financial reporting pdf documents. All sentence texts are preprocessed with the following steps: removing stop words, deleting punctuation, and using word stemming to replace word in text. We have implemented two classifiers: Logistics Regression and Deep Attention Model. As the Deep Attention Model, the input vector is word2vec, as the logistics regression, the tf-idf vector and word2vec are concatenated as 400 dimensions for input vector features.

3.2 Pre-trained Language Models for Sub-task2

As sub-task2, we have implemented different PLM models: BERT, Roberta, Albert, DistillBert, and XLNet with related PLM's tokenizer. The sentence label classification has been fine-tuned by adding dropout, linear layer and Relu function after PLM's output as shown in the Figure 2.

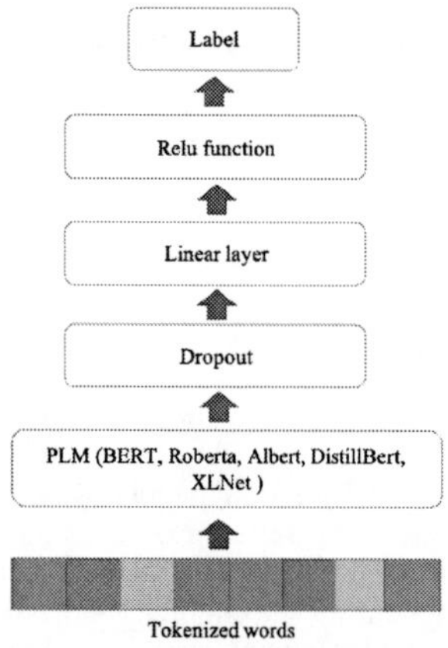

Figure 2: Structure of proposed method for sub-task2.

Input layer	Model	Accuracy
Word2vec trained via train & test data	Logistics Regression	73.84%
Word2vec trained via train & test data + tf-idf vector	Logistics Regression	81.53%
Word2vec trained via train & test data pdf documents + tf-idf vector	Logistics Regression	87.69%
Word2vec trained via train & test data pdf documents	Deep attention model	81.5315%

Table 2: Validation result of each model for sub-task1

4 EXPERIMENT AND RESULT

4.1 Experiment Design

In order to select the best classifier model in the training stage, the label data are split into train and valid data with ratio 9:1 for both two sub-tasks. In the training stage, we mainly test two models: Logistics Regression, Deep Attention Model for sub-task1. We have tested different vector combination for Logistics Regression and Deep Attention Model. As sub-task2, we have implemented the pre-trained models with hugging face library and fine tuning the model with adding linear layer. After the validation stage, the best performance models are selected to predict the test data for final submission.

Input layer	Model	Accuracy
Train & Valid data	BERT	92.1%
Train & Valid data	Roberta	94.0%
Train & Valid data	ALBert	92.29%
Train & Valid data	Distil Bert	91.7%
Train & Valid data	XLNet	93.6%

Table 3: Validation result of each model for sub-task2

Input layer	Model	Accuracy
Word2vec trained via train & test data + tf-idf vector	Logistics Regression	66.2%
Word2vec trained via train & test data pdf documents + tf-idf vector	Logistics Regression	74.48%
Word2vec trained via train & test data pdf documents	Deep Attention Model	75.17%

Table 4: Test result of each model for sub-task1

Input layer	Model	Accuracy
Train & Valid data	BERT	89.75%
Train & Valid data	Roberta	94.63%
Train & Valid data	Distil Bert	89.267%
Train & Valid data	XLNet	92.68%

Table 5: Test result of each model for sub-task2

4.2 Result and Discussion

The result for each model in the experiment is shown in the Table 2 and Table 3. In the validation stage, as sub-task1 we could find that the Logistics Regression based on word2vec and tf-idf vectors achieved better than other classifiers. As the test stage, we submitted 3 model prediction results for test terms. The final score is shown as Table 4 . It can conclude that the Deep Attention Model outperforms than other models in test stage although the accuracy of deep attention model is worse than Logistics Regression's result in the validation stage. As sub-task2, we have implemented different PLM, we found that the Roberta model is the best in the validation stage. In test leader board, Roberta model outperforms obviously better than other three models as shown in Table 5.

5 CONCLUSION

This paper mainly presents kaka team how to tackle the FinSim4 shared tasks. We approach the two tasks using different modes. As sub-task1, we implemented Logistics Regression and Deep Attention Model with different word vectors. As sub-task2, several PLM are implemented with fine tuning to classify the sentences into sustainable or unsustainable class. The experimented result show that our methods could effectively solve the goal of the two tasks. However, our method still needs to be improved to achieve better performance in the following direction. Firstly, it is better to do more parameter tuning in each model to improve the accuracy. Secondly, as sub-task1, there is significant gap between our score and the best result in the final test leaderboard, we could make more efforts in feature engineer like text similarity for models.

Acknowledgments

We would like to thank organizers for holding this shared task and also building the training data. This work is financially supported by the Jiangxi Double Thousand Plan-Long term young innovation project (grant nos.0299/09030022).

References

[Araci, 2019] Dogu Araci. Finbert: Financial sentiment analysis with pre-trained language models, 2019.

[Devlin *et al.*, 2018] Jacob Devlin, Ming-Wei Chang, Kenton Lee, and Kristina Toutanova. Bert: Pre-training of deep bidirectional transformers for language understanding, 2018.

[Dosovitskiy *et al.*, 2020] Alexey Dosovitskiy, Lucas Beyer, Alexander Kolesnikov, Dirk Weissenborn, Xiaohua Zhai, Thomas Unterthiner, Mostafa Dehghani, Matthias Minderer, Georg Heigold, Sylvain Gelly, Jakob Uszkoreit, and Neil Houlsby. An image is worth 16x16 words: Transformers for image recognition at scale, 2020.

[Jeffrey Pennington and Manning, 2014] Richard Socher Jeffrey Pennington and Christopher D. Manning. Glove: Global vectors for word representation. In *Proceedings of the 2014 Conference on Empirical Methods in Natural Language Processing (EMNLP)*, page 1532–1543, Doha, Qatar, October 2014. Association for Computational Linguistics.

[Lample and Conneau, 2019] Guillaume Lample and Alexis Conneau. Cross-lingual language model pretraining, 2019.

[Liu *et al.*, 2019] Yinhan Liu, Myle Ott, Naman Goyal, Jingfei Du, Mandar Joshi, Danqi Chen, Omer Levy, Mike Lewis, Luke Zettlemoyer, and Veselin Stoyanov. Roberta: A robustly optimized bert pretraining approach, 2019.

[Mikolov *et al.*, 2013] Tomas Mikolov, Ilya Sutskever, Kai Chen, Greg Corrado, and Jeffrey Dean. Distributed representations of words and phrases and their compositionality, 2013.

[Organizer,] FinSim4-ESG Organizer. Shared task finsim4-esg. https://sites.google.com/nlg.csie.ntu.edu.tw/finnlp-2022/shared-task-finsim4-esg?authuser=0.

[Radford and Narasimhan, 2018] Alec Radford and Karthik Narasimhan. Improving language understanding by generative pre-training. In *Technical report, OpenAI*, 2018.

[Sanh *et al.*, 2019] Victor Sanh, Lysandre Debut, Julien Chaumond, and Thomas Wolf. Distilbert, a distilled version of bert: smaller, faster, cheaper and lighter, 2019.

[Tian and Chen, 2021] Ke Tian and Hua Chen. aiai at the finsim-2 task: Finance domain terms automatic classification via word ontology and embedding. In *The 1st Workshop on Financial Technology on the Web (FinWeb) The Web Conference*, page 320–322, Ljubljana Slovenia, April 2021. Association for Computing Machinery.

[Tian and Peng, 2019a] Ke Tian and Zi Jun Peng. aiai at finnum task: Financial numeral tweets fine-grained classification using deep word and character embedding-based attention model. In *The 14th NTCIR Conference*, pages 198–202, Tokyo, Japan, June 2019.

[Tian and Peng, 2019b] Ke Tian and Zi Jun Peng. aiai at FinSBD task: Sentence boundary detection in noisy texts from financial documents using deep attention model. In *Proceedings of the First Workshop on Financial Technology and Natural Language Processing*, pages 88–92, Macao, China, August 2019.

[Vaswani *et al.*, 2017] Ashish Vaswani, Noam Shazeer, Niki Parmar, Jakob Uszkoreit, Llion Jones, Aidan N. Gomez, Lukasz Kaiser, and Illia Polosukhin. Attention is all you need, 2017.

[wikipedia,] wikipedia. tf-idf. https://en.wikipedia.org/wiki/Tf\OT1\textendashidf.

[Yang *et al.*, 2019] Zhilin Yang, Zihang Dai, Yiming Yang, Jaime Carbonell, Ruslan Salakhutdinov, and Quoc V. Le. Xlnet: Generalized autoregressive pretraining for language understanding, 2019.

Knowledge informed sustainability detection from short financial texts

Boshko Koloski[1,2] , **Syrielle Montariol**[1] , **Matthew Purver**[1,3] , **Senja Pollak**[1]
[1]Jožef Stefan Institute
[2]International Postgraduate School Jožef Stefan
[3]Queen Mary University of London
{boshko.koloski, senja.pollak}@ijs.com, m.purver@qmul.ac.uk

Abstract

Nowadays in the finance world, there is a global trend for responsible investing, linked with a growing need for developing automated methods for analysing Environmental, Social and Governance (ESG) related elements in financial texts. In this work we propose a solution to the FinSim4-ESG task, consisting in classifying sentences from financial reports as sustainable or unsustainable. We propose a novel knowledge-based latent heterogeneous representation that relies on knowledge from taxonomies, knowledge graphs and multiple contemporary document representations. We hypothesize that an approach based on a combination of knowledge and document representations can introduce significant improvement over conventional document representation approaches. We perform ensembling, both at the classifier level and at the representation level (late-fusion and early-fusion). The proposed approaches achieve competitive accuracy of 89% and are 5.85% behind the best score in the shared task.

1 Introduction

In this work we develop a *knowledge-backed* approach for the detection of **sustainability** on premises of a given short textual document (i.e. a sentence). More specifically, we propose a solution to the shared task of the FinSim4-ESG workshop, where the task is to classify a given sentence extracted from a company financial report as either sustainable or unsustainable.

Investors have ever-increased interest in the assessment of the **Environmental, Social and Governance** (ESG) criteria, as non-financial factors describing the company's position on social well-being [Nagy *et al.*, 2016]. ESG criteria cover a company's environmental impact (Environmental), their relationships with their community including employees, suppliers and customers (Social), and their leadership structures including executive pay, shareholder rights, audits and controls (Governance). These *ESG* factors are usually reported as a structured output in the companies annual reports. The companies reporting these factors have moved from only a dozen in the 1990s to more than 6000 in 2014 [Serafeim and Yoon, 2022]. In a study by [Amel-Zadeh and Serafeim, 2018] using survey data from mainstream investment organizations, the authors provide insights into why and how investors use reported ESG information and highlight that relevance to investment performance is the most frequent motivation, followed by client demand, product strategy, and then ethical considerations. Also social media impacted the way of interaction between companies, employees and potential customers. Publishing posts that reveal a certain way of operation that leads to company's miss-behaviour can have a wild response from the customers. Aula [2010] studied the impact of social media on the reputation risk and the ambient publicity. An instance of such event is the H&M's *thrash-gate* scandal - where a company producing and selling clothes was charged of damaging and disposing them as waste instead of reusing them. The story sparked a public outrage and a sever impact on the company. Recently [Guo *et al.*, 2020] highlighted the high correlation of the company's volatility on the market based on the ESG factors. These works showcase how social monitoring of posts can be a powerful asset in the way of achieving a more sustainable and environmentally friendly companies and market.

The field of natural language processing (NLP) has seen increased interest in ESG-related automated analysis. For example, [Mehra *et al.*, 2022] propose fine-tuning a generic BERT model [Devlin *et al.*, 2018] on ESG corpus (ESG-BERT), and use this model for detecting positive or negative change in companies stock values based on the related sections of their 10-Q filings. [Serafeim and Yoon, 2022] showed that ESG ratings can be used to predict market reactions to ESG news, particularly when there is disagreement amongst raters.

The remainder of this work is structured as follows: Section 2 describes the related work, Section 3 presents the dataset. Section 4 presents the proposed method, followed by the results in Section 5 and the final remarks and conclusions in Section 6.

2 Related work

In the FinSim4-ESG shared task, the goal is to classify a given sentence. as either sustainable or unsustainable. A sentence is defined as sustainable if it mentions any ESG factor from a dedicated ESG taxonomy, unsustainable otherwise. We treat this problem as **binary document classification**.

Proceedings of the Fourth Workshop on Financial Technology and Natural Language Processing (FinNLP), pages 228 - 234
December 8, 2022 ©2022 Association for Computational Linguistics

To be able to learn to classify the documents, initial approaches focused on lexicons or used machine learning techniques. For the financial domain, the collection of financial dictionaries by [Loughran and McDonald, 2011] has been widely used. Later, machine learning approaches have been proposed where models need a numerical representation of documents as input. Initial methods for document classification relied on hand-crafted features or on word frequency counts using various weighting schemes (e.g. TF-iDF [Sammut and Webb, 2010]). For example, [Qiu *et al.*, 2006] represent past annual reports with TF-IDF weighted word stems and various feature selection methods in order to predict Return On Equity (ROE) ratio classes with a linear SVM classifier. Weighted (TF, TF-IDF and logarithm damp weighting) *unigrams and bigrams* are used as features in a study by [Kogan *et al.*, 2009], where a support vector machine for regression (SVR) with linear kernel is trained to predict volatility of stock returns. [Balakrishnan *et al.*, 2010] use a linear SVM classifier to predict subsequent performance based on narrative parts of 10-K reports, based on both word-level and document-level features.

The democratisation of neural-networks introduced denser and more robust document representations, where the models from this paradigm are tasked to predict the next word or the missing word in the sequence. Contemporary state-of-the-art models such as BERT [Devlin *et al.*, 2018] are based on the transformer architecture [Vaswani *et al.*, 2017]. This model learns to generate document representations by being pre-trained on a big corpora from a general domain on the task of Masked Language Modeling, where a portion of the corpora is masked and the model is tasked to predict the words missing. The pre-trained model is then fine-tuned on data from a downstream task such as document classification; this is the transfer learning setting. In this study, we utilize two different variants of the BERT model family: FinBERT [Yang *et al.*, 2020], a model pre-trained on financial data, and LinkBERT [Yasunaga *et al.*, 2022], a model that modifies the initial BERT learning paradigm by taking into account background knowledge.

Taxonomies and ontologies are increasingly used for machine reasoning over the last few years. In our study we use Tax2Vec [Škrlj *et al.*, 2021] which is based on knowledge derived from *taxonomies*, aiming at improving short documents classification. Recently [Koloski *et al.*, 2022] studied the inclusion of *knowledge graphs* as banks of large factual knowledge. In their work, they have proposed heterogeneous representation ensembles that are based on knowledge graphs and contextual and non-contextual document representations. These proposed representations achieve nearly state-of-the art results on various tasks such as classification of short texts in the scope of the depression detection from short documents (social media posts) [Tavchioski *et al.*, 2022]. In the financial domain, automatic classification of a given list of financial terms against a domain ontology was proposed in the scope of FinSim2 [Mansar *et al.*, 2021].

In terms of ESG-related NLP, in addition to ESG-BERT by [Mehra *et al.*, 2022], [Armbrust *et al.*, 2020] studied the effect of the environmental performance of a company on the relationship between the company's disclosures and financial performance, [Sokolov *et al.*, 2021] focused on automated ESG scoring, while [Purver *et al.*, 2022 accepted] performed a diachronic analysis of ESG terms in UK annual reports.

3 Data

The shared task consisted of two phases: development of methods and official evaluation. In the first phase the organizers released *2265* training documents. For our internal evaluation purposes we created custom splits of the data into *1812 (80%)* documents for training, *226 (10%)* for development and *227 (10%)* for testing. We give description of the data in Table 1.

	Training data	Development data	Test data
sustainable	978 (54 %)	122 (54%)	123 (59 %)
unsustainable	834 (46 %)	104 (46 %)	104(41 %)
All	1812	226	227

Table 1: Data distribution in our training set.

In the second phase the organizers released a test set consisting of *205* documents.

4 Methodology

In this section, we present the different methods we used to generate sentence representations. We classify them into 3 categories: standalone, which are either knowledge or text-based, high-level, which are ensembles of representations and models learned on top of the standalone, and fine-tuned BERT models.

4.1 Standalone representations

We derive standalone representations via two different paradigms: textual-driven and knowledge-driven. The former rely only on either contextual or non-contextual word features while the latter is based on features obtained from some knowledge base or taxonomy.

Non-contextual textual features

Following [Koloski *et al.*, 2021], we extract *stylometric* and *latent semantic analysis* based features.

Stylometric features were built on top of word and character frequencies statistic descriptions - maximum and minimum word size, number of characters, number of words, number of vowels, etc.

Latent Semantic Analysis [Dumais *et al.*, 1988] was built on top of top-*n* word and n-grams features, TF-IDF weighted and represented in a latent space of *d* dimensions. We generate multiple combinations of n-gram features n and final dimension space d:

- LSA - *n=2500, d = 512*
- LSA_1 - *n=5000, d = 256*
- LSA_2 - *n=5000, d = 128*
- LSA_3 - *n=10000, d = 512*

Contextual textual features

For the contextual features we use *sentence-transformers* [Reimers and Gurevych, 2019] representations. The method is constructed on top of a *BERT* model, using BERT representations as input to a Siamese network that learns sentence representation as an intermediate task while it predicts sentence similarity.

Taxonomy-based representation

Leveraging background data in form of taxonomy has proven successful for classification of short documents. Here, we use the *Tax2Vec* model [Škrlj *et al.*, 2021][1] where the words from a given document are mapped to the terms of the WordNet taxonomy [Fellbaum, 1998]; then, a term-weighting heuristic is applied for the construction of the final taxonomy-enriched feature space. We use the default parameters *max-features = 10*, *heuristic = "pagerank"*, *disambiguation-window = 2* and *start-term-depth = 3*.

Knowledge graph based representation

Factual knowledge about concepts and relations linking those concepts together are stored in large knowledge bases. We consider a knowledge-backed document representation from the Wikidata5m [Vrandečić and Krötzsch, 2014] knowledge graph. We follow the approach proposed in [Koloski *et al.*, 2022] to extract and generate knowledge graph based document representations. To obtain the representations of the entities, we utilize three different embedding methods:

- TransE [Bordes *et al.*, 2013] - embedding method based on simple tensor factorization, capable of capturing the *antisymmetry*, *inversion*, *transitivity* and *composition* property of relations.
- DistMult [Yang *et al.*, 2014] - embedding method based on neural tensor factorization, capable of capturing the *symmetry* property of relations.
- RotatE [Sun *et al.*, 2019] - embedding method based on complex-space tensor factorization, capable of capturing the *symmetry*, *antisymmetry*, *inversion*, *transitivity*, and *composition* property of relations.

Classifier learning for the standalone representations

For the above representations, we consider learning Stochastic Gradient Descent classifier with a search on the hyper-parameters space proposed in the autoBOT, an auto-ML model [Škrlj *et al.*, 2021]: [2]

- loss : *hinge*, *log* or *modified-huber*
- class-weight : *balanced*
- penalty: *elasticnet*
- power-t $\in \{0.1, 0.2, 0.3, 0.4, 0.5\}$
- alpha $\in \{0.01, 0.005, 0.001, 0.0005, 0.0001, 0.00005\}$
- l1-ratio $\in \{0, 0.2, 0.4, 0.5, 0.6, 0.8, 1\}$
- Early-stopping criteria $\in \{8, 32\}$

[1]https://github.com/SkBlaz/tax2vec

[2]https://github.com/SkBlaz/autobot/blob/master/autoBOTLib/learning/hyperparameter_configurations.py

4.2 Fine-tuned BERT variants

We use several *state-of-the-art* BERT variants[3] and fine-tune them for our task.

- **FinSim** [Yang *et al.*, 2020] A contextually pre-trained BERT model on a large scale financial corpora with more than 4.9 billion tokens from corporate reports, conference call transcripts and financial analysts reports.
- **LinkBERT** [Yasunaga *et al.*, 2022] A knowledge-informed BERT model pre-trained on two joint self-supervised objectives: *MLM* (masked language modeling) and *DPR* (document relation prediction). In the former, a part of the input sentence is masked and the model is tasked to predict this masked token. In the latter, given two paragraphs, the model is tasked to predict whether they come from documents that are linked, whether they are subsequent in the same document of whether they are not related at all. During training, the model considers the graph of links between Wikipedia documents.

We train the models with a reproducible seed of *42* and a learning rate of $5e^{-5}$ for *10* epochs with *32* documents in a single batch.

4.3 Higher-level representations

Early-fusion

In order to explore the expressiveness of the joint representations, we construct two different approaches for fusion of representations:

Naive concatenation - We concatenate all the generated representations previously described in the *standalone representations* subsection.

Construction of latent spaces - We first concatenate all the generated representations, then we perform singular-value-decomposition **(SVD)** to obtain a new *joint latent space*. We reduce the proposed space to $d \in \{256, 512, 1024\}$ dimensions.

Late-fusion

Finally, we build ensembles on top of the standalone models (i.e. **late-fusion**). For the final ensemble we use the fine-tuned *FinSim*, *LinkBERT* and the *jointSVD* predictions. The final prediction is based on the majority vote (i.e. the class selected by at least two out of three methods).

5 Results

In this section we report the results of our internal evaluation (with our own splits) together with the final evaluation using the test set of the shared task.

5.1 Internal evaluation

We perform a thorough internal evaluation on our custom data split described in Section 3. We train all our models on the *train* split and optimize the hyper-parameters using the *development* split. For all models we report the evaluation with respect to the F1-score. We use the *test* split for the selection

[3]Implementation and checkpoints from the *huggingface* library.

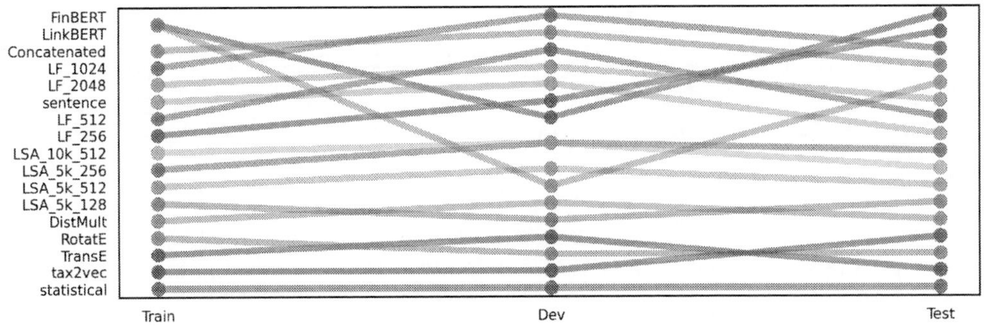

Figure 1: Ranking of the various document representations per split in the dataset (in the internal evaluation phase).

of the final models for submission. Among the knowledge-based methods, the **DistMult** method performs best, achieving a score of 70.91% on the test set, outscoring the *RotatE* by 3.09% and the *TransE* method by 6.83%. The *DistMult* method also outscores the *tax2vec* method by 0.62%.

Method	Dims	Train	Dev	Test
Knowledge based				
TransE	512	71.96	76.10	64.08
DistMult	512	*81.16*	*85.6*	*70.91*
RotatE	512	74.12	72.72	67.82
tax2vec	10	70.18	70.11	70.29
Text based				
statistical	10	59.23	60.38	55.05
LSA	512	89.20	92.43	*88.61*
LSA_1	256	85.53	90.16	85.95
LSA_2	128	83.42	85.59	85.36
LSA_3	512	89.78	*92.41*	88.10
sentence transformers	768	*95.32*	*93.98*	*91.20*
Fine-tuned BERTs				
LinkBERT	512	***100.0***	*92.85*	***95.59***
FinBERT	512	***100.0***	88.50	92.51
Higher level				
Concatenated	3737	*97.52*	96.0	93.49
Latent-fusion	256	93.54	93.0	*94.89*
Latent-fusion	512	94.89	94.69	92.11
Latent-fusion	1024	97.50	***96.32***	93.50
Latent-fusion	2048	95.57	94.40	92.24

Table 2: Internal evaluation of our models in terms of F1-score (%) on our internal data split. The *italic* scores represent the best-performing for each representation paradigm while the **bold** entries represent the best scores all-around.

As the *stylometric* features score the lowest, the next in line are the *LSA*-based features. They improve the scores by nearly 30% compared to the basic statistical features, achieving a score of 88.10%. The best performing methods for this category of methods that did not require fine tuning use a sentence-transformers trained on top of *distilBERT* [Sanh *et al.*, 2019], improving the performance over the *LSA*-based representation by 3%.

The *end2end* fine-tuned BERT models outperform the score of the sentence-transformers by 1.31% for the FinBERT variant and achieve the best score with LinkBERT, improving over FinBERT by 3.08% - reaching a score of 95.59% on our test set.

Finally, the higher level representations improve the performance over our standalone representations by 2.29% for the simple concatenated representations, while the latent representation improves over the naive concatenation by 0.14% - reaching a score of 94.89%.

The ranking of different representations is given in Figure 1, while Figure 2 represents the critical distance diagram between models. We also include the distribution of concepts found in the Knowledge Graph per label in the training set in Figure 3. We see that the distribution of concepts are extremely similar between sustainable and unsustainable sentence, despite unsustainable sentence supposedly not including any reference to ESG-related concepts. However, this analysis is not representative of the distribution of concepts in a full company financial reports, as the sentences in the train set might to have been sampled from reports in an uniform way; some bias might exist due to the sentence selection process during the annotation.

5.2 Final evaluation

We submitted two different approaches for the final evaluation. We opted for the deep latent representation from our standalone representations for the first submission. For the second submission we chose the ensemble of models *LinkBERT, FinBERT* and *latent fusion*, with arbitrary wheights of 2/4 for LinkBERT and 1/4 for the other two.

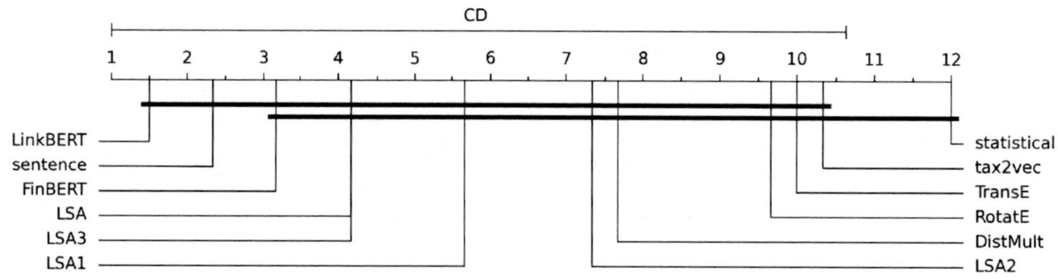

Figure 2: Critical distance plot representing the results of the Nemenyi test. Two classifiers are statistically significantly different in terms of F1-score if a difference between their ranks (shown in brackets next to the classifier name) is larger than the critical distance (CD).

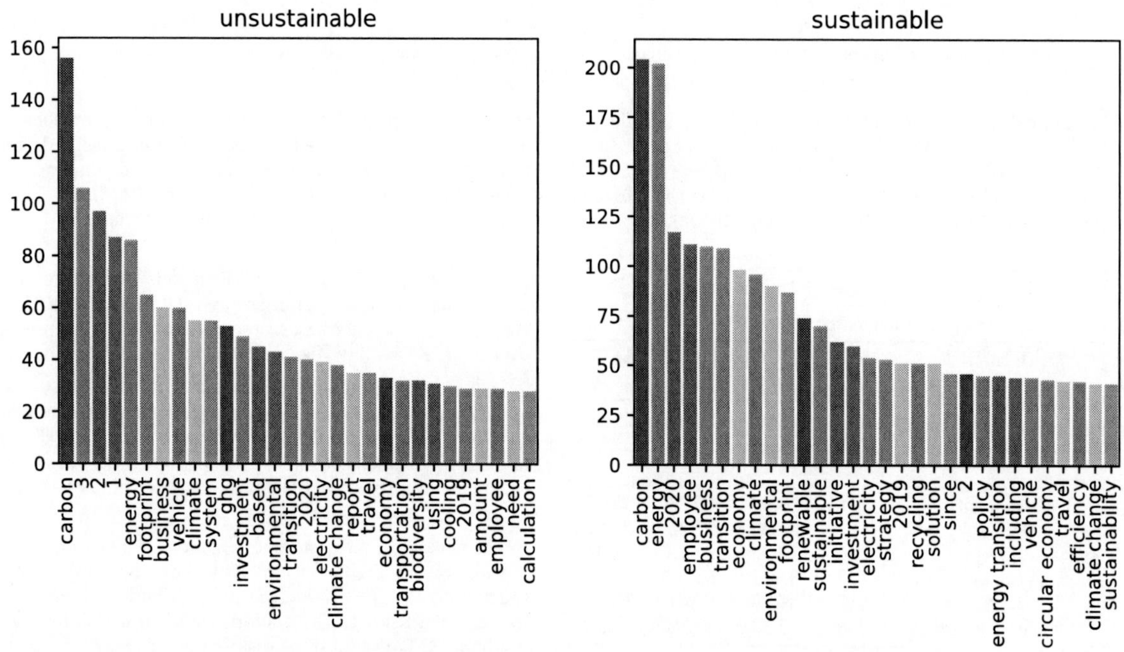

Figure 3: Distribution of extracted concepts from the WikiData5m knowledge graph in the knowledge-enrichment representations, by the respective label in the training set.

Latent representations (early-fusion)			
	precision	recall	f1-score
sustainable	0.86	0.92	0.89
unsustainable	0.91	0.84	0.88
weighted avg	0.89	0.88	0.88
Ensemble of models (late-fusion)			
sustainable	0.83	0.97	0.90
unsustainable	0.96	0.80	0.88
weighted avg	**0.90**	**0.89**	**0.89**

Table 3: Classification report of the final submissions. The **bold** entries represent the best scores between the two fusion approaches with respect to the average scores.

The *ensemble*-based approach achieves an accuracy of ***88.29%*** while the joint latent representation scores ***88.78%***. More granular report of the classification on the final test set is given in Table 3.

6 Conclusions and further work

In this work we developed a system for classification of *ESG* sentences. We used two representation paradigms: text-based and knowledge-based. In the text-based approaches we fine-tuned two BERT variants: *LinkBERT* and *FinBERT*. On top of the standalone representations we built ensembles on two different verticals: at the representation level, where we concatenated the representations and transformed them into a new latent space via SVD, and at the model level, where we stacked various models together for prediction of final labels. Our models scored competitively good, achieving nearly 89% in terms of accuracy. For further work, we consider training deep neural networks on top of the sentence representations to obtain more expressive deep representations that would improve classification performance. We also consider performing feature importance analysis on the representation-level ensembles, to see how representations in the heterogeneous stacks affect the classification on instance level. We also want to include domain-specific knowledge graphs or ontologies and explore their impact on the performance of the models. We also consider using background knowledge as a source for data augmentation, since for various use cases it contributes to better performance [Tang *et al.*, 2022; Shorten *et al.*, 2021; Cashman *et al.*, 2020]. Finally, we want to perform recursive dimensionality reduction to produce better fused document representations.

Availability

The code is available at https://gitlab.com/boshko.koloski/formicca-finsem-esg.

Acknowledgements

The authors acknowledge the financial support from the Slovenian Research Agency for research core funding (No. P2-0103), as well as for funding of the research project *Quantitative and qualitative analysis of the unregulated corporate financial reporting* (No. J5-2554).

References

[Amel-Zadeh and Serafeim, 2018] Amir Amel-Zadeh and George Serafeim. Why and how investors use esg information: Evidence from a global survey. *Financial Analysts Journal*, 74(3):87–103, 2018.

[Armbrust *et al.*, 2020] Felix Armbrust, Henry Schäfer, and Roman Klinger. A computational analysis of financial and environmental narratives within financial reports and its value for investors. In *Proceedings of the 1st Joint Workshop on Financial Narrative Processing and MultiLing Financial Summarisation*, pages 181–194, Barcelona, Spain (Online), December 2020. COLING.

[Aula, 2010] Pekka Aula. Social media, reputation risk and ambient publicity management. *Strategy & leadership*, 2010.

[Balakrishnan *et al.*, 2010] Ramji Balakrishnan, Xin Ying Qiu, and Padmini Srinivasan. On the predictive ability of narrative disclosures in annual reports. *European Journal of Operational Research*, 202(3):789–801, 2010.

[Bordes *et al.*, 2013] Antoine Bordes, Nicolas Usunier, Alberto Garcia-Duran, Jason Weston, and Oksana Yakhnenko. Translating embeddings for modeling multirelational data. In C.J. Burges, L. Bottou, M. Welling, Z. Ghahramani, and K.Q. Weinberger, editors, *Advances in Neural Information Processing Systems*, volume 26. Curran Associates, Inc., 2013.

[Cashman *et al.*, 2020] Dylan Cashman, Shenyu Xu, Subhajit Das, Florian Heimerl, Cong Liu, Shah Rukh Humayoun, Michael Gleicher, Alex Endert, and Remco Chang. Cava: A visual analytics system for exploratory columnar data augmentation using knowledge graphs. *IEEE Transactions on Visualization and Computer Graphics*, 27(2):1731–1741, 2020.

[Devlin *et al.*, 2018] Jacob Devlin, Ming-Wei Chang, Kenton Lee, and Kristina Toutanova. Bert: Pre-training of deep bidirectional transformers for language understanding. *arXiv preprint arXiv:1810.04805*, 2018.

[Dumais *et al.*, 1988] Susan T Dumais, George W Furnas, Thomas K Landauer, Scott Deerwester, and Richard Harshman. Using latent semantic analysis to improve access to textual information. In *Proceedings of the SIGCHI conference on Human factors in computing systems*, pages 281–285, 1988.

[Fellbaum, 1998] Christiane Fellbaum. *WordNet: An Electronic Lexical Database*. Bradford Books, 1998.

[Guo *et al.*, 2020] Tian Guo, Nicolas Jamet, Valentin Betrix, Louis-Alexandre Piquet, and Emmanuel Hauptmann. Esg2risk: A deep learning framework from esg news to stock volatility prediction, 2020.

[Kogan *et al.*, 2009] Shimon Kogan, Dimitry Levin, Bryan R Routledge, Jacob S Sagi, and Noah A Smith. Predicting risk from financial reports with regression. In *Proceedings of Human Language Technologies: The 2009 Annual Conference of the North American Chapter of the Association for Computational Linguistics*, pages 272–280. Association for Computational Linguistics, 2009.

[Koloski *et al.*, 2021] Boshko Koloski, Timen Stepišnik-Perdih, Senja Pollak, and Blaž Škrlj. Identification of covid-19 related fake news via neural stacking. In *International Workshop on Combating Online Hostile Posts in Regional Languages during Emergency Situation*, pages 177–188. Springer, 2021.

[Koloski *et al.*, 2022] Boshko Koloski, Timen Stepišnik Perdih, Marko Robnik-Šikonja, Senja Pollak, and Blaž Škrlj. Knowledge graph informed fake news classification via heterogeneous representation ensembles. *Neurocomputing*, 496:208–226, 2022.

[Loughran and McDonald, 2011] Tim Loughran and Bill McDonald. When is a liability not a liability? textual analysis, dictionaries, and 10-ks. *The Journal of Finance*, 66(1):35–65, 2011.

[Mansar *et al.*, 2021] Youness Mansar, Juyeon Kang, and Ismail El Maarouf. The finsim-2 2021 shared task: Learning semantic similarities for the financial domain. In *Companion Proceedings of the Web Conference 2021*, WWW '21, page 288–292, New York, NY, USA, 2021. Association for Computing Machinery.

[Mehra *et al.*, 2022] Srishti Mehra, Robert Louka, and Yixun Zhang. ESGBERT: Language model to help with classification tasks related to companies' environmental, social, and governance practices. In *Embedded Systems and Applications*. Academy and Industry Research Collaboration Center (AIRCC), mar 2022.

[Nagy *et al.*, 2016] Zoltán Imre Nagy, Altaf Kassam, and Linda-Eling Lee. Can esg add alpha? an analysis of esg tilt and momentum strategies. *The Journal of Investing*, 25:113 – 124, 2016.

[Purver *et al.*, 2022 accepted] Matthew Purver, Matej Martinc, Riste Ichev, Igor Lončarski, Katarina Sitar, Valentinčič Aljoša, and Senja Pollak. Tracking changes in ESG representation: Initial investigations in uk annual reports. In *Proceedings of the First Computing Social Responsibility Workshop -NLP Approaches to Corporate Social Responsibilities (CSR-NLP I) 2022, co-located with LREC 2022*, 2022, accepted.

[Qiu *et al.*, 2006] Xin Ying Qiu, Padmini Srinivasan, and Nick Street. Exploring the forecasting potential of company annual reports. *Proceedings of the American Society for Information Science and Technology*, 43(1):1–15, 2006.

[Reimers and Gurevych, 2019] Nils Reimers and Iryna Gurevych. Sentence-bert: Sentence embeddings using siamese bert-networks. In *Proceedings of the 2019 Conference on Empirical Methods in Natural Language Processing*. Association for Computational Linguistics, 11 2019.

[Sammut and Webb, 2010] Claude Sammut and Geoffrey I. Webb, editors. *TF–IDF*, pages 986–987. Springer US, Boston, MA, 2010.

[Sanh *et al.*, 2019] Victor Sanh, Lysandre Debut, Julien Chaumond, and Thomas Wolf. Distilbert, a distilled version of bert: smaller, faster, cheaper and lighter. *arXiv preprint arXiv:1910.01108*, 2019.

[Serafeim and Yoon, 2022] George Serafeim and Aaron Yoon. Stock price reactions to esg news: The role of esg ratings and disagreement. *Review of accounting studies*, pages 1–31, 2022.

[Shorten *et al.*, 2021] Connor Shorten, Taghi M Khoshgoftaar, and Borko Furht. Text data augmentation for deep learning. *Journal of big Data*, 8(1):1–34, 2021.

[Škrlj *et al.*, 2021] Blaž Škrlj, Matej Martinc, Nada Lavrač, and Senja Pollak. autobot: evolving neuro-symbolic representations for explainable low resource text classification. *Machine Learning*, Apr 2021.

[Sokolov *et al.*, 2021] Alik Sokolov, Jonathan Mostovoy, Jack Ding, and Luis Seco. Building machine learning systems for automated ESG scoring. *The Journal of Impact and ESG Investing*, 1(3):39–50, January 2021.

[Sun *et al.*, 2019] Zhiqing Sun, Zhi-Hong Deng, Jian-Yun Nie, and Jian Tang. Rotate: Knowledge graph embedding by relational rotation in complex space. In *International Conference on Learning Representations*, 2019.

[Tang *et al.*, 2022] Zhenwei Tang, Shichao Pei, Zhao Zhang, Yongchun Zhu, Fuzhen Zhuang, Robert Hoehndorf, and Xiangliang Zhang. Positive-unlabeled learning with adversarial data augmentation for knowledge graph completion. *arXiv preprint arXiv:2205.00904*, 2022.

[Tavchioski *et al.*, 2022] Ilija Tavchioski, Boshko Koloski, Blaž Škrlj, and Senja Pollak. E8-IJS@LT-EDI-ACL2022 - BERT, AutoML and knowledge-graph backed detection of depression. In *Proceedings of the Second Workshop on Language Technology for Equality, Diversity and Inclusion*, pages 251–257, Dublin, Ireland, May 2022. Association for Computational Linguistics.

[Vaswani *et al.*, 2017] Ashish Vaswani, Noam Shazeer, Niki Parmar, Jakob Uszkoreit, Llion Jones, Aidan N Gomez, Łukasz Kaiser, and Illia Polosukhin. Attention is all you need. *Advances in neural information processing systems*, 30, 2017.

[Vrandečić and Krötzsch, 2014] Denny Vrandečić and Markus Krötzsch. Wikidata: a free collaborative knowledgebase. *Communications of the ACM*, 57(10):78–85, 2014.

[Yang *et al.*, 2014] Bishan Yang, Wen-tau Yih, Xiaodong He, Jianfeng Gao, and Li Deng. Embedding entities and relations for learning and inference in knowledge bases. *arXiv preprint arXiv:1412.6575*, 2014.

[Yang *et al.*, 2020] Yi Yang, Mark Christopher Siy Uy, and Allen Huang. Finbert: A pretrained language model for financial communications. *CoRR*, abs/2006.08097, 2020.

[Yasunaga *et al.*, 2022] Michihiro Yasunaga, Jure Leskovec, and Percy Liang. Linkbert: Pretraining language models with document links, 2022.

[Škrlj *et al.*, 2021] Blaž Škrlj, Matej Martinc, Jan Kralj, Nada Lavrač, and Senja Pollak. tax2vec: Constructing interpretable features from taxonomies for short text classification. *Computer Speech & Language*, 65:101104, 2021.

TCS_WITM_2022@FinSim4-ESG: Augmenting BERT with Linguistic and Semantic features for ESG data classification

Tushar Goel, Vipul Chauhan, Suyash Sangwan, Ishan Verma, Tirthankar Dasgupta, Lipika Dey
TCS Research
New Delhi India
(t.goel, chauhan.vipul, suyash.sangwan, ishan.verma, dasgupta.tirthankar, lipika.dey)@tcs.com

Abstract

Advanced neural network architectures have provided several opportunities to develop systems to automatically capture information from domain-specific unstructured text sources. The FinSim4-ESG shared task, collocated with the FinNLP workshop, proposed two sub-tasks. In sub-task1, the challenge was to design systems that could utilize contextual word embeddings along with sustainability resources to elaborate an ESG taxonomy. In the second sub-task, participants were asked to design a system that could classify sentences into sustainable or unsustainable sentences. In this paper, we utilize semantic similarity features along with BERT embeddings to segregate domain terms into a fixed number of class labels. The proposed model not only considers the contextual BERT embeddings but also incorporates Word2Vec, cosine, and Jaccard similarity which gives word-level importance to the model. For sentence classification, several linguistic elements along with BERT embeddings were used as classification features. We have shown a detailed ablation study for the proposed models.

1 Introduction

Sustainability disclosures have started gaining traction in Financial world. Sustainability disclosures reflects the procedures that an organization follow to fulfill its commitment towards Environment, Social and Governance (ESG) factors. Investors are increasingly considering the ESG commitments of organizations to aid their investments decisions. ESG information is not commonly part of financial reporting but organizations have started making ESG disclosures either as a part of their annual report or as a separate sustainability report altogether.

Recently, European Union has proposed new guidelines making ESG disclosures mandatory for companies providing ESG driven investment products. Companies in EU must comply with increasing obligations related to ESG in order to have their businesses qualify as sustainable and to be noticed by investors on the EU market. Several institutions, such as the Sustainability Accounting Standards Board (SASB), the Global Reporting Initiative (GRI), and the Task Force on Climate-related Financial Disclosures (TCFD) are also working to form standards and define standards to facilitate incorporation of ESG factors into the investment process. Organization need to align their disclosures to various ESG taxonomies available to facilitate effective utilization of the disclosures. Since, ESG domain and the allied taxonomies are still evolving, there is a need to have automated systems that can elaborate the existing taxonomies and also aid the organization to align their disclosures to the existing standards. The FinSim4-ESG shared task is one of the few attempts that primarily focused on automatically learning effective and precise semantic models adapted to the ESG domain. Specifically it addressed the task of automatic categorization of ESG terms into pre-defined categories to enhance the existing taxonomy and to create a language model that can understand the language of sustainability and segregate sustainable sentences from unsustainable ones. The specific details of the shared task is described in section 3.

In this paper, we propose to augment the transformer based BERT architecture with semantic similarity features to address the ESG term classification task. The base BERT model is first fine-tuned on a set of ESG document to facilitate capture of ESG language context. The embedding obtained from the resultant model is then augmented with semantic similarity features like Word2Vec, Cosine and Jaccard similarity to perform the classification task of segregating domain terms into fixed number of class labels. In a similar way, for sentence classification task, various lexical features are used along with BERT embeddings. Dimensionality reduction techniques are also incorporated into the experiments. For training the model, we have used the

Proceedings of the Fourth Workshop on Financial Technology and Natural Language Processing (FinNLP), pages 235 - 242
December 8, 2022

$BERT_{base}$ architecture. We have conducted multiple experiments with the model architecture such as taking combination of proposed features with different classifiers in both sub-tasks. Our experiments shows that a combination of ESG fine tuned BERT with Word2Vec, cosine and jaccard similarity with a Logistic Regression classifiers gives the best result for term classification. For sentence classification we exploited linguistic and NLP-based features like presence of specific named entities (like organisation, date), word-count in the document, etc. Our experimental results showed that when we combine these features along with fine-tuned BERT-base classifier, it lead to an increase of about 2% in system's accuracy.

2 Related Work

Rising sustainability awareness amongst consumers, investors and regulators is forcing organizations to pay attention towards Environment, Social or Governance (ESG) factors. Researchers around the world have conducted experiments to study the effect of ESG factors on financial performance of organizations. The last three editions of the FinSim proposed the challenge to automatically learn effective and precise semantic models for the financial domain (Mansar et al., 2021; El Maarouf et al., 2020; Kang et al., 2021). (Chersoni and Huang, 2021) solve the financial hypernym detection task by using the logistic regression classifier trained on a combination of word embeddings, semantic and string similarity metrics and won the challenge. (Nguyen et al., 2021) approached the task as a semantic textual similarity problem. They used a siamese network with pre-trained language model encoders to derive term embeddings and computed similarity scores between them while (Goel et al., 2021) leverage the use of given documents by extracting sentences corresponding to each term and then used a transformer based BERT architecture to perform a classification task. A number of approaches like use of publicly available knowledge graphs to generate explicit features (Portisch et al., 2021), customize word embeddings (Pei and Zhang, 2021), word ontology (Tian and Chen, 2021), pre-trained sentence embedding extracted from Universal Sentence Encoder along with cosine similarity (Anand et al., 2020) and use of static word embeddings (Fu et al., 2014; Nguyen et al., 2017) have also been proposed to automatically map financial concepts with its most relevant hypernym.

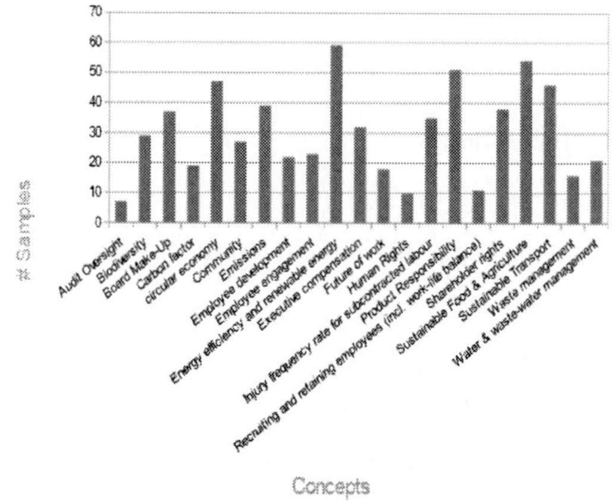

Figure 1: Sub-task1 Data Distribution

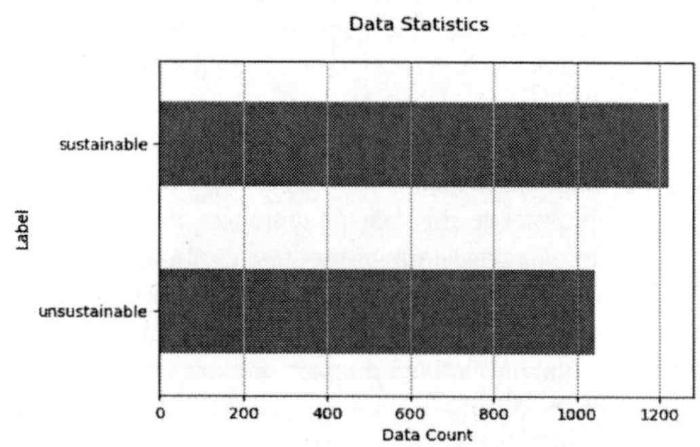

Figure 2: Sub-task2 Data Distribution

3 Shared Task Detail and Dataset Description

The FinSim4-ESG 2022 task focused on elaboration of an ESG taxonomy (ESG related concepts representations) based on the data like companies sustainability reports, annual reports, and environment reports, and make use of them to analyze how an economic activity complies with the taxonomy. The current edition proposed two sub-tasks :

- **Sub-task1** - Given a list of carefully selected terms from the sustainability domain such as "low-carbon", "Greenhouse gas emissions", the task was to design a system which can automatically classify them into the most relevant ESG-concept. For example, given the set of concepts "Future of Work", "Human Rights", "Biodiversity", "Community", "Waste Management", the most relevant concept of "Palm Oil" is "Biodiversity". The training data consisted of 647 unique terms with corresponding concepts. There were 25 unique concepts in the shared task but for few concepts data was insufficient like terms corresponding to concept "Diversity & Inclusion" were not present in the training data. Hence, we considered 641 unique terms which corresponded to 21 unique concepts for our experiments. Moreover, As shown in Figure 1, the training data was also imbalanced wherein concepts such as "Energy Efficiency and Renewable Energy" had 9.2% data and concept "Audit Oversight" had only 1.09% data. For test data, there were 145 terms to be classified into the correct concepts.

- **Sub-task2** - In this sub-task, the participants were asked to create an automated system which could classify sustainable and unsustainable sentences. Here, a sentence is considered sustainable if and only if it semantically mentions the Environmental or Social or Governance related factors. For example, a sentence "At Vauban Infrastructure Partners, we integrate in our daily work practices to avoid, reduce or offset our carbon emissions." is a sustainable sentence. For this purpose, the organisers provided the list of labeled sentences from the sustainability reports and other documents. The training data consisted of 2265 sentences, out of which 1223 sentences were sustainable and the remaining 1042 sentences were unsustainable. The dataset was balanced with a ratio of 0.852 as shown in Figure 2. There were 205 sentences in the test data which needs to be classified into their respective label categories.

4 Proposed Approach

The proposed approach can be divided into three main stages namely feature extraction stage, dimensionality reduction stage and classification stage as shown in Figure 3. For both sub-tasks, the input text is first subjected to feature extraction module where different NLP and text mining techniques are applied to obtain various Linguistic and Semantic features along with BERT embeddings. A combination of these features are then subjected to dimensionality reduction where a subset of features are selected as final input variables for classification

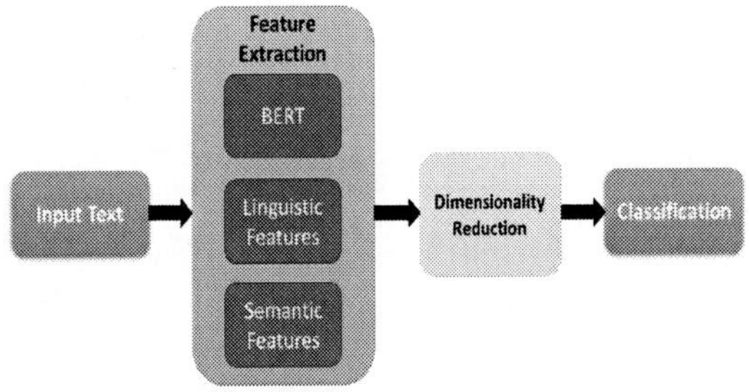

Figure 3: Proposed approach pipeline

module. The detailed description of the activities in each stage is explained next.

4.1 Feature Extraction for Sub-task1

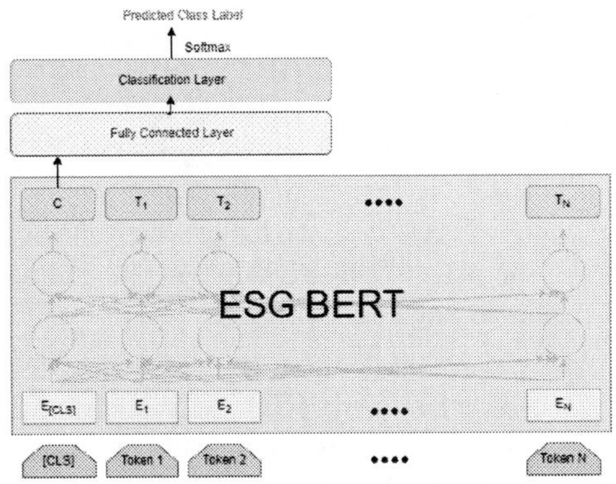

Figure 4: ESG BERT Architecture

- **ESG BERT** - BERT (Bidirection Encoder Representation from Transformers) is a state of the art model for language modeling (Devlin et al., 2018). The official BERT Repository[1] contains various pre-trained models that can be further used for the downstream task. In this work, ESG-BERT model[2] pre-trained on Sustainability corpora has been utilised to achieve better capability of understanding domain specific vocabulary. The model is fine-tuned further on the downstream task of concept classification as shown in Figure 4. Experiments show that the Fully Connected (FCN) layer added between the classification layer and BERT output layer benefited the model in learning the representation for the downstream task. The output of the FCN layer represents the term by an embedding vector.

[1] https://github.com/google-research/bert
[2] github.com/mukut03/ESG-BERT

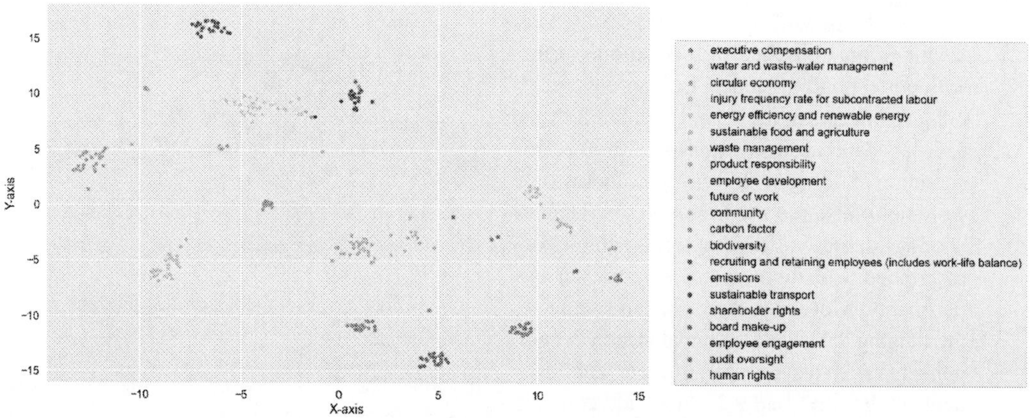

Figure 5: ESG BERT Embedding Plot

This vector has been used as one of the feature in our system for the classification. A tsne-plot of ESG BERT embedding of terms in training data is shown in Figure 5. The cluster segregation for different concepts can be seen clearly in the figure which shows the potential of ESG-BERT based embedding in classifying ESG concepts.

- **Cosine Similarity (CS)** - Semantic similarity between the terms and the concepts plays an important role in the classification. The ESG-BERT fine-tuned in the previous experiment is further used to obtain the cosine similarity between the terms and the pre-defined concepts. For each term, the embedding vector of the term is compared against the embedding vectors of each concept. Cosine similarity is used as the metric for comparing the vectors. This results into a N dimensional vector for each term where N is the number of concepts. Each value in this vector represents cosine similarity of a term with $concept_i$.

- **Word2Vec Features** - The organizers of the shared task have provided a set of 190 sustainability reports of various companies. The corpus extracted from these reports contains about 33 thousand unique tokens. These tokens are used to train the 100 dimensional domain-specific Word2Vec (Mikolov et al., 2013) word embeddings. For terms composed by multiple words, we simply represent them by summing the vectors of the individual words.

- **Jaccard Similarity** - It was observed that out of 641 samples, there were 326 samples with at least one word overlapping (excluding stopwords) between term and concept. Based on (Keswani et al., 2020) approach of pointing out "concept inclusion", we computed *Jaccard Similarity* as a N dimensional feature vector(one feature for each concept), where each values in this feature reflect the syntactic similarity between the terms and concepts.

Dimensionality Reduction with Principal Component Analysis (PCA) - The combination of embeddings and features used in our experiments results into large number of features as compared to number of samples. The performance of any machine learning model can suffer from the curse of dimensionality where the number of features becomes larger than the number of samples in the dataset. To tackle this issue, we have empirically reduce the dimensions of the features using Principal Component Anaysis (PCA) (Martinez and Kak, 2001) and found that reduction to 200 dimensions are giving the best results.

4.2 Feature Extraction for Sub-task2

Data pre-processing is a crucial first step before applying any text machine learning model. Firstly, we remove all the punctuations and convert the tokenized words into lower-case format. Then to clean the noise present in the sentences we removed stopwords. Subsequently, the cleaned data is subjected to feature extraction step. In this step, raw text data is transformed into feature vectors. We tried following different ideas to obtain relevant features from the dataset:

- **Count vector**- Count vector is the matrix notation of the dataset in which every row represents a sentence from the corpus, every column represents a term from the corpus, and every cell represents the frequency count of a particular term in a particular sentence.

- **Character level, N-gram level, Word level TF-IDF vectors as features**- This vector represents the relative importance of a character/n-gram/word to the given output class. TF-IDF stands for Term Frequency – Inverse Document Frequency. This weighting has been widely used for feature extraction in text data. Term frequency (TF) is equal to the frequency of a given word in the given sentence. Inverse Document Frequency (IDF) measures the information provided by the word. It is equal to the inverse of number of sentences containing the word. Hence, $tfidf(w, s) = tf(w, s) * idf(w, S)$ where w is the given word, s is the given sentence and S is the corpus containing all sentences. TF-IDF gives higher value to the words which are less frequent among sentences and vice versa.

- **Sentiment polarity as a feature**- We used TextBlob[3] to extract sentiment polarities of each input sentence.

- **Text based features**- A number of other text based features are extracted using NLTK[4] and SpaCy[5] to aid the text classification models. Some exmaples are-
  - **NLTK features**-
    - **Word count of the sentences**- Total number of words in the sentence.
    - **Punctuation count of the sentences**- Total number of punctuation marks in the sentence.
    - **Frequency distribution of POS tags**- Total number of nouns, verbs, adjectives, adverbs, and, pronouns in the sentence.
  - **SpaCy features**- We extracted Named Entities using SpaCy. Some of the extracted named entities are- Organisations, Places, Money, Date, and, Person.

[3]https://github.com/sloria/TextBlob
[4]https://github.com/nltk/nltk
[5]https://spacy.io/

Dimensionality reduction: We used correlation and p-values to select the final feature set. We compare the correlation between different pairs of features and remove one of the two features that have a correlation higher than 0.9. Now from the remaining set of features we remove different features randomly and measure the p-value in each case. These measured p-values are used to decide whether to keep a feature or not. Finally the feature set giving maximum p-value is selected.

Embedding models: With so many rampant advances taking place in NLP, it can sometimes become overwhelming to be able to objectively understand the differences between the different models. We experimented with different word and sentence level embeddings like Word2Vec (both CBOW and Skip-gram), GloVe (Pennington et al., 2014), FastText (Joulin et al., 2016), ELMo (Peters et al., 2018), InferSent[6], BERT, and ESG BERT. Finally fine-tuned ESG BERT embeddings performed best on our classification task. Therefore ESG BERT vectors are appended with above set of selected feature vectors which are then passed to the classification model.

4.3 Classification Model

Sub-task1 features and Sub-task2 features are used to train classifiers for their respective classification tasks. A classification model takes vectors generated from task dependent features corresponding to each task data as an input and generate the predicted results corresponding to each input. To find the best classifiers, we test several widely used classification methods including Logistic Regression, Gradient Boosting and XGBoost Classifier (all in the standard scikit-learn implementation). We gradually augmented the models by adding the features one by one and computed the scores. From the experimental studies, we found that linear classifier performed the best. Hence, we selected Logistic Regression as the classifier in our submitted systems. This observation is consistent with findings in the FinSim 2020 and FinSim 2021 shared tasks, that models learning linear boundaries perform better for these tasks (Mansar et al., 2021) (El Maarouf et al., 2020).

5 Metrics

The most important part of any system is to choose the most accurate model. The metrics used for

[6]https://github.com/facebookresearch/InferSent

S.No.	Model	Accuracy	MR
1	Baseline 1	0.4920	2.2146
2	Baseline 2	0.775	1.4728
3	BERT + CL	0.7596	1.5038
4	BERT FCN + CL	0.7751	1.4573
5	ESG BERT + CL	0.7905	1.4582
6	ESG BERT FCN + CL	0.7906	1.4573
7	ESG BERT FCN + LR	0.8139	1.341
8	ESG BERT FCN + Word2vec + LR	0.8217	1.34
9	ESG BERT FCN + CS + Jaccard + LR	0.8139	1.33
10	ESG BERT FCN + Word2vec+ CS + Jaccard +LR*	**0.8217**	**1.3255**
11	ESG BERT FCN + Word2vec+ CS + Jaccard + PCA 100 + LR	0.8154	1.379
12	ESG BERT FCN + Word2vec+ CS + Jaccard + PCA 150 + LR	**0.8217**	1.35
13	ESG BERT FCN + Word2vec+ CS + Jaccard + PCA 200 + LR**	**0.8217**	**1.3215**

Table 1: Sub-task1 Evaluation results on the validation data ('*' and '**' represent *TCSWITM_1* and *TCSWITM_2* submission respectively.)

S.No.	Model	Accuracy	Recall
1	TFIDF	0.61	0.59
2	Wod2Vec (CBOW)	0.61	0.59
3	Word2Vec (SkipGram)	0.79	0.78
4	GloVe	0.77	0.75
5	FastText	0.81	0.79
6	ELMo	0.83	0.82
7	InferSent	0.80	0.78
8	BERT	0.92	0.91
9	ESG BERT	0.93	0.92
10	ESG BERT+NLP based features (TCSWITM_1)	**0.95**	**0.94**

Table 2: Sub-task2-Evaluation results on Validation data

the evaluation is provided by the organizers. For Sub-task1, the evaluation metric used is Accuracy and Mean Rank. The model is required to predict the concepts in the ranking order (from the most probable to the least probable) for each term. The Accuracy and Mean Rank is defined as follows -

$$Accuracy = \frac{1}{n} * \sum_{i=1}^{n} I(y_i = y_i^l[0])$$

$$MeanRank = \frac{1}{n} * \sum_{i=1}^{n} rank_i$$

Note that $rank_i$ corresponds to the rank of the correct label.

For Sub-task2, the evaluation metric considered is Accuracy and Recall. Recall (also known as sensitivity) is the fraction of relevant (here sustainable) instances that were correctly retrieved.

6 Experiments and Results

Sub-task1 - We were provided with 641 data samples which included terms and their corresponding concepts for model development and validation. We had split the data in 80:20 train-validation split using 5 fold cross validation technique which results into 5 sets containing 512 data points for training and 129 data points for validation. All proposed models were trained and validated on the generated training and validation dataset respectively. The test set provided contained a list of 145 terms without their concepts in json format. Table 1 shows the performance on validation set for sub-task1 and Table 2 shows the performance on validation set for sub-task2 in terms of mean rank and accuracy whereas Table 3 shows the evaluation results of hidden test data for both the tasks.

Baseline 1 is a distance-based classifier using custom embeddings (Mikolov et al., 2013) whereas

Baseline 2 uses logistic regression classifier over these custom embeddings (Mikolov et al., 2013) given in FinSim4-ESG shared task. BERT (pre-trained on general English corpora[7]) based classification model is fine-tuned on the downstream task by adding a classification layer (CL). It can be seen from the Table 1 that the performance has been improved by BERT pre-trained on Sustainability corpora (ESG) after incorporating a Fully Connected Layer (FCN). In the further experiments, Embedding from the resultant BERT model is used as features in Logistic Regression (LR) classifier. The concatenation of BERT features with Word2vec, Cosine Similarity (CS) and Jaccard resulted into the best Mean Rank as shown in Table 1. The ablation study confirmed the gravity of these features. As the data was limited as compared to the features, employing dimension reduction technique (PCA) benefited the performance by improving feature selection. This can also be seen in the test data results in Table 3.

Model	Accuracy	MR
Sub-task1 Baseline1	0.4620	2.2758
Sub-task1 Baseline2	0.7448	1.5241
Sub-task1 TCSWITM_1	0.7724	1.4620
Sub-task1 TCSWITM_2	**0.7793**	**1.4482**
Sub-task2 Baseline1	0.4976	NA
Sub-task2 Baseline2	0.8195	NA
Sub-task2 TCSWITM_1	**0.8731**	NA

Table 3: Evaluation results on Hidden Test data

From Table 3, it can be observed that ESG-BERT combined with all other features along with PCA outperforms other models in terms of mean rank and accuracy. It is clear from the table that all our models performs better than the baseline models.

We have also observed misalignment amongst the terms and concepts in the given training data. For example, the alignment given in the training data is "CO2 Equivalent Emissions Indirect, Scope 3" - *Biodiversity*, "Accident spills" - *Energy efficiency and renewable energy*, "Gender diversity" - *Recruiting and retaining employees (incl. work-life balance)* etc. But as per our understanding the ideal assignment should be "CO2 Equivalent Emissions Indirect, Scope 3" - *Emissions*, "Accident spills" - *Injury frequency rate* and "Gender diversity" - *Diversity & Inclusion.*

Sub-task2- We split the data in 80:20 train-validation split using 5 fold cross validation technique which results into 5 sets. All proposed models were trained and validated on the generated training and validation dataset respectively. Sentence embeddings performed better than word based embeddings as shown in Table 2. One of the main reason is that word embeddings like Word2Vec and GloVe are unable to encode unknown or out-of-vocabulary words. Moreover word based embeddings don't take into consideration the order of words in which they appear which leads to loss of syntactic and semantic understanding of the sentence. Finally we used BERT-based features as our main feature set. BERT-based features when combined with above set of rule-based and NLP-based features (like presence of specific NERs (like organisation, date entity), and, word count of document, etc.) provided a significant improvement in performance of the classification system.

7 Conclusion

As part of FinSim4-ESG shared task on Learning Semantic Similarities for Financial Domain, we attempt to solve the problems of finding the most relevant ESG concept for each given domain term and classify a given sentence into sustainable or unsustainable based on provided training data. In sub-task1, in order to utilize contextual word embeddings along with sustainability resources to elaborate an ESG taxonomy, we proposed the use of semantic similarity features along with BERT embeddings to segregate domain terms into a fixed number of class labels. For sub-task2, several linguistic and NLP features along with BERT embeddings were used for classification. In our experiments we observed that linear classifier models like logistic regression performs the best. We have also compared our models with the given baseline accuracy and found that their performance is far superior to it. We have also shown a detailed ablation study for the proposed models. In future, we are planning to use better data augmentation techniques and explore the possibility of using the ontology hierarchy and definitions available as part of the EU taxonomy.

[7]https://huggingface.co/bert-base-uncased

References

Vivek Anand, Yash Agrawal, Aarti Pol, and Vasudeva Varma. 2020. Finsim20 at the finsim task: Making sense of text in financial domain. In *Proceedings of the Second Workshop on Financial Technology and Natural Language Processing*, pages 104–107.

Emmanuele Chersoni and Chu-Ren Huang. 2021. Polyu-cbs at the finsim-2 task: combining distributional, string-based and transformers-based features for hypernymy detection in the financial domain. In *Companion Proceedings of the Web Conference 2021*, pages 316–319.

Jacob Devlin, Ming-Wei Chang, Kenton Lee, and Kristina Toutanova. 2018. Bert: Pre-training of deep bidirectional transformers for language understanding. *arXiv preprint arXiv:1810.04805*.

Ismail El Maarouf, Youness Mansar, Virginie Mouilleron, and Dialekti Valsamou-Stanislawski. 2020. The finsim 2020 shared task: Learning semantic representations for the financial domain. In *Proceedings of the Second Workshop on Financial Technology and Natural Language Processing*, pages 81–86.

Ruiji Fu, Jiang Guo, Bing Qin, Wanxiang Che, Haifeng Wang, and Ting Liu. 2014. Learning semantic hierarchies via word embeddings. In *Proceedings of the 52nd Annual Meeting of the Association for Computational Linguistics (Volume 1: Long Papers)*, pages 1199–1209.

Tushar Goel, Vipul Chauhan, Ishan Verma, Tirthankar Dasgupta, and Lipika Dey. 2021. Tcs_witm_2021@ finsim-2: Transformer based models for automatic classification of financial terms. In *Companion Proceedings of the Web Conference 2021*, pages 311–315.

Armand Joulin, Edouard Grave, Piotr Bojanowski, and Tomas Mikolov. 2016. Bag of tricks for efficient text classification. *arXiv preprint arXiv:1607.01759*.

Juyeon Kang, Ismail El Maarouf, Sandra Bellato, and Mei Gan. 2021. Finsim-3: The 3rd shared task on learning semantic similarities for the financial domain. In *Proceedings of the Third Workshop on Financial Technology and Natural Language Processing*, pages 31–35.

Vishal Keswani, Sakshi Singh, and Ashutosh Modi. 2020. Iitk at the finsim task: Hypernym detection in financial domain via context-free and contextualized word embeddings. *arXiv preprint arXiv:2007.11201*.

Youness Mansar, Juyeon Kang, and Ismail El Maarouf. 2021. The finsim-2 2021 shared task: Learning semantic similarities for the financial domain. In *Companion Proceedings of the Web Conference 2021*, pages 288–292.

Aleix M Martinez and Avinash C Kak. 2001. Pca versus lda. *IEEE transactions on pattern analysis and machine intelligence*, 23(2):228–233.

Tomas Mikolov, Kai Chen, Greg Corrado, and Jeffrey Dean. 2013. Efficient estimation of word representations in vector space. *arXiv preprint arXiv:1301.3781*.

Kim Anh Nguyen, Maximilian Köper, Sabine Schulte im Walde, and Ngoc Thang Vu. 2017. Hierarchical embeddings for hypernymy detection and directionality. *arXiv preprint arXiv:1707.07273*.

Nhu Khoa Nguyen, Emanuela Boros, Gaël Lejeune, Antoine Doucet, and Thierry Delahaut. 2021. L3i_lbpam at the finsim-2 task: Learning financial semantic similarities with siamese transformers. In *Companion Proceedings of the Web Conference 2021*, pages 302–306.

Yulong Pei and Qian Zhang. 2021. Goat at the finsim-2 task: Learning word representations of financial data with customized corpus. In *Companion Proceedings of the Web Conference 2021*, pages 307–310.

Jeffrey Pennington, Richard Socher, and Christopher D Manning. 2014. Glove: Global vectors for word representation. In *Proceedings of the 2014 conference on empirical methods in natural language processing (EMNLP)*, pages 1532–1543.

Matthew E. Peters, Mark Neumann, Mohit Iyyer, Matt Gardner, Christopher Clark, Kenton Lee, and Luke Zettlemoyer. 2018. Deep contextualized word representations. pages 2227–2237, New Orleans, Louisiana. Association for Computational Linguistics.

Jan Portisch, Michael Hladik, and Heiko Paulheim. 2021. Finmatcher at finsim-2: hypernym detection in the financial services domain using knowledge graphs. In *Companion Proceedings of the Web Conference 2021*, pages 293–297.

Ke Tian and Hua Chen. 2021. aiai at the finsim-2 task: Finance domain terms automatic classification via word ontology and embedding. In *Companion Proceedings of the Web Conference 2021*, pages 320–322.

Ranking Environment, Social And Governance Related Concepts And Assessing Sustainability Aspect Of Financial Texts

Sohom Ghosh[1,2] and **Sudip Kumar Naskar**[2]
[1]Fidelity Investments, Bengaluru, India
[2]Jadavpur University, Kolkata, India
{sohom1ghosh, sudip.naskar}@gmail.com

Abstract

Understanding Environmental, Social, and Governance (ESG) factors related to financial products has become extremely important for investors. However, manually screening through the corporate policies and reports to understand their sustainability aspect is extremely tedious. In this paper, we propose solutions to two such problems which were released as shared tasks of the FinNLP workshop of the IJCAI-2022 conference. Firstly, we train a Sentence Transformers based model which automatically ranks ESG related concepts for a given unknown term. Secondly, we fine-tune a RoBERTa model to classify financial texts as sustainable or not. Out of 26 registered teams, our team ranked 4th in sub-task 1 and 3rd in sub-task 2. The source code can be accessed from https://github.com/sohomghosh/Finsim4_ESG.

1 Introduction

These days a lot of investors have become socially responsible and environmentally conscious[1]. They tend to choose stocks and funds which do not harm the environment[2]. Keeping this in mind, organizations are also putting in efforts to increase their Environmental, Social, and Governance (ESG) ratings. They tend to publish reports mentioning the ESG aspect of their policies. However, reading through all such reports is time-consuming and inefficient. This brings in the need for an automated system for mapping terms to ESG concepts and classifying financial texts as sustainable or not. FinNLP workshop of IJCAI-2022 conference hosted a shared task with these problems. We present an example of this in Figure 1. Our team LIPI participated in the shared task and ranked 4th and 3rd in sub-tasks 1 and 2 respectively. In this paper, we describe our solutions.

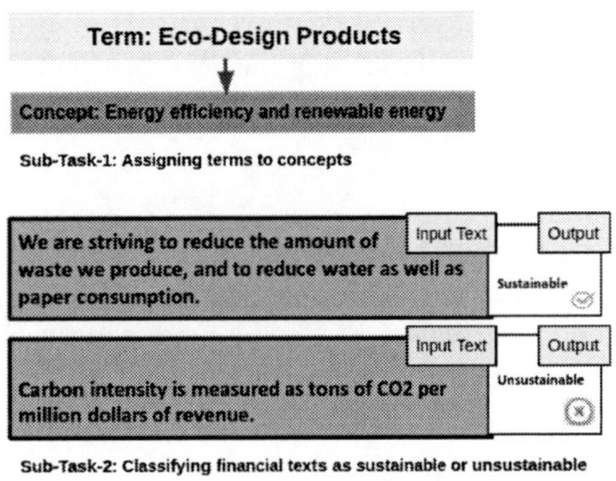

Figure 1: FinSim-4 ESG Sub-Tasks

2 Related Works

The sub-task of mapping terms with high level concepts is similar to hypernym detection. For the Natural Language Processing (NLP) community, Hypernym detection has been an active area of research. Several SemEval tasks ((Bordea et al., 2015), (Bordea et al., 2016), (Augenstein et al., 2017), (Camacho-Collados et al., 2018)) were organized on this topic. Subsequently, three editions of FinSim ((Maarouf et al., 2020), (Mansar et al., 2021), (Kang et al., 2021)) shared task were held which adapted the task of hypernym detection for the financial domain. This year while organizing FinSim-4, this was extended to ESG insights.

With the rising popularity of green investing, understanding the sustainability aspect of financial texts has become extremely important. Smeuninx et al. (Smeuninx et al., 2020) studied the readability of annual reports of several organizations. They highlighted how formula-based readability scores classified these texts as complex documents. They also mentioned the need for NLP based techniques

[1]https://news.gallup.com/poll/389780/investors-stand-esg-investing.aspx (accessed on 10 June 2022)

[2]https://bwdisrupt.businessworld.in/article/Sustainable-Investing-To-Surge-To-125-B-In-India-By-2026-Report/09-06-2022-432078/ (accessed on 10 June 2022)

Proceedings of the Fourth Workshop on Financial Technology and Natural Language Processing (FinNLP), pages 243 - 249
December 8, 2022 ©2022 Association for Computational Linguistics

to comprehend the readability of such documents. Luccioni et al. (Luccioni et al., 2020) fine-tuned RoBERTa-base (Liu et al., 2019) model to develop a question-answering based tool, ClimateQA for extracting sections related to climate from financial reports.

Guo et al. (Guo et al., 2020) proposed a framework ESG2Risk for predicting stock prices by analyzing ESG related events from financial news. They specifically used sentiments from these events.

Nugent et al. (Nugent et al., 2020) pre-trained a BERT (Devlin et al., 2019) model with financial news articles from Reuters News Archive for predicting ESG related controversies. Furthermore, they used it for mapping financial news into one of the United Nations Sustainable Development Goals.

3 Problem Statements

The fourth edition of FinSim presented two sub-tasks. They are as follows:

3.1 Sub-Task 1:

Given a set J consisting of n tuples of terms and their high level concepts i.e. $J = \{(t_1, c_1), (t_2, c_2), ...(t_n, c_n)\}$ where c_i represents the high level concept corresponding to the ith term t_i and $c_i \epsilon$ set of concepts mentioned in Table 1. For a given unknown term, the task was to develop a system to rank these concepts.

The evaluation metrics for this sub-task were accuracy and mean rank. As per the evaluation script shared by the organizers, the rank of an instance was calculated by checking the presence of the true value in the first three elements of the predicted ranked list.

3.2 Sub-Task 2:

Given a set F consisting of n tuples of financial texts and their sustainability labels i.e. $F = \{(f_1, l_1), (f_2, l_2), ...(f_n, l_n)\}$ where l_i represents the sustainability label corresponding to the ith financial text f_i and $l_i \epsilon$ {sustainable, unsustainable}. We need to develop a system to classify an unknown financial text as sustainable or not.

The evaluation metric for this sub-task was accuracy.

Concept	Count
Energy efficiency and renewable energy	59
Sustainable Food & Agriculture	54
Product Responsibility	51
Circular economy	47
Sustainable Transport	46
Emissions	39
Shareholder rights	38
Board Make-Up	37
Injury frequency rate for subcontracted labour	35
Executive compensation	32
Biodiversity	29
Community	27
Employee engagement	23
Employee development	22
Water & waste-water management	21
Carbon factor	19
Future of work	18
Waste management	16
Recruiting and retaining employees	11
Human Rights	10
Audit Oversight	7
Injury frequency rate	2
Board Independence	2
Share Capital	2

Table 1: Distribution of concepts

4 Data

The data sets provided by the organizers consist of a set of 190 documents in PDF format, 651 terms mapped to 24 concepts and 2265 financial texts labelled as sustainable or unsustainable. We provide more details about the data set in the following sections.

4.1 Data Description

For sub-task 1, the number of instances for each concept has been mentioned in Table 1. For sub-task 2, out of 2,265 financial texts 1,223 were sustainable whereas 1,042 were unsustainable. We maintained a training to validation split of 80% to 20% for both the sub-tasks.

4.2 Data Augmentation

Firstly for sub-task 1, we started by using 80% of 651 instances for training. To bring in more context, we collected the definitions for each of the 24 concepts from various websites. For each term

(t_i, concept c_i) pair, we obtained the corresponding concept definition d_i. Since, each term t_i present here were mapped to a concept definition d_i, we had only positive instances i.e. similarity score of 1.0 corresponding to the (t_i, d_i) pair. Subsequently, we thought of adding negative samples in the training process as well. For each term, concept definition pair (t_i, d_i), we experimented by randomly paring t_i with 1, 5 or 15 concepts definitions. Later, we grouped the concepts manually. This is presented in Table 2. We could group 20 out of 24 concepts. The remaining four were singleton sets. For randomly selecting concept definitions for term t_i, we tried out the following sampling methods:

- Select any concept definition d_j such that concept $c_j \neq$ concept c_i, and assign a similarity score of 0.0 to the (t_i, d_j) pair.
- Select any concept definition d_j such that concept $c_j \notin$ the group where concept c_i is present, and assign a similarity score of 0.0 to the (t_i, d_j) pair.
- Select any concept definition d_j, if concept c_j $\notin$ the group where concept c_i is present assign a similarity score of 0.0 to the (t_i, d_j) pair, else assign a similarity score of 0.5 to the (t_i, d_j) pair.

5 System Description

As per the rules, for every team, the number of submissions for each sub-task was restricted to two. We describe each of our submissions here. We pictorially depict our methodology in Figure 2.

5.1 Sub-Task 1, System -1

We fine-tuned a sentence transformer (Reimers and Gurevych, 2019) model[3] (SBERT-UN) which was pre-trained with United Nations (UN) sustainable development goals. For each of the terms in the training set, we randomly picked five concept definitions from different groups as mentioned in section 4.2. Our objective was to minimize the Multiple Negatives Ranking Loss as well as the Online Contrastive Loss. This was trained for 15 epochs with a batch size of 20.[4]. For sub-task 1, among all our submissions, this performed the best in terms of both accuracy and mean rank. This is similar to the solution (Chopra and Ghosh, 2021) presented at FinSim-3.

5.2 Sub-Task 1, System -2

This is a RoBERTa-base (Liu et al., 2019) based classifier. We fine-tune the pre-trained RoBERTa-base model so that its [CLS] token learns how to classify terms into 24 pre-defined concepts or classes. It's hyper-parameters are as follows: maximum length = 16, batch size = 256, epochs = 60, learning rate = 0.00002. We use the checkpoint created at 57th epoch as this was the best performing one.

5.3 Sub-Task 2, System -1

This system consists of the pre-trained FinBERT (Araci, 2019) fine-tuned for classifying financial texts as sustainable or unsustainable. It's hyper-parameters are as follows: maximum length = 128, batch size = 256, epochs = 60, learning rate = 0.00002. We use the checkpoint created at the 8th epoch as this performed the best on the validation set.

5.4 Sub-Task 2, System -2

It consists of the pre-trained RoBERTa-base (Liu et al., 2019) fine-tuned for the task of classifying financial texts as sustainable or not. It's hyper-parameters are as follows: maximum length = 128, batch size = 256, epochs = 60, learning rate = 0.00002. We use the checkpoint created at the 12th epoch as this performed the best on the validation set. Among all our submissions, this performed the best on the test set.

6 Experiments and Results

We initiated by fine-tuning the all-mpnet-base-v2 model (Song et al., 2020) using sentence transformer architecture. Our objective was to reduce the Multiple Negatives Ranking Loss as well as the Online Contrastive Loss for the task of Information Retrieval[4]. We also studied the effect of changing this model with the SBERT-UN model, adding negative samples and concepts as it is. We further experimented with different sampling methods as mentioned in section 4.2. Furthermore, we fine-tuned a RoBERTa-base (Liu et al., 2019) based model to classify terms into 24 pre-defined concepts or classes.

[3]https://huggingface.co/Rodion/sbert_uno_sustainable_development_goals

[4]The details are available at https://www.sbert.net/examples/training/quora_duplicate_questions/README.html

Group-1	Group-2	Group-3	Group-4
Carbon factor	Employee development	Injury frequency rate	Audit Oversight
Emissions	Recruiting and retaining employees	Injury frequency rate for subcontracted labour	Shareholder rights
Energy efficiency and renewable energy	Future of work	Human Rights	Executive compensation
	Employee engagement		Share Capital

Group-5	Group-6	Group-7
Waste management	Sustainable Transport	Board Independence
Water waste-water management	Sustainable Food Agriculture	Board Make-Up

Table 2: Concepts divided into groups

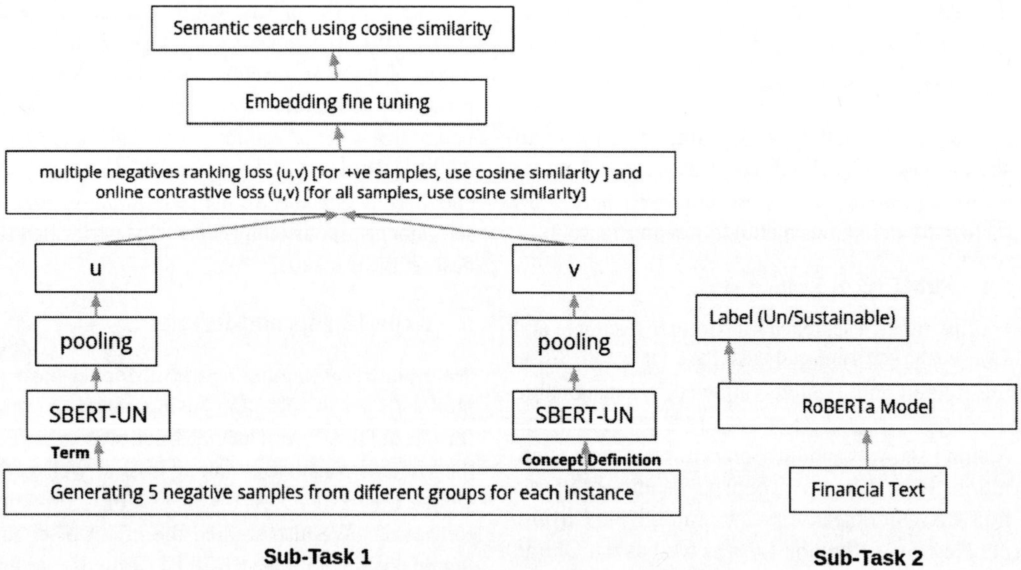

Figure 2: Methodology Sub-Task 1 and 2

Subsequently, we extracted texts from the documents provided in PDF format and fine-tuned a SBERT-UN model using Masked Language Modeling. However, this did not improve the performance. We also tried adding the definitions of 73 terms obtained from DBpedia (Auer et al., 2007). However, this did not yield any substantial improvement in the results. We present the result of subtask 1 in Table 3. The SBERT-UN model trained with negative samples (SL. No. 8) performed the best in the validation as well as the test set.

For sub-task-2, we fine-tuned four models for classifying financial texts into two classes sustainable and unsustainable. These models are: RoBERTa-base (Liu et al., 2019), FinBERT (Araci, 2019), SBERT-UN and SBERT-UN fine-tuned for sub-task 1. We present the results in Table 4. FinBERT (Araci, 2019) performed the best in the validation set whereas RoBERTa-base (Liu et al., 2019) performed the best in the test set. Each of these models was trained for a maximum of 128 input tokens with a batch size of 256, a learning rate of 0.00002 and for 60 epochs.

We present the test set results in Table 5.

7 Conclusion and Future Work

In this paper, we elaborate on our team LIPI's approach toward solving the FinSim-4-ESG sub-tasks. As per the official report, out of 28 registered teams, 6 and 8 teams participated in sub-task 1 and 2 respectively. For sub-task 1, our team ranked 4th whereas for sub-task 2, our team ranked 3rd.

In future, we would like to collect more data and work towards improving the model performance. Developing a user-friendly tool for assigning terms to concepts and automatically evaluating the sustainable aspect of financial texts are other directions of future work.

Disclaimer

The opinions expressed in this paper are of the authors'. They do not reflect the opinions of their affiliations.

References

Dogu Araci. 2019. Finbert: Financial sentiment analysis with pre-trained language models. *arXiv preprint arXiv:1908.10063*.

Sören Auer, Christian Bizer, Georgi Kobilarov, Jens Lehmann, Richard Cyganiak, and Zachary Ives. 2007. Dbpedia: A nucleus for a web of open data. In *The Semantic Web*, ISWC'07/ASWC'07, page 722–735, Berlin, Heidelberg. Springer-Verlag.

Isabelle Augenstein, Mrinal Das, Sebastian Riedel, Lakshmi Vikraman, and Andrew McCallum. 2017. SemEval 2017 task 10: ScienceIE - extracting keyphrases and relations from scientific publications. In *Proceedings of the 11th International Workshop on Semantic Evaluation (SemEval-2017)*, pages 546–555, Vancouver, Canada. Association for Computational Linguistics.

Georgeta Bordea, Paul Buitelaar, Stefano Faralli, and Roberto Navigli. 2015. SemEval-2015 task 17: Taxonomy extraction evaluation (TExEval). In *Proceedings of the 9th International Workshop on Semantic Evaluation (SemEval 2015)*, pages 902–910, Denver, Colorado. Association for Computational Linguistics.

Georgeta Bordea, Els Lefever, and Paul Buitelaar. 2016. SemEval-2016 task 13: Taxonomy extraction evaluation (TExEval-2). In *Proceedings of the 10th International Workshop on Semantic Evaluation (SemEval-2016)*, pages 1081–1091, San Diego, California. Association for Computational Linguistics.

Jose Camacho-Collados, Claudio Delli Bovi, Luis Espinosa-Anke, Sergio Oramas, Tommaso Pasini, Enrico Santus, Vered Shwartz, Roberto Navigli, and Horacio Saggion. 2018. SemEval-2018 task 9: Hypernym discovery. In *Proceedings of The 12th International Workshop on Semantic Evaluation*, pages 712–724, New Orleans, Louisiana. Association for Computational Linguistics.

Ankush Chopra and Sohom Ghosh. 2021. Term expansion and FinBERT fine-tuning for hypernym and synonym ranking of financial terms. In *Proceedings of the Third Workshop on Financial Technology and Natural Language Processing*, pages 46–51, Online. -.

Jacob Devlin, Ming-Wei Chang, Kenton Lee, and Kristina Toutanova. 2019. BERT: Pre-training of deep bidirectional transformers for language understanding. In *Proceedings of the 2019 Conference of the North American Chapter of the Association for Computational Linguistics: Human Language Technologies, Volume 1 (Long and Short Papers)*, pages 4171–4186, Minneapolis, Minnesota. Association for Computational Linguistics.

Tian Guo, Nicolas Jamet, Valentin Betrix, Louis-Alexandre Piquet, and Emmanuel Hauptmann. 2020. Esg2risk: A deep learning framework from esg news to stock volatility prediction.

Juyeon Kang, Ismail El Maarouf, Sandra Bellato, and Mei Gan. 2021. FinSim-3: The 3rd shared task on learning semantic similarities for the financial domain. In *Proceedings of the Third Workshop on Financial Technology and Natural Language Processing*, pages 31–35, Online. -.

Sl. No.	Base Model	Data Augmentation	Mean Rank	Accuracy
1	all-mpnet-base-v2	No (only positives)	1.4692	0.6923
2	all-mpnet-base-v2	Yes (1 negative per positive)	1.5769	0.7000
3	sbert_un	No (only positives)	1.5308	0.6769
4	sbert_un	Yes (1 negative per positive)	1.4769	0.7308
5	sbert_un	Yes (1 negative per positive) + concepts	1.4615	0.7154
6	sbert_un	Yes (1 negative per positive) - concept definitions + concepts	1.4846	0.7462
7	sbert_un	Yes (1 negative per positive) [out of group sampling]	1.4385	0.7462
8	sbert_un	Yes (5 negative per positive) [out of group sampling]	**1.4308**	**0.7615**
9	sbert_un	Yes (15 negative per positive) [out of group sampling]	1.5308	0.7000
10	sbert_un	Yes (5 negative per positive) [out of group sampling] {batch size = 40, epoch = 30}	1.4154	0.7462
11	sbert_un	Yes (5 negative per positive) [out of group sampling] {batch size = 40, epoch = 20}	1.4615	0.7462
12	roberta classifier	-	1.4846	0.7538
13	sbert_un	Yes (1 negative per positive) [same group & out of group sampling]	1.4615	0.7462
14	sbert_un	Yes (5 negative per positive) [same group & out of group sampling]	1.5000	0.7385
15	baseline-1	-	2.5308	0.3769
16	baseline-2	-	1.6846	0.7154

Table 3: Results of Sub-Task 1 on the validation set.
NOTE: Where not mentioned, definitions of concepts were used with batch size of 20 for 15 epochs.

Sl. No.	Model	Accuracy
1	roberta-base	0.9338
2	finbert	**0.9426**
3	sbert_un	0.8653
4	sub-task1 finetune	0.8543

Table 4: Results of Sub-Task 2 on the validation set.

ST	Sub.	Accuracy	Mean Rank
1	1	**0.7103**	**1.5172**
1	2	0.7034	1.6689
2	1	0.9219	-
2	2	**0.9317**	-

Table 5: Test set results for sub-tasks (ST) 1 and 2. Sub.: Submission

Yinhan Liu, Myle Ott, Naman Goyal, Jingfei Du, Mandar Joshi, Danqi Chen, Omer Levy, Mike Lewis, Luke Zettlemoyer, and Veselin Stoyanov. 2019. Roberta: A robustly optimized bert pretraining approach.

Alexandra Luccioni, Emily Baylor, and Nicolas Duchene. 2020. Analyzing sustainability reports using natural language processing.

Ismail El Maarouf, Youness Mansar, Virginie Mouilleron, and Dialekti Valsamou-Stanislawski. 2020. The FinSim 2020 shared task: Learning semantic representations for the financial domain. In *Proceedings of the Second Workshop on Financial Technology and Natural Language Processing*, pages 81–86, Kyoto, Japan. -.

Youness Mansar, Juyeon Kang, and Ismail El Maarouf. 2021. *The FinSim-2 2021 Shared Task: Learning Semantic Similarities for the Financial Domain*, page 288–292. Association for Computing Machinery, New York, NY, USA.

Tim Nugent, Nicole Stelea, and Jochen L. Leidner. 2020. Detecting esg topics using domain-specific language models and data augmentation approaches.

Nils Reimers and Iryna Gurevych. 2019. Sentence-

BERT: Sentence embeddings using Siamese BERT-networks. In *Proceedings of the 2019 Conference on Empirical Methods in Natural Language Processing and the 9th International Joint Conference on Natural Language Processing (EMNLP-IJCNLP)*, pages 3982–3992, Hong Kong, China. Association for Computational Linguistics.

Nils Smeuninx, Bernard De Clerck, and Walter Aerts. 2020. Measuring the readability of sustainability reports: A corpus-based analysis through standard formulae and nlp. *International Journal of Business Communication*, 57(1):52–85.

Kaitao Song, Xu Tan, Tao Qin, Jianfeng Lu, and Tie-Yan Liu. 2020. Mpnet: Masked and permuted pre-training for language understanding. *arXiv preprint arXiv:2004.09297*.

Using Transformer-based Models for Taxonomy Enrichment and Sentence Classification

Parag Dakle, Shrikumar Patil, SaiKrishna Rallabandi, Chaitra Hegde, Preethi Raghavan
Fidelity Investments, AICoE, Boston
{paragpravin.dakle, shrikumarrajendra.patil, saikrishna.rallabandi, chaitra.vishwanathahegde, preethi.raghavan}@fmr.com

Abstract

In this paper, we present a system that addresses the taxonomy enrichment problem for "Environment, Social and Governance" issues in the financial domain, as well as classifying sentences as sustainable or unsustainable, for FinSim4-ESG, a shared task for the FinNLP workshop at IJCAI-2022. We first created a derived dataset for taxonomy enrichment by using a sentence-BERT-based paraphrase detector (Reimers and Gurevych, 2019) (on the train set) to create positive and negative term-concept pairs. We then model the problem by fine-tuning the sentence-BERT-based paraphrase detector on this derived dataset, and use it as the encoder, and use a Logistic Regression classifier as the decoder, resulting in test Accuracy: 0.6 and Avg. Rank: 1.97. In case of the sentence classification task, the best performing classifier (Accuracy: 0.92) consists of a pre-trained RoBERTa model (Liu et al., 2019a) as the encoder and a Feed Forward Neural Network classifier as the decoder.

1 Introduction

Taxonomies classify, categorize and organize information hierarchically and are typically designed and curated by domain experts. They require frequent manual and automated updates to capture a domain sufficiently and to be considered complete. However, it is not to feasible to manually edit taxonomies to reflect changing concepts and evolving human knowledge. The taxonomy enrichment task helps address this problem by developing methods to add new terms to an existing taxonomy. The FinNLP shared task 1 defines this problem on a ESG taxonomy. Given a list of concepts and terms, the task is to rank the concepts given the term. In case of shared task 2, we are asked to classify a given sentence from sustainability reports and other documents as either sustainable or unsustainable.

In approaching these problems, we leverage large-scale pre-trained language models for token and sentence representations. We explore transfer learning through transformer models like BeRT (Devlin et al., 2018), DistillBeRT (Sanh et al., 2019), RoBeRTa (Liu et al., 2019b) as well as generative text to text transformers like T5 (Raffel et al., 2019) especially since training data is very limited for both tasks.

Like most NLP tasks in FinTech, the task 1 has limited amount of data. We addressed this limitation by creating a dataset derived from the train set and used a paraphrase detector to create positive and negative instances of <term, concept> pairs. We then fine-tune sentence-BERT (Reimers and Gurevych, 2019) on this derived dataset and use it as the encoder in our model. The decoder is a logistic regression classifier. This gives us a ten-fold cross-validated accuracy of 0.89 on the train set. However at test time, the performance varies and resulting accuracy is 60.6%. We describe the different approaches to modeling this problem that led to this final system and hypothesize reasons for the train-test performance discrepancy in the final system.

Shared task 2 is a binary sustainability classification task. We experimented with various models starting with a tf-idf based classifier to transformer based RoBeRTa (Liu et al., 2019b) based classifier. The RoBeRTa based model resulted in a ten-fold cross-validated accuracy of 0.96 and test-set accuracy of 0.92.

2 Related Works

2.1 Taxonomy Enrichment

Taxonomy enrichment is the task of extending an existing taxonomy with new terms. Word embeddings derived from language models are popularly used for this task (Jurgens and Pilehvar, 2016; Nikishina et al., 2021). Using word vector representations, it may be modeled as a hypernym classification task (SemEval 2018) or an embedding

Proceedings of the Fourth Workshop on Financial Technology and Natural Language Processing (FinNLP), pages 250 - 258

similarity task. Graph based representations are also used for taxonomy completion tasks (Zeng et al., 2021).

We explore the taxonomy enrichment problem using embedding similarity by modeling the problem as a paraphrase detection task. In the taxonomy enrichment task, we are given a list of terms and corresponding concepts. Our approach uses word2vec to get sentence embeddings for terms; we use (Reimers and Gurevych, 2019) which learns semantic representation of the given sentence using contrastive loss trained on various open-source datasets (Bowman et al., 2015; Williams et al., 2018).

2.2 Sustainability Classification

Pre-trained language models such as BERT(Devlin et al., 2018) and Roberta(Liu et al., 2019b) have achieved state-of-the-art performance on classification tasks. In our experiments, we found that Roberta (Liu et al., 2019a) performs better than other models.

3 Problem Statement

3.1 Sub-task 1: Taxonomy Enrichment

Given a set T of n terms $\{t_1, t_2, .., t_n\}$ and a set C of m concepts $\{c_1, c_2, .., c_m\}$, the task of taxonomy enrichment is to find a many-to-one mapping M between the terms and the corresponding concepts.

3.2 Sub-task 2: Sentence Classification

Given a set of k sentences $S = \{s_1, s_2, .., s_k\}$, the aim of this sub-task is to classify each sentence in S into one of two classes - *sustainable* or *unsustainable*.

Concept	#instances
Energy efficiency and renewable energy	59
Sustainable Food & Agriculture	54
Product Responsibility	51
circular economy	47
Sustainable Transport	46
Emissions	39
Shareholder rights	38
Board Make-Up	37
Injury frequency rate for subcontracted labour	35
Executive compensation	32
Biodiversity	29
Community	27
Employee engagement	23
Employee development	22
Water & waste-water management	21
Carbon factor	19
Future of work	18
Waste management	16
Recruiting and retaining employees (incl. work-life balance)	11
Human Rights	10
Audit Oversight	7
Injury frequency rate	2
Board Independence	2
SHARE CAPITAL	2
Total	**646**

Table 1: Label distribution in the training set for taxonomy enrichment sub-task 01

4 Data Description

The training dataset for sub-task 1 contains 646 annotated term-concept pairs. The total number of unique concepts are 25. Table 1 shows the label distribution in the training set for sub-task 1. Since the released training data did not contain any validation set, 10-fold cross validation was used for training. The data was first shuffled and then split into 10 parts. For each fold, 9 parts containing 582 term-concept pairs and one fold containing 65 term-concept pairs were selected as the training and validation set respectively.

The training dataset for sub-task 2 contains 2265 annotated sentences. Table 2 shows the label distribution in the training set for sub-task 2. On an average a sentence in the training set had a length of 162 characters or 25 tokens. Similar to sub-task 1, for this sub-task also 10-fold cross validation was used. Each fold contains 2038 sentences in the training set and 227 sentences in the validation set. In addition to the training sets for both sub-tasks, the shared task also provided a set of 190 annual reports and sustainability reports of financial companies.

5 Taxonomy Enrichment Task

5.1 Preliminary Experiments and Results

- Baseline 1 (B_1): A Word2Vec model trained on the given reports is used to generate term and concept embeddings. The similarity scores or distance between each term embed-

Class	#instances
Sustainable	1223
Unsustainable	1042
Total	**2265**

Table 2: Label distribution in the training set for sentence classification sub-task 02

ding and concept embedding is computed using the vector norm of the difference between the two embeddings. For each term, scores for all concepts are computed and the top k concepts are used as predicted concepts.

- Baseline 2 (B_2): A Word2Vec model trained on the given reports is used to generate term embeddings. Next, a Logistic Regression classifier is trained using these embeddings to do multi-class classification over the concepts. The final model consists of a Word2Vec model as the encoder and the trained Logistic Regression classifier as the decoder.

- Pre-trained DistilBERT (DistilBERT^P): This baseline is similar to Baseline 1 except that a pre-trained DistilBERT-base model is used as the encoder.

- Fine-tuned DistilBERT (DistilBERT^F): A pre-trained DistilBERT model was further fine-tuned on the sentences from the reports using the Masked Language Modelling task. The aim of this baseline is to see if training on the sentences in the given reports results in richer term and concept embeddings.

- Pre-trained Sentence-BERT (SentBERT^P): A pre-trained Sentence-BERT paraphrase detector (paraphrase-MiniLM-L3-v2) is used as the encoder to generate term and concept embeddings. The generated embeddings are then used to compute cosine distances between a term and all concepts. The top k ranked concepts are then selected as the predicted concepts.

- Pre-trained Sentence-BERT + Logistic Regression (SentBERT$^P_{LR}$): This baseline is similar to Baseline 2 except that a pre-trained Sentence-BERT paraphrase detector is used as the encoder to obtain term and concept embeddings.

Baseline	Accuracy	Mean Rank
Baseline 1	0.47	2.27
DistilBERT^P	0.34	2.72
DistilBERT^F	0.45	2.28
SentBERT^P	0.56	2.04
Baseline 2*	0.76	1.46
SentBERT$^{P*}_{LR}$	**0.79**	**1.41**

Table 3: Statistics showing the results of various baselines for sub task 01. First four scores are reported on the training set with no training. The last two models marked with * report the average scores with 10-fold cross validation on the training set.

For pre-trained DistilBERT and Sentence-BERT baselines, numerous variants were tested in the same setting for each of the baselines. However, we only report the best of the variants here due to space restrictions. We also tried using an approach similar to Wang et al. (2021) which encodes corrupted sentences into fixed-sized vectors and requires the decoder to reconstruct the original sentences from this sentence embedding, using RoBERTa as the encoder and decoder, on the sentences from the given reports to learn embeddings. Using this encoder to get embeddings, we train a Logistic Regression classifier, which gave similar performance to the baselines, and the model did not learn anything from the auto-encoder recontruction on the sentences from the reports to learn better embeddings.

Table 3 shows the results of the initial experiments and that SentBERT$^P_{LR}$ gave the best accuracy of 0.79 and a mean rank of 1.41.

5.2 Derived Dataset

In the SentBERT$^P_{LR}$ system, the weights of the Logistic Regression model are learnt during the training phase. There is no change in the weights of the Sentence-BERT model, thus, the training process has no impact on the generated embeddings. In order to enrich the generated embeddings, we propose training the encoder on a simple task of The following steps were followed for creating the derived dataset:

1. Obtain top 5 concept predictions for each term in the train set using the SentBERT^P model.

2. From the predictions create a dataset containing positive and negative samples.

3. A positive sample is the correct term-concept

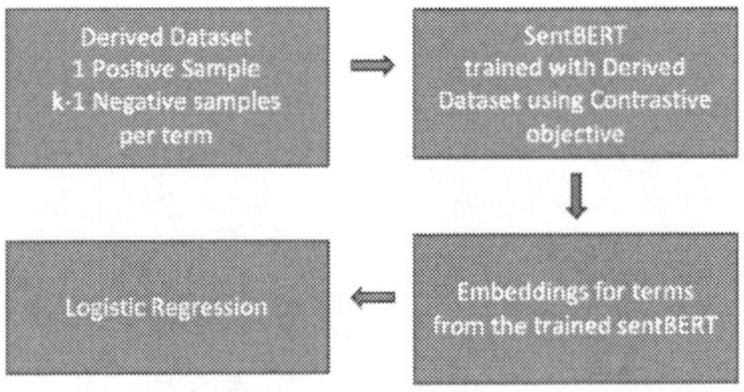

Figure 1: Proposed overall model for sub task 01

mapping.

4. A negative sample is a mapping between a term and an incorrectly predicted concept in the top k predictions.

5.3 System Description

The initial experiments using SentBERT^P show that although the embeddings generated by the model are richer, there is still room for improvement. The model, trained on paraphrase detection data, manages to capture the *hypernym* relation to some extent. If further fine-tuning of the model is carried out, it should ensure two things - correct neighbourhood relationship between term and concept embedding vectors in the current embedding space should be maintained, and missing neighbourhood relationships between correct term-concept vectors should be established. Previous work of Hadsell et al. (2006) proposed a contrastive loss function for this task. Contrastive loss given by equation 1. Here Y is the label of an instance, D_W is the distance between the concept and the term. The first section of the addition on the right side of the equation relates to the scenario when the model sees a positive example. The second section of the addition relates to the scenario when a negative example is seen. The constant m is the margin around the term within which a concept is considered a valid mapping. For all experiments, the value of m was set to 0.5.

$$L = (1-Y)\frac{1}{2}(D_W)^2+(Y)\frac{1}{2}\{max(0,m-D_W)\}^2 \quad (1)$$

The trained SentBERT model, SentBERT^F is then used with a Logistic Regression classifier as shown in figure 1. The system takes a term as input, generates term embedding using SentBERT^F as the encoder, and uses the embedding and a Logistic Regression classifier to predict the concept class.

Baseline	Accuracy	Mean Rank
SentBERT$^P_{LR}$	0.79 (Avg.)	1.41 (Avg.)
fold-0	0.8	1.46
fold-1	0.81	1.38
fold-2	0.70	1.61
fold-3	0.84	1.24
fold-4	0.75	1.55
fold-5	0.81	1.41
fold-6	0.80	1.38
fold-7	0.90	1.1
fold-8	0.78	1.5
fold-9	0.73	1.51
SentBERT$^F_{LR}$	**0.89** (Avg.)	**1.24** (Avg.)
fold-0	0.83	1.43
fold-1	0.90	1.2
fold-2	0.86	1.36
fold-3	0.90	1.21
fold-4	0.93	1.18
fold-5	0.92	1.15
fold-6	0.86	1.27
fold-7	0.93	1.09
fold-8	0.87	1.26
fold-9	0.87	1.28

Table 4: Statistics showing the impact of fine-tuning the SentBERT^P model on the derived dataset for sub task 01. The experiments were carried out with 10-fold cross validation.

5.4 Results and Analysis

Table 4 show the results of SentBERT$^F_{LR}$ on 10-fold training dataaset. Fine-tuning the SentBERT^P model results in a 10% increase in the average accuracy of the previous best model. This increase also results in a 0.17 reduction in the mean rank across 10-folds. The predictions obtained on the test set using a model trained on a random fold were submitted as part of the shared task. The predictions received an accuracy of 0.6 and a mean rank of 1.97. At this point, test labels have not been released and thus, error analysis cannot be carried out on the test set resulting in the usage of the validation set for a single fold for error analysis.

For error analysis, the fold with the lowest accuracy on the corresponding fold test set was used (fold-0). The size of the test set for fold-0 is 65 and of these 13 (20%) were classified incorrectly. Table 5 shows the distribution of the test set in terms of concepts and of these how many were incorrect.

Concept	Total Count	Incorrect Count
Energy efficiency and renewable energy	10	**4**
Board Make-Up	6	0
Carbon factor	5	**2**
Executive compensation	5	**2**
Product Responsibility	5	**1**
Sustainable Food & Agriculture	4	0
Shareholder rights	4	0
Employee engagement	4	0
Community	3	**1**
Emissions	3	0
Human Rights	2	**1**
Waste management	2	0
Biodiversity	2	0
Sustainable Transport	2	0
circular economy	2	0
Water & waste-water management	2	0
Injury frequency rate for subcontracted labour	2	**2**
Future of work	1	0
Employee development	1	0

Table 5: Concept distribution of the test set instances along with the corresponding counts for number of instances that were incorrectly classified in sub task 01.

Of the 17 concepts in the train set, 7 concepts had incorrectly classified instances. Figure 2 shows the confusion matrix for the incorrectly predicted classes. From the confusion matrix it can be seen that the model primarily has difficulty in understanding the difference between Emissions and the concepts *Energy efficiency and renewable energy* and *Carbon factor*.

6 Sentence Classification

In sub-task 2, we holdout 20 percent of the data (463 instances of 2265) as validation set to evaluate performance of our various approaches and fine-tune the hyperparameters. We use rest of the data

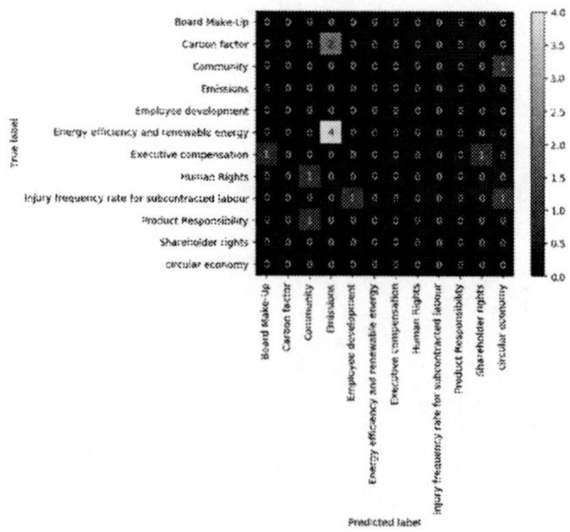

Figure 2: Confusion matrix for the incorrectly predicted classes.

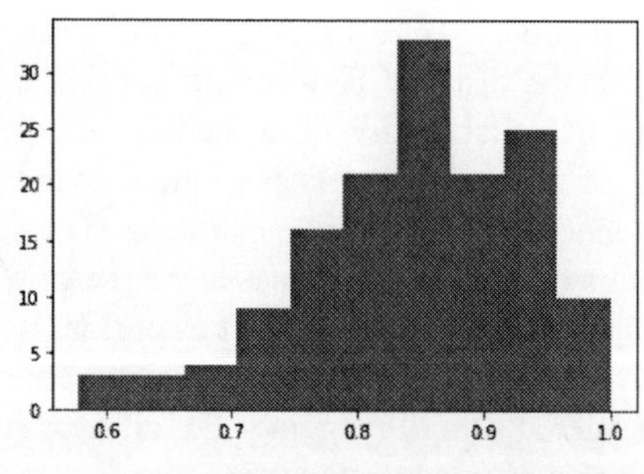

Figure 3: Histogram plot of Pair wise similarity for sentences in the train set with the test set in sub task 01.

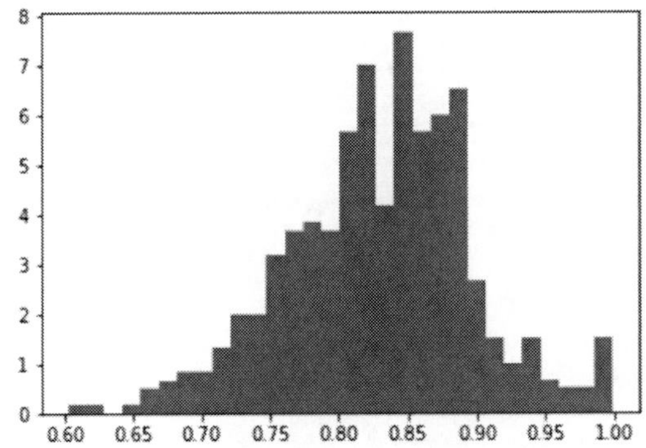

Figure 4: Histogram plot of Pair wise similarity for sentences in Val set with train set in sub task 02.

for training. We have built the following systems for sub task 02:

- Baseline 1 (B_1): We generate Term Frequency and Inverse Document frequency for the given data. Next, a Logistic Regression classifier is trained to perform binary classification.
- Baseline 2 (B_2): This baseline is similar to Baseline 1 except that a Naive Bayes model is used as the classifier.
- Leveraging Pretrained LMs: The world of NLP has extensively benefited from the development of large pretrained Language Models(LMs). Architectures such as ELMO (Peters et al., 2018), various extensions of BERT (Devlin et al., 2018; Liu et al., 2019b), XLNET (Yang et al., 2019), GPT (Brown et al., 2020), T5 (Raffel et al., 2019), etc have demonstrated dramatic improvements over conventional approaches. We were interested in leveraging such pretrained LMs in identifying if the given sentence is sustainable or unsustainable. To accomplish this we have built multiple systems where we finetune a pretrained LM using the data from sub task 02, as can be seen in table 6.

6.1 Discussion

As can be seen from the results in table 6, RoBERTa based model achieves the best performance among all the approaches we have tried. Using the Sentence Bert (Reimers and Gurevych, 2019) employed for sub task 01, we calculate the pairwise similarity between all the sentences of train set and held out validation set. The histogram plot of the similarity can be seen in figure 4. Here is an example pair of sentences from train and val sets that has high similarity score(0.91):

Model	Accuracy	Precision	Recall	F1
Baseline 01	85	85	86	85
Baseline 02	77.26	83.9	75.42	75.03
BERT	92.4	92	92	92
T5	93.3	93.5	93.3	93.3
RoBERTa	**96**	**96**	**96**	**96**

Table 6: Statistics showing the results on Val set for various models for Subtask 02.

- *Val Sentence*: In 2020, as part of our **commitment** to carbon neutrality, we began focusing Scope 2 REC purchases on a country-by-country basis, depending on where the electricity is being used.
- *Train Sentence*: In 2020, as part of our **approach** to carbon neutrality, we began focusing Scope 2 REC purchases on a country-by-country basis, depending on where the electricity is **actually** being used.

It has to be noted that these sentences differ only in the words highlighted in bold and are almost identical to each other. Since the sentences seem very similar across the train and val sets, we were interested in seeing if the model was biased towards sentences it has already seen during training. To alleviate this and further validate our results from pretrained LMs, we performed 10 fold cross validation to prevent model over fitting to a section of training data. The results from cross validation can be found in table 7. We have submitted this system to the shared task and obtained joint third position on the leader board with accuracy of 92.6 percent.

6.2 Error Analysis

To understand the type of errors being made by our model, we have performed word level attribute analysis on the trained model. For this, we have used the open source package transformers-interpret[1]. Here are the types of errors being made by our model.

[1]https://github.com/cdpierse/transformers-interpret

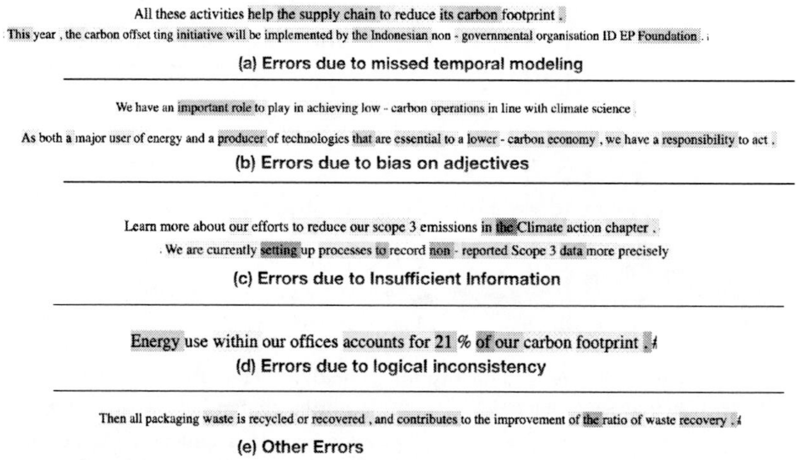

Figure 5: Error Analysis - Categorization of errors made by our model for sub task 02.

- *Errors due to missed Temporal Modeling*: These are the errors due to the model being unaware of the temporal context of a sentence. Examples of this type of errors are given in (a) of figure 5.

- *Errors due to bias on Adjectives*: We have noticed that attention in our model is biased towards adjective words which might be misleading the prediction when the context is ambiguous. Examples of this type of errors are given in (b) of figure 5.

- *Errors due to insufficient information*: There are sentences that lack the information required to make a prediction even for humans. We depict examples of this error type in (c) of figure 5.

- *Errors due to logical inconsistency*: There are a few errors where the model misses the logical consistency. For instance, in the example shown in (d) of figure 5, the model considers 21 as a positive attribute towards making the decision.

- Other Errors: Example of this type of errors are mentioned in (e) of figure 5.

6.3 Observations

The sentences in test and train sets have high degree of similarity. There are instances where the sentences are nearly identical as mentioned in the discussion sub section. In addition, there are also sentences which are paraphrases of each other. Here is an example pair of sentences from train and test sets:

Fold	Accuracy	Precision	Recall	F1
Fold 01	95	95	96	95
Fold 02	94	94	93	93
Fold 03	92.4	92	92	92
Fold 04	93.3	93.5	93.3	93.3
Fold 05	96	96	96	96
Fold 06	95	95	96	95
Fold 07	95	95	95	94
Fold 08	91.4	91	91	91
Fold 09	93.3	93.5	93.3	93.3
Fold 10	96	96	96	96

Table 7: Results of 10 fold Cross Validation using Roberta Model on Subtask 02

- *Train Sentence:* Our operational carbon footprint (occupied offices and business travel) will be net zero from 2030.

- *Test Sentence:* From 2030, our operational footprint (occupied offices and business travel) will operate with net zero carbon emissions.

Given the high levels of similarity, we hypothesize that architectures that can model paraphrasing can perform well on this sub task. It might be interesting to employ models that can generate paraphrases of original sentences to augment the

Task	Accuracy	Mean Rank
Sub Task 01	60.08	1.97
Sub Task 02	92.68	-

Table 8: Test Results of our submissions to the shared task.

training data and achieve competitive performance even in low resource scenarios.

7 Test Submission

As part of the shared task, we have made submissions to both the subtasks. Our team name is Jetsons and we have presented the results of our systems from both sub tasks in the table 8. We are nearly 24 percentage points off from the best system in sub task 01. We are in joint third position in sub task 02.

8 Conclusion

In this paper, we presented our submission to the sub tasks of FinSim4-ESG. We first present a system that addresses the taxonomy enrichment problem for "Environment, Social and Governance" issues in the financial domain. We first created a derived dataset for taxonomy enrichment by using a sentence-BERT-based paraphrase detector to create positive and negative term-concept pairs. We employ a Logistic Regression classifier as the decoder, resulting in test Accuracy: 0.6 and Avg. Rank: 1.97. We then present our approach to the sub task of sentence classification. Our best performing model, a finetuned version of RoBERTa model achieves 96 percent on validation set and 92.3 on test set.

References

Samuel R. Bowman, Gabor Angeli, Christopher Potts, and Christopher D. Manning. 2015. A large annotated corpus for learning natural language inference. In *Proceedings of the 2015 Conference on Empirical Methods in Natural Language Processing*, pages 632–642, Lisbon, Portugal. Association for Computational Linguistics.

Tom Brown, Benjamin Mann, Nick Ryder, Melanie Subbiah, Jared D Kaplan, Prafulla Dhariwal, Arvind Neelakantan, Pranav Shyam, Girish Sastry, Amanda Askell, et al. 2020. Language models are few-shot learners. *Advances in neural information processing systems*, 33:1877–1901.

Jacob Devlin, Ming-Wei Chang, Kenton Lee, and Kristina Toutanova. 2018. Bert: Pre-training of deep bidirectional transformers for language understanding. *arXiv preprint arXiv:1810.04805*.

Raia Hadsell, Sumit Chopra, and Yann LeCun. 2006. Dimensionality reduction by learning an invariant mapping. In *2006 IEEE Computer Society Conference on Computer Vision and Pattern Recognition (CVPR'06)*, volume 2, pages 1735–1742. IEEE.

David Jurgens and Mohammad Taher Pilehvar. 2016. Semeval-2016 task 14: Semantic taxonomy enrichment. In *Proceedings of the 10th international workshop on semantic evaluation (SemEval-2016)*, pages 1092–1102.

Yinhan Liu, Myle Ott, Naman Goyal, Jingfei Du, Mandar Joshi, Danqi Chen, Omer Levy, Mike Lewis, Luke Zettlemoyer, and Veselin Stoyanov. 2019a. Roberta: A robustly optimized BERT pretraining approach. *CoRR*, abs/1907.11692.

Yinhan Liu, Myle Ott, Naman Goyal, Jingfei Du, Mandar Joshi, Danqi Chen, Omer Levy, Mike Lewis, Luke Zettlemoyer, and Veselin Stoyanov. 2019b. Roberta: A robustly optimized bert pretraining approach. *arXiv preprint arXiv:1907.11692*.

Irina Nikishina, Natalia Loukachevitch, Varvara Logacheva, and Alexander Panchenko. 2021. Evaluation of taxonomy enrichment on diachronic wordnet versions. In *Proceedings of the 11th Global Wordnet Conference*, pages 126–136.

Matthew E Peters, Mark Neumann, Mohit Iyyer, Matt Gardner, Christopher Clark, Kenton Lee, and Luke Zettlemoyer. 2018. Deep contextualized word representations." arxiv preprint. *arXiv preprint arXiv:1802.05365*.

Colin Raffel, Noam Shazeer, Adam Roberts, Katherine Lee, Sharan Narang, Michael Matena, Yanqi Zhou, Wei Li, and Peter J Liu. 2019. Exploring the limits of transfer learning with a unified text-to-text transformer. *arXiv preprint arXiv:1910.10683*.

Nils Reimers and Iryna Gurevych. 2019. Sentence-bert: Sentence embeddings using siamese bert-networks. In *Proceedings of the 2019 Conference on Empirical Methods in Natural Language Processing*. Association for Computational Linguistics.

Victor Sanh, Lysandre Debut, Julien Chaumond, and Thomas Wolf. 2019. Distilbert, a distilled version of bert: smaller, faster, cheaper and lighter. *arXiv preprint arXiv:1910.01108*.

Kexin Wang, Nils Reimers, and Iryna Gurevych. 2021. Tsdae: Using transformer-based sequential denoising auto-encoder for unsupervised sentence embedding learning.

Adina Williams, Nikita Nangia, and Samuel Bowman. 2018. A broad-coverage challenge corpus for sentence understanding through inference. In *Proceedings of the 2018 Conference of the North American*

Chapter of the Association for Computational Linguistics: Human Language Technologies, Volume 1 (Long Papers), pages 1112–1122, New Orleans, Louisiana. Association for Computational Linguistics.

Zhilin Yang, Zihang Dai, Yiming Yang, Jaime Carbonell, Russ R Salakhutdinov, and Quoc V Le. 2019. Xlnet: Generalized autoregressive pretraining for language understanding. *Advances in neural information processing systems*, 32.

Qingkai Zeng, Jinfeng Lin, Wenhao Yu, Jane Cleland-Huang, and Meng Jiang. 2021. Enhancing taxonomy completion with concept generation via fusing relational representations. In *Proceedings of the 27th ACM SIGKDD Conference on Knowledge Discovery & Data Mining*, pages 2104–2113.

Author Index

Association for Computational Linguistics
209 N. Eighth Street
Stroudsburg, Pennsylvania 18360

ISBN 978-1-7138-9109-3

CURRAN ASSOCIATES INC.
proceedings.com